INTERNATIONAL CONFLICT RESOLUTION AFTER THE COLD WAR

Committee on International Conflict Resolution

Paul C. Stern and Daniel Druckman, *Editors*

Commission on Behavioral and Social Sciences and Education

National Research Council

NATIONAL ACADEMY PRESS
Washington, D.C.

NATIONAL ACADEMY PRESS • 2101 Constitution Avenue, NW • Washington, D.C. 20418

NOTICE: The project that is the subject of this report was approved by the Governing Board of the National Research Council, whose members are drawn from the councils of the National Academy of Sciences, the National Academy of Engineering, and the Institute of Medicine. The members of the committee responsible for the report were chosen for their special competences and with regard for appropriate balance.

This study was supported by Grants No. B6083 and B6728 from the Carnegie Corporation of New York to the National Academy of Sciences. Any opinions, findings, conclusions, or recommendations expressed in this publication are those of the author(s), and the Carnegie Corporation does not take responsibility for any statements or views expressed.

Library of Congress Cataloging-in-Publication Data

International conflict resolution after the cold war / Committee on International Conflict Resolution ; Paul C. Stern and Daniel Druckman, editors.
     p. cm.
Includes bibliographical references.
   ISBN 0-309-07027-9 (pbk.)
   1. Pacific settlement of international disputes. 2. Mediation, International. I. Stern, Paul C., 1944- II. Druckman, Daniel. III. National Research Council (U.S.). Committee on International Conflict Resolution.
   JZ6010 .I57 2000
   327.1'7—dc21
00-010212

Additional copies of this report are available from National Academy Press, 2101 Constitution Avenue, N.W., Lockbox 285, Washington, D.C. 20055; (800) 624-6242 or (202) 334-3313 (in the Washington metropolitan area); Internet, http://www.nap.edu

Suggested citation: National Research Council (2000) *International Conflict Resolution After the Cold War*. Committee on International Conflict Resolution. Paul C. Stern and Daniel Druckman, editors. Commission on Behavioral and Social Sciences and Education. Washington, DC: National Academy Press.

THE NATIONAL ACADEMIES

National Academy of Sciences
National Academy of Engineering
Institute of Medicine
National Research Council

The **National Academy of Sciences** is a private, nonprofit, self-perpetuating society of distinguished scholars engaged in scientific and engineering research, dedicated to the furtherance of science and technology and to their use for the general welfare. Upon the authority of the charter granted to it by the Congress in 1863, the Academy has a mandate that requires it to advise the federal government on scientific and technical matters. Dr. Bruce M. Alberts is president of the National Academy of Sciences.

The **National Academy of Engineering** was established in 1964, under the charter of the National Academy of Sciences, as a parallel organization of outstanding engineers. It is autonomous in its administration and in the selection of its members, sharing with the National Academy of Sciences the responsibility for advising the federal government. The National Academy of Engineering also sponsors engineering programs aimed at meeting national needs, encourages education and research, and recognizes the superior achievements of engineers. Dr. William A. Wulf is president of the National Academy of Engineering.

The **Institute of Medicine** was established in 1970 by the National Academy of Sciences to secure the services of eminent members of appropriate professions in the examination of policy matters pertaining to the health of the public. The Institute acts under the responsibility given to the National Academy of Sciences by its congressional charter to be an adviser to the federal government and, upon its own initiative, to identify issues of medical care, research, and education. Dr. Kenneth I. Shine is president of the Institute of Medicine.

The **National Research Council** was organized by the National Academy of Sciences in 1916 to associate the broad community of science and technology with the Academy's purposes of furthering knowledge and advising the federal government. Functioning in accordance with general policies determined by the Academy, the Council has become the principal operating agency of both the National Academy of Sciences and the National Academy of Engineering in providing services to the government, the public, and the scientific and engineering communities. The Council is administered jointly by both Academies and the Institute of Medicine. Dr. Bruce M. Alberts and Dr. William A. Wulf are chairman and vice chairman, respectively, of the National Research Council.

iv

Contents

Preface

In 1995 the National Research Council organized the Committee on International Conflict Resolution to respond to a growing need for prevention, management, and resolution of violent conflicts in the international arena; a concern about the changing nature and context of such conflicts in the post-Cold War era; and a need to expand knowledge in the field. The committee's primary goal was to advance the practice and theory of conflict resolution by using the methods and critical attitude of social science to examine the effectiveness of various approaches that have been advanced for preventing, managing, and resolving international conflicts. Its research agenda was designed in part to complement the work of the Carnegie Corporation of New York's Commission on Preventing Deadly Conflict, which sponsored a large number of specialized studies and issued its final report in December 1997.

The committee's work was organized around a central question: How effective are various techniques and concepts for managing, preventing, and resolving conflicts in the international arena? In the early 1990s many observers had begun to wonder to what extent the conventional wisdom about international conflict resolution, developed from practice and scholarship over many decades, was still valid after the passing of the Cold War and global bipolarity. Some had argued that previously underutilized techniques and strategies—such as types of track two diplomacy, the promotion of democracy in divided countries, and the establishment of truth commissions—were particularly well suited for dealing with the conflicts that were occurring during the early years of the post-Cold War period. Practitioners felt the need for an assessment of such claims, and the committee aimed to help fill this need with respect to selected conflict resolution techniques.

The committee invited a series of chapter-length studies focused on particular approaches to conflict resolution. We wanted each study to address pressing concerns of conflict management practitioners and also to be intellectually rigorous in drawing conclusions. Thus, topics were selected on the basis of three criteria: the perceived need of international conflict resolution practitioners for additional knowledge, the availability of new information and analyses for advancing knowledge, and the likelihood that knowledge or insights to be generated were not already being made available from other projects or research programs.

The committee went to great lengths to bridge a gap that exists between scholarship and practice by involving both scholars and practitioners at each phase of development of its activities. Each study survived a three-stage process of review by practitioners and scholars, designed to enhance its usefulness to both audiences. First, the topics were chosen by consensus of the committee's members. Both scholars and practitioners served on the committee; the practitioners included individuals with experience working on behalf of national governments, international organizations, and nongovernmental organizations. Second, the authors, who were selected for their knowledge of their topics and their ability to address both practical and analytical issues, presented the ideas for their chapters to seminars for scholars and practitioners selected to represent the audience for the chapter. Each author thus had the benefit of the perspectives of both groups before beginning to write in earnest. Finally, after the author had prepared a complete paper, it was subjected to blind review by three to five reviewers, again including both scholars and practitioners, who judged the draft paper on its practical value and appropriate use of evidence. We believe this effort has resulted in a set of studies that scholars and practitioners will find enlightening and useful.

We strove to achieve the highest-possible quality of analysis by pressing authors to be explicit about definitions of the concepts or techniques they examined, to discuss criteria for judging the effectiveness of each technique, and to evaluate the strength of the evidence supporting their conclusions. We asked them to consider whether their conclusions apply equally across world regions, historical periods, and types of conflict and to assess whether success depends on external conditions, present or past, including the operation of other conflict resolution techniques. Thus, the chapters address critical analytical issues and clarify concepts, as well as try to summarize the lessons of experience.

There are limits to what can be expected from a volume such as this. Drawing conclusions about the effectiveness of interventions in historical processes is very challenging, for the methodological reasons discussed in Chapter 2. It is also risky in a rapidly changing world. The chapters are current only to their dates of completion—in 1999, in most cases. Moreover, the study is selective. It does not cover the full range of techniques and concepts in use for international conflict resolution and does not draw overall conclusions about international conflict resolution as a field or a practice.

Despite these limits, we believe that the studies in this volume, by virtue of their thorough and critical examination of the relevant evidence, will add appreciably to both practitioners' and scholars' understanding. They will enable conflict resolution practitioners in governments, international organizations, nongovernmental organizations, and academic centers to better diagnose conflict situations and make informed choices about whether, when, and how to intervene. We believe these studies will also advance a second goal of the committee, which is to improve the quality of future analytical efforts to understand international conflict and conflict resolution.

We express our appreciation to the Carnegie Corporation of New York for its generous support of the committee's activities. We also thank the many practitioners and scholars who participated in the committee's seminars on the topics covered in this book and to those who participated in reviewing papers, whose names are listed separately. Our gratitude goes to Heather Schofield, who managed the logistics of this project from its inception to its near completion, and to Brian Tobachnick, who carried it the rest of the way. We also owe a debt to Barbara Bodling O'Hare, who did the copy editing, and to Eugenia Grohman and Christine McShane, who managed the review and editorial processes.

Finally, we wish to thank the following individuals for their participation in the review of the papers in this volume: Harry Barnes, Carter Center, Atlanta, Georgia; Cynthia Chataway, York University, Toronto, Canada; Thomas Cook, Northwestern University; Chester A. Crocker, Georgetown University; David Crocker, University of Maryland, College Park; Abram de Swaan, Amsterdam School for Social Science Research, Amsterdam, Netherlands; Kimberly Elliott, Institute for International Economics, Washington, D.C. ; Robert Gallucci, Georgetown University; Larry Garber, U.S. Agency for International Development; Ambassador Maynard Glitman, Jeffersonville, Vermont; Richard Herrmann, Ohio State University; Donald Horowitz, Duke University School of Law; Herbert C. Kelman, Harvard University; Russell Leng, Middlebury College; Ambassador Samuel Lewis, McLean, Virginia; David Malone, International Peace Academy, New York, New York; Michael Mastanduno, Dartmouth College; John W. McDonald, Institute for Multi-Track Diplomacy, Washington, D.C.; Stephen Morrison, Center for Strategic and International Studies; Brian Pollins, Ohio State University; Jonathan Pool, Esperantic Studies Foundation, Seattle, Washington; Dean G. Pruitt, State University of New York at Buffalo; Dennis Sandole, George Mason University; Timothy Sisk, University of Denver; Richard Soudriette, International Foundation for Election Systems, Washington, D.C.; Stephen Stedman, Stanford University; Philip Tetlock, Ohio State University; James Wall, University of Missouri, Columbia; Ronald Watts, Queen's University, Kingston, Ontario, Canada; Thomas G. Weiss, City University of New York Graduate Center; and Aristide Zolberg, New School for Social Research, New York, New York.

Alexander L. George, *Chair*
Paul C. Stern, *Study Director*
Committee on International Conflict Resolution

1

Conflict Resolution in a Changing World

Committee on International Conflict Resolution

The world has transformed rapidly in the decade since the end of the Cold War. An old system is gone and, although it is easy to identify what has changed, it is not yet clear that a new system has taken its place. Old patterns have come unstuck, and if new patterns are emerging, it is still too soon to define them clearly. The list of potentially epoch-making changes is familiar by now: the end of an era of bipolarity, a new wave of democratization, increasing globalization of information and economic power, more frequent efforts at international coordination of security policy, a rash of sometimes-violent expressions of claims to rights based on cultural identity, and a redefinition of sovereignty that imposes on states new responsibilities to their citizens and the world community.[1]

These transformations are changing much in the world, including, it seems, the shape of organized violence and the ways in which governments and others try to set its limits. One indication of change is the noteworthy decrease in the frequency and death toll of international wars in the 1990s. Subnational ethnic and religious conflicts, however, have been so intense that the first post-Cold War decade was marked by enough deadly lower-intensity conflicts to make it the bloodiest since the advent of nuclear weapons (Wallensteen and Sollenberg, 1996). It is still too soon to tell whether this shift in the most lethal type of warfare is a lasting change: the continued presence of contested borders between militarily potent states—in Korea, Kashmir, Taiwan, and the Middle East—gives reason to postpone judgment. It seems likely, though, that efforts to prevent outbreaks in such hot spots will take different forms in the changed international situation.

A potentially revolutionary change in world politics has been a de facto redefinition of "international conflict." International conflict still includes the old-fashioned war, a violent confrontation between nation states acting through their own armed forces or proxies with at least one state fighting outside its borders. But now some conflicts are treated as threats to international peace and security even if two states are not fighting. Particularly when internal conflicts involve violations of universal norms such as self-determination, human rights, or democratic governance, concerted international actions—including the threat or use of force—are being taken to prevent, conclude, or resolve them just as they sometimes have been for old-fashioned wars. In this sense some conflicts within a country's borders are being treated as international.

There are various prominent recent examples. They include the delayed international military responses to genocide in Rwanda, ethnic cleansing in Bosnia, and repression in East Timor; the unprecedented military response of NATO to repression in Kosovo; the establishment and enforcement of no-fly zones in Iraq; and the use of economic sanctions against South Africa and Yugoslavia. Threatened or enacted coups d'état against democratically established governments have also sometimes been treated as international conflicts, as in Haiti. Similarly, threats of the violent dissolution of states or of their dissolution into violence have triggered international concern, as in Bosnia, Albania, and Somalia.

How important are such recent developments? In particular, do they make any important difference in how the actors on the world scene should deal with international conflicts? Do the tools developed for managing international conflicts under the old world system still apply? Are they best applied in new ways or by new entities? Are there new tools that are more appropriate for the new conditions? How do the old and new tools relate to each other?

This book is devoted to examining these questions. This chapter begins the examination by identifying the major strategies of conflict resolution, old and new, that are relevant in the emerging world system. We use the term *conflict resolution* broadly to refer to efforts to prevent or mitigate violence resulting from intergroup or interstate conflict, as well as efforts to reduce the underlying disagreements. We presume that conflict between social groups is an inevitably recurring fact of life and that the goal of conflict resolution is to keep conflicts channeled within a set of agreed norms that foster peaceful discussion of differences, proscribe violence as a means of settling disputes, and establish rules for the limited kinds of violence that are condoned (e.g., as punishment for violations of codes of criminal conduct).

The new world conditions are validating some past conflict resolution practices that can now be more precisely defined and conceptualized and are bringing to prominence some techniques that had not been taken very seriously by diplomatic practitioners in the recent past. We consider the implications of these new developments for the practice of conflict resolution. What knowledge base can conflict resolution practitioners rely on in a world in which their accumulated experience may no longer fully apply? What can the careful examination of historical experience and other sources of insight offer them? We identify the ways in which a careful and judicious examination of empirical evidence can be of use to conflict resolution practitioners and the limitations of generalizations from past experience. Finally, we introduce the rest of the book, in which contributors address the above questions in the general case and in the context of a set of conflict resolution techniques that are likely to be important in the coming years.

TRADITIONAL AND EMERGING STRATEGIES FOR INTERNATIONAL CONFLICT RESOLUTION

The major practices of international conflict management during the Cold War period—the practices of traditional diplomacy—reflected the state system dominant in world politics for centuries. It made sense to treat international conflict as occurring between nation states that acted in a unitary fashion on the basis of stable and discrete national interests rooted in geopolitics, natural resources, and other enduring features of countries. If the behavior of states was dictated by such interests, it followed that conflict between states reflected conflicting interests. Such conflicts were often perceived as zero sum: the more one state gained, the more its adversary lost.

In the world of national interests the chief methods of international conflict management were the traditional diplomatic, military, and economic means of influence, up to and including the threat or use of force. These tools of *power politics*—the same tools that states used to engage in international conflict—were the main ones employed in efforts to address conflict.[2] Thus, states or coalitions of states tried to prevent or mitigate violence by using threats of armed force (deterrence, coercive diplomacy, defensive alliances such as NATO); economic sanctions and other tangible nonmilitary threats and punishments, such as the withdrawal of foreign aid; and direct military force to establish demilitarized zones. States were also sensitive to the delicate balance of nuclear power that could be jeopardized by this kind of coercive diplomacy. For this reason, in particular, they sought security regimes (see Jervis, 1983) that provided norms devised to reduce the risks of escalation. The implicit understandings gained through an extended arms control negotiation process served to reduce the chances of superpower military confrontations during this period.

Negotiation in the world of national interests meant balancing or trading the competing interests of states against one another or finding common interests that could be the basis for agreement even in the face of other conflicting interests. A search for common interests was characteristic of Cold War-era negotiations aimed at preventing military confrontations between the United States and the Soviet Union. For example, the negotiations to end the Cuban missile crisis and to develop confidence-building measures for avoiding accidental nuclear war were based on the common interest in reducing the risk of confrontations that might escalate to nuclear warfare. Such negotiations could proceed because it was possible to identify shared interests that cut across or partially overrode the conflicting ones.[3]

The traditional diplomatic strategies of influence were refined and elaborated greatly during the Cold War period. They continue to be relevant in the post-Cold War world, although their application is sometimes a bit different now (see Chapters 3 through 6). In deploying and threatening force to address and possibly resolve conflicts, there has been increased emphasis during the post-Cold War period on multilateral action (e.g., NATO intervention in Kosovo; the alliance that reversed the Iraqi invasion of Kuwait). States have increasingly looked to regional international organizations to advance conflict resolution goals, especially where unilateral state action might create new kinds of conflict and where influential nations within regions see merit in strengthening their regions' institutions. Thus, for example, the Conference on Security and Cooperation in Europe (CSCE), begun in the 1970s, matured in the 1990s into a formal organization—the Organization for Security and Cooperation in Europe (OSCE)—that has intervened in various ways in conflicts across a broad region, although not by force (see Chapter 14).

Military organizations are now increasingly being used in new ways and for new conflict resolution purposes. Armed force is infrequently used in direct interventions, even in Europe, where regional organizations are particularly strong (exceptions are the NATO air campaign in Bosnia and the Russian interventions in Chechnya and Tajikistan). Peace-keeping missions still sometimes physically separate adversaries to prevent further violence, but they also provide humanitarian relief, resettle refugees, and rebuild infrastructure.

Another new development is that states and associations of states are no longer the only actors that can use techniques of influence like those of traditional diplomacy. For example, in the 1980s, even before the end of the Cold War, transnational corporations, pressured by negative publicity about their investments, and even local governments used their economic power to exert pressure against apartheid in South Africa. Small peace-oriented nongovernmental organizations (NGOs) can sometimes threaten states' interests, for example, by threatening prospects for international assistance with a bad human rights report or deciding to leave a country because humanitarian relief efforts are being thwarted.

A striking development since the end of the Cold War has been the emergence from relative obscurity of three previously underutilized strategies for international conflict resolution. These strategies all deviate from the zero-sum logic of international conflict as a confrontation of interests (see Table 1.1). The observation that these strategies are now more widely used is not meant to imply that they are always used effectively. Also, the strategies are often used together, and sometimes the distinctions among them may be blurred. One strategy may be called *conflict transformation*. This is the effort to reach accommodation between parties in conflict through interactive processes that lead to reconciling tensions, redefining interests, or finding common ground. This strategy departs radically from the logic of enduring national interests by making two related presumptions: that interests and conflicts of interest are to some degree socially constructed and malleable, and that it is possible for groups to redefine their interests to reduce intergroup tension and suspicion and to make peaceful settlements more possible. Certain intergroup conflicts, particularly those associated with the politics of identity, are seen as having significant perceptual and emotional elements that can be transformed by carefully organized intergroup processes so as to allow reconciliation and the recognition of new possibilities for solution.

TABLE 1.1 Strategies and Tools for Conflict Resolution

Strategy	Tools that Feature the Strategy
Power politics	Threats of force
	Defensive alliances
	Economic sanctions
	Bargaining as a tradeoff of interests
	Power mediation
Conflict transformation	Problem-solving workshops
	Alternative dispute resolution
	Reconciliation by truth commissions
Structural prevention	Electoral system design
	Autonomy
	Legal guarantees of free speech and association
	Civilian control of military organizations
Normative change	OSCE invocation of human rights norms

NOTE: These strategies and tools are often used in combination; moreover, the conceptual distinctions among them are sometimes blurred in use.

The conflict transformation approach is seen in its purest form in a set of techniques pioneered in the 1960s by academics and NGOs under such names as interactive conflict resolution, citizen diplomacy, and problem-solving workshops (e.g., Fisher, 1997; Saunders, 1999; also see Chapters 7 and 8). This approach features facilitated meetings at which members of groups in conflict seek to understand each other's positions and world views in order to create an atmosphere more conducive to the peaceful resolution of disputes. The intent is that over the course of the meetings the participants will come to reinterpret the relationship between their groups and the possible futures of that relationship and that this change in the perceptions of a small number of individuals will lead either directly (through concrete peace proposals) or indirectly (e.g., through the rise to power of people who accept new ideas) to a more peaceful future for the groups. In recent years, conflict transformation strategies have also been promoted by NGOs that are spreading ideas such as alternative dispute resolution to emerging democracies in Eastern Europe and elsewhere. The so-called truth commissions in South Africa and some Latin American countries use a strategy of conflict transformation when they work to construct a shared understanding of history that can be a basis for emotional reconciliation, tension reduction, and the creation of a more cooperative political climate (see Chapter 9).

A second previously underutilized strategy for conflict resolution is sometimes called *structural prevention* to distinguish it from "operational prevention," which involves dealing with immediate crises likely to erupt quickly into deadly violence.[4] Structural prevention involves creating organizations or institutionalized systems of laws and rules that establish and strengthen nonviolent channels for adjudicating intergroup disputes, accommodating conflicting interests, and transforming conflicts by finding common ground.

Structural prevention typically focuses on the problems of culturally divided states, especially those with weak democratic traditions, deep ethnic divisions, and histories of collective violence perpetrated by one group against another or by past governments against civilian populations. Various tools are available for structural prevention, including institutions for transitional justice, truth telling, and reconciliation (Chapter 9); electoral and constitutional design (see Chapter 11); autonomy arrangements within federal governance structures (Chapter 12); laws and policies to accommodate linguistic and religious differences (Chapter 13); training for law enforcement officials in following the rule of law; institutions assuring civilian control of military organizations; and the development and support of institutions of civil society. Such institutions, including a free and pluralistic press, a set of NGOs dedicated to their members' common and peaceful purposes, organizations for alternative dispute resolution, and the like, serve in part as arenas for the integrative negotiation of differences.

The third strategy is *normative change*, defined as developing and institutionalizing formal principles and informal expectations that are intended to create a new context for the management of conflict. Norms may also define responsibilities for states to prevent violent conflict. Although norms were established to manage conflict between states during the Cold War, a notable feature of the post-Cold War period is the effort to use international norms to regulate or prevent conflict within states.

In previous eras the principle of noninterference in the internal affairs of sovereign states provided that sovereigns had license to control conflicts within their borders, free from outside influence. Although this norm was often breached by great powers acting in their own national interest within their spheres of influence, it was rarely overturned in favor of universal principles that held all states responsible to common standards. This situation began to change in the later decades of the Cold War, when norms such as human rights, democratic control, and the self-determination of peoples were increasingly invoked against states that abused their citizens. In Europe the Helsinki Final Act of 1975 was an historic watershed in this regard, permitting oversight by the 35 signatories of human rights conditions in each of their territories. Efforts like those of the Helsinki Watch groups in the former Soviet bloc, the disinvestment movement against apartheid, the democracy movement, and the indigenous peoples' movements in the Americas showed the potential of universal norms to galvanize world opinion for conflict resolution.

Of course, we are a long way from a world in which what is good for humanity consistently outweighs the prerogatives of states. Nevertheless, there are signs that universal norms, many of which are stated in the United Nations Charter and other international documents, are becoming embodied in transnational institutions that can exert influence on states. For example, human rights norms have, through the operations of the CSCE and OSCE, provided increasing leverage for the international community to curb organized state violence against minority groups. Continuing dialogue about the tension in international law between the norm of noninterference on the one hand and those of human rights and self-determination of peoples on the other may be leading toward a new international consensus on how to provide for the rights of minorities.[5] Within the OSCE, for example, norms seem to be emerging that under certain conditions favor working out autonomy arrangements in preference to secession or submergence of minorities within unitary state structures (see Chapter 14). And the growing international acceptance of norms of democratic decision making are making it more legitimate for states, international donors, and NGOs to support structural prevention institutions in fragile states and to act against the perpetrators of coups d'état.

It is too soon to be sure that the increased prominence of these new strategies of international conflict resolution is an enduring feature of a new world system. However, it seems likely that many of the forces that have made these strategies more attractive are themselves enduring. If intrastate conflicts continue to pose serious threats to global security, if nonstate interests remain important, and if global integration makes foreign policy increasingly difficult to organize exclusively around coherent and unitary notions of national interest, conflict resolution is likely to rely more than in the past on the transnational activities of nonstate actors and on techniques that do not depend on traditional definitions of national interest. Nation states are likely to remain important actors in international relations for some time to come, however, and the possibility of violent interstate conflict remains a serious concern. But recent events presage a more complex multidimensional arena of international conflict in which both state interests and nonstate actors are important parts of the mix.

Under such conditions some recent trends are likely to stabilize. For example, NGOs with humanitarian and conflict resolution missions have a good chance to remain prominent players in world politics. Their comparative advantage lies in using conflict resolution tools that do not depend directly on power politics. Although NGOs can facilitate negotiations that trade off interests, states are probably better positioned to do this. NGOs are uniquely able to contribute by deploying the emerging tools of conflict resolution, as they have increasingly done in recent years. They have promoted conflict transformation by sponsoring interactive conflict resolution activities (see Chapters 7 and 8), providing training in informal dispute resolution techniques, and supporting various institutions of civil society that participate in democratic debate. They have contributed to structural prevention by advising on constitutional design and the rule of law, monitoring elections, and delivering information on other countries' experiences with particular structural prevention techniques (e.g., Chapter 11, written by two staff members of the International Institute for Democracy and Electoral Assistance, summarizes knowledge on some constitutional design issues). The roles for NGOs in structural prevention are sometimes more prominent than the roles for states. And they have contributed to the development and enforcement of new international norms by promoting and monitoring conditions of human rights, treatment of minorities, and democratic governance (e.g., free and fair elections) and by arguing for international organizations to use their resources and influence to hold states to universal norms.

The recently increased acceptance of NGOs in international conflict resolution, as evidenced by their increasing use as conduits for international aid, is attributable in considerable part to their increasing political clout within democratic systems as well as to the potential that diplomats see in the emerging techniques of conflict resolution and to the advantages NGOs have in using those techniques. Their continued importance will depend not only on their usefulness to diplomats in the aid-donor states but also on their acceptance by the parties to the conflicts they want to resolve. Thus, to be effective, these NGOs must be accepted by their potential clients as democratic, accountable, and true to the humanistic principles they espouse. They must also find ways to ensure that their activities do not make conflicts worse (see Chapter 10).

WHAT WORKS IN A CHANGED WORLD?

If the post-Cold War world is qualitatively different from what came before, does it follow that what practitioners know about conflict resolution is no longer reliable? A provisional answer comes from the results of a previous investigation by a National Research Council committee that reviewed the state of knowledge relevant to preventing major international conflict, including nuclear war. Between 1985 and 1987 this group commissioned 14 comprehensive review articles covering major areas of knowledge about international conflict (National Research Council, 1989, 1991, 1993). By the time the reviews were published, the Cold War was over and it seemed timely to reexamine the reviewers' conclusions on the basis of the very surprising international events of the period around 1989. Stern and Druckman (1995) identified 104 propositions that the authors of the reviews judged to be supported by the evidence available at the time. Each proposition was coded in terms of how well it stood up against a list of five political surprises of the period.[6]

The Stern-Druckman investigation reached conclusions that may also apply to knowledge about conflict resolution techniques. First, the great majority of the propositions (about 80) were not tested by the surprising events. Thus, these conclusions from historical experience remained as well supported as before. Second, of the propositions that were tested by events, most were supported by the events that occurred. This knowledge was also unchanged by the shift in the world system. Third, however, some of the most critical events of 1989 were not addressed by any of the propositions. Available knowledge about the international system had virtually nothing to say about the conditions under which an international epidemic of democratization would break out, or a great empire would peacefully liquidate itself, or a new historical era would dawn without a great-power war. So, although much of what passed as knowledge before 1989 was still reliable knowledge after that time, much of what in retrospect was important to understand about 1989 had never been seriously analyzed by the community of specialists. The main lessons of the end of the Cold War were not that previous knowledge was wrong but that there was no knowledge about some of the most important phenomena of the new era.

The results of that analysis suggest that, although it makes sense to look carefully and critically at what is known about the traditional strategies and tools of conflict resolution that have received considerable attention from scholars and practitioners, it is especially important to examine what is known about less familiar strategies and tools that received limited attention in the past and that may be of major importance under the new conditions. This book does not attempt to comprehensively review knowledge about the effectiveness of the conflict resolution techniques based mainly on the influence of tools of traditional diplomacy. Instead, the contributors were asked to examine only a few of these techniques and only in some areas of their application: threats of force by the United States (Chapter 3), economic sanctions (Chapter 4), methods for controlling "spoilers" in peace processes (Chapter 5), and the issues of timing and ripeness in negotiation and mediation (Chapter 6). Generally, what the contributors find is that the new conditions in the world have not invalidated past knowledge about how and under what conditions these techniques work. However, the new conditions do call for some modification and refinement of past knowledge and suggest that the old tools sometimes need to be thought of and used in new ways. Each of the above chapters includes a summary of the state of knowledge about the conditions favoring effective use of the techniques it examines.

Much closer attention is paid to the emerging strategies of conflict resolution and to the techniques that embody them, about which much less has been written. For most of the conflict resolution techniques that involve conflict transformation, structural prevention, and normative change, there is no systematic body of past knowledge from the previous era that is directly relevant to current needs.[7] Practitioners' experience in implementing these techniques has not been seriously applied to post-Cold War conditions, and international relations scholarship did not pay much attention to them in the past. Therefore, careful examination of what is known about the effectiveness of these techniques is particularly needed at this time.

Fortunately, these techniques, though underutilized, are not new. Each has a history that may hold lessons for conflict resolution in today's divided states. For example, one type of structural prevention strategy is to offer autonomy—special status and governance rights—for certain culturally identified subunits in a unitary or federal state. There is a fairly long history of happy and unhappy examples of autonomy that may hold valuable lessons for the current era. But it is only very recently that scholars have looked to cases like Scotland, Puerto Rico, the Soviet republics and autonomous regions, Catalonia, Greenland, the Native American reservations of the United States and Canada, the French overseas territories and departments, and the like to find lessons that might be informative in places like Chechnya, Bosnia, and Hong Kong (see Chapter 12). In the past, when such structural arrangements were the subject of scholarly attention, it usually came from specialists in domestic politics (e.g., comparative researchers on federalism) or international law, not international relations scholars, so the questions have been framed differently and the answers discussed in a community that rarely interacts with specialists in international conflict resolution.

The same situation holds for constitutional design. The world is full of constitutions and electoral systems, and their consequences for conflict management in their home countries are available for historical examination. However, until recently, relatively little systematic attention was paid to the question of how electoral system design shapes the course of conflict in a society (see Chapter 11 for a review and analysis of the evidence).

This book gives detailed attention to several nontraditional conflict resolution techniques in order to shed light on the potential for using techniques that employ the strategies of conflict transformation, structural prevention, and normative change as part of the toolbox of international conflict resolution. It devotes chapters to evaluating the effects on conflict of interactive conflict resolution workshops (Chapters 7 and 8), truth commissions (Chapter 9), "engineered" electoral systems (Chapter 11), autonomy arrangements (Chapter 12), language policy within states (Chapter 13), and the various conflict resolution activities of the OSCE (Chapter 14) and humanitarian NGOs (Chapter 10). The intent is to draw out lessons—what George (1993) calls generic knowledge—about the conditions under which each type of intervention in fact reduces the likelihood of violent conflict and about the processes that lead to such outcomes.

Our primary intent in conducting this exercise is to provide useful input to the decisions of conflict resolution practitioners—decision makers in national governments, international organizations, and NGOs—who must consider a wider-than-ever panoply of policy options, some of which they have not seriously considered before. The contributors to this volume were asked to summarize available knowledge with an eye to informing these decisions. We also hope, of course, to advance knowledge among specialists about the functioning and effectiveness of the various techniques of international conflict resolution. But the rationale for developing this knowledge is more than the curiosity of science. It is also to help in efforts to reduce both organized and nonorganized violence in the world.

THE CHALLENGE OF DEVELOPING USABLE KNOWLEDGE

Conflict resolution practitioners need many kinds of knowledge to achieve their objectives. Some essential knowledge is highly situation specific and can come only from examining features of particular conflict situations in the present—the political forces currently affecting the parties in conflict, the personalities of the leaders, the contested terrain or resources, and so forth. Other kinds of essential knowledge apply across situations. They tell what to expect in certain kinds of conflicts or with certain kinds of parties, leaders, or contested resources. These kinds of knowledge are generic, that is, cross-situational, and therefore subject to improvement by systematic examination of the past.[8]

Types of Usable Knowledge

The chapters in this book are organized around problems in conflict resolution and techniques or classes of techniques for addressing them. Problems are situations encountered repeatedly, though in different contexts, in the conduct of the practice of diplomacy or conflict resolution, such as deterring aggression, mediating disputes, managing crises, achieving cooperation among allies, and so forth. Practitioners typically consider several specific policy instruments and strategies for dealing with each of these generic problems. In this process they can benefit from several types of knowledge about them.

First, *general conceptual models* identify the critical variables for dealing effectively with the phenomenon in question and the general logic associated with successful use of strategies or techniques to address a type of problem. For example, deterrence theory in its classical form (e.g., Schelling, 1960; George and Smoke, 1974) provides a conceptual model of a strategy of conflict management. It presumes that the target of a deterrent threat is rational and thus, if well informed, can make a reasonably accurate calculation of the costs and risks associated with each possible response to the threat, and it prescribes the characteristics of threats that are effective with rational actors. A conceptual model is the starting point for constructing a strategy or response for dealing with a particular conflict situation.

Second, practitioners need *conditional generalizations* about what favors the success of specific strategies they might use. This kind of knowledge normally takes the form of statements of association—that a strategy is effective under certain conditions but not others. Although conditional generalizations are not sufficient to determine which action to take, they are useful for diagnostic purposes. A practitioner can examine a situation to see whether favorable conditions exist or can be created for using a particular conflict resolution technique. Good conditional generalizations enable a practitioner to increase the chances of making the right choice about whether and when to use a technique.

Third, practitioners need *knowledge about causal processes and mechanisms* that link the use of each strategy to its outcomes. For example, one indication that an electoral system in a culturally divided society is channeling conflict in nonviolent directions is that each major party is running candidates from several ethnic groups. When party conflicts are no longer reflections of raw ethnic conflict, future political conflicts are likely to be less highly charged. Knowledge about such mechanisms is useful for monitoring the progress of a conflict resolution effort and for deciding whether additional efforts should be made to support previous ones.

Fourth, in order to craft an appropriate strategy for a situation, practitioners need a correct *general understanding of the actors* whose behavior the strategy is designed to influence.[9] Policy specialists and academic scholars agree on this fundamental point: to act effectively in the international arena it is necessary to see events—and, indeed, assess one's own behavior—from the perspective of the others acting in the situation. Only by doing so can a practitioner diagnose a developing situation accurately and select appropriate ways of communicating with and influencing others. Faulty images of others are a source of major misperceptions and miscalculations that have often led to major errors in policy, avoidable catastrophes, and missed opportunities. Area specialists in academia can make useful, indeed indispensable, contributions to developing and making available such knowledge, as can diplomats and other individuals on the scene of a conflict who have personal knowledge about the major actors.

All of these types of knowledge are generic in that they apply across specific situations. It is important to emphasize, however, that although such knowledge is useful, even indispensable to practice, a conflict resolution practitioner also needs accurate situation-specific knowledge in order to act effectively. Skilled practitioners use their judgment to combine generic and specific knowledge in order to act in what are always unique decision situations.

Developing Knowledge

The contributors to this volume have attempted to develop the first three kinds of knowledge described above: general conceptual models of conflict situations, knowledge about the conditions favoring the success of particular conflict resolution techniques, and knowledge about the causal processes that lead them to succeed or fail. In doing this they have had to grapple with other important but difficult issues: defining success for a technique of conflict resolution, setting reasonable expectations and time lines for evaluating success, identifying indicators of success, and deciding how to make general inferences when historical evidence is imperfect and when one can never know what the outcome would have been if practitioners had acted differently or if events beyond their control had played out differently.

Each contributor to this volume was asked to carefully define a technique or concept of conflict resolution and to evaluate the available historical and other evidence regarding the conditions for its success. In Chapter 2, Stern and Druckman discuss the challenges of making such evaluations. They identify the difficulties of making valid inferences about efforts to change the course of history and discuss strategies by which knowledge can be developed in the face of these challenges. The other contributors tried to meet the challenges, each by examining a particular technique, concept, institution, or problem. They tried to be aware of the limitations involved in using historical evidence to derive causal inferences about relationships between concepts or variables and tried to look dispassionately at historical experience and other sources of insight in order to evaluate the state of knowledge and, if possible, develop conclusions about "what works" in conflict resolution.

Most of the contributors used some form of structured case comparison to do their work.[10] They defined the technique or concept they studied, identified a number of indicators of success and factors that may affect the likelihood of success, and then examined the available historical evidence to identify associations of conditions and outcomes (contingent generalizations) and causal mechanisms that might lead to those outcomes. The results of their efforts have been sets of propositions or empirically based hypotheses about the conditions and mechanisms by which particular efforts at international conflict resolution yield results that can be considered successful.

Uses of Generic Knowledge

It is our hope and expectation that the knowledge developed by the contributors will be of practical value. We do not expect that it will be prescriptive in the sense of providing a standard set of procedures that tell practitioners what to do in particular situations. However, it is intended to be useful to practitioners when they combine it with specific knowledge about what kind of situation is at hand. Generic knowledge also has diagnostic value for practitioners because it describes the characteristics to look for in situations that make a difference in terms of which actions will be effective. After a practitioner has accurately diagnosed a situation, knowledge about what works in which situations comes more strongly into play.

However, even with the perfect diagnosis of a situation, generic knowledge cannot be expected to provide prescriptions for action, for several reasons. First, this kind of knowledge will never be solidly established in the fashion of a law of physics. For one thing, human actors can defy the laws said to govern their own behavior; for another, world conditions continually change in ways that may invalidate conclusions from past experience. Second, the many tradeoffs in any decision situation make general knowledge an imperfect guide to action. Sometimes, all the aspects of success cannot be achieved at once and choices must be made. Sometimes, conflict resolution outcomes are not the only ones relevant to practitioners, who must then weigh those outcomes against other desired outcomes (e.g., for government officials, continued domestic support for the government).

Despite such limitations, we believe the kinds of knowledge developed in this volume will prove useful to conflict resolution practitioners. They can help practitioners identify options for action they might not otherwise have considered, think through the implications of each course of action, and identify ways of checking to see if actions, once taken, remain on track. However, one must recognize that practitioners may resist accepting conclusions developed by systematic analysis. Many practitioners mistrust such conclusions and prefer to trust their own experiential knowledge and that developed by other practitioners. Anticipating this possibility, we have involved current or former practitioners in discussion about each of the studies presented in Chapters 3 through 14 from the earliest phases and in the review of the chapters. We hope that this sort of interaction between researchers and practitioners will, over time, improve mutual respect for and understanding of the kinds of knowledge that direct experience and systematic analysis taken together can provide. Bridging the gap between scholarship and practice remains an overriding challenge for international conflict resolution (George, 1993).

We believe this volume will also be of value for scholars of international relations and conflict resolution. For them it will collect useful knowledge, raise important issues for the future development of knowledge, and generate a variety of propositions to examine and hypotheses to test in future research in this area.

ABOUT THE STUDIES

The remainder of this book consists of 13 studies, one methodological and 12 substantive, concerned with particular techniques of conflict resolution. In Chapter 2, Paul Stern and Daniel Druckman set the context for the substantive studies by discussing the general problem of making and validating inferences about international conflict resolution techniques. They identify the inherent difficulties of this task and show how progress can be made in the face of these obstacles. They conclude that a systematic approach based on social scientific concepts and techniques can produce useful generalizations about which techniques work under which conditions and thus raise the level of understanding available to conflict resolution practitioners.

The main challenges of evaluation defined in Chapter 2 concern developing analytical concepts, selecting cases for analysis, measuring outcomes and the factors affecting them, and making inferences about cause and effect. The conceptual challenges include defining and classifying interventions, defining success, and setting reasonable expectations for the effects of an intervention. The problems of case selection include delineating the relevant universe of cases and drawing a representative sample of them—for instance, the universe of known cases may not be representative of all actual cases. Measurement problems include taking into account events that cannot be observed, such as closed negotiations or unpublicized mediation efforts. Key inference problems are raised by the lack of adequate comparison situations and the need to compare actual events with imagined, or counterfactual, ones; the need to take into account the effects of other events that occur at the same time as the intervention; the need to consider indirect effects of the interventions; and the need to sort out the overlapping and conflicting effects of the multiple efforts that are often made to resolve a conflict.

The authors then consider ways of meeting these challenges. With regard to the conceptual challenges, they emphasize the importance of clear definitions and taxonomies of intervention types and of conceptual frameworks that link concepts together and generate hypotheses about the conditions under which interventions have particular consequences over a short and longer span of time. With regard to sampling, suggestions are made to carefully develop purposive sampling frames guided by theory as an alternative to the sort of random sampling that only has meaning in the context of a specified universe of cases. On measurement, ways are presented to deal with incomplete information, improve reliability, and construct appropriate indicators of various outcomes, rather than attempting to measure "success" as a unitary variable. The chapter discusses the strengths and weaknesses of the main available systematic methods of making inferences: experiments (including quasi-experiments) and simulations, multivariate analysis, and enhanced case study methods such as the approach of structured and focused case comparison.

The authors reach three important conclusions. First, they conclude that theory development, including taxonomies and hypotheses about causes, outcomes, contingencies, and causal mechanisms, is critically needed to advance knowledge about what works in international conflict resolution. Second, a dialogue between theory and experience, with progress in each leading to refinements in the other, is the best route to improved understanding. Third, a strategy using multiple sources of data and methods of analysis, referred to as "triangulation," is preferred for increasing confidence in evaluative conclusions.

Many of the substantive studies in Chapters 3 through 14 take up the challenges defined in Chapter 2, making new contributions to knowledge by clarifying concepts; defining types of interventions; stating explicit hypotheses about causes, effects, and causal mechanisms; defining outcome indicators; and so forth. In this respect these chapters may be previews of the directions that the field is likely to take during the first decade of the new millennium.

Below, we briefly summarize the topics and findings of the 12 substantive studies in this book. The summaries are not intended to substitute for the studies; rather, they are intended as a guide to the reader. We group the summaries under the four strategies of conflict resolution previously identified: traditional diplomacy and power politics, conflict transformation, structural prevention, and normative change. This classification is artificial in some cases because some conflict resolution approaches employ more than one of these strategies. For example, truth commissions may promote conflict transformation while also recommending structural prevention measures. These complexities are mentioned below and are more evident in the chapters that follow.

Traditional Diplomacy and Power Politics

Chapters 3 through 6 assess conflict resolution techniques strongly rooted in traditional diplomacy. Chapter 3, for example, focuses on the use and threat of force. It examines the limited ability of the United States, despite its military dominance in the post-Cold War era, to achieve diplomatic objectives through threats of force and limited (exemplary) uses of force. Barry Blechman and Tamara Cofman Wittes explain this paradox of power by identifying a number of conditions that, although neither necessary or sufficient for the success of a U.S. threat, favor the effectiveness of a threat when present.

The authors group these "enabling conditions" into two broad categories: those that make a threat sufficiently credible and those that make it sufficiently potent to overcome the reluctance of foreign leaders to comply with the demand. They conclude that the credibility and the potency of a threat together shape the targeted leaders' evaluation of the likely costs of complying or not complying.

Blechman and Wittes examine eight major post-Cold War cases: Panama (1989-1990), Iraq (1990-1996), Somalia (1992-1995), Macedonia (1992-1996), Bosnia (1992-1996), Haiti (1994-1996), Korea (1994-1996), and Taiwan (1996). To a large extent they find that the enabling conditions were present in those cases in which U.S. threats of force secured compliance with the demands and absent in cases where the threats proved ineffectual. The authors go beyond this correlation to suggest how the enabling conditions operated to produce the outcomes in the eight cases.

The authors draw three noteworthy conclusions from their case analyses. First is the critical importance of how much is demanded of the target. The greater the demand made, the greater the reluctance to comply. Thus, in six of seven cases of success the demand made was a relatively modest one—compliance was relatively easy. A second finding was that coupling threats with positive incentives for compliance increased success. Positive incentives were employed in six of seven success cases. A third important lesson concerned the degree of public support for the policy in the United States. Potent threats are harder to sustain because they imply greater risks, triggering the U.S. public's aversion to suffering combat casualties. This aversion, seen as a legacy of the Vietnam War, constrains American presidents from making threats that are sufficiently credible and potent to achieve ambitious objectives. The authors' review of available evidence reveals that Bosnian Serb leaders, Haitian paramilitary leaders, Saddam Hussein, and the Somali warlord Muhammad Farah Aideed all believed they would be able to force a U.S. retreat by inflicting a relatively small number of casualties on U.S. forces. U.S. officials often have great difficulty breaking through such preconceptions of American weakness. The authors conclude that, as long as this situation continues, the targets of U.S. threats are likely to perceive them as signs of weakness rather than determination and, as a result, are likely to continue to be willing to withstand these threats until their perceptions are changed by strong military action.

The findings of this study suggest these possible implications for U.S. policy: (1) pick fights carefully, making demands that are not likely to be perceived as difficult to meet; (2) seek to demilitarize U.S. policy somewhat, relying to a greater extent on skillful diplomacy and positive incentives, backed in most cases by threats of force; and (3) when nonmilitary instruments of policy seem likely to be ineffectual but the president still perceives the situation to require action, act decisively. In this situation the authors suggest that U.S. officials make demands clear and urgent, make demonstration of military power incontrovertible, and make the threat sufficiently credible and potent to persuade the adversary to accept the demands.

In Chapter 4, Bruce Jentleson evaluates the success or failure of efforts to achieve diplomatic objectives by the use of economic sanctions. The chapter clarifies several conceptual and methodological issues and identifies lessons drawn from a comprehensive assessment of experience with economic sanctions.

Jentleson discusses the use of sanctions both for deterrence and for coercing states to reverse past actions ("sanctions for conflict resolution"). His analysis reinforces the findings of previous writers on deterrence and coercive diplomacy, including Blechman and Wittes in Chapter 3, that the task of deterrence is easier than the task of compellence and that the success of sanctions, either for deterrence or coercive diplomacy, depends on the threat being perceived by the target as sufficiently potent to induce it to accept the demands on it. Again, as in earlier studies, Jentleson finds that the stronger the demand, the more credible and more potent the threat must be to achieve compliance. Jentleson concludes that the effectiveness of sanctions depends on "proportionality"—that is, the more far reaching the demand made on the target, the less likely sanctions are to be effective.

Jentleson's analytical framework stresses two main sets of factors, the political economy of relations among the key actors and the design of the strategy by which sanctions are imposed. The key aspects of political economy are the extent of multilateral cooperation and the problem of alternative trade partners, the target state's economic and political capability to defend against sanctions, and the sender state's ability to limit its own domestic constraints. The crucial components of strategy design are the definition of objectives, the targeting strategy, measures for sanctions enforcement, and the broader policy of which sanctions are a part.

Proceeding from this framework, Jentleson assesses whether and how the post-Cold War environment has affected the efficacy of sanctions. The main pattern he identifies is "a paradoxical one of greater target state vulnerability to the potential coercive potency of sanctions on the one hand but more problematic political viability on the other." He traces this "vulnerability-viability paradox" to three major systemic changes—the end of Cold War bipolarity, economic globalization, and greater global democratization. These trends increase vulnerability because of reduced geopolitical incentives for great powers to protect target states against other powers, the greater economic openness of virtually all economies, and increased political openings for target state domestic elites hurt by sanctions to serve as "transmission belts" and pressure their governments for policy change. At the same time, the "political viability" of sanctions has become more problematic in several respects: (1) international coalitions in support of sanctions are harder to build in some cases than before; (2) the economic impact of sanctions on nontarget citizens in target states and on nearby countries now can raise tough ethical issues and humanitarian concerns; and (3) domestic politics in the sending state can create deep divisions as regards the state's sanctions policies. We thus have the dilemma, as Jentleson states it, that "in some respects sanctions have more potential efficacy than before. In other respects it is more problematic to tap that efficacy."

Given this dilemma, Jentleson advocates a policy of "sanctions realism," which he describes in detail as "less frequent but more concerted use of sanctions." He places great emphasis on the importance of multilateral cooperation, which he finds much more important for effective sanctions in the post-Cold War era than before. Consequently, unilateral U.S. sanctions are less effective than they were during the Cold War era. The threat of serious Western collective action in pursuing sanctions is vital to the sanctions being sufficiently credible and formidable to elicit compliance. Jentleson advocates that U.S. policy makers be selective in pushing allies for joint action on sanctions in return for eliciting sanctions cooperation on issues on which fundamental shared interests exist, such as nonproliferation of weapons of mass destruction, deterrence of interstate aggression, and prevention of terrorism. U.S. leaders should recognize that allied cooperation is least likely when it pursues sanctions that are largely externalizations of U.S. domestic politics. With regard to sanctions strategy, Jentleson emphasizes the greater potential efficacy of comprehensive and decisive sanctions over partial and incremental ones and the need to take enforcement more seriously, both to reduce leaks in sanctions and to buttress credibility. He also cautions strongly against turning to sanctions as a "default option" and stresses the need to integrate them into a well-formulated influence strategy that may include other coercive measures as well as positive incentives.

In Chapter 5, Stephen Stedman addresses the problem of dealing with "spoilers" in peace processes—local actors who attempt to disrupt efforts to terminate conflicts. Stedman examined the activities of spoilers in several recent conflicts and drew the lesson that it is important to distinguish between different types of spoilers. As noted above, it is important for policy makers in dealing with conflict situations to have a correct image of the adversary. Stedman presents an analysis of types of spoilers that can be used to classify spoilers and judge how best to interact with them in order to advance the peace processes they may try to derail. His typology focuses on important differences in the motives of spoilers and in their objectives; classifies spoilers as "limited," "greedy," or "total"; identifies three strategies for managing spoilers (withdrawal, a "departing-train" strategy involving a threat to move the peace process forward without involving the spoiler, and the use of inducements to address a spoiler's grievances); and evaluates these strategies in terms of their potential for success with different types of spoilers.

Stedman finds that a correct classification of the type of spoiler is critical for choosing the most effective strategy for neutralizing the spoiler's effort to disrupt a peace process. He provides practitioners with a framework that can assist them in classifying future spoilers and with propositions that lead to advice on how to proceed once the spoiler has been correctly classified. Thus, the chapter requires the practitioner to use actor-specific knowledge to classify the spoiler; with that task done, Stedman's analysis offers recommendations about the strategy to follow in dealing with a spoiler. Stedman also discusses the difficulty and uncertainty involved in correctly classifying spoilers.

In Chapter 6, I. William Zartman provides a major clarification and extension of earlier writings on the concept of "ripeness" and its role in bringing the parties to a conflict into serious negotiations. Unlike the other substantive chapters in this book, Zartman's is primarily an elaboration of a theory as the basis for an empirical analysis of the effectiveness of a conflict resolution technique. Ripeness focuses attention on the timing rather than the substance of proposals for conflict settlement. Zartman maintains that more attention is needed to the timing question because those who focus on substantive aspects of negotiation have generally ignored or downplayed timing. Zartman reemphasizes that ripeness and the related notion of the mutually hurting stalemate are perceptual phenomena, necessary but not sufficient for the opening of productive negotiations. Not all ripe moments are seized, and some kinds of negotiations can take place in the absence of ripeness. In addition to a perceived stalemate, a perceived possibility of a way out through negotiation or mediation is also necessary for productive negotiations to begin.

Zartman summarizes references to ripeness in accounts by scholars and diplomatic practitioners and reviews the literature on the ripeness concept, presenting and analyzing a series of propositions about timing and ripeness. He notes the important refinements of the ripeness concept by a number of authors, including Stephen Stedman, who took the concept "beyond a single perception into the complexity of [the] internal dynamics" of each side to a conflict. This refinement expands the concept of the perception of ripeness to include a country's patrons, its military officers, changes in leadership, and domestic rivalries.

Zartman notes a number of problems with the emphasis on the need for ripeness. One is that increased pain may increase resistance rather than reduce it. He postulates that "cultural" differences may explain this variation: some parties to a conflict may act as "true believers" who treat increased pain as a justification for intensified struggle. Zartman says that "in the current era, cases of resisting reactions . . . come particularly from the Middle East." For example, he sees the United States in the Iran hostage crisis as having acted under the logic of the hurting stalemate, exerting increased pressure in the hope that the Iranian leaders would perceive a stalemate and agree to negotiate; Iran, however, saw the U.S. strategy as indicating the opposite of the contrition Iran required as a basis for negotiation. Zartman concludes that negotiations with true believers take longer to come to fruition because ripe moments are harder to find.

Zartman discusses various suggestions for "ripening" conflicts to bring about negotiations as a conflict resolution technique. He emphasizes that, when ripeness exists, practitioners need all their skills to turn it into a successful peacemaking process. Ripeness, when created, only provides an opportunity for substantive knowledge and techniques of negotiation to come into play.

Conflict Transformation

Chapters 7 through 10 discuss conflict resolution techniques that rely heavily on the strategy of conflict transformation. Chapters 7 and 8 focus on unofficial efforts by citizens outside government who use organized processes of dialogue, analysis, and the like to change conflictual relationships. The chapters examine these processes of "interactive conflict resolution" to assess how these "public" peace processes can work together with official processes. Interactive conflict resolution is a well-defined and systematic approach used in small unofficial meetings of members of groups in tension or violent conflict to stimulate their talk together about the problems that divide them and the relationships that underlie these problems. The objective, as Harold Saunders argues in Chapter 7, is different from official processes of conflict resolution. It is primarily to redefine problems and develop new frameworks of interaction. Interactive conflict resolution is especially useful for subjects that are taboo on official agendas and when formal contacts between official representatives are politically impossible. It can help to pave the way for negotiation, address the obstacles to progress, and work in the larger society where peace will be made.

The two chapters approach the same topic from quite different standpoints. Chapter 7 examines it from the standpoint of its practitioners, explaining what interactive conflict resolution activities try to do and providing the experience-based judgments of practitioners about how and why it succeeds or fails. Chapter 8 complements Chapter 7 by examining interactive conflict resolution from an analyst's point of view. It approaches the issue of evaluation theoretically and methodologically with a conceptual analysis of the ways that workshops might transform conflict and a set of hypotheses that can be tested in evaluations of the technique by future analysts.

In Chapter 7, Harold Saunders points to the difficulty of using standard instruments to evaluate public peace processes and sets as the criterion improvement in the practical capacity to make and build peace. He sees processes as successful if they help to define and diagnose the problem, establish a strategic and operational framework, and design a tactical framework or possible course(s) of action. Saunders and his collaborators present six case examples: early experiences with Israelis and Palestinians in the 1980s, meetings of a group of political leaders from opposing parties in Northern Ireland that came together to create a bill of rights, an expanded process in the Middle East, a six-year process in Tajikistan, a series of dialogues in newly independent Estonia, and a program of training workshops in Cyprus.

The experience of 30 years has produced a significant track record for interactive conflict resolution. According to Saunders, the work of citizens outside government in a multilevel peace process is increasingly fruitful as one moves across a spectrum from quasi-official situations—those in which the primary task is to develop analysis of conflict not available to government, provide a channel of communication where none exists, or find a particular solution to a problem in negotiation—to those situations where the main task is to analyze the dynamics of relationships and design ways to work in the body politic to change them.

Saunders finds that the contribution of interactive conflict resolution increases as the capacities of government diminish. Governments, Saunders concludes, desperately need this added tool for peace making and peace building. He concludes that projects that "work" are those that create well-designed opportunities for individuals in conflict to develop the capacity to take responsibility for applying what they have learned in new ways. As their skills increase, their sense of possibility increases. Saunders also concludes that policy makers working to resolve conflict in divided countries can extend the reach of peace making and peace building by consciously seeking ways of bringing both governmental and unofficial work under the same conceptual umbrella. If citizens' groups add a capacity for conflict resolution to the capabilities of governments, the overall ability to make and sustain peace within civil society can be enhanced.

In Chapter 8, Nadim Rouhana examines the major theoretical and methodological issues in analyzing and evaluating processes of interactive conflict resolution. He develops a conceptual framework that links the activities of problem-solving workshops to their microobjectives for the workshop participants and their macrogoals in terms of the larger conflict. Rouhana argues that it is important to develop taxonomies of practice in order to identify which methods work in what types of conflict, at what stage of conflict, and under what conditions. In his view it is necessary to develop programs that provide training in intervention techniques that are explicitly based on theoretical foundations and guided by research findings.

Problem-solving workshops, if they are to achieve their microobjectives, must generate new learning among the participants, who must retain part of that learning when they return to the conflict arena and demonstrate that learning in their political discourse and behavior. Learning can be measured by increased cognitive complexity and humanization in participants' understandings of the adversary and by their ability to generate new options.

Problem-solving workshops that are successful at the macro level tend to be those that create visions of peace before official processes begin, help to overcome obstacles during negotiations, and help to create supportive dynamics in the society that can sustain peaceful relations once formal negotiations have concluded. Rouhana suggests that workshops may contribute through their exploratory function, their innovative function, their capacity to legitimate discussion among adversaries, by accumulating public support over time, by clarifying what can and what cannot be agreed, and by preparing the terrain for political action.

Rouhana examines how the effects of interactive conflict resolution may relate to the dynamics of conflict, proposes ways to conceptualize these effects, and examines how the impact of these processes on the dynamics of conflict can be assessed. He offers three tentative conclusions about how to enhance the effect of interactive conflict resolution workshops on the larger conflict. First, third parties can take on a more active role in increasing the impact of the problem-solving workshop, provided that the role itself is carefully coordinated with participants and is part of the design of the problem-solving workshop. Second, future workshops will have broader societal impact if conceived of as a joint learning opportunity for both participants and third party, on whom equal responsibility rests for transfer of insights into the broader societal context. And third, problem-solving workshops can be used as laboratories for conflict analysis. Understanding of the political needs of each party, their internal dynamics, their limitations and constraints, and the views of the other party of these constraints is important material to transmit to experts, publics, and decision makers.

In Chapter 9, Priscilla Hayner considers official truth seeking—one of the available mechanisms for confronting past crimes of a prior regime or its armed opposition—as a mechanism for resolving and preventing violent conflict. Official truth-seeking efforts are sometimes advocated as a way to heal the wounds of past conflicts—to transform a conflictual atmosphere into one more conducive to peaceful intergroup relations. Hayner notes an irony in this expectation that official truth seeking has come to be seen as a peace-making tool, considering that the process of digging into such sensitive issues as the past crimes of powerful actors can easily lead to further conflict and even to threats of violence. This potential is sometimes seen in the fear felt by victims and witnesses when providing testimony to a truth commission.

The chapter summarizes the experience of over 20 truth commissions and considers three ways they may help with conflict resolution. First, the proposal to establish a truth commission may represent one of the positive components of a peace accord that entices the parties to a conflict (or perhaps one of the parties) to agree to a peace. Nevertheless, the negotiation of a mandate for a truth commission is often very difficult. Whether a truth commission is adopted, and what shape it takes, depends on the perceived interests of the parties, perceptions about whether truth seeking would spark new violence, and whether indigenous mechanisms are available to deal with past abuses. This positive effect of a truth commission happens, when it does, before the commission takes any action. However, the factors that determine whether a truth commission comes into being also affect its mandate, which in turn affects the chances of future violence.

Second, a truth commission may defuse conflicts over the past through reconciliation, that is, by conflict transformation. Hayner identifies several indicators that reconciliation may be occurring (e.g., acceptance of a shared history, reduced conflict about "the past," apologies by perpetrators) and some conditions that affect the likelihood that reconciliation will occur (e.g., the existence of prior social ties between the sides). She also identifies conditions that improve the chances that a truth commission's activities will lead to reconciliation. These include the extent to which the commission reaches out to all victims, provides for their security and psychological support, holds hearings in public, makes efforts to be fair in its process and its report, and invites the participation of all segments of society, including perpetrators.

Third, a truth commission's report may lead to the adoption of reforms to mitigate conflicts and protect rights—that is, truth seeking may resolve conflict through mechanisms of structural prevention. Two classes of reforms are judged relevant for conflict prevention: those that hold those responsible for abuses to account (including legal and institutional reforms) and those that strengthen institutions for democratic conflict management (e.g., by strengthening the judicial system so that conflicts and grievances can be addressed within the formal system of dispute resolution, or increasing political representation of disenfranchised groups). The chapter identifies several conditions conducive to a truth commission's efforts to advance effective structural reform. One is the strength of the commission (its resources, funding, breadth of investigation, etc.). Another is the extent to which careful advance thought was given to the kinds of structural reforms that may be needed. A third is the strength of the forces internationally and especially within the society that can be brought to bear on implementing good recommendations.

The chapter concludes that, although truth commissions tend to focus mainly on their immediate products, "the real effect on conflict resolution will be in how the process of truth seeking is undertaken," the impact on public policy, and the responses of public actors. Truth commissions make their strongest contributions to preventing violence when (1) civilian authorities are willing and able to implement the commission's conclusions and recommendations; (2) perpetrators are weak and have incentives to acknowledge and apologize for past wrongs; (3) human rights groups and other elements of civil society are strong and support the commission and its recommendations; (4) the international community supports the commission and its recommendations; (5) the commission has a strong mandate and adequate resources; and (6) the old regime is no longer strongly supported or feared. These conclusions imply that international support for strong truth commissions, civil society organizations, and domestic institutions for peaceful conflict management can all contribute to peace making in transitional countries.

In Chapter 10, Janice Gross Stein considers what might be called a new pathology of conflict transformation—a set of new challenges faced by NGOs seeking to mitigate violence in the context of "complex humanitarian emergencies." In many recent internal conflicts, humanitarian assistance has been systematically diverted by those who perpetrate violence against civilians and used to sustain their capacity to continue the violence. Humanitarian assets thus fuel rather than resolve the conflicts. Stein's analysis suggests that complex humanitarian emergencies are likely to continue and that NGOs will continue to engage on behalf of vulnerable populations. Given the privatization of assistance and the retreat of the major powers as well as the United Nations from involvement in many world regions in recent years, Stein expects that NGOs will play an even larger role in the regulation of conflicts than they have in the past. They will continue to face situations in which a security vacuum exists and the perpetrators of violence will be tempted to use humanitarian aid as a weapon.

Stein assesses the troubling evidence that humanitarian NGOs have at times contributed inadvertently to the escalation of violence rather than to conflict resolution. The central challenge for NGOs is to find ways of minimizing the negative externalities of assistance as aid flows to the most vulnerable populations. NGOs have developed a set of practical tactics to minimize the diversion of assistance: they select foods that are less attractive to looters, "monetize" food, collaborate to standardize physical costs, and work to improve the sharing of information. These strategies can reduce the scope of diversion but never eliminate the political incentives to tax assistance to fuel conflict.

Stein examines three explicit strategies, some of them counterintuitive, which could contribute to the mitigation of violence, and offers three recommendations to NGOs and international organizations. First, she calls on humanitarian NGOs to think politically and coordinate with diplomatic and military institutions. NGOs must acknowledge that their actions in a complex emergency can have profound political consequences. Even as they insist on the imperative of legitimate authorities assuming responsibility, they must explicitly analyze the political consequences of their strategies to mitigate violence—relief delivery, refugee protection, election monitoring, postwar reconstruction, peace building—and plan for these consequences. Stein calls on NGOs to (1) improve their analytical capacity so that they can participate more effectively at global policy tables; (2) improve their capacity to monitor the consequences of their actions so that they can properly assess the consequences of their strategic choices (e.g., by developing diagnostics for early identification of systematic diversion); (3) enhance the knowledge and skills required for effective negotiation with implementing partners, international institutions, and political leaders; and (4) develop a specialized understanding of the political economy of the humanitarian assistance marketplace that will enable them to press for more flexible rules of engagement in complex emergencies.

Second, Stein recommends that the UN secretary-general consider providing security from private markets when (and only when) public security for humanitarian operations is unavailable from global or regional institutions. Paid, volunteer, or professionally trained security personnel, employed without regard to national origin and beholden to their employer rather than to any single government, could reduce the likelihood of systematic diversion of humanitarian assets to fuel violence.

Third, Stein advocates that NGOs be prepared to consider seriously the option of temporary withdrawal when assistance intended for humanitarian purposes is being diverted into renewed cycles of conflict. Such a strategy requires coordination among the principal NGOs that are providing assistance and a clearly stated set of conditions for return.

Structural Prevention

Chapters 11 through 13 discuss conflict resolution techniques that rely primarily on the strategy of structural prevention: creating organizations or institutions that are intended to direct social conflict into nonviolent channels. In Chapter 11, Ben Reilly and Andrew Reynolds consider "whether the choice of a legislative electoral system in a culturally plural society can affect the potential for future violent conflict." They conclude that electoral system design can have a marked influence but that the most helpful electoral system for conflict resolution must be selected to suit the society.

The chapter classifies the great variety of electoral systems in use in the modern world and discusses them in the context of four broad strategies of constitutional design for divided societies, each of which features a particular electoral system. It finds that the appropriate electoral system design depends on factors specific to the country, including "the way and degree to which ethnicity is politicized, the degree of conflict, and the demographic and geographic distribution of ethnic groups. In addition, the electoral system that is most appropriate for initially ending internal conflict may not be the best one for long-term conflict management." The chapter notes that electoral systems are often chosen by historical accident (e.g., adopting the system of a colonizing country) and only rarely designed on the basis of careful diagnosis of a country's situation. Moreover, not all imaginable options are politically viable.

The authors discuss the strengths and weaknesses of each strategy of electoral system design and its appropriateness for particular kinds of countries, thus making it possible to diagnose a country's situation for the purpose of choosing an electoral system. For example, "centripetal" electoral systems that seek to encourage vote swapping among ethnic groups, usually by establishing multimember districts and an alternative vote electoral system in which voters rank their preferences, seem to work well for conflict management in countries where a small number of ethnic groups are geographically intermixed or a very large number live in segregation—that is, in countries where it is practicable to devise multiethnic electoral districts. As another example, systems that allocate seats by ethnic category tend to ensure ethnic representation but also entrench ethnic divisions; as a result, they seem advisable only in countries where these divisions are already very deep.

Reilly and Reynolds note that new and established democracies have different requirements in electoral system design. For instance, the need for inclusiveness may decline, and the need for geographic accountability may increase, as democracy becomes more firmly established. As a result, a system that works well for an initial election or two in a transitional democracy may not seem so good when the democracy becomes established.

The fact that each electoral system has strengths and weaknesses implies that electoral design involves tradeoffs. It is necessary for the designers to choose among desiderata for the electoral system. Consequently, for a system to work well over time, the involvement of local actors in making the design decisions is key. Electoral system designers must also choose between achieving a system that seems optimal and staying with electoral features that are familiar to the electorate. The evidence suggests the value of making moderate changes that take advantage of what familiar systems do well and changing only what they do not.

In Chapter 12, Yash Ghai considers autonomy as a strategy for conflict management. He defines a variety of autonomy arrangements "that allow ethnic or other groups claiming a distinct identity to exercise direct control over affairs of special concern to them while allowing a larger entity to exercise those powers which cover common interests." The chapter documents the great variety of possible autonomy arrangements—a fact that creates broad opportunities for negotiation and compromise. The variety, Ghai notes, also creates a danger that negotiation will lead to agreement on arrangements that are too complex to make operational, creating a conflict between immediate and long-term conflict management objectives.

Ghai enumerates the various arguments for and against autonomy and the variety of criteria for success. He concludes that "autonomy can play an important, constructive role in mediating relations between communities in multiethnic states . . . but it is not an easy device to operate," requiring great political and technical skills. To make autonomy work, it is necessary to recognize both the particular needs of the group granted autonomy and the common needs of the whole. Success does not depend on particular provisions of an autonomy arrangement: similar provisions have "produced quite different results in different countries."

The success of autonomy arrangements can be assessed in terms of the purposes of granting autonomy, such as to acknowledge a group's identity, to facilitate harmonious relations with other communities and the central government, to end a dispute, and to maintain the integrity of the state. It can also be judged by the extent to which interests are accommodated, by the durability of the arrangements, and by the ways it transforms preexisting relations (e.g., by leading to fair resolution of future disputes, improving ethnic relations, overcoming extreme positions, integrating rebels into society). Different parties have different expectations and apply different criteria of success.

Ghai finds that autonomy arrangements are most likely to be made at times of regime change, when the international community is involved, in countries with strong democratic traditions, when the area claiming autonomy is small and relatively unimportant to the central state, when sovereignty is not an issue (i.e., secession is not considered an option), when there are more than two ethnic groups, and when the grounds for autonomy are not explicitly ethnic. He finds that success, in terms of many of the above criteria, is most likely to be achieved under the following conditions: when autonomy is negotiated in a participatory manner, when the arrangement provides for consultation and negotiation, when flexibility is built in, when there are independent dispute settlement mechanisms in the political and judicial arenas, and when several specific issues of institutional design are carefully addressed. Although history provides exceptions to most of the above generalizations, flexibility and independent dispute settlement mechanisms appear to be critical design criteria for lasting autonomy arrangements. The best way to meet the criteria seems to be situation dependent. For instance, what can work in a federation created by aggregation of independent units may not work in a federation created by the breakup of an empire. Also, success is more likely in countries with established traditions of peaceful political bargaining and judicial independence. The evidence implies that international involvement may increase the chances of success in countries lacking these traditions.

In terms of the social and political consequences of autonomy arrangements, Ghai finds that such arrangements typically begin as asymmetric, establishing special arrangements with the state for only certain regions or communities. Typically, national governments that grant meaningful autonomy feel pressure to offer similar opportunities to other regions, with the result that successful autonomy arrangements tend toward symmetry. There are exceptions for communities that are clearly and historically distinct, such as Greenland or Corsica, whose autonomy does not have this effect. A major conclusion is that true autonomy prevents secession, mainly by reducing the stridency of minority groups: cases in which autonomy preceded secession overwhelmingly involved refusals of the central government to respect autonomy provisions or the dissolution of the central state for reasons unrelated to autonomy.

Serious problems arise with autonomy when the autonomous community wants superior power to other groups or when it wants unique powers not given to other communities in order to mark its special status. Such problems with the theory of autonomy adopted in a country may overshadow the practical problems of managing the arrangements.

In Chapter 13, David Laitin considers the roles of language conflict and language policy in intergroup violence in multiethnic countries. The chapter considers two questions: What is the effect of language differences within a country on the potential for violent conflict between language groups there? What are the effects of policies for addressing language differences on the likelihood of such violence?

On the first question, Laitin finds that, unlike some other bases of intergroup conflict that are rooted in group identity, language differences do not increase the likelihood of violence; under some conditions, in fact, he concludes that language conflict can help contain violence. Laitin analyzed data from the Minorities at Risk database (Gurr, 1993) on 268 politically active communal groups and found that rebellion of a minority group against the state is most intense when both groups have the same language. Controlling for levels of economic development and democracy in a country, for whether or not a minority group has an established rural base, and for levels of religious grievance, language difference has no overall effect on levels of violence but mitigates violence when religious grievances are strong. Laitin, relying on game theoretical analyses and case studies, explains these findings in terms of the ease of subverting oppressive language laws, the difficulties of organizing rebellion by minority-language entrepreneurs, and the tendency of language conflicts to be "fought out in translation committees, school boards, and bureaucracies." Religious conflict is much more incendiary for several reasons—among them, that religious groups' hierarchies can impose discipline and organize resistance and that there is much more social resistance to bireligionism than to bilingualism as a way for a minority to get along in a society.

The analysis of language policies, again relying on multicountry statistical comparisons, identifies five classes of language policies and reaches two main conclusions. One is that political bargaining over language grievances reduces the threat of violence regardless of the language policy a state has in effect and even if it is perceived as unfair. It is the refusal to bargain that predisposes to violence. The other conclusion is that there is no clear benefit of one language policy over another for defusing violence. For instance, in countries where several languages are recognized, there is no greater violence by minorities whose languages are not recognized than by those whose languages are. For international actors Laitin suggests that language policies that are unfair do not justify international intervention on the grounds of incipient violent conflict.

Normative Change

Several studies in this book conclude that the success of international conflict resolution techniques as varied as economic sanctions, truth commissions, and autonomy depends on international support. They suggest that creating international norms that can provide such support may in itself be an important strategy for international conflict resolution. In Chapter 14, P. Terrence Hopmann sheds some light on this hypothesis through his analysis of the efforts of the OSCE to prevent and resolve conflicts. He argues that the OSCE has developed into a security regime for the Eurasian region. It has created many of the conditions necessary for regional cooperation to maintain European security since the end of the Cold War. It has articulated shared values and constructed an institutional framework within which all members may attend to the security needs of one another, exchange information, and facilitate the peaceful resolution of differences. It has also emphasized the development of common political, economic, and social principles based on the ideas of liberal democracy and market economies in an effort to create a "zone of peace." Finally, the OSCE has created a set of structures intended to prevent conflicts, to mediate cease-fires in times of violent conflicts, to manage and resolve the underlying issues that have produced violence, and to assist states and regions that have experienced violence to rebuild their security. Thus, Hopmann's analysis shows that the OSCE has used the strategies of structural prevention and normative change.

The chapter assesses the contribution of the OSCE to limiting the escalation of conflict and to promoting the abatement and resolution of conflict in the aftermath of violence. It pays particular attention to (1) monitoring, early warning, and conflict prevention to head off incipient violence; (2) negotiating cease-fires in ongoing conflicts; and (3) preventing the reignition of violence and assisting the resolution of underlying issues in conflict situations.

With respect to conflict prevention, Hopmann concludes that the OSCE experienced considerable success in Crimea. By intervening rapidly the OSCE mission was able to strengthen moderate forces on both sides and helped avert violence. With respect to negotiating cease-fires, the OSCE mission in Chechnya can be viewed as having played a positive role in bringing an end to the intense fighting between Russian and Chechen forces in the mid-1990s, but it fell short of its goal of restoring a secure environment within which Chechens could reestablish anything approximating a normal livelihood. With respect to prevention of the renewal of violence and conflict resolution, Hopmann concludes that it is necessary to establish an identity formula that guarantees the protection of the identity of the vulnerable group. In Transdniestria the OSCE was unable to achieve a long-term resolution of the conflict even though it did help prevent an escalation to violence.

Hopmann concludes that a real strength of the OSCE is its broad approach to security, linking the "human dimension" to virtually all of its efforts to prevent escalation and to facilitate the abatement and resolution of conflict. He finds that the OSCE has contributed significantly to strengthening democratic processes and institutions in countries undergoing transformation. The OSCE has also proven to be remarkably flexible in reacting to potential crises, which has enabled it to react rapidly.

SOME RECURRING THEMES

Although the studies in this volume cover widely diverse topics in international conflict resolution, a few themes arise repeatedly. It is worth noting these recurring themes because the fact that they have emerged independently in these studies may reveal important features of international conflict and conflict resolution in the post-Cold War period. The themes may suggest important issues for practitioners to consider when they apply conflict resolution techniques, even those not reviewed in this book; they may also suggest promising hypotheses for researchers to explore.

Perhaps the most frequently recurring theme is the need for international coordination and support for conflict resolution processes. This theme appears in studies focused on traditional techniques of diplomacy (see Chapters 4 and 5 on economic sanctions and response to spoilers), conflict transformation (see Chapters 9 and 10 on truth commissions and humanitarian relief activities), structural prevention (Chapter 12 on autonomy arrangements), and normative change (Chapter 14 on the OSCE). Studies in this volume repeatedly and independently find that, across a broad range of conflict techniques, success is more likely if international support can be organized behind the efforts. The pervasiveness of this theme may reflect a general truth about the end of global bipolarity: coordination is difficult when there are no opposing alliances to facilitate it. The studies suggest that states and other actors in the international system that want to promote conflict resolution need to do more work to build the bases for international coordination in support of conflict resolution efforts.

Another frequently recurring theme is the need for strong internal institutions for nonviolent dispute settlement in divided societies. This theme appears explicitly in studies of conflict transformation (see Chapters 7 through 9 on interactive conflict resolution and truth commissions) and structural prevention (Chapter 12, autonomy arrangements). It is also implicit in the study of electoral systems (Chapter 11), which presumes that elections are an institution for nonviolent dispute settlement. The frequent focus on internal institutions for conflict resolution may reflect an increased international recognition of the threat of internal conflict. It is worth noting that the themes of internal institutions and international coordination are related: the studies of autonomy and of truth commissions both note that appropriate international assistance may help compensate for weaknesses in internal conflict management institutions.

Some recurring themes are associated with particular strategies of conflict resolution. For example, the studies of traditional diplomatic techniques (Chapters 3 through 6) confirm that basic principles of power politics, such as set forth in past work on deterrence and coercive diplomacy, operate as well in the present era as in the past. What may have changed, as the studies of economic sanctions and the threat and use of force both report (Chapters 4 and 3), is the ability of states to exercise these tools. Because of increased difficulty in applying these techniques, both of these studies advocate that those who would employ them be more selective in their use and, when they do act, that they do so in a concerted and decisive manner.

The studies of conflict transformation (Chapters 7 through 10) reveal another recurring theme: that there are new and important roles for NGOs in international conflict resolution. NGOs can be important both for building support for peace within societies, as indicated in the studies of interactive conflict resolution, and in responding to complex humanitarian emergencies. The studies of electoral systems and truth commissions reveal yet another potential role for NGOs—as a carrier of lessons about peace making from one country to another. These studies together suggest that international conflict resolution may benefit from improved skills of various kinds within NGOs, including skills in conflict analysis and in coordination with governments and other NGOs.

The studies of structural prevention recurrently emphasize the importance of involvement of a spectrum of local actors in institutional design. This theme appears in the studies of electoral design, autonomy, and truth commissions (Chapters 11, 12, and 9) and is implicit in the study of language conflict (Chapter 13). These studies suggest that, in an era in which internal conflicts have gained greater importance, it is important for the parties to be actively involved in conflict resolution: participatory approaches are preferable to imposed solutions from above, and although outside technical assistance can be helpful, lasting success may depend on giving local actors the final say. Chapter 5 on spoilers addresses options for external actors when some of the parties will not participate.

The structural prevention studies raise two other recurring, and related, themes. One is that the institutions that can be agreed on in a peace settlement may not be best for long-term conflict management in the society. This finding appears in the studies of truth commissions, electoral systems, and autonomy arrangements. The other theme is that the success of structural prevention often depends on flexibility and willingness to keep bargaining. This theme appears in the studies of language conflict and autonomy. Both themes suggest that it may be very important to design flexibility into institutional arrangements that are intended to prevent future conflict.

We do not know enough yet to say that these recurring themes reflect enduring features of the emerging world system or that the lessons they may suggest are the right ones to draw from recent history. However, these studies, completed a decade into a new era of world politics, do suggest what some of the main issues may be in international conflict resolution in this era. Many of these, such as international coordination for conflict resolution, support of internal institutions for dispute settlement, strengthening the NGO role, devolving decision making power to local actors, and designing flexible institutions, are quite different from the main conflict resolution issues of the Cold War period. To the extent that such issues emerge as critical, they will require new work from analysts and new understanding and skills from practitioners. We hope the studies in this book will help analysts and practitioners better understand and address the problems of conflict resolution in this new era.

NOTES

[1]Among the many scholarly works that address these changes and assess their potential implications are those of Ruggie (1993), Joseph (1998), Held et al. (1998), Russett (1993), Doyle (1997), Keck and Sikkink (1998), Ratner (1998), and Gurr (1993).

[2]Researchers in the peace studies tradition often note the apparent contradiction between these opposed uses of the same tools of power politics. They typically stand these techniques in opposition to those they see as embodying the true spirit of international conflict resolution, which they define in terms of the use of nonviolent means in a spirit of dialogue and cooperation. For example, see Burton (1990) and Laue (1991).

[3]Strategies of so-called integrative negotiation or integrative bargaining departed from zero-sum thinking with the notion that there may be ways to accommodate both parties' interests in a negotiation. See, for example, Homans (1961), de Callieres (1963), and Pruitt (1986). In practice, integrative negotiation often involves adding inducements to bring one or both parties to recalculate interests enough to support an agreement. Thus, although integrative negotiation allows for nonzero-sum outcomes, in many applications it follows the logic of stable interests.

[4]The distinction between structural and operational prevention was made in the report of the Carnegie Commission on Preventing Deadly Conflict (1997). That report used the term *structural prevention* broadly to include all strategies that can obviate the need for operational prevention. We use the term more narrowly to include only efforts to modify structural conditions within states so as to improve opportunities for nonviolent conflict resolution. For example, although truth commissions do not engage in operational prevention, not everything they do is structural prevention in our usage. When they recommend modifications in the national judiciary or policing systems to prevent future human rights abuses, they are recommending structural prevention in this narrower sense. However, when their efforts are directed toward emotional reconciliation or establishing a common understanding of the past, they are using the strategy of conflict transformation. These changes, even if they are long lasting, are psychological rather than structural.

[5]The norm of territorial integrity is also undergoing an interesting transformation. The cases of the former Soviet Union and Yugoslavia are making clear an emerging international consensus that, when division of a state becomes unavoidable, the division should be made along the lines of extant provincial subdivisions.

[6]The surprises were: "(1) The Soviet empire, and then the Soviet Union, disintegrated without any major international or civil war. They effectively dismantled themselves. (2) The probability of strategic nuclear war between great powers diminished greatly. (3) Authoritarian regimes in many countries around the world, especially regimes that had been controlled or strongly supported by one of the superpowers, were replaced by new regimes voicing commitments to democracy. (4) Local wars erupted in areas where superpowers or superpower conflict would have not permitted them before [e.g., Kuwait, Yugoslavia, Nagorno-Karabakh]. . . . (5) Communist insurgencies faded or reached accommodations with regimes in a number of countries, although not all (for example, Peru)" (Stern and Druckman, 1995:109).

[7]Arms control agreements during the Cold War often involved structural prevention of conflict, but it was conflict between states, and its relevance to the current spate of substate conflicts has not been clearly defined. On normative change, the spread of adherence to human rights norms during the last decades of the Cold War probably holds lessons for the current period. See, for example, Mastny (1992) and Lauren (1998).

[8]The term *generic knowledge* and much of the discussion in this section are adapted from George (1993). However, unlike George, who restricts the term to knowledge about which strategies work under which conditions, we consider that other kinds of knowledge, for example, about the parties to a conflict, also may be generic in the sense of being applicable across situations.

[9]George (1993) uses the term *actor-specific behavioral models* to refer to this kind of knowledge.

[10]The method of structured, focused case comparison has been described in detail elsewhere (see George, 1979; Bennett and George, forthcoming). Although the contributors were not asked to follow this method in a formal way, most of them worked in that spirit.

REFERENCES

Bennett, A., and A.L. George
   Forth-   *Case Study and Theory Development.* Cambridge, Mass.: MIT Press.
   coming
Burton, J.W.
   1990   *Conflict: Resolution and Prevention.* New York: St. Martin's Press.
Carnegie Commission on Preventing Deadly Conflict
   1997   *Preventing Deadly Conflict: Final Report.* Washington, D.C.: Carnegie Commission
           on Preventing Deadly Conflict.
de Callieres, F.
   1963   *On the Manner of Negotiating with Princes.* Notre Dame, Ind.: University of Notre
           Dame Press.
Doyle, M.
   1997   *Ways of War and Peace.* New York: Norton.
Fisher, R.J.
   1997   *Interactive Conflict Resolution.* Syracuse, N.Y.: Syracuse University Press.
George, A.L.
   1979   Case studies and theory development: The method of structured, focused com-
           parison. In *Diplomacy: New Approaches in History, Theory, and Policy*, P.G. Lauren,
           ed. New York: The Free Press.
   1993   *Bridging the Gap: Theory and Practice in Foreign Policy.* Washington, D.C.: United
           States Institute of Peace Press.
George, A.L., and R. Smoke
   1974   *Deterrence in American Foreign Policy: Theory and Practice.* New York: Columbia
           University Press.
Gurr, T.R.
   1993   *Minorities at Risk: A Global View of Ethnopolitical Conflicts.* Washington, D.C.:
           United States Institute of Peace Press.
Held, D., A. McGrew, D. Goldblatt, and J. Perraton
   1998   *Global Transformations: Politics, Economics, and Culture.* Stanford, Calif.: Stanford
           University Press.
Homans, G.
   1961   *Social Behavior.* New York: Harcourt, Brace, and World.

Jervis, R.
1983   Security regimes. In *International Regimes*, S.D. Krasner, ed. Ithaca, N.Y.: Cornell University Press.
Joseph, R.A., ed.
1998   *State, Conflict, and Democracy in Africa.* Boulder, Colo.: Lynne Rienner.
Keck, M., and K. Sikkink
1998   *Activists Beyond Borders.* Ithaca, N.Y.: Cornell University Press.
Laue, J.
1991   Contributions of the emerging field of conflict resolution. Pp. 300-332 in *Approaches to Peace: An Intellectual Map*, W.S. Thompson and K.M. Jensen, eds. Washington, D.C.: United States Institute of Peace.
Lauren, P.G.
1998   *The Evolution of International Human Rights: Visions Seen.* Philadelphia: University of Pennsylvania Press.
Mastny, V.
1991   The Helsinki Process and the Reintegration of Europe, 1986-1991: Analysis and Documentation. New York: New York University Press.
National Research Council
1989   *Behavior, Society, and Nuclear War*, vol. 1, P.E. Tetlock, J.L. Husbands, R. Jervis, P.C. Stern, and C. Tilly, eds. Committee on the Contributions of Behavioral and Social Science to the Prevention of Nuclear War. New York: Oxford University Press.
1991   *Behavior, Society, and Nuclear War*, vol. 2, P.E. Tetlock, J.L. Husbands, R. Jervis, P.C. Stern, and C. Tilly, eds. Committee on the Contributions of Behavioral and Social Science to the Prevention of Nuclear War. New York: Oxford University Press.
1993   *Behavior, Society, and International Conflict*, vol. 3, P.E. Tetlock, J.L. Husbands, R. Jervis, P.C. Stern, and C. Tilly, eds. Committee on International Conflict and Cooperation. New York: Oxford University Press.
Pruitt, D.G.
1986   Achieving integrative agreements in negotiation. Pp. 463-478 in *Psychology and the Prevention of Nuclear War*, R.K. White, ed. New York: New York University Press.
Ratner, S.R.
1998   International law: The trials of global norms. *Foreign Affairs* 110 (Spring):65-80.
Ruggie, J.G.
1993   *Multilateralism Matters: The Theory and Praxis of an Institutional Form.* New York: Columbia University Press.
Russett, B.
1993   *Grasping the Democratic Peace: Principles for a Post-Cold War World.* Princeton, N.J.: Princeton University Press.
Saunders, H.H.
1999   *A Public Peace Process: Sustained Dialogue to Transform Racial and Ethnic Conflicts.* New York: St. Martin's Press.
Schelling, T.C.
1960   *The Strategy of Conflict.* Cambridge, Mass.: Harvard University Press.
Stern, P.C., and D. Druckman
1995   Has the earthquake of 1989 toppled international relations theory? *Peace Psychology Review* 1:109-122.
Wallensteen, P., and M. Sollenberg
1996   The end of international war? Armed conflict 1989-1995. *Journal of Peace Research* 33:353-370.

2

Evaluating Interventions in History: The Case of International Conflict Resolution

Paul C. Stern and Daniel Druckman

When decision makers at any level organize interventions to prevent, mitigate, or resolve international conflicts, they are attempting to change the course of history.[1] They therefore need to learn lessons from history about why past interventions had the results they did—that is, they need to have the interventions evaluated in a relatively systematic way.

Opinions are sometimes quite polarized about whether and how a scientific approach to evaluation can help conflict resolution practitioners. One extreme view, sometimes attributed to social scientists, follows from a simple model of how science gains knowledge and how that knowledge is used. Classical thinking about infectious disease illustrates this model. Each disease is caused by a specific microorganism, and the microbiologist's task is to identify that organism so that applied scientists can find effective vaccines and treatments. When a disease follows the classic pattern, every case is sufficiently alike that, once it is correctly diagnosed, the prescribed prevention or treatment will be universally effective. Various scientific methods are used to identify infectious agents, develop vaccines and treatments, and evaluate their effectiveness and safety.

Conflict resolution practitioners are like physicians in that they work to prevent or control noxious situations.[2] Few of them, however, believe that violent international conflict follows the classical model of infectious disease in which each condition has a single cause and a small number of effective treatments that can be identified and evaluated by scientific analysis and applied independent of the situation.[3] Practitioners are typically suspicious or even contemptuous of generalizations put forth as "scientific." The extreme view sometimes attributed to them is that, because each international conflict situation is unique, scientific approaches that seek general laws cannot provide useful insights. In this view, useful knowledge is highly case specific. It requires detailed understanding of the cultural, political, and historical contexts affecting the parties to a conflict and experiential knowledge about the parties, their motives, and their susceptibility to influence. In this view, useful knowledge can be gained but not from systematic scientific investigation.

Neither of these extreme views is satisfactory—and neither actually describes what competent scholars or practitioners do. International relations scholars do more than apply standard scientific techniques of measurement and analysis when they try to understand the causes of international conflict and its cessation. They know that the phenomena are difficult to categorize and quantify and virtually impossible to manipulate in the style of experimental microbiology. The best a scientifically oriented international relations scholar can hope to do is to apply some of the methods of social science, such as event analysis, comparative case study research, simulation, and modeling, and make inferences carefully and judiciously, understanding the limitations of each method. In making inferences, competent social scientists act a bit like practitioners, taking advantage of detailed knowledge about specific cases and their contexts to temper the conclusions that may seem at first glance to flow from their analyses.

Similarly, skilled practitioners do more than rely on case-specific knowledge to guide their actions. They typically search history for similar situations and are influenced by their judgments of what was effective in those situations. For example, a foreign minister's expressed desire to avoid "another Munich," "another Vietnam," or "another Somalia" is likely to be more than rhetoric used to justify a decision in the face of political opposition. A practitioner who sees striking similarities between a current situation and the situation preceding a well-known policy failure of the past is likely to treat very seriously the notion that the approach that failed before would fail if tried again (e.g., Khong, 1991). Thus, skilled practitioners benefit from acting a bit like social scientists: examining a body of presumably relevant evidence, drawing tentative conclusions from it, and making inferences about the likely effects of the interventions they are contemplating in the new situation. They temper those inferences, of course, with their specific knowledge of the current situation. But to the extent that they believe history holds lessons for them, they are acting like empirical social scientists and ought to find it useful to have thorough and carefully considered analyses available. There are serious dangers, of course, in relying on single historical analogies for policy guidance (Neustadt and May, 1984). Practitioners can gain more reliable insights from more sophisticated social science approaches, such as the careful analysis and comparison of several relevant cases (George, 1979).

It is possible to move beyond caricatures of social science and diplomatic practice by distinguishing among three types of knowledge, all of them useful to conflict resolution practitioners. One is case-specific knowledge of the current situation facing the parties to a conflict; the historical, cultural, and geopolitical contexts of the conflict; the internal dynamics of the decision-making groups for each party; the political pressures affecting decision makers on each side; and so forth. A second, which George (1993) calls generic knowledge, crosses situations and focuses on particular strategies of intervention. It takes the form of propositions that, under certain kinds of conditions, a particular type of intervention can be expected to yield certain kinds of outcomes. To make such generic knowledge useful in practice requires not only that the propositions be correct but also that the practitioner can accurately classify the situation at hand as to the types of conditions present. Thus, making generic knowledge useful requires case-specific knowledge. George (1993) also discusses "actor-specific behavioral models," which include general propositions about the behavior of a particular actor, such as the state leader who is the target of an influence attempt. These propositions take the form that under certain kinds of conditions the target actor can be expected to behave in certain ways. When an actor-specific behavioral model is correct, it offers a form of generic knowledge about an actor. As with generic knowledge about intervention strategies, generic knowledge about actors must be combined with case-specific knowledge to be of practical value.

It may be presumed that case-specific knowledge comes only from practical experience and that generic knowledge comes only from systematic research and analysis—that specific knowledge is "practical" and generic knowledge is "theoretical." We do not accept either of these presumptions. For example, generic studies of actors and strategies can create typologies of situations that are very useful for building case-specific knowledge—the concepts tell observers what to look for in a situation. And generic knowledge can be greatly informed by the introspection of experienced practitioners who have developed useful practical distinctions among situations and working hypotheses about how conditions affect outcomes that can be tested and refined by systematic research. Thus, we are suspicious of theory in this field that does not have a strong basis in practice, and we accept the aphorism attributed to psychologist Kurt Lewin that there is nothing so practical as a good theory.[4]

Our concern here is with how systematic analysis can help distill the

lessons of history and thus aid the practice of international conflict resolution. Social scientific analysis can make practical contributions in several
ways. It can help diplomatic practitioners check their tentative judgments about the lessons of history against the evidence and confirm or
refine their judgments accordingly. For instance, it can test inferences
from history against a wider range of relevant historical evidence and
thus help keep practitioners from making errors because of gaps in their
experience or overreliance on single historical analogies. Analytical studies can critically examine the assumptions underlying conventional wisdom about which interventions work under which conditions and may
sometimes reveal weaknesses in policy thinking and suggest ways to
refine it. By examining historical cases systematically, analytical studies
can identify the conditions that have been favorable to the success of a
particular strategy in the past and thus help practitioners identify aspects
of a new situation that are especially important to consider in making
policy choices. They may also identify past situations that practitioners
have not considered that may have useful lessons to teach.

Although social science can be useful to conflict resolution practitioners, it does not replace judgment. An analogy to the way medicine uses
biological science can help clarify what social science can and cannot
offer. Medicine is a practice that has a scientific base. Physicians use
biological science in diagnosis to tell what signs, symptoms, and test results are the best indicators of the nature of a patient's disease. To make
an accurate diagnosis, however, a clinician must also rely on case-specific
knowledge and clinical judgment. This includes not only the specific
patient's test results but also clinical knowledge about how to interpret
evidence (e.g., patients' reports of symptoms) and judgment about how,
in a particular case, to combine evidence from different sources (symptoms, physical examination, lab tests) that may not all point to the same
diagnosis.

In treatment, physicians also draw on both scientific knowledge and
clinical knowledge and judgment. Scientific research can tell which treatments are generally most effective and identify special conditions under
which the usual treatment is contraindicated and an alternative treatment
should be tried. But case-specific knowledge is required, among other
things, to determine whether special conditions apply and to decide
whether the patient will accept the usual treatment or might, because of
other medical conditions or personal characteristics, respond better to an
alternative treatment.

Social science can aspire to be useful to conflict resolution practitioners in the same ways that biological science is useful to physicians. It can
develop and refine taxonomic categories that make it easier to accurately
diagnose conflict situations, and it can develop empirically supported

general propositions about the conditions under which and the processes by which particular interventions are likely to ameliorate particular kinds of conflict situations. But practitioners still have to rely on their judgment and experience as well as case-specific information (e.g., field reports) to diagnose situations, interpret ambiguous information, select interventions and combinations of interventions, and choose the right time to act. They must also judge how to deal with constraints on choosing the best-quality policy, such as the need for policy support, the limits on resources for policy analysis, and the impacts of decisions on other policy goals and domestic politics. And they must make choices about how risky a policy to adopt, how to resolve value conflicts embedded in policy choices, and the relative value of expected short- and long-term benefits. George (1993) provides a more detailed discussion of the major types of judgments practitioners must make for which social science can presently offer little assistance.

The medical analogy is imperfect in that the social science of international conflict resolution is not as well developed as the biological science of disease. Because of the nature of international conflict, there are reasons to believe it never will be. The next section identifies and critically discusses the key challenges of taking a social scientific approach to evaluating interventions for international conflict resolution. It identifies the most serious obstacles to achieving a quality of knowledge that meets rigorous scientific standards. The following section suggests ways to make progress in the face of these obstacles. It proposes strategies for developing useful evaluations of conflict resolution techniques even in the face of the impossibility of achieving the highest levels of verification. We conclude that a systematic approach to learning from the experience of conflict resolution based on social scientific techniques and concepts can yield useful generalizations about what works under which conditions and thus make a modest but important contribution to practitioners' skill. We also identify strategies for developing and validating these generalizations.

CHALLENGES OF EVALUATION

Compared with evaluating the efficacy of a medicine for malaria, it is very difficult to draw firm conclusions about the effectiveness of an intervention to reduce, eliminate, or transform an international conflict. This section identifies the major difficulties that face a social scientist who would like to evaluate such an intervention. Although none of these methodological difficulties of evaluation are unique to international conflict resolution, the scale of the difficulties and their conjunction around this particular kind of social intervention make the evaluation of international conflict resolution efforts different from the evaluation of many other kinds of social interventions.

Conceptual Challenges

In the standard model of social science, researchers develop and test hypotheses about relationships among variables, including causal relationships. For conflict resolution interventions the key variables are the types of intervention; the consequences of those interventions, judged in terms of success; and the factors that may ultimately influence these consequences. A researcher must define each of these with sufficient clarity to allow other researchers and practitioners to duplicate the researcher's procedures or ratings of events and situations. It is difficult to achieve this level of clarity with the phenomena of international conflict for several reasons, as this section shows.

Defining the Intervention

Interventions in international conflicts can be considered analogous to treatments in scientific experiments, but neither practitioners nor researchers are as precise in defining types of interventions as scientific canons prescribe. For social scientific analysis it is critical to define each type of intervention precisely enough to know how to classify each specific case. But the terms that describe international conflict resolution activities are not nearly this precise. A single term often refers to a family of related procedures with varying objectives rather than to a single "treatment." For example, peacekeeping missions consist of many activities serving many functions in local, regional, and international contexts: peacekeepers may be stationed between combatants as an interposition force following a cease-fire, may defend the victims of international aggression, may monitor elections following a peace agreement, may restore law and order in the absence of government authority, may quell civil disturbances, and may establish safe havens or "no-fly" zones. The definition of peacekeeping has expanded with the increasing number of operations over the past decade (Diehl et al., 1998). Similarly, the term *interactive conflict resolution* and related terms such as *problem-solving workshops* and *interactive problem solving* have referred to a variety of interventions that have some overall similarities but also considerable differences in their operations and objectives (see Fisher, 1997; Saunders, Chapter 7; Rouhana, Chapter 8). Some aim to develop concrete proposals for immediate action by the parties to a conflict, while the immediate goals of others are limited to improving mutual understanding and establishing informal lines of communication. Even the traditional conflict resolution approaches of negotiation and mediation refer to a variety of forms and processes. Negotiation may be formal or informal; it may be bilateral, trilateral, or multilateral or it may occur as part of conference diplomacy. Mediation may take the form of facilitation, good offices, the use of ombudsmen, or even slip into arbitration; it may be practiced by parties who can and do use material inducements or threats or by mediators who have little power of this sort.

Should activities with such different content be lumped together for evaluation? Perhaps not, because the factors that affect success may not be the same for all of them. The use of a common umbrella term like *peacekeeping* or *mediation* suggests some similarity of purpose (various peacekeeping missions aim to improve relations among conflicting groups in a region, and various forms of mediation seek to help the parties to a conflict find a common ground that can lead to lasting agreements). But is such a common purpose a good enough guide for classifying interventions? If not, how should classification be done? The challenge is a serious one.

Umbrella terms are particularly appropriate if there is a useful conceptual model to go with them. For instance, theories of deterrence provide a conceptual model within which it is possible to understand a variety of policies as instances of the same general concept and to offer postulates about which deterrence strategies are likely to work well in which situations. If a single conceptual model can do this for peacekeeping or interactive conflict resolution, it would demonstrate the usefulness of the umbrella terms.

Defining Success

Conflict resolution interventions are generally intended to alter the course of events in a particular direction, usually from violent to nonviolent interactions or, more ambitiously, to transform relationships from hostile and unstable to friendly and enduring (i.e., they may aim for "negative peace," defined as the reduction of violence, or "positive peace" defined in terms of transforming relationships; Galtung, 1969). The absence of violent conflict is the most obvious observable criterion for success of a conflict resolution technique. But it is not the only possible criterion, and it may not be the best one. Some analysts have recommended measuring success in terms of specific changes in a peace process that indicate progress toward a negotiated settlement or a lasting peace. For example, Stedman (1997; Chapter 5) defines success as the weakening of actors opposed to the peace process vis-à-vis those engaged in it. Such process-based criteria can be assessed independently of the intensity of violence in the short term and may be preferable indicators under some conditions. For instance, some spurts of extremist violence during the

Israeli-Palestinian peace process during the 1990s occurred as a direct consequence of progress in peace talks and had the immediate effect of bringing the negotiating parties closer together.

Some observers, stressing international norms of human rights, self-determination, or democratic participation, suggest that conflict resolution efforts should not be considered successful without improvements in these aspects of the well-being of people affected by the conflict. Sometimes, the violence of civil war has been greatly reduced by the establishment of a repressive and authoritarian regime (e.g., Zaire in the 1960s), but many observers would not consider this outcome a success or an instance of true conflict resolution. This is a good example of the achievement of negative peace without positive peace.

The definition of success may also vary with the standpoint of the judge. The principals to the conflict, various interested third parties, and representatives of international and nongovernmental organizations may all have different criteria of success. Sometimes, what looks like a resolution from a certain external standpoint may look quite different from the inside. U.S. interventions to resolve the conflicts in Guatemala and the Dominican Republic in the 1950s and 1960s may have looked like conflict resolution from Washington, but to many Latin American observers the result was an imposed repression. Also, elites and general populations in a country in conflict may see success differently. A settlement that seems successful to national leaders or to outsiders who claim to see the big picture may seem not to be a resolution at all to members of populations forced to sacrifice as part of the settlement. Historical examples include populations that were moved between Greece and Turkey after World War I and between India and Pakistan after partition; the Bosnian conflict of the mid-1990s is likely also to seem unresolved from the perspective of groups that feel aggrieved by the settlement. If different parties have different definitions of success, which one is an analyst to use? The issue here is that many settlements have winners and losers, and in such cases the winners are likely to consider the settlement more successful than the losers do.

It is also difficult to define success when an intervention has multiple or competing goals. An example was the economic sanctions against South Africa under apartheid. One goal was to reduce intergroup violence; another was to achieve adherence to international norms, such as human rights. The two goals were not entirely compatible. For some participants in the embargo, a period of increased internal violence in South Africa was an acceptable price to pay for changes that would establish human rights and, eventually, majority rule.

To the extent that there is no consensus on what constitutes success, it is difficult to judge whether it has been achieved. A possible solution to the problem of defining success is to define multiple criteria and to judge the effectiveness of an intervention separately against each criterion. We return to this possibility later.

Setting Reasonable Expectations—How Much, How Soon?

Closely related to the challenge of defining success is that of setting reasonable expectations—deciding how high to set the bar. The challenge here is to be clear about how much change to expect from an intervention. Some interventions are expected to do only part of the job of resolving conflict or preventing violence, so it is unfair to judge them failures simply because the whole job remains incomplete. For example, an economic sanction may be designed to get a party to negotiate. If the negotiation then fails to yield a settlement, it is unreasonable to judge the sanction a failure. Similarly, a single problem-solving workshop with a few members from the opposing sides in a civil war cannot reasonably be expected to end the war by itself, though it may contribute to that result by improving communication. If an intervention is expected only to contribute to conflict resolution and not resolve the conflict by itself, evaluation requires clarity about what it is expected to contribute.

It is also important to set the appropriate time for assessment. How long should it take for an intervention, such as economic sanctions, to work? What looks like failure at one time might later turn into success. On the other hand, a settlement that looks successful in the short run may lead directly to violent conflicts in the future. The classic example is the 1919 Treaty of Versailles, which brought to a close the "war to end all wars" but generated resentment that contributed to World War II. A more recent example may be the consociational governmental arrangements in Lebanon that seemed to be successfully managing conflict into the 1970s but that may have contributed to conflict later on, when the formulas for group representation no longer fit the distribution of the groups in the population.

Thus, evaluation requires setting reasonable expectations as to what a particular intervention should accomplish and over what period of time. Observers may disagree not only about the appropriate definition of success to apply in an evaluation but also on how much change the intervention should reasonably be expected to accomplish and on the time period that should pass before pronouncing success or failure.

Identifying Relevant Characteristics and Contingencies

Scholars and practitioners are well aware that the consequences of any intervention depend not only on the intervention itself but also on the way it is carried out and on external contingencies that may influence its outcomes. The latter may include unexpected events in other parts of the world, domestic political and economic forces in the countries in conflict or those intervening, personal characteristics of leaders, and so forth. The relevant contingencies may include both preexisting conditions and events that intervene in time between the intervention and its expected effects. Evaluation efforts should seek to determine the effects of an intervention holding such contingencies aside or, better, to specify how the outcomes depend on the conjunction or interaction of the intervention with particular contingencies. But which factors are likely to be important? It is difficult to know this a priori; consequently, specifying the important contingencies is a continuing challenge.

Selecting Cases for Analysis

Generalizations in social science are supposed to apply to some universe of cases. The standard social scientific approach to developing empirical generalizations is to define or enumerate the universe of cases of interest and, if there are too many cases to study them all, to investigate a representative sample of cases—that is, a sample that approximates the entire population in terms of the distributions of the key independent and dependent variables that will eventually become part of the explanation. There are formidable difficulties in applying this scientific approach to the study of international conflict resolution; however, other case selection strategies can help in developing useful generalizations (see below).

Enumerating the Universe of Cases

The appropriate universe of cases is determined in part by the choice of how broadly or narrowly to frame the topic under analysis. This so-called frame of comparison issue (Collier and Mahoney, 1996) is typically discussed in terms of how broadly or narrowly the independent variable (the type of intervention) is defined. This might be called the conceptual framing of the topic. A narrowly conceived topic makes research easier because the universe of cases is smaller, and, because the cases are likely to be more homogeneous in their cause-and-effect relationships, these relationships are easier to discern. However, conclusions drawn about a narrowly defined universe are not intended to apply outside that narrow frame. A more detailed discussion of such tradeoffs appears in Collier and Mahoney (1996). It is sometimes useful to divide a type of intervention into subtypes, to study each separately, and then to compare results to see if the subtypes follow different processes or produce different outcomes.

Topics are also framed historically. In recent years, for example, researchers have been concerned about whether the end of the Cold War has so changed the international context that pre- and post-1989 conflict resolution efforts should be treated as parts of different universes. As with decisions about conceptual framing, the choice of a historical frame presents a tradeoff in which a narrowly defined research task is easier but yields more limited results. Comparing different time periods can illuminate both the similarities and the differences between them.

Even if an analytical problem is given a clear frame conceptually and historically, it may still be difficult to enumerate the universe of cases. Interventions such as negotiation are so widespread that it is virtually impossible to locate all cases, although this may be less of a problem for official intergovernmental talks. Further complicating this issue is the fact that many negotiations and third-party activities are kept secret, based on the assumption that secrecy may contribute to effectiveness. Recent evidence suggests that secrecy enhances flexibility in negotiation (Druckman and Druckman, 1996).

Moreover, it can be difficult to determine accurately whether an intervention was a serious effort at conflict resolution or only a symbolic action. Often threats, economic sanctions, and the delivery of foreign aid are publicly represented as if the intent is to help resolve conflict in the target country when the main objective is something else, such as to placate public opinion in the country that took the initiative. It may be inappropriate to treat a purely symbolic effort analytically as part of the same universe as a serious intervention, even if symbolic efforts may have an impact on the conflict.

Getting an Appropriate Sample

A serious difficulty in the study of diplomatic activity is that the universe of known cases may be a biased sample of the full universe of cases. For instance, successful third-party mediations tend to be widely publicized, but many failures are kept hidden. If the known cases are biased toward success and lacking in cases that exemplify the routes to failure, a representative sample of the known cases would have the same biases. A similar problem of bias arises if all cases can be identified but the subset with adequate data for analysis forms a biased sample (e.g., if data are systematically lacking on mediations involving authoritarian governments). These possibilities can make it quite difficult to determine whether a sample of conflict resolution interventions is appropriate for drawing inferences about the universe of instances in which a technique was used.

Even when one can be fairly certain that all cases of a particular type of intervention are known, there remain serious problems in selecting an appropriate sample of them. One solution, only rarely available, is to examine the entire universe of cases. For example, Blechman and Wittes (Chapter 3) examine what they say are all cases between 1989 and 1997 in which the United States threatened to use force against another state to advance its international political objectives. Although there can be no objection to this sampling strategy, it does not lead to unequivocal conclusions. Typically, one can examine the universe of cases only when it is quite small—and in such cases the data are typically rich enough to be consistent with more than one explanation for the available cases. Thus, the conclusions are likely to be only tentative, even regarding the cases examined. The conclusions should be considered even more suspect if they are to be generalized to future cases because with a small number of cases—even when this number includes all cases that exist—little is likely to be known about whether the outcomes are contingent on conditions that were common to all past cases but might not hold in the future. In short, sometimes there is not enough historical experience to draw firm conclusions, even by examining all of the cases.

When all cases cannot be examined, sampling theory prescribes random selection from the universe to assure representativeness—at least when large sample sizes can be analyzed. Large-sample analyses have occasionally been carried out on international conflict resolution techniques (e.g., Bercovitch, 1997, on mediation; Druckman, 1997, on negotiation), but typically only a few instances of the use of an international conflict resolution technique are available for study or resources are insufficient to study a large sample. In such situations the statistical theory of randomization warns that randomly selected small samples may not closely approximate the population because the presence or absence of a particular extreme case can have a strong effect on the sample average. For testing simple bivariate hypotheses, sample sizes in the dozens are typically necessary to assure representativeness and meaningful results; examining multivariate relationships involving complex contingencies may require samples in the hundreds.

Because of these difficulties of case selection, the strategy of representative sampling often fails to bring the benefits to the study of international relations that it brings, for instance, to survey research. Thus, it is not clear that a representative sample is always the most useful one for building generic knowledge. Because of this and for theoretical reasons, researchers sometimes use purposive sampling, in which cases are selected on theoretical grounds according to a taxonomy that specifies the important types of cases that should be considered and the variables that should be observed. There is a lively debate among methodologists about whether purposive samples have inherent limitations, particularly when selection is based on the values of an outcome variable, such as in a study restricted to "successful" interventions. Discussions of the issue of selection bias can be found in Achen (1986), Geddes (1990), King et al. (1994), and Collier and Mahoney (1996). We return to this issue in a later section.

A serious problem with reasoning from small samples, even if they are randomly selected, is that any factor that is constant in all of the cases studied will not show up as important in the results of the study. For example, the Cold War international regime is a constant in all pre-1989 studies of conflict resolution techniques, so these studies cannot determine whether bipolarity in the international system moderates the effectiveness of the techniques studied. The problem is a general one: it is always appropriate to ask whether new historical conditions invalidate the conclusions of past research.

Researchers should therefore be cautious and self-critical about claims that the cases they examine appropriately represent the intervention type about which they wish to generalize. They should be especially alert to the possibility that their samples may not include variation on particular variables that may prove important to the success of an intervention technique. This may happen because of limitations of the sample or because the universe of known cases has limited variation.

Observing and Measuring Interventions and Outcomes

A characteristic problem with historical data is that the events usually cannot be directly observed or measured as they happen. They must typically be observed indirectly and with hindsight, making it impossible to have the sorts of reliable and dispassionate observations that scientists rightly prize. Thus, interpretation is required to determine which interventions were used and what their outcomes were. Researchers may have access to press accounts, to documentary evidence, and to the recollections of actual participants, but these different sources of evidence have characteristic biases and sometimes tell quite different stories. Moreover, experience suggests that understanding of what happened sometimes changes as new sources of information become available. Analyses of recent historical events are particularly vulnerable to unrecognized biases and gaps in the available data because the normal processes of research and academic debate have not yet revealed them. Measurement problems are especially severe in evaluating what happened in the course of events that were not widely observed, such as closed negotiations or unpublicized mediation efforts, and how events might have been affected by the perceptions of parties in a conflict situation who are not available for interviews or whose recollections are suspect.

Challenges of Inference

Making causal inferences about conflict resolution efforts—the main objective of evaluation—is risky business. The strongest evidence that social science can provide about causation comes from controlled experiments, and history does not lend itself to such experimentation. It is rarely possible to achieve the necessary control and when it is, this is usually unethical or politically unacceptable. Consequently, analysts usually rely on various forms of nonexperimental data—events occurring in time without careful manipulation and control. They examine interventions, outcomes, and extrinsic events and attempt to infer causation.

In this approach the main challenge of inference is that, although interventions always precede outcomes, they may not cause them. Events outside the control of the intervening actors may lead a conflict to intensify despite a set of interventions that would otherwise have been effective or to diminish even though the deliberate interventions have had no effect. Such associations between events are called spurious. Because each international conflict situation is unique in some way, it is difficult to draw firm conclusions from historical experience and particularly to make judgments about the causal efficacy of interventions. This section discusses some of the reasons for these difficulties. A later section discusses ways to address them.

Comparing Events with Counterfactuals

To support a conclusion that an intervention had a particular effect requires answering the following question: What would have happened if the intervention had not been tried when it was? It implies a comparison between what actually happened after the intervention and alternative histories in which the intervention was not tried, or was tried earlier or later in the conflict, or a different intervention was tried. This involves comparisons with hypothetical or counterfactual worlds, which history does not provide (Tetlock and Belkin, 1996). As discussed in the next section, social scientists have developed an array of techniques that attempt to find appropriate comparison conditions from the real world as a substitute for controlled experimentation and for the counterfactual worlds that would provide the most convincing answer to the "what if . . ." question: for example, simulation (Guetzkow and Valadez, 1981), quasi-experimentation (Cook and Campbell, 1979), analysis of coded sets of events data (Bercovitch, 1986), focused case comparisons (Faure, 1994; Putnam, 1993), process tracing (George and Bennett, 1998), and surveys. Each of these analytical strategies is problematic, but each has different limitations. Used together, the social science approaches can reduce the difficulties posed by the need to make inferences about counterfactuals.

A particularly difficult challenge in making inferences concerns comparisons between what actually occurred after an intervention and what would have happened if the intervention had been considered but not used. This comparison is difficult for two reasons. First, it can be extremely difficult to find cases in which an intervention was considered but not used because there may be no record of the rejected alternative. Second, such cases are unlikely to be fully comparable to ones in which the intervention was used because they will tend systematically to have characteristics that the decision makers believe predispose the technique to failure.

Assessing the Roles of Extrinsic Events

Evaluation requires determining how much an outcome should be attributed to specific conflict resolution efforts and how much to events independent of those efforts. For example, an outcome may be predetermined by an antecedent condition and would have come about even if the intervention being studied had not been used. Once a peace process gets to a certain point, for instance, it may become inevitable that the parties will seek mediation and that it will be successful. If the conflict is then satisfactorily resolved, the mediation may deserve a small part of the credit but not much. Or the form of a new democracy's electoral system may be strongly determined by its history. If the system put in place is a historical accident rather than a choice, the consequences, whether peaceful or not, cannot reasonably be attributed only to the structure of the electoral system.

Outcomes may also be affected by events subsequent to a conflict resolution effort that are not part of that effort but affect the outcomes. Consider, for example, the assassination of Israeli Prime Minister Rabin in the midst of his negotiations with the Palestinians. That event probably changed the course of the negotiations—in fact, the assassin intended that it do so, although he may not have achieved the result he desired. But this dramatic turn of events makes it very hard to discern the roles of the various interventions that had been intended to move the negotiation process forward. Would they have yielded the same outcome if the assassination had not happened?

The longer the time between an intervention and its expected effect, the harder it is to evaluate the intervention because there is more time in which intervening events can occur and influence outcomes. Thus, the inference problem is especially serious with techniques that are expected or intended to have delayed effects, such as economic sanctions, efforts to build civil society in emerging multiethnic democracies, and interactive problem-solving workshops.　To evaluate the effects of such delayed-effect techniques, it is important to postulate causal mechanisms that the intervention might set in place—to offer hypotheses or predictions about how the intervention will change the course of the conflict—and to identify indicators that can be used to assess the hypotheses or predictions. Such hypotheses make it possible to observe whether history is following a path postulated to lead to conflict resolution and thus to conduct partial or interim evaluations.[5]　For example, one way that problem-solving workshops may be effective over the long run is by establishing relationships of trust between potentially influential members of communities in conflict that years later facilitate agreements between the communities, when the participants in the workshops have risen to decision-making positions.　It is possible to observe indicators of the operation of this causal mechanism: continued informal communication between workshop alumni from opposing sides after a workshop ends; back-channel communication between these alumni when they later have the opportunity to participate in formal negotiations; an increase in alumni in prominent leadership positions during periods just before breakthroughs in the negotiation process; and so forth. The explanatory strategy of comparing a theoretically predicted course of events with the flow of history has been called *process tracing* or *monitoring* (George, 1997).

Assessing Contingent Relationships

Even if extrinsic events do not affect outcomes on their own, an intervention's outcomes are usually contingent on its context. Thus, practitioners want to know the conditions under which an intervention is likely to succeed. However, social scientific analysis of this issue is challenging. Taking a purely empirical approach may not be fruitful because there are normally a very large number of potentially relevant events going on relative to the number of interventions available for study. Thus, history normally leaves us with multiple, sometimes conflicting, explanations based on different causal variables and each consistent with events. In quantitative methodology this problem is often referred to as an overspecification or overdetermination problem or a shortage of degrees of freedom: there are a large number of variables available to explain the outcomes of interventions compared with the number of historical cases to test the explanations against (Campbell, 1975).

Since it is not possible to create new historical events to solve this problem, other approaches are needed. One way to increase the ratio of cases to variables is to simulate events or processes. The simulation can be construed as an experiment using an analog to the historical process of interest. By replicating the simulation a number of times, it is possible to evaluate the effects of an intervention on any number of cases. However, inferences from simulations depend on the assumptions that the variables being studied are among the important ones determining the consequences of the intervention and that their effects are not modified in major ways by other variables not included in the simulation. We discuss simulation in more detail in a later section.

Researchers also develop and test theories about how or under what conditions particular interventions work. Such theories focus attention on a small set of variables and presume that the others make no difference to the effects of an intervention. For example, deterrence theory posits that deterrent threats are more effective when they are made by an actor who has both the capability and the commitment to carry them forward and when the recipient perceives the threat as sufficiently credible and potent (George and Smoke, 1974). This set of hypotheses contains few enough variables to allow testing against historical data. Theory can also help by making a series of intermediate predictions—predictions about the process an intervention is expected to set in motion. Such predictions allow each case to support a larger number of hypothesis tests. We discuss this approach, sometimes referred to in terms of "causal mechanisms" and "process tracing," in more detail below. The challenge for theory is to develop the necessary hypotheses about the contingencies that matter for particular conflict resolution techniques or about the processes they set in motion. One value of the analyses in this book may be to help build such theories and hypotheses.

Accounting for Indirect Effects of Interventions

Peace processes sometimes take a twisting course in which the short-term effects of an intervention in turn alter events in the future, sometimes in the opposite direction. For example, progress in a peace process may lead to subsequent violence by "spoilers"—groups that are not participating in the process or that do not want it to succeed (Stedman, 1997; Chapter 5). The effects of the peace process on such spoilers can turn back on the peace process, sometimes derailing it but at other times increasing the resolve of the participants to reach a settlement. One implication of indirect effects is that there may be several causal paths to the same outcome (sometimes called *equifinality* or *plurality of causes*). For example, a program of interactive conflict resolution workshops may help advance the peace process in several distinct ways and might be counted successful if it moves the process along any one of these causal paths (Saunders, Chapter 7). Similarly, there may be several possible outcomes from the same set of initial conditions. These possibilities are important for evaluation efforts to consider, though they can make it extremely difficult to attribute causation.

Accounting for Actors' Perceptions

Sometimes an intervention is misperceived (e.g., a threat is not believed or an inducement is viewed as a threat). Such possibilities are discussed extensively in the literatures on the effectiveness of deterrent threats (e.g., George and Smoke, 1974; Jervis, 1976; Lebow, 1981) and on crisis decision making (Holsti, 1989; Tetlock, 1998). When misperception can be documented, it is misleading to blame the failure on the intervention technique, although it may be very useful to advise practitioners on how to act so that their intentions are correctly perceived.

The Context of Multiple Interventions

In most conflicts there are numerous interested third parties, and each of them may be doing several things at once to address the conflict. This situation makes it hard to assess the effect of any single intervention because the intervention cannot be meaningfully abstracted from other simultaneous interventions that may or may not be coordinated with it (see Kriesberg, 1996). In fact, diplomats often do several things at once specifically because they believe one intervention will make another more effective. Again, the challenge is to build theories of enough specificity to give guidance on how to examine the evidence. There are normally too many variables and too few cases to draw conclusions based on a purely empirical approach that examines all of the combinations of interventions and other factors that may influence the course of a peace process.

MEETING THE CHALLENGES

The above challenges are serious enough to indicate that social scientists should be modest about how much insight they can offer practitioners. The phenomena of international conflict are too complicated and too resistant to normal scientific methods to make it possible to produce simple lawlike generalizations. Nevertheless, each of the above challenges has faced other social scientific endeavors in the past, and some of the strategies that have been tried in other fields are available in this one. Even where these standard strategies have only limited value, there are ways to address the challenges effectively enough for careful analysis to add something useful to practitioners' understanding.

Conceptual Challenges

We have noted that a lack of generally accepted concepts is a major problem for evaluating international conflict resolution efforts. For instance, concepts like peacekeeping and track two diplomacy do not have the same meaning to all observers, and their meanings may shift over time. Other social scientific fields have faced this sort of problem and have made progress, even while conceptual debates have continued. For example, the study of group cohesion has been characterized by conceptual disagreements since the 1940s. Social psychologists have disagreed about whether cohesion is a single attribute (e.g., morale) or a collection of them (e.g., morale, shared understandings, teamwork, productivity). They have also disagreed about whether it applies only (or primarily) to small groups or also to larger units such as organizations or even nations. The field has progressed because social scientists developed several competing concepts of cohesion with enough clarity and specificity to allow reliable measurements of each and with enough theoretical elaboration to generate testable hypotheses about how the various aspects of cohesion are expected to affect group behavior. With careful measurement of each clearly defined concept and with sets of testable hypotheses, it became possible to continue the conceptual arguments with an empirical referent. That is, it became possible to assess the usefulness of each concept of cohesion for understanding and predicting group performance. Eventually, a widely shared concept of cohesion may be adopted, but in the meantime much is being learned about group processes and performance (for a discussion of these issues, see National Research Council, 1988).

This intellectual history, which has analogs in several other social scientific fields, holds some lessons for the newer field of international conflict resolution with its many loosely defined concepts, such as peacekeeping and mediation. The most general lesson is that for a field to progress it must develop its concepts with sufficient clarity to allow for reliable measurement and must develop theories and hypotheses with enough specificity to allow for empirical assessment. Four types of conceptual advances are important.

First, the terms that define *interventions* need clear referents if the interventions are to be evaluated meaningfully. An important first step is developing taxonomies. For example, Diehl et al. (1998) have identified a variety of activities that have been called peacekeeping. This kind of taxonomic effort helps highlight important issues such as whether different kinds of missions require different kinds of training for peacekeepers. A continuing discussion of the peacekeeping concept is beginning to clarify the meanings of the term in the post-Cold War setting (e.g., Druckman and Stern, 1997). Some writers have identified a number of distinct types of nontraditional diplomacy, or "tracks" (Diamond and McDonald, 1991).

Useful taxonomies of interventions are those that embody, at least implicitly, propositions that the variations between taxonomic types are associated with variations in outcomes, either generally or under certain conditions. To the extent that a taxonomy implies testable hypotheses, it takes an important step toward developing theory that can guide further analysis and refinement of the taxonomic categories (see Bennett and George, forthcoming, on taxonomic theory).

Several of the chapters in this volume, particularly those that cover relatively new interventions in the library of conflict resolution techniques, deal explicitly with conceptual and taxonomic issues. For example, Reilly and Reynolds (Chapter 11) attempt a classification of electoral systems into four broad categories that they believe are useful for finding the appropriate electoral structure for managing conflicts in different types of divided societies. Stedman (Chapter 5, also 1997) develops a typology of "spoilers" to peace agreements that he believes will help practitioners choose the best strategy for defeating spoilers and advancing peace processes. Ghai (Chapter 12) presents a classification of types of autonomy and decentralization of power, and Hayner (Chapter 9) develops a classification of transitional justice mechanisms and, within that, defines attributes that can be used to classify various truth-seeking efforts.

Second, the undifferentiated *concept of "success"* must be specified. Because success has so many possible meanings, it is useful to identify the various outcomes that signify success to at least some of the potential evaluators of an intervention. In this way an intervention can be evaluated separately against each outcome. Analytical efforts can focus on whether an intervention has particular outcomes rather than on whether it was a "success." Of course, evaluating whether a particular outcome has occurred and whether it is an effect of the intervention or of other factors presents challenges of measurement and inference. We discuss these below.

The evaluation of peacekeeping missions provides an illustrative example. An exchange of views among analysts (Druckman and Stern, 1997) has identified a number of meanings of success: accomplishing the mission's mandate, containing the conflict in the host state or region, advancing acceptance in the target area of larger values such as world peace and justice, and (especially for humanitarian missions) reducing human suffering among the local population. Because practitioners from different countries or organizations, such as the United Nations, nongovernmental organizations, or national military organizations, may have different goals for the intervention or different perspectives on success, they may disagree on whether a particular intervention was successful. However, with the help of careful analysis, they may come to agree on what its outcomes were. Systematic analysis of what is responsible for each of the outcomes of peacekeeping missions can help inform practitioners' judgments about whether and how to support particular peacekeeping missions, in light of their objectives.

Third, it is important to define *reasonable expectations* for an intervention: to select a time horizon for evaluation and—when the time horizon is long—to identify interim indicators of progress. If these choices are to be other than arbitrary, it is necessary to have a theory of the peace process and of how a particular intervention might affect it, or at least a set of working hypotheses about how the intervention might affect the peace process over time. Interactive problem-solving workshops provide a good example. Many of the desired effects, such as an overall decrease in intergroup hostility or the development of reliable channels for nonviolent resolution of grievances, take a long time to become manifest. The process is intended to change relationships and ways of thinking among the participants and, eventually, among the communities in conflict. It is fair for a practitioner to ask that evaluation not be finalized for years or even decades, but it also fair to ask in return whether there is any way to make an interim evaluation. Those who support slow-acting interventions should be prepared to estimate how long it will take for them to bear fruit and what the course of their progress might be, so that even if it is not possible to reach a final conclusion for many years, it is possible to judge whether the process is moving along as expected.

Fourth, it is important to develop *conceptual frameworks* that identify contingencies that may shape the outcomes of an intervention or processes by which it may have its effects. This is because the limits of historical data make it virtually impossible for a purely inductive approach to yield useful understanding of how, when, and by what mechanisms an intervention works. Conceptual frameworks link concepts together and form the basis for theory.

Central to meeting the conceptual challenges is the task of developing theory, or at least the elements of theory. Among these elements are taxonomies of interventions, outcomes, and contingencies that matter. Taxonomies are a step prior to the development of theories in that they are necessary for stating hypotheses or theoretical propositions of the form that intervention A will have outcome B under conditions C and D but not E and F. A well-developed theory also includes a sufficiently explicit conception of the process surrounding an intervention so as to embody expectations of what outcomes should be observable after defined amounts of time or at particular well-defined stages of a successful process or of how the intervention can be expected to change the trajectory of a conflict situation. The knowledge gained from exploring such propositions, hypotheses, and expectations about contingent relationships and temporal processes can provide practitioners with a useful diagnostic guide for action. They are also necessary, although not sufficient, for rigorous evaluation.

Selecting Cases for Analysis

We have already noted that the standard approach in social science to making generalizations about a set of phenomena is to observe a representative sample of those phenomena and presume that what holds for the sample holds also for the population. This strategy works well when the population is easily enumerated and it is possible to choose a large representative sample within which the important variables are well measured for all cases. Unfortunately, it is rare for any of these conditions to be met for studies of international conflict resolution techniques. Even examining the entire universe of cases—a viable strategy when the universe is small—has limitations because the data often allow for multiple explanations, making interpretation inconclusive. For such reasons it is important to develop reliable methods of purposive sampling.

Advocates of purposive sampling in the case analysis research tradition hold that statistically representative samples, which in most instances are impracticable to obtain, are not necessary for making useful inferences from case study data (e.g., Bennett and George, forthcoming) and that samples can be appropriate for making inferences if there is no way of knowing whether they are representative or even, in some cases, if they are known not to be statistically representative. They propose that understanding can be greatly advanced by analyzing samples of cases that cover the expected range of variations on the theoretically important factors or variables or that focus on cases that are critical for resolving important theoretical questions.

There is much to be said for this argument, especially in the early stages of theory development. It is easier to meet this criterion of an appropriate sample than to meet the criterion of representativeness because it is not necessary to enumerate the universe of cases. However, the researcher must specify the variables with respect to which the sample must be appropriate—the potentially important factors affecting the outcomes of an intervention and the important outcome variables. The claim that a sample study contributes to knowledge normally rests on a theoretical presumption that it has examined the range of variations on one or more of the variables that matter and therefore illuminates the contingencies that affect outcomes. It is advantageous for theory development to be explicit about which variables matter, and it is especially important when generalizations are being offered on the basis of a small sample of cases.

As yet there is no general theory of purposive sampling beyond the admonition to select the sample to suit the research objectives. It often makes sense to include cases generally considered successful and cases generally considered unsuccessful, but beyond that what should the logic of purposive sampling be? Does the region of the world matter? How important is the identity of the intervening actor or that actor's past relationships to the parties in a conflict? How important are conditions affecting countries adjacent to the location of the conflict, and which conditions are the important ones?

Researchers who use purposive sampling resolve these questions by making judgments based on explicit or implicit theoretical propositions. The results of their studies often lead them to modify these propositions. Thus, the questions get resolved in stages. If researchers are explicit about the theoretical presumptions that provide their rationales for selecting samples, others can question their judgment. Meanwhile, their analyses will produce tentative results. The combination of empirical results and critical debate is likely, over time, to lead to better rationales for case selection, improved theory, and more complete knowledge of the phenomena in question.

We have noted that the usefulness of samples of any kind may be compromised by a lack of sufficient data about possible cases. Sometimes, interventions occur that analysts never learn about because they were secret or unpublicized. Sometimes there is not enough information about a particular intervention to determine whether it was indeed a member of the class being examined. Sometimes more complete data are available for some kinds of cases (e.g., those publicized as successful) than for others. The best way to address such problems is through a combination of awareness of the possibility and openness in analysis. Analysts should look for hidden cases, explain their case selection, and leave it to future reviewers and readers to consider whether addition of other cases to the analysis or more detailed research on some of the cases would have altered the conclusions.

Observing and Measuring Interventions and Outcomes

Although it can be difficult to be sure an intervention is what it seems (to classify the independent variable), the central measurement challenge lies in measuring outcomes (the dependent variables). Changing the focus from "success" to outcomes is a first step, but it is not always easy to agree on whether particular outcomes have occurred or on which outcomes are relevant to success.

Dealing with Incomplete Information

Often, key information about an intervention, its context, and the outcomes is missing, and sometimes researchers are unsure how incomplete the information is. It is sometimes known or reasonably suspected that government agencies have classified files on a matter or that certain key participants are hiding or distorting information in order to defend political positions or personal reputations. It makes sense for analysts, in addition to specifying the sources of their information, to speculate about the kinds of information that may be missing and the kinds of distortion the available information may contain. It is also useful for analysts to make efforts to develop information from sources that vary in their perspective on the conflict, so that each information source can be used as a check on the others.

Achieving Reliable Measurement

One problem is to specify particular outcomes well enough that observers with access to the same information will agree on whether they occurred—to achieve what methodologists call *interobserver reliability*. Reliability is relatively easy to achieve for certain indicators of successful outcomes, such as a signed agreement or a reduction in the number of deaths in communal violence, but these are rarely the only outcomes of interest. It can be difficult for observers to agree, for example, about whether a peace process is stalled or still moving forward, whether or not the police force in an emerging democracy is making progress in upholding norms of human rights, or whether an absence of violence indicates conflict resolution or conflict suppression.

There are two main strategies for arriving at adequate interobserver reliability. One is to rely on operational definitions—standard procedures that an observer can follow to decide on whether an outcome has occurred. This approach is easy to imagine for an outcome variable like deaths from violence. An observer could consult official records or, in the absence of those, reports coming from the different sides to a conflict and use a prearranged formula for arriving at an estimate when the reports disagree. Not everyone would agree with the result, but the procedures for arriving at it would be explicit, so that criticisms could be focused on those.

For many important outcomes, using operational definitions is not feasible because there is nothing approaching agreement on a procedure for measuring the outcome in question. In such instances it is possible to use another strategy, directly comparing the assessments of expert judges. This is what analysts do in an informal way when they interview the important practitioners involved on all sides of a peace process in order to construct a story of how it developed and to determine which interventions were responsible for the results. This strategy is most successful at demonstrating interobserver reliability when the interviewer can develop a set of specific questions or probes to elicit each informant's judgment about whether particular outcomes were present at particular times.

An important complication in evaluating outcomes, especially when relying on expert judgment, is that all observers do not have access to the same information. Often, important parts of a peace process are private—for instance, deliberations among negotiators on one side of a negotiation are seen only by that side, and the progress of a problem-solving workshop is rarely recorded electronically, so only those present know what happened. Those present at important private moments have relevant information others lack, but they also often have motivations that can distort their memories and their reports, so that others may suspect the accuracy of their accounts. There is no standard procedure for addressing this problem, but it helps to be aware of it, to search for corroboration from participants whose incentives to distort may be different, and to temper conclusions when it appears that much of the available information is biased in one way or another. It may be possible to assemble a group of experts at the same place and time or to confront each of them with other experts' judgments in an effort to move toward a consensus of expert judgment, as is done in Delphi panels (Frei and Ruloff, 1989).

There are well-known tradeoffs between reliability and validity. Attempts to maximize agreement between coders in order to enhance reliability (accuracy), as in mechanical coding, may result in a distortion of the concept being assessed, thereby detracting from validity (meaning). For example, it is possible to obtain highly reliable measures of concessions in a bargaining experiment, where concessions can be defined as the numerical difference between an offer made at one time and the offer the next time. It is much more difficult to reliably quantify a concession made in an international negotiation, as it must be inferred from suggestions, exploratory proposals, and packages that combine several offers. Coding is typically an interpretive exercise and tends to result in a loss of intercoder agreement, although possibly enhancing validity. The extent to which it enhances validity depends, however, on the adequacy of the coding categories and on the sampling of appropriate materials. Analysts often invent coding systems to capture the essence of a phenomenon and thus enhance validity. To enhance reliability they tend to adopt standard categories that can be used repeatedly. Standard categories may be applicable across intervention types (e.g., discussions in formal negotiations and problem-solving workshops) but may sacrifice validity. Analysts often observe that the coding categories that seem most useful are not the same from one type of data to another.

Developing Indicators of Success

We have noted that evaluation is complicated by the fact that short- and long-term definitions of success may be quite different. This difficulty can be addressed in part by focusing on particular outcomes rather than overall "success." Evaluations can be separated according to time horizon, with outcomes at different times analyzed separately. As noted, it is important to have short-term indicators of progress even for interventions intended mainly to have long-term effects. This is so partly to provide interim indications of progress and also to allow for meaningful evaluation even in cases in which intervening events not brought about by the intervention throw the process of conflict resolution off its intended course.

One way to develop interim indicators of progress for interventions that have a long time horizon is to postulate mechanisms believed to lead from the intervention to the desired long-term results and identify indicators that can be used to tell whether events are moving along the desired track. For instance, practitioners of interactive problem-solving workshops as a way to improve intergroup communication over the long term might postulate that one mechanism leading to long-term effects such as formal agreements between the parties is through improved communication and trust between workshop participants from opposing sides and their advancement over time to more influential positions in their groups. One could assess whether this mechanism is operating by examining various indicators, such as improved communication between the participants immediately after the workshop, continued communication between them a year or two later, the rise of workshop participants to positions of increased influence, and evidence of sensitivity to and accommodation of the opposite group in the policies they influence. Using such indicators of intermediate progress improves on an outcomes-only approach to evaluation by adding a process element to the evaluation and by strengthening the case for a causal link between the intervention and long-term outcomes.

Another important measurement issue is that of setting realistic expectations for interventions. This issue is especially important for evaluating interventions that are intended to contribute to a peace process but are not expected to produce peace by themselves; however, the issue has not received much attention to date. A first step is to raise the issue—to ask practitioners in interviews and to discern from their writings what their expectations have been for the short- and long-term effects of particular interventions. Their own expectations constitute one reasonable test of success. Of course, different practitioners may have different expectations, even for the same intervention. Conducting a dialogue among reflective practitioners on what expectations are reasonable can lead to more defensible indicators.

Practitioners' own expectations are an imperfect guide for the analyst, however. One reason is that practitioners may state unrealistically high expectations to get political support for intervening or unrealistically low ones to increase the chances that the intervention will be judged successful. Also, they may have expectations unrelated to the peace process that influence their statements. For instance, undertaking an intervention or claiming success may benefit a practitioner's career or the standing of the government agency or nongovernmental organization he or she represents. In such cases an intervention may be successful from the practitioner's viewpoint even if it has no effect on the conflict, and the practitioner's view of reasonable expectations may differ from the one an analyst would want to adopt.

In the course of the project leading to this book, we have encouraged scholars and practitioners to interact around the questions of interim indicators and reasonable expectations and have asked authors to address the issues explicitly. The chapters that follow help clarify these issues for several conflict resolution techniques. A good example is Hayner's (Chapter 9) indicators that postconflict truth-seeking efforts are producing reconciliation between past adversaries.

Inferences from Data

Social scientists have developed many analytical techniques for analyzing claims about cause-and-effect relationships, and numerous textbooks have been written that classify the techniques and assess the strengths and weaknesses of each. The texts and typologies they present usually emphasize applications in a particular discipline. For discussing the challenges of inference about the effects of international conflict resolution interventions, it is useful to group the methods into three broad categories: experiments and simulations, multivariate analyses, and case study methods. This section discusses the possibilities and limitations of each.

Experiments and Simulations

The distinguishing feature of experimental methods is that a researcher deliberately manipulates an independent variable—a variable that is hypothesized to have an effect—and, controlling for other variables that might affect the outcome, observes the consequences. All conflict resolution efforts are experiments in the sense that they are deliberate and intended to have an effect. Experimental methodology is devoted to identifying ways to conduct and collect data on experiments in order to support strong conclusions about cause and effect and rule out alternative hypotheses for explaining the observed outcomes. There is little experimental research on international conflict resolution because actual conflict situations do not permit experimental controls and because, for most types of intervention, conceptual models are not yet sufficiently well developed even to conduct laboratory simulations (negotiation processes are an exception to this generality).

The conditions for drawing strong conclusions from experiments are rarely, if ever, met with international conflict resolution interventions. The main condition is that all variables that might affect the outcome are either explicitly manipulated or adequately controlled. Adequate control may be achieved either by holding a variable constant—a condition researchers may be able to approximate only in the laboratory—or by randomly assigning each situation in which an intervention might be tried to receive either the intervention or some control or comparison condition. Because these conditions are rarely met for studies conducted outside the laboratory, an alternative approach referred to as quasi-experimentation has been developed (Cook and Campbell, 1979). Quasi-experimental research involves using surrogates for experimental manipulation. For example, a quasi-experimental study might compare the consequences of an intervention in one situation to the consequences in another situation that is comparable in important ways. A researcher might compare the consequences of different efforts to mediate the same conflict at different times, thus achieving control over some of the important variables extraneous to the negotiation strategy (Stedman, 1991, used this strategy as part of his study of mediation in Zimbabwe in the 1970s). Quasi-experimental research methodology makes explicit the limitations of each research design and the most important threats to valid inference about causation that arise with each type of research design. It thus helps researchers evaluate the extent to which these threats can be ignored in a particular study, taking into account its features and the pattern of results obtained (see Robson, 1993). Classical experiments, in which cases are randomly assigned to intervention conditions, generally do a better job than quasi-experiments in ruling out alternative hypotheses; for quasi-experiments and other research methods, it is important to specify each rival hypothesis and seek evidence to rule it out.

Experimental evidence is sometimes used to draw conclusions about international conflict resolution. Researchers subject individuals or small groups to controlled manipulation of variables believed to affect behavior in actual international conflict resolution situations, and use the results to test hypotheses about the effects of those variables. This strategy obtains the chief advantage of experimental method—the ability to rule out rival

hypotheses about causation within the experiment—at the cost of correspondence with real-world conflicts. In methodologists' language it
achieves stronger internal validity (the ability to infer causation) at a cost
in external validity (the ability to apply conclusions from the situation
studied to other situations).

A laboratory experiment, such as a study of the effects of stress on the
accuracy of perception, may have very strong internal validity and potential relevance to real-world conflicts but be highly questionable in terms
of its external validity. One approach used to increase external validity is
the simulation experiment. An attempt is made to preserve the rigorous
features of experiments (random assignment, controls) while representing key aspects of the conflict setting of interest. By building in aspects of
the actual setting, it is believed that the results will be relevant to that
setting. Of course, this is an empirical issue that is best evaluated by
comparing findings obtained in simulations with those obtained in the
field (for more on these issues see Guetzkow and Valadez, 1981).

Experimental research on conflict resolution has been most useful for
identifying particular aspects of complex interventions that are critical
sources of variation in outcomes. This progress has come primarily in
research on small-group interventions such as negotiation, mediation,
and interactive problem-solving workshops. Simulations typically include considerable detail to enhance external validity and a careful experimental design to allow statistical separation of the key variables pos-
ited to affect processes and outcomes and to enhance internal validity.
For example, studies simulating the conflict between the Greek and Turkish Cypriots have explored hypotheses about the impact of focusing on
values in negotiation. It was possible in a simulated setting to compare
interventions using Burton's (1986) idea of confronting value differences
in prenegotiation sessions ("facilitation") with Fisher's (1964) notion of
focusing only on interests ("fractionation"). Facilitation was found to
produce more cooperative negotiations than fractionation (Druckman et
al., 1988), and further experimentation uncovered the specific factors or
mechanisms that accounted for the positive effects of facilitation (Druckman and Broome, 1991).

Experimental research on mediation has provided insights into the
ways that mediators' role definitions, their tactics, and aspects of the negotiating situation influence their effectiveness. Some studies show that when
a mediator is seen as having no stake in the outcome and when hostility
between parties is high, pressure tactics (leverage) are more effective than
rewards in producing concessions (Harris and Carnevale, 1990; Carnevale
and Henry, 1989). Other experiments show that mediators are more likely

to be taken seriously if they suggest compromises early in the talks rather than later because the implications for who gives up what are clear and do not favor one party over the other (Conlon et al., 1994). Also, agreements are likely to be more effective if the mediators encourage the parties to generate and test hypotheses about the sources of the conflict and to take ownership of any agreements that result (Kressel et al., 1994).

An illustrative finding on interactive problem solving comes from a simulation by Cross and Rosenthal (1999), who recruited Palestinians and Israelis to participate in a discussion of several issues that divided these groups. Forty dyads were randomly assigned to one of four approaches to organizing the discussion: distributive bargaining, in which participants emphasize group positions and bargain about them; integrative bargaining, in which they identify interests and then seek to expand the alternatives; interactive problem solving, in which they identify needs and engage in joint problem solving; and a control condition in which participants receive no instructions on how to discuss the issues. Participants using the interactive problem-solving approach became less hawkish in their attitudes than those in the other conditions, and those using the integrative bargaining approach, to the researchers' surprise, became more hawkish than those in all the other conditions. The study examined only attitudes, not negotiating behavior or outcomes.

These examples illustrate how experimentation can be used to investigate the effects of well-defined aspects of conflict resolution interventions on attitudes and behaviors. Experimentation is well suited for clarifying the mechanisms responsible for effects and thus contributing to an explanation of why an intervention works the way it does. The usefulness of the approach is limited because the criteria for conducting strong experiments are too stringent for collecting and evaluating data on some types of conflict resolution interventions (e.g., the design of national electoral systems, peacekeeping missions). Further, it is difficult to simulate the many aspects of international interventions. Nevertheless, experiments can make useful contributions to knowledge as part of a multimethod research strategy (e.g., Hopmann and Walcott, 1977, compared experimental simulations with the coded results of an actual arms control negotiation). Insights from other research approaches can be evaluated in a more precise way with experiments, experimental hypotheses can be studied in field contexts, and the results from experiments can be compared to those obtained from other methods in a search for conclusions that do not depend on the research method. The classical experiment is also a benchmark or a point of comparison in evaluating the results of nonexperimental methods of analysis.

Multivariate Data Analysis Methods

These methods measure aspects of the historical record of past international conflicts and conflict resolution efforts and search for regularities in that record that qualify as generic knowledge. Researchers who use these methods typically examine a number of aspects of each of several interventions of a particular type. Their measurements may be qualitative, such as simple tabulations of whether particular conditions were present or absent, or they may involve numerical measurements (e.g., numbers of people killed) or the development of indicators (e.g., measures of attitudes derived from surveys or analyses of public statements). Techniques of multivariate data analysis are designed to investigate the strengths of associations and sometimes the temporal ordering of events or indicators in order to support some hypotheses and rule out others concerning the causes of these associations and temporal orderings. Although most often used on datasets involving large numbers of separate events, the approach can also be applied to small numbers of events if many observations have been made of each. Thus, even case materials, if properly prepared, can be subjected to multivariate analysis.

A common use of multivariate analysis for research on international conflict resolution begins with the compilation of so-called events data on conflicts and on the efforts that have been made to resolve them. For example, Bercovitch and colleagues (e.g., Bercovitch, 1989, 1986; Bercovitch and Wells, 1993; Bercovitch and Langley, 1993) have assembled a dataset on more than 300 mediation attempts since the end of World War II. Each case is coded in terms of such indicators as type of mediator (e.g., individual, organization), mediator's resources, mediator's status, strategies used, types of issues, duration and intensity of the dispute, timing of intervention, complexity of the dispute, and outcome (impasse, partial settlement, full settlement). These researchers used quantitative techniques to analyze the coded data and test hypotheses about relationships between the outcome of the intervention and conditions that may affect the outcome, such as the use of directive or passive mediation strategies, the nature of the issues as ideological or interest based, power imbalances between the parties, and early versus late intervention. They also developed and tested various causal models of the connections among features of the disputes and the mediation outcome (Bercovitch and Langley, 1993). This analytical approach makes it possible to examine the outcomes of mediation as a function not only of the mediation itself but also prior contextual conditions (features of the dispute)—something that is difficult to examine by simulation.

The multivariate approach has also been used to study negotiation. Using primary sources (interviews with delegates) and secondary sources (published accounts), it is possible to code each of a series of negotiation cases in terms of such characteristics as the issues (large or small), parties (strong or weak), conditions (public or private), processes (bargaining or problem solving), and outcomes (impasse, partial agreement, comprehensive agreement). Researchers have used such data to define distinct types of negotiations (Chasek, 1997) and to organize them along such dimensions as the size of the negotiation (bilateral, trilateral, multilateral) and the complexity of the issues (Druckman, 1997). Such analyses provide an empirical basis for developing typologies based on profiles of negotiation characteristics. They may also enable practitioners to consult the historical record for past cases that may be instructive for present purposes.

Multivariate datasets like these can be compiled for a wide variety of interventions. For instance, they have been used to illuminate the effectiveness of economic sanctions (Hufbauer et al., 1990), the factors conducive to ethnic conflicts (Gurr, 1993), and the relationship of language policy to communal conflict (Laitin, Chapter 13). In all cases their usefulness depends on the relevance of the variables chosen, the validity of the coding, and the level of detail. The chief strength of the approach is that statistical analysis allows researchers to consider numerous possible causal mechanisms using more cases than they can evaluate with the unaided mind. The chief weakness is that much of the richness of each case is lost when the case is reduced to a list of indicators. There is obviously a tradeoff between breadth and depth in case analysis, and multivariate data analysis normally exhibits both the strengths and the weaknesses of breadth.

The above examples use a cross-sectional approach—that is, they analyze multivariate data in which each case is assigned a single value for each characteristic being coded, without regard to time. While the cross-sectional approach can, with sufficient data, probe complex contingent relationships among variables, it is limited for investigating causal mechanisms because the operation of these can only be assessed across time. It is possible to apply statistical techniques of causal modeling to test the consistency of the data with a hypothesis about causal mechanisms (e.g., Bollen, 1989; Stevens, 1996), but the strength of the inferences from these techniques, even with sufficient data, is always limited by the lack of a temporal dimension.

Multivariate analysis can also consider change over time—and examine causal mechanisms more directly—by analyzing data arranged in a time series, in which the same variable is coded at many points in the history of a case to allow the study of temporal processes. In one such time series approach, historical data are used to "postdict" known outcomes. The goal is to develop a conceptually coherent account of a conflict resolution process that is consistent with the known outcome. For example, in a study of base rights negotiation between Spain and the United States in 1975-1976, Druckman (1986) showed that the agreement resulted from a sequence of identifiable crises and turning points. The approach can also be used to identify a mechanism for the operation of an intervention that is consistent with the observed chain of events. Hopmann and Smith (1978) showed that the outcomes of the 1962-1963 partial nuclear test ban talks resulted from certain actions taken by nations outside the negotiations. This multivariate time series research design is quite useful for identifying how the temporal pattern of interactions between the conflicting parties and interventions by external actors led to the ultimate outcome. Postdiction can be considered as something like an experiment in that theory can be tested by comparing the actual outcome with "predictions" made on the basis of the theory and the initial conditions.

Historical data that are coded by time of occurrence can be used to evaluate the impacts of planned interventions and to trace the processes by which these impacts occur. The research approach is referred to in the technical literature as interrupted time series analysis. An example is a study of five mediation efforts in the conflict between Armenia and Azerbaijan between 1990 and 1995. Mooradian and Druckman (1999) demonstrated that each mediation effort had limited effects on the time series of events. However, the historical pattern of continuous violence was altered dramatically after Azerbaijan's major military offensive in 1993-1994, apparently due to a hurting stalemate suffered by both sides. The pattern of conflictual events before the offensive (October 1992 to March 1993) changed to a cooperative trend following the fighting (May 1994 to September 1994), only to turn again to conflict by October 1994. A long time series of events enables the analyst to ascertain the extent to which each intervention alters the trend and to consider whether the effects are immediate or delayed. Inference is complicated by the fact that the multiple interventions are not independent of each other—for example, the effect of a successful intervention may be due in part to the fact that past efforts failed. In addition, the validity of the time series is sometimes hard to establish.

Many of the problems of inference involved in time series analyses have been addressed by quantitative methodologists. For example, they have developed techniques for differential weighting of distant and recent events (referred to as exponential smoothing), compensating for the dependence of events on similar events in the recent past (statistical controls for autocorrelation), accounting for possible explanatory factors that are associated with each other (stepwise regression for unique variance explained), and taking account of changes in the estimated subjective probabilities of events (Bayesian analysis, Markov chain processes; see Frei and Ruloff, 1989, for discussion of these techniques). These techniques have been used in sophisticated forecasting methodologies (e.g., Duncan and Job, 1980) and model-fitting analyses of interactive processes (e.g., Druckman and Harris, 1990; Patchen and Bogumil, 1995, 1997). They have not, however, solved some of the fundamental conceptual and measurement problems of multivariate time series analysis, such as the need to compare events with counterfactuals, the lack of valid measures for some important variables, and the lack of sufficient size or variation in the sample of historical events.

Multivariate analysis techniques, like other methods, have their characteristic strengths and weaknesses. As already noted, their chief strength is that they can simultaneously consider more cases, and more aspects of a single case, than a human analyst can comprehend. This capability is particularly useful for analyzing the effects of contextual factors on conflict resolution efforts because the potential effects are numerous and because useful indicators are available for many contextual variables. In such situations, multivariate analysis can reveal patterns that might otherwise go unnoticed. The chief limitations of the approach are those of the available data and concepts. The methods can only be applied when a sufficient number of historical cases (or a sufficient richness of data on a single case) exist for quantitative comparison—normally, dozens of data points are necessary to test a single bivariate hypothesis, and more are needed to test hypotheses involving a conjunction of several variables. Also, the available data must include reasonably valid measures of the variables that are central to the desired analysis. Sometimes the variables for which valid measures are available for numerous cases are not the ones of the greatest theoretical or practical interest, and sometimes the variables of greatest interest are not well enough conceptualized to allow for valid measurement. In such instances, multivariate analysis has obvious limitations.

Multivariate analysis is particularly useful at the current state of theory development for uncovering patterns that deserve further analysis by other analytical methods. When patterns evident in cross-sectional studies suggest causal hypotheses, it may be useful to explore those hypotheses further by using simulation experiments or detailed analyses of individual cases through time. Similarly, patterns that emerge from time series data are also worth further examination by other methods, particularly intensive examination of case material. A major value of quantitative research approaches is through the discipline they impose on thinking. The measurement efforts that these approaches demand (e.g., specifying operational definitions, developing valid indicators) force researchers to be precise about their concepts and may thus sharpen analysis and raise the level of debate among scholars and practitioners.

Enhanced Case Study Methods: Structured, Focused Case Comparisons and Process Tracing

The case study is one of the classical methods of political science, and its uses and limitations for making inferences are well known (e.g., Smelser, 1976; Ragin, 1987; Collier, 1993; Collier and Mahoney, 1996; King et al., 1994). Our interest here is in refinements of the traditional case study approach that have been developed over the past two or three decades to increase the rigor of the approach and overcome some of its limitations, particularly the problem of noncomparability across cases and the difficulty of using case material to test hypotheses. Traditional case studies can be useful by demonstrating that a particular case is inconsistent with an existing theory and thus stimulating scholarly research and rethinking by practitioners. However, the contribution of traditional case studies to cumulative knowledge has been limited by noncomparability across cases: there is typically no way to test the conclusions from one case study against evidence from other case studies because they fail to include information needed for the comparison.

The focus here is on two particular refinements to the case study approach: the method of structured, focused case comparisons, and process tracing. Both methods improve on the traditional case study by being more theoretically explicit. By stating in advance which variables are worth examining and which processes are worth tracing (and by implication which are not), these approaches make it possible to focus case-based research and thus to build knowledge cumulatively.

Structured, focused case comparisons differ from the traditional case study approach in that cases are selected and case descriptions developed with particular theory-guided questions or conceptual issues in mind (Lijphart, 1971; George and Smoke, 1974; George, 1979; Collier, 1993; Putnam, 1993; Faure, 1994). The method requires that an analytical protocol be developed before the case studies are conducted that defines the variables of interest and some of the researcher's key questions about them. This allows the researcher to compare the cases on the central issues of interest. The structured, focused case comparison method cannot, as a rule, be applied to previously completed case studies because they usually lack information demanded by the protocol.

A well-known application of the structured, focused case comparison approach has been to test deterrence theory. Researchers select a set of cases they judge to represent successful and failed deterrence and then examine the historical evidence on each case to answer theoretically relevant questions such as whether the deterrent threat was credible, whether it was clearly communicated, whether the leaders of the target country followed principles of rational decision making, and the like (George and Smoke, 1974; Lebow, 1981). This research has focused especially on deterrence failures because a failure that occurred when all of the theoretical conditions for success were in place would call into question the principles of deterrence theory and because of the difficulties of establishing deterrence successes (when a deterrent is successful, the result is often that nothing observable happens). Blechman and Wittes's paper (Chapter 3) in this volume on the use of threats of force uses a form of structured, focused case comparison.

The structured, focused case comparison method requires a theory or conceptual framework that is sufficiently well specified to generate the list of factors or variables that must be considered in each case. The method is particularly attractive when a testable hypothesis exists along with unambiguous indicators of the relevant variables that are obtainable from available historical information. It also requires that several relevant cases are available. Sometimes, useful results can be obtained with fewer than a dozen cases—a contrast to the requirements of the multivariate quantitative approach.

Compared to traditional case study research, structured and focused case comparisons have the advantage of comparability: the same information is collected about each case using the same methods. Because only selected information is needed about each case, it may be possible to do more structured comparisons with a given set of resources than unstructured comparisons, but the method can miss information on aspects of the cases that are not presumed in advance to be important. This is both the advantage and the disadvantage of research methods informed by explicit conceptualization. Structured and focused case comparisons can to some extent overcome this problem by being flexible about the way information is extracted from cases. Flexibility allows insights to be discovered in individual cases that may have been missed in the answers to structured questions. These insights can then be examined by collecting the necessary information on the other cases under study.

Compared to the multivariate analysis approach, structured and focused case comparisons examine fewer variables and fewer cases (the selection being made on theoretical grounds) but provide much more detailed information on the variables they do examine. Because of these differences, the multivariate approach has a comparative advantage for exploratory analysis, like traditional case studies; in contrast, structured and focused case comparison is comparatively well suited to testing hypotheses from theory and refining the theories it tests. It is sometimes possible to treat a set of case comparisons as a source of events data and to apply multivariate quantitative analysis to the case-based data. For example, Table 3.1 summarizes the results of Blechman and Wittes's analysis of the uses of threats of force by the United States since the end of the Cold War by coding a number of key variables, usually as present or absent. Such a table of categorical data can be analyzed statistically in the manner of cross-sectional events-data analysis, although this particular data table may be small enough for adequate analysis by inspection.

Just as structured case comparison is a sort of qualitative analog to cross-sectional events-data research, the process-tracing approach is a sort of qualitative analog to time series data analysis. In the process-tracing approach (Bennett and George, forthcoming), a researcher postulates one or more processes or "causal mechanisms" by which a set of initial events, including a conflict resolution intervention, might lead to a set of outcomes.[6] The historical record is then searched for evidence that the postulated processes did or did not occur. The process-tracing approach can allow for multiple tests of the same hypothesis in a single case, thus dampening the criticism that a single case study cannot test a hypothesis because a single test is never statistically convincing. However, repetitions of similar conditions in the course of the same conflict are not independent in a statistical sense. This situation presents a threat to the validity of cause-and-effect generalizations drawn from process-tracing studies, analogous to threats to validity in quantitative time series research. Process tracing could, in principle, be used in a way that allows statistical tests of the relative explanatory power of different theories; however, we are not aware of any such applications. It is important to note that, for drawing inferences about learning and other experience-dependent processes, statistical nonindependence between events is not a problem and in fact is necessary for a case to be informative (Bennett and George, forthcoming).

An important difference between enhanced case study approaches and multivariate data analysis is that the former requires an explicit theory or conceptual framework while the latter does not. The enhanced case study approaches are an improvement over traditional case studies precisely because of their greater conceptual explicitness. It is useful to make a similar distinction regarding how multivariate quantitative research is conducted. This approach can be employed as a form of nearly pure empiricism by simply analyzing whatever indicators are available across a set of cases to see what regularities emerge. However, the results will be unsatisfying if the available indicators do not include measures of the important variables affecting outcomes. Thus, multivariate analysis is likely to yield more useful results if concepts are made explicit—if an effort is made at the start to specify the key variables and to develop indicators for them. This form of multivariate analysis is enhanced in much the same way as enhanced case study methods are.

We are suggesting here that there can be some convergence between case-based and multivariate quantitative approaches. We further believe that progress in understanding depends on such convergence. Both case study and multivariate research approaches to international conflict resolution were initially used in an exploratory mode to examine the available evidence (either case material or quantitative indicators) and to search for empirical regularities. This empiricist strategy has not led to strongly supported generic knowledge, but it has generated hypotheses that can be tested with more carefully focused research, using either case-based or quantitative research modes. It has also led to refinements in understanding, in which bivariate hypotheses about relationships between interventions and outcomes give way to conditional generalizations. These are statements or propositions that specify the conditions (sometimes called moderating variables) under which such relationships are likely to occur. Propositions about these conditions contribute to more nuanced knowledge, as exemplified by contingent theories of conflict resolution (Fisher, 1997).

Because of the limitations of each approach, progress seems most likely if both methods are used. One promising way to do this is to apply quantitative methods to data gathered by case study methods. This has occasionally been done with traditional case study data (e.g., the work of Ember and Ember, 1992, using ethnographic data from the Human Relations Area Files) and with enhanced case study material (e.g., quantitative scaling of data from negotiation cases; Druckman, 1997). The approach can be applied to several of the topics in this book, including the use of threats of force (Chapter 3), electoral system design (Chapter 11), and language policy (Chapter 13). Quantifying case study data may make for more precise comparisons between theories in terms of how well they explain available data and may also show more clearly where the data are inconclusive. Following a similar logic, statistical techniques of time series analysis can be applied to data from process-tracing case studies. It is also possible for quantitative researchers to build on the results of case comparisons by designing large-N studies that focus on the key variables identified in case-based research.

Another promising strategy for combining research methods is to use the results of multivariate studies to guide the development of protocols for structured case comparisons and process-tracing studies. Whenever multivariate research identifies a statistical regularity, it generates a hypothesis that could be tested in case-based research. Case study researchers may find the indicators from multivariate research too restrictive for their way of thinking, but they have the option to add depth to these variables in their protocols. We believe that this sort of interplay between methods is much more likely to be productive than a continuation of arguments about which method is superior, such as have frequently appeared in the literature on research methodology in international relations.

CONCLUSION

The challenges of evaluating efforts at international conflict resolution and our suggestions for how to meet those challenges are summarized in Table 2.1. This work leads to three major conclusions. First, theory development is key to addressing many of the most serious challenges of building knowledge about what works in international conflict resolution. This point has also been emphasized by others (e.g., Lijphart, 1971; Eckstein, 1975; George, 1979; Bennett and George, forthcoming). Second, understanding is most likely to progress through a dialogue between theory and

TABLE 2.1 Challenges of Evaluation and Strategies for Meeting Them

Challenges	Strategies
Conceptualization	
Defining the intervention	Develop and improve taxonomy of interventions
Defining "success"	Enumerate outcomes of interest
Setting reasonable expectations (how much? how soon?)	State hypotheses about process
Identifying relevant contingencies	Develop hypotheses about contingencies
Case Selection	
Enumerating the universe of cases	Frame the topic conceptually and historically; look for hidden and incomplete cases
Getting an appropriate sample	Specify bases of sample selection
Observation and Measurement	
Dealing with incomplete information	Develop multiple information sources
Achieving reliable measurement	Develop operational definitions; seek expert agreement
Developing indicators of success	Develop interim and long-term indicators
Making Inferences	
Comparing events with counterfactuals	Use multiple analytical methods (experimentation, multivariate analysis, case study)
Assessing the roles of extrinsic events	
Assessing contingent relationships	
Accounting for indirect effects of interventions	Develop and test hypotheses about contingencies
Accounting for actors' perceptions	Develop and test hypotheses about mechanisms and processes
Assessing the context of multiple interventions	

experience, with progress in each leading to refinements in the other. Third, the empirical research enterprise should use a strategy of "triangulation" (Campbell and Fiske, 1959; Cook, 1985) that relies on multiple sources of data and multiple modes of analysis to correct for the characteristic sources of error or bias in each and to help analysis converge on results that can be accepted with reasonable confidence.

Theory Development

The practical concern with how best to develop generic knowledge about what works in international conflict resolution leads to a perhaps surprising conclusion: there is a critical need to develop theory. This conclusion follows from the recognition that improvements in the quality of theory would help meet each of the major challenges of evaluation.

The needed theories would combine three elements. First, *taxonomies*, which can focus on types within a kind of intervention (e.g., peacekeeping missions), characteristics of interventions (e.g., strategies of coercive diplomacy, strength and speed of the application of economic sanctions, procedures used in problem-solving workshops), external contingencies (types of conditions affecting the link from intervention to outcomes), and types of outcomes (e.g., types of deterrence failures). The most useful taxonomies are presented with enough specificity to allow each phenomenon to be reliably classified. Second, postulates about *causal mechanisms and processes* that specify the ideal working of one or more types of intervention, including the processes by which intervention changes the course of a conflict and the outcomes that may result. Third, *contingent generalizations*—propositions or hypotheses that link the outcomes of a particular type of intervention to the characteristics of the intervention and the external contingencies that shape these outcomes. Ideally, theory also specifies the processes by which these characteristics and contingencies have their effects, thus linking contingent generalizations to causal mechanisms. This is a very demanding set of requirements given the current state of knowledge, but it is an appropriate list of objectives for theories.

Theories with all three elements would incorporate most of the suggestions in Table 2.1 and in this chapter for how to meet the challenges of evaluation. They would thus help meet the most fundamental challenge of evaluating conflict resolution interventions, posed by the fact that a tremendous number of events may be consequential for the outcomes of an intervention, especially if the outcomes are delayed in time. Without some guidance from theory about which events to examine and which aspects of those events matter, a researcher or practitioner faces an unsorted mountain of relevant and irrelevant detail and must make the inevitable choices about what is and is not worth considering on the basis of unstated theoretical presumptions. The history of science shows that more progress is made when such presumptions are made explicit so they can be tested and refined through cumulative research.

Well-specified theory also helps meet many of the more specific challenges to developing generic knowledge. It helps meet the major conceptual challenges by providing clear definitions of the types of interventions, the outcomes that might be considered indicators of their success or effectiveness, and the characteristics and external contingencies that may influence the relationships between interventions and outcomes. By explicitly identifying processes and causal mechanisms, a well-specified theory helps analysts focus their attention selectively on those events that follow an intervention that are postulated to have important effects on its eventual outcomes. Well-specified theory helps meet the challenges of case selection by clarifying which cases fall within the universe of any particular type of intervention. By specifying the important variables affecting outcomes, theory provides a rationale for purposive sampling and a basis for judging the appropriateness of samples selected in other ways. It helps solve the problem of a shortage of cases relative to explanatory variables by reducing the number of the latter and by postulating processes that lead to multiple testable hypotheses about each case. Finally, by specifying ideal outcomes and the processes that lead to them, theory can provide clear expectations about the course of a conflict after intervention, thus helping both researchers and practitioners evaluate progress and consider the next steps.

Knowledge about the techniques and concepts of international conflict resolution is not nearly well enough developed to strongly confirm a theory about even one of the techniques. Nevertheless, enough thinking and study have been done to state fairly well specified theories about many of them and subject those theories to focused empirical analysis. Pressing ahead with clear theoretical statements is, we believe, essential to developing generic knowledge about international conflict resolution techniques. Although many of these theoretical statements will be incomplete or wrong at first, they will nevertheless be useful for advancing knowledge. Deterrence theory provides a good example of what can be gained. Fairly well specified statements of deterrence theory have been available for several decades (e.g., Brodie, 1959; Schelling, 1960), allowing a cumulation of focused research using a variety of methods (e.g., George and Smoke, 1974; Lebow, 1981; Jervis et al., 1985; National Research Council, 1989). Although the early theoretical statements can now be said to have been incomplete, they sharpened debate about the historical evidence and encouraged researchers to look more closely at history to test the theory. As a result, practitioners of deterrence now have a more sophisticated understanding than before of which factors to consider in their domestic situation, in the target country, and in the international context before making threats. We believe that theory about other techniques and concepts can usefully follow this model and that several of the contributions to this volume make advances in that direction.

Theoretical statements need not closely approach the ideal presented here in order to be useful. Even partial theoretical statements—partial taxonomies, for example, or limited sets of hypotheses about the ways that certain contingencies affect the outcomes of intervention—help both research and practice by directing attention to particular variables that may be important to the outcomes of conflict resolution interventions. To the extent that a theory is supported by evidence, it has identified variables worth considering. Both analysts and practitioners can economize on time and effort by looking at those variables first and considering what theory says about them. Of course, to the extent that a theory is incomplete or wrong, it may direct attention to the wrong variables. Scholars and practitioners need to take theories only as seriously as the supporting evidence implies. They are not absolute guides to action, only interim statements that summarize and systematize available knowledge and that may have suggestive implications about what is likely to work in new historical situations.

Well-supported theoretical propositions have several uses for practitioners. They help practitioners assess situations by identifying the factors to consider in deciding whether, when, and how to use a particular type of intervention. They suggest scenarios leading from interventions to outcomes, both desired and otherwise, that practitioners may examine for their relevance to the situation at hand. They suggest what must be put into an intervention if it is to achieve a desired outcome and identify external conditions that are likely to lead to undesirable outcomes. Theories thus help practitioners identify policy opportunities and anticipate policy pitfalls. In all these ways, well-supported theories have diagnostic value for practitioners. Even theoretical propositions that are merely plausible can have diagnostic value if used with caution.

A Dialogue of Theory and Experience

Theories such as deterrence theory have advanced practical knowledge primarily because of how they help make sense of historical experience. Advances in formal theory by themselves may have very limited practical value because such theories may make opposing predictions depending on the specifics of a case. Wilson (1989), for example, shows that game theory models predict different outcomes of deterrence attempts depending on the structure of information and the parties' interaction—variables whose values can be determined only by observation of particular cases. From the researcher's standpoint, a useful theory is one that, by focusing attention on particular contingencies, causal mechanisms, or distinctions between situations or classes and characteristics of interventions, leads to empirically supported generic statements that distinguish between favorable and unfavorable conditions for particular types of intervention and explanatory accounts of the processes by which conflicts are resolved. Such theories are also useful to practitioners by focusing their attention on aspects of conflict situations that are likely to be important to their decisions and offering ways to think through the possible consequences of their choices. Experience tests and refines theories, thus making them more useful over time.

Good theory gives practitioners advantages they are not likely to gain from unaided reflection on their experience and past cases. Consider, for example, the development of theory about how the structure of electoral systems may affect the course of communal conflict in multicultural societies. Because each electoral system is unique, it would be hard for a practitioner in such a country to make sense of historical evidence from over 200 other countries without theoretical concepts that make it possible to classify those systems and consider their outcomes. Concepts like vote-seat proportionality, geographic accountability, consociationalism, and centripetalism and the theories in which they are embedded (Lijphart, 1984; Horowitz, 1985; Reilly and Reynolds, Chapter 11) offer useful ways of thinking about how any specific proposed electoral design is likely to shape the ethnic composition of political parties, interparty competition, and the potential for interethnic cooperation, communal violence, and peaceful transfers of power. Of course, there is no definitive theory in this field. Nevertheless, the theories that exist, and even the debate among them, are useful to practitioners by identifying causal mechanisms and historical trajectories from the past that may represent models to emulate or pitfalls to avoid. The theories not only point out good and bad examples but also specify what about them is good or bad.

It is important to be explicit about the ways in which theory can and cannot help practitioners of international conflict resolution. No matter how well a theory is established, it cannot eliminate the need for practitioners to exercise judgment based on their experience and knowledge. It will always be necessary, at a minimum, for practitioners to classify current conflict situations into theoretically meaningful types based on available information and their judgments of the parties, to define their policy objectives, to make tradeoffs between competing objectives and between short- and long-term objectives, to judge how to proceed given the possibility of unforeseen events that might intervene, and to decide whether aspects of the current situation make it so different from past experience as to question the applicability of the theory to the particular case. A detailed discussion of practitioners' judgment can be found in George (1993).

What good theory can do for practitioners is help them think through the decisions they face. Theory provides diagnostic categories for classifying conflict situations, and it advises on which aspects of a conflict situation are diagnostically important. It offers generic knowledge about the conditions that favor the use of particular interventions in particular kinds of situations and about the effects of implementing the interventions in specific ways. It also provides information on how strongly such generalizations are supported by historical and other evidence. By offering accounts of the processes and causal mechanisms that lead from interventions to outcomes, it gives practitioners ways of checking on the progress of their conflict resolution efforts. A theory of causal mechanisms may also help a practitioner think of new approaches to conflict situations designed to influence those mechanisms.

Thus, it makes sense for practitioners to use theories as guides to thinking and action but not as sources of prescriptions for action. A theory that is well supported by evidence may provide a better guide to action than an individual practitioner's experience; it certainly provides an important supplement to that experience. A theory may also mislead—either because it is in error or because it does not apply to the situation at hand—but a theory built on careful analysis of the relevant cases is less likely to mislead than an implicit theory based only on the limited and perhaps biasing experiences of a few practitioners. Theories can be useful and can be made more useful by careful research. However, they cannot eliminate the need or the responsibility for practitioners to make careful judgments appropriate to particular situations.

It is useful to distinguish between theory development and the evaluation of interventions. Theory is intended to produce knowledge that applies to a number of cases, referred to here as generic knowledge. Theories include propositions that specify contingent relationships among variables or causal processes or mechanisms to explain these relationships. Evaluations are intended to throw light on whether particular interventions were or were not effective and why. Evaluation depends on theory development, which provides indicators or criteria of success and a body of propositions describing the conditions under which success or failure (under those criteria) can be expected and the processes leading to those outcomes. Thus, theory provides the concepts needed to evaluate an intervention and explain the reasons for its outcomes.

Triangulation

Using several distinct research approaches or sources of information in conjunction is a valuable strategy for developing generic knowledge. This strategy is particularly useful for meeting the challenges of measurement and inference. The nature of historical phenomena makes impossible controlled experimentation with real-life situations—the analytical technique best suited to make strong inferences about causes and effects. Thus, making inferences requires using experimentation in simulated conditions and various other methods, each of which has its own advantages and limitations but none of which alone can provide the level of certainty desired about what works and under what conditions. We conclude that debates between advocates of different research methods (e.g., the quantitative-qualitative debate) are unproductive except in the context of a search for ways in which different methods can complement each other. Because there is no single best way to develop knowledge, the search for generic knowledge about international conflict resolution should adopt an epistemological strategy of "triangulation" (Campbell and Fiske, 1959), sometimes called "critical multiplism" (Cook, 1985, 1993). That is, it should use multiple perspectives, sources of data, constructs, interpretive frameworks, and modes of analysis to address specific questions on the presumption that research approaches that rely on certain perspectives, constructs, and so forth can act as partial correctives for the limitations of research approaches that rely on different ones. An underlying assumption is that robust findings (those that hold across studies that vary along several dimensions) engender more confidence than replicated findings (a traditional scientific ideal but not practicable in international relations research outside the laboratory). Thus, when different sources of data or different methods converge on a single answer, one can have increased confidence in the result. When they do not converge, one can make interpretations that take into account the known biases in each research approach. A continuing critical dialogue among analysts using different perspectives, methods, and data is likely to lead to an understanding that better approximates reality than the results from any single study, method, or data source. For more detailed theoretical discussion of triangulation approaches to understanding, see Cook (1985, 1993).

A Final Word

Practitioners who wish to resolve international conflicts need to learn the lessons of history, but history provides no definitive or comprehensive text. This situation is inevitable in a continually changing international system. A particular challenge in learning lessons from history is the tendency of individuals to assimilate new information to old ways of thinking and the related tendency of organizations to reject information that calls current policies into question. Both these tendencies may lead practitioners to discount or misinterpret new information that does not accord with their preexisting views. Because inferences from history always involve comparisons with unrealized, or counterfactual, worlds, there is plenty of room for reinterpreting available knowledge to fit preconceptions or policy commitments, thus undermining the potential value of new knowledge.[7] Nevertheless, careful analysis of historical and other evidence, together with the development of clear diagnostic concepts and empirically tested theories of peace processes, can make a modest but significant contribution to practitioners' ability to understand and intervene to resolve conflicts. The following chapters are intended as part of that contribution.

ACKNOWLEDGMENTS

We are indebted to Alexander George, Thomas Cook, Ronald Fisher, David Laitin, Dean Pruitt, and Philip Tetlock for helpful comments on drafts of this paper.

A shorter version of this paper appeared in *International Studies Review*, 2000, 2:33-63.

NOTES

[1]It is useful to offer a few working definitions. We use the term *intervene* broadly to include any action undertaken to change the course of a conflict process. Interventions by force are only one type. *International conflict* includes violent conflicts between states as part of a larger class. Our concern is with significant intercommunal conflicts that have the potential to (1) generate violence that crosses state boundaries, (2) cause intrastate violence that generates international concern, or (3) result in violations of international norms about the appropriate uses of force to secure justice or order in states. Thus, our concern is with intercommunal conflict that is or may become violent. The parties to international conflict may be states, international organizations, or other collective actors that are defined or that mobilize themselves as ethnic, cultural, religious, socioeconomic, political, or national entities. *International conflict resolution efforts* are activities that aim to decrease the level of violence in international conflicts, to reduce the likelihood that conflicts will result in violence, or to provide or strengthen mechanisms or institutions for the peaceful expression and resolution of intercommunal grievances so that they will not turn violent.

These efforts aim to change history at least in the narrow sense of altering the course of events and the pattern of forces that have, over an extended period of time, shaped the interaction between the parties to a conflict. They may also seek or produce broader historical changes affecting relationships of additional parties or the international system. It might be said that all social interventions are efforts to change the course of history in the sense that all social relationships have historical contexts. However, interventions in international conflict processes are quintessentially historical: they aim to change the long sweep

of relationships among classical historical actors such as states, nations, and social movements in ways likely to be noticed by world historians.

[2]We adopt this analogy from George (1993).

[3]Medical science is finding that few diseases follow this model. Smallpox and yellow
fever may follow it, but cancer may be a more apt analogy for international conflict. There
are many types of cancer, many paths the disease may take through time, and many points
at which medical intervention may do some good. As with international conflict, the multifaceted nature of cancer makes it very hard to understand and treat. We are indebted to
David Laitin on this point.

[4]By *theory* we mean a conceptual model that defines a set of actors and conditions
(such as intervention strategies, outcome conditions, and factors other than the intervention
that affect outcomes) and postulates associations and causal relationships among them. To
the extent that evidence is consistent with a theory and inconsistent with alternatives, confidence is increased that the postulated associations and causal relationships constitute generic knowledge about the actors or conditions. A theory is practical to the extent that it
produces reliable generic knowledge that can be used, along with case-specific knowledge,
to enable a practitioner to identify the intervention most likely to yield a desired outcome in
a particular situation.

[5]Such hypotheses and theories may be deductive in origin or they may be developed
inductively from studies of the historical paths that led from an intervention to expected or
unexpected outcomes. Inductively generated hypotheses can be tested on additional cases. An
example from the negotiation literature is the work of Druckman (1995) on "situational levers."

[6]The search for causal mechanisms has increasingly been recognized as an important
aspect of explanation and an important complement to the search for contingent generalizations in understanding international historical processes (e.g., Elster, 1983; Dessler, 1991;
Little, 1991; Bennett and George, forthcoming). Whereas cross-sectional analyses tend to
focus on establishing associations among variables, the search for causal mechanisms focuses on explaining such associations.

[7]We are indebted to Philip Tetlock for emphasizing these points.

REFERENCES

Achen, C.H.
   1986   *The Statistical Analysis of Quasi-Experiments.* Berkeley: University of California
           Press.
Bennett, A., and A.L. George
   Forth-   *Case Study and Theory Development.* Cambridge, Mass.: MIT Press.
   coming
Bercovitch, J.
   1986   International mediation: A study of incidence, strategies, and conditions of suc-
           cessful outcomes. *Cooperation and Conflict* 21:155-168.
   1989   International dispute resolution. In *Mediation Research: The Process and Effectiveness
           of Third Party Intervention,* K. Kressel and D. Pruitt, eds. San Francisco: Jossey-Bass.
   1997   Mediation in international conflict: An overview of theory, a review of practice.
           In *Peacemaking in International Conflict,* I.W. Zartman and J.L. Rasmussen, eds.
           Washington, D.C.: United States Institute of Peace Press.
Bercovitch, J., and J. Langley
   1993   The nature of the dispute and the effectiveness of international mediation. *Jour-
           nal of Conflict Resolution* 37:670-691.

Bercovitch, J., and R. Wells
   1993   Evaluating mediation strategies: A theoretical and empirical analysis. *Peace and Change* 18:3-25.
Bollen, K.A.
   1989   *Structural Equations with Latent Variables.* New York: Wiley.
Brodie, B.
   1959   *Strategy in the Missile Age.* Princeton, N.J.: Princeton University Press.
Burton, J.W.
   1986   The history of international conflict resolution. In *International Conflict Resolution: Theory and Practice*, E.E. Azar and J.W. Burton, eds. Boulder, Colo.: Lynne Rienner.
Campbell, D.T.
   1975   Degrees of freedom and the case study. *Comparative Political Studies* 8:178-193.
Campbell, D.T., and D. Fiske
   1959   Convergent and discriminant validation by the multitrait-multimethod matrix. *Psychological Bulletin* 56:81-105.
Carnevale, P.J., and R.A. Henry
   1989   Determinants of mediator behavior: A test of the strategic choice model. *Journal of Applied Social Psychology* 19:481-498.
Chasek, P.
   1997   A comparative analysis of multilateral environmental negotiations. *Group Decision and Negotiation* 6:437-461.
Collier, D.
   1993   The comparative method. In *Political Science: The State of the Discipline II*, A.W. Finifter, ed. Washington, D.C.: American Political Science Association.
Collier, D., and J. Mahoney
   1996   Insights and pitfalls: Selection bias in qualitative research. *World Politics* 49(1):56-91.
Conlon, D.E., P. Carnevale, and W.H. Ross
   1994   The influence of third party power and suggestions on negotiation: The surface value of a compromise. *Journal of Applied Social Psychology* 24(12):1084-1113.
Cook, T.D.
   1985   Post-positivist critical multiplism. Pp. 21-62 in *Social Science and Social Policy*, R.L. Shotland and M.M. Mark, eds. Beverly Hills, Calif.: Sage.
   1993   A quasi-sampling theory of the generalization of causal relationships. In *New Directions for Program Evaluation: Understanding Causes and Generalizing About Them*, vol. 57, L. Sechrest and A.G. Scott, eds. San Francisco: Jossey-Bass.
Cook, T.D., and D.T. Campbell
   1979   *Quasi-Experimentation: Designs and Analysis Issues for Social Research in Field Settings.* Boston: Houghton Mifflin.
Cross, S., and R. Rosenthal
   1999   Three models of conflict resolution: Effects on intergroup expectations and attitudes. *Journal of Social Issues* 55(3):561-580.
Dessler, D.
   1991   Beyond correlations: Toward a causal theory of war. *International Studies Quarterly* 35:337-355.
Diamond, L., and J.W. McDonald
   1991   *Multi-track Diplomacy: A Systems Guide and Analysis.* Grinnell: Iowa Peace Institute.

Diehl, P.F., D. Druckman, and J. Wall
  1998   International peacekeeping and conflict resolution: A taxonomic analysis with
         implications. *Journal of Conflict Resolution* 42:33-55.
Druckman, D.
  1986   Stages, turning points, and crises: Negotiating military base rights, Spain and the
         United States. *Journal of Conflict Resolution* 30:327-360.
  1995   Situational levers of position change: Further explorations. *Annals of the Ameri-
         can Academy of Political and Social Science* 542:61-80.
  1997   Dimensions of international negotiations: Structures, processes, and outcomes.
         Group Decision and Negotiation 6:395-420.
Druckman, D., and B.J. Broome
  1991   Value differences and conflict resolution: Liking or familiarity? *Journal of Conflict
         Resolution* 35:571-593.
Druckman, D., and J.N. Druckman
  1996   Visibility and negotiating flexibility. *Journal of Social Psychology* 136:117-120.
Druckman, D., and R. Harris
  1990   Alternative models of responsiveness in international negotiation. *Journal of Con-
         flict Resolution* 34:235-251.
Druckman, D., and P.C. Stern
  1997   Evaluating peacekeeping missions. *Mershon International Studies Review* 41:151-
         165.
Druckman, D., B.J. Broome, and S.H. Korper
  1988   Value differences and conflict resolution: Facilitation or delinking? *Journal of
         Conflict Resolution* 32:489-510.
Duncan, G.T., and B. Job
  1980   Probability Forecasting in International Affairs. Final report to the Defense Ad-
         vanced Research Projects Agency.
Eckstein, H.
  1975   Case studies and theory in political science. Pp. 79-138 in *Handbook of Political
         Science*, vol. 7, F. Greenstein and N. Polsby, eds. Boston: Addison-Wesley.
Elster, J.
  1983   *Explaining Technical Change: A Case Study in the Philosophy of Science.* Cambridge:
         Cambridge University Press.
Ember, C.R., and M. Ember
  1992   Resource unpredictability, mistrust, and war: A cross-cultural study. *Journal of
         Conflict Resolution* 36(2):242-262.
Faure, A.M.
  1994   Some methodological problems in comparative politics. *Journal of Theoretical Poli-
         tics* 6:307-322.
Fisher, R.
  1964   Fractionating conflict. In *International Conflict and Behavioral Science: The Craigville
         Papers*, R. Fisher, ed. New York: Basic Books.
Fisher, R.J.
  1997   *Interactive Conflict Resolution.* Syracuse, N.Y.: Syracuse University Press.
Frei, D., and D. Ruloff
  1989   *Handbook of Foreign Policy Analysis.* Boston: Martinus Nijhoff.
Galtung, J.
  1969   Peace, violence and peace research. *Journal of Peace Research* 6:167-191.
Geddes, B.
  1990   How the cases you choose affect the answers you get. In *Political Analysis*, vol. 2,
         J.A. Stimson, ed. Ann Arbor: University of Michigan Press.

George, A.L.
  1979   Case studies and theory development: The method of structured, focused comparison. In *Diplomacy: New Approaches in History, Theory, and Policy*, P.G. Lauren, ed. New York: Free Press.
  1993   *Bridging the Gap: Theory and Practice in Foreign Policy.* Washington, D.C.: United States Institute of Peace Press.
  1997   The role of the congruence method for case study research. Paper presented at the convention of the International Studies Association, Toronto, March.
George, A.L., and A. Bennett
  1998   Process tracing with notes on causal mechanisms and historical explanation. Paper presented at the Diplomatic History and International Relations Theory Conference, Arizona State University, January.
George, A.L., and R. Smoke
  1974   *Deterrence in American Foreign Policy: Theory and Practice.* New York: Columbia University Press.
Guetzkow, H., and J.J. Valadez
  1981   *Simulated International Processes: Theories and Research in Global Modeling.* Beverly Hills, Calif.: Sage.
Gurr, T.R.
  1993   *Minorities at Risk: A Global View of Ethnopolitical Conflict.* Washington, D.C.: United States Institute of Peace Press.
Harris, K.I., and P.J. Carnevale
  1990   Chilling and hastening: The influence of third party power and interests in negotiation. *Organizational Behavior and Human Performance* 47:138-160.
Holsti, O.R.
  1989   Crisis decision making. Pp. 8-84 in *Behavior, Society, and Nuclear War*, vol. 1, P.E. Tetlock, J.L. Husbands, R. Jervis, P.C. Stern, and C. Tilly, eds. New York: Oxford University Press.
Hopmann, P.T., and T.C. Smith
  1978   An application of a Richardson process model: Soviet-American interactions in the test-ban negotiations, 1962-63. In *The Negotiation Process*, I.W. Zartman, ed. Beverly Hills, Calif.: Sage.
Hopmann, P.T., and C. Walcott
  1977   The impact of external stresses and tensions on negotiations. Pp. 301-323 in *Negotiations: Social Psychological Perspectives*, D. Druckman, ed. Beverly Hills, Calif.: Sage.
Horowitz, D.L.
  1985   *Ethnic Groups in Conflict.* Berkeley: University of California Press.
Hufbauer, G.C., J.J. Schott, and K.A. Elliott
  1990   *Economic Sanctions Reconsidered*, 2nd ed. Washington, D.C.: Institute for International Economics.
Jervis, R.
  1976   *Perception and Misperception in International Politics.* Princeton, N.J.: Princeton University Press.
Jervis, R., R.N. Lebow, and J.G. Stern
  1985   *Psychology and Deterrence.* Baltimore: Johns Hopkins University Press.
Khong, Y-F.
  1991   The lessons of Korea and the Vietnam decisions of 1965. Pp. 302-349 in *Learning in U.S. and Soviet Foreign Policy*, G.W. Breslauer and P.E. Tetlock, eds. Boulder, Colo.: Westview.

King, G., R.O. Keohane, and S. Verba
  1994   *Designing Social Inquiry: Scientific Inference in Qualitative Research.* Princeton, N.J.:
          Princeton University Press.
Kressel, K., E.A. Frontera, and S. Forlenza
  1994   The settlement orientation vs. the problem-solving style in custody mediation.
          Journal of Social Issues 50:67-84.
Kriesberg, L.
  1996   Coordinating intermediary peace efforts. *Negotiation Journal* 12:341-352.
Lebow, R.N.
  1981   *Between Peace and War: The Nature of International Crisis.* Baltimore: Johns Hop-
          kins University Press.
Lijphart, A.
  1971   Comparative politics and comparative method. *Americal Political Science Review*
          65(3):682-693.
  1984   *Democracies: Patterns of Majoritarian and Consensus Government in Twenty-One
          Countries.* New Haven, Conn.: Yale University Press.
Little, D.
  1991   *Varieties of Social Explanation: An Introduction to the Philosophy of Social Science.*
          Boulder, Colo.: Westview Press.
Mooradian, M., and D. Druckman
  1999   Hurting stalemate or mediation? The conflict over Nagorno-Karabakh, 1990-95.
          Journal of Peace Research 36(6):709-727.
National Research Council
  1988   *Enhancing Human Performance: Issues, Theories, and Techniques.* Committee on
          Techniques for the Enhancement of Human Performance, D. Druckman and J.A.
          Swets, eds. Washington, D.C.: National Academy Press.
  1989   *Perspectives on Deterrence.* Committee on Contributions of the Behavioral and
          Social Sciences to the Prevention of Nuclear War, P.C. Stern, R. Axelrod, R. Jervis,
          and R. Radner, eds. Washington, D.C.: National Academy Press.
Neustadt, R.E., and E.R. May
  1984   *Thinking in Time: The Uses of History for Decision Makers.* New York: Free Press.
Patchen, M., and D.D. Bogumil
  1995   Testing alternative models of reciprocity against interaction during the Cold War.
          Conflict Management and Peace Science 4:163-195.
  1997   Comparative reciprocity during the Cold War. *Peace and Conflict* 3:37-58.
Putnam, R.D.
  1993   *Making Democracy Work: Civic Traditions in Modern Italy.* Princeton, N.J.: Princeton
          University Press.
Ragin, C.
  1987   *The Comparative Method: Moving Beyond Qualitative and Quantitative Strategies.*
          Berkeley: University of California Press.
Robson, C.
  1993   *Real-World Research.* Oxford: Blackwell.
Schelling, T.C.
  1960   *The Strategy of Conflict.* Cambridge, Mass.: Harvard University Press.
Smelser, N.J.
  1976   *Comparative Methods in the Social Sciences.* Englewood Cliffs, N.J.: Prentice-Hall.
Stedman, S.J.
  1991   *Peacemaking in Civil War: International Mediation in Zimbabwe, 1974-1980.* Boulder,
          Colo.: Lynne Rienner.
  1997   Spoiler problems in peace processes. *International Security* 22(2):5-53.

Stevens, J.
  1996   *Applied Multivariate Statistics for the Social Sciences*, 3rd ed.   Hillsdale, N.J.:
         Lawrence Erlbaum.
Tetlock, P.E.
  1998   Social psychology and world politics. Pp. 868-912 in *Handbook of Social Psychol-
         ogy*, D. Gilbert, S. Fiske, and G. Lindzey, eds. New York: McGraw-Hill.
Tetlock, P.E., and A. Belkin, eds.
  1996   *Counterfactual Thought Experiments in World Politics*. Princeton, N.J.: Princeton
         University Press.
Wilson, R.
  1989   Deterrence in oligopolistic competition. Pp. 157-190 in *Perspectives on Deterrence*,
         Committee on Contributions of Behavioral and Social Science to the Prevention
         of Nuclear War, P.C. Stern, R. Axelrod, R. Jervis, and R. Radner, eds. Washington,
         D.C.: National Academy Press.

3

Defining Moment:
The Threat and Use of Force in
American Foreign Policy Since 1989

Barry M. Blechman and Tamara Cofman Wittes

The use of military force has been a difficult subject for American leaders for three decades. Ever since the failure of American policy and military power in Vietnam, it has been hard for U.S. policy makers to gain domestic support for the use of force as an instrument of statecraft. U.S. military power has been exercised throughout this 30-year period, but both threats of its use and the actual conduct of military operations have usually been controversial, turned to reluctantly, and marked by significant failures as well as successes. The American armed forces are large, superbly trained, fully prepared, and technologically advanced. Since the demise of the Soviet Union, U.S. forces are without question the most powerful, by far, on the face of the earth. Their competence, lethality, and global reach have been demonstrated time and again. Yet with rare exceptions, U.S. policy makers have found it difficult to achieve their objectives by threats alone. Often, they have had to use force, even if only in limited ways, to add strength to the words of diplomats. And, at more times than is desirable, the failures of threats and limited demonstrative uses of military power have confronted U.S. presidents with difficult choices between retreat and "all-out" military actions intended to achieve objectives by the force of arms alone.

In the 1980s most U.S. military leaders and many politicians and policy makers drew a strong conclusion from the failure of U.S. policy in Vietnam. This viewpoint was spelled out most clearly by then Secretary of Defense Caspar Weinberger in 1984: force should only be used as a last resort, he stated, to protect vital American interests, and with a commitment to win. Threats of force should not be used as part of diplomacy.

They should be used only when diplomacy fails and, even then, only when the objective is clear and attracts the support of the American public and the Congress.[1]

General Colin Powell, former chairman of the Joint Chiefs of Staff, was and remains a proponent of what was called the Weinberger doctrine. "Threats of military force will work," he says, "only when U.S. leaders actually have decided that they are prepared to use force." In the absence of such resolution, U.S. threats lack credibility because of the transparency of the American policy-making process. For this reason "the threat and use of force must be a last resort and must be used decisively."[2] Powell (1992a, 1992b) has argued that any use of force by the United States should accomplish U.S. objectives quickly while minimizing the risks to U.S. soldiers.

Other U.S. policy makers have taken a more traditional geopolitical view, believing that the U.S. failure in Vietnam needs to be understood on its own terms. Regardless of what was or was not achieved in Southeast Asia in the late 1960s and early 1970s, the United States, they believe, can and should continue to threaten and to use limited military force in support of diplomacy, to achieve limited ends without resorting to all-out contests of arms. In the words of then Secretary of State George Shultz in December 1984, "Diplomacy not backed by strength will always be ineffectual at best, dangerous at worst" (Shultz, 1985). Moreover, Shultz insisted, a use of force need not enjoy public support when first announced; it will acquire that support if the action is consonant with America's interests and moral values. In 1992 Les Aspin, then chairman of the House Armed Services Committee and later secretary of defense, branded the Weinberger doctrine an "all-or-nothing" approach. He asserted that the United States should be willing to use limited force for limited objectives and that it could pull back from such limited engagements without risk.[3] From this perspective, force should be used earlier in a crisis, rather than later, and need not be displayed in decisive quantities. The "limited objectives" school describes the threat of force as an important and relatively inexpensive adjunct to American diplomatic suasion.

As the Soviet Union disintegrated and the Cold War came to an end, this debate began to wane. U.S. policy makers began to wrestle with an array of problems that were individually less severe than the threat posed by the USSR but collectively no less vexing. The military situation changed drastically as well. U.S. military power reigned supreme, and the risk that a limited military intervention in a third nation could escalate into a global confrontation quickly faded. During both the Bush and first Clinton administrations, it became increasingly evident not only that there were many situations in which limited applications of force seemed helpful but that in the complicated post-Cold War world, opportunities for the pure application of Secretary Weinberger's maxims were rare. During this eight-year period, numerous challenges to American interests emerged that were too intractable for diplomatic solutions, that resisted cooperative multilateral approaches, and that were immune not only to sweet reason but to positive blandishments of any sort. Unencumbered by Cold War fears of sparking a confrontation with the powerful Soviet Union, American policy makers turned frequently to threats and the use of military power to deal with these situations, sometimes in ways that conformed to the Weinberger guidelines but more often suggesting that, rightly or wrongly, the press of world events drives policy makers inevitably toward Secretary Shultz's prescriptions for limited uses of force in support of diplomacy.

The United States sometimes succeeded in these ventures and sometimes failed. Success rarely came easily, however; more often, the United States had to go to great lengths to persuade adversaries to yield to its will. Even leaders of seemingly hapless nations, or of factions within devastated countries, proved surprisingly resistant to American threats. Often, U.S. leaders had to make good on threats by exercising U.S. military power. These further steps usually worked, but even when the United States conducted military operations in support of its post-Cold War policies the results were not always as clean and easy, or their consequences as far reaching, as decision makers had hoped. Given the overwhelming superiority of U.S. military power during this period, these results are hard to understand.

Indeed, even the greatest military success of the U.S. armed forces in the post-Cold War period—the expulsion of the Iraqi occupation army from Kuwait in 1991—became necessary because U.S. diplomacy, including powerful threats of force, failed. Despite the most amazing demonstration of U.S. military capabilities and willingness to utilize force if necessary to expel the Iraqi military from Kuwait, despite the movement of one-half million U.S. soldiers, sailors, and air men and women to the region, the call-up of U.S. reserve forces, the forging of a global military alliance, even the conduct of a devastating air campaign against the Iraqi occupation army and against strategic targets throughout Iraq itself, Saddam Hussein refused to comply with U.S. demands and his troops had to be expelled by force of arms. The United States was not able to accomplish its goals through threats alone. The Iraqi leader either disbelieved the U.S. threats, discounted U.S. military capabilities, or was willing to withstand defeat in Kuwait in pursuit of grander designs.

Why was this the case? Why has it been so difficult for the United States to realize its objectives through threats of using military force alone? Why have U.S. military threats not had greater impact in the post-Cold

War period, and why have limited uses of force, in support of diplomacy and in pursuit of political aims, not been able to accomplish U.S. goals more often? Is this situation changing as it becomes indisputably clear that the United States is the only remaining military superpower? Or have history and circumstance made U.S. military superiority an asset of only narrow utility in advancing the nation's interests through diplomacy?

To answer these questions, we examined all the cases during the Bush and first Clinton administrations in which the United States utilized its armed forces demonstratively in support of political objectives in specific situations. There are eight such cases, several of which include multiple uses of force. In two of the cases, Iraq and Bosnia, threats or uses of force became enduring elements in defining the limits of the relationship between the United States and its adversary.

Actually, the U.S. armed forces have been used demonstratively in support of diplomatic objectives in literally more than a thousand incidents during this period, ranging from major humanitarian operations to joint exercises with the armed forces of friendly nations to minor logistical operations in support of the United Nations (UN) or other multinational or national organizations. Moreover, the deployment and operations of U.S. forces in Europe, and in Southwest and East Asia on a continuing basis throughout the period, are intended to support U.S. foreign policy by deterring foreign leaders from pursuing hostile aims and by reassuring friends and allies. In some cases the presence of these forces, combined with the words of American leaders, may have been sufficient to deter unwanted initiatives. The presence of U.S. troops in South Korea, for example, is believed to deter a North Korean attack. We did not look at such cases of continuing military support of diplomacy in which "dogs may not have barked."[4] Instead, we looked only at the handful of specific incidents in which U.S. armed forces were used deliberately and actively to threaten or to conduct limited military operations in support of American policy objectives in specific situations.[5]

We did not examine such military threats prior to the Bush administration because, as noted above, the Cold War placed significant constraints on U.S. uses of force. We believe that the demise of the USSR altered the global political and military environments so fundamentally as to make prior incidents irrelevant to understanding the effectiveness of contemporary military threats. The puzzle we seek to explain is the frequent inability of the United States to achieve its objectives through threats and limited uses of military power *despite* the political and military dominance it has enjoyed since 1989.

We supplemented published information about the cases we considered with interviews with key U.S. policy makers during this period, including individuals who served in high positions in the Pentagon and at the State Department. At times these individuals are quoted directly. More often, their perspectives provide background and detail in the accounts of the incidents.[6]

We have concluded that the U.S. experience in Vietnam and subsequent incidents during both the Carter and first Reagan administrations left a heavy burden on future American policy makers. There is a generation of political leaders throughout the world whose basic perception of U.S. military power and political will is one of weakness, who enter any situation with a fundamental belief that the United States can be defeated or driven away. This point of view was expressed explicitly and concisely by Mohamed Farah Aideed, leader of a key Somali faction, to Ambassador Robert Oakley, U.S. special envoy to Somalia, during the disastrous U.S. involvement there in 1993-1995: "We have studied Vietnam and Lebanon and know how to get rid of Americans, by killing them so that public opinion will put an end to things."[7]

Aideed, of course, was proven to be correct. And the withdrawal from Mogadishu not only was a humiliating defeat for the United States but it also reinforced perceptions of America's lack of resolve and further complicated U.S. efforts to achieve its goals through threats of force alone.

This initial judgment, this basic "default setting" conditioning foreign leaders to believe that U.S. military power can be withstood, has made it extremely difficult for the United States to achieve its objectives without actually conducting military operations, despite its overwhelming military superiority. With the targets of U.S. diplomacy predisposed to disbelieve American threats, and to believe they can ride out any American military initiative and drive away American forces, it has been necessary for the United States in many incidents to go to great lengths to change these individuals' minds. *Reaching this defining moment, the point at which a foreign decision maker comes to the realization that, despite what may have happened in the past, in the current situation U.S. leaders are committed and, if necessary, will persevere in carrying out violent military actions, has become a difficult challenge in U.S. diplomacy.* It also creates a large obstacle to resolving conflicts and protecting U.S. interests while avoiding military confrontation.

HOW THREATS ARE EVALUATED

There is a rich literature on the use of force in world affairs and a considerable body of writing on the particular problems of the use of American military power in the post-Cold War period. Some voices in this debate include Gacek (1995), George (1995; George and Simons, 1994), Jentleson (1997), Damrosch (1993), the Aspen Strategy Group (1995), and

Muravchik (1996). There is also a large body of memoirs and contemporary histories testifying to the perceptions of American decision makers in particular incidents. Some examples are Baker (1995), Powell with Persico (1995), Quayle (1994), Schwarzkopf with Petre (1992), Woodward (1991), and Bush and Scowcroft (1998).

The authors of this literature have made any number of observations as to the conditions that facilitate the effective use of military threats. Typically, these conditions are not proposed as prerequisites for effective threats but merely as elements that make it more likely that threats will succeed. We therefore term these variables *enabling conditions*. The large number suggested in the literature, many of which differ from one another only in nuance, can be grouped into two broad categories. Most enabling conditions shape the credibility of the U.S. threat in the minds of the targeted foreign leaders; these include both conditions pertaining to the context in which the U.S. threat is made and to the character of the threat itself. Quite apart from the credibility of the U.S. threat, however, some demands are more difficult for foreign leaders to comply with than others, and some of the enabling conditions directly affect this perception of how costly it would be to comply with the demands. Together, the credibility of the threat and the degree of difficulty of the demands shape the targeted leader's evaluation of the likely cost of complying, or of not complying, with U.S. demands. The balance between the cost of compliance and the cost of defiance represents the *potency* of the U.S. threat.[8] These relationships are expressed in Figure 3.1 and are discussed further below.

Enabling Conditions

The *context* in which a threat is made and the *character* of the threat itself together shape the *credibility* of the threat. The *degree of difficulty* of a demand is evaluated through this credibility screen to determine the likely costs of compliance and noncompliance.

Context of the Threat

In previous work on this subject, Stephen Kaplan and Barry Blechman determined that coercive uses of military power by the United States were most likely to be successful when the United States acted in an appropriate historical context, when there was *precedent* for its demands and actions. This stands to reason. We know from experience that reaffirmations of long-standing positions are more likely to be taken seriously than declarations of new demands, particularly when the credibility of the traditional claim has already been tested through force of arms and found to be genuine. Targets of new claims of U.S. vital interests may

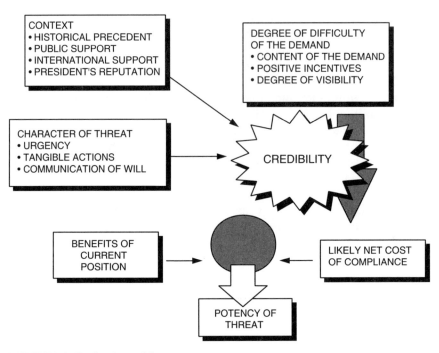

FIGURE 3.1 Evaluation of threats.

quite naturally want to test the claimant's seriousness. Such a challenge, when it occurs, means that the threat is ineffective, and the goals of the U.S. demands must be asserted through direct military action. Precedents may also have negative effects; as we shall see, the fact that U.S. military power was resisted successfully in Vietnam and elsewhere by weaker military powers seems to have adversely affected the credibility of U.S. military threats in recent years (Blechman and Kaplan, 1978; Jervis et al., 1985; Schelling, 1966).[9]

A second contextual factor believed to shape the credibility of U.S. military threats is the presence or absence of broad *public support* for military action and, particularly, whether or not there is wide support among members of Congress. Obviously, as in the case of Vietnam, domestic dissent raises the possibility either that the United States will not act on its threats if challenged or that, even if it does act, the force of public opinion will sooner or later, probably sooner, compel a retreat. This does not necessarily mean that any dissent negates a president's threats; the effect of dissent presumably depends on the importance attributed to it by the intended target. Nonetheless, because since Vietnam there has only rarely been broad public support for U.S. initiatives involving the threat or use of military force—at least prior to the actual and successful conduct of the operation—there is usually evidence that foreign leaders can cite in persuading themselves and their people that the Americans can be made to back down.[10]

The presence or absence of *third-nation support* for the U.S. position is a third contextual factor that seems to influence perceptions of the credibility of a U.S. threat. Allies' protests can curtail the willingness of the United States to act on its threats or to persevere in any military action needed to respond to a challenge, for fear of incurring high costs in more important relationships. This factor has become increasingly important in assessments of threats or uses of force in recent years, as the United States has become increasingly reluctant to act without allies in the new types of situations that have emerged following the Cold War. As with all the enabling conditions, what matters is not the reality of allied support but the targeted leader's perception of this factor. In explaining Saddam Hussein's disbelief of American threats during the Persian Gulf conflict, for example, former Secretary of Defense Richard Cheney cited Hussein's belief that the United States could never carry out military operations in Iraq itself because—in Hussein's view—the Arab nations allied with the United States would make clear that in such circumstances they would have to leave the coalition.[11]

A final contextual factor often said to influence the credibility of U.S. threats is the reputation of the president and other high-level U.S. officials. The scholarly literature is mixed in its assessments of the importance of this factor, however, and the case studies examined for this project shed no light on the subject—no discernible difference could be seen in responses to threats by Presidents Bush or Clinton that would seem to pertain to the incumbent's reputation. More basic attributes of U.S. credibility and of the situation itself seem to have been more important.

Character of the Threat

Other factors contributing importantly to the credibility of threats reflect the manner in which they are conveyed. A sense of *urgency* must be part of the threat or the targeted leader can believe that a strategy of delay and inaction will be effective in avoiding compliance. The establishment of deadlines appears to be particularly important (George and Simons, 1994). In 1989 Panamanian strongman Manuel Noriega understood well that the United States would prefer to see him removed from power and democracy restored. But because the United States endorsed negotiations by the Organization of American States (OAS) with Noriega and never articulated an "either-or" threat of Noriega's forcible removal, he apparently interpreted U.S. rhetoric as bluster and dismissed stepped-

up American military exercises in the Panama Canal Zone as "mere posturing" (Grant, 1991; Kempe, 1990; Treaster, 1989).

Verbal threats are also more effective when accompanied by *tangible
military actions*—steps that indicate the seriousness of the U.S. undertaking. Not only can movements or other actions by military units demonstrate actual capabilities, thus lending verisimilitude to threats, but by
demonstrating the U.S. president's willingness to pay a price for the situation, they add credibility to his verbal demands. In this respect the
greater the commitment demonstrated by the action, the more likely the
threat is to be successful. Thus, Blechman and Kaplan (1978) found the
deployment of forces on the ground in the potential theater of operations
to be a more effective means of making threats credible than the movement of naval forces, as ground deployments demonstrate a willingness
to pay the political price by putting U.S. soldiers, or air men and women,
at risk. Similarly, the mobilization of military reserves has been an effective means of adding credibility to threats. Disrupting the lives of U.S.
citizens by placing them on active duty, separating them from their families and workplaces, indicates indisputably the president's willingness to
pay a high political price to get his way.

Difficulty of the Demand

The context and character of a threat determine its credibility in the
mind of the target. But whether a foreign leader chooses to comply with
a U.S. demand is also conditioned by the degree of difficulty of the demand itself. To be effective, a demand must obviously be specific, clearly
articulated, and put in terms that the target understands. There is no
shortage of cases in which the targets of military threats simply did not
understand what was being asked of them and therefore could not have
acted to satisfy U.S. demands even if they had wanted to.[12]

In addition, a demand can be more or less onerous for the targeted
leader to contemplate. In part this evaluation will depend on the demand's specific *content*: What is, in fact, being demanded? At the extreme, some demands may not be *satisfiable* by the target. In some cases
the United States (and other nations) have misread situations, demanding
actions that the target of a threat was not capable of delivering. This may
have been the case in U.S. relations with the Soviet Union over the Middle
East in the 1960s and 1970s, for example, where the United States threatened repeatedly but seems to have misjudged the Soviet Union's ability to
influence certain Arab nations and factions (Whetten, 1974).

The inclusion of *positive incentives* in the overall U.S. diplomatic strategy is an important way of improving the targeted leader's perception of
a U.S. demand. Not only do positive incentives change perceptions of the

content of a demand itself, they also provide a political excuse for the target to do what it might have wanted to do anyway: back down and accept the U.S. demand.

A targeted leader's perception of the difficulty of a demand also will be affected by the *degree of visibility* of the retreat required. Regardless of substance, an act of compliance that can be taken invisibly is far easier to accept, as it may not convey additional political costs. A retreat that is visible and humiliating may often be perceived as something to be resisted at any cost.[13]

It has been demonstrated in many studies that threats or limited uses of force are more likely to be effective when the behavior demanded of a target requires only that the target not carry out some threatened or promised action. This is a subset of the visibility factor: deterrent threats are more likely to succeed than compellent threats; the latter require the target to carry out a positive and therefore usually visible action. In the case of deterrent threats, on the other hand, it is usually unknown, and unknowable, whether or not in the absence of U.S. threats the target would have carried out the action being deterred. Would the Soviet Union have attempted to seize West Berlin in the late 1950s or early 1960s if the United States had not threatened to contest such an initiative with military force? No one can say with certainty. Thus, deterrent threats may appear to be more successful because they are sometimes used to deter actions that would not be carried out in any event. Moreover, in those deterrent cases in which the initial threatened action would otherwise have been carried out, it is easier politically for the target to back down, as it need not be done in public; the target can always claim that, regardless of the U.S. threat, it would not have acted in any event. When the U.S. threat requires a positive act on the part of the target (e.g., withdrawal from Kuwait), the retreat is publicly evident and could have dire consequences in national or regional politics.

Potency of the Threat

All of these enabling conditions—context of the threat, character of the threat, and degree of difficulty of a demand—contribute to a targeted leader's understanding of the cost of complying, or of not complying, with U.S. demands. In Alexander George's phrase, an effective threat must be *potent* relative to the demand. This means that the target must perceive that the threat, if carried out, would result in a situation in which the target would be worse off than if it complied with the U.S. demand. If, for example, the demand is that a ruler give up the throne, the only potent threat is likely to be that otherwise the ruler will be killed (or that a situation would be created in which the ruler might be killed). Any threat less potent would likely be seen—even if it were carried out—as resulting in a situation no worse, and possibly better, than that which would have resulted from satisfying the demand. This evaluation, of course, will be filtered through the target's perception of the credibility of the threat—how likely it is that the anticipated punishment will be carried out. If the threat is perceived to be wholly incredible, the anticipated cost of non-compliance will be low. If the context and character of the threat add verisimilitude, however, the difficulty of the demand will be weighed carefully relative to the cost of noncompliance, and a sufficiently potent threat should produce compliance in a rational opponent.

CASE STUDIES

All these enabling conditions were examined for each of the eight major cases in which military force was threatened or used in limited ways in support of diplomacy during the Bush and first Clinton administrations. Although the authors examined each case extensively, only a brief summary of each can be presented in this paper; the summaries highlight the key findings.

Panama (1989-1990)[14]

The Panamanian dictator Manuel Noriega was an agent of U.S. policy in Central America for many years. In the late 1980s, however, his value declined with settlement of the Nicaraguan insurgency, and he became increasingly and more openly involved with the Colombian drug cartels. After he was indicted in the United States in February 1988 for drug trafficking and money laundering, first the Reagan administration and then the Bush administration decided to seek his removal from office. As tensions grew between the two countries in 1988 and 1989, the Panamanian Defense Forces, one key source of Noriega's power, began to harass U.S. military personnel in the country and in the Canal Zone, as well as to step up repression of the democratic opposition in Panama.

Because of the upcoming presidential election, the U.S. government did not initiate serious pressures against Noriega until 1989. Beginning in April of that year, however, the United States tried to make clear that it considered Noriega an illegitimate ruler and that it wanted him to step down. It renewed economic sanctions against Panama, gave Panamanian opposition parties $10 million in covert assistance toward their effort in the scheduled May presidential elections, and provided election observers. After Noriega manipulated the elections, the United States initiated a variety of diplomatic actions, including recalling its ambassador. The Bush administration worked through the OAS to negotiate Noriega's resignation and also carried out a series of military exercises and other actions in the Canal Zone intended to make the U.S. military presence there more visible. Noriega continued to refuse to comply with U.S. demands, however, and survived a coup in which the United States played a minor role. When a U.S. naval officer was murdered in December 1989, President Bush quickly authorized the U.S. armed forces to invade Panama, capture Noriega, and bring him to the United States for trial.

In this case, therefore, both diplomacy and military threats failed, necessitating the direct use of military force in war to accomplish the U.S. objective. Why was this the case? The main reasons appear to be related to the context and character of the threat itself. Despite any number of statements by U.S. leaders indicating that they believed Noriega should step down and that they considered him an illegitimate ruler, it was never stated clearly and definitively that the United States would be willing to invade the country and throw Noriega out if he did not comply with the demand to relinquish office.[15] In short, no cost was ever specified for noncompliance with U.S. demands; hence, a *potent* threat was never made. The United States demanded that Noriega leave office and, although a threat to expel him by force might have been inferred from U.S. statements, it was never stated explicitly. Nor was any deadline set for his compliance with the demand to relinquish office; Noriega was permitted to defer action for months without any obvious penalty. Likewise, U.S. verbal demands were not directly supported by tangible military actions. Although reinforcements were sent to the Canal Zone and some exercises were held there, they were all downplayed by U.S. officials and explained by a general concern for the security of the Canal Zone in light of deteriorating U.S.-Panamanian relations (Buckley, 1991). Colin Powell has stated that the limited military actions taken by the United States in 1988 and 1989 probably reinforced Noriega's preexisting perception that the United States was irresolute and that he could persevere.[16] When the invasion force was assembled, it was done in secrecy and never displayed publicly or brandished in support of an ultimatum that Noriega surrender or face forceful expulsion. This approach, of course, was dictated by the Weinberger maxims of how to use military power effectively.

It was harder for U.S. officials to threaten effectively in this case because the demand was extremely difficult for the target to contemplate. Noriega was being told to relinquish office; this was not a deterrent, but rather a compellent, situation. Only a clear and potent threat might have had a chance of success and, as noted earlier, in this case the target really did not understand that he faced a serious threat of U.S. action.

In the Panama case, in short, there was no defining moment because of the U.S. failure to make clear its compellent threat. The United States did not explicitly state the action it was prepared to take if its demand was not satisfied. Nor did it demonstrate a credible willingness to enforce the demand. No deadline for action by Noriega was established. The U.S. target, Noriega, never had to contemplate the seriousness of the U.S. resolve until it was too late for him to yield. U.S. leaders failed to press him into a defining moment.

U.S. Relations with Iraq (1990-1996)[17]

Eight months after the successful military operation in Panama, the Bush administration faced a far greater challenge in the Persian Gulf. In this case the threat of force was a central element of the U.S. strategy from nearly the outset of the crisis. President Bush and all other senior officials stated repeatedly and unequivocally that, if Saddam Hussein did not withdraw Iraqi forces from Kuwait, the United States was prepared, with the help of its allies, to expel them by force of arms. The threat was made increasingly credible throughout the remainder of 1990 by the mobilization and deployment of an enormous U.S. and allied military force in the region, an operation that could have left no question in Hussein's mind about the president's willingness to run huge political risks to implement the threat. Furthermore, the president's credibility was strengthened by the forging of a broad coalition that backed the American action, including Arab nations as well as traditional U.S. allies, by authorization of the allied military action by the UN and of U.S. military action by Congress, and by the establishment of a clear deadline for compliance that imparted a definite sense of urgency. Finally, the United States initiated an air campaign prior to launching its ground offensive, providing even more evidence of its military prowess and will and offering a final opportunity for Iraq to withdraw from Kuwait rather than being thrown out.

The context and character of the U.S. threat would have predicted success. Yet all these measures failed; in the end, U.S. and allied armies had to invade Kuwait and compel the Iraqi retreat by force of arms. Why? Because of the opacity of the Iraqi regime, the answer may never be clear, although several possibilities come to mind.

Despite their visible display in the theater of operations, Hussein may still have underestimated U.S. military capabilities relative to Iraq's. He may have believed that the war would be far less one sided, causing sufficient U.S. casualties for President Bush to end (or to be forced by U.S. and allied opinion to end) the hostilities short of the full expulsion of Iraqi forces from Kuwait. If so, he would have been counting heavily on the considerable opposition in the United States to the use of force prior to the authorizing legislation, as well as the obvious fragility of the coalition that had been brought together for the war (Bengio, 1992). He also simply may not have understood the extent of U.S. and allied power. Then Secretary of Defense Richard Cheney believes, for example, that Hussein's subordinates were afraid to bring him bad news or negative evaluations, as he was known to treat such messengers as traitors.[18]

Alternatively, the U.S. threat might simply not have been potent enough relative to the demand being made. The United States never threatened to unseat Hussein or to destroy his regime if Iraqi occupation forces were not withdrawn from Kuwait.[19] The threat was deliberately restricted to the destruction or expulsion of Iraqi forces in Kuwait, in part because Arab coalition members would not or could not support a more ambitious threat to destroy the Iraqi regime. From Hussein's perspective, in the context of his strategic vision, a military defeat while retaining power might have seemed preferable to an ignoble retreat. He might first have miscalculated and believed that the United States would not act to expel him from Kuwait but, subsequently, when he realized the error, figured that in terms of his overall goals in the region, and in terms of the likelihood of his being able to hold on to power in Baghdad, it would be better to be defeated militarily by the overwhelming forces that had been arrayed against him than to knuckle down to U.S. demands (Stein, 1992). If this was the case, only a credible threat to destroy Hussein and his regime would have been potent enough to have achieved the objective—liberating Kuwait—without the direct use of military forces in war. In the absence of such a potent threat, Hussein never had to face a defining moment.

Because of this ambiguous outcome—military triumph for the United States but political survival for Saddam Hussein—threats and uses of force have remained a central element in U.S. relations with Iraq since the Gulf War ended. Immediately following the war, the United States and its allies, acting through the UN, intervened on the ground to protect the Kurds in Iraq's north and established no-fly zones in both the north and the south to protect the Kurds and the Shi'a minority, respectively, from Iraq's air force. Both actions were accompanied by covert support for rebellious elements in the two regions intended to destabilize the Hussein regime. The no-fly zones have been enforced through combat air patrols and, occasionally, by air and missile strikes against radars, surface-to-air missiles, and command facilities.

The last such incident during the first Clinton administration took place in September 1996, when the United States once again struck at air defense sites in the south of Iraq, this time in response to an Iraqi intervention in a conflict between two Kurdish factions in the north. The United States maintained that the Iraqi military action was unacceptable and responded both by reinforcing its forces in the Gulf region and by launching cruise missile attacks on newly rebuilt Iraqi air defense sites in the south. (The United States took no action directly in the Kurdish region.) When Hussein seemed to defy U.S. injunctions regarding the need for Iraq to respect the no-fly zone in the south, the United States threatened more devastating air strikes against Iraq (and moved aircraft into the region that would be capable of carrying them out), and Hussein seemed to comply with the U.S. demand.

In an odd incident earlier in the Clinton administration, the United States launched cruise missile attacks against Iraq in retaliation for a plot by Iraqi intelligence agents to assassinate former President Bush during a visit to Kuwait. The plot was uncovered before the assassination attempt could be made, but the United States retaliated anyway to punish Iraq and deter future incidents. The cruise missile attacks, which included a strike on an Iraqi military intelligence headquarters said to be implicated in the plot, were intended to indicate to Hussein that such acts of terror and similar covert operations would not be tolerated.

An even more dramatic threat of American military force in the Persian Gulf took place in August 1994 when, in response to the movement of Iraqi armored forces toward Kuwait, the United States deployed substantial quantities of naval and land-based air and ground forces to the Persian Gulf and stated that it would resist any new invasion with force. The United States had been building up its capabilities and facilities in the Gulf ever since the 1991 war and used the occasion of the Iraqi armored movements to reinforce its presence there so as to deter any new invasion of Kuwait. The Iraqi units withdrew soon after the U.S. reinforcements arrived, and the Clinton administration claimed that its threats had succeeded. This claim is uncertain, however, as many observers maintained that the Iraqi leader could not possibly have contemplated an invasion given the experience in 1991, the much weaker state of the Iraqi armed forces, and the much greater preparedness of the United States and its allies three years later.

This sequence of incidents presents interesting evidence about the difficulty of utilizing military threats. In each episode the United States was apparently successful: the no-fly zones have generally been respected; there have been no publicly known Iraqi terrorist plots directed against American targets since U.S. retaliation for the planned assassination of President Bush; and there have been no further overt threats against Kuwait since 1994. Yet in the larger strategic sense the United States has failed. U.S. interests would be served most effectively either by the fall of the Hussein regime or by a radical change in Hussein's behavior such that he complies willingly with U.S. wishes. But the Hussein regime continues to skirt UN resolutions and the terms of the agreement that ended the war, continues to terrorize its minority populations, continues to behave belligerently toward Kuwait and other states in the region and, periodically, continues to challenge the United States politically. In short, the United States has had to settle for a lesser objective: containment. In the words of one U.S. official, U.S. diplomacy and military activity have served at best "to put Hussein back in the box."

This failure has occurred despite the fact that most of the enabling conditions surrounding U.S. policy are positive. There is now precedent for the actions, the U.S. public is very supportive, and the allies have generally cooperated (when they have not, the United States has been willing to act unilaterally). All the enabling conditions that determine the context and character of the threats are positive. While the demands made have varied in their degree of difficulty, none have been onerous. The failure, then, appears to be the result of the *potency* of the threat relative to the demand. As in the Gulf War, the United States and its allies have not been willing to make and, if necessary, carry out the one threat that might accomplish their long-term strategic interest. It is evident that the United States is not willing to topple the Hussein regime through force of arms or even to enforce its more far-reaching demands.

The weakness of the U.S. and allied position became evident in the 1996 incident. In response to Iraq's military action against a Kurdish faction in the north, which U.S. leaders termed unacceptable, the United States was only willing to stage symbolic attacks against Iraqi air defense facilities in the south—far from the scene of the Kurdish conflict. This time most of the allies were unwilling to go along with the action, and open dissent weakened the coalition. The crisis worsened for a time as Hussein seemed to defy U.S. demands about the southern no-fly zone. While he ultimately gave in, the broader U.S. strategic objective of containment was threatened. Hussein reasserted control over significant territory in the north and dismantled the Kurdish opposition. Once again, U.S. demands were not sufficiently potent to bring Hussein to a defining moment.[20]

Somalia (1992-1995)[21]

The disastrous U.S. intervention in Somalia probably did more to undermine worldwide perceptions of the efficacy of U.S. military power than any event in recent memory. Among other things, American actions in Somalia influenced the calculations of leaders in Haiti and Bosnia as they confronted U.S. threats simultaneously.

In Somalia, largely as a result of inattention at political levels, the United States allowed its military forces to transform their original humanitarian mission into a coercive activity intended to enforce a peaceful settlement of the underlying political conflict by disarming factions in a particular section of the country. When one faction resisted and killed 24 members of the Pakistani component of the UN peacekeeping force, the United States launched a low-level military offensive directed specifically against that faction. When U.S. forces suffered a tactical defeat in October 1993, Washington suddenly curtailed its objectives and announced that it would withdraw virtually all U.S. forces from the country.[22]

Once U.S. forces assumed the larger political role, the mission became extremely difficult. Most of the enabling conditions with respect to the context of the threat were negative. There was no significant precedent for U.S. involvement in Somali politics, and the American public did not support the mission beyond its initial humanitarian boundaries. Other countries with troops participating in the UN mission were extremely reluctant to undertake any actions implying a threat of conflict. The degree of difficulty of the demand escalated sharply once the U.S. offensive against Mohamed Farah Aideed began. Finally, because of the shift in objectives, the U.S. demands were unclear—to U.S. officials and the U.S. public as well as to the Somali targets. Also, the Somali leaders were constrained by their mutual competition, as well as by internal conflicts within their respective factions, making it unclear whether compliance with U.S. demands was ever feasible.

Nonetheless, the character of the threat suggested potency. A clear sense of urgency was implied, and positive inducements for compliance were supplied—yet the threat and use of force both failed. The clearest reason was noted previously and stated by the faction leader, Aideed, to the U.S. negotiator. Based on his understanding of recent U.S. history, he believed that the United States could not sustain a campaign against him in the face of casualties. The lack of precedent for the U.S. action in Somalia and the dissension already evident in the United States and among its allies served to confirm his preexisting view that the United States could not sustain its threats against even nominal opposition. The U.S. threat was not credible because contextual factors reinforced the target's preexisting judgment about U.S. credibility.

Macedonia (1992-1996)[23]

The deployment of U.S. and other nations' ground forces to Macedonia to deter any extension of the Bosnian war to that nation, or any internal ethnic conflagration, represents an apparent success for U.S. military threats. Despite their reluctance to become involved in Bosnia itself, first the Europeans and then the United States were willing to deploy troops to Macedonia as a means of guaranteeing their involvement should the conflict spread. As noted, the deployment also was intended to strengthen warnings to Serb leaders not to tighten oppression of the Albanian population in Kosovo, a secondary aim that was ultimately not achieved, as evidenced by the 1999 Serbian offensive in Kosovo. In a way the unwillingness of U.S. leaders to take decisive action in Bosnia at the time made Macedonia seem more important in the eyes of Washington decision makers. It was a means of demonstrating some "on-the-ground" involvement and a willingness to prevent a widening conflict, thereby, it was hoped, earning some credits with the Europeans.

In this case, virtually all the enabling conditions were positive. There was support in the Congress, unanimity among the allies, the demand was stated clearly and reinforced by military actions, and the threat (automatic involvement in any extension of the Bosnian conflict) was potent relative to the demand. Its self-implementing nature intrinsically conveyed a sense of commitment and urgency.[24]

Of course, the U.S. threat with respect to Macedonia had another great advantage. It was intended to deter hostile actions whose likelihood was not clear. Whether or not the Serbs or anyone else might have tried to extend the Bosnian conflict to Macedonia absent the allied deployment of ground forces there is anyone's guess. The threat might have worked because the degree of difficulty of the demand was low. Compliance with the demand required no visible action; in fact, it might have required no action at all.

Bosnia (1992-1996)

The Bosnian war and its accompanying humanitarian tragedies bedeviled both the Bush and the Clinton administrations. Throughout the conflict, threats and limited applications of force have been used for tactical purposes, with mixed results. Early in the conflict, the United States and its allies established a no-fly zone to protect their humanitarian shipments and forces, and the threat of selective air strikes was employed to remind the Serbs of these rules—generally with some tactical success. On the other hand, the United States and its allies, working through the UN, threatened and used limited amounts of force repeatedly in efforts to protect the so-called safe areas from Serb encroachments and subsequent mass murders. These efforts failed miserably, climaxing with the occupation of Zepa and Srebrenica in 1995 and the murder of thousands of their residents.

On the strategic level, from the earliest days of the Clinton administration, U.S. leaders repeatedly threatened a deeper level of involvement in the conflict if Serb forces did not comply with various resolutions. The United States also deployed a considerable number of forces to the Adriatic and to Italian air bases, helping to enforce sanctions against Serbia and an arms embargo in Bosnia, as well as carrying out the limited strikes mentioned above. But the vagueness of the U.S.

strategic threats encouraged Serb intransigence and continued Serb efforts to seize additional territory. The appearance of a lack of American resolve was compounded by clear indications that the United States was not willing to deploy ground forces to Bosnia and that the allies were willing to deploy troops but not to place them in danger, as would be required by any serious effort to compel Serb compliance with Western demands. It was not until August 1995, following the atrocities in Zepa and Srebrenica and the successful Croat offensive against the Serbs, that the United States and its allies made a serious effort to pressure the Serbs into entering peace negotiations by carrying out repeated air strikes against a variety of targets. Soon thereafter the Dayton talks were begun and the peace agreement now being implemented was concluded. Whether the Serbs were brought to the peace table by the Croat offensive, the new allied will to end the conflict suggested by the air campaign, or their own weariness with war and sanctions is anyone's guess. Whether the peace will last is an even greater unknown. In the post-Dayton phase, of course, the United States and its allies again used military force, deploying ground troops of the Implementation Force, or IFOR, throughout Bosnia to help keep the peace. IFOR was successful in ensuring that the parties observed the military aspects of the Dayton Accords and completed its mission in December 1996. (It has been succeeded, of course, by a smaller force known as the Stabilization Force, or SFOR.)

In the end, therefore, U.S. strategic threats appear to have been successful in persuading the Serbs to stop fighting and start talking, or at least were coincident with success. But this one success capped a long period of clear failure, consistent with the negative values of most of the enabling conditions in this case. All the contextual variables were negative: there was no precedent for U.S. involvement in the former Yugoslavia, the Congress and the American people were starkly divided as to the wisdom of U.S. involvement, and the allies were obviously reluctant to risk the lives of their soldiers. The credibility of the threat was strengthened by the deployment of forces, but the actual uses of these forces were so limited as to convey a message of reluctance and weakness rather than of strength. This is certainly the view of Undersecretary of Defense Walter Slocombe, who has said that "UNPROFOR's mistake was tolerating hostile behavior. It should have slapped down the people who were shooting at them."[25]

Similarly, the enabling conditions pertaining to the final demand made of the Serbs were mainly negative. The U.S. demand to halt the war was not articulated clearly until the final air offensive, and no sense of urgency was conveyed until then. The U.S. objective was to compel participation in a peace process, rather that deter certain actions, requiring a positive and visible step by the target. And that target—Serbia's president—often was unable to deliver the Serb leaders in Bosnia even when he wanted to meet the U.S. demands.

The enabling conditions only turned positive, for the most part, following the massacres at Zepa and Srebrenica and the beginning of the massive NATO air strikes. As the air strikes continued, they not only raised the cost of noncompliance but also encouraged the development of a sense of urgency among Serb leaders. At this point, the choice became more clear to the Serbs—peace or destruction of the military infrastructure of the Bosnian Serbs. Given other conditions at the time, particularly the successful Croatian ground offensive that was changing the entire strategic situation and the evident weariness with the war in Serbia, the U.S. threats at last gained the potency necessary to achieve their objective. Then Secretary of Defense William Perry, in fact, believes that he can identify the defining moment: a visit by the chiefs of the U.S., British, and French armed forces to Bosnian Serb military leaders in Belgrade, on July 23, 1995, to convey the new resoluteness of the NATO nations in the aftermath of the Srebrenica massacres.[26]

The picture that thus emerges with respect to the efficacy of U.S. military threats in Bosnia is mixed. For the most part the threats failed, mainly because the element central to their potency—a willingness to deploy U.S. ground troops and to utilize European forces already on the ground—was missing. Seeing the disarray in the United States and the dissension among the allies, the Serbs had little reason to comply. Only when the NATO allies, reacting to the murders in Srebrenica and the Croat offensive, made clear that they would be willing to act more forcefully did the Serbs perceive a real cost to their noncompliance and begin to take the allies' threats seriously.

Haiti (1994-1996)[27]

Haiti presents a similar picture: ineffective threats and excessively limited military actions showed U.S. irresoluteness for a considerable period of time but were followed by a potent threat that finally achieved its objective.

The crisis in Haiti actually began in 1991, when a military coup expelled the country's first elected president, Jean Bertrand Aristide. The United States pursued a diplomatic strategy to reinstall the president, accompanied by sanctions, for more than two years. Only when the Governor's Island agreement that would have permitted Aristide to regain office failed in the fall of 1993, and the Haitian military government turned back a U.S. ship delivering the lead element of a UN peacekeeping force, did the United States threaten to overthrow the military government and reinstall Aristide by force, if necessary.

The turning away of the U.S. ship followed closely on the defeat of U.S. forces in Somalia, a coincidence that was particularly harmful to the efficacy of U.S. threats (Ribadeneira, 1994; Downie, 1993a, 1993b). For the next eight months the United States made numerous demonstrations of its military capabilities through deployments of Navy and Marine forces off the island and by staging exercises intended to show practice for an invasion. Yet the Haitian ruler, General Raoul Cedras, with virtually no means of defending himself if the United States did invade, refused to back down. Finally, President Clinton received authorizations to utilize military force from the OAS and the UN and set a deadline for the invasion. Still, the Haitian ruler refused to back down. It was only when he received word that U.S. airborne troops had left their bases and that the operation was actually under way that he accepted a U.S. offer, conveyed by a delegation chaired by former President Jimmy Carter, to step down with some semblance of dignity and a guarantee of safety.

It should have been easier to make effective threats in the Haitian case than in Bosnia. While U.S. opinion tended to oppose the use of American forces in both cases, there was ample precedent for U.S. interventions in Haiti and the Caribbean and most other hemispheric nations were supportive. The demand was clear, the target could easily comply, the threat was potent relative to the demand, and U.S. military power was displayed with great visibility. There were also positive inducements for compliance: U.S. representatives offered to provide for the personal safety of the Haitian dictator and his family.

Why, then, was it so difficult to make a threat that worked? Why was it necessary to actually launch a huge invasion force before Cedras would believe that President Clinton was truly committed to his ouster? Two factors relating to the context of the U.S. threat seem to have been essential. First, the opposition of much of the American public and Congress to invasion plans may have conveyed hope to Cedras that Clinton could not possibly go through with his threats. Indeed, knowing that he would be defeated, Clinton did not seek congressional authorization for the invasion. Second, particularly in view of this opposition, Cedras may have taken heart from the recent American behavior in Somalia, as well as from his success in compelling the ship carrying UN peacekeepers to withdraw.[28] He may have believed that, even if the United States did invade, all his forces would have to do would be to inflict some casualties and the Americans would withdraw. If this is the case, the persuasiveness of the Carter mission, which made clear both the magnitude and commitment of the U.S. effort and provided positive inducements for compliance, was essential in increasing the potency of the U.S. threat and bringing Cedras to his defining moment.

Korea (1994-1996)²⁹

The Korean case is probably the most successful use of military threats during this period. Essentially, in this case, threats of military force were used as one element in a strategy that concentrated mainly on using economic instruments—both positive and negative—to halt the North Korean nuclear weapons program. While threats were not the most prominent element of the strategy, they clearly played a role, enforcing boundaries on Pyongyang's choices. According to Walter Slocombe, when Pyongyang tried to counter the U.S. threat to impose economic sanctions by stating that such an action would constitute an act of war, the United States made clear that it was willing to escalate along with North Korea through visible efforts to increase its readiness for war on the peninsula.³⁰

The threats generally were vague in character and articulated indirectly. Neither the president nor other high-ranking U.S. officials threatened explicitly to destroy North Korea's nuclear facilities, but the administration let it be known that it was considering military options and reinforced the message by strengthening its presence in South Korea with air defense missiles and other items. Consultations with the U.S. commander in Korea to discuss possible military options were held with a fair amount of publicity. The fact that prominent Republicans, such as former National Security Advisor Brent Scowcroft, were calling for military strikes reinforced the message that the administration could not rule out direct military action if negotiations failed.

Enabling conditions in this case were generally positive for effective threats. The U.S. interest and willingness to use force in Korea had strong precedent, public opinion and the Congress supported the need to do something about North Korea's nuclear weapons program, the demand was clear, and the threat was supported by visible military actions. The major negative condition was that the U.S. ally, South Korea, was reluctant to see the crisis get out of control, as it faced the possibility of major casualties if combat resumed on the peninsula.

In the end, North Korea probably ended its nuclear program because it had gotten what it wanted—an economic payoff and, more importantly, the beginning of a dialogue with the United States that might lead eventually to normal relations. Still, U.S. officials believe that Pyongyang took the U.S. threats seriously and that they played some role in bringing about the so-far positive outcome.

Taiwan (1996)[31]

The final case is an odd one—more symbolic than real. In 1996 China staged a series of military exercises and missile tests near Taiwan as the latter moved toward an election in which opposition parties were campaigning on a platform that demanded independence from the mainland. The Chinese actions were apparently intended to intimidate the Taiwanese and to remind all other parties—particularly the United States—that China would not tolerate de facto Taiwanese independence indefinitely and especially would not tolerate overt steps toward a de jure sovereign status. In response, the United States sent an aircraft carrier task group through the straits that separate Taiwan from the mainland and later in the crisis deployed a second carrier near the island. The U.S. actions apparently were intended to remind China of the American interest in preventing Taiwan's unification with the mainland by force.

Both parties' actions, of course, were shadowboxing. China was probably not seriously contemplating invading Taiwan. It does not have the means to accomplish that goal, and Taiwan could probably defend itself against an invasion without U.S. help. Moreover, the fallout from such an action would set back China's economic development immensely, as well as antagonize neighboring states (especially Japan) and trigger massive armament programs on their parts—a counterproductive outcome from China's perspective.

But if China's threat was not serious, neither was that of the United States. Despite a great deal of hype in the news media, both countries apparently understood that they were playing on a stage, making points for world opinion and for domestic audiences. Both Chinese and American statements explicitly discounted any risk of a U.S.-Chinese military confrontation and anticipated continued relations in the future (Burns, 1996). In this sense the U.S. threats were effective—the target, however, was not China but rather Taiwan and domestic U.S. audiences.

CONCLUSION

The results of the case studies discussed above are summarized in Table 3.1. The cases are arrayed in rows, moving chronologically from top to bottom. The outcomes of each case and a description of the enabling conditions constitute the columns.

Overall, the use of military power by the United States clearly failed in only one of the cases—Somalia. U.S. threats to use military force clearly succeeded in three—Macedonia, North Korea, and Taiwan. In the four other cases—Panama, Iraq, Bosnia, and Haiti—the use of military power ultimately succeeded, but either success came only with great difficulty,

at considerable cost to other U.S. interests, or the United States was successful only in achieving its immediate objectives, not its longer-term
strategic goals. In Panama, Bosnia, and Haiti, success came only after
long periods of failure, with high costs for the administration domestically and internationally; in Iraq each individual use of military power
was successful, but the strategic situation remains unchanged and unsatisfactory from an American perspective; in Bosnia and Haiti the underlying political conflicts remain unresolved and easily reversible.

With respect to the enabling conditions, none alone appear to be a
sufficient condition for success; nor can it be said for certain that any one
condition—other than that the target indeed be able to fulfill the demand—
is a prerequisite for success. Still, one noteworthy partial correlation can be
seen between the difficulty of the demand and positive outcomes. In all
seven successes (counting individual uses of force within cases as well as
overall cases) but one, fulfillment of the U.S. objective demanded relatively
little of the target. Typically, the actions required of the targets also tended
to be less visible in these cases (with the exceptions of the action required of
North Korea and of the Bosnian Serbs with respect to entering the Dayton
negotiations). The U.S. posture in six of the seven successful uses of military power also included positive incentives, further reducing the difficulty
of the demand as perceived by the target.

Enabling conditions pertaining to the credibility of U.S. threats (as
determined by the context and character) present a less consistent pattern. There was precedent for U.S. action in only half of the cases, and the
results were mixed in those cases with precedents and those without.
Third-nation support and whether or not a sense of urgency was conveyed present no clear pattern. Tangible military actions were taken in all
cases and hence shed no light.

The presence or absence of public support is more interesting. It was
present in the three clear successes and absent in the one clear failure. The
remaining four cases, which had mixed results, were also split with respect to public support. Public support for a threat evidently cannot
guarantee its success, but an evident lack of public support apparently
can make it difficult to make threats credibly. In Somalia and Haiti, as
well as Bosnia for most of the conflict, the evident lack of public support
in the United States for the policies being pursued by the administration—at least at the price level that potentially would be implied if the
relevant threat had been carried out—seems to have given great comfort
to the target of the U.S. action and encouraged him to attempt to stay the
course. Evidence of public dissension was probably a factor encouraging
Hussein to defy U.S. threats as well, and each of the former officials
interviewed cited this factor as greatly complicating the use of military
power by the United States.

TABLE 3.1 Outcomes and Enabling Conditions

Case	Credibility						Degree of Difficulty			Outcome
	Precedent	Public Support	Third-Nation Support	Urgency	Tangible Military Actions	Articulated Content	Visibility	Positive Incentive	Potency	
I. Panama	+	+	+	-	+	- 3	-	-	-	YB
II. Iraq										
(Strategic Outcome)										
DS/DS^a	-	+	+	+	+	+ 2	-	-	-	YB
South no-fly	-	+	-	+	+	+ 2	-	-	+	YB
Kurds	-	+	-	+	+	- 2	-	+	-	YB
Terror	+	+	+	+	+	+ 1	+	-	+	S
VW^b	+	+	+	+	+	+ 1	+	+	+	S
III. Somalia	-	-	-	+	+	- 2	-	-	-	F
IV. Macedonia	-	+	+	+	+	+ 1	+	+	+	S

										Outcome
V. Bosnia										
(Strategic Outcome)	-	-	+	+	+	-	-		+	YB
Lift/no-fly	+	+	+	+	+	+	-	2	-	YB
Sanctions	-	-	+	-	+	+	+	2	-	YB
Safe/weapons[c]	-	-	+	-	+	+	+	2	-	F
Dayton	-	-	+	+	+	+	-	2	+	S
IFOR	+	+	+	+	+	+	+	1	+	S
VI. Haiti	+	-	+	-	+	+	-	3	+	YB
VII. North Korea	+	+	+	+	+	+	-	1	+	S
VIII. Taiwan	+	+	-	-	+	+	+	1	+	S

[a]Desert Shield/Desert Storm.
[b]Valiant Warrior (1994).
[c]Safe Havens/Weapons Exclusion Zones.

Notes: The *enabling conditions* are generally labeled positive, meaning that they favored a successful outcome from the U.S. perspective, or negative, meaning the opposite. The one exception is the content of the demand made, which is ranked from 1 (least difficult for the target) to 3 (most difficult for the target). *Outcomes* are categorized as a success (S), failure (F), or "yes, but" (YB), meaning that the outcome eventually favored the United States but that getting there left a great deal to be desired. The Iraq and Bosnia cases are rated both for their strategic outcome and for specific uses of force within each case.

Looking beyond the scoreboard of results to the cases themselves, the question of potency also appears to be especially important. Potent threats relative to the cost of noncompliance were made in each of the clearly successful cases (Macedonia, North Korea, and Taiwan) and were not made in the one clear failure (Somalia). In the case of Iraq, as in Panama and in all but the so-far-final stage of the Bosnian conflict, the unwillingness of the United States to make threats that would clearly offer the target the prospect of an unacceptable cost seems to have been an important reason for the failure of U.S. policy.

The problem that the United States faces, therefore, is very clear. It is rare that it can both make potent threats and retain public support. Potent threats imply greater risks. And the American public's aversion to risk, particularly the risk of suffering casualties, is well known; the legacy of Vietnam is real. This is particularly true in the types of conflict situations that have arisen since the end of the Cold War—where there is little precedent for American action, where American interests are more abstract than tangible, where the battle lines are uncertain, and where none of the contending parties wear a particularly friendly face.

Recognizing this public aversion to casualties, or predicting such opposition in particular cases, American presidents have been reluctant to step as close to the plate as has been required to achieve U.S. objectives in many post-Cold War conflicts. They have made threats only reluctantly and usually have not made as clear or potent a threat as was called for by the situation. They have understood the need to act in the situation but have been unwilling or perceived themselves as being unable to lead the American people into the potential sacrifice necessary to secure the proper goal. As a result, they have attempted to satisfice—taking some action but not the most effective possible action to challenge the foreign leader threatening U.S. interests. They have sought to curtail the extent and potential cost of the confrontation by avoiding the most serious type of threat and therefore the most costly type of war if the threat were challenged.

The American public's sensitivity to the human and economic costs of military action is a clear legacy of the Vietnam experience. But it has been reinforced since then by sharp reactions—by the public and elected officials—to the suicide bombing of U.S. Marines in Beirut and to the deaths of U.S. soldiers in Mogadishu. Both Presidents Bush and Clinton have been keenly cognizant of this sensitivity, and their attempts to threaten to use military power have been hesitant as a result.

This syndrome would impair the effectiveness of U.S. coercive diplomacy under any circumstances, but its deleterious effects are magnified by the impact of those same historical events on foreign leaders. Vietnam syndrome is not solely an American disease—its symptoms are visible abroad, when potential targets of U.S. threats see the American public's sensitivity to casualties as a positive factor in their own reckoning of the risks and benefits of alternative courses of action. A review of the evidence reveals that Bosnian Serb leaders, Haitian paramilitary leaders, Saddam Hussein, and Somalia's late warlord all banked on their ability to force a U.S. retreat by inflicting relatively small numbers of casualties on U.S. forces. That places American presidents attempting to accomplish goals through threats in a dilemma. Domestic opinion rarely supports forceful policies at the outset, but tentative policies only reinforce the prejudices of foreign leaders and induce them to stand firm.

Vietnam's legacy abroad pushes foreign leaders' defining moments back, requiring greater demonstrations of will, greater urgency, more tangible actions by U.S. forces, and greater potency for threats to succeed. But Vietnam's legacy at home makes it much harder for U.S. presidents to take such forceful actions without significant investments of political capital.

As a result of this dilemma, American officials have often been unable to break through the preconceived notions of U.S. weakness held by foreign leaders to bring about a defining moment. Indeed, the cases in which decisive U.S. actions were taken only after long periods of indecision (especially Panama, Bosnia, and Haiti) may have only reinforced foreign leaders' preconceptions about America's lack of will. Until U.S. presidents show a greater ability to lead on this issue, or until the American people demonstrate a greater willingness to step up to the challenges of exercising military dominance on a global scale, foreign leaders in many situations will likely continue to see American threats more as signs of weakness than as potent expressions of America's true military power. As a result, they will likely continue to be willing to withstand American threats—necessitating either recourse to force to achieve American goals or embarrassing retreats in the pursuit of American interests abroad.

This suggests that American presidents have several options when considering potential uses of military power in support of diplomacy:

• They can pick their fights carefully, choosing to make public demands of other nations mainly in situations in which the actions they require will not be perceived by the target as excessively difficult, and when they can leaven their threats with positive incentives to encourage compliance, as in the cases of Taiwan and North Korea.

• They can seek to "demilitarize" U.S. policy somewhat. Strategies close to those used in the Korean case may be more appropriate, and more effective, than the quick recourse to military threats seen in most of the other cases. Threats and limited military force have a clear role but more as reinforcing elements in policies dominated by economic, diplomatic, and political factors than as the primary policy instrument. In Haiti it was ultimately a skilled diplomatic team backed by force, not the force itself, that secured Cedras's removal from power. Given domestic constraints on U.S. ability to use military power, in threats or in actuality, Presidents Bush and Clinton may have leaned too heavily on the armed forces to advance American interests in the immediate post-Cold War world. Policies that deemphasize the role of force may be more appropriate more often.

• When nonmilitary instruments of policy seem likely to be ineffectual but the U.S. president still perceives an imperative to act, and the foreign leader seems likely to perceive compliance with U.S. demands as onerous, the president must act decisively. In these situations the demand must be clear and urgent, the demonstration of military power incontrovertible, and the threat itself potent relative to the target's alternatives. The ultimate achievement of U.S. objectives in Desert Storm and at the end of the Bosnian and Haitian scenarios demonstrates that presidential decisiveness can be effective, even at the later stages of a crisis. Most importantly, in Colin Powell's words, "The president himself must begin the action prepared to see the course through to its end. . . . He can only persuade an opponent of his seriousness when, indeed, he is serious."[32]

NOTES

A version of this article appeared in *Political Science Quarterly* (1999) 114:1-30.

[1]Remarks by Secretary of Defense Caspar W. Weinberger to the National Press Club, November 28, 1984; published as Department of Defense News Release No. 609-84.

[2]Interview by Barry Blechman with General Colin Powell, February 21, 1997.

[3]Les Aspin, chairman of the House Armed Services Committee, address to the Jewish Institute for National Security Affairs, Washington, D.C., September 21, 1992.

[4]A database listing all uses of the American armed forces since the end of the Cold War was prepared by DFI International for the U.S. Air Force. It is based largely on official unpublished documents prepared by the major U.S. Air Force commands and other official data. For additional information, please contact Oliver Fritz, DFI International, 11 Dupont Circle, NW, Washington, DC 20036, U.S.A.

[5]In principle, there may also have been cases in which the United States achieved its ends through verbal threats alone, threats not backed by deliberate military activity. Some have suggested, for example, that President Bush was successful in preventing greater Serbian oppression in Kosovo through verbal warnings alone. In that specific case, however, President Bush's warnings were given weight both by U.S. military activity in support of the UN Protection Force (UNPROFOR) in Bosnia and in enforcing the embargo on arms shipments to the region and by the deployment of U.S. troops to Macedonia. Overall, the authors could not identify any cases of verbal threats unaccompanied by military activity during this period, successful or unsuccessful, and would be grateful for any suggestion of such incidents.

[6]The individuals interviewed include Richard Cheney (secretary of defense, 1989-1993); William Perry (secretary of defense, 1994-1997); Walter Slocombe (undersecretary of defense for policy, 1994-present); Colin Powell (chairman of the Joint Chiefs of Staff, 1989-1993); Strobe Talbott (deputy secretary of state, 1994-present); James Steinberg (director of policy planning, Department of State, 1994-1996).

[7]Letter from Robert Oakley to Barry Blechman, August 7, 1997.

[8]This term was first suggested by Alexander George. See his discussion of credibility and of the magnitude of demands in George and Simons (1994).

[9] Some scholars argue that forceful precedents are useful only when they reflect core U.S. interests; for example, see George and Smoke (1974).

[10]For discussion of the role that public opinion plays in America's ability to take effective military action abroad, see Jentleson (1997) and Holl (1995).

[11]Interview by Barry Blechman with Richard Cheney, January 15, 1997. See also Stein (1992) and George and Simons (1994).

[12]Lauren (1994) suggests that ultimatums are the most explicit and precise method of communicating demands and that they may lessen the chances of misperception or miscalculation by the opponent.

[13]On the effect that degree of difficulty and "losing face" have on the effectiveness of threats, see George and Simons (1994).

[14]Sources used for this case study include contemporaneous news reports, Powell with Persico (1995), Baker (1995), Grant (1991), Woodward (1991), and Kempe (1990).

[15]President Bush even stated in a news conference on October 13, 1989, that using force in Panama was "a stupid argument that some very erudite people make" (transcript printed in *New York Times,* October 14, 1989).

[16]Interview by Barry Blechman with General Colin Powell, February 21, 1997.

[17]Sources used in this case study included for the Persian Gulf crisis, Freedman and Karsh (1993), BBC World Service (1991), Bengio (1992), Baker (1995), Woodward (1991), and Powell with Persico (1995). For the post-1991 incidents, sources included Foreign Broadcast Information Service (FBIS) transcripts of statements by Iraqi officials, statements by U.S. officials, and contemporaneous Western news reports.

[18]Interview by Barry Blechman with Richard Cheney, January 15, 1997.

[19]There have been some suggestions, however, that the United States made such a threat to deter the Iraqis from using chemical weapons. See James Baker's comments on his Geneva meeting with Tariq Aziz in January 1991, in *The Gulf War,* a BBC/WGBH Frontline coproduction, written and produced by Eamonn Matthews (Seattle: PBS Video, 1996).

[20]The consequences of this failure were seen throughout 1997 and early 1998. In late 1997 Hussein barred U.S. citizens from the UN teams inspecting Iraq for weapons of mass destruction in compliance with the agreements ending the war; he also refused to permit inspections of certain types of sites, such as presidential palaces. Although Hussein seemed to relent on the first issue, in January 1998 Iraqi officials refused to allow a particular inspection team, led by an American claimed to be a spy, to carry out its work. The United States and some of its allies threatened once again to carry out air strikes, and eventually the UN Secretary General, Kofi Annan, was able to negotiate an acceptable resolution of the conflict.

[21]Primary sources for this case study include FBIS transcripts of Radio Mogadishu broadcasts, contemporaneous news reports, Baker (1995), Powell with Persico (1995), and Blechman and Vaccaro (1995).

[22]U.S. forces initially entered Somalia in December 1992 as part of a multilateral mission, UNITAF, intended to secure the delivery of food and other relief supplies that would end the famine and prepare the way for a broader UN force. Having accomplished this limited mission, in May 1993 UNITAF gave way to UNOSOM II, which included only 4,500

U.S. troops. UNOSOM II's mission included disarming the various clan factions that were making the reestablishment of a central government impossible. U.S. forces and the entire UN peacekeeping mission had withdrawn from Somalia by March 1995.

[23]This and the following case study on Bosnian policy are based on public statements by President Clinton and then Secretary of State Warren Christopher, news reports, and extensive FBIS transcripts of Croatian, Bosnian Serb, Serbian, and Bosnian TV and radio broadcasts containing statements by leaders of these groups.

[24]There have been virtually no complaints from the Congress about the Macedonian deployment despite the fact that U.S. troops serve under UN command—a hot issue among conservatives. Of course, the support would probably disappear quickly if the troops in Macedonia appeared in danger of entering combat.

[25]Interview by Barry Blechman with Walter Slocombe, January 27, 1996.

[26]Interview by Barry Blechman with William Perry, January 21, 1997.

[27]Sources for this case study included Powell with Persico (1995), contemporaneous U.S. news reports, and FBIS transcripts of Port-au-Prince Radio Metropole.

[28]According to a wire service report (Downie, 1993a), Haitian paramilitaries demonstrating in Port-au-Prince chanted, "We're going to make a second Somalia here!" and UN envoy Dante Caputo said that the Haitians were "trying to create an atmosphere where it would be a disaster, a blood bath, if foreign troops came."

[29]Sources for this case study included *The Public Perspective* (1994); statements by President Clinton, Secretary of Defense Perry, and other U.S. officials; and contemporaneous news reports.

[30]Interview by Barry Blechman with Walter Slocombe, January 27, 1996.

[31]Sources for this case study included public statements by President Clinton, Secretary of State Christopher, and Secretary of Defense Perry; transcripts of State Department press conferences; and Chinese Foreign Ministry statements, including press conferences by Foreign Minister Qian Qichen.

[32]Interview by Barry Blechman with General Colin Powell, February 21, 1997.

REFERENCES

Agence France Presse
    1996a US postpones visit by Chinese defense minister. *Agence France Presse*, March 22.
    1996b No firm date for Christopher-Qian meeting. *Agence France Presse*, March 22.
Aspen Strategy Group
    1995   *The United States and the Use of Force in the Post-Cold War Era.* Queenstown, Md.: Aspen Institute.
BBC World Service
    1991   *Gulf Crisis Chronology.* Essex, U.K.: Longman Current Affairs.
Baker, J.A.
    1995   *The Politics of Diplomacy.* New York: Putnam.
Bengio, O., ed.
    1992   *Saddam Speaks on the Gulf Crisis: A Collection of Documents.* Tel Aviv, Israel: Moshe Dayan Center.
Blechman, B.M., and S.S. Kaplan
    1978   *Force Without War.* Washington, D.C.: Brookings Institution.
Blechman B., and J.M. Vaccaro, eds.
    1995   *Towards an Operational Strategy of Peace Enforcement: Lessons from Interventions and Peace Operations.* Washington, D.C.: DFI International.
Buckley, K.
    1991   *Panama: The Whole Story.* New York: Simon & Schuster.

Burns, R.
  1996   Fallout from Taiwan tensions: U.S. cancels China talks. *The Record*, March 23.
Bush, G., and B. Scowcroft
  1998   *A World Transformed*. New York: Alfred Knopf.
Damrosch, L.F., ed.
  1993   *Enforcing Restraint: Collective Intervention in Internal Conflicts*. New York: Council on Foreign Relations Press.
Downie, A.
  1993a   U.S. diplomats in Haiti threatened, ship delayed. *Reuters*, October 11.
  1993b   Tense standoff in Haiti over U.S. troopship. *Reuters North American Wire*, October 12.
Freedman, L., and E. Karsh
  1993   *The Gulf Conflict, 1990-1991*. Princeton, N.J.: Princeton University Press.
Gacek, C.
  1995   *The Logic of Force*. New York: Columbia University Press.
George, A.L.
  1995   The role of force in diplomacy: A continuing dilemma for U.S. foreign policy. In *Force and Statecraft*, 3rd ed., G. Craig and A.L. George, eds. New York: Oxford University Press.
George, A.L., and W.E. Simons, eds.
  1994   *The Limits of Coercive Diplomacy*, 2nd ed. Boulder, Colo.: Westview.
George, A.L., and R. Smoke
  1974   *Deterrence in American Foreign Policy: Theory and Practice*. New York: Columbia University Press.
Grant, R.L.
  1991   *Operation Just Cause and the U.S. Policy Process*. RAND Note N-3265-AF. Santa Monica, Calif.: RAND Corp.
Holl, J.
  1995   We the people here don't want no war. In *The United States and the Use of Force in the Post-Cold War Era*. Aspen Strategy Group. Queenstown, Md.: Aspen Institute.
Jentleson, B.
  1997   Who, why, what and how: Debates over post-Cold War military intervention. In *Eagle Adrift: American Policy at the End of the Century*, R.J. Lieber, ed. New York: Longman's.
Jervis, R., R.N. Lebow, and J.G. Stein
  1985   *Psychology and Deterrence*. Baltimore: Johns Hopkins University Press.
Kempe, F.
  1990   *Divorcing the Dictator: America's Bungled Affair with Noriega*. New York: Putnam.
Lauren, P.G.
  1994   Coercive diplomacy and ultimata: Theory and practice in history. In *Limits of Coercive Diplomacy*, 2nd ed., A.L. George and W.E. Simons, eds. Boulder, Colo.: Westview.
Muravchik, J.
  1996   *The Imperative of American Leadership*. Washington, D.C.: American Enterprise Institute.
Powell, C.L.
  1992a   Why generals get nervous. *New York Times*, October 8:A35.
  1992b   U.S. force: Challenges ahead. *Foreign Affairs*, 72(Winter 1992-1993):32-45.
Powell, C., with J.E. Persico
  1995   *My American Journey*. New York: Random House.

The Public Perspective
   1994   North Korea. *The Public Perspective*, 5(July/August):5.
Quayle, D.
   1994   *Standing Firm: A Vice-Presidential Memoir.* New York: Harper Collins.
Ribadeneira, D.
   1994   Life as usual for Haiti troops: At military headquarters in capital, no signs of
           concern. *The Boston Globe*, May 15:9.
Schelling, T.
   1966   *Arms and Influence.* New Haven: Yale University Press.
Schwarzkopf, H.N., with P. Petre
   1992   *It Doesn't Take a Hero: General H. Norman Schwarzkopf, the Autobiography.* New
           York: Bantam Books.
Shultz, G.
   1985   The Ethics of Power. Address given at the convocation of Yeshiva University,
           New York City, December 9, 1984. *Department of State Bulletin*, February:1-3.
Stein, J.G.
   1992   Deterrence and compellence in the Gulf, 1990-1991: A failed or impossible task?
           International Security, 17(Fall):2.
Treaster, J.B.
   1989   After Noriega: Noriega military command belittles general. *New York Times*,
           December 27:A14.
Whetten, L.L.
   1974   *The Canal War: Four Power Conflict in the Middle East.* Cambridge, Mass.: MIT
           Press.
Woodward, B.
   1991   *The Commanders.* New York: Simon & Schuster.

4

Economic Sanctions and Post-Cold War Conflicts: Challenges for Theory and Policy

Bruce W. Jentleson

T he sanctions literature is among the most contentious and inconclusive in international relations. Survey the studies of major sanctions cases—from pre-Cold War ones like the 1935-1936 League of Nations sanctions against Mussolini's Italy, to Cold War-era ones like the U.S. sanctions against Cuba, the 1960s-1970s United Nations (UN) sanctions against Rhodesia, the 1981-1983 Siberian gas pipeline and the 1980s antiapartheid sanctions, and post-Cold War cases like Iraq, Serbia, Haiti, Libya, and Iran—and one finds some studies that claim success while others of the very same cases conclude that the sanctions were failures.

The basic theoretical debate is often cast as traditionalists versus revisionists. Traditionalists see little efficacy in sanctions. "It would be difficult to find any proposition in the international relations literature more widely accepted," as David Baldwin puts it in his critique of the traditionalists, "than those belittling the utility of economic techniques of statecraft." Among the works Baldwin cites are studies by Henry Bienen and Robert Gilpin, who accept "the nearly unanimous conclusion of scholars that sanctions seldom achieve their purposes and more likely have severe counterproductive consequences"; Charles Kindleberger, that "most sanctions are not effective"; Klaus Knorr, on their "uncertain effectiveness and decidedly low utility when used for purposes of coercing other states"; Margaret Doxey, that "in none of the cases analyzed in this study have economic sanctions succeeded in producing the desired political result"; Johan Galtung, that "the probable effectiveness of economic sanctions is, generally, negative"; and Donald Losman, that the cases he studied "failed to accomplish their political ends, and it seems unlikely that economic measures alone will fare better in the future." Among more recent authors, Robert Pape takes this view quite strongly, titling his article "Why Economic Sanctions Do Not Work."[1]

In his *Economic Statecraft*, often cited as the leading revisionist work, Baldwin questions whether sanctions are held to an "analytical 'double standard' . . . prone to accentuate the negative and downplay the positive aspects of such measures."[2] Among other studies that are or lean toward revisionism are those by M.S. Daoudi and M.S. Dajani, concluding that sanctions "are useful and effective political weapons in international politics"; Barry Carter, that "there is persuasive historical evidence that sanctions can sometimes be an effective tool for achieving foreign policy objectives"; Lisa Martin, that "sanctions can be a useful foreign policy tool"; Jonathan Kirshner, that "one fundamental conclusion is clear . . . [monetary sanctions] have demonstrated considerable power"; and Elizabeth Rogers, that "economic sanctions are more effective than most analysts suggest."[3]

Perhaps the best example of the inconclusiveness over sanctions is the study *Economic Sanctions Reconsidered* (by Gary Hufbauer, Jeffrey Schott, and Kimberly Ann Elliott; hereafter referred to as the HSE study), which is cited by both traditionalists and revisionists as supporting their arguments.[4] Revisionists hail the 34 percent success rate in the HSE study as higher than traditionalists claimed, while traditionalists raise methodological issues about the validity of the 34 percent rate and question, even if it is valid, just how impressive it is.

The uncertainties of the sanctions efficacy debate have become even more problematic in the post-Cold War era because of the frequency with which sanctions are used, as a veritable weapon of choice, in many different cases by many different actors. Some cases have involved the United States acting unilaterally; others have involved multilateral action by the UN and regional organizations such as the Organization of American States and the Organization for African Unity; still others have involved other international actors, as with Greece against Macedonia and Russia against various ex-Soviet states. All told, sanctions have been used in pursuit of a broad range of objectives related to international conflict prevention, conflict management, and conflict resolution. Yet as one recent study put it, "contemporary scholarship and policy analysis [lag] behind the current plethora of sanctions episodes . . . [and] scholars and policy makers readily acknowledge that judgments about current sanctions cases are made on the basis of ill-defined generalizations."[5] Of course, there cannot be a single theory or strategy, foolproof and universal. But we can do better in developing middle-range and conditional generalizations that balance the desirability of parsimony of explanation with the complexity of the range of factors that affect the policy utility of sanctions.

This study seeks to move toward this goal and to do so in a manner that has the theoretical significance as well as the policy relevance needed to help "bridge the gap."[6] It begins with a discussion of the main conceptual and methodological issues that complicate empirical research and theory development on sanctions. The next section reviews the theoretical debate and Cold War-era record through an analytical framework of sanctions as a coercive bargaining strategy, encompassing both the political economy of the relationships among the major actors and the design of the strategy by which sanctions are imposed.

The third section analyzes the use of sanctions thus far in the post-Cold War era in the context of the broader systemic changes—strategic, economic, political—that mark our transitional period. Three major empirical patterns are identified: the increased frequency with which sanctions are being used, the increased economic impact they are having, and their mixed record of policy success and failure. The central dynamic is what I term the "vulnerability-viability" paradox of shifts in the post-Cold War political economy both conducive and counter to sanctions' efficacy, heightening target state vulnerability on the one hand but making the political viability of sanctions more problematic on the other. The fourth section then considers the challenges this analysis poses for both theory and policy in an effort to move toward greater "sanctions realism" that recognizes both the scope and the limits, the possibilities as well as the requisites, for sanctions to be an effective strategy for international conflict prevention, management, and resolution.

CONCEPTUAL AND METHODOLOGICAL ISSUES IN SANCTIONS RESEARCH

As noted, one of the striking aspects of the literature on sanctions is the extent to which there is debate even over what constitutes success and failure, let alone the policy strategies for achieving success and the theories for explaining when and why success is most likely to be achieved. The HSE study sought to resolve these analytical differences with an ordinal scale of "success score" rankings. In the HSE study the two measures were "the extent to which the policy objective sought by the sender state was in fact achieved" and "the contribution made by the sanctions (as opposed to other factors, such as military action)." Each was coded on a scale from 1 to 4: for the policy result, running from failed (1) to successful (4); for the sanctions contribution, from zero or negative contribution (1) to significant contribution (4). The two codings were multiplied and scores of 9 and above were deemed successes and 8 or below failures.[7] However, far from resolving the methodological problems, the HSE methodology itself has been the subject of extensive debate, with serious questions raised about its own reliability and validity.[8]

All of this is indicative of a number of inherently difficult conceptual and methodological issues that complicate research on economic sanctions: (a) the lack of a consensual definition of the basic term of investigation, "economic sanctions"; (b) the need to differentiate among the different types of objectives that sanctions can have; (c) selection bias problems in identifying sets of cases for analysis; (d) the problem of establishing reliable and valid criteria for measuring policy outcomes as a dependent variable; (e) the independent variable problem of attributing causality for whatever impact is measured to sanctions vis-à-vis other aspects of the overall foreign policy strategy; and (f) setting a standard for what constitutes an acceptable rate of success.

Establishing a Working Definition of Economic Sanctions

One of the problems for research on economic sanctions is that there is no common accepted definition in the literature. Some definitions are broad and encompassing; some are narrow; some, as Kim Richard Nossal laments, are "idiosyncratic, often sloppy."[9] The most useful working definition in my view is of sanctions as *the actual or threatened denial of economic relations by one or more states (sender[s]) intended to influence the behavior of another state (target) on noneconomic issues or to limit its military capabilities.* The key elements this definition seeks to convey are that (a) this is a coercive act, as distinct from inducements and other more positive influence efforts; (b) that the instrument is economic, most often trade relations but also monetary relations, investments, credits, foreign aid, and foreign assets; and (c) that the objective is impact on noneconomic policy, such as foreign policy behavior or domestic politics, but excluding trade disputes and other economic bargaining objectives.

As such this is a narrower definition than some, such as Baldwin's "economic statecraft," which holds to element b but by including positive inducements among the instruments and trade and other economic bargaining cases among the objectives not to elements a or c.[10] On the other hand, it is broader in its scope of objectives than those, such as Pape's, that principally focus on whether sanctions can achieve the same goals as military force.[11]

Objectives of Sanctions

Here, too, as with the definition of sanctions, and even within the noneconomic parameter of point c above, there is huge variation in the literature in the terms of conceptualization of the objectives of sanctions.[12]

TABLE 4.1 Typology of Sanctions' Objectives

	Limited	Extensive
Containment	Military capabilities	Economic warfare
Antiaggression	Policies (e.g., terrorism, proliferation)	Wars, invasions
Domestic Political Influence	Democratization, human rights	Regime change

Consistent with the purposes of this paper, my focus is on those objectives that pertain most directly to conflict prevention, conflict resolution, and conflict management—on " 'what works' . . . for preventing, mitigating, resolving, or nonviolently managing conflicts of concern to the international community."[13]

Table 4.1 sketches a typology based on the purpose and scope of sanctions' objectives. The principal distinctions are among three different purposes: *containment*, limiting the target state's military and other relevant capabilities so as to constrain its capacity for causing conflicts; *antiaggression*, deterring or compelling the target state to refrain from or cease military or other aggressive actions; and *domestic political influence*, coercing change in the target state's domestic politics or policies. The subdistinctions in each of these between limited and extensive objectives are consistent with the more general literature about the need for proportionality between means and ends.[14] Containing a target's military capabilities is a more limited objective than broader economic warfare; coercing change in aggressive policies such as terrorism or proliferation of weapons of mass destruction is more limited than deterring it from launching or compelling it to end a war or invasion; pressuring for democratization or protecting human rights is more limited than forcing a change in the governing regime.

Case Selection

The question of what constitutes a sanctions case is important for both comparative case analyses and aggregate data studies. Even within the definitional parameters set above, there are three other methodological issues about how and what to count. One is the problem of how substantial the action must be to constitute a case. We know to include "big" cases like Iraq, Cuba, Haiti, and Serbia. But what about instances that involve more limited measures? For example, in May 1998 Turkey suspended a $145 million arms purchase with France because of a resolution passed by the French National Assembly recognizing the Armenian "genocide" of 1915. Was this a sufficient action to be considered a sanctions case? There is no definitive answer.

Second is the question of what to do about cases in which sanctions were invoked but did not have to be imposed because the threat sufficed for the desired coercive effect. The problem here is akin to that for general studies of deterrence, when the standing deterrence posture may have impact even if no explicit threats are made. While such cases are inherently harder to identify empirically, their exclusion can bias the sample from which conclusions about efficacy are drawn.[15]

Third is the question of how to count cases like the U.S. sanctions against Cuba that have gone on for many years. Is this a single case? Should it be analytically split over time? These questions are important as we need to know the time frame in order to know at what point(s) to take the measures of success or failure.

Dependent Variable Measurement: Assessing Policy Outcomes

Consistent with the HSE approach we can cast the dependent variable as a measurement of the extent to which the sender achieves its objectives at an acceptable cost. The operationalization of such terms, though, in a methodologically sound manner is more complicated than their 1 to 4 ordinal scale depicts. Three factors are key—differentiation, net assessment, and relativity—each of which has its own problems to be overcome.

Differentiation: The measure of success and failure needs to be differentiated in two respects. One is that multiple objectives often are pursued, with some achieved to a greater degree than others. The objectives in Table 4.1 are not at all mutually exclusive; many sanctions cases involve more than one of these types of objectives. Objectives thus need relative weights on a case-specific basis. And this must be done despite the frequent discrepancy, and at times even inverse relationship, between the emphasis on an objective in public rhetoric and its genuine policy importance. The other is the need for the measure to be cast in nondichotomous terms even as applied to success/failure on a particular objective. It is hard enough to find cases of total victory in war, let alone with a less directly coercive policy instrument like economic sanctions. We thus need to have measures that pick up on degrees of success/failure and that work with ranges and not strict yes/no conceptions of outcomes.

A caveat, though, is that too minimalist criteria must be avoided. While our analytical measures must be gauged to register whether something is achieved even when everything is not, too low a bar should not be set. It is one thing to acknowledge degrees of success, but some midpoint needs to be defined, a threshold established, so that a claim of some degree of success is not necessarily sufficient for a positive bottom line.

Net assessment: Net assessments take into account costs incurred as well as gains made. It would be of sufficient concern if the only consequence of ineffective sanctions were nonpositive—that is, that they simply did not achieve the objectives for which they were intended. However, they also can be not just nonpositive but also net negative in terms of the costs they end up carrying in one or more of four respects: *backfiring* and having a politically integrative effect strengthening the will of an embattled people to resist; *misfiring* and inflicting a humanitarian crisis on the civilian populace, making the "civilian pain" much greater than any "political gain";[16] *cross-firing*, straining relations with key allies; and *shooting in the foot* with high self-inflicted costs.

The argument that costs incurred can actually have a beneficial effect as a show of resolve is often made.[17] It is said to be part of U.S. leadership responsibilities to be willing to bear costs to take actions that, even if others do not join in, convey a message of resolve. Or in the Wilsonian version of the argument, it is holding high the mantle of democratic values. Credibility, though, is not just about resolve; it also is about judgment. It therefore cannot be too readily assumed that incurring costs will be a credibility-enhancing demonstration of fortitude. Incurring costs can deter, but it does not necessarily do so. It also may convey weakness, damage prestige, and erode credibility.

Relativity: The assessment must be relative to other available policy options. What sanctions did or did not achieve and at what cost must be compared to the pros and cons of available alternative policy strategies. As Baldwin rightly stresses, "policy making involves making decisions, and decision making involves choosing among alternative courses of action. The advantages and disadvantages of various policy options acquire significance primarily by comparison with the options."[18] This also is a point to which policy makers give great emphasis. If not sanctions, then what? Business as usual has a derogatory ring to it, both strategically and within domestic politics. The caution here is that sanctions not become a default option, resorted to based more on the negatives of other options than any systematic or convincing analysis of the probable efficacy of sanctions themselves. If an American president's choice genuinely is between sanctions and a policy response with a high likelihood of war, the relative merits of the sanctions option are obvious. But while the sanctions option often gets justified in this way, the reality is often more complicated. As Alexander George argues with respect to coercive diplomacy, the relative attractiveness of a particular policy option compared to others must not be confused with an assessment of its own feasibility and utility.[19] Thus, the question regarding relativity to other policy options should be asked but the answer not assumed a priori.

In addition to the methodological complexity that these factors add up to, there are rigorous data requirements if analytical reliability and validity are to be achieved. This is another of the methodological problems with the HSE study. The empirical evidence on which the HSE authors base their case codings is exceedingly limited, quite unsystematic, often very selective, and mostly from secondary sources.

Independent Variable: Attributing Causality

Once we have a measure of impact, the next question is the extent to which sanctions get credit for the success or blame for the lack thereof relative to other components of the sender state's overall strategy. Here too the HSE construct ("the contribution made by sanctions") has significant empirical and analytical deficiencies that leave two main problems that can undermine the validity of the causal analysis.

One is a *false positive* reading—that is, cases in which success is achieved but mistakenly attributed to sanctions rather than one of the other policies involved in the situation. This is one of the main bases for Pape's critique of the HSE study—that the principal or even exclusive credit for many of the HSE study's successes should go to the use of military force, covert action, and other such policies rather than to sanctions. While some of Pape's criticisms are stronger than others, the problem remains that many outcomes are overdetermined in their causality, making it hard to reliably establish where the credit lies. Moreover, part of the problem here as well is the data quality one, with much more systematic data gathering and analysis required if we are to have the empirical base needed to determine how and why key policy decisions were made.

The bigger problem is with *false negatives*. Here there are two subtypes: (1) cases of policy failure in which sanctions did their job, but other policies that were part of the overall strategy did not, and (2) cases in which sanctions did fail but could have worked had mistakes of strategy and implementation not been made in the ways in which they were used. Sensitivity to reaching falsely negative conclusions and keeping analytically open to the possibility that sanctions may have worked had they been done right, whether in themselves or as they fit into an overall foreign policy strategy, is a no less crucial consideration for drawing appropriate policy lessons from certain failure cases than is caution about reaching premature analytical closure around a false positive. I come back to this point later with regard to some key post-Cold War cases.

This does get into the realm of counterfactual analysis, of trying to make claims and offer explanations about what could have happened. While there is no strict singular method for doing counterfactual analysis, as Philip Tetlock and Aaron Belkin state, it must be done substantively and according to explicit criteria if we are to be able "to distinguish plausible from implausible, insightful from vacuous arguments."[20] These are methodological challenges worth tackling, both with regard to sanctions and other areas of foreign policy strategy, because important insights and policy lessons can be gained.[21]

Reasonable Expectations for the Success Rate of Sanctions

Even once all these conceptual and methodological problems are worked out and one has confidence in the success rate that is measured, the question is: Measured against what? What are "reasonable expectations" for the percentage of successes needed for sanctions to be considered an effective strategy?[22] In baseball a batter who hits .300—that is, three successes out of 10 tries—is considered to have had an excellent year. But in football a quarterback needs a passing completion rate of more than 50 percent to be considered as having had even a good season. In gymnastics a 9 out of 10 is actually a little low.

Even taking the HSE study's 34 percent success rate on its face, there are differing views of whether it meets expectations. Elizabeth Rogers sees it as "respectable" compared to other coercive foreign policy strategies, such as military intervention and covert action.[23] Others, though, see a one in three success rate for a strategy that carries such significant costs as much less acceptable.

ANALYTICAL FRAMEWORK: SANCTIONS AS A COERCIVE BARGAINING STRATEGY

The working definition given earlier conveys a conceptualization of economic sanctions as a coercive bargaining strategy. There are strong similarities with Alexander George's concept of coercive diplomacy, as well as with Thomas Schelling's work on political-military bargaining.[24] All these strategies have coercive components but are used in ways and kept at levels that entail inducing rather than fully and forcefully imposing compliance.

For sanctions this means both having economic impact and conveying political credibility. Sanctions need to hurt. The target state needs to feel their economic impact if and when imposed or, if still at the stage of a threat, be convinced that it will. The HSE study showed a differential in the average level of economic impact between success (2.4 percent of

TABLE 4.2 Sanctions as Coercive Bargaining: An Analytical Framework

Main Factors	Dimensions
Political economy of sanctions	Alternative trade partner cooperation Target state defense Sender state constraints
Design of sanctions' strategy	Objectives Targeting Enforcement Broader policy context

gross domestic product [GDP]) and failures (1.0 percent). In addition, T. Clifton Morgan and Valerie Schwebach subjected the HSE data to more rigorous analysis and found their own relationship between costs imposed and effectiveness.[25] This is not to say that the efficacy of sanctions neatly correlates to economic impact. Kirshner's comparison of the 1960-1962 U.S. sanctions against the Dominican Republic and the 1987-1989 sanctions against Panama is an example of greater political influence in the case with lesser, albeit still significant, economic impact.[26] It stands to reason, though, that if a target state has to take into account significant economic impact, whether felt or anticipated, this will affect its political decisions. In addition, beyond the immediate material impact of sanctions, political credibility comes into play as a matter of conveying a strong sense of the sender state's will and capacity to do what is necessary to gain compliance. It must be clear that the sender state will stay the course of the sanctions as imposed and ratchet them up to an increased level if need be, as well as take other coercive actions as necessary. Nor is it enough for the sender to claim credibility; the key is the target state's perceptions.

Two main sets of factors are key to the efficacy of sanctions as a coercive bargaining strategy: the *political economy* of the relationships among the key actors and the *design of the strategy* by which sanctions are imposed (Table 4.2). Each is discussed along with illustrative and substantiating Cold War-era examples.

The Political Economy of Sanctions

Here there are three dimensions: (1) the alternative trade partner dilemma and the likelihood of multilateral cooperation, (2) the target state's "sanctions defense" capacity, and (3) the domestic constraints on the sender state.

The Alternative Trade Partner Dilemma

Historically, the most frequent cause of the failure of sanctions has been other states acting as alternative trade partners for the target state. "A country menaced with an interruption of trade with a given country," as Albert O. Hirschmann stated as the general proposition in his classic 1945 work, *National Power and the Structure of Foreign Trade*, "has the alternative of diverting trade to a third country: by so doing it evades more or less completely the damaging consequences of the stoppage of trade with one particular country. The stoppage or the threat of it would thus lose all its force."[27]

There are two main reasons why the need for multilateral cooperation from prospective alternative trade partners is so important. First, even if a premium must be paid or some efficiency is lost, the ability to trade with an alternative partner substantially reduces the economic impact that sanctions can have. This has been true even in cases of extreme economic dependence, as in the Cold War-era Soviet-Yugoslavia and U.S.-Cuba cases.[28] Second, alternative trade partners also can have a political effect that plays into the political credibility and influence conversion problem. If, as in the Yugoslavian and Cuban cases, the alternative trade is provided by states that are adversaries of the sender, the target can feel it has the safe haven of a protector. From this more secure position there is less pressure to be compelled into submission or even to be deterred from future provocations. And if the alternative trade comes from the sender state's own allies, the threat to sustain the sanctions or escalate the level of confrontation loses much of its credibility. The message of resolve is much less credible if other states, especially allies, do not show solidarity.[29]

Multilateral cooperation on sanctions can be achieved in three ways: shared interests, sender state leverage, and institutionalized cooperation. "Identity of interests," as the old adage from Thucydides has it, "is the surest of bonds, whether between states or individuals."[30] The surest of bonds, perhaps, but not the most common, not even among Cold War allies, as was evident in the 1981-1983 Siberian gas pipeline case with the major intraalliance differences and disputes stemming from divergences between the United States and key Western European allies over both the economic interests at stake and divergent foreign policy strategies for relations with the Soviet Union.[31]

In this and other cases sender states resorted to imposition of secondary sanctions, claims of extraterritoriality, and other modes of leverage seeking to coerce cooperation. An interesting contrast in this regard is between the 1962-1963 "Friendship" oil pipeline case, when the United States was able to coerce its European allies to reduce their oil trade with the Soviet Union, and the 1981-1983 Siberian gas pipeline case, in which comparable cooperation could not be coerced. In the 1960s case U.S. leverage was sufficient in both its political and economic sources to get Italy to cut back on its imports of Soviet oil and Germany to block its exports of wide-diameter pipe.[32] However, in the early 1980s, Reagan administration efforts to coerce European compliance through the secondary sanctions of the extraterritorial application of U.S. law set off bitter charges and countercharges, and the Reagan administration eventually had to accede, lifting the secondary sanctions with but a few face-saving concessions by the allies.[33]

The third main strategy is through multilateral institutions. One of the problems with East-West energy trade issues like the Soviet pipelines was that they largely fell outside the framework of the Coordinating Committee on Multilateral Export Controls (COCOM), which was the semiformal NATO-like organization established in 1949 to coordinate Western alliance policy on dual-use exports and other militarily relevant and strategically significant trade. While conflicts did occur within COCOM, going back even to the 1950s, for the most part the norms, procedures, and structures established through COCOM provided the basis for managing these differences and maintaining prevailing Western multilateral cooperation, including in some instances by the United States making compromises with an eye to sustaining COCOM.[34]

The United Nations played a very limited role in sanctions prior to the post-Cold War era. It is vested by its charter with sanctions authority: if the UN Security Council determines under Article 39 the "existence of any threat to the peace, breach of the peace, or act of aggression," under Article 41 it can authorize "complete or partial interruption of economic relations" and under Article 42 it can enforce these through "such action by air, sea or land forces as may be necessary." But the UN only used this authority twice during the Cold War era—in 1966 for comprehensive sanctions against Rhodesia following the white minority regime's unilateral declaration of independence and in 1979 for an arms embargo against South Africa. While in both cases the UN's role was an important one, this did not make for much of a frequency rate. One factor constraining UN action was the Security Council's veto threat from one or the other superpower. Another was the disinclination to intervene even through sanctions on human rights and other intrastate issues that was rooted in the "sovereignty as sacrosanct" strict constructionism that was a legacy of postcolonialism.[35]

The one other institution that had some success in facilitating cooperation on sanctions was the European Community in the Falklands War case. Lisa Martin shows how Britain worked through the EC to gain cooperation with its sanctions. This was more the exception, however, than the rule.[36] The issue was the extreme one of a war, not just a foreign policy dispute or human rights violation. And the EC, for all its problems and rivalries, generally was well ahead of other regional organizations in its capacity for collective action.

Target State Characteristics and Sanctions Defense Capacity

One key aspect of a target state's sanctions defense capacity is the extent to which it can mobilize its own economy for domestic substitution. This can reduce the immediate disruptive effects as well as the ongoing economic impact. In some cases sanctions have even served as the functional equivalent of high tariffs, "protecting" domestic industry from foreign competition. Thus in Rhodesia, while sanctions ultimately did help bring down the white minority regime, the domestic substitution capacity by which it increased domestic manufacturing capacity from 602 products presanctions to 3,837 five years later was one of the reasons it took 14 years and the added pressure of a number of other forces, most particularly the guerrilla war.[37]

In other cases this economic self-defense may be less economywide and more the bastion of the governing regime and supporting elites through black markets, sanctions busting, and other profiteering. U.S. sanctions against Noriega in Panama, for example, wreaked the most damage "to the Panamanian economy since Henry Morgan, the pirate who sacked Panama City in 1671," yet Noriega well insulated himself and his cronies.[38] The pattern can be seen in post-Cold War cases such as Haiti and Iraq.

The other aspect of target state self-defense against sanctions is the relative political will it can muster to bear whatever costs are imposed and thus block any significant conversion of economic impact to political influence. It is in this regard that the political effects in fact often end up backfiring. Johan Galtung, writing in the early days of the sanctions against Rhodesia, assailed as "naïve theories of economic warfare" those theories that "do not take into account the possibility that value deprivation may initially lead to *political integration* and only later—perhaps much later, or even never—to political disintegration."[39]

It is in this sense that it is argued that nondemocracies are harder to influence through sanctions than are democracies. However, we need to get beyond this categorical distinction as there are cross-cutting patterns in both political regime categories. The key element is not just the formal domestic political structure but the extent to which the political system is apt to react to sanctions in the politically integrative dynamic that Galtung warned about or is open to sanctions having a more undermining effect on regime support. This means getting at the permeability of the regime as indicated by the degree of independent activity of domestic actors that can act as "transmission belts," carrying the economic impact of the sanctions into the target's core political structures.[40]

The likelihood of transmission belt effects depends on two factors. One is the role of key elites (e.g., political, the military, business) and whether they calculate their interests as served by or at risk from sanctions. As an economic assessment this depends on the degree of internationalization of elite economic interests. This may be a general macroeconomic internationalization or it may be more particularistic; the latter is what financial assets freezes and other sanctions targeted at the financial sector in part are intended to get at. However, if target state elites are not substantially engaged in the international economy, be it through trade or investment or finance, they are less likely to have enough to lose to spur them to bring pressure on their government. They may even stand to gain from import substitutions, black markets, or other economic opportunities induced by sanctions. In addition, if the sanctions are seeking to bring about democratic or other political reforms that in themselves are inconsistent with elite interests, elites have an added political calculus for blocking the transmission.

The other key factor is whether there is a reasonably strong internal political opposition and whether it is strengthened or undermined by sanctions. The effect can be strengthening both as a show of international solidarity and through economic disruptions on which the opposition can capitalize; it also, though, may backfire, cutting the opposition off from outside contact and providing nationalist cover for the regime to increase repression.[41]

One of the main reasons for the limited efficacy of sanctions during the Cold War was that so few states had "activatable" transmission belts. This was true of the Soviet Union and other communist countries but not just communist countries. In Latin America few elites did much transmission of the human rights sanctions. Their interests were with the regime. Moreover, they knew that in the Cold War context there were limits to how much the United States would push and pressure them. So too with other semiauthoritarian, semidemocratic U.S. Third World allies.

South Africa was the Cold War-era case that best demonstrates the transmission belt effect. The sanctions "affected key sectors of the South African economy . . . thus creating the powerful effect of chilling business confidence." Moreover, "South African whites, who consider themselves European, were shunned by these countries. The non-economic sanction of banning sports-crazy South Africa from international sporting events had a particularly potent negative effect on the psyche of South African whites." At this juncture the elites shifted from buttressing the regime against international pressure to transmitting that pressure internally "to abandon apartheid and to opt for a negotiated transition to democracy."[42]

Another factor often cited is the sender/target state bilateral relationship. When this relationship is already highly adversarial, target states are more apt to resist sanctions. Daniel Drezner shows how this comes through as calculations of relative gains based on "conflict expectations" in his study of Russian sanctions against other states in the formerly Soviet space.[43] HSE and others take this argument further to claim that sanctions generally work better against allies than adversaries. While there is some logic to this it does not generalize to countersanctions and claims of extraterritoriality, which as in the U.S.-European relationship consistently touch a nerve.

Sender State's Domestic Constraints

The third dimension to the political economy of sanctions gets at the sender state's motivations. On the one side are any strategic calculations that lead it to see benefits in sanctions even if they are unilateral and even in the face of a well self-defending target. On the other hand are domestic constraints from interest groups and bureaucratic actors that seek to block the enactment of sanctions, impede their imposition, or prompt their lifting.

For much of the Cold War there was a strategic logic for the United States to still impose sanctions unilaterally when multilateral cooperation was not possible. More often than not the case was a strong one for acting even when other states would not because of the responsibilities of global leadership. On the political side there were few domestic constraints, both because of the Cold War consensus and the general lesser importance of trade to the American economy than for Europe or Japan. However, over the course of the Cold War, as the former weakened and the latter grew, the calculus became more ambivalent.

Take, for example, grain trade with the Soviet Union. When in 1963 President Kennedy proposed the first major grain sale ($250 million) to the Soviets, the reaction even in the farmbelt was lukewarm at best. At that time farm income was increasing at a rate of 11.8 percent, and exports constituted only 21 percent of total grain output. There was, though, a strong sentiment, as expressed by 10 farm belt members of the House Agriculture Committee, that "the vast majority of American farmers, like the vast majority of all Americans, are unwilling to sell out a high moral principle, even for solid gold."[44] Yet in 1980 when President Carter imposed the grain embargo against the Soviets in retaliation for their invasion of Afghanistan, it set off a wave of prairie fever that was among the key factors in his overwhelming defeat in the 1980 presidential election.

Now the domestic political economy was very different: exports accounted for 40 percent of total grain output; exports to the Soviet Union were 15.6 percent of total grain exports; and the agricultural sector no longer was prosperous, indeed was in a deep recession. Ronald Reagan felt this pressure, too, and notwithstanding the rest of his tough anti-Soviet positions ("Why shouldn't the Western world quarantine the Soviet Union," one of his 1980 campaign stump speeches went, "until they decide to behave like a civilized nation?"), promised to lift the grain embargo if elected. He not only lifted the embargo but also signed a trade agreement with the Soviets pledging not to impose one ever again—this on the one American export on which the Soviets relied heavily and in the same year that he proclaimed the Soviet Union an "evil empire."

Another example involved Iraq in the period prior to the Gulf War.[45] In 1988, following Saddam Hussein's chemical weapons warfare against the Kurds in northern Iraq, the Senate passed an anti-Iraq sanctions bill by a unanimous vote. The Reagan administration actually opposed the bill, both because of the trade benefits and because of the strategic rationale for trading with Iraq, at least as the administration saw the relationship in terms of the enemy of my enemy as my friend. It thus did little to oppose, and even tacitly supported, efforts by groups with trade interests at stake to head off the bill in the House of Representatives. Iraq had become the twelfth-largest overall market for American agricultural exports, and as House Agriculture Committee Chairman E. "Kika" de la Garza (D-Tex.) put it, while "I in no way wish to condone the use of chemical weapons by Iraq . . . in light of the difficulties our nation's farmers have faced over the past few years, I am deeply concerned over any possible loss of a major market." The U.S. Chamber of Commerce urged that the United States "set aside the emotions of the moment" and ponder the economic costs of sanctions. The U.S.-Iraq Business Forum, whose member companies included major oil companies and other Fortune 500 companies, asserted that while "morality is an essential ingredient in foreign policy in a democratic society . . . morality detached from reality is stupidity." The sanctions bill died in the House.

Design of Sanctions' Strategy

When it comes to military strategy, questions of strategy design are asked as a matter of course. They also should be, but often are not, when it comes to sanctions. Here they involve four main components: the definition of objectives, as already initially discussed; targeting strategy; measures for enforcement; and the broader policy context of which sanctions are a part.

Sanctions' Objectives

The different objectives identified in Table 4.1 play into the political economy of sanctions (Table 4.2) in distinct ways. Military containment objectives have two inherent advantages but also one major disadvantage. The advantages are that target states have fewer self-defense options because of limited ability to domestically substitute for the sophisticated technologies and unique materiel denied and that the strong national security rationale can help limit the domestic constraints in the sender state. The disadvantage is that these sanctions are especially vulnerable to the target state finding even one alternative trade partner that can provide it with the military capability it is seeking, such as equipment and technologies for nuclear and other weapons of mass destruction.

On the other hand, economic containment poses difficulties along all three political economy dimensions. Its economic warfare requires even broader cooperation from alternative trade partners yet provides a weaker sense of shared interests. Its image of the enemy "trying to choke us" feeds right into target state leaders' nationalistic appeals. Domestically for the sender state it means taking on a wider range of interest groups yet with a weaker claim to an overriding strategic rationale.

Because the antiaggression and domestic political influence objectives require not only affecting capabilities but also influencing policy behavior, their success requires both having economic impact and converting that impact into political influence. This makes them more reliant on the transmission belts in the target state by which economic denial is converted into policy or political change. Moreover, they have the same difficulties of proportionality as do other limited coercive strategies. This is reflected in the HSE study's findings of a 50 percent sanctions success rate for "modest policy change" but only a 23 percent success rate for "high policy."

Targeting Strategy

One of the main points of agreement in the literature is that sanctions that are comprehensive in scope as well as decisive in their imposition are more effective than partial ones ratcheted up incrementally.[46] The usual arguments for an incremental approach are that it constitutes a measured method of conflict management and that it is easier to get multilateral cooperation. The critique, though, is that this approach undermines the coercive capacity of sanctions by limiting their immediate economic disruptive impact, by making the political message one of less than firm resolve, by providing time for the target to build up its defensive counter-measures (e.g., stockpiling oil or other strategic commodities), and by the onset of "sanctions fatigue."

The specific and intentional policy choice to target sanctions at certain sectors deemed economically strategic is different from just keeping sanctions partial. Past cases of sectoral targeting show oil sanctions to have been the most successful. The lessons of the 1973 sanctions by the Organization of Petroleum Exporting Countries (OPEC), which as the London-based International Institute of Strategic Studies put it were a success "at the highest level of politics," still are with us.[47] Conversely, in the Mussolini-League of Nations case, it was the unwillingness of the British and the French to embargo oil that doomed the sanctions. Mussolini himself was quoted as having told Hitler three years later that, if his oil supply had been embargoed, "I would have had to order a withdrawal from Abyssinnia [Ethiopia] in a week."[48]

The various sanctions targeted at the financial sector also appear associated with a number of successes. HSE found a 41 percent success rate for financial sanctions, compared to 25 percent for trade sanctions. Three factors explain this greater efficacy: (1) greater target state vulnerability because of the limited domestic substitution capacity for foreign capital; (2) the ability to target financial sanctions, as through freezes of foreign assets, at transmission belts in the regime and at its key supporters; and (3) a tendency for domestic constraints in the sender state to be weak—in fact, financial sanctions often are in the interest of groups seeking to recover assets or debts. Examples include South Africa, where the currency crisis set off by the credit crunch was "the last nail in the coffin that drove [President Frederick] de Klerk to negotiate with the ANC [African National Congress],"[49] and the 1979-1981 crisis over the American hostages held in Iran, in which the financial sanction of freezing over $11 billion in Iranian assets was "one of the key elements in their [the hostages'] eventual release."[50]

Enforcement

Leaky sanctions not only mitigate economic impact but also undermine political credibility. For if you tell me you are going to hurt me, but I know that for all your tough talk I am able to get around your threats, you won't be very credible in my eyes the next time you make a threat. Yet enforcement often has been a problem. The UN's role in the enforcement of sanctions during the Cold War era was more on paper than in practice. It had set up a mechanism called the Collective Measures Committee back in 1951-1952 to address the enforcement problem, but its recommendations were buried under the general paralysis of such type of action by the Cold War.[51] In the U.S.-Soviet case there was serious leakage of technology transfer controls, especially of dual-use technologies, reaching the Soviets in the late 1970s to early 1980s.[52] This also was a major problem with Iraq in the 1980s, as Saddam Hussein's regime took advantage of lax Western enforcement to establish a global front company network and other means for acquiring weapons of mass destruction-related technologies, thus both acquiring proscribed capabilities and drawing damaging conclusions about Western credibility.[53]

Broader Policy Context

HSE used the term "companion policies" to make the point that sanctions rarely if ever are used on their own and thus, aside from all the above sanctions-specific criteria, their effectiveness in part depends on the other components that constitute the broader policy context. Analytically, the false positive and false negative methodological problems often come from not taking this broader policy context into account and attributing credit to or placing blame on sanctions that should go to another aspect of policy.

In policy terms this can cut one of two ways. One relates to questions of credibility and whether the broader policy context leads the target state to perceive sanctions as either a step away from or a step toward the use of military force. The sign-of-weakness perception is risked when sanctions come out of a policy debate that expresses doubts about if not rejection of more coercive measures; the sign-of-resolve perception is more likely when sanctions are arrived at perhaps as a first step and within a broader policy message of other tougher steps likely to follow if there is no compliance.

The other key aspect of the broader policy context is how the stick of sanctions links to whatever carrots are being offered as inducements. Here the problem can either be that the inducements are too much and/or too quick for the stick to have the credibility it needs or that they are insufficient to provide balance to the bargaining strategy.

SANCTIONS IN THE POST-COLD WAR ERA: PATTERNS AND ANALYSIS

Given the profound changes that have come with the end of the Cold War, how have sanctions been affected? In this section four major patterns are identified: the increased frequency with which sanctions are being used; the substantially greater economic impact that sanctions are having; their mixed policy record of success and failure; and changes in the political economy of sanctions along the lines of what I term the "vulnerability-viability paradox."

TABLE 4.3 Major Post-Cold War Economic Sanctions

Year Imposed[a]	Target	Principal Sender(s)[b]	Principal Objectives
1990-1991	Iraq	UN	Military containment, antiaggression
1990	China	U.S.	Domestic political influence (human rights)
1990	El Salvador	U.S.	Antiaggression (civil war), domestic political influence (human rights)
1990	Lithuania	USSR	Domestic political influence (revoke independence)
1990	Suriname	Netherlands	Domestic political influence (regime change)
1990	Zaire	U.S., EU, Belgium	Domestic political influence (human rights)
1991	Former Yugoslavia	UN	Military containment (arms embargo)
1991	Kenya	U.S., Western Europe	Domestic political influence (democratization)
1991, 1993	Haiti	U.S., OAS, UN	Domestic political influence (regime change)
1991	Thailand	U.S.	Domestic political influence (democratization)
1992	Peru	U.S.	Domestic political influence (democratization)
1992	Somalia	UN	Antiaggression (civil war)
1992	Liberia	UN	Antiaggression (civil war)
1992	Malawi	U.S., Western Europe	Domestic political influence (democratization)
1992	Syria	U.S.	Antiaggression (terrorism)
1992	Serbia	UN	Antiaggression (ethnic war)
1992	Turkmenistan	Russia	Domestic political influence (Russian ethnic minority)
1992	Latvia	Russia	Domestic political influence (Russian ethnic minority)
1992	Azerbaijan	Armenia	Antiaggression (war)
1992	Azerbaijan	U.S.	Antiaggression (war)
1992	Algeria	EU	Domestic political influence (democratization)
1992	Cambodia (Khmer Rouge)	UN	Domestic political influence (democratization)
1992	Cameroon	U.S.	Domestic political influence (democratization)
1992	Equatorial Guineau	EU, Spain	Domestic political influence (democratization)
1992	Estonia	Russia	Domestic political influence (human rights)
1992	Peru	U.S.	Domestic political influence (democratization, human rights)

TABLE 4.3 Continued

Year Imposed[a]	Target	Principal Sender(s)[b]	Principal Objectives
1992	Togo	U.S., EU	Domestic political influence (democratization)
1992-1993, 1996	Libya	UN (1992-1993), U.S.	Antiaggression (terrorism, proliferation)
1992, 1995, 1996	Iran	U.S., Europe, and Japan (some)	Military containment, economic containment, antiaggression
1993	Guatemala	U.S., OAS, Germany	Domestic political influence (block regime change)
1993	Nigeria	U.S., British Commonwealth	Domestic political influence (democratization, human rights)
1993	Sudan	U.S.	Antiaggression (terrorism)
1993	Mauritania	U.S.	Domestic political influence (workers' rights)
1993	Rwanda	UN	Antiaggression (civil war)
1993	Kazakhstan	Russia	Domestic political influence (ethnic minority)
1993	Macedonia	Greece	Domestic political influence (national identity)
1993	Angola-UNITA	UN	Antiaggression (civil war)
1993, 1996	China	U.S.	Antiaggression (proliferation)
1993, 1996	Pakistan	U.S.	Antiaggression (proliferation), domestic political influence, democratization
1993	India	U.S.	Antiaggression (proliferation)
1994	Gambia	U.S., UK	Domestic political influence (democratization)
1994	North Korea	U.S.	Antiaggression (proliferation)
1994	Albania	Greece	Domestic political influence (human rights)
1995	Afghanistan	U.S.	Domestic political influence (drugs, democratization)
1995	Saudi Arabia, Qatar, United Arab Emirates	U.S.	Domestic political influence (workers' rights)
1995	Maldives	U.S.	Domestic political influence (workers' rights)
1995	Colombia	U.S.	Domestic political influence (drug cartels)
1995	Peru, Ecuador	U.S.	Antiaggression (border war)

Continued on next page

TABLE 4.3 Continued

Year Imposed[a]	Target	Principal Sender(s)[b]	Principal Objectives
1996	Paraguay	U.S., OAS, Mercosur	Domestic political influence (block regime change)
1996	Nations trading with Cuba	U.S.	Domestic political influence (regime change)
1996	Nations trading with Iran, Libya	U.S.	Antiaggression (terrorism)
1996	Burma (Myanmar)	U.S.	Domestic political influence (human rights)
1996	Burundi	East African nations	Domestic political influence (regime change)
1996	Turkey	EU	Domestic political influence (human rights)
1996	Niger	U.S., France	Domestic political influence (democratization)
1997	Palestinian Authority	Israel	Antiaggression (terrorism)
1997	Kenya	World Bank	Domestic political influence (corruption)
1997	Sierra Leone	ECOWAS	Domestic political influence (democratization)
1998	India, Pakistan	U.S.	Antiaggression (proliferation)

NOTE: EU, European Union; OAS, Organization of American States; UNITA, Union for the Total Independence of Angola; ECOWAS, Economic Community of West African States Monitoring Group.

[a]Many of these cases had preexisting sanctions as well; dates are for new sanctions imposed in the 1990s.

[b]Cases in which both the United States and an international institution or other countries are listed indicate more extensive unilateral U.S. sanctions.

Frequency of Use

While some of the methodological issues noted earlier regarding case identification and selection complicate fully accurate case counting, the basic pattern of sanctions being used with great frequency is clear. Table 4.3, covering the 1990-1999 period, includes 59 sanctions cases. This list follows the same counting rule as in the HSE study of including newly initiated and ratcheted up sanctions but not those ongoing with minimal change from an earlier period. The 1990s total of 59 is substantially greater than the 37 for the 1970s, the highest previous total for a decade. No wonder so many see sanctions as the post-Cold War weapon of choice.

Three reasons explain this initial pattern of frequency of use. First, it

is indicative of the nature and scope of conflict that has been characteriz-
ing the post-Cold War international system. The initial euphoria circa
1989 of "the end of history," "a new world order," and the like did not last
very long. The post-Cold War era is all too replete with its own extensive
agenda for conflict prevention, management, and resolution.

Second is the relativity calculus, that sanctions are even more attractive as an alternative to military intervention than in earlier periods. Major powers find themselves on the one hand with weaker claims to international legitimacy for using military force than during the Cold War and
greater need in this less realpolitik age for such legitimacy. Thus, for
example, it was one thing for Russia to impose sanctions on Lithuania but
would have been quite another had it invaded. And when the United
States went beyond sanctions to military action in Haiti, it did so only
after getting a separately legitimizing UN resolution. While as we will see
it is often a mistake to view sanctions as a preferred alternative to military
intervention, the point here is explanatory not evaluative.

Third is the shift in the U.S. domestic political dynamics of sanctions.
The number and range of groups pressuring for sanctions have increased
quite substantially. These particularly include ethnic and other "identity"
groups (e.g., the American Israel Public Affairs Committee (AIPAC) on
Iran and Libya, the Cuban American National Foundation on Cuba), human rights groups on a number of issues, and the conservative Christian
right on religious freedom and human rights issues. Pressures from prosanctions groups have been targeted most intensely on Congress, contributing to a shift in Congress's role to being even more "directive" and
"prescriptive" than in the past, leaving less executive discretion for deciding whether to actually impose sanctions and instead "mandating, rather
than simply authorizing their use . . . [and] identifying the precise conditions for their removal."[54] The same politics underlie the increased imposition of sanctions by state and local governments using pension fund
holdings and their procurement contracts with companies trading and
investing in offending countries as a form of intra-U.S. countersanctions
(e.g., Burma).

In some cases the Clinton administration sought to oppose or at least
temper these pressures; in others it welcomed or at least went along with
them. The business community has been the principal source of opposition to sanctions, emphasizing the much greater costs to the American
economy than in the past given the greater relative importance of trade.
In some cases (e.g., China, India-Pakistan) opposition has also come from
the general foreign policy community. While the antisanctions forces have
been gaining some ground and the dynamic has begun to shift, the prosanctions forces have tended to dominate thus far.

Greater Economic Impact: On Target States
But Also Civilian Populaces

A second main post-Cold War pattern is the increased economic impact sanctions have been having on their targets. Whereas the overall average impact on gross national product (GNP) in the original HSE study was less than 2 percent and only 2.4 percent in HSE's success cases, double-digit effects are seen in a number of post-Cold War cases, much of which remains attributable to sanctions even taking into account self-induced factors such as corruption and internal inefficiencies.

For example, in Iraq the original 1990 sanctions had the immediate effect of cutting off 97 percent of Iraqi oil exports and over 90 percent of its imports and caused a 40 percent decline in civilian production.[55] Later, in the initial aftermath of the 1991 Gulf War, there was a miniboom as Saddam Hussein drew on accumulated stocks of industrial equipment, hidden cash reserves, materials stolen from Kuwait, and smuggling and transshipment routes through then-ally Jordan. And for a period thereafter Saddam was able to use rationing to provide Iraqis with food and other basic needs.[56] But these compensatory measures provided only partial and temporary relief. By 1993 GDP had fallen by more than half, from $40 billion (in 1990) to $17 billion. Food imports had to be cut to about one-third of prewar levels, and the resulting shortages and black markets drove inflation up to 170 percent overall and to such astronomical levels as 350 percent for eggs, 2,857 percent for bread, and 2,222 percent for infant formula. Through both official devaluations and black market activity the Iraqi dinar plummeted from about one-third to the dollar before the Gulf War to over 3,000. Salaries of government employees were cut to the equivalent of $1 to $2 a month. From electricity to telephone service to drinking water to hospitals, the basic economic infrastructure of Iraq severely deteriorated. "Every day is worse than before," one Iraqi told a foreign correspondent in mid-1994.[57] Overall estimates are of Iraq having lost $120 billion in oil sales because of the sanctions.

In the case of Iran, as one economist put it, the sanctions "did not, by any means, create the current economic situation, but they have made a bad situation worse."[58] Iran's economic problems were rooted most fundamentally in the softness of international oil markets and in the corruption and inefficiencies of the Iranian political system. Inflation, for example, hit 100 percent in 1994; imports were down to $12 billion, lower even than nonadjusted 1977 figures. Even though the sanctions imposed by the United States in 1995 were not fully supported by other major Western nations, because the Iranian economy was so tied to the dollar the immediate impact was quite substantial. A wave of dollar buying was set off, and the Iranian rial took an immediate plunge of 50 percent, recov-

ering somewhat but still down by about one-third later in the year. Inflation went up even higher, indeed to the highest rates since the Iran-Iraq
war, and hit consumer goods especially hard. Hard currency reserves
also were being stretched, making servicing of Iran's large debt ($4.5
billion to $6 billion) more difficult, which in turn made foreign investors
and creditors more wary of providing new capital.[59] This has begun to
change in recent years for a number of reasons, notably the improved
outlooks in the oil and gas sector, the political and economic reforms
initiated since 1997 by President Mohamed Khatemi, and the increased
willingness of European and other governments and companies to buck
U.S. efforts to claim extraterritoriality and impose secondary sanctions.
But the likely decreasing future economic impact that sanctions will have
is a separate point from the impact they have had.

   With Serbia in the Bosnia conflict, while also guarding against over-
attribution to the effects of sanctions relative to other factors such as the
Milosevic regime's mismanagement of the economy, the overall economic
picture was characterized by one observer as "terrible": "Inflation skyrocketed. Necessary agricultural supplies and fertilizers virtually disappeared, as did fuel, spare parts and supplies for all industry. Production
fell sharply while unemployment jumped. Average salaries plummeted.
. . . [B]y 1993 close to 80 percent of the population had fallen below the
poverty line."[60] GDP fell from $26.6 billion in 1990 to $10 billion in 1994.
With sanctions lost trade was estimated at $20 billion.[61] If sanctions were
not lifted, the national bank governor direly warned in August 1994, "it's
all over for us." Effects lingered even after the Dayton Accords were
signed and the sanctions lifted, with the average monthly wage in mid-
1996 only about $100, an 80 percent drop, and even then often months late
in payment.[62]

   In the India-Pakistan cases sanctions had less economic impact but
still had some. The sanctions were primarily U.S. ones and were limited
mostly to aid, loans, and investment financing and export credits. Nor
were even these maintained for very long, first being relaxed to allow
agricultural exports and then mostly lifted after less than six months.
Still the economic impact was not inconsequential. In the month after
the sanctions were imposed, the Indian rupee dropped about 19 percent
in value, and the Bombay Stock Exchange fell about 30 percent. While
still more self-reliant than most post-Cold War economies, India had
been opening up more and more. The Bharatiya Janata Party (BJP) government had plans on the books for 50 projects involving over $600
million in foreign investment and was looking to increase these even
further. The Pakistani economy was weaker and more vulnerable generally. Prime Minister Nawaz Sharif defiantly told his people to "let them
eat grass," but fortunately for all concerned things never got to such a

point. This is not to say that sanctions have substantial economic impact in all cases. But the pattern of much greater economic impact than in the past is quite pronounced.

A second point, though, is the huge collateral costs being borne by civilian populaces. The number of cases in which sanctions have caused or contributed to major humanitarian crises for the civilians in a target state bearing the brunt of the economic impact, and that economic impact being so severe as to push living standards below (in some cases further below) subsistence levels, is unprecedented. The Haiti case poses this dilemma particularly sharply. Sanctions hit the already weak Haitian economy very hard. One former U.S. ambassador assessed the sanctions as having "set the Haitian economy back 15 years." Per capita GDP, while falling by about 1 to 2 percent prior to sanctions, plummeted 25 percent in the ensuing two years. Unemployment was running 60 to 70 percent and inflation 60 percent at the time of the U.S. invasion. The agriculture sector was in "complete disarray," including an estimated 400,000 to 500,000 displaced people. The assembly sector, a major urban employer, lost 36,000 jobs as 140 plants shut down. The loss of export earnings left Haiti $76 million in arrears to the World Bank and the Inter-American Development Bank. Yet while the vast majority of the Haitian people were enormously vulnerable to this further economic deprivation, because the sanctions were so poorly targeted the regime and its supporters were minimally affected. A former Aristide government official recounts how in Creole this led to such take-offs on *anbago* (embargo) as *anba gwo*, meaning "under the heels of the rich and powerful."[63]

In the case of Serbia a system was set up under UN auspices to consider requests for humanitarian exemptions for specific goods and shipments. The UN Security Council established terms of reference to guide consideration by the sanctions committees of the individual cases. One problem, though, was the sheer volume of such cases, which went from 2,000 in 1992 to 18,000 in 1993 and 34,000 by 1995.[64] A second problem was that many of the shipments that were approved under humanitarian auspices were diverted to other purposes, including reselling on the black market and using the hard currency for arms purchases.

The Iraq case also is often raised, and the debate over how much responsibility falls on the international community and how much on Saddam Hussein has been a difficult one. Numerous reports by the UN and nongovernmental organizations have documented the deterioration of basic standards of subsistence, health, and nutrition for the Iraqi people. In mid-1993 the UN's Food and Agriculture Organization (FAO) warned that "a vast majority of the Iraqi population" was facing "persistent deprivation, severe hunger and malnutrition" and that "larger numbers of Iraqis now have food intakes lower than those of populations in disaster-stricken African countries." In mid-1995 another UN report found the Iraqi hospitals had lost 75 percent of their pre-1990 staff and that waste-water facilities in Baghdad were running at 30 percent capacity. In late 1996 the United Nations International Children's Emergency Fund (UNICEF) estimated that 4,500 children under the age of 5 were dying every month. Another FAO report in 1997 found food shortages and mal-nutrition to have become more "severe and chronic."[65]

But provisions were offered all along to allow for humanitarian relief, with the caveat of UN control of the funds to assure that Saddam did not divert them for weapons of mass destruction or other such purposes, yet Saddam did not accept these terms until late 1996 with UN Security Council Resolution 986. Meanwhile, there were ample reports that he and his cronies manipulated the humanitarian supplies that were coming into Iraq, using them to reward supporters and punish opponents as well as reselling them at huge markups. His regime also was still finding the money to clandestinely import missile guidance systems and other weap-ons of mass destruction items. Still the humanitarian issue presents itself, and the Iraqi people have continued to suffer.

The other misfired economic impact has been the high collateral costs borne by third-party front-line states deprived of their natural trade part-ners. The lost revenues to Turkey from pipeline transit charges on Iraqi oil and other trade have been estimated at $20 billion. Among other effects, these losses contributed to the economic hardships and anti-Western re-sentments that helped the Islamist Refah party come to power in 1996-1997. In the Serbia case Macedonia was particularly hard hit, sanctioned from its largest trade partner and with its land and river links to the rest of Europe cut off at the same time that to its south Greece imposed sanc-tions on it. In both cases these costs came on top of other factors compli-cating the stability of countries important in their own right to U.S. for-eign policy.

Assessments of Success and Failure

As to whether this greater economic impact is being converted into policy success, for a number of reasons, including the methodological problems raised earlier, the record of sanctions success and failure is more mixed and ambiguous than proponents or opponents often ac-knowledge. There are few major successes but some limited and qualified ones. There are numerous failures but some that raise the false negative question of whether sanctions could have worked had mistakes not been made in the strategy design and implementation. And there are other cases for which contending assessments of success or failure exist. A few cases are summarized below as examples.

Iraq: Limited and Qualified Success

With regard to the first major phase of sanctions imposed on Iraq, those immediately following its August 1990 invasion of Kuwait, the assessment is largely negative. The sanctions as first established by UN Security Council Resolutions 661 and 665 did have value as an immediate response to Saddam's invasion and one expressing the broadest possible multilateral support. But the extent of the foreign policy influence objective of compelling Saddam to withdraw from Kuwait was disproportionate to the limited instrument that even comprehensive and UN-mandated multilateral sanctions constituted. Saddam also was able to draw on the wealth he plundered from the Kuwaiti economy as a target state defense for ameliorating the economic impact of sanctions at least in the short term.

As to the post-Gulf War sanctions, some success can be attributed with regard to the military containment objective. While the problem of Iraqi weapons of mass destruction has yet to be fully resolved, the basic terms of "give up your weapons and we'll give you your oil," as Ambassador Rolf Ekeus, the first chair of the United Nations Special Commission on Iraq (UNSCOM) put it, were crucial to UNSCOM's disarmament work.[66] The more general economic denial that has cost Iraq an estimated $120 billion in lost oil revenues has also been a factor, for as Eric Melby observes, those revenues "in all likelihood would result once again in significant Iraqi expenditures for offensive military weapons."[67] It therefore is one of the less uncertain counterfactuals to conclude that without sanctions Iraq would be even more of a military threat than it still is.

Sustaining this success over time, though, has grown harder and harder. The collapse of UNSCOM in 1998 raised concerns about the unfinished business of the Iraqi threat of weapons of mass destruction as well as possible new unchecked advances. While UNSCOM's collapse is more attributable to flaws in and failures of other aspects of U.S. and Western strategy, it exemplifies the problems that arise when the time that sanctions can buy is not used effectively. Moreover, the resumption by Russia of its role as an alternative trade partner for Iraq, reportedly providing a range of military equipment, including missiles, is a sanctions problem. While some such sales had been reported earlier, they apparently were stepped up substantially in early 1999 as sanctions fatigue increasingly set in and other policy disputes had their repercussions.[68] Thus, the success of the Iraq sanctions at military containment is best assessed as substantial but eroding.

While claims of success also are made for the foreign policy objective of limiting Saddam's regional influence—the helping "keep Saddam in the box" contention made by the Clinton administration—this too is time sensitive. Over time Russia, France, Turkey, and some Arab states, including Egypt, have been pushing harder for lifting many of the sanctions and for an overall shift to a less coercive and more cooperative strategy. For each of these countries the motives have been a mix of economic interests, geopolitical regional interests, and part of a broader diplomatic fencing with the United States related to other issues in the respective bilateral relationships. Whatever the particulars and irrespective of the relative merits of one position or the another, the point was that the status quo was becoming less and less tenable.

As to the regime change goal (i.e., to help bring down Saddam), sanctions have had some backfiring effects. One cannot really call it a politically integrative effect in the terms Galtung coined back in the Rhodesia case, given the nonvolitional nature of politics under a dictator as brutal as Saddam. Nevertheless, sanctions have served as a rallying point and scapegoat for channeling popular discontent into anti-Americanism. They also ended up having perverse effects on the 1995-1996 covert strategy being worked with the Kurds in northern Iraq. The further weakening of the Kurdish economy that sanctions caused set off a competition for limited economic resources that exacerbated the long-standing factional rivalry between the Kurdish Democratic Party (KDP) and the Patriotic Union of Kurdistan (PUK). The KDP-PUK splits had so widened that by mid-1996 the PUK struck an alliance of convenience with Iran, in turn prompting the PUK to actually invite Saddam and his military forces in to fight on their side, all of which created a major crisis for U.S. policy.

In summary, the Iraq case exemplifies the need for differentiation among the various objectives that sanctions have so as to take into account both what has and what has not been achieved. It is based on this analysis, as well as a net assessment weighing costs incurred against gains made along the lines noted earlier, that the success claimed for Iraqi sanctions is only limited and qualified.

Iran: Mixed Assessment and the "Cross-Fire" Problem

The Iran case involves a wide array of sanctions with a range of objectives, many of which have been U.S. unilateral ones, some of which are multilateral albeit none UN authorized. Some success can be claimed for military containment, as Iran has been partially restrained in building conventional and nonconventional military capacities. This was due in part to the overall economic impact from the full package of sanctions as noted earlier and the budget shortfalls and credit, forcing a scaling back of planned weapons purchases by about 35 percent.[69] It also was due to the extent to which there has been substantial Western multilateral cooperation on arms, dual-use exports, and weapons of mass destruction-related exports. While there have still been intraalliance differences, there has been enough of a sense of shared interests and strong enough multilateral institutional mechanisms such as the Group of Seven (G-7), the Nuclear Suppliers Group, and the Wassenaar Agreement for cooperation to prevail on military-related sanctions. The greater problem has been with North Korea, China, and Russia, the latter a particular problem with regard to nuclear and missile technology. This is a major item on the debit side of the sanctions assessment. Still it seems a balanced assessment that "Iranian efforts to acquire nonconventional weapons and expand and modernize its armed forces have been delayed and that some success can be claimed. . . . [T]o the extent that U.S. policy toward Iran has prevented Teheran from becoming more of a threat than it now is."[70]

For the broader economic containment and foreign policy influence the United States has sought, there has been much less success, largely because of limited multilateral cooperation. When it comes to oil and gas, there is a fundamental divergence of interests between the United States on one side and Europe and Japan on the other. The United States is much less dependent overall on imports for its oil and gas consumption than are its allies. The difference is especially marked in terms of the importance of the Persian Gulf per se as reflected in respective rates for OPEC oil as a percentage of total oil imports at about 50 percent for the United States, 85 percent for Europe, and 80 percent for Japan.

This was why the Iran-Libya Sanctions Act (ILSA) focused its threat of countersanctions particularly against European and other investments in the Iranian energy sector. ILSA supporters claim that it has been effective, that its coercive threat helped dissuade major investments by European and other companies that had more to lose from penalties against their trade with the United States than to gain from trade and investments with Iran. Such assessments, though, seriously undervalue the costs in intraalliance tensions. ILSA was widely seen as a combination of big power bullying and as the United States playing out its own domestic politics (AIPAC laid claims to having virtually written ILSA). A major test of ILSA came in late 1997 when a $2 billion natural gas development deal was announced by the French company Total, with Russia's Gazprom and a Malaysian company as partners. The Clinton administration took no punitive action, making its own calculation of having more to lose than to gain from doing so. The same calculation has been made on a number of ensuing oil and gas deals, albeit with various partially face-saving compromises.

It should also be stressed that these differences were not just from divergent economic interests; they also reflected very real differences in foreign policy strategy. The United States has pushed for "dual containment," the allies for "critical dialogue." At various times the Europeans have stepped back from critical dialogue in reaction to particular incidents, such as the Salman Rushdie *fatwa* and the "Mykonos" trial, in which German courts found the Iranian government guilty of complicity in the assassination of an Iranian dissident leader in a Berlin restaurant by that name. But stepping back has not led to backing off. President Khatami's election in 1997 was seen by many as further opening up new possibilities for critical dialogue and undercutting the argument for dual containment.

Serbia: Success? Failure? Contending Assessments

The case of Serbia shows how different analysts provide fundamentally contrasting success/failure assessments. Susan Woodward and Sonja Licht are among those who see sanctions as having been more negative than positive all along because of their unintended impact of reinforcing Milosevic's political ideology as well as the economic position of his state apparatus in allocating scarce goods while weakening and demoralizing the opposition.[71] On the other hand, others see a discernible pattern in Milosevic's actions of responding to sanctions when they were seriously applied but reverting and deviating when he could. David Owen, the former British foreign minister who was one of the lead international negotiators in 1993-1994, writes that, "I had no doubt then, and never have doubted since that it was the prospect of financial sanctions which Milosevic most feared: the chance of avoiding any further economic misery was too attractive domestically for him to go on humoring Karadzic as he obstructed virtually any deal."[72] General Rupert Smith, commander of the UN peacekeeping troops in Bosnia, made a similar point, that Milosevic's shift to greater willingness to enforce the sanctions against the Bosnian Serbs as he was supposed to, substantially weakened Karadzic.[73]

Haiti: Failure, But a False Negative?

There is no disagreement about the Haiti sanctions having failed. They did not bring down the military junta led by General Raul Cedras and restore the democratically elected regime of Jean-Bertrand Aristide. It took U.S. military intervention to do that. But the question is whether sanctions did not work because they could not work or whether they could have worked had they been done differently. The plausibility of the question is based primarily on sanctions having been imposed partially and incrementally rather than comprehensively and decisively. Haiti was the epitome of target state economic vulnerability—a small country with a weak economy, dependent on the United States for almost 70 percent of its trade, and pretty conducive to enforcement given its mostly island geography. From the start a Bush administration official stressed its particular vulnerabilities to an oil cutoff and to sanctions against its manufacturing assembly industry, which employed 35,000 people. He predicted a 60 percent chance that the sanctions would achieve their objective of bringing Aristide back to power within just two months.[74] Yet six months into the sanctions exemptions were granted for American-owned assembly plants. "The mood of optimism among many who supported the coup," *The New York Times* reported at the time, "turned to bravado and frankly expressed glee."[75] Moreover, in accommodating its own economic interests the United States weakened its standing for leaning on the Europeans or Latin Americans.

Nor was it until June 1993 that the Haiti sanctions finally became more comprehensive. The United States now banned from its ports all foreign ships still doing business with Haiti and froze financial and other assets of the major coup leaders. The United Nations now imposed an oil embargo. There is at least a correlation between these steps and the signing shortly thereafter of the Governor's Island agreement setting the terms for ending the coup. But a little more than a month after the agreement was signed, the oil embargo was lifted. While intended as a carrot, this was exploited by the junta to enhance its antisanctions defenses by stockpiling oil and other key commodities and then abrogating the agreement a few months later. Other factors also entered into the junta's decision to abrogate the agreement, but it is hard to dismiss the on-off pattern of the sanctions. Even then the U.S. and international responses kept moving only incrementally. The UN oil embargo was reimposed, but it would be another six months or so until enforcement was seriously tightened. The assets freeze was broadened to include another 41 individuals, but it was not until January 1994 that the list really expanded (another 523 names were added).[76] Elliott and Hufbauer make the case that "carefully crafted financial sanctions, swiftly applied, might have captured the attention of the economic elite, without whose support the military would not be able to rule. The Haitian elite keeps little of its wealth in Haiti and enjoys spending time and money in the United States and Europe. A global assets freeze, coupled with a travel ban, would have hit primarily that class."[77] But it was a long time coming. Meanwhile the regime and its supportive elites stayed well insulated, continuing to make large sums of money off the sanctions-facilitated black market, while the suffering deepened for the masses of Haitian people the sanctions were supposed to be helping.

Another factor in raising the false negative question stems from the weakness of the broader policy context, specifically the absence until the very end of a credible threat to use military force. Without this backdrop the message conveyed by the sanctions to the Haitian regime and its supportive elites was of sanctions being resorted to as a way of avoiding more serious action than a sense that more coercive steps lay on the horizon if the sanctions were not complied with.

India-Pakistan Nuclear Proliferation: Failures as Foreign Policy Influence

The 1998 case of nonproliferation sanctions against India and Pakistan is unequivocal in terms of sanctions as prevention. The Glenn amendment and other sanctions that the United States had on the books did not dissuade India from nuclear weapons testing. The "nuclear nationalism" motivations were quite strong, making for a case of disproportionality with sanctions inherently inadequate for the objectives in question, especially given the intense domestic political reactions on both sides.[78] Once India had tested, threats of U.S. sanctions were sorely inadequate to prevent Pakistan from following suit. This was especially so when the G-7, which by coincidence was holding its annual summit just after the Indian nuclear tests, balked at a genuinely collective stance. This undermined the credibility of sanctions even more than their economic effects, showing that even on an issue like nuclear nonproliferation Western multilateral cooperation was problematic. Still it is worth thinking through whether had the G-7 taken serious and decisive collective action against India and cast the issue as one in which Pakistan could make significant diplomatic and economic gains, Pakistan might have made a different calculation. Whatever threads of credibility may have been left were stripped bare when under domestic political pressure the United States waived its agricultural sanctions against India.

Political Economy of Post-Cold War Sanctions and the "Vulnerability-Viability" Paradox

Other cases also could have been cited and also would have fallen short of definitively substantiating either the sanctions-don't-work or yes-they-do schools. All told, while some definite patterns can be identified, the overarching one is a paradoxical one of greater target state vulnerability to the potential coercive potency of sanctions on the one hand but more problematic political viability in a number of respects on the other. This "vulnerability-viability" paradox is a consequence of the three major systemic changes that mark the transition to the post-Cold War era—the strategic changes of the end of bipolarity, the economic changes of globalization, and the political changes of the spread of democratization—which cut in both directions, conducive to and counter to the efficacy of sanctions.

On the target state vulnerability side, these broad systemic forces have made for a weakening of target state defenses in three respects. First, in economic terms, while the impact of globalization does vary across countries, few if any countries have been able to stay sufficiently insulated or isolated so as to not face major GDP effects from disruptions set off by economic sanctions. Broad global trends toward greater economic interdependence, openness, and transnational economic activity have been one of the strongest forces of the post-Cold War international system. The importance of trade, investment, finance, and other international economic relations has been increasing for virtually all states at least in relative terms. Notwithstanding the normal benefits of these trends, the effect here is to make for greater susceptibility to economic impact from sanctions. Nor is this just a matter of initial disruptive effects. Autarky and domestic substitution are not as viable as target state defenses as they were in earlier less economically globalized periods.

A number of recent cases from Africa show this dynamic with respect to aid conditionality. Larry Diamond cites Malawi, where the joint decision by international donors in May 1992 to freeze $74 million in aid "compelled" the Banda dictatorship to liberalize. A national referendum on multiparty elections was called, which the regime lost, and then was "severely crushed" in actual multiparty elections. Conversely but consistently, in Togo in 1991, less than a week after French President Francois Mitterand weakened the French stance on aid conditionality, a coup was launched to stop the democratic transition. More generally, as Diamond concludes from these and other cases, "if aid dependence is extreme enough, as it is in much of Africa, and the donor community is sufficiently united . . . even a regime in which hard-liners predominate may have little choice but to give in to the pressure (or face financial collapse)."[79]

Second is the strategic context of the end of bipolarity. While alternative trade partners still can be a significant factor, absent the geopolitical incentives of the Cold War, it is much more difficult for target states to find a protector, as Tito's Yugoslavia was able to get from the West and Castro's Cuba from the Soviet Union. Also there is the increased use by the United Nations of its sanctions authority, broadening the coalition and establishing its legitimacy in ways only the UN can. Indeed, the UN has authorized more sanctions in the 1990s than in its entire previous history—for example, against Iraq, all of the former Yugoslavia (arms embargo), Somalia, Serbia, Libya, Haiti, the National Union for the Total Independence of Angola (UNITA), and Rwanda. The same holds true albeit in more limited ways for regional multilateral organizations, such as the Organization for Security and Cooperation in Europe (OSCE), the Organization of American States (OAS), and the Organization for African Unity (OAU), all of which used sanctions in the 1990s.

Third is the spread of democracy and the consequent fostering of transmission belts in places they did not previously exist. One does not have to become a democratic triumphalist, with the attendant underestimations of the instabilities and uncertainties that the institutionalization of democracy will continue to face for a long time to come to acknowledge the trend in this direction.[80] The effect of this trend combined with the economic globalization one is that more groups in target states have interests at risk to sanctions, and these groups are more likely to be in a position to transmit their concerns about those interests in a politically meaningful way.

The Guatemala 1993 and Paraguay 1996 cases provide examples. Both involved efforts to turn back antidemocracy coups. Guatemala stood to lose $67 million in direct aid, trade, and investment benefits under both the GSP (Generalized System of Preferences) and the CBI (Caribbean Basin Initiative) and a World Bank loan. For Paraguay, even more than its economic relations with the United States, the threat from its Mercosur partners, with which total trade had grown from $4 billion in 1990 to $13 billion in 1995, risked becoming a major economic disruption.[81] In both cases key elites acted as transmission belts:

> Most important, it seems, was the concern of business leaders that Guatemala's rising exports to the United States and Europe could be devastated if threatened sanctions were imposed. Within hours of an American threat to cut Guatemala's trade benefits, business leaders who in the past had supported authoritarian rule began pressing government and military officials to reverse Mr. Serrano's actions.[82]

> Paraguay's business and professional classes are now reliant upon external markets and supplies. . . . [The sanctions] send shivers through the country's commercial classes, and helped convince Oviedo's fellow officers that he could not prevail. . . . [T]he recent episode presents in stark terms the powerful links between commercial ties and democratic stability in the Western Hemisphere.[83]

This constitutes a very significant shift in the Latin American political economy. Economic elites and the military had long been far more inclined toward authoritarian than democratic rule. It may well be that their intrinsic preferences still are not particularly prodemocracy. But the combination of the generally more moderate nature of the democratic forces and the new calculus of their self-interests based on the greater importance of international economic relationships has made these elites more susceptible to international influence.

On the other hand, other aspects of these same systemic trends have made the political viability of sanctions more problematic. Economic globalization also has intensified the political gain/civilian pain tradeoff from sanctions misfiring and setting off humanitarian crises through their massive effects on civilian populaces. Some have questioned whether in such cases sanctions are to be seen as "an alternate to war or an alternative form of war. . . . If the harm they [the sanctions] cause is like that caused by war, are they, in fact, morally superior to war? And even if the harm caused does not compare with that caused by war, how can one justify imposing even a lesser harm on the civilian population?"[84]

There are also cross-cutting trends with regard to alternative trade partners. While Russia and China are no longer U.S. adversaries, they are still rivals for influence in post-Cold War geopolitics, as evident in cases like Iraq, Iran, and India-Pakistan. Within the Western alliance, without the overriding rationale of a common enemy and first-order security threat, Europe and Japan are more inclined to take foreign policy initiatives that may be inconsistent with those of the United States and to give salience to their economic interests. The Persian Gulf again is a prime example, particularly the Iran case. In this case and especially in the Cuba case the intraalliance feuding set off by the U.S. secondary sanctions and claims of extraterritoriality has been exacerbated by the extent to which U.S. policies are seen as being heavily motivated by domestic politics. Moreover, there are more and more countries that, thanks to the diffusion of technology and capital that have come with economic globalization, are in a position to act as alternative trade partners. They may not be able to totally replace the United States or other major industrial countries, but they can assuage some of the economic impact. Malaysia, for example, was among those pursuing major energy-sector investments in Iran, through its state-owned Petronas Company. South Africa was pursuing arms sales exports to Syria. Numerous other examples could be cited as well.

With regard to the UN and regional multilateral organizations, there are both limits and exceptions to the trend identified earlier. In cases like Libya the UN sanctions were far less than the United States sought. And in other cases the UN has not acted in large part because of the resistance of member states that feared further strengthening precedents legitimizing international action to intervene in domestic affairs. The Nigeria case in part exemplifies this. The push for sanctions came in response to the nullification by the military regime of the June 1993 presidential election, clearly won by the opposition candidate Chief Moshood Abiola, and the ensuing brutal violations of human rights, including the execution of the internationally renowned dissident Ken Saro-Wiwa and the assassination of the wife of Chief Abiola. Yet the most that came out of the UN General Assembly in the Nigeria case was a nonbinding resolution calling on the

UN Human Rights Commission to "give urgent attention" to the situation in Nigeria—and even that drew 42 abstentions and 12 negative votes, the latter coming from 10 African countries as well as China and Iran.

As to the democratization trend, those types of regimes that had been least permeable still are—for example, highly personalized dictatorships as in Iraq and Cuba and a strong single-party state as in China. Sanctions against these regimes and others like them thus continue to be limited in what they can achieve. The boomerang effect of sanctions setting off politically integrative reactions also remains possible in a number of political systems, especially when the sanctions have domestic political influence objectives and are imposed overtly and "loudly."

It is in large part because of this vulnerability-viability paradox and the ways in which both proponents and opponents of sanctions can argue that the post-Cold War political economy favors their positions that sanctions are more politically contentious than they have ever been. In the past there were specific case controversies, like over the 1980 Soviet grain embargo. In recent years, though, it has been one case after—actually, on top of—another. Opposition to sanctions comes principally from the business community. Some of its estimates of the costs incurred are open to question and are taken up below as a separate analytical point that bears on net assessments of unilateral sanctions. The relevant point here is that the increased opposition in itself reflects the greater relative importance of trade in the American domestic political economy. Just since 1980 exports as a share of U.S. GDP increased almost 50 percent, from 8.5 to 12.3 percent. Moreover, exports have accounted for a disproportionate one-third share of overall economic growth, including a startling 65.3 percent in the recession year 1990. Exports also tend to be associated with higher-paying jobs, with an estimated 5 to 15 percent differential.[85]

More general foreign policy considerations also motivate opponents of sanctions, as manifested along one or both of two lines of argument. One is a questioning of the conception of interests underlying sanctions when they are motivated by a particular issue seen as being given undue emphasis in the context of the overall set of issues and interests in the bilateral relationship (e.g., the China case). The other is more a question of the utility of sanctions in those cases in which they are seen as a weak substitute for the use of military force or other more concerted coercive action, in effect raising the proportionality problem between the nature of the issue and the instruments selected (e.g., Iraq).

The strongest support for sanctions has come from ethnic and other "identity" groups. The Jewish-American lobby was a key force behind the Iran sanctions, both unilateral and extraterritorial secondary; so, too, with the Cuban-American lobby and Helms-Burton. In precisely these ways these cases also exemplify the interaction effect across different dimensions of the political economy of sanctions, as one of the reasons for European and Japanese ire about the Iran and Cuba sanctions was their blatancy as externalized domestic politics. Human rights groups also tend to be prosanctions. Their role is particularly noteworthy in the ways that they have taken the politics of sanctions to the state and local levels. This started in the 1980s with the antiapartheid sanctions, and its success in that case became a model that has been emulated and expanded.

Sanctions at this level usually are through prohibitions on state and local government pension fund holdings and contracting with companies trading and investing in offending countries, in effect a form of intra-U.S. secondary sanctions. In the Burma case, for example, cities such as San Francisco, Boulder, Ann Arbor, Chapel Hill, and Madison (Wisconsin) imposed their own sanctions, and a number of state governments considered similar action.[86]

These and other opponents of sanctions also make their own claims about the national interest and invoke core national principles. Issues like relations with Iran or how best to facilitate a democratic transition in Cuba do not have consensual answers, and politics aside there is room for serious policy debate. So too with human rights and other issues that raise difficult questions about tradeoffs and prioritization between values and other interests.[87] We "don't want to make the gross national product the be-all and end-all of American foreign policy and trade relationships," stated one Christian right leader. "There are other American values which are higher." Again the politics are obvious, but there is a debate to be had.

In summary, target states generally are more vulnerable than they used to be. Their economies are more open, they are less likely to find a great power protector, and they are more likely to feel pressure from domestic elites. Sanctions can hit and they can hurt more than in previous eras. They unquestionably have potential coercive potency. But their political viability is problematic in a number of respects. International coalitions are harder to build than before on some issues; on others not harder but also not much easier. The very economic impacts that sanctions now can have raise tough ethical issues and deep humanitarian concerns. Domestic U.S. politics are deeply divided and highly contentious, a more salient issue for groups on both sides.

It would be one thing if we could simply conclude either that sanctions really just do not work or that they are push-button easy to wield. It would be even easier if we could just say that the patterns are largely the same as during the Cold War. But none of these hold up. The post-Cold War political economy of sanctions definitely has changed in significant ways, but these changes do not cut strictly one way or the other. In some respects sanctions have more potential efficacy than before. In other respects it is more problematic to tap that efficacy—thus the paradox and the policy dilemmas.

TOWARD A STRATEGY OF "SANCTIONS REALISM":
CHALLENGES FOR THEORY AND POLICY

One thing we can be sure of is that international conflict prevention and resolution will remain crucial in the post-Cold War era. The post-Cold War world, as we most assuredly know by now, is not one in which history is over, or war is obsolescent, or some new order will spring forth like Athena from Zeus's head. Security threats, other interstate conflicts, ethnic conflicts and civil wars, and violations of democracy and human rights will be with us far into the foreseeable future. The international community thus needs as many tools of statecraft at its disposal as possible.

Sanctions can and should be one of those tools. The post-Cold War changes that have made target states more vulnerable mean that sanctions *can* work, but they do not guarantee that sanctions *will* work. Problems of political viability also have increased, which is why this is cast as a paradox. And when sanctions do fail, it is not just that success is not achieved but that significant costs and consequences have to be borne, economic of course but also often strategic, political, and humanitarian.

Sanctions thus can neither be written off nor turned to as a default option—not by the United States, the United Nations, or others in the international community. What is needed is a strategy of "sanctions realism," one that takes into account both the scope and the limits, the possibilities and the requisites, for sanctions' efficacy. Doing this poses challenges for policy that not only have political aspects but also could be informed and facilitated by further theory development and scholarly research in the sanctions literature. We thus come back to the coercive bargaining framework that has guided our analysis as the basis for drawing policy implications.

Post-Cold War Political Economy of Sanctions:
"Mini-Maxing" the Vulnerability-Viability Paradox

The crucial change giving sanctions more potential efficacy than before is the heightened vulnerability of target states especially to the economic impact of sanctions and also, albeit with some exceptions, to the political conversion of that economic impact. But the concomitant increase in problems of political viability constrains the capacity to actualize this potential. The key policy challenge thus is a "mini-max" one; that is, how to manage this vulnerability-viability paradox so as to minimize the problems impeding the latter and maximize the potentiality of the former.

Maximizing the Prospects for Multilateral Cooperation

Of all the factors identified, the most important in the post-Cold War context is multilateral cooperation. In those cases in which false negative questions were raised, one of the key issues was the alternative trade partner problem and the greater likely efficacy if there had been greater multilateral cooperation. The difficult but essential question is the malleability of this factor. Could greater multilateral cooperation have been achieved and, if so, how? Or is the lack thereof to be treated as a limiting parameter? The policy lessons fundamentally depend on which is true. The answer is perhaps the single most important sanctions-related area for further research, both at the case level and more broadly regarding theories of cooperation.

The most contentious conflicts over sanctions in the post-Cold War era have been intra-Western. Some of this is inevitable given differences in interests, both economic and geopolitical. And it must be added that "ally bashing" often has its political benefits at home, be it by or of the United States. But surely the scope and intensity of these battles can be scaled back.

The basic terms for an intraalliance sanctions strategy compromise that maximizes shared interests are for the less frequent but more concerted use of sanctions. The threat of serious Western collective action on sanctions is vital to sanctions having the credibility needed as part of making the threat sufficiently formidable to deter and prevent. The allies would need to be more willing to acknowledge that sanctions can work and to agree that when sanctions are used they will be backed by strong unity, including follow through on their enforcement and maintenance. For their part they cannot take freedom of foreign policy action to the point of free riding on U.S.-supplied security. On issues such as nonproliferation, deterrence of interstate aggression, antiterrorism, and ethnic conflict in Europe, there are fundamental shared interests at stake. They are not always sufficiently recognized as such, but they are.

The U.S. part of the strategic compromise would be to be more selective on when it pushed its allies for joint action on sanctions. In particular it would recognize that cooperation is least likely when sanctions are largely externalizations of American domestic politics in the garb of security or foreign policy concerns and/or when the means of leverage are secondary sanctions based on claims of extraterritoriality. We have seen that these types of and approach to sanctions have a long history of being highly contentious within the Western alliance. The post-Cold War context makes this even more the case, especially when the political motivations are as unmistakable as they were in the Helms-Burton Act and ILSA.

There is an argument to be made that secondary sanctions targeted at the firm level can have impact.[88] If forced to choose, few foreign firms would opt for their business in the Soviet or Cuban or even Iranian markets over doing business with and in the United States. This speaks to the continued quasi-monopsonistic power the United States has because of the sheer size of the American market. One of the key factors such an argument inadequately takes into account, though, is the interceding of those foreign firms' own governments to pass their own domestic laws prohibiting compliance with U.S. extraterritorial assertions. Moreover, the reverberations and fallout are quite high collateral costs in their own right. American leverage is far from insubstantial, but it is a more finite asset than it used to be and thus strategically wise not to expend it indiscriminately.

On sanctions seeking military containment objectives, Russia and China also enter the picture. It would indeed be unrealistic to ignore the differences of interests that are inherent to the mix of cooperation and rivalry in these post-Cold War relationships. The target states with which the United States is most concerned regarding proliferation and military capabilities generally—Iran and Iraq, Pakistan and India—are states with which Russia and China have their own strong geopolitical interests to pursue, both viz their respective rivalries with the United States and with each other. This will not be easy to resolve. It means striking a balance between not risking broader damage to the strategic relationship from conflict on one particular issue but also not being prone to Russia or China playing on this concern for reverse leverage.

Another key is to strengthen and expand the United Nations and regional institutions. The UN Security Council needs to act more expeditiously and firmly in imposing sanctions, including using its authority to authorize interdiction and other military operations to enforce sanctions. Also, the gap between the sanctions imposed by the Security Council and the UN's capacity to effectively monitor and enforce them needs to be closed. One approach could be, as John Stremlau proposed, the creation of a new Collective Measures Committee, building on the useful but still-born ideas of the early 1950s, the mandate of which would be "seeking the removal of the structural obstacles to implementing sanctions resolutions and to proposing ways to improve the chances that sanctions will succeed."[89] The Collective Measures Committee also could be one of the mechanisms for providing assistance to national governments in improving their capacities to enforce their sanctions. Most UN sanctions resolutions even when making sanctions mandatory have left to individual states the decisions and procedures for enforcing compliance. Thus, as Christopher Joyner writes, "the real effectiveness of international sanctions essentially turns on decision-makers in national governments."[90] Such efforts also need to include more effective coordination against global front companies and other methods of sanctions busting. These have been favorite target state strategies for undercutting the economic impact of sanctions, especially as it affects themselves. Additionally there is the credibility-undermining effect if official statements are claiming tough sanctions yet the target knows it is getting what it needs clandestinely.

Minimizing Target State Defenses

Another part of the policy challenge is making sanctions effective against governments that lack transmission belts or, for that matter, much of any kind of openness and permeability. Sanctions against regimes like Saddam Hussein's in Iraq will continue to be limited in the impact they can have especially for foreign policy influence and domestic political change objectives. Yet the range of states so excluded from the reach of sanctions has been diminishing. China, for example, is likely to continue to be highly resistant to pressures on domestic political issues but much less incontrovertibly resistant for other objectives. The failure of sanctions in cases like Haiti and Nigeria, dictatorships to be sure, had more to do with the strategy as pursued than with inherent limits based on the nature of the regime. More generally, economic globalization and the interests thus created in the international economy for elites and other groups, combined with the opening up of more and more political systems through democratization, will continue to create increased opportunities for transmission belt effects.

The Political Gain/Civilian Pain Dilemma

To be sure, as a number of recent cases have shown, flawed sanctions can end up doing significant damage to the states and peoples they are supposed to help. Surely if the "civilian pain" side of the calculus is much higher than the "political gain" one, sanctions must be assessed as net negative. The same can be argued if the political gain is relatively high but the civilian pain of achieving it also is. Precisely because sanctions now can have so much greater economic impact than in the past, the humanitarian issues and ethical considerations are difficult.

Yet so too can that be said of the consequences of inaction. As in the case of Nigeria, amidst the failure to impose anything more than partial sanctions, the military regime considered itself free to intensify and spread its repression. The point here is similar to the other side of the coin with "ripeness" theory—that waiting for a process to reach the point when it seems opportune to take action also risks allowing "rotting" to set in.

Clearly there are difficult moral choices all around. Sanctions with high misfiring collateral costs can pose grave humanitarian-socioeconomic crises; inaction by sanctions can pose its own humanitarian-human rights crises. The optimizing strategy again would be for the threat of sanctions to be sufficiently credible that it could be invoked without sanctions actually being imposed or to make sanctions as effective as possible as quickly as possible. The former point relates to the discussion above of maximizing the credibility of the threat that sanctions will be multilateral. The latter point ties in to the discussion of targeting strategy below.

The United States and the Debate Over Unilateral Sanctions

The United States, in particular the U.S. Congress, has been using unilateral sanctions more in recent years than ever before. This has engendered increasingly intensive debate, with strong opposition from the U.S. business community.[91] Many of the issues raised are very political and do not relate directly to the particular concern herein with sanctions and international conflict resolution. Two points, though, seem most pertinent.

First, even if one accepted the argument as made during the Cold War about the utility of unilateral U.S. sanctions for message-sending/leadership-asserting purposes, its salience is significantly less today. For sanctions to convey the credibility needed to coerce behavioral changes in targets, it is much more important in the post-Cold War context that the international community speak with a single voice than there be one loud voice amidst multilateral cacophony. There are times when the United States needs to take the initial action unilaterally in an effort to set the pace and get others to follow. But that is tactically different than simply going its own way. Messages as received are not necessarily the same as messages as sent and intended. Unilateral sanctions may convey isolation and disunity rather than resolve. To the extent that the United States or any other sender state is constrained by domestic political pressures from imposing sanctions, it risks being saddled with the "bluffer's dilemma." For when, as Bruce Russett and Harvey Starr argue in a more general context, a government is prevented "from pursuing certain policies or using certain capabilities, the credibility of that government declines in the eyes of other states. Its ability to influence them shrinks as its reputation as a 'bluffer' grows."[92]

Second, though, is the what's-the-alternative question. The business community's response has focused almost exclusively on establishing rigorous criteria to circumscribe the use of unilateral sanctions.[93] It is insufficient, however, to simply claim a trickle-down-like effect of contributing to a nation's growth, having a "moderating influence," and "contribut[ing] by example."[94] An array of alternatives need to be presented and pursued, such as voluntary codes of conduct, clear corporate policies that establish the importance of human rights and the rule of law, and cooperation between multinational corporations and nongovernmental organizations on democratization and other programs in these areas. Incentives can at times work better than sanctions for conflict resolution but only if they do not become blank checks and their conditions are enforced.

A number of calls are being made for process reform in U.S. policy, for a more deliberative process with more access and check points for assessing the range of interests at stake and the groups affected. Some even call for "sanctions impact" statements akin to environmental impact statements and a comparable process of review prior to action. Disciplining Congress's tendency to invoke sanctions with more rhetoric than analysis, and the executive branch's tendency to fall back on them as a default option, would be a positive development. But the real contribution will come only if the deliberative process can help forge the political will to meet the requisites for making sanctions more effective when they are used, for thinking analytically about what the limits of using them are, and for doing more to develop alternatives.

Key Elements of Effective Design of Sanctions' Strategy

The post-Cold War cases largely reinforce the basic patterns and conditions as identified analytically and from earlier periods regarding objectives, targeting, enforcement, and the broader policy context.

Objectives

First, with respect to objectives, the general rule of proportionality is again borne out. The basic parameter of greater effectiveness for limited objectives over extensive ones still holds. Sanctions at their most are a strategy of measured coerciveness. The "fit" between strategy and objectives therefore is most congruent with respect to objectives that are limited in scope.

As to the three types of objectives, none are inherently nonachievable through sanctions. The important analytical point is that each has somewhat different requisites. In many cases seeking domestic political influence, universal multilateral cooperation may not be necessary. Even if some trade seeps in, so long as the sanctions coalition includes the states that are the target's principal trading partners and that politically are most relevant, both the economic impact and the political credibility of the sanctions can be sufficient to have an impact (e.g., sanctions by the OAS and Mercosur against Paraguay). For antiaggression objectives the requisite coalition tends to be a bit broader as all the major global powers are likely to come into play in one aspect or another.

For military containment the requisites are at once easier and more difficult. As noted, intra-Western cooperation has been more readily achieved. But Russia and China play larger roles. Ultimately, the objective is to prevent the target state from acquiring certain military capabilities. Sanctions with less than universal cooperation still may succeed in slowing the acquisition, imposing additional costs, and even limiting the level of capability, but only with full multilateral cooperation can actual denial be achieved.

Economic Strategic Targeting

One of the strongest conclusions to be drawn from recent cases is the fundamental flaws in partial incremental sanctions. This was the most frequently used targeting strategy and consistently contributed to the limits and inefficacy of the sanctions. We already discussed the Haiti case and the questions as to whether sanctions imposed comprehensively and decisively might have worked. The 1993 sanctions against Nigeria raise similar questions. Whereas Nigerian oil exports amounted to over $1 billion a year and accounted for 90 percent of Nigeria's export earnings and 80 percent of government revenue, the sanctions as imposed in a limited fashion by the United States, Britain, and some Commonwealth countries did not include oil. Had comprehensive sanctions been imposed that included oil, would the military regime still have resisted or would it have conceded to the pressure? The Nigerian economy already was in quite bad shape. Unemployment was estimated to be as high as 40 percent in Lagos; inflation exceeded 50 percent; the currency had to be devalued; and debt rescheduling negotiations with the International Monetary Fund were not going well. Given their economic vulnerabilities and with Abiola having demonstrated what noted Africanist scholar Crawford Young assesses as "a remarkably broad distribution of electoral support,"[95] there could have been some transmission belt effect of business and other influential groups whose interests stood to be negatively affected by the sanctions reinforcing the political opposition with their own pressure. General Abacha also may not have felt as free to act if he were convinced the international community genuinely intended to impose significant costs.

These and other cases strongly support the greater strategic logic of comprehensive decisive sanctions. They are a more formidable threat both economically and in terms of credibility, they hit harder if imposed, and they recognize that time often is not on the side of sanctions. The HSE study and other past studies stressed this, and it is even truer in recent cases where we have seen severe humanitarian crises and a neutron-bomb-like effect of destroying the target's economy but leaving the regime standing. Moreover, the longer sanctions last the harder they are to maintain as sanctions fatigue sets in. Front-line states grow especially restless because of the costs they must bear. Leakage increases over time. Black markets get organized.

To be sure, the main question posed is political: if it is so difficult to get multilateral cooperation with limited sanctions, how could cooperation be expected with comprehensive ones? But there is an argument to be made that the economic costs to sanctioning states may actually be less, not more. If the strategy works and the sanctions achieve their objective more quickly, the larger "unit" costs but for a shorter period of time can end up being less than smaller unit costs stretched out over a much longer period of time through the graduated sanctions approach. Moreover, there is the possibility that the greater credibility of the more decisive threat can actually achieve the goal without ever having to get to the point of actual imposition.

Also one of the lessons learned from cases like Haiti and Serbia, in which financial assets were targeted only very late in the game, was the importance of doing this more fully and more quickly. Financial sanctions can be strategically targeted at the assets of the target regime and its principal supporters. They can also be aimed fairly well so as to reduce collateral costs. And they can be more effectively enforced than trade sanctions (although not totally so given banking havens and other money-laundering mechanisms). The key, though, is "quick, decisive action" so as to "prevent the target from moving funds and enlisting the cooperation of banks and governments that are unwilling to make such disclosures."[96]

Enforcement

The cases discussed above also show the problems entailed in effective enforcement of sanctions. Even in the context of the 1999 NATO war against Serbia over Kosovo, proposals for strict and intrusive enforcement of sanctions were so controversial they had to be scaled back. On the other hand, the Serbia-Bosnia sanctions case shows what can be achieved when there is the will to impose strict enforcement and resources are committed. To be sure, the mechanisms of the "sanctions assistance missions" (SAMs) was far from watertight. Even once they started to be firmed up in 1993, goods got through. There was also the problem of how to allow for humanitarian exemptions yet make sure they were in fact humanitarian and then not diverted to other purposes, including reselling on the black market and using the hard currency for arms purchases. The UN Security Council established terms of reference to guide consideration by the sanctions committees of the individual cases, but the sheer volume of such cases was a problem in itself. Still, the SAMs were effective overall and showed that with enough resources sanctions can be effectively enforced even under very difficult geographic and political circumstances.

Broader Policy Context

Finally, as to the broader policy context the point here remains what has been emphasized throughout. To the extent that sanctions are seen as a means for evading tougher action in a conflict situation that requires it, their chances for success are reduced substantially. They can be an effective part of a broader coercive strategy, indeed in some situations the lead part, but this needs to be manifested positively and assertively, not resorted to as a default option. A number of examples could be cited here, but the Iraqi case especially makes the point that, even in a case with such extensive multilateral support and such comprehensive sanctions, the overall success of sanctions requires that the other pieces of the overall strategy be sound and functional.

Further Considerations for a Research Agenda

A number of questions and areas where a stronger understanding of the theoretical dimensions and underpinnings of sanctions would be beneficial already have been stated. Others are implied, and hopefully inspired, by the overall discussion.

There are two further points on a research agenda. One is the need to work through the conceptual and methodological issues that have been identified. We will not be able to have better theories about the efficacy of sanctions unless we have sounder empirical bases for developing and testing those theories. Reliability and validity problems plague both the dependent variable assessment of the impact of sanctions and the independent variable analysis of causal attribution. Part of what is needed is an empirical database that allows for what Alexander George calls "process tracing." We need to have both the quantity and the quality of data to allow for cases to be analyzed in depth and questions about the extent of the impact of sanctions to be answered more systematically.[97]

Finally, more and better research and theorizing are needed on alternatives to sanctions. It is not enough to just recognize where sanctions will not work when there are issues to be dealt with; what can work also

must be identified and acted on. What about incentives, carrots, inducements? To what extent are these alternatives to sanctions? To what extent
are they potential complements? If complements, what are the key conditions for tapping their synergy? In more specific terms, what are the possibilities and conditions for such options as voluntary codes of corporate
conduct, cooperation between multinational corporations and nongovernmental organizations on civil society/democratization programs, and
other ideas and strategies that reach out to other areas of study?

Conclusions

While it is often easier to get action on sanctions when conflicts are
active and threats are imminent and the need for policy action is more
explicitly evident, sanctions as conflict resolution strategies have the difficulties inherent in all efforts to compel policy change or reverse a new
status quo. As with other strategies, sanctions also need to follow more of
a conflict prevention approach. Yet doing this with sanctions involves
many of the same difficulties as with other forms of preventive statecraft.
Most especially there is the problem of political will. Policy makers tend
to prefer to act only when absolutely necessary, which usually means
later rather than earlier. They are more attuned to the immediate costs
that a policy incurs and the short-term risks that it runs than to arguments
about longer-term costs and benefits. Bureaucracies are even harder than
usual to move when the issue is not clear and present. And that is within each government, let alone adding on the need for multilateral
coordination.

Yet even in such terms preventive statecraft *does* have a strong logic,
as another study I have been involved with strongly shows.[98] Whereas
the costs of waiting to act tend to be assumed to be less than the costs of
acting preventively, in sanctions cases as well as all too many other post-
Cold War conflicts, the costs have proven to be much greater than expected and arguably more than those for preventive action would have
been. This also comes back to the basic tenet of compellence being more
difficult than deterrence or other forms of prevention. It also is the case
that many interests dismissed as being of insufficient importance to warrant action end up cascading to greater importance as their conflicts intensify and spread, thus calling into question this part of the original
calculus as well.

It is always easiest if either a foreign policy strategy that is difficult is
not all that necessary or if one that is necessary is not all that difficult. The
use of economic sanctions for international conflict resolution in the post-
Cold War era is both difficult and necessary. Heightened target state
vulnerability creates opportunities, while more problematic political vi-

ability poses challenges. Sanctions realism requires prudent weighing of where the constraints of political viability are so unmalleable as to need to be treated as limiting parameters, combined with strategic assessments of the optimal strategies for maximizing the efficacy of sanctions for conflict resolution within those parameters. It needs to be recognized both that sanctions can be net negative, not just nonpositive, and that inaction and delayed action risk a worsening of the conflicts. These are difficult analyses but necessary ones in a world in which conflict resolution requires as many effective strategies as possible.

NOTES

[1]David A. Baldwin, *Economic Statecraft* (Princeton, N.J.: Princeton University Press, 1985), pp. 55-57. See also Henry Bienen and Robert Gilpin, "An Evaluation of the Use of Economic Sanctions to Promote Foreign Policy Objectives, with Special Reference to the Problem of Terrorism and the Promotion of Human Rights," a report prepared for the Boeing Corporation, April 2, 1979; Charles P. Kindleberger, *Power and Money: The Economics of International Politics and the Politics of International Economics* (New York: Basic Books, 1970), p. 97; Klaus Knorr, *The Power of Nations: The Political Economy of International Relations* (New York: Basic Books, 1974), pp. 205-206; Margaret P. Doxey, *Economic Sanctions and International Enforcement* (New York: Oxford University Press, 1971), p. 139; Johan Galtung, "On the Effects of Sanctions, with Examples from Rhodesia," p. 409; Donald L. Losman, *International Economic Sanctions: The Cases of Cuba, Israel and Rhodesia* (Albuquerque: University of New Mexico Press, 1979), p. 140; Robert A. Pape, "Why Economic Sanctions Do Not Work," *International Security*, 22 (Fall 1997), pp. 90-136.

[2]Baldwin, *Economic Statecraft*, p. 144.

[3]M.S. Daoudi and M.S. Dajani, *Economic Sanctions: Ideals and Experience* (Boston: Routledge and Kegan-Paul, 1983), p. 12; Barry E. Carter, *International Economic Sanctions: Improving the Haphazard U.S. Legal Regime* (New York: Cambridge University Press, 1988), p. 233; Lisa L. Martin, *Coercive Cooperation: Explaining Multilateral Economic Sanctions* (Princeton, N.J.: Princeton University Press, 1992), p. 250; Jonathan Kirshner, *Currency and Coercion: The Political Economy of International Monetary Power* (Princeton, N.J.: Princeton University Press, 1995), p. 166; Elizabeth S. Rogers, "Using Economic Sanctions to Control Regional Conflicts," *Security Studies*, 5 (Summer 1996), p. 72.

[4]Gary Clyde Hufbauer, Jeffrey J. Schott, and Kimberly Ann Elliott (hereafter HSE), *Economic Sanctions Reconsidered*, two volumes (Washington, D.C.: Institute for International Economics, 1990).

[5]George A. Lopez and David Cortright, "Economic Sanctions in Contemporary Global Relations," in D. Cortright and G.A. Lopez, eds., *Economic Sanctions: Panacea or Peacekeeping in a Post-Cold War World?* (Boulder, Colo.: Westview Press, 1995), p. 4.

[6]The term and the approach are based on Alexander L. George, *Bridging the Gap: Theory and Practice in Foreign Policy* (Washington, D.C.: United States Institute of Peace Press, 1993).

[7]HSE, *Economic Sanctions Reconsidered*, vol. 1, pp. 41-42.

[8]Pape, "Why Economic Sanctions Do Not Work," and the two follow-up exchanges, Kimberly Ann Elliott, "The Sanctions Glass: Half-Full or Completely Empty?," and Robert A. Pape, "Why Economic Sanctions *Still* Do Not Work," *International Security*, 23 (Summer 1998); and David A. Baldwin and Robert A. Pape, "Evaluating Economic Sanctions," *International Security* 23 (Fall 1998), pp. 189-198.

[9]Kim Richard Nossal, "International Sanctions as International Punishment," *International Organization*, 43 (Spring 1989), p. 304.

[10]Baldwin, *Economic Statecraft*, pp. 55-57.

[11]Pape, "Why Economic Sanctions Do Not Work," pp. 93-97.

[12]The variation is in the number of objectives, the basis for differentiation, and other ways. For example: modest policy change, destabilization, disruption of military adventures, military impairment, other major policy changes (HSE, *Economic Sanctions Reconsidered*); policy change, costs imposition, demonstration of resolve, domestic politics (Baldwin, *Economic Statecraft*); primary, secondary, tertiary [James Barber, "Economic Sanctions as a Policy Instrument," *International Affairs* (London), 55 (July 1979)]; formal, undisclosed, implicit [Sidney Weintraub, ed., *Economic Coercion and U.S. Foreign Policy: Implications of Case Studies from the Johnson Administration* (Boulder, Colo.: Westview Press, 1982)]; instrumental, symbolic-expressive [Johan Galtung, "On the Effects of International Sanctions, with Examples from the Case of Rhodesia," *World Politics*, 19 (April 1967)]; compliance, subversion, deterrence, international symbolism, domestic symbolism [James M. Lindsay, "Trade Sanctions as Policy Instruments: A Re-examination," *International Studies Quarterly*, 30 (June 1986)]; punishment to compel, to deter, for retribution (Nossal, "International Sanctions as International Punishment"); take or defend territory, change military behavior, change ruling regime or internal political structure (Pape, "Why Economic Sanctions *Still* Do Not Work").

[13]National Research Council, Committee on International Conflict Resolution, "Draft Guidelines for Commissioned Papers" (n.d.).

[14]Alexander L. George, *The Limits of Coercive Diplomacy* (Boston: Little Brown, 1971); Thomas S. Schelling, *Arms and Influence* (New Haven: Yale University Press, 1966).

[15]Alexander George and Richard Smoke, *Deterrence in American Foreign Policy: Theory and Practice* (New York: Columbia University Press, 1974); Richard Ned Lebow and Janice Gross Stein, *When Does Deterrence Succeed and How Do We Know?*, Occasional Paper #8 (Ottawa: Canadian Institute for International Peace and Security, 1990). Elizabeth S. Rogers ["Using Economic Sanctions to Control Regional Conflicts," *Security Studies*, 5 (Summer 1996), p. 50] makes a similar point regarding sanctions cases.

[16]Thomas G. Weiss, David Cortright, George A. Lopez, and Larry Minear, eds., *Political Gain and Civilian Pain: Humanitarian Impact of Economic Sanctions* (Lanham, Md.: Rowman and Littlefield, 1997).

[17]Baldwin draws on conceptual and theoretical work on credibility particularly by Schelling to argue that the willingness to bear costs is "a standard indicator of the intensity of one's resolve" and thus in certain situations is "a desirable attribute in a policy alternative" (*Economic Statecraft*, p. 107). Lisa Martin (*Coercive Cooperation*) also finds a direct and strong relationship between the sender's self-imposed costs and its ability to gain the cooperation of other states.

[18]Baldwin, *Economic Statecraft*, p. 15.

[19]George, *The Limits of Coercive Diplomacy*, p. 250.

[20]Philip E. Tetlock and Aaron Belkin, eds., *Counterfactual Thought Experiments in World Politics: Logical, Methodological and Psychological Perspectives* (Princeton, N.J.: Princeton University Press, 1997), pp. 5, 17.

[21]See, for example, Bruce W. Jentleson, ed., *Opportunities Missed, Opportunities Seized: Preventive Diplomacy in the Post-Cold War World* (Lanham, Md.: Rowman and Littlefield, 2000).

[22]My thanks to Paul Stern for his input on this point, drawing on his work with Daniel Druckman (see Chapter 2).

[23]Rogers, "Using Sanctions to Control Regional Conflicts," p. 49.

24George, *Limits of Coercive Diplomacy*; Schelling, *Arms and Influence and the Strategy of Conflict* (Cambridge, Mass.: Harvard University Press, 1960).

25T. Clifton Morgan and Valerie Schwebach, "Fools Suffer Gladly: The Use of Economic Sanctions in International Crises," *International Studies Quarterly*, 41 (March 1997), pp. 27-50.

26Jonathan Kirshner, "The Microfoundations of Economic Sanctions," *Security Studies*, 6 (Spring 1997).

27Albert O. Hirschman, *National Power and the Structure of Foreign Trade*, rev. ed. (Berkeley: University of California Press, 1980), p. 14.

28NATO nations, which as of 1948 accounted for only 38.5 percent of Yugoslavian imports and 30 percent of its exports, by 1954 had increased their shares to 78.5 and 71.5 percent, respectively. In the Cuba case the Soviet bloc's share of Cuban trade soared from 2 to 77.4 percent.

29Thus, for example, in the case of Rhodesia, the passage by the U.S. Congress in 1971 of the Byrd amendment authorizing imports of Rhodesian chrome, and thus defecting from the sanctions initiated by its closest ally Britain and endorsed by the United Nations, led the *Rhodesian Herald* to editorialize on this "wonderful boost for Rhodesian morale . . . a signal to the world that sanctions are not important enough to warrant serious sacrifices" [Harry R. Strack, *Sanctions: The Case of Rhodesia* (Syracuse, N.Y.: Syracuse University Press, 1978), p. 164].

30Cited in Hans J. Morgenthau, *Politics Among Nations*, 5th ed. (New York: Alfred A. Knopf, 1985), p. 10.

31Bruce W. Jentleson, *Pipeline Politics: The Complex Political Economy of East-West Energy Trade* (Ithaca, N.Y.: Cornell University Press, 1986).

32While "my heart is completely with the iron and steel industry," as West German Foreign Minister Gerhard Schroeder put it, "I must choose here between the interests of foreign policy and the interests of our economy" (Jentleson, *Pipeline Politics*, p. 118). See also Angela Stent, *From Embargo to Ostpolitik: The Political Economy of West German-Soviet Relations, 1955-1980* (New York: Cambridge University Press, 1981).

33French Foreign Minister Claude Cheysson spoke of a "progressive divorce" because "we no longer speak the same language." West German Chancellor Helmut Schmidt angrily pledged that "the pipeline will be built." Even conservative British Prime Minister Margaret Thatcher argued that "the question is whether one very powerful nation can prevent existing contracts from being fulfilled" (Jentleson, *Pipeline Politics*, p. 195).

34Following Stalin's death in 1953, there were major differences over whether to reduce the scope of export controls through the NATO-like COCOM. In August 1954 for the first time since its inception, COCOM cut its embargo lists. It did so at European insistence and over American objections. The number of exports under total embargo was cut from 320 to 226 items, and the number under any form of COCOM control fell from 514 to 315. The most extensive decontrol was in general industrial equipment; the least extensive was of monitors and other items with direct military significance. Interests still coincided on military containment but not on economic containment. Indeed no less a figure than Winston Churchill was pushing for increased trade in response to the "peaceful coexistence" overtures of the post-Stalin Soviet leaders. "The more trade there is through the Iron Curtain," Churchill argued, "the more the two great divisions of the world mingle in the healthy and fertile activities of commerce, the greater is the counterpoise to purely military calculations. Other thoughts take up their places in the minds of men." Jentleson, *Pipeline Politics*, pp. 76-81, and Michael Mastanduno, *Economic Containment: COCOM and the Politics of East-West Trade* (Ithaca, N.Y.: Cornell University Press, 1992).

35The UN Charter's Article 2(7) has been the touchstone for this view: "Nothing contained in the present Charter shall authorize the United Nations to intervene in matters which are essentially within the domestic jurisdiction of any state."

[36]Martin, *Coercive Cooperation*.

[37]Strack, *Sanctions: The Case of Rhodesia*, pp. 86, 90; Losman, *International Economic Sanctions*, p. 102; R.B. Sutcliffe, "The Political Economy of Rhodesian Sanctions," *Journal of Commonwealth Political Studies* (July 1969).

[38]Kirshner, "Microfoundations of Economic Sanctions," p. 52.

[39]Johan Galtung, "On the Effects of International Economic Sanctions, with Examples from the Case of Rhodesia," *World Politics*, 19 (April 1967), p. 407.

[40]Kirshner's "microfoundations" concept similarly seeks to get at the role of elites and "how groups within the target state are affected differentially" (Kirshner, "Microfoundations of Economic Sanctions," p. 33).

[41]On the internal opposition effect, see Ivan Eland, "Economic Sanctions as Tools of Foreign Policy," in Cortright and Lopez, *Economic Sanctions: Panacea or Peacebuilding?*, pp. 31-35, and Weiss et al., "Economic Sanctions and Their Humanitarian Impacts: An Overview" and "Toward a Framework for Analysis" in *Political Gain and Civilian Pain*, pp. 30, 42-43.

[42]Eland, "Economic Sanctions as Tools of Foreign Policy," p. 33, and Jennifer Davis, "Sanctions and Apartheid: The Economic Challenge to Discrimination," pp. 173-184, in Cortright and Lopez, *Economic Sanctions: Panacea or Peacebuilding?*; also Larry Diamond, *Promoting Democracy in the 1990s: Actors and Instruments, Issues and Imperatives* (Washington, D.C.: Carnegie Commission on Preventing Deadly Conflict, 1995), p. 55.

[43]Daniel Drezner, "Allies, Adversaries and Economic Coercion: Russian Foreign Economic Policy Since 1991," *Security Studies*, 6 (Spring 1997), pp. 65-111.

[44]Congressional Quarterly, *1963 Almanac*, p. 328, cited in Jentleson, *Pipeline Politics*, p. 48.

[45]Bruce W. Jentleson, *With Friends Like These: Reagan, Bush and Saddam, 1982-1990* (New York: W.W. Norton, 1994), chap. 2.

[46]Among those supporting this view are HSE, *Economic Sanctions Reconsidered*; Cortright and Lopez, *Economic Sanctions*; and Rogers, "Using Sanctions to Control Regional Conflicts."

[47]International Institute of Strategic Studies, *Strategic Survey 1973* (London, 1973), pp. 1-2. Japan went so far as to publicly split with the United States, rejecting the basic principles of U.S. Middle East policy and coming out in favor of Israeli withdrawal from the occupied territories as a precondition to peace negotiations. During the Yom Kippur War, Britain embargoed arms and spare-parts sales to all belligerents, a policy that primarily hurt Israel. West Germany protested the American use of its ports for loading military cargo bound for Israel. Only Portugal allowed the United States to use its bases for the airlift. The European Economic Community foreign ministers issued a communiqué adopting a pro-Arab interpretation of UN Security Council Resolution 242. The *Times of London* labeled this policy "a surrender to Arab blackmail," while OPEC cited it as a reason for canceling the additional oil production cutbacks scheduled for the following month. See also Hans Maull, "The Strategy of Avoidance: Europe's Middle East Policies After the October War," in J.C. Hurewitz, ed., *Oil, the Arab-Israeli Dispute and the Industrial World* (Boulder, Colo: Westview Press, 1976), p. 118.

[48]Together Britain and France held a near monopoly over Italy's oil supply. Yet in their effort to maintain nonadversarial relations with Mussolini to balance Hitler, according to A.J.P. Taylor they "inquired of Mussolini whether he would object to his oil being cut off. When he told them that he would, they successfully resisted oil sanctions." Anthony Eden later would write in his diary, "Looking back the thought comes again, should we not have shown more determination in pressing through with sanctions in 1935, and if we had, would we not have called Mussolini's bluff and at least postponed this [second world] war?

The answer, I am sure, is yes" [George W. Baer, "Sanctions and Security: The League of Nations and the Italian-Ethiopian War, 1935-36," *International Organization,* 27 (Spring 1973)]; Frederick Hartmann, *The Relations of Nations* (New York: Macmillan, 1973), p. 369; A.J.P. Taylor, *Origins of the Second World War* (Hammondsworth, Great Britain: Penguin, 1965), p. 127.

49According to a "white establishment" figure, as quoted in Allister Sparks, "A New South Africa: The Role of Sanctions," *Washington Post,* October 5, 1993, p. A19. The financial squeeze on South Africa was first ratcheted up by the decision by a private-sector actor, Chase Manhattan Bank, not to roll over short-term loans. But the Chase decision itself was shaped by the sanctions being imposed by the U.S. and other governments in that these sanctions were limiting South Africa's capacity to earn enough hard currency to service its debt. See also Neta C. Crawford and Audie Klotz, eds., *How Sanctions Work: Lessons from South Africa* (New York: St. Martin's Press, 1999).

50Benjamin J. Cohen, *In Whose Interest? International Banking and American Foreign Policy* (New Haven, Conn.: Yale University Press, 1986); see also Carswell, *Foreign Affairs (1980-81),* p. 251.

51John Stremlau, *Sharpening International Sanctions: Toward a Stronger Role for the United Nations* (Washington, D.C.: Carnegie Commission for Preventing Deadly Conflict, 1996), pp. 57-58.

52U.S. Department of Defense, *Soviet Acquisition of Western Technology* (Washington, D.C.: U.S. Government Printing Office, 1982), and *Soviet Acquisition of Western Technology: An Update* (Washington, D.C.: U.S. Government Printing Office, 1985).

53Jentleson, *With Friends Like These;* Kenneth R. Timmerman, *The Death Lobby: How the West Armed Iraq* (Boston: Houghton Mifflin, 1991); Alan Friedman, *Spider's Web: The Secret History of How the White House Illegally Armed Iraq* (New York: Bantam Books, 1993).

54National Association of Manufacturers, *A Catalog of New U.S. Unilateral Economic Sanctions for Foreign Policy Purposes, 1993-1996* (Washington, D.C.: NAM, 1997); President's Export Council, "Unilateral Economic Sanctions: A Review of Existing Sanctions and Their Impacts on U.S. Economic Interests with Recommendations for Policy and Process Improvements," June 1997 (mimeograph); Dianne E. Rennack and Robert D. Shuey, Congressional Research Service, *Economic Sanctions to Achieve U.S. Foreign Policy Goals: Discussion and Guide to Current Law,* CRS Report 97-949 F, updated June 5, 1998.

55"How to Choke Iraq," *New York Times,* December 7, 1990, p. A18.

56Patrick Clawson, *How Saddam Hussein Survived: Economic Sanctions, 1990-93* (Washington, D.C.: National Defense University Press, 1993); Paul Lewis, "Hussein Rebuilds Iraq's Economy Undeterred by the U.S. Sanctions," *The New York Times,* January 23, 1993, pp. 1, 14.

57Caryle Murphy, "In Iraq, Every Day Worse Than the Day Before," *Washington Post,* July 24, 1994, p. A1; Michael Kelly, "Mob Town," *New York Times Magazine,* February 14, 1993, p. 18; Paul Lewis "Iraq Reeling After 4 Years of Sanctions," *New York Times,* July 29, 1994; "Data Base," *U.S. News and World Report,* August 7, 1995.

58Eliyahu Kanovsky, "Iran's Fragile Economy: Problems and Prospects," *PolicyWatch,* #201, Washington Institute for Near East Policy, May 22, 1996; see also Elaine Sciolino, "Fear, Inflation and Graft Feed Disillusion Among Iranians," *New York Times,* May 30, 1995, pp. A1, A8.

59Nora Boustany, "Economic Woes Strain Iran's Islamic Government," *Washington Post,* October 5, 1994, pp. A25, A26; Daniel Southerland, "2-Month-Old Trade Embargo Begins to Take Toll on Iran," *Washington Post,* August 9, 1995, pp. F1, F2.

60Sonja Licht, "The Use of Sanctions in the Former Yugoslavia: Can They Assist in Conflict Resolution?," in Cortright and Lopez, *Economic Sanctions,* p. 156.

61Cited in Lopez et al., "Toward a Framework for Analysis," in *Political Gain and Civilian Pain,* p. 45.

[62]*Facts on File*, August 11, 1994, p. 561; Chris Hedges, "Isolated and Corrupt, Serbia's Economy Stagnates," *New York Times*, July 8, 1997, p. 10.

[63]Werleigh, "The Use of Sanctions in Haiti," in Cortright and Lopez, *Economic Sanctions: Panacea or Peacebuilding?*, p. 169; Sarah Zaidi, "Humanitarian Effects of the Coup and Sanctions in Haiti," in Weiss et al., *Political Gain and Civilian Pain.*

[64]Stremlau, *Sharpening International Sanctions*, p. 45.

[65]Eric Hoskins, "The Humanitarian Impact of Economic Sanctions and War in Iraq," in Weiss et al., *Political Gain and Civilian Pain;* Barbara Crossette, "UNICEF Head Says Thousands of Children Are Dying in Iraq," *New York Times*, October 29, 1996, p. A8; UN Food and Agriculture Organization (FAO), "Special Report: FAO/WFP Food Supply and Nutrition Assessment to Iraq," October 3, 1997, p. 1.

[66]Ambassador Rolf Ekeus, "UNSCOM Progress Report," speech at the Washington Institute for Near East Policy, January 29, 1997.

[67]Eric D.K. Melby, "Iraq," in Richard N. Haass, ed., *Economic Sanctions and American Diplomacy* (Washington, D.C.: Brookings Institution, 1998), p. 120.

[68]See, for example, Con Coughlin, "Russian Weapons Experts Confirm Baghdad Connection," *Sunday Telegraph* (London), February 21, 1999; Jamie Dettmer, "Russian Arms Sales to Iraq," *Washington Times*, February 22, 1999, and "Russia Becomes Saddam's Military Superstore," *Insight*, March 15, 1999, all available electronically through IRAQ NEWS, sam11@ erols.com.

[69]Between 1991 and 1995 planned annual arms imports were set at $2 billion per year, but actual figures were only $1.3 billion. The numbers for arms sales agreements as announced compared to actual acquisitions were as follows: 1,000 to 1,500 tanks but only 184 actually acquired; 100 to 200 aircraft versus 57; 200 to 300 artillery pieces versus 106 (Clawson, "Iran," pp. 94-95, and Eisenstadt, *Iranian Military Capabilities*, pp. 36-37).

[70]Eisenstadt, *Iranian Military Capabilities*, pp. 90, 93.

[71]Susan L. Woodward, "The Use of Sanctions in Former Yugoslavia: Misunderstanding Political Realities," and Sonja Licht, "The Use of Sanctions in the Former Yugoslavia: Can They Assist in Conflict Resolution?," in Cortright and Lopez, *Sanctions: Panacea or Peacebuilding?*, pp. 141-152, 153-160.

[72]David Owen, *Balkan Odyssey* (New York: Harcourt Brace, 1995), p. 144.

[73]See sources in Stedman, "The Former Yugoslavia," in Haass, *Economic Sanctions and American Diplomacy*, p. 196, fn. 42.

[74]Rose, "Haiti," in Haass, *Economic Sanctions and American Diplomacy*, p. 61.

[75]Ibid., p. 63.

[76]Ibid., p. 81, note 33.

[77]Kimberly Ann Elliott and Gary Clyde Hufbauer, " 'New' Approaches to Economic Sanctions," in Arnold Kanter and Linton F. Brooks, eds., *U.S. Intervention Policy for the Post-Cold War World* (New York: W.W. Norton, 1994), pp. 153-154.

[78]See, for example, Stephen P. Cohen, "Nuclear Breakout: How Should Washington Respond to the South Asian Bombs?," Brooking Institution Policy Brief, June 11, 1998.

[79]Diamond, *Promoting Democracy in the 1990s*, p. 78.

[80]Of 193 countries and territories included in Freedom House's annual survey, 140 (72 percent) are ranked as either "free" or "partly free." This includes 36 that are new democracies since 1989, with only eight backsliders in the same period (Freedom House, *Freedom in the World: The Annual Survey of Political Rights and Civil Liberties, 1997-98*).

[81]Mercosur followed up by amending its charter to suspend any member country that "abandons the full exercise of republican institutions" [Strobe Talbott, "Democracy and the National Interest," *Foreign Affairs*, 75 (November/December 1996), p. 54].

[82]Jim Golden, "Guatemala's Counter-Coup: A Military About-Face," *New York Times*,

June 3, 1993, p. A3; see also Francisco Villagran de Leon, "Thwarting the Guatemala Coup," *Journal of Democracy*, 4 (October 1993), pp. 115-124.

83Richard Feinberg, "The Coup That Wasn't," *Washington Post*, April 30, 1996, p. A13; see also Thomas W. Lippman, "Joint Effort Helps Head Off Coup Threat in Paraguay," *Washington Post*, April 26, 1996, p. A30.

84Drew Christiansen, and Gerard F. Powers, "Economic Sanctions and the Just War Doctrine," in Cortright and Lopez, *Economic Sanctions: Panacea or Peacebuilding?*, pp. 101, 104.

85J. David Richardson and Karin Rindal, *Why Exports Really Matter!* (Washington, D.C.: Institute of International Economics, 1995), pp. 1, 7.

86Paul Blustein, "Thinking Globally, Punishing Locally," *Washington Post*, May 16, 1997, pp. G1, G2.

87For a view on the constitutionality issues raised by state and local sanctions, see David Schmahmann and James Finch, "The Unconstitutionality of State and Local Enactments in the United States Restricting Business Ties with Burma (Myanmar)," *Vanderbilt Journal of Transnational Law*, 30 (March 1997), pp. 175-207.

88See, for example, George E. Shambaugh, "Dominance, Dependence and Political Power: Tethering Technology in the 1980s and Today," *International Studies Quarterly*, 40 (December 1996), pp. 559-588.

89Ibid., p. 40 passim.

90Christopher C. Joyner, "Collective Sanctions as Peaceful Coercion: Lessons from the United Nations Experience," *The Australian Year Book on International Law 1995*, vol. 16, p. 257.

91National Association of Manufacturers, *Catalog of New U.S. Unilateral Economic Sanctions*; President's Export Council, "Unilateral Economic Sanctions"; Mobil Oil Company, "Sanctions: Our Perspective," *New York Times*, September 16, 1997.

92Bruce Russett and Harvey Starr, *World Politics: The Menu for Choice* (San Francisco: Freeman, 1981), pp. 237-238.

93The National Association of Manufacturers report goes no further than conceding that sanctions "may be" used in "clearly defined cases of national or international emergency" and even then only if it can be demonstrated that success is likely and that other states and firms will cooperate; NAM, *Catalog*, p. iv.

94Mobil, "Sanctions: Our Perspective."

95Crawford Young, "The Impossible Necessity of Nigeria: A Struggle for Nationhood" (review of Wole Soyinlea, *The Open Sore of a Continent: A Personal Narrative of the Nigerian Crisis*), *Foreign Affairs*, 75 (November/December 1996), p. 143.

96Stremlau, *Sharpening International Sanctions*, p. 63.

97In this regard a project recently proposed by David Baldwin for constructing a new, more comprehensive and more systematic dataset on economic sanctions cases is of particular note (David A. Baldwin, "Evaluating Economic Sanctions," August 1998 proposal currently under development).

98Jentleson, *Opportunities Missed, Opportunities Seized.*

5

Spoiler Problems in Peace Processes

Stephen John Stedman

eace making in civil war is a risky business.[1] The biggest source of
risk comes from spoilers—leaders and parties who believe the
emerging peace threatens their power, world view, and interests
and who use violence to undermine attempts to achieve it.[2] By signing a
peace agreement, leaders put themselves at risk from adversaries who
may exploit a settlement, from disgruntled followers who see peace as a
betrayal of key values, and from excluded parties who seek either to alter
the process or destroy it. By implementing a peace agreement, peace
makers are vulnerable to attack from those who oppose their efforts. And
most important, the risks of peace making increase the insecurity and
uncertainty of average citizens who have the most to lose if war is
renewed.

When spoilers succeed, as they did in Angola in 1992 and in Rwanda
in 1994, the results are catastrophic. In both cases the casualties of failed
peace were infinitely higher than the casualties of war. When Jonas
Savimbi refused to accept the outcome of United Nations (UN)-moni-
tored elections in 1992 and plunged Angola back into civil war, approximately 300,000 people died. When Hutu extremists in Rwanda rejected
the Arusha Peace Accords in 1994 and launched a genocide, over 800,000
Rwandans died in less than three months.

If all spoilers succeeded, the quest for peace in civil wars would be
dangerously counterproductive. But not all spoilers succeed. In Mozambique the Mozambique National Resistance (RENAMO), a party known
as the "Khmer Rouge of Africa," stalled in meeting its commitments to
peace and threatened to boycott elections and return to war. In the end,
however, RENAMO joined parliamentary politics, accepted losing an elec-

tion, and disarmed, thus ending a civil war that had taken 800,000 lives. In Cambodia the peace process was able to overcome the resistance from the real Khmer Rouge, the party that has provided the sobriquet for fanatic parties elsewhere.

The crucial difference between the success and failure of spoilers is the role played by international actors as custodians of peace. Where international custodians have created and implemented coherent, effective strategies for protecting peace and managing spoilers, damage has been limited and peace has triumphed. Where international custodians have failed to develop and implement such strategies, spoilers have succeeded at the cost of hundreds of thousands of lives.

This study begins to develop a typological theory of spoiler management and pursues the following research objectives: (1) to create a typology of spoilers that can help custodians choose robust strategies for implementing peace, (2) to describe various strategies that custodians have used to manage spoilers, (3) to propose which strategies will be most effective for particular spoiler types, (4) to sensitize policy makers to the complexities and uncertainties of correctly diagnosing the type of spoiler, and (5) to compare several successful and failed cases of spoiler management in order to refine and elaborate my initial propositions about strategies.

This research is a first step toward understanding spoiler problems in peace processes and evaluating the effectiveness of different strategies of spoiler management. The findings of this study are provisional. As more case studies of spoiler management emerge, as new research develops on the case studies examined below, and as more theoretical attention is trained on the problem, some of the findings will need to be reconsidered and revised. Moreover, this study addresses only the strategies and actions of external actors who oversee peace processes; the topic of spoiler management from the perspective of domestic parties committed to peace is beyond the scope of this study.

This paper argues that spoilers differ by the goals they seek and their commitment to achieving those goals. Some spoilers have limited goals; others see the world in all-or-nothing terms and pursue total power. Furthermore, some spoilers are willing to make reasoned judgments concerning the costs and benefits of their actions, whereas others show high insensitivity to costs and risks and may hold immutable preferences. Custodians have a range of strategies to deal with spoilers, from ones that rely heavily on conciliation to ones that depend greatly on the use of coercion. The case studies discussed below suggest three major findings. First, the choice of an appropriate strategy requires correct diagnosis of the type of spoiler and thoughtful consideration of constraints posed by other parties in the peace process. Second, to make good diagnoses, policy makers must overcome organizational blinders that lead them to misread intentions and motivations. Third, implementation of a successful strategy depends on the custodian's ability to create an external coalition for peace, the resources that the coalition brings to its responsibility, and the consensus that the coalition forms about the legitimacy (or lack thereof) of spoiler demands and behavior.

SPOILERS: A PRELIMINARY TYPOLOGY

Peace processes create spoilers. This is a statement about definition and causality. In war there are combatants, who can be identified in myriad ways—for example, rebels, bandits, pariahs, rogues, or terrorists—but not as spoilers. Spoilers exist only when there is a peace process to undermine, that is, after at least two warring parties have committed themselves publicly to a pact or have signed a comprehensive peace agreement.[3] Peace creates spoilers because it is rare in civil wars for all leaders and factions to see peace as beneficial. Even if all parties come to value peace, they rarely do so simultaneously, and they often strongly disagree over the terms of an acceptable peace. A negotiated peace often has losers: leaders and factions that do not achieve their war aims. Nor can every war find a compromise solution that addresses the demands of all the warring parties. For example, the most perfectly crafted power-sharing institutions in the world are useless if one of the parties does not want to share power.[4] Even the best-designed settlements may be attacked by leaders and parties who decide that the kind of peace in question is not in their interest.

Custodians of peace processes confront several different spoiler problems, which differ on the dimensions of the *position* of the spoiler (inside or outside an agreement); the *number* of spoilers; the *type* of spoiler (limited, greedy, or total); and the *locus* of the spoiler problem (leader, followers, or both).

Position of the Spoiler

Spoilers can be inside or outside a peace process. An inside spoiler signs a peace agreement and signals a willingness to implement a settlement, yet fails to fulfill key obligations to the agreement. Examples include President Juvenal Habyarimana of Rwanda, who failed to implement the Arusha Accords to end his country's internal war; the Khmer Rouge (KR) in Cambodia, which signed the Paris Peace Accords and then refused to demobilize its soldiers and chose to boycott elections; and the Union for the Total Independence of Angola (UNITA), which signed the Bicesse Accords in 1991 but returned to war in 1992 when it lost the election. Outside spoilers are parties who are excluded from a peace process or who exclude themselves and use violence to attack the peace process—for example, the Committee for the Defense of the Revolution (CDR) in Rwanda, which committed genocide to prevent implementation of the Arusha Accords.

Inside spoilers tend to use strategies of stealth; outside spoilers often use strategies of overt violence. Spoilers who have signed peace agreements for tactical reasons have an incentive to keep their threat hidden and to minimize the amount of violence they use; they want the peace process to continue as long as it promises to strengthen them against their adversary. Inside spoilers need to comply enough to convince others of their goodwill but not so much that it weakens their *offensive* military capability. Outside spoilers, on the other hand, tend to use overt violence as a strategy toward undermining peace. Favorite tactics include the assassination of moderates who stand for a negotiated peace, massacres that coincide with any progress in reaching a negotiated settlement, and the creation of alliances with conservative members in the armed forces and police to sabotage any agreement.

Number of Spoilers

The presence of more than one spoiler creates a compound challenge for custodians. Any strategy a custodian chooses to deal with one spoiler has implications for the strategy selected to deal with other spoilers. Actions taken to marginalize one spoiler may inadvertently strengthen another. To give an example from the case studies, in Rwanda the stability of the peace process was endangered because Habyarimana refused to fulfill his obligations to the peace agreement he had signed. The UN threatened to withdraw its peacekeeping operation in order to coerce Habyarimana into implementing the agreement. Yet Habyarimana was only one of two spoilers. The CDR, former members of Habyarimana's regime, rejected the peace agreement and conspired against the peace process from outside. The UN strategy succeeded in pressuring Habyarimana but emboldened the CDR to attack the peace process.

Types of Spoilers

Recent work on civil war termination suffers from a flawed attenuated portrayal of combatants and their aims. At one extreme are analyses that posit that parties are solely motivated by insecurity and only seek party survival.[5] According to this view, the only reason for parties in civil wars to fight is their fear that, if they make peace and disarm, their adversary will take advantage and eliminate them. The lack of an overarching authority that can enforce a political settlement in civil war means that warring parties cannot credibly commit to making peace, either in the short term (through disarmament) or the long term (through a constitution). Thus, any party that violates or opposes a peace agreement does so out of fear, not some other motivation. Scholars who embrace this view believe that spoiler behavior can be addressed only by reducing the spoiler's fears through international guarantees. Like those international relations theorists steeped in the security dilemma, these writers believe that the central theme of civil war termination "is not evil but tragedy."[6]

At another extreme are those who assert that all parties in civil war seek total power.[7] This, however, is too facile; all parties in civil war seek power, but not all parties seek total power. Some parties desire exclusive power and recognition of authority; some want dominant power; some seek a significant share of power; and some desire to exercise power subject to democratic controls. This should not be surprising: power is a means or resource to realize other goals. Some goals—for instance, the permanent subjugation or elimination of an ethnic group, race, or socio-economic class—need more power than the goals of creating a democratic political regime or gaining recognition of political equality among races or ethnic groups. That parties differ in their goals and commitment to total power can be seen by all of the parties that have accepted and lived with compromise solutions to civil wars (in Colombia, Zimbabwe, Namibia, El Salvador, South Africa, and Mozambique). Similarly, not every winner of a civil war creates a totalitarian regime or slaughters its opponents.[8] A thought experiment makes the point: if you had to be on the losing side of a civil war, would you rather surrender to Abraham Lincoln or Hafez al-Assad, to Nelson Mandela or Mao Zedong?

Successful management of spoiler problems requires the recognition that parties in civil wars differ in their intentions, motivations, and commitment—dimensions that are crucial for understanding why some parties undermine peace agreements. Spoilers vary by type: limited, greedy, and total. These types differ primarily on the goals that the spoiler pursues and secondarily on the spoiler's commitment to achieving its goals. At one end of the spectrum are limited spoilers, who have limited goals—for example, recognition and redress of a grievance, a share of power or the exercise of power constrained by a constitution and opposition, and basic security of followers. Limited goals do not imply limited commitment to achieving those goals, however. Limited goals can be nonnegotiable and hence subject to heavy sacrifice.

At the other end of the spectrum are total spoilers, who pursue total power and exclusive recognition of authority and hold immutable preferences: that is, their goals are not subject to change. Total spoilers are led by individuals who see the world in all-or-nothing terms, who often suffer from pathological tendencies contrary to the pragmatism necessary for compromise settlements of conflict. Total spoilers often espouse radical ideologies; total power is a means for achieving the radical transformation of society.

The greedy spoiler lies between the limited spoiler and the total spoiler. The greedy spoiler holds goals that expand or contract based on calculations of cost and risk. A greedy spoiler may have limited goals that expand when faced with low costs and risks; alternatively, it may have total goals that contract when faced with high costs and risks.

The spoiler type poses different problems for peace processes. Total spoilers are irreconcilably opposed to any compromise peace; any commitment to peace by a total spoiler is tactical—a move to gain advantage in a struggle to the death. Limited spoilers can conceivably be included in peace processes, if their limited nonnegotiable demands can be accommodated by other parties to the conflict. Greedy spoilers can be accommodated in peace processes if their limited goals are met and they are constrained from making added demands.[9]

Locus of the Spoiler Problem

A key issue concerns the possibility of change in type. For example, can a total spoiler become a limited spoiler? The answer depends on the locus of spoiler behavior—that is, whether it is the leader or the followers. If the impetus for spoiler behavior comes from the leader, the parties can change type if their leadership changes. This seems particularly relevant for total spoilers because their total goals and commitment are so extreme. A change in leadership may be enough to alter a party from a total spoiler to a limited spoiler. For instance, a negotiated settlement to Zimbabwe's civil war became possible only when Abel Muzorewa replaced Ian Smith as leader of Zimbabwe-Rhodesia. Likewise, the willingness of the South African government to implement the Namibian peace process was aided by the incapacitation and replacement of President P.W. Botha. Long-time observers of Cambodia argued that the KR would never accept a negotiated peace as long as Pol Pot was in power. Other cases, however, suggest that there are times when followers are the locus of spoiler behavior. As one of the cases below suggests, in Rwanda in 1994, Habyarimana was reluctant to fulfill his commitments to the Arusha Accords for fear that his followers would attack him.

STRATEGIES OF SPOILER MANAGEMENT

Custodians of peace processes are defined here as international actors whose task is to oversee the implementation of peace agreements. Implicit in their role is the cultivation and protection of peace and the management of spoilers. International custodians can be international organizations, individual states, or formal or ad hoc groups of concerned third parties. Custodians can be tightly organized or loosely coordinated. With the exception of the implementation of the Dayton Peace Agreement on Bosnia and implementation of the South African peace settlement, the chief custodian of peace processes in the 1990s was the United Nations.

Custodians of peace processes in the 1990s pursued three major strategies to manage spoilers. In order of conciliation to coercion, the strategies were (1) inducement, or giving the spoiler what it wants; (2) socialization, or changing the behavior of the spoiler to adhere to a set of established norms; and (3) coercion, or punishing spoiler behavior or reducing the capacity of the spoiler to destroy the peace process. These strategies are general conceptual types; in practice each takes on a specific configuration likely to be more complex than the general version of it identified here. It should also be noted, as will be evident in some of the cases to be examined, that international actors can employ more than one strategy—either simultaneously (with different priority and emphasis) or in sequence.

Inducement as a strategy for managing spoilers entails taking positive measures to address grievances of factions that obstruct peace. Custodians attempt to induce the spoiler into joining a peace process or fulfilling its obligations to an existing agreement by meeting the spoiler's demands, which can be of several types. Spoilers may insist that their behavior is based on (1) fear, and demand greater protection; (2) fairness, and demand greater benefits; or (3) justice, and demand legitimation or recognition of their position. The custodian must assess the veracity and significance of such claims.

Inducement can be rigorously applied by meeting costly demands made by spoilers, as the UN did in Mozambique in 1993-1994. Or it can be something as lax and questionable as offering a spoiler a continued role in negotiations, even when the spoiler has returned to war, as in the case of Angola in 1992, or when the spoiler has committed genocide, as in Rwanda in 1994. Indeed, the frequency of inducement attempts in peace processes suggests that it is a "default mode"—that is, a convenient strategy that is applied without adequate consideration of whether it is an appropriate strategy for the type of spoiler in question.

The strategy of *socialization* requires custodians to establish a set of norms for acceptable behavior by parties that commit to peace or seek to join a peace process. These norms then become the basis for judging the demands of the parties (are they legitimate or not?) and the behaviors of the parties (are they acceptable in the normative framework?). In turn this strategy relies on two components to elicit normatively acceptable behavior: the material and the intellectual. The material component involves custodians carefully calibrating the supply of carrots and sticks to reward and punish the spoiler. The intellectual component emphasizes regular persuasion by custodians of the value of the desired normative behavior. Normative standards can include commitment to the rules of democratic competition and adherence to the protection of human rights. The intellectual component can be aimed at both elites (the attempt to inculcate appropriate values) and citizens (the attempt to educate the mass of citizens into norms of good governance, democratic competition, and accountability, as a means of pressuring elites).

A strategy of coercion relies on the use or threat of punishment to deter or alter unacceptable spoiler behavior or reduce a spoiler's capability to disrupt the peace process. The strategy of coercion has several variations. The use of *coercive diplomacy*, or the use of threat and demand, has been used infrequently against spoilers in peace processes, the notable exception being the use of NATO air strikes against Bosnian Serbs in 1995.[10] Likewise, the *use of force to defeat a spoiler* has been attempted infrequently—most notably, in Somalia, when the UN decided to hold Somali warlord Mohammed Farah Aideed responsible for an ambush by his forces against Pakistani peacekeepers, and in Sri Lanka, when an Indian peacekeeping force attempted to forcibly disarm Tamil rebels and capture their leader, Velupillai Prabakaran.[11]

Two more common variations of the coercion strategy are what I call the "departing-train" strategy and the "withdrawal" strategy. The departing-train strategy combines a judgment that the spoiler's demands and behavior are illegitimate with the assertion that the *peace process will go irrevocably forward*, regardless of whether the spoiler joins. In Cambodia the strategy was linked to the holding of an election, thereby setting a deadline for joining the process and promising a change in the status quo. The departing-train metaphor implies that the peace process is like a train leaving the station at a preordained time and that, once set in motion, anyone not on board will be left behind. The departing-train strategy may require active measures to protect the parties of peace and limit the ability of the spoiler to attack the peace process.

The withdrawal variation of the coercive strategy assumes that the spoiler wants an international presence during the peace process. This strategy aims to punish the spoiler by threatening to withdraw international support and peacekeepers from the peace process. This was the dominant strategy pursued by the UN in Rwanda and the Implementation Force in Bosnia; it was also used in a tertiary manner in Mozambique. The strategy is a blunt instrument in that the punishment—withdrawal—promises to hurt parties that have fulfilled their obligations and reward any spoiler that opposes international engagement.

Matching Strategies to the Type of Spoiler

A correct diagnosis of spoiler type is crucial for the choice of an appropriate strategy of spoiler management. Total spoilers cannot be accommodated in a peace settlement; they must be defeated or so marginalized that they can do little damage. A limited spoiler can be accommodated by meeting its nonnegotiable demands. A greedy spoiler with limited goals may be accommodated, but such accommodation may whet its appetite to demand more concessions. A total spoiler, because it defines the war in all-or-nothing terms and holds immutable preferences, cannot be appeased through inducements, nor can it be socialized; moreover, both strategies risk strengthening the spoiler by rewarding it. Two versions of the coercive strategy are also dangerously counterproductive for managing total spoilers. Coercive diplomacy is unlikely to succeed given the cost insensitivity of total spoilers; they call bluffs and test wills. If custodians fail to carry through on threats or fail to establish escalation dominance, the spoiler's position may be strengthened. By showing the inadequacy of international force, the spoiler adds to its domestic reputation for coercive strength. The withdrawal strategy also backfires against a total spoiler, who has everything to gain if custodians abandon the peace process.

Two strategies are appropriate for managing a total spoiler: the use of force to defeat the spoiler or the departing-train strategy. Because few custodians are willing to use force to defeat a total spoiler, they should strengthen the parties of peace so that they can defend themselves. The departing-train strategy can do this by legitimizing the parties of peace and delegitimizing the spoiler, by depriving the spoiler of resources— both capital and weapons—for war, and by redeploying peacekeepers to protect the parties of peace.

A limited spoiler can be included in a peace process if its demands are acceptable to the conflict's other parties. Thus, inducement may be an appropriate strategy for managing a limited spoiler, but the strategy depends on the bargaining range established by the other parties that have already committed to peace. If the demands of the limited spoiler cannot be accommodated through inclusion, the custodian may have to choose socialization or coercion. The danger is that the threat or use of force may prompt a counterescalation of violence by the limited spoiler.

The greedy spoiler requires a long-term strategy of socialization. Because the spoiler is not total, there is at least a possibility of bringing it into the peace process. In the short term the greedy spoiler presents a serious dilemma. As inducements alone will serve to whet the appetite of the greedy spoiler, the legitimacy and illegitimacy of its demands must be clearly distinguished. Moreover, depending on the cost insensitivity and risk taking of the spoiler, coercion may be necessary to impose costs and create a strong sense of limits to the spoiler's demands. On the other hand, sole reliance on a coercive strategy ignores that even the greedy spoiler has legitimate security goals that can only be met through inducements.

Limitations of the Custodian

Policy makers often have concerns other than a specific conflict at hand; a strategy that may be the best from a perspective of solely managing a conflict may not be the best for a policy maker considering a range of interests. This is certainly true for U.S. policy makers when it comes to conflict resolution in small, unimportant (to U.S. national interests), and faraway countries. Even the UN considers its actions in light of its organizational interests and the need to protect the reputation and institution of peacekeeping. The optimal strategy to end a conflict and manage a spoiler may be too costly or risky for external actors.

The UN has special limitations as a peace custodian. Although it possesses formal authority, its agent on the ground (the special representative of the secretary-general) is constrained by the direction and will of its Security Council. Special representatives must borrow leverage through coalition building; their ability to induce or punish, even their ability to rule credibly on the legitimacy or illegitimacy of demands, depends on the support of member states. In some cases, such as the Salvadoran and Cambodian peace processes, the UN relied on groups of friends—formal associations of all member states that have an interest in the peace process and therefore bring their power, energy, and attention to implementing peace. In other cases the special representative has relied on ad hoc groupings of interested states, usually working with their diplomatic representatives on site.

In managing a spoiler, member states that are patrons of the spoiler are the biggest potential liability (and source of possible leverage). On the one hand, such patrons, if they are sincerely interested in making peace, may supply the special representative with assets of leverage, credibility, and trust. On the other hand, such patrons may be slow to acknowledge that their client is acting as a spoiler and may be reluctant to declare their client's demands illegitimate. Almost every patron of a spoiler has personal networks and domestic groups that support the spoiler. Pressures from these groups, as well as prior policy commitments to the spoiler, lead the patron to continue to support the spoiler even in the face of outrageous behavior.

The Fog of Peace Making

The typology of spoiler problems described so far reflects two fundamental attributes of peace processes: complexity and uncertainty. The

typology suggests that custodians face numerous uncertainties that require skilled diagnosis, including (1) the goal of a spoiler; (2) the intent
behind acts of noncooperation or aggression; (3) the degree of commitment of the spoiler; (4) the degree of leadership command and control of
followers; (5) the degree of unity within the spoiler; and (6) the likely
effects of custodial action on the spoiler's willingness to continue aggression, on the other parties to the peace process, and on interested external
actors.

Custodians must interpret why a particular party attacks a peace
process or refuses to meet its obligations to implement a peace agreement.
Several interpretations are possible. A party that has signed an agreement
but refuses to fulfill its obligations may be motivated by fear. It may
desire an agreement but fears putting its security into the hands of its
adversary. This causes it to stall on its commitments or cheat on agreements by creating a fail-safe option. A party that has signed an agreement
may cheat because it is greedy and desires a better deal; it may want a
negotiated settlement to succeed but also wants to increase its chances of
maximizing its return in the settlement. A failure to fulfill its obligations
may be a means of seeking advantage in an election that could determine
partially the division of spoils and power of the settlement; alternatively,
holding back from commitments may be a way to strengthen its bargaining position in the result of losing an election. Finally, a party may cheat
because it has signed a peace agreement for tactical reasons; if the agreement seems as though it will bring the party to power, the party will
abide by it; however, if the agreement seems like it will not bring the
party to power, the party will cheat to overturn it. In such a case the
spoiler is motivated by total goals and defines the stakes as all or nothing.

When external spoilers use violence to attack the peace process, a
custodian must judge the intention behind the violence. Is it an attempt
by the spoiler to force its way into negotiations—to alter a process so that
its demands are included in a settlement? Or is it an attempt to weaken
the commitment of the internal parties as a means to destroy a negotiated
settlement? Again, the action must be connected to a judgment about the
spoiler's motivation. Is the spoiler motivated by limited grievances that
can be incorporated into an agreement? Or is it motivated by total goals
that are unalterably opposed to agreement? Custodians of peace processes must make judgments about the commitment of a spoiler to its
preference. Spoilers may vary in their sensitivity to costs and risks; greedy
parties may seek only limited opportunities to maximize their goals, or
they may be willing to incur high costs and take large risks to improve
their position.

The above interpretations assume a unified party—that the leader's
behavior reflects a group consensus about its aims. But if a warring group is

divided, a leader may sign an agreement but be reluctant to implement it for fear that an act of compromise could prompt a rebellion of hard-liners. Alternatively, a party's aggressive behavior may or may not be evidence of a leader's willingness to make peace; it could be the result of rogue elements that are opposed to settlement and seek to wreck an agreement.

Custodians of peace face uncertainty about the effects of actions they take toward a spoiler. Will they encourage the spoiler to desist from attacking the peace process? Or will they encourage the spoiler to continue its resistance? If divisions between hard-liners and moderates within the spoiler become evident, there will be uncertainty about how one's actions will affect the relative strengths of the factions. A custodian's actions likewise will have uncertain effects on the other parties to the conflict. Custodians may have to limit their use of coercion against a spoiler for fear of upsetting a fragile balance of power that might lead other internal parties to eschew a peaceful settlement. Custodians may be constrained in the use of inducements by the bargaining range permitted by the other parties to the conflict. A custodian's failure to respond to spoiler behavior by one party may trigger a mimetic response by other parties to the conflict. If a custodian is lenient toward a spoiler, will it encourage other parties to cheat as well? If it acts aggressively toward a spoiler, might it encourage other parties to act aggressively in the belief that they have an ally that tips the balance of power against the spoiler? All of this is to say that the strategy that custodians pursue toward a specific spoiler must take into account the positions of other internal parties to the conflict and perhaps even the need to work with those parties to coordinate action.

CASE STUDIES OF SPOILER MANAGEMENT

This paper is a first step in developing a typological theory of spoiler management. The initial framework discussed above posits a typology of spoilers based on their intentions—limited, greedy, and total; it then describes a range of strategies available for managing spoilers—inducement, socialization, and coercion, with several variations of the latter strategy. It is suggested that the general appropriateness of a strategy depends on the type of spoiler: inducement for limited spoilers, socialization for greedy spoilers, and departing train for total spoilers. The framework places a heavy burden on the ability of custodians to diagnose correctly the type of spoiler they face.

This section examines five case studies of spoiler management in the 1990s as a way of refining, elaborating, and modifying the initial theory. The case studies serve the function of identifying complexities of various kinds that affect success or failure in dealing with spoiler problems that are not anticipated or explainable by the initial theory. The method of structured, focused comparison precludes an investigation into all possible cases of spoiler management. Rather, I have chosen to present here the results of five important recent cases as an initial exploration of successful management and failed management.

The cases—Rwanda, Angola, Mozambique, and Cambodia toward the KR and the State of Cambodia—have reached stages where judgment is possible about the effectiveness of the chosen strategies. For example, even though at the time of my research, the war in Angola had not been brought to a close, I treat the period of 1991-1993 as a distinct stage in the war. Regardless of negotiations that took place after 1993, I am confident that most scholars would agree that, between the signing of the Bicesse Accords in May 1991 and the resumption of all-out civil war in 1993, the custodians of peace utterly failed to manage the spoiler problem presented by Jonas Savimbi. With respect to Cambodia, some may argue that when the research was undertaken the war continued between the KR and the coalition of the Cambodian People's Party and FUNCINPEC (National Unified Front for an Independent, Neutral, Peaceful, and Cooperative Cambodia). While this is true, it was also possible to make an informed judgment about the relative strengths of the forces and their likely chances of victory. In contrast to some cases not studied here—for example, Burundi, Northern Ireland, and Bosnia—judgment of success and failure was premature.

The five cases examined here include variations in outcome—successful management of the spoiler (RENAMO in Mozambique and the KR in Cambodia) and failed management of the spoiler (the CDR in Rwanda, UNITA in Angola. and the State of Cambodia [SOC] in Cambodia). The judgment of successful management or failed management of the spoiler is based on whether the spoiler has been relatively weakened or strengthened vis-à-vis its opponents. The cases also vary in the mix of strategies chosen to manage the spoiler and the type of spoiler. In terms of primary strategy, Cambodia (against the KR) is an example of the departing-train version of the coercion strategy. Rwanda is an example of the withdrawal version of the coercive strategy. Angola and Cambodia (against the SOC) are examples of inducement; Mozambique is an example of a mixed inducement and socialization strategy. In terms of spoiler type, the KR and CDR are examples of total spoilers, UNITA and the SOC are greedy spoilers, and RENAMO is a limited spoiler. My judgment of spoiler type is based on evidence of intentions at the time.

Several limitations of the cases should be pointed out. First, they all took place after the end of the Cold War. Although this increases the relevance of lessons for policy makers who must grapple with the difficulties of peace making unconstrained by superpower rivalry, the findings are bounded by the historical era. Second, the primary custodian in all of the cases is the UN. There is variation among the cases, however, in the roles played by individual states as interested actors or subcustodians who support the peace process. Third, not all combinations of strategy and spoiler type are covered in the cases, given the relatively few cases of spoiler management in the 1990s. For instance, neither coercive diplomacy nor use of force to defeat the spoiler is included. Fourth, these cases are not completely independent of one another. Strategies for managing a particular spoiler were sometimes the result of lessons derived from another case. Some UN personnel worked on more than one case. Some spoilers themselves likely drew lessons for their strategy based on evaluating the efficacy of custodians in other cases.

Following the method of structured, focused comparison of Alexander L. George,[12] the case studies address the following general questions:

1. What was the spoiler's behavior? What demands did the spoiler make? What was the rhetoric of the spoiler?

2. How did external parties interpret the empirically verifiable observations of the spoiler? What were the custodian's judgments about the intentions and motivation of the spoiler?

3. What evidence existed for interpreting spoiler intentions and evaluating the organizational unity of the spoiler? What evidence did the custodian have? What evidence did it cite to support its interpretations? Was other evidence ignored or disregarded?

4. What strategy did the custodian choose to manage the spoiler? What was the theory behind the strategy?

5. Did the custodian implement the strategy effectively? What was the effect of the strategy—on the spoiler and on other parties in the conflict?

6. Did the custodian reevaluate the strategy during its implementation? Did the custodian reconsider its initial diagnosis of spoiler type?

Case 1. Rwanda: Threatened Withdrawal

The Arusha Peace Accords, signed in August 1993 by President Juvenal Habyarimana of Rwanda and officials from the Rwandan Patriotic Front (RPF), a rebel force composed of mostly Tutsi exiles, promised to end a three-year civil war in which approximately 10,000 people had been killed. The accords pledged an end to violent conflict between the Hutu ethnic group, which formed approximately 70 percent of the population, and the Tutsi ethnic group, which comprised nearly 30 percent.[13] Simultaneously, the accords attempted to end Hutu political hegemony over the Tutsi; integrate thousands of Tutsi exiles into Rwandan life; and democratize the Rwandan government, which had been dominated for over 20 years by a small elite group of Hutu close to Habyarimana. The accords also contained elaborate provisions for power sharing in government; integration of the two armies; a detailed plan for the return of some soldiers to civilian life; procedures for democratization of Rwandan politics; and the establishment of a coalition transition government, the Broad Based Transitional Government (BBTG). The accords were the culmination of 14 months of negotiation and mediation by the Tanzanian government, in conjunction with the Organization of African Unity and the governments of France, Belgium, and the United States. The UN was to oversee the accords' implementation.

The mediators of the agreement apparently anticipated resistance from Hutu extremists in the army and government, who had rallied under the banner of the CDR.[14] The RPF vetoed provisions that would have given the CDR a role in a new Rwandan government, arguing that it was not an independent political party and that its extreme belief in ethnic superiority was contrary to the spirit of settlement. A further point of contention concerned representation in the army: Arusha allotted 50 percent of the officer corps and 40 percent of the rest of the army to the RPF. Although the formula alleviated RPF security fears, it was contested by the CDR. Nonetheless, the Rwandan government's negotiating team reached agreement with the RPF on those terms.

The accords contained one major flaw: they lacked a strategy to deal with the CDR. The United States and France advocated inclusion of the CDR in the peace process. Instead, the RPF and the government signatories to the accords hoped for a robust UN peacekeeping force that "would neutralize the extremists."[15] Chastened by its recent experience in Somalia, however, the UN had no intention of robust peacekeeping. Indeed, some UN diplomats foresaw implementation as a relatively easy task. The force that was deployed to Rwanda was not only less than the parties had agreed to but also less than what the UN Assistance Mission to Rwanda (UNAMIR) force commander, General Romeo Dallaire, believed necessary.

Between the signing of the peace accords in August 1993 and the full deployment of UNAMIR in February 1994, tension and uncertainty grew in Rwanda. The accords aided the growth of moderate Hutu politicians who could provide an ethnic bridge to the mostly Tutsi RPF. Habyarimana's party seemed divided; the CDR, resolutely opposed to compromise with the RPF, emerged as a possible competitor to Habyarimana. In October 1993 a coup attempt in neighboring Burundi by Tutsi officers against its recently elected Hutu president triggered acts of genocide in that country. Between 50,000 and 100,000 people died, including Burundi's president. In Rwanda the coup bolstered Hutu extremist resistance to the Arusha compromise, sowed suspicion among moderate Hutu politicians toward the RPF, and emboldened Hutu extremists to publicly advocate extermination of the Tutsi as a final solution to Rwanda's ethnic problem.[16]

UNAMIR's top officials, Special Representative Jacques-Roger Booh-Booh and General Dallaire, confronted several challenges: Habyarimana's unwillingness to fulfill his obligations to the Arusha Accords and form the BBTG, low-level political violence and ethnic killings, growing public incitement of ethnic hatred—especially by the popular radio station Radio Mille Collines—and evidence of a CDR plan to commit genocide if the BBTG were installed. On January 11, 1994, Dallaire cabled the UN Department of Peacekeeping to inform it that a high-level government defector had told UNAMIR about the formation of militias specially trained to carry out a genocide, the creation of lists of targets of Hutu moderates for assassination, a plan to kill Belgian peacekeepers in order to drive the UN out of Rwanda, and a specific threat that the BBTG would be attacked upon installation.

Although Dallaire requested better equipment that would improve UNAMIR's capacity to respond in the case of crisis, his request was ignored. He also sought permission to begin independent searches for arms caches but was told to do so only in conjunction with local authorities—some of whom were implicated in the January 11 warning. In the words of the definitive account of this period, UN headquarters was prepared to approve only "what the traffic would bear."[17]

Habyarimana's role in the plot and his motivations for stalling on implementing the Arusha Accords were uncertain; analysts disagreed on whether Habyarimana was himself an extremist who was only tactically committed to the peace process or a pragmatic peace maker whom ethnic extremists had boxed in. The faction that was implicated in the January warning to Dallaire included members of Habyarimana's own elite troops, the Presidential Guard, several close presidential advisers, and the president's wife. Habyarimana's behavior could be construed as supporting either interpretation. His prevarication might have been evidence that he hoped events would strengthen the extremists for a return to war. Alternatively, it was possible that he feared for his life if he implemented the accords and therefore "buying time, without knowing exactly for what purpose, became a kind of survival reflex."[18] U.S. officials close to the situation believed that there was no split between Habyarimana and the extremists; therefore, the key to dealing with the extremists was to get Habyarimana to install the BBTG. They assumed that he would deliver his followers to the peace process.[19]

No coordinated unified international approach was taken toward the extremists. Booh-Booh adamantly opposed CDR demands for inclusion in the peace process, only to reverse himself and argue for their participation. France continued to have cordial relations with both Habyarimana and officials implicated in the January warning. Arms supplies from France arrived in Rwanda in January 1994 in violation of the Arusha Accords and, according to UNAMIR officials, again in April after the beginning of the genocide. Representatives of donor nations in Kigali failed to voice clear consistent concerns about the government's violence and human rights violations. Even the radio broadcast of genocidal threats did not yield a consensus toward the extremists. The failure of international actors to assert unified minimal standards of human rights "probably succeeded only in eroding the credibility of diplomatic suasion."[20]

In late March 1994 a strategy emerged for dealing with the stalled implementation that proved completely counterproductive. The UN threatened to withdraw its peacekeeping mission unless the warring parties fulfilled their obligations to the peace plan. Pushed by the United States and endorsed by the UN, the strategy bore little connection to any of the problems in Rwanda: the presence of extremists who had pledged to attack the parties of peace, the uncertainty about whether Habyarimana was allied to the extremists, or Habyarimana's reluctance to carry out Arusha. Although the U.S. government clearly saw the Rwandan government as the main culprit,[21] the strategy threatened to punish all of the parties for its obstruction. On April 5 the UN Security Council announced that the mandate for UNAMIR would be extended but warned that its patience had worn out; if the parties did not comply with Arusha, the UN would leave.

On April 6 the strategy, combined with growing diplomatic pressure, wrested from Habyarimana a commitment to install the BBTG. In a meeting in Arusha with the regional mediators and representatives of France and the United States, he agreed to implement the accords, only to be assassinated on his return to Kigali later that night. Immediately, the Presidential Guard and CDR assassinated almost all of the Hutu moderates, and their militias began killing Tutsi throughout the country. In addition to assassinating the moderate Hutu prime minister, Agathe Uwilingiyimana, the Presidential Guard killed 10 Belgian peacekeepers who had failed to protect her.

In the ensuing two months of genocide the UN and its member states reduced the number of peacekeepers in Rwanda. Its approach became one of appeasement by inaction. For two months the UN and the United States urged the RPF and the Presidential Guard to establish a cease-fire and return to negotiations. In doing so they conveyed a clear message: committing genocide was not enough to disqualify a party in Rwanda from a legitimate place at the bargaining table.

The UN's failure to manage the spoiler problem in Rwanda resulted from poor diagnosis, which was caused in part by organizational blinders. The poor diagnosis was threefold: incorrect assessment of the number of spoilers, their types, and the locus of the spoiler problem. The UN targeted Habyarimana, who was a spoiler but a limited one whose hesitations stemmed from fear of his former followers. Habyarimana did not control the CDR, a total spoiler that sought to destroy the entire process. The threat of withdrawal forced Habyarimana to reveal that he was a limited spoiler who preferred peace. But the same threat had no leverage on the CDR; in fact, the threat signaled to it a basic lack of international commitment to the implementation.

The only strategy that might have avoided the cataclysm of April 1994 would have been one that combined protection for the parties of peace—the moderate Hutu parties, the RPF, and Habyarimana—through a larger, more proactive peacekeeping force; clear credible threats against the use of violence by extremists; and the defanging of extremists by reducing their capability to attack the peace process. The international community would have had to diagnose that there were two spoilers, not one; that the CDR was a total spoiler; and that the locus of the spoiler problem resided with Habyarimana's followers. The goal then would have been to protect the coalition for peace, marginalize the Hutu extremists, and create the opportunity for Habyarimana to distance himself from the extremes to join the middle.

That such a strategy was not articulated and attempted was overdetermined. Beyond the obvious intelligence failure in detecting Habyarimana's position, myriad factors led to an absence of critical judgment. Right from the planning for implementation, the UN and its member states were only minimally committed to the peace process. The choice of the withdrawal strategy stemmed from the Clinton administration's desire to show Congress that the UN had the discipline to say *no* to peacekeeping operations that seemed troubled.[22] Organizational politics and the frailty of individual decision making combined to ignore the warnings of spoilers committed to genocide. Mediators could not overcome the basic contradiction in their analysis: on the one hand, Arusha excluded Hutu extremists who threatened the peace process; on the other hand, those same extremists would not really act when the peace process was implemented. The UN and its member states did not want to face up to the implications of an accurate diagnosis of the problem and failed to even create a unified disciplined message of disapproval to the extremists.

Case 2. Cambodia I:
The Khmer Rouge and the Departing-Train Strategy

The Paris Peace Accords, signed on October 23, 1991, brought to a close four years of negotiations aimed at ending Cambodia's civil war. Several factors contributed to the settlement. The war had reached a stalemate among the major combatants—the National United Front for an Independent, Neutral, Peaceful and Cooperative Cambodia (FUNCINPEC), the royalist party of Prince Norodom Sihanouk; the KR; the State of Cambodia (SOC); and the Khmer People's National Liberation Front (KPNLF). The external patrons of the warring parties (China, Russia, Vietnam, and the United States) had tired of the stalemate and wished to divest themselves of their clients. The countries of the region coalesced around a framework that called for multiparty elections, demobilization and disarmament of the parties, and UN implementation of the agreement. The warring parties consented to the agreement as a result of their sponsors' coercion and remained deeply suspicious of one another as well as distrustful of the international consortium—the Core Group, consisting of the permanent five member countries of the UN Security Council and interested regional states, including Japan and Australia—that brokered the agreement.

The party to the settlement that commanded the most scrutiny was the KR. Responsible for the deaths of nearly 2 million Cambodians during its three years in power, the KR survived because of its military prowess, support from China, and diplomatic recognition from the Association of Southeast Asian Nations (ASEAN) and the United States. Inclusion of the KR in the peace process evolved from the recognition by the United States and others that the KR could not be defeated militarily and the hope that peace would marginalize it.[23]

Between November 1991 and May 1992 the KR complied sporadically with the Paris settlement. Immediately after the accords were signed but before deployment of the UN Transitional Authority in Cambodia (UNTAC), a KR spokesman, Khieu Samphan, attempted to open a political office in Phnom Penh, only to be attacked by SOC-instigated rioters. Samphan retreated to Bangkok, and the KR demanded 1,000 peacekeepers to provide security in Phnom Penh. At about the same time, Sihanouk proposed a SOC-FUNCINPEC coalition government as a means of isolating the KR, which was a violation of the spirit and law of the Paris Peace Accords. As a result of these two incidents, a lobby was created that argued the KR was ready to implement the accords but was frightened into noncompliance by its antagonists. Some experts suggested there were two Khmer Rouges: a "moderate" KR that wanted peace and a "hardline" KR that wanted war. Other analysts argued that KR commitment to the accords was always tactical and the belligerence of its adversaries provided it with a convenient excuse for spoiler behavior. Evidence of KR intentions, based on interviews of its top officials and lowly foot soldiers, suggests that the party was committed to the peace process insofar as it promised to return it to power.[24] The KR interpreted the Paris Peace Accords as giving UNTAC the right to dismantle the SOC's administration and expel all ethnic Vietnamese from Cambodia. If UNTAC carried out such a program, the KR would benefit from the crisis that would ensue for the SOC.

The KR's inconsistent behavior between November 1991 and May 1992 provided evidence for different interpretations about its intentions. The KR frequently violated the cease-fire, restricted UN mobility in its areas, boycotted joint military consultations, and attacked a UN helicopter in February 1992, wounding a peacekeeper. When UNTAC began in March 1992,[25] the KR "adopted a posture of cautious cooperation, despite engaging in numerous ceasefire violations."[26] On the positive side, it allowed some UNTAC civilians into its areas. Samphan actively represented the KR on the Supreme National Council (SNC), a transitional body composed of representatives of the warring parties, and cooperated on several humanitarian initiatives with the UN.[27] On the negative side, the few military observers allowed into KR territory were so limited in their activities that "at times they seemed more [like] hostages than monitors."[28]

The issue of KR noncompliance surfaced publicly in May and June 1992. On May 30, 1992, a group of KR soldiers refused to allow a UN armed convoy, accompanied by the secretary-general's special representative, Yasushi Akashi, and his force commander, General John Sanderson, to enter KR territory in western Cambodia. Instead of insisting on UNTAC's right of passage, Akashi retreated. When cantonment, demobilization, and disarmament of all of the warring parties began in June, the KR insisted that it would not comply because Vietnamese forces were still present in Cambodia in violation of the Paris Peace Accords and because UNTAC had not established effective control over SOC. The KR insisted that it would demobilize only if UNTAC dismantled SOC administrative structures and vested the SNC with the power to run the country.

UNTAC officials debated the use of force to gain KR compliance. French General Michel Loridon, UNTAC's deputy force commander, believed that a show of strength would compel the KR to meet its obligations and would establish a reputation among the other factions that the UN would enforce compliance. If the UN did not act, Loridon maintained, it would lose credibility with all of the parties. He asserted that UNTAC had the legal authority to enforce compliance and did not need to seek a Chapter 7 mandate to do so.[29] Human rights organizations and nongovernmental organizations in Cambodia supported Loridon's call for toughness against the KR.[30]

Akashi and Sanderson opposed the use or threat of force against the KR for six reasons. First, Sanderson drew no distinction between threatening the KR with force to gain compliance and going to war with the KR.[31] This dovetailed with Akashi's assessment that the troop contributors to the mission, as well as the Core Group, would oppose fighting a

war. Second, Sanderson thought that UNTAC was not organized for offensive operations and would thus prove ineffective. Third, both Akashi
and Sanderson argued that any attempt to use force would destroy the
Core Group's consensus; it was unlikely that the group would immediately agree to condemn KR behavior and condone the use or threat of
force. Fourth, they believed that, if the Core Group disintegrated, the
operation would collapse. Fifth, they thought that any use of force would
undermine the attempt to negotiate compliance, which was Akashi's preferred approach and which meshed with Sanderson's belief in the "good
Khmer Rouge-bad Khmer Rouge" line; as long as there was a good KR,
there was a possibility of earning its voluntary compliance. Sixth, Akashi
feared that using force against the KR would upset the balance of the
peace process. FUNCINPEC and KPNLF derived some of their power
from the KR counterbalance to the SOC; to weaken the KR might tempt
the SOC to seek an outright victory.

Akashi sought to discuss with the KR its noncompliance. He quickly
realized that the KR interpreted two key components of the Paris Peace
Accords in ways counter to their spirit. First, the KR believed that an
injunction for the removal of all "foreign forces" meant all foreigners,
regardless of their status as combatants. At stake was the political status
of non-Khmer Cambodians, especially ethnic Vietnamese who lived in
Cambodia. Second, the KR insisted that the accords required the complete
destruction of SOC administrative structures. Akashi realized that meeting the first demand would violate human rights and pander to ethnic
extremism and that meeting the second demand was impossible: UNTAC
did not have the administrative personnel or know-how to replace the
SOC. The likely result would be chaos, which, although satisfying KR
aspirations, would destroy the peace process.[32] Akashi chose not to appease KR demands and began to build a strategy for managing the party's
spoiler behavior. He met with local representatives of KR patrons—Thailand and China—to create a unified approach to the problem, privately
condemned KR noncompliance at SNC meetings, and warned then-UN
Secretary-General Boutros Boutros-Ghali that pressure would likely have
to be applied in the future.

In diagnosing the problem in a letter to Boutros-Ghali in July 1992,
Akashi described the KR rejection of UNTAC's efforts to address its concerns and stated that KR behavior had demonstrated that it was not sincerely committed to the peace process. He attributed KR noncompliance
to its attempt "to gain what it could not get either in the battlefield or in
the Paris negotiations, that is, to improve its political and military power
to such an extent that the other parties will be placed at a distinct disadvantage when UNTAC leaves."[33] Akashi then chronicled acts of bad faith

by the KR and asserted that Samphan "is little more than a glorified mouthpiece of . . . Pol Pot," who "seems to be dedicated to the doctrine of simultaneously 'talk and fight.' "[34] He argued that the circumstances dictated a strategy of "patient persuasion" and "sustained pressure." He insisted that UNTAC "adhere to an impartial stand, while criticizing any acts in violation of the Paris Agreement." Although doubting KR good faith, Akashi asserted that keeping an open door to its participation would prevent turning KR followers into a "permanent disgruntled minority."[35]

Akashi pointed out that leverage over the KR could come from Thailand and China. He expressed skepticism about the former because of the unwillingness of the Thai government to control several army generals who collaborated with the KR in illegal timber and gem trading across the Thai border. Akashi also argued that China's influence over the KR waned after the signing of the peace accords and its cessation of assistance to the KR. He requested that, if KR noncompliance continued, Boutros-Ghali should mobilize economic pressure against the KR: "This should not however involve any spectacular action, but rather a steady strengthening of our border checkpoints adjacent to the DK [KR] zones, in order to control the inflow of arms and petroleum and the outflow of gems and logs, a major source of DK's [KR's] income."[36]

By leaving open the door to the KR to rejoin the peace process, Akashi hoped to contain its dispute with UNTAC and to limit its hostility to the peace process. An aggressive stance toward the KR would make targets of all UNTAC's personnel. If KR opposition could be contained, UNTAC could redeploy its peacekeepers to protect the election, which would go forward without the KR. The Australian foreign ministry promoted Akashi's strategy in a September 1992 policy paper that became the basis of the international response to the KR.[37] It sought a concerted response from the Core Group, based on the judgment that KR "demands are not in strict accord with the actual terms of the Paris Agreements."[38]

Although Sanderson was loathe to try to enforce KR compliance with the peace process, he reconfigured the peacekeepers to protect the strategic objective of holding the elections. He redeployed his battalions in ways that could contain KR attacks and reinterpreted the traditional peacekeeping doctrine of neutrality and impartiality, going so far as to use military units of all of the factions (save the KR) to assist UNTAC in providing security during the election. Sanderson justified using soldiers from the other parties by insisting that these armies were not deployed against the KR per se but rather against any force determined to disrupt the election. In a rather ingenious formulation, he described the changed military mission as "an interposition strategy, but not between opposing forces. Rather, it was between a highly moral act sanctioned under international law and supported by international consensus, and any person or group which might threaten it."[39]

To help establish an atmosphere where civilians would feel secure participating in an election, UNTAC created a radio station in December 1992. Although its purpose was to convince voters of ballot secrecy and to explain UNTAC's mission and activities, it also aimed to neutralize KR propaganda. The establishment of Radio UNTAC overcame objections of the UN Secretariat, among others, that an independent media outlet would endanger UNTAC's perceived neutrality.

From September 1992 to May 1993, the scheduled month for elections, UNTAC held firm in its strategy. The Core Group clearly signaled that the peace process would go forward without KR participation. China and Thailand acceded to a nonbinding UN Security Council resolution to impose economic sanctions on the KR. And as the election date drew near, both China and Thailand explicitly supported the elections. Although the KR increased attacks against UNTAC during March and April 1993, it did not unleash a military offensive against the elections, which were held as planned.

UNTAC's strategy for dealing with the KR was imaginative and effective and serves as the prototype of the departing-train strategy for managing spoilers. When faced with KR attempts to undermine peace, UNTAC emphasized that the peace process would not exclude the KR nor would it be held hostage by it. UNTAC tried first to address the KR's specific demands, but when such demands threatened the core agreement of the peace process, UNTAC sought international consensus to delegitimize KR demands and to approve the strategy of continuing the peace process in its absence. UNTAC reconfigured itself militarily to protect the electoral process from KR attack but left open the door to the KR if it wanted to reengage the peace process.

Case 3. Cambodia II: The SOC and Inducement

The motivation of the KR was difficult to gauge because its grievance toward UNTAC's lack of control over the SOC had some merit. UNTAC faced an ongoing problem of SOC obstruction of its mandate. It never established control of SOC's administrative structures, given the lack of qualified personnel in the numbers that were needed, SOC's tendency to ignore and sabotage UNTAC directives, and UNTAC's unwillingness to assert its administrative prerogatives as outlined in the Paris Peace Accords. An equally pressing matter of control concerned the SOC's police and security forces. Throughout UNTAC's life span, SOC police intimidated civil society organizations and physically assaulted and assassinated members of the opposition. While UNTAC reconfigured its military mission to protect the election from KR attack, SOC security personnel waged a low-level reign of terror against its party's electoral competition.

Despite warnings and protest by some UNTAC human rights officials, Akashi did not perceive the SOC as a potential spoiler and was unprepared when it attempted to undermine the peace process immediately after the May 1993 election. The election results devastated the SOC. Despite the SOC's use of intimidation, assassination, and fraud, FUNCINPEC beat SOC's political party, the Cambodian People's Party (CPP), which disputed the election results and attempted to grab power. The president of the SOC, Hun Sen, charged that the election was fraudulent; some CPP officials declared secession for one region of the country; and SOC-orchestrated riots throughout Cambodia threatened UNTAC officials. At the very moment that UNTAC had seemingly achieved success, the SOC threatened to tear down the whole edifice of peace in Cambodia.

From the beginning of implementation of the Paris Peace Accords, Akashi, the UN, and the Core Group focused mostly on the KR as a threat to peace and ignored the potential for the SOC to be a spoiler. Moreover, KR spoiler behavior created incentives and excuses for the SOC to undermine the peace process. Unless both spoilers carried out their commitments to the peace process, each could claim that its behavior was a function of the other. Witnessing violence or lack of commitment by their opponent, they asserted that playing by the rules would leave them vulnerable. This rationale can become a barrier for peace makers who seek to determine the real motivation behind acts of violence and subversion. In cases of mimetic spoilers, peace makers tend to accept a situational explanation for spoiler behavior—an explanation that may be correct and will seem reasonable—and overlook the possibility that such an explanation may also be a facade for a party already committed to tactical subversion of the peace process.

The departing-train strategy toward the KR increased Akashi's perception that UNTAC was dependent on the SOC and thus limited in its options for controlling it. That UNTAC was dependent on the SOC is not in doubt; if the SOC left the peace process, there would be no elections and the parties would return to war. But Akashi failed to comprehend the SOC's dependence on UNTAC. UNTAC had greatly strengthened the SOC, which had a stake in holding the election and gaining international legitimacy and support. If the SOC had to wage another war against the KR, it would do so from a stronger position with international support and FUNCINPEC's abandonment of its former coalition partner. Akashi also misread command-and-control relations within the SOC. He told aides of his fear that Hun Sen had only tenuous control over hard-liners, who if pushed too hard would rebel against Hun Sen and return to war. Akashi's staff, however, believed Hun Sen to be firmly in control of his followers.

Although the accords contained numerous references to administrative control, the UN interpreted UNTAC's mandate in a limited way. UNTAC was "urged to rely on 'codes of conduct and guidelines for management' " and to avoid issuing binding directives.[40] Akashi, under the advice of Boutros-Ghali, envisioned UNTAC exerting control by monitoring and supervising existing administrative structures.[41] Moreover, Akashi worried about UNTAC's lack of domestic legitimacy; he envisioned the SNC as a governing body that could make hard decisions, referee the peace process, and therefore provide domestic legitimacy for actions against spoilers. Although the SNC did assist the strategy against the KR by ruling that its demands were illegitimate, it proved much less effective toward the SOC.

For the most part, UNTAC refrained from attempting to enforce compliance with its administrative directives. Akashi did not want to use the prerogative of replacing or repositioning SOC bureaucrats. His restraint in the face of SOC obstruction prompted the head of UNTAC administration, Gerald Porcell, to resign in February 1993. At the time Porcell lamented that as long as UNTAC did not "have the political will to apply the peace accords, its control cannot but be ineffective."[42]

UNTAC was also lax in holding the SOC accountable for human rights violations. Although UNTAC's mandate for creating an environment conducive to human rights was the most ambitious ever for a UN peacekeeping operation, its enforcement of violations was "dilatory, sporadic, and improvised."[43] Akashi interpreted UNTAC's human rights mandate narrowly. He believed that rigorous action to enforce human rights would endanger UNTAC's neutrality; moreover, he felt that a broad interpretation of human rights "seemed to be based on unrealistically high standards in the context of Cambodia's reality."[44]

As violence increased and the political climate deteriorated at the end of 1992, Akashi acceded to the establishment of a special prosecutor's office. But as William Shawcross notes, "the office languished as Akashi, Sanderson, and other UNTAC officials began to fear that prosecutorial zeal might destroy the entire mission's fragile links with the Phnom Penh regime."[45] Akashi was indirectly supported in this in February 1993 when ASEAN and China exerted pressure to limit the human rights component of UNTAC to education and training.[46]

Between May 1992 and May 1993, UNTAC pursued a de facto policy of inducement against the SOC. It usually did not act against SOC violations; when it did, it sought to deter SOC obstruction through private persuasion. Akashi asserted that the parties need not adhere strictly to all of their commitments. As he later wrote, "too rigid, legalistic interpretations of the agreements would have hindered my work."[47] He believed that, although the accords were "based on the concepts of Western democracy, Asian methods and procedures should be used in the negotiations."[48] Such methods found public reprimand (or acknowledgment of violation of agreements) distasteful.

In May 1993 UNTAC's tacit strategy of inducement became explicit in its response to SOC's attacks immediately after the election. UNTAC's support of the election results wavered. Within the first 48 hours, Akashi attempted to console Hun Sen and promised to investigate fully his charges of electoral fraud. He also sought out the leader of FUNCINPEC, Prince Norodom Ranariddh, to urge him to be conciliatory toward the CPP.

In the two weeks after the election the CPP resorted to violence "to blackmail both FUNCINPEC and UNTAC in an attempt to reverse the election results."[49] As Shawcross writes, the CPP attempt at blackmail was largely successful.[50] Fearing a return to open civil war, the UN acceded to a power-sharing arrangement mediated by Sihanouk that provided the SOC with more power and cabinet positions than its electoral performance deserved. Akashi acknowledged that the deal was "unorthodox by universal democratic principles," but he defended it on the basis of the "practical wisdom" of combining FUNCINPEC's political appeal with the administrative experience and power of the CPP.[51]

Akashi believed that compliance on most of the dimensions of the peace process, including demobilization and disarmament, and human rights protection, was secondary to compliance with holding an election. The election became a Holy Grail for UNTAC; Akashi defined the mission's success solely on the basis of achieving it, and the myriad goals of UNTAC's mandate—promotion and protection of human rights, disarmament and demobilization, and administrative control during the transition—were made subservient to this quest. In the end this even included rejecting a "strict adherence" to the results of the election; Akashi and UNTAC did not insist that the political outcome of the election accurately reflect the electoral outcome for fear that it would undermine the triumph of holding the election.

In hindsight it is possible to hazard a judgment about the effectiveness of UNTAC's strategies for managing the spoiler problems in the Cambodian peace process. The strategy it chose to deal with the KR has been vindicated. The KR's power declined; in the summer of 1996 a severe factional split decimated the party. In June 1997 an internal rebellion by soldiers who wanted to end the war deposed Pol Pot. Time has not been so kind in evaluating UNTAC's strategy toward the SOC. For instance, the

SOC's steadily increasing grip on power since 1993 caused several Cambodian experts in 1996 to warn of a "creeping coup."[52] Such warning turned prophetic in July 1997 when Hun Sen and the SOC attacked FUNCINPEC, sent Prince Ranariddh into exile, and assassinated FUNCINPEC officials and prodemocracy advocates. As the United States, ASEAN, and the UN engaged in collective hand wringing, the SOC skillfully manipulated an internationally negotiated and implemented peace process to triumph in a war that it could not win on the battlefield.

Case 4. Angola: UNITA and the Failure of Inducement

In May 1991 the two main antagonists in the Angolan civil war, the government of Angola and UNITA, signed a peace agreement in Bicesse, Portugal. The agreement, mediated by Portugal, the United States, and the Soviet Union, called for an 18-month transition period during which each party would canton its troops, demobilize some of them, and then join the remainder in a unified Angolan army. At the end of this period, elections would determine the presidency and composition of a national assembly. The agreement contained no provisions for power sharing, nor was there a provision for the election's loser to receive a share of ministerial portfolios or provincial governorships in the highly centralized state structure. Although each party had been urged to consider various power-sharing options, both vetoed them in the belief that they would win the elections.

The government of Angola reluctantly accepted a role for the UN to monitor and assist implementation of the peace agreement. The role and size of the UN presence were the result of hard bargaining between UNITA, which wanted a large UN force with an active mandate to implement the agreement, and the government of Angola, which perceived a large UN presence as an infringement on its sovereignty.

The UN operation in Angola was done on a small budget with little independent latitude. The parties themselves were left to carry out the demobilization, and they failed. By May 1992 about 70 percent of the estimated 160,000 soldiers had been processed at assembly points, but only 6,000 had been demobilized. By the elections on September 29-30, substantially more government troops had demobilized than had UNITA soldiers; nonetheless, both sides had intact armies. Between January and September 1992 there were numerous violations of the cease-fire, with UN monitors estimating that at least 16 skirmishes could have escalated into major combat between the parties.[53] That they did not was attributed to the parties' determination to see the process through to elections and their command and control over their armed forces.

Until late summer 1992 the United States and the United Nations were more apprehensive about the Angolan government's willingness to abide by the peace process than they were about UNITA's. The biggest worry for U.S. policy makers regarding Angola was that the government might not accept an electoral defeat and would throw the peace process into crisis.[54] Nonetheless, UNITA's president, Jonas Savimbi, provided signs that *he* might be the obstacle to ending the war. Under cover of the agreement, UNITA stationed soldiers throughout the country—especially in areas it had previously not engaged—and cached arms for quick access. In addition, rumors suggested that UNITA was holding back armed battalions across the Zaire border. A top Savimbi aide defected and informed the United States of a plan for a quick strike offensive to take the country by force.

The transition period had upset the balance of power between the two militaries. The cantonment process had worked decisively in UNITA's favor; UNITA's army maintained its discipline and remained a unified force that could be mobilized quickly for fighting purposes. The government's army, on the other hand, suffered from poor morale; desertion and drunkenness were rife. Savimbi's generals informed him that Angola could be taken by a military surprise attack—a sentiment that Savimbi relayed to officials in Washington in August, two months before the elections.[55]

As elections drew near, U.S. policy makers grew alarmed about Savimbi's potential as a spoiler. Reports circulated that his standing among Angolan voters was declining, raising the possibility that Savimbi would lose the election. Then-Assistant Secretary of State for Africa Herman Cohen and his Portuguese counterpart traveled to Angola at the beginning of September to persuade Savimbi and President Eduardo dos Santos to share power after the elections. While Savimbi responded enthusiastically to the plan, dos Santos privately expressed interest but felt he could not publicly commit to such a deal. In the end no contingency plan was formed in case Savimbi lost the election.

The elections were peaceful. The UN took multiple intricate precautions to prevent fraud: representatives of the competing parties were present at the 5,800 polling stations and at every municipal, provincial, and national electoral center. Party representatives signed off on results sheets at each level, a process that added days to the vote counting. There were numerous logistical foul-ups, but international observers judged the elections to be free from intimidation and fraud. The results jibed with the UN electoral unit's quick count, thus confirming that fraud did not occur.[56] In the legislative elections the ruling Movement for the Popular Liberation of Angola (MPLA) outpolled UNITA by a margin of five to three. Dos Santos received about 49.5 percent to Savimbi's 40 percent for the presidency; as no candidate received 50 percent of the vote, a runoff election would have to be held in 30 days.

Problems emerged as soon as the preliminary results were reported. The first results came from Luanda, an MPLA stronghold; not surprisingly, they showed the MPLA and dos Santos with a large majority. Savimbi and UNITA immediately cried foul and issued a bombastic five-page memo (in English) declaring that the MPLA was engaged in massive fraud and warning in veiled terms that UNITA would resume the war if it lost the election. When returns from the central provinces (UNITA's stronghold) did not offset MPLA's early lead, UNITA withdrew its generals from the joint command of the newly established united Angolan army. Savimbi retreated to a redoubt, refused to meet any foreign officials or take a phone call from Cohen, denounced the UN, and repeatedly ignored international calls for reasonableness. His army then launched attacks throughout the Angolan countryside, quickly seizing large amounts of territory and destroying government arms depots.

The international response to Savimbi was scattershot. The UN at first insisted on the primacy of the elections and condemned Savimbi for obstructing them. The United States initially urged Savimbi to use the established mechanisms for investigating his electoral grievances, making its appeal over Voice of America because Savimbi would not speak with U.S. officials. As the UN attempted to press Savimbi to honor the election results and participate in a presidential runoff election, South Africa's foreign minister, Pik Botha, visited Savimbi and unilaterally put forward a plan to shelve new elections and to provide for a government of national unity. Policy makers in Washington quickly chose a similar option: to press the MPLA into a power-sharing agreement to appease Savimbi.

The U.S. response established the international strategy toward Savimbi. By initially equivocating, the United States failed to challenge him; then by interpreting his actions as understandable and reasonable, it chose a strategy of inducement, which served only to encourage further aggression. Savimbi continued his attempts to defeat the Angolan government and to avoid serious negotiations. A year later, in November 1993, Savimbi returned to negotiations, but only after the rearmed Angolan military had rolled back UNITA's gains, the United States had granted diplomatic recognition to the Angolan government, the UN had imposed sanctions against UNITA, and 300,000 Angolans had died.

Washington's strategy of inducement toward Savimbi was disputed by U.S. officials in Angola, including Ambassador-designate Edmund De Jarnette. From the beginning of the crisis he and others stationed in Luanda diagnosed the problem as stemming from Savimbi's personality and ambitions. They believed he was motivated by a desire to win complete power in Angola. These officials counseled giving Savimbi an ultimatum to return to the peace process, backed by a threat to use U.S.

military force. From the onset of the crisis through 1993, De Jarnette argued that an inducement strategy toward Savimbi would fail.

U.S. officials in Washington, however, believed that Savimbi did not want to overturn the peace process but simply wanted a better deal. Long-standing ties between Savimbi and the Defense Department and intelligence agencies were part of the problem; individuals who knew Savimbi and had been romanced by him could not bring themselves to find him at fault. Likewise, negotiators who had worked hard to get an agreement could not believe that one of the signatories was rejecting a compromise solution outright. And those in Washington who were swayed by the analysis of the U.S. diplomats in Luanda were stymied by the tight connections between Savimbi's Washington lobbyists and the Bush administration.

A top U.S. policy maker admitted in retrospect that the strategy of inducement toward Savimbi was "clutching at straws" but insisted that a tougher policy was out of the question.[57] The Bush administration was preoccupied with the November 1992 presidential election and then with the humanitarian crisis and intervention in Somalia in December. Moreover, Savimbi's Washington connections precluded any use of coercion. Inducement failed in Angola because U.S. policy makers erroneously believed that limited incentives would satisfy Savimbi. Furthermore, they were not prepared when inducement emboldened Savimbi to continue his spoiler behavior. In part, Savimbi's personality defined the conflict in all-or-nothing terms; a combination of racism, paranoia, and megalomania led him to believe that the MPLA had stolen the election from him and that he had the right to rule all of Angola. In October 1992, at the time that he rejected the elections, anything less than an absolute firm stand against his pursuit of war and a credible threat of force and sanctions against UNITA had little chance of persuading Savimbi to return to the peace process. The initial choice of inducement convinced Savimbi that the international community would likely defer to his return to war. Inducement proved that the U.S. and South African governments saw Savimbi's demands and actions as legitimate. There was little international support for rallying behind the sanctity of the Bicesse peace process.

The change in power positions of the MPLA and UNITA also worked against the inducement strategy. By October 1992 the peace process had greatly strengthened UNITA; Savimbi was confident that UNITA could win the war, and he underestimated the resolve and capability of the MPLA to fight. If Savimbi had been militarily weak in October 1992 and the international community held a monopoly on rewards, inducement might have brought him back into the fold. Savimbi, however, continued to have uninterrupted sources of revenue through UNITA's control of diamond mines and support from some of his neighbors—Mobutu in

Zaire and rogue elements in the South African defense forces—who would continue to supply him with arms, ammunition, and fuel to fight the war.

Case 5. Mozambique: RENAMO and Successful Inducement

In October 1992 the government of Mozambique signed a peace agreement with RENAMO, a South African-trained and -assisted guerrilla movement. Although RENAMO was unable to defeat the Mozambican government, it had rendered most of the country ungovernable. RENAMO's use of terror, indiscriminate killing of civilians, press-ganging of child soldiers, and destructive capacity had earned it the appellation the "Khmer Rouge of Africa." Upon assuming the task of implementing the peace accords, the UN, having witnessed Savimbi's return to war in Angola and being concerned about the character of RENAMO and its leader, Afonso Dhlakama, doubted the sincerity of RENAMO's commitment to the negotiated settlement.[58]

The tardy deployment of UN peacekeepers and establishment of an administrative capacity to oversee cantonment and demobilization of troops provided RENAMO and the government with an excuse to stall on their obligations under the peace treaty.[59] But as the necessary UN units and personnel arrived in Mozambique and eliminated the excuse, UN Special Representative Aldo Ajello found himself stymied by the warring parties' continuing noncooperation—especially RENAMO, which embarked on a three-month boycott of the implementation process.[60]

To bring RENAMO back into the fold, Ajello pursued two policies. First, the peace accord's mediators stressed that Dhlakama, in addition to searching for security assurances, placed a high priority on the issue of legitimacy—that his movement had fought for a just cause, had domestic roots, and was not simply a puppet of South Africa—and hungered for recognition as a Mozambican nationalist who had fought for democracy. Much of RENAMO's behavior belied such a self-image, and Dhlakama's vision of democracy was not multiparty pluralism where parties do not return to war if they lose an election or eliminate their adversary if they win. A key task for Ajello therefore was to socialize RENAMO into the rules of democratic competition and to make its legitimacy contingent on fulfilling its commitment to peace. The subcustodians of the peace process—the representatives of the countries supporting the UN Observation Mission in Mozambique—assisted Ajello by continuously reinforcing Dhlakama's desire for legitimacy. Leaders of neighboring countries overcame their distaste for RENAMO, met with Dhlakama, and treated him as a legitimate national leader.

Second, Ajello understood that it was crucial to wean RENAMO from its military raison d'être. To do so he fulfilled a promise that mediators

made to Dhlakama to provide financial assistance to RENAMO to transform it into a democratic party. Italy, Ajello's home country, gave him a
$15 million fund to assist RENAMO's renovation. This fund, combined
with the flexibility to use it in conjunction with gaining incremental compliance to the accords, gave Ajello enormous leverage with RENAMO.
This leverage was amplified because of the unique context of the Mozambican case. Unlike Angola, where Savimbi bankrolled his spoiler behavior
through the illegal diamond trade, or Cambodia, where the Khmer Rouge
replenished its weapons and ammunition through illicit gem and timber
deals, Mozambique's paucity of accessible valuable commodities deprived
RENAMO of resources if it chose to reject peace.

Although Ajello's use of inducements kept RENAMO engaged in the
peace process, it also encouraged Dhlakama to continue voicing grievances and making demands on the UN. Ajello resolved several incidents
involving cantonment and demobilization by acceding to RENAMO demands that were not contained in the peace accords.[61] Eventually, Ajello
grew frustrated with RENAMO's tactics and threatened withdrawal.
Ajello used a visit by Secretary-General Boutros-Ghali to Mozambique in
October 1993 to convince RENAMO that continuation of the peace process was conditional on RENAMO meeting its obligations. The withdrawal threat yielded short-term results; RENAMO pledged anew its
commitment to peace, and UN officials reported progress on implementing key provisions of the agreement.

Ajello discovered, however, that the closer the peace process came to
the election in October 1994, the more the UN's threat of withdrawal
declined in credibility. Having spent $800 million on the peace process,
the UN could not convince RENAMO of its pledge to walk away without
at least holding elections.[62] Ajello therefore relied increasingly on inducement, even though the risk of whetting Dhlakama's appetite grew more
dangerous as the elections drew near. What would happen, for example,
if RENAMO lost the elections and demanded that the results be annulled
in the hope of being rewarded for its obstructionist behavior?

The UN had sought to make the actions of a postelection spoiler
irrelevant by fully demobilizing both armies and creating a new unified
army. Demobilization, however, was incomplete; both RENAMO and the
government had armies at the time of the elections in October 1994. Neither side, however, had anything close to the amount of troops wielded
by the parties in Angola in October 1992; RENAMO and the government
had several thousand troops held in reserve.[63] If the loser decided to
defect from the peace process, it would still possess a destructive capacity
but not a force capable of winning the civil war in a short period.

Given the UN and U.S. experience of Savimbi's overturn of the elections in Angola in 1992, as well as the use of violence by the SOC to

blackmail UNTAC after the Cambodian elections, it is remarkable that as late as June 1994, four months before the Mozambican elections, neither the UN nor the U.S. embassy in Maputo had contingency plans in case the loser of the election rejected the results.[64] Instead of thinking strategically about the possibility, the United States unsuccessfully urged the parties to consider a power-sharing pact that would establish a South African-style government of national unity after the election. On the other hand, the governments of states in the region, very much chastened by the experience of Savimbi in 1992, began consultations on responses if Dhlakama rejected the results.

RENAMO did attempt to boycott the elections and reject the results. Because the United Nations had not set a limit on how far inducement would go, diplomats from the neighboring countries of Zimbabwe and South Africa had to meet with Dhlakama and warn in no uncertain terms that they would not accept any obstruction of the elections. The UN and United States followed the warning with both an appeal to Dhlakama's desire to be a legitimate national actor and democrat and a promise to investigate any alleged electoral fraud. RENAMO rejoined the elections, withdrew its charges of fraud, and took its seats in the newly elected Mozambican parliament.

SPOILER MANAGEMENT:
EVALUATING SUCCESS AND FAILURE

The case studies discussed here suggest several general findings about managing spoilers in peace processes. First, they illustrate that spoiler type, number of spoilers, and locus of the spoiler problem are key variables that affect the robustness of strategies for managing spoilers. Second, the cases underscore the need for custodians to diagnose correctly the spoiler problem, a task made difficult by the fog of peace making. Third, the cases show that quite often the very rules, beliefs, and frames that custodians use to cope with the complexity of peace processes defeat them. Fourth, the cases of successful spoiler management demonstrate that spoilers need not destroy peace—if custodians create robust strategies, seek international consensus behind the strategy, and recognize the much maligned force of normative power.

Diagnosis and Treatment

The case studies in this paper demonstrate that the creation of an effective strategy of spoiler management rests first on correct diagnosis of the spoiler problem and the selection of an appropriate strategy to treat the problem. Choice of strategy depends on judgment about the intentions of the spoiler and awareness of constraints posed by other parties to the conflict.

The failure to manage spoilers in Rwanda, Angola, and Cambodia (SOC) stemmed from poor diagnosis and the choice of a strategy that was inadequate to the problem at hand. In contrast, common to the successful cases—Cambodia (KR) and Mozambique—was early identification of a potential problem, a good diagnosis, and the selection of an appropriate strategy to treat the problem. By examining the specific strategies—withdrawal, departing train, and inducement—we can begin to understand the conditions that favor or mitigate against their effectiveness.

Withdrawal

Custodians used the threat of withdrawal as a primary strategy in Rwanda and as a secondary strategy in Mozambique. In Rwanda the strategy pressured Habyarimana, a limited spoiler, into implementing the Arusha Accords but provided a green light for the CDR, a total spoiler, to commit genocide to stop implementation. In Mozambique the strategy created a short-term sense of urgency among the warring parties to fulfill their obligations to peace before the opportunity to end the war disappeared.

These two cases suggest that the withdrawal strategy's effectiveness depends in part on the type of spoiler at which it is aimed, the number of spoilers in the peace process, and the credibility of the threat. The withdrawal strategy is a coercive strategy that aims to punish recalcitrance by taking away the opportunity for peace. For the strategy to have its intended effect, the target must view the withdrawal of international engagement as a punishment. Moreover, for the threat to be credible, the custodian must seem indifferent to ending the war. Against a total spoiler like the CDR in Rwanda, the strategy cannot work because the spoiler does not view withdrawal as punishment. Indeed, the strategy can backfire if it signals to the total spoiler that the custodian lacks a commitment to peace.

The withdrawal strategy is a blunt instrument of spoiler management. The strategy can work only if all parties to an agreement are equally culpable in failing their obligations and all spoilers are limited spoilers who want a settlement to succeed. The threat of withdrawal can then provide a test of motivation: if the parties are really committed to the peace process, the possibility of losing international support might provoke them into beginning the implementation process. Where not all parties are spoilers, as in Rwanda, the strategy punishes even those parties committed to peace. Where one party is a total spoiler, as in Rwanda, the withdrawal strategy gives it a veto on the peace process.

The Departing Train

The departing-train strategy succeeded in Cambodia against the KR, a total spoiler. Success derived from the ability of the custodians to learn the spoiler's intentions, the strong degree of international consensus and unity behind a judgment that the spoiler's demands were illegitimate, the deployment of force to protect the peace process, and the custodian's willingness to stand firm in implementing the peace process.

The departing-train strategy was developed by UNTAC in Cambodia to deal with the KR. Evidence suggests that the KR was a total spoiler and that a coercive strategy was necessary, but UNTAC judged that it was constrained from using either force to defeat the KR or coercive diplomacy to threaten it. The use of force against the KR ran the risk of escalation, which could have endangered the overall UNTAC mission. Moreover, use of force against the KR could have weakened FUNCINPEC, which used the existence of the KR as leverage against the SOC. The departing-train strategy held out the possibility of continuing the peace process while marginalizing the KR. UNTAC ruled that KR demands were illegitimate, continued the peace process without the KR, and established a deadline—the election—for it to join the process. UNTAC then redeployed its force to protect the election.

The departing-train strategy requires that external actors take a stand on the spoiler's demands: Are they legitimate and important enough to halt the progress at compromise that the other parties have made? For the strategy to work, external actors (including current or former patrons of the spoiler) must concur that, if the spoiler's demands are met, peace may be unattainable. Having made a decision that the peace process will go on without the spoiler, external actors must find ways to protect the parties of peace. Attempts can be made through the spoiler's patron to warn the spoiler of dire implications if it escalates its attacks, and the custodian can deploy military forces to protect people and processes such as elections.

The departing-train strategy also depends on the custodian's ability to convince all parties that the peace process will proceed without everyone on board. International consensus is crucial for sustaining such credibility. In Cambodia the commitment of China and Thailand to the election timetable clearly conveyed to the KR that the peace train was departing.

The Cambodian case suggests two limitations of the strategy. First, the strategy is a gamble that the parties to the peace process will be strengthened sufficiently to deal with the spoiler on their own after international disengagement from the process. The strategy's long-term success rests on the ability of the parties favoring peace to form a strong enough front to withstand future challenges. For example, when UNTAC departed in 1993, the KR had not been eliminated, but it had been marginalized. Subsequent developments have vindicated the strategy: a factional split in the KR all but destroyed it in 1997. Second, the strategy can make the custodian dependent on the parties that get on the train. In Cambodia, for example, the strategy against the KR required that the SOC be part of the peace process. UNTAC's sense of dependence on the SOC constrained it from opposing the SOC's behavior as a greedy inside spoiler.

Inducement

Inducement was attempted against the SOC in Cambodia, UNITA in Angola, and RENAMO in Mozambique. Although the strategy failed in the first two cases, inducement toward RENAMO largely succeeded, albeit in conjunction with a heavy emphasis on socialization of RENAMO and an implied threat by regional actors that established the limits of inducement.

The three cases of inducement suggest that this strategy can only succeed with limited spoilers. Toward the SOC, a greedy spoiler, the inducement strategy backfired by strengthening the SOC and weakening FUNCINPEC. The only strategy that might have managed the SOC would have been a strong socialization effort that would have established strong norms of human rights, democracy, and good governance, as well as systematic use of carrots and sticks to gain compliance. In the case of UNITA, another greedy spoiler, inducement whetted its appetite for power. Thus, even if UN and U.S. policy makers were correct in 1992 that Savimbi was not a total spoiler but simply greedy, the only strategy that would have managed him would have been a socialization strategy with a heavy dose of coercion. This relates to the second aspect of spoiler type: commitment to achieving goals. Savimbi's insensitivity to risk and cost meant that he would fulfill his obligations to the peace process only if the price of not doing so was extremely high.

The Angolan and Mozambican cases suggest that leadership personality is a key variable behind successful inducement. Unlike Savimbi, Dhlakama did not characterize his conflict in all-or-nothing terms. UN and U.S. policy makers came to believe that Dhlakama's goal was not total power in Mozambique but rather to gain legitimacy for his movement, for the war he waged, and for the people and region that supported him.[65] When faced with Dhlakama's continuous demands for money and recognition of various grievances, UN Special Representative Ajello believed that financial resources would keep Dhlakama and RENAMO in the peace process. Moreover, the neighboring countries (especially Zimbabwe and South Africa), the United States, and the UN continued to focus on the legitimacy theme—to try to socialize Dhlakama and RENAMO into playing by the rules and transforming themselves into democratic politicians. The message was clear: Dhlakama's newly recognized legitimacy depended on his willingness to meet his obligations. When the moment of truth came and Dhlakama's commitment wavered, the neighboring states, the UN, and the United States delivered a strong unambiguous signal: if he returned to war, his legitimacy would be lost and there would be a high cost to pay.

The Mozambican case suggests several requirements for a successful inducement strategy. First, the spoiler must be a limited type. Diagnosing Dhlakama's type was not easy, however; the view that he sought limited goals was disputed by veteran Mozambique watchers and was at odds with RENAMO's past brutal behavior. Second, external actors must be unified in establishing the legitimacy and illegitimacy of spoiler demands and behavior. Again, this seems deceptively simple. At the time many in the human rights community disputed the legitimacy of RENAMO as an actor. The United States, the UN, and neighboring countries all had to reverse their characterization of Dhlakama both as a puppet of the former apartheid regime in South Africa and as a leader with no domestic constituency.[66] Third, inducement is aided if the custodian, by acting in coordination with others, is the sole source of rewards to the spoiler. Unlike Savimbi in Angola, Dhlakama had no independent source of capital if he chose to return to war. Fourth, in civil wars where the goal is the establishment of sustained peace, inducement is most likely best carried out in conjunction with a concerted international effort to socialize the spoiler into accepting the basic rules of good governance and democracy. Fifth, inducement must be accompanied, if necessary, by a credible threat to establish its limits and break any cycle of grievance, reward, new grievance, reward, new grievance. Even in the case of a limited spoiler like RENAMO, inducement can encourage increased obstructionist behavior in the hope of getting more rewards. If a limited spoiler continues to undermine peace, it will run the risk of prompting its opponent to view it as a total spoiler for whom no concession will gain its commitment.

Organizational Blinders

In addition to pointing to the crucial role of good diagnosis and choice of appropriate treatment, the case studies provide a vivid reminder of the uncertainties, complexity, and ambiguity of peace processes—what I refer to earlier as the "fog of peace making." But the case studies also provide evidence that several organizational rules, beliefs, and frames that custodians use to cope with uncertainty can contribute to poor diagnosis and in extreme cases to avoiding the spoiler problem. Such organizational blinders include (1) prior commitments of the organization to the spoiler, (2) organizational doctrine, (3) organizational Holy Grails, (4) organizational interests, and (5) organizational roles.

Prior Commitments

In several of the cases, prior commitments between individual states and spoilers blocked a correct interpretation of the intention and behavior of the spoiler. In the case of Angola the U.S. government had long been a patron of Savimbi, had supplied him with arms and supplies, and had cultivated his friendship. When Savimbi rejected the election results and returned to war in late 1992, the initial tendency of the United States was to believe Savimbi's versions of events, to discount interpretations that Savimbi intended to win complete power, and to emphasize that even-handedness was still called for because the MPLA was no better than UNITA. Savimbi's impressive network of friends, supporters, and representatives in Washington buttressed the psychological commitment to him. While this commitment led U.S. policy makers to benign interpretations of Savimbi's actions, or at least to assertions that there were no good guys in the conflict, the personal networks served to constrain the influence of those who sought a more aggressive policy toward Savimbi.

The Angolan case is similar to France's relationship to the CDR and Presidential Guard in Rwanda. First, the French military's prior organizational commitment to the Presidential Guard led it to demonize the RPF—to see it as the all-or-nothing party, a "Khmer Noir," an image that reinforced and legitimized the Hutu extremist version of the conflict. Second, the prior relationship caused the French military to ignore clear signs that the CDR was planning genocide. Third, the personal network of relationships extended high into the Mitterand government, thus paralyzing conflicting policy tendencies in the French foreign ministry.

Doctrine

Beyond prior ties to the spoiler, the ability of organizations to interpret the intentions and behavior of spoilers and to fashion effective responses is constrained by their doctrines. The UN, for example, approaches its custodial role with several assumptions. First, its representatives assume that the parties are acting in good faith when they sign a peace agreement. This leads UN personnel to downplay violations by signatories to agreements. Second, its representatives tend to be slavish in their devotion to the troika of traditional peacekeeping values: neutrality, impartiality, and consent. Such values, when followed blindly, constrain attempts to challenge spoiler behavior, as custodians fear being seen as partial to the victim. Even when spoiler behavior is recognized as such, the doctrine insists on reestablishing consent and not forcefully challenging violations.

In the successful cases of spoiler management, custodians took a stand on the merits of issues under dispute. In Cambodia, UNTAC rejected KR grievances as illegitimate. UNTAC's success stemmed from its ability to garner international consensus against KR interpretations of the Paris Peace Accords. In the case of Mozambique the regional custodians of the peace process confronted RENAMO when it attempted to withdraw from the election at the last moment and threatened to return to war.

The successful cases of spoiler management, however, do not diminish the more significant point that doctrine poses constraints; they simply show that custodians had to reinterpret their actions so as not to appear to be in conflict with their principles and had to triumph in intraorganizational battles over the doctrinal implications of their actions. For instance, in Cambodia General Sanderson succeeded in employing soldiers from the warring factions to protect the election against the KR by redefining the meanings of impartiality and neutrality. Radio UNTAC, which earned universal praise for its role in combating KR propaganda, was established only over strenuous objections from UN headquarters that such a radio station would imperil UNTAC's neutrality.

Holy Grails

A third organizational blinder is the tendency of custodians when faced with complexity and uncertainty to redefine their goals and standard of success to one overriding accomplishment, a Holy Grail. When implementing peace, the UN often drops its commitments to various components of the peace agreement in order to focus on holding an election. When spoilers plunge their countries into war, the UN focuses on obtaining a cease-fire.

For example, when faced with KR intransigence in Cambodia, UNTAC narrowed its mission to holding an election rather than fulfilling complete implementation of the Paris Peace Accords. This redefinition of mission was an appropriate response to a spoiler's attempt to veto the Paris agreements. Yet UNTAC became so focused on attaining the election that it ignored SOC violence and obstruction during the electoral campaign. The need to reach an election took precedence over how the parties conducted themselves during the election. When an election finally took place, UNTAC acquiesced to SOC blackmail and encouraged its quest for a coalition deal that was disproportionate to its electoral result. UNTAC feared that the SOC's threat would nullify the achievement of the election, so it compromised the quality of the election to appease the SOC.

When spoilers in Rwanda and Angola attacked and plunged their countries back into civil war, the UN responded by insisting on a cease-fire and return to negotiations. In both cases, spoilers were willing to kill hundreds of thousands of people to demonstrate that they did not want a negotiated settlement, yet the UN responded by pleading with them to return to negotiations.

Organizational Interests

An overriding sense of organizational interest can also prevent custodians from recognizing and effectively managing spoilers. In Rwanda, like Angola before it, the UN's interpretation of the conflict and its consideration of an appropriate response were based heavily on "what the traffic would bear." Faced with information that requires costly and risky action, the UN and many of its member states chose to ignore the information.

Organizational Roles

The conceptions that mediators and UN special representatives have of their roles can lead them to misinterpret evidence of spoiler intention. Both mediators and special representatives invest enormous time and energy into negotiating and implementing peace; therefore, when faced with spoiler behavior, they assume spoiler motivation and behavior to be negotiable—a judgment that confirms the continuing relevance of their role as peace maker. They tend to seek out any evidence that confirms the basic willingness of the parties to still reach agreement and ignore compelling evidence that suggests one of the parties may reject peace completely. They tend to grab at any straw that seems to hold out the promise of a settlement. Even when confronted with compelling evidence of bad faith and the preference of one or more of the parties for war, they are likely to insist that there are no alternatives to negotiation. In some cases the mediators or special representatives seem unwilling to place the responsibility for continued hostilities on the parties themselves and instead blame their own organizations for not providing the one request that would have made the difference between war and peace. Finally, there is the perverse tendency of custodians to so value an agreement that they blame the victim rather than the spoiler.

The Need for International Agreement and Coordination

A common denominator among the successful cases of spoiler management is unity and coordination among external parties in defining the problem, establishing legitimacy for the strategy, and applying the strategy. Although this is not a surprising finding, it is nonetheless a robust one, and external parties to a peace process ignore it at their peril.

Spoilers often exist because external patrons provide them with guns, ammunition, capital, and sanctuary. External patrons may also help internal spoilers survive by supporting their claims to legitimacy—support that can play havoc with a strategy such as the departing train, where the key to putting pressure on the spoiler is to declare its grievances illegitimate and to insist that the peace process itself embodies the best chance for resolving the conflict. In the cases of successful spoiler management, external support for the spoiler had either dried up or been severely curtailed. Inducement succeeded with RENAMO because its external patron, South Africa, wanted a peaceful settlement to the war. Unlike UNITA or the KR, RENAMO did not have easy access to illegal markets to finance a continuation of the war.

International unity and cooperation require cultivation, time, resources, and pressure. It is therefore better if both are institutionalized in the peace process, as with the Core Group in Cambodia.[67]

The Legitimating Function of Spoiler Management

Another key aspect to spoiler management is the development of an international consensus about what are legitimate and illegitimate solutions to a country's civil war. The successful strategies of spoiler management all have in common a unified stance by external actors about which spoiler demands should be met and which should be rejected. For example, the departing-train strategy in Cambodia depended on the willingness of international actors to define limits of accommodation for the spoiler. In Cambodia even the former patrons of the KR agreed that their client's demands were illegitimate and that the peace process could move forward without them. In Mozambique external actors agreed to legitimate RENAMO as a nationalist party, socialize it into an agreed set of rules of behavior, and establish limits on how far it would be appeased.

By contrast, in the failed cases of spoiler management, no international consensus formed about legitimate and illegitimate solutions to the civil wars. In Rwanda external actors failed to create a common stance toward the Hutu extremists and wavered about the content of the Arusha Peace Accords. In Angola little attempt was made to rally international support against UNITA's return to war. Indeed, the strategy that emerged from the United States insisted that legitimacy was irrelevant to ending the war and proceeded to pressure the party that had won the election.

The finding that legitimization is an integral part of spoiler management is important in two regards. First, it counters the adage that solutions to internal conflicts must come from the participants themselves. In this study successful management of internal conflict has resulted from the willingness of external actors to take sides as to which demands and grievances are legitimate and which are not. Second, it shows that when external consensus is used in conjunction with a coherent larger strategy, the setting of a normative standard can be an effective tool for conflict management. This last point is crucial. For all the lip service they pay to the power of norm setting, when it comes to protecting peace and managing spoilers the member states and many UN personnel seldom act like they mean it.

CONCLUSION

How confident can policy makers and theorists be in the conclusions presented above? Although the set of cases is small and necessarily incomplete, I believe the conclusions derived here are robust. The successful cases of spoiler management were tough cases. Few analysts in 1991 predicted that the KR would be so weakened that it would cease to exist seven years later; similarly, most experts on Southern Africa were skeptical that RENAMO could be transformed from a killing machine into a loyal democratic opposition party.

While more work needs to be done on refining the strategies of spoiler management presented above, and while more cases can add to our knowledge about necessary conditions for such strategies to succeed, I believe the analysis of peace making here is sound. The period after a peace agreement is reached is a time of uncertainty and vulnerability for peace makers and citizens alike. International actors who seek to bring deadly civil wars to a close must anticipate violent challenges to peace processes. Instead of thinking generally about the possible threats to peace, they must ask, "*Who* are the threats to peace?" The custodians of peace must constantly probe the intentions of warring parties: they must look for evidence that parties that sign peace agreements are sincere in their commitment to peace, and they must search out and make good use of intelligence about the warring parties' goals, strategies, and tactics. The emphasis of this paper on individual typing of leaders and attributing permanent traits to some of them raises important questions about the weight of personality and situation as motivations of spoiler behavior. But I believe that the analysis begins to correct an analytic trend that asserts that all behavior by leaders in civil war is situationally determined.

The research presented here strongly suggests that international consensus about norms and coordination behind a strategy of aggressive management of spoilers can provide the difference between successful and failed implementation of peace agreements. Custodians must judge what is right or wrong, just or unjust, and fair or unfair in peace processes. They can do so either explicitly by creating an international consensus about what is appropriate for the warring parties or tacitly by not taking action in the face of violent attacks and spoiler behavior.

Is the post-Cold War international environment conducive to forging such consensus and coordination? The answer is mixed. A large gap currently exists between international proclamation of norms—human rights, rule of law, democracy, and good governance—and behavior in warfare that makes a mockery of such norms—wanton killing of noncombatants, ethnic cleansing, war crimes, and atrocities. The establishment of international consensus about norms writ large seems disarmingly easy; in the cases presented above the establishment of consensus about norms in a specific case was much harder. States seem much more likely to proclaim norms when they view compromise on their freedom of maneuver in the abstract; in actual cases, national foreign policies still define situations differently, ascribe motivations differently, judge self-interest differently, and waver in applying universal normative standards.

Likewise the present age presents difficult problems for international coordination in applying a strategy of spoiler management. Economic globalization and the weakening of state control over trade and borders weaken state control over private economic actors who trade with and profit from potential spoilers in civil wars. Cutting off spoilers from resources and capital may be more difficult in the post-Cold War era than previously. Similarly, a proliferation of nongovernmental organizations involved in the implementation of peace accords in civil wars increases the difficulty of establishing and coordinating strategies toward spoilers.

ACKNOWLEDGMENTS

I thank the following people for their comments, criticisms, and suggestions: Howard Adelman, Nichole Argo, Michael Brown, Cynthia Chataway, Juergen Dedring, Michael Doyle, Daniel Druckman, William Durch, Page Fortna, Alexander L. George, Charles L. Glaser, Robert Jervis, Elizabeth Kier, Stephen Low, Dianne McCree, James Morrow, Michael O'Hanlon, Jerrold Post, Tonya Putnam, Donald Rothchild, Timothy D. Sisk, Janice Gross Stein, Paul Stern, and Saadia Touval. I also thank the current and former policy makers and diplomats who spoke with me off the record about their peace-making experiences. A slightly different version of this paper has been published in the fall 1997 issue of *International Security* (vol. 22, no. 2, pp. 5-53).

NOTES

[1]For analysis of various risks in peace making, see Stephen John Stedman, *Peacemaking in Civil Wars: International Mediation in Zimbabwe, 1974-1980* (Boulder, Colo.: Lynne Rienner, 1991), pp. 14-16, 231-232.

[2]Stephen John Stedman, "Negotiation and Mediation in Internal Conflicts," in Michael E. Brown, ed., *The International Dimensions of Internal Conflict* (Cambridge, Mass.: MIT Press, 1996), pp. 369-371.

[3]For example, in South Africa prior to 1990 there was no public agreement among the antagonists to peacefully resolve their conflict. Only after the release of Nelson Mandela in 1990 and the reaching of several public agreements that committed the African National Congress and South African government to a process of negotiation can one speak of a South African peace process. Similarly, in the case of Cambodia, even though negotiations dragged on for several years, only after the parties formally committed themselves to the Paris Peace Accords can one speak of a Cambodian peace process.

[4]Timothy D. Sisk, *Power Sharing and International Mediation in Ethnic Conflicts* (Washington, D.C.: United States Institute of Peace, 1996), concludes that successful power sharing depends on "a core of moderate, integrated elites [that have] a deeply imbued sense of interdependence and shared or common destiny" (p. 117). Most recommendations for power sharing in civil wars simply assume the parties are willing to share power.

[5]Barbara F. Walter, "The Resolution of Civil Wars: Why Negotiations Fail," Ph.D. dissertation, University of Chicago, 1994.

[6]This is a paraphrase of a quote from Robert Jervis, *Perception and Misperception in International Politics* (Princeton, N.J.: Princeton University Press, 1976), p. 66.

[7]Richard K. Betts, "The Delusion of Impartial Intervention," *Foreign Affairs*, vol. 73, no. 6 (November/December 1994), pp. 20-33.

[8]Roy Licklider's estimates that 81 percent of civil wars in the twentieth century that were fought over identity issues and ended through the victory of one side did not result in genocide [Roy Licklider, "The Consequences of Negotiated Settlements in Civil Wars, 1945-1993," *American Political Science Review*, vol. 89, no. 3 (September 1995), pp. 681-690].

[9]The notion of intentions as combining goals and commitment comes from Jervis, *Perception and Misperception*, pp. 48-54. The appellation of "greedy" comes from Charles L. Glaser but differs from his definition [Charles L. Glaser, "Political Consequences of Military Strategy: Expanding and Refining the Spiral and Deterrence Models," *World Politics*, vol. 44, no. 4 (July 1992), pp. 497-538]. Glaser substitutes motivation of players for intentions of players, the difference being the internal source of aggressive behavior—greed or insecurity. In my use of the term, "greedy" does not imply that the spoiler acts out of greed but rather that it expands its goals and is willing to incur high costs and risks to reach them.

[10]Using my definition, it is a tough call whether the Bosnian Serbs were a spoiler at that point. One could argue that the public peace process had achieved the commitment of the Bosnian and Bosnian Croat parties and therefore that the Bosnian Serbs were spoilers.

[11]Again, it is difficult to determine whether Aideed was a spoiler by my definition. One could argue that the Addis Ababa agreements between the various clan factions in Somalia constituted a formal peace process and that therefore Aideed was a spoiler. Likewise, although Indian diplomats claimed that Prabakaran provided his consent to the peace agreement in 1987, he never signed the agreement.

[12]Alexander L. George, "Case Studies and Theory Development," paper presented to the Second Annual Symposium on Information Processing in Organizations, Carnegie-Mellon University, Pittsburgh, October 15-16, 1982.

[13]Another group, the Twa, comprises 1 percent of Rwanda's population. A common

figure for the respective populations is 85 percent Hutu and 14 percent Tutsi. Based on new calculations, Howard Adelman estimates that the percentage of Tutsi was greatly underreported, hence the 70 and 30 percent figures here (private communication, Howard Adelman, October 10, 1996).

[14]Howard Adelman and Astri Suhrke, with Bruce Jones, *The International Response to Conflict and Genocide: Lessons from the Rwanda Experience, Study 2, Early Warning and Conflict Management* (Copenhagen: Joint Evaluation of Emergency Assistance to Rwanda, March 1996), p. 25.

[15]Howard Adelman, "Preventing Post-Cold War Conflicts: What Have We Learned? The Case of Rwanda," paper presented to the International Studies Association Meeting, San Diego, April 17, 1996, p. 7.

[16]Prunier, *The Rwanda Crisis: History of a Genocide* (N.Y.: Columbia University Press, 1995), pp. 198-203.

[17]Adelman et al., *The International Response*, p. 68.

[18]Ibid., p. 203.

[19]Anthony Marley, U.S. Department of State, presentation at the Fourteenth Annual Africa Conference, Paul H. Nitze School of Advanced International Studies, Johns Hopkins University, Washington, D.C., April 7, 1995. Lieutenant Colonel Marley (retired) was the U.S. military attaché to the Arusha peace process.

[20]Adelman et al., *The International Response*, p. 32.

[21]Michael Barnett, "The Security Council, Peacekeeping, and Indifference in Genocide in Rwanda," *Cultural Anthropology*, vol. 12, no. 4 (December 1997), pp. 551-578. At the time, Barnett was a Council on Foreign Relations fellow with the U.S. Mission to the United Nations.

[22]Ibid.

[23]Stephen Solarz, "Cambodia and the International Community," *Foreign Affairs*, vol. 69, no. 2 (Spring 1990), pp. 99-115.

[24]See especially Steven Heder, "The Resumption of Armed Struggle by the Party of Democratic Kampuchea: Evidence from National Army of Democratic Kampuchea 'Self-Demobilizers,' " in Steven Heder and Judy Ledgerwood, eds., *Propaganda, Politics, and Violence in Cambodia: Democratic Transition Under United Nations Peacekeeping* (Armonk, N.Y.: M.E. Sharpe, 1996), pp. 73-113.

[25]Although the Paris Peace Accords were signed in October 1991, the operational plan for UNTAC was not presented to the UN Security Council for approval until February 19, 1992. On February 28 the Security Council approved the mission, and on March 15 the secretary-general's special representative to Cambodia, Yasushi Akashi, arrived in Phnom Penh. A small UN holding operation was deployed as a bridge between the signing of the Paris Peace Accords and the arrival of UNTAC.

[26]James A. Schear, "Beyond Traditional Peacekeeping: The Case of Cambodia," in Donald Daniel and Bradd Hayes, eds., *Beyond Traditional Peacekeeping* (New York: St. Martin's, 1995), p. 253. Schear was an assistant to Akashi in Cambodia.

[27]Ibid.

[28]Trevor Findlay, *Cambodia: The Legacy and Lessons of UNTAC* (Oxford, U.K.: Oxford University Press, 1995), p. 51.

[29]Under the UN Charter, a Chapter 7 operation permits enforcement against identified threats to peace and does not require the warring parties' consent.

[30]Steven R. Ratner, *The New UN Peacekeeping: Building Peace in Lands of Conflict After the Cold War* (New York: St. Martin's Press and the Council on Foreign Relations, 1995), pp. 170-171; Michael Doyle, *UN Peacekeeping in Cambodia: UNTAC's Civil Mandate*, International Peace Academy Occasional Paper Series (Boulder, Colo.: Lynne Rienner, 1995), p. 67; and Findlay, *Cambodia*, pp. 37-38.

[31]John Sanderson, "UNTAC: Successes and Failures," in H. Smith, ed., *International Peacekeeping: Building on the Cambodian Experience* (Canberra: Australian Defence Studies Centre, 1994), pp. 16-31.

[32]Heder, "The Resumption of Armed Struggle."

[33]"Document 43: Letter Dated 27 July 1992 from the Special Representative of the Secretary-General for Cambodia to the Secretary-General Concerning the Situation in Cambodia," in *The United Nations and Cambodia: 1991-1995*, UN Blue Books Series, vol. 2 (New York: UN Department of Public Information, 1995), p. 206.

[34]Ibid., p. 207.

[35]Ibid.

[36]Ibid.

[37]"Document 44: 'Cambodia: Next Steps,' Australian Paper Dated 16 September 1992," in *The United Nations and Cambodia*, p. 208.

[38]Ibid.

[39]General John Sanderson, as quoted in Jianwei Wang, *Managing Arms in Peace Processes: Cambodia* (Geneva: UN Institute for Disarmament Research, 1996), p. 71.

[40]Doyle, *UN Peacekeeping in Cambodia*, p. 37.

[41]Ibid.

[42]Gerald Porcell, as quoted in Findlay, *Cambodia*, p. 63.

[43]Ibid., p. 64.

[44]Ibid., p. 66.

[45]William Shawcross, *Cambodia's New Deal*, Contemporary Issues Paper No. 1 (Washington, D.C.: Carnegie Endowment for International Peace, 1994), p. 59.

[46]Ibid., pp. 59-60.

[47]Yasushi Akashi, "UNTAC in Cambodia: Lessons for U.N. Peace-keeping," Charles Rostov Annual Lecture on Asian Affairs, Paul H. Nitze School of Advanced International Studies, Johns Hopkins University, Washington, D.C., October 14, 1993, p. 12.

[48]Ibid., p. 13.

[49]Shawcross, *Cambodia's New Deal*, p. 26.

[50]Ibid., pp. 27-28.

[51]Yasushi Akashi, "The Challenge of Peace-keeping in Cambodia: Lessons to Be Learned," paper presented to the School of International and Public Affairs, Columbia University, November 29, 1993, p. 8.

[52]Michael Doyle, "Peacebuilding in Cambodia," Occasional Paper, International Peace Academy, New York, January 1997.

[53]Thomas Ohlson and Stephen John Stedman, with Robert Davies, *The New Is Not Yet Born: Conflict Resolution in Southern Africa* (Washington, D.C.: Brookings Institution, 1994), p. 111.

[54]Confidential interview.

[55]Ibid.

[56]Margaret Anstee, *Orphan of the Cold War: The Inside Story of the Collapse of the Angolan Peace Process, 1992-1993* (New York: St. Martin's Press, 1996), p. 205.

[57]Confidential interview.

[58]Eric Berman, *Managing Arms in Peace Processes: Mozambique* (Geneva: UN Institute for Disarmament Research, 1996), p. 81.

[59]Chris Alden, "The UN and the Resolution of Conflict in Mozambique," *Journal of Modern African Studies*, vol. 33, no. 1 (1995), pp. 112-114, and Stephen M. Hill, "Disarmament in Mozambique: Learning the Lessons of Experience," *Contemporary Security Policy*, vol. 17, no. 1 (April 1996), pp. 133-134.

[60]Alden, "The UN and the Resolution of Conflict," pp. 113-114.

61Mats Berdal, "Disarmament and Demobilization After Civil Wars," Adelphi Paper No. 303 (London: Institute for International and Strategic Studies and Oxford University Press, 1996), p. 43.

62Michael Doyle refers to this problem as the "obsolescing bargain of peacekeeping": as long as few resources are committed, UN influence is high; as soon as the UN commits substantial resources and personnel, its influence wanes (Doyle, UN Peacekeeping in Cambodia, pp. 82-83).

63Hill, "Disarmament in Mozambique," p. 137.

64My impression from interviews with UN and U.S. officials in Maputo at the time is of an unwillingness to seriously consider the possibility that a loser might overturn the election. The refrain I received from both UN and U.S. officials was that "this is not Angola." When pushed to describe the differences that mitigated against a Savimbi-type outcome, the same officials stated that the elections would take place in October only if both armies were fully demobilized, thus rendering moot any obstructionist behavior. In the end this proved not to be the case.

65This is an ongoing theme of Cameron Hume, Ending Mozambique's War: The Role of Good Offices (Washington, D.C.: United States Institute of Peace, 1995). Hume was the U.S. State Department delegate to the Rome peace talks.

66Donald Rothchild's recent work on mediation emphasizes that the granting of legitimacy can be an effective tool in resolving internal conflicts but that there are often high domestic and international costs for actors to declare previously rogue leaders or factions legitimate [Donald Rothchild, Managing Ethnic Conflict in Africa: Pressures and Incentives for Cooperation (Washington, D.C.: Brookings Institution, 1997), chap. 9].

67This is the thrust of much of Michael Doyle's latest work on peacekeeping [Michael W. Doyle, "Strategies of Enhanced Consent," in Abram Chayes and Antonia Handler Chayes, eds., Preventing Conflict in the Post-Communist World: Mobilizing International and Regional Organizations (Washington, D.C.: Brookings Institution, 1996), pp. 483-506].

6

Ripeness: The Hurting Stalemate and Beyond

I. William Zartman

There are essentially two approaches to the study and practice of negotiation (and its facilitated form, mediation).[1] One, of longest standing, holds that the key to a successful resolution of conflict lies in the substance of the proposals for a solution. Parties resolve their conflict by finding an acceptable agreement—more or less a midpoint—between their positions, either along a flat front through compromise or, as more recent studies have highlighted, along a front made convex through the search for positive-sum solutions or encompassing formulas (Walton and McKersie, 1965; Young, 1975; Pruitt, 1981; Zartman and Berman, 1982; Raiffa, 1982; Pillar, 1983; Lax and Sebenius, 1986; Fisher and Ury, 1991; Pruitt and Carnevale, 1993; Hopmann, 1997).

The other holds that the key to successful conflict resolution lies in the timing of efforts for resolution. Parties resolve their conflict only when they are ready to do so—when alternative, usually unilateral, means of achieving a satisfactory result are blocked and the parties find themselves in an uncomfortable and costly predicament.[2] At that point they grab on to proposals that usually have been in the air for a long time and that only now appear attractive.

It is obvious that the second school does not claim to have the sole answer (since it refers to the first) but rather maintains that substantive answers are fruitless until the moment is ripe. The same tends not to be true of the first school, which has long ignored the element of timing and has focused exclusively on finding the right solution regardless of the right moment. To be sure, attention to the question of timing does not obviate the analysis of substance, and in particular it does not guarantee successful results once negotiation has begun. But more attention is needed to the timing question precisely because the analysis of substance has ignored it.

This chapter presents the state of current understanding of the most specific aspect of timing and the initiation of negotiations—the theory of "ripeness." Because the metaphor of ripeness is easy to comprehend, the idea has resonated with practitioners. However, the apparent simplicity of the notion has also led to some confusion and misunderstanding among those who have written about it. To improve and advance understanding of the role of timing in the initiation of negotiations, it is necessary to make the implications of ripeness theory clearer.

To do so, this chapter begins with the presentation of the theory indicating necessary, even if not sufficient, elements in beginning negotiations and implications of the theory for both analysis and practice. It then discusses the experience and testimony of practitioners who have used the concept in their negotiations and mediation. Next it presents and evaluates refinements to the theory, followed by two types of remaining problems: the inherent, persistent resistance to the perception of ripeness and the tantalizing "other side of the moon" with its prospects for negotiation. In the process it carries the theory to its next extension, dealing with the continuation of negotiations toward a successful conclusion. Finally, the chapter addresses implications for practitioners in the absence of ripeness, specifically on the need and policies for ripening. As the argument proceeds, each discussion is summarized by definitional or hypothetical propositions.

RIPENESS THEORY IN PRACTICE

The notion of ripeness is critical for policy makers in the post-Cold War era who seek to mediate disputes in the international arena. It is also highly relevant for conflicting parties themselves as they assess their courses of action. Several aspects of the timing question need to be anchored in theory and practice. First, the concept and theory of ripeness need clarification, indicating what they do and do not cover. Second, the ways of recognizing ripeness need to be identified. Third, new questions raised by the concept and theory need to be addressed, so that further use and development can be accomplished.

The idea of a ripe moment lies at the fingertips of diplomats. "Ripeness of time is one of the absolute essences of diplomacy," wrote John Campbell (1976:73). "You have to do the right thing at the right time." "The success of negotiations is attributable not to a particular procedure chosen but to the readiness of the parties to exploit opportunities, confront hard choices, and make fair and mutual concessions," wrote then

Secretary of State George Shultz (1988), without indicating specific moments. Few diplomats have tried to identify what it is that provides that essence or readiness, leaving its identification to a sense of feel. Henry Kissinger (1974) did better, recognizing that "stalemate is the most propitious condition for settlement."

Conversely, practitioners are often heard to say that certain policies, including mediation initiatives, should not be pursued because the conflict just is not yet ripe. In mid-1992, in the midst of ongoing conflict, the Iranian deputy foreign minister noted that "the situation in Azerbaijan is not ripe for such moves for mediation" (Agence France Presse, May 17, 1992). Indeed, the notion comes out of the lexicon of practitioners, used with significant effect but only implicit content, and has only recently been taken up by analysts in an effort to make its meaning more explicit. These views can be summarized in a proposition: Proposition 1. *Ripeness is a necessary but not sufficient condition for the initiation of negotiations, bilateral or mediated.*

Even before turning to a detailed examination of the meaning and dynamics of ripeness, it is important to understand its strength and its limitations. Ripeness is only a condition: it is not self-fulfilling or self-implementing. It must be seized, either directly by the parties or, if not, through the persuasion of a mediator. Not all ripe moments are so seized and turned into negotiations, hence the importance of specifying the meaning and evidence of ripeness so as to indicate when conflicting or third parties can fruitfully initiate negotiations.

At the outset, confusion may arise from the fact that not all "negotiations" appear to be the result of a ripe moment. Negotiation may be a tactical interlude, a breather for rest and rearmamant, a sop to external pressure, without any intent of opening a sincere search for a joint outcome—thus the need for quotation marks or for some elusive modifier such as "serious" or "sincere" negotiations. It is difficult at the outset to determine whether negotiations are indeed serious or sincere, and indeed "true" and "false" motives may be indistinguishably mixed in the minds of the actors themselves at the beginning. Yet it is the outset that is the subject of the theory. The best that can be done is to note that many theories contain a reference to a "false" event or an event in appearance only, to distinguish it from an event that has a defined purpose. Indeed, a sense of ripeness may be required to turn negotiations for side effects (Ikle, 1964) into negotiations to resolve conflict. In any case, unless the moment is ripe, as defined below, the search for an agreed outcome cannot begin.

It therefore follows that ripeness is not identical to its results, which are not part of its definition, and is therefore not tautological. It has its own identifying characteristics that can be found through research independent of the possible subsequent resolution or of efforts toward it. It also follows that ripeness theory is not predictive in the sense that it can tell when a ripe moment will appear in a given situation. It is predictive, however, in identifying the elements necessary (even if not sufficient) for the productive inauguration of negotiations. This type of analytical prediction is the best that can be obtained in social science, where stronger predictions could only be ventured by eliminating free choice (including the human possibility of blindness and mistakes). As such it is of great prescriptive value to policy makers seeking to know when and how to begin a peace process—and that is no small beer.

Components of Ripeness

Ripeness theory is intended to explain why, and therefore when, parties to a conflict are susceptible to their own or others' efforts to turn the conflict toward resolution through negotiation. The concept of a ripe moment centers on the parties' perception of a mutually hurting stalemate (MHS), optimally associated with an impending, past, or recently avoided catastrophe (Zartman and Berman, 1982; Zartman, 1983, 1985/ 1989; Touval and Zartman, 1985). The idea behind the concept is that, when the parties find themselves locked in a conflict from which they cannot escalate to victory and this deadlock is painful to both of them (although not necessarily in equal degrees or for the same reasons), they seek a way out. The catastrophe provides a deadline or a lesson indicating that pain can be sharply increased if something is not done about it now; catastrophe is a useful extension of the notion of an MHS but is not necessary to either its definition or its existence. In different images the stalemate has been termed the *plateau*, a flat and unending terrain without relief, and the catastrophe the *precipice*, the point where things suddenly and predictably get worse. If the notion of mutual blockage is too static to be realistic, the concept may be stated dynamically as a moment when the upper hand slips and the lower hand rises, both parties moving toward equality, with both movements carrying pain for the parties.[3]

The other element necessary for a ripe moment is less complex and controversial: the perception of a way out. Parties do not have to be able to identify a specific solution, only a sense that a negotiated solution is possible for the searching and that the other party shares that sense and the willingness to search too. Without the sense of a way out, the push associated with the MHS would leave the parties with nowhere to go. These elements can be combined in a definitional proposition: Proposition 2 (Definitional): *If the (two) parties to a conflict (a) perceive themselves to be in a hurting stalemate and (b) perceive the possibility of a negotiated solution (a way out), the conflict is ripe for resolution (i.e., for negotiations toward resolution to begin).*

The basic reasoning underlying the MHS lies in cost-benefit analysis, based on the assumption that, when parties to a conflict find themselves on a pain-producing path, they prepare to look for an alternative that is more advantageous. This calculation is fully consistent with public choice notions of rationality (Sen, 1970; Arrow, 1963; Olson, 1965) and public choice studies of negotiation (Brams, 1990, 1994; Brams and Taylor, 1996), which assume that a party will pick the alternative it prefers and that a decision to change is induced by means of increasing pain associated with the present (conflictual) course. In game theoretical terms it marks the transformation of the situation in the parties' perception from a prisoners' dilemma into a chicken dilemma game (Brams, 1985; Goldstein, 1998). It is also consistent with prospect theory, currently in focus in international relations, which indicates that people tend to be more risk averse concerning gains than losses of equal magnitude and therefore that sunk costs or investments in conflict escalation tend to push parties into costly deadlocks or MHSs (Kahneman and Tversky, 1979; Bazerman et al., 1985; Stein and Pauly, 1992; Mitchell, 1995).

The ripe moment is necessarily a perceptual event, not one that stands alone in objective reality; it can be created if outside parties can cultivate the perception of a painful present versus a preferable alternative and therefore can be resisted so long as the party in question refuses or is otherwise able to block out that perception. As with any other subjective perception, there are likely to be objective referents or bases to be perceived. These can be highlighted by a mediator or an opposing party when they are not immediately recognized by the parties themselves, but it is the perception of the objective condition, not the condition itself, that makes for an MHS. Since such a stalemate is a future or contingent event, referring to the impossibility of breaking out of the impasse—"It can't go on like this"—any objective evidence is always subject to the recognition of the parties before it becomes operative. If the parties do not recognize "clear evidence" (in someone else's view) that they are in an impasse, an MHS has not (yet) occurred, and if they do perceive themselves to be in such a situation, no matter how flimsy the "evidence," the MHS is present. The relationship between objective and subjective components can be summarized in a proposition: Proposition 3: *An MHS contains objective and subjective elements, of which only the latter are necessary and sufficient to its existence.* The first three propositions can be combined into a model expressing a theory of ripeness in which ripeness is located as both a dependent and an independent variable (see Figure 6.1).

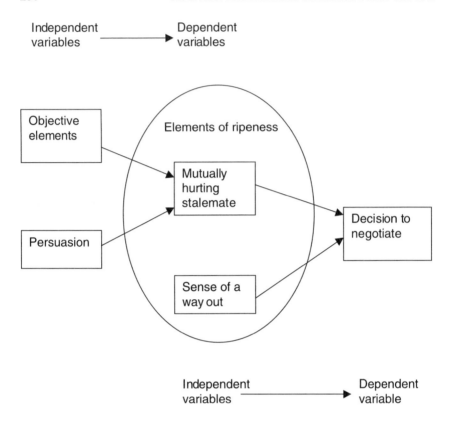

FIGURE 6.1 Factors affecting ripeness, elements of ripeness, and the decision to negotiate.

Identifying the Components

Since an MHS is a subjective matter, it can be perceived at any point in the conflict, early or late. Nothing in the definition of an MHS requires it to take place at the height of the conflict or at a high level of violence. The internal (and unmediated) negotiations in South Africa between 1990 and 1994 stand out as a striking case of negotiations opened (and pursued) on the basis of an MHS perceived by both sides on the basis of impending catastrophe, not of present casualties (Ohlson and Stedman, 1994; Sisk, 1995; Zartman, 1995b; Lieberfield, 1999a, 1999b). However, the greater the objective evidence, the greater the subjective perception of a stalemate and its pain is likely to be, and this evidence is more likely to come late, when all other courses of action and possibilities of escalation have been exhausted. In notable cases a long period of conflict is required before the MHS sinks in, whereas few if any studies have been made of early settlements and the role of long-range calculations. Indeed, given the infinite number of potential conflicts that have not reached the "heights," evidence would suggest that perception of an MHS occurs either at a low level of conflict, where it is relatively easy to begin problem solving in most cases, or in salient cases at rather high levels of conflict, a distinction that could be the subject of broad research. While the optimum situation would arguably be the first, where the parties to a conflict perceive ripeness before much escalation and loss of life have occurred, there is as yet little evidence—but a lot of methodological problems—in this regard, and such wisdom would still leave unanswered the question of how the importance of an issue would be established. In any case, as suggested, conflicts not treated "early" appear to require a high level of intensity for an MHS perception to kick in and negotiations toward a solution to begin.

As the notion of ripeness implies, an MHS can be a very fleeting opportunity, a moment to be seized lest it pass, or it can be of a long duration, waiting to be noticed and acted on by mediators. In the citations below the moment was brief in Bosnia but longer in Angola. In fact, failure to seize the moment often hastens its passing, as parties lose faith in the possibility of a negotiated way out or regain hope in the possibility of unilateral escalation. By the same token, the possibility of long duration often dulls the urgency of rapid seizure. Behind the duration of the ripe moment itself is the process of producing it through escalation and decision. The impact of incremental compared with massive escalation (Mitchell, 1995; Zartman and Aurik, 1991), and the internal process of converting members impervious to pain (hawks) into "pain perceivers" (doves) (Stedman, 1997; Mitchell, 1995) are further examples of research questions opened by the concept of ripeness.

The other component of a ripe moment—a perception by both parties of a way out—is less difficult to identify. Leaders often indicate whether they do or do not feel that a deal can be made with the other side, particularly when there is a change in that judgment. The sense that the other party is ready and willing to repay concessions with concessions is termed *requitement* (Zartman and Aurik, 1991). This element is also necessary (but, alone, insufficient) since, without a sense of the possibility of a negotiated exit from an MHS, fruitful negotiations cannot take off. Conversely, cases abound in which the absence of this component prevented otherwise promising beginnings to a negotiation. These elements of evidence and indication can be summarized in a proposition: Proposition 4: *If the parties' subjective expressions of pain, impass, and inability to bear the costs of further escalation, related to objective evidence of stalemate, data on numbers and nature of casualties and material costs, and/or other such indicators of an MHS can be found, along with expressions of a sense of a way out, ripeness exists.*

Research and intelligence on ripeness are needed to ascertain whether its defining components exist at any time and whether it is or can be seized by the parties or mediator(s) in order to begin negotiations. Thereafter, further research questions are needed to find out whether that moment can be prolonged or whether its favorable predispositions can be transferred to the process of negotiation itself (Mooradian and Druckman, 1999). Researchers would look for evidence, for example, whether the rapidly shifting military balance in the Burundian civil war has given rise to a perception of an MHS by the parties, as well as a sense by authoritative spokesmen for each side that the other is ready to seek a solution to the conflict, or, to the contrary, whether it has reinforced the conclusion that any mediation is bound to fail because one or both parties believes in the possibility or necessity of escalating out of the current impasse to achieve a decisive military victory. Research and intelligence would be required to learn why Bosnia in the war-torn summer of 1994 was not ripe for a negotiated settlement and mediation would fail and why it was ripe in November 1995 and mediation could use that condition to achieve agreement (Touval, 1996; Goodby, 1996). Similarly, research would indicate that there was no chance of mediating a settlement in the Ethiopia-Eritrean conflict in the early 1980s and early 1990s, or in the Southern Sudan conflict in the early 1990s, the skills of President Carter notwithstanding, because the components of ripeness were not present (Ottaway, 1995; Deng, 1995). The relationship of mediator tactics to ripeness can be summarized in a proposition: Proposition 5: *(a) Once ripeness has been established, specific tactics by mediators can seize the ripe moment and turn it into negotiations; (b) If only objective elements of ripeness exist, specific tactics by mediators can bring the conflicting parties to feel/understand the pain of their mutual stalemate and turn to negotiations.*

RIPENESS IN ACTION

While ripeness has not always been used to open negotiations, there have been occasions when it has come into play, as identified by both analysts and practitioners. A number of studies beyond the original examination (Zartman and Berman, 1982; Zartman, 1983, 1985/1989, 1986; Touval and Zartman, 1985; Zartman and Aurik, 1991) have used and tested the notion of ripeness regarding negotiations in Zimbabwe, Namibia and Angola, Eritrea, South Africa, Philippines, Cyprus, Iran-Iraq, Israel, Mozambique, and elsewhere (Touval, 1982; Haass, 1990; Stedman, 1991; Kriesberg and Thorson, 1991; Sisk, 1995; Druckman and Green, 1995; Zartman, 1995a; Norlen, 1995; Hampson, 1996; Goodby, 1996; Taisier and

Matthews, 1999; Salla, 1997; Pruitt, 1997; Aggestam and Jönson, 1997; Mooradian and Druckman, 1999; Sambanis, in press). Touval's (1982) work on the Middle East was particularly important in launching the idea. In general, these studies have found the concept applicable and useful as an explanation for the successful initiation of negotiations or their failure, while in some cases proposing refinements to the concept.

Other diplomatic memoirs have specifically referred to the idea by its MHS component. Chester Crocker, U.S. Assistant Secretary of State for Africa between 1981 and 1989, patiently mediated an agreement between Angola and South Africa for the withdrawal of Cuban troops from Angola and of South African troops from Namibia, then to become independent. For years an MHS, and hence an agreement, eluded the parties. "The second half of 1987 was the great turning point. . . .This was the moment when the situation 'ripened' " (Crocker, 1992:363). Military escalations on both sides in southern Angola heightened the conflict and the chances for further military damage; "a battle of perceptions was underway" (p. 370). Bloody confrontations in southeastern Angola beginning in November 1987 and in southwestern Angola in May 1988 ended in a draw. "By late June 1988, the cycle of South African and Cuban military moves in 1987-88 was nearly complete. The Techipa-Calueque clashes in southwestern Angola confirmed a precarious military stalemate. That stalemate was both the reflection and the cause of underlying political decisions. By early May, my colleagues and I convened representatives of Angola, Cuba, and South Africa in London for face-to-face, tripartite talks. The political decisions leading to the London meeting formed a distinct sequence, par-alleling military events on the ground, like planets moving one by one into a certain alignment" (Crocker, 1992:373).

In his conclusion, Crocker identifies specific signs of ripeness while qualifying that "correct timing is a matter of feel and instinct" (p. 481). He details the maintenance of the status quo at Cuito Carnevale despite massive Cubans reinforcements at the end of 1987, which led to a change from a "climate [that] was not conducive" in December to a meeting at the end of January when "negotiation was about to change for good" (pp. 373-374). The American mediation involved building diplomatic moves that paralleled the growing awareness of the parties, observed by the mediator, of the hurting stalemate in which they found themselves.

At the United Nations, Assistant Secretary General for Political Affairs Alvaro de Soto also endorsed the necessity of ripeness in his mission to mediate a peace in El Salvador. After chronicling a series of failed initiatives, he pointed to the importance of the Farabundo Marti National Liberation Front's (FMLN) November 1989 offensive, the largest of the war, which penetrated the main cities, including the capital, but failed to dislodge the government.

The silver lining was that it was, almost literally, a defining moment—the point at which it became possible to seriously envisage a negotiation. The FMLN had been reviewing their long-term prospects and strategy since 1988, adjusting their sights in the process. They were coming to the view that time was not entirely on their side. . . . [T]he offensive showed the FMLN that they could not spark a popular uprising. . . . The offensive also showed the rightist elements in government, and elites in general, that the armed forces could not defend them, let alone crush the insurgents. . . . However inchoate at first, the elements of a military deadlock began to appear. Neither side could defeat the other. As the dust settled, the notion that the conflict could not be solved by military means, and that its persistence was causing pain that could no longer be endured, began to take shape. The offensive codified the existence of a mutually hurting stalemate. The conflict was ripe for a negotiated solution. (de Soto, 1999:356)

In his parting report, Under-Secretary-General of the United Nations Marrack Goulding (1997:20) specifically cited the literature on ripeness in discussing the selection of conflicts to be handled by an overburdened UN: "Not all conflicts are 'ripe' for action by the United Nations (or any other third party). . . . It therefore behooves the Secretary-General to be selective and to recommend action only in situations where he judges that the investment of scarce resources is likely to produce a good return (in terms of preventing, managing and resolving conflict)."

In Yugoslavia, Secretary of State James Baker looked for a ripe moment during his quick trip to Belgrade in June 1991 and reported the same day to President George Bush that he did not find it: "My gut feeling is that we won't produce a serious dialogue on the future of Yugoslavia until all the parties have a greater sense of urgency and danger" (Holbrooke, 1998). Holbrooke calls this "a crucial misreading," as he did the later moment created by the Croatian Krajina offensive in August 1995. Holbrooke had his own image of the MHS (or the upper hand slipping and the underdog rising): "The best time to hit a serve is when the ball is suspended in the air, neither rising nor falling. We felt this equilibrium had arrived, or was about to, on the battlefield [in October 1995]." Trying to instill in Bosnian President Izetbegovic a perception, Holbrooke and his team pointed out "that the [Croat-Bosniac] Federation had probably reached its point of maximum conquest. . . . [I]n all wars, there were times for advance and times for consolidation, and in our opinion this was a time for consolidation [through negotiation]. . . . 'If you continue the war, you will be shooting craps with your nation's destiny' " (Holbrooke, 1998:193). It took the Croatian offensive, coupled with NATO bombing, to create an MHS composed of a temporary Serb setback and a temporary Croat advance that could not be sustained. As a State Department official stated: "Events on the ground have made it propitious to try again to get the negotiations started. The Serbs are on the run a bit. That won't last forever. So we are taking the obvious major step" (*New York Times*, August 9, 1995, p. A7). Many other statements by practitioners could be cited. In brief, alert practitioners do not seem to have difficulty identifying the existence or importance of an MHS for the opening of negotiations, although not all practitioners are so alert.

PROPOSED REFINEMENTS TO THE THEORY

The notion of ripeness is a simple idea that has been born out in a number of studies but that has also been subject to frequent, sometimes curious, misunderstandings. Many of these should be able to be eliminated by careful attention to the concept, while others have suggested further study and refinement.

The most important refinements carry the theory to a second level of questions about the effects of each side's pluralized politics on both the perceptions and the uses of ripeness. What kinds of internal political conditions are helpful both for perceiving ripeness and for turning that perception into the initiation of promising negotiations? A careful case study by Stedman (1991) of the Rhodesian negotiations for independence as Zimbabwe takes the concept beyond a single perception into the complexities of internal dynamics. Stedman specifies that some but not all parties must perceive a hurting stalemate, that patrons rather than parties may be the agents of perception, that the military element in each party is the crucial element in perceiving the stalemate, and that the way out is as important an ingredient as the stalemate in that all parties may well see victory in the alternative outcome prepared by negotiation (although some parties will be proven wrong in that perception). Stedman also highlights the potential of leadership change for the subjective perception of an MHS where it had not been seen previously in the same objective circumstances and of the threat of domestic rivals to incumbent leadership, rather than threats from the enemy, as the source of impending catastrophe, points also applied by Lieberfield (1999a, 1999b) in his more recent comparison of the Middle East and South Africa.

The original formulation of the theory added a third element to the definition of ripeness—the presence of a valid spokesman for each side; it has been dropped in the current reformulation because as a structural element it is of a different order than the other two defining perceptual elements. Nonetheless, it remains of second-level importance, as Stedman and Lieberfield point out. The presence of strong leadership recognized as representative of each party and that can deliver that party's compliance to the agreement is a necessary (while alone an insufficient) condition for productive negotiations to begin or, indeed, end successfully. The discussion of leadership conditions for ripeness to be perceived and used illustrates not only a fruitful area for further research but also the way in which the basic concept can give rise to ancillary questions of importance that build on the original theory.

Other studies have used and discussed the notion of ripeness in a search for alternatives and restatements, although the result has generally been a reaffirmation of the concept. Kriesberg and Thorson (1991), particularly in the chapters by Hurwitz and Rubin, emphasize the elusiveness and perceptional quality of the concept and its possible misuse as an excuse for inaction. Haass (1990) restates the components of ripeness as time pressure, appropriate power relations, acceptable formula (way out), and acceptable process, emphasizing in the rest of his work the elusiveness of the moment and the need to prepare or position for it in its absence. The latter discussion of alternative policies in the absence of ripeness is a useful extension, although in the attempt to restate the concept, it loses its precision and its distinction from resolution. A number of commentators (Licklider, 1995; Walter, 1997; Kleiboer, 1994, 1997; Kleiboer and 't Hart, 1995) allege tautology in the concept, confusing ripeness with final results. Kleiboer proposes instead the notion of willingness, which in fact repeats the perceptional aspect of ripeness without the causal component of the MHS.

There have been a number of attempts to reformulate the concept of ripeness. Druckman and Green (1995:299) have defined ripeness as the intersection of an insurgency's "calculation that its effective power was increasing while its legitimacy remained constant, and a government calculation that its power was decreasing while its legitimacy remained unchanged." The discussion reaffirms many aspects of MHS—its perceptional (calculated) quality, its objective base, its bilateral character, its initiating reference, and its researchable nature—but it adds the element of legitimacy, not only constant but high. Indeed, the stalemate is to be found on the level of legitimacy in this reformulation in addition to the more dynamically evolving stalemate on the level of power. More testing is needed of this additional element.

Goodby (1996) has defined ripeness entirely differently, focusing on the susceptibility of the situation to change through external (mediator's) inputs. Seeking to distinguish ripe moments from other stalemates, even mutually hurting ones, that "the parties to the conflict may be able to live with," Goodby (1996:502) draws on catastrophe theory (Forrester, 1961; Sandefur, 1990; Nicholson, 1989; Lachow, 1993) to distinguish between nonlinear stable, unstable, and metastable situations, the third—when "small external inputs can have large effects on the system"—being ripe for negotiation. From the perception of a third party, if small external efforts can accomplish major changes, the situation is ripe for resolution (i.e., for the third party to assist negotiations toward resolution). Firm indicators for metastability remain to be developed.

Pruitt (1997) and Pruitt and Olczak (1995) have extended the notion of ripeness into the negotiations themselves under the name of "readiness theory." Pruitt starts with the elements that ripeness theory seeks to explain (i.e., motivation to cooperate and requitement toward a way out) and posits them as push and pull factors driving negotiation to its conclusion. In identifying the sources of the first, which he terms motivational ripeness (presumably as opposed to objective referents to ripeness), he adds the positive factor of mutual dependence in achieving the goal to the negative elements already contained in the MHS (unattainable victory, unacceptable costs in escalation). Motivational ripeness is the parties' "willingness to give up a lot now in exchange for substantial concessions from the other rather than waiting [until] later in the hope that the other can be persuaded to make these concessions unilaterally." Like the original formulation, Pruitt's discussion also underlines the point that parties can come to this willingness/perception for different reasons, at different speeds, and even at different times, as well as the need for both parties to sense that there is a way out (and hence to sense that the other party so senses). The need for—presumably perceived—mutual dependence as an element in ripeness has not been tested beyond the initial proposal and could be done so fruitfully.

Spector (1998) has also written of "readiness," in a different sense, referring to negotiators' and mediators' capacity to negotiate, which is necessary even when ripeness is present. Skill and resources, including identity, interests, and strategies, are necessary components without which the parties are unlikely to be able to seize the ripe moment. Additional studies (Crocker et al., 1999; Maundi et al., 2000) have developed this notion.

Such discussions miss some of the original points and emphasize others in an effort to better grasp the essence of ripeness theory. The value of these efforts is highlighted by the question: Are they formulating a different concept, adding new terms or precision to the old original concept, or expressing the concept itself in different terms? For the most part it would seem that the emendations have either helped refine aspects of the concept or expressed the same thing differently, rather than offering an alternative concept or theory.

Some of the commentary on ripeness theory raises the relationship between parsimony in theory building and complexity in human action. This is a problem that dogs any attempt at social science theorizing and, carried to its extreme, is merely a matter of two different levels of discourse and analysis that can never meet. However, the present formulation of ripeness theory has sought to leave room for other undeniably important aspects of mediation and negotiation by referring to necessary but not sufficient components of ripeness. Other elements do play a role, often of varying importance. One has been identified from the outset: the substantive search for a formula for agreement between the parties. Another of particular importance is the authoritative structure of each side, most notably the presence of a valid spokesman who can represent a party and deliver its concurrence and compliance as negotiations proceed. Others could be added, and the effort to advance a clear and unambiguous theory, which is necessary to testing and application, in no way eliminates such facilitating variables.

Problems: Resistant Reactions

There are other intriguing problems raised by ripeness theory. One complication with the notion of a hurting stalemate arises when increased pain increases resistance rather than reducing it. Thus, under some conditions, an MHS does not create an opening for negotiation but makes it more difficult (it must be remembered that, while ripeness is a necessary precondition for negotiation, not all ripeness leads to negotiation.) Although this may be considered "bad," irrational, or even adolescent behavior, it is a common reaction and one that may be natural and functional. The reinforcing reaction to hurt in a stalemate can be tied to four different levels of situations or contexts. First is the normal response to opposition: "Don't give up without a fight," and "If at first you don't succeed, try, try again." The imposition of pain to a present course in conflict is not likely to lead to a search for alternative measures without first being tested. The theory itself takes this into account by referring to the parties' being locked into a stalemate from which they cannot escalate an exit, implying efforts to break out before giving in. Nonetheless, since the ripe moment is tied to perception, nothing indicates when and how the switch from breaking-out perceptions to giving-in perceptions will occur. In other words, while the theory indicates that an MHS is a necessary and identifiable element, nothing (other than tautological definitions) indicates when it will occur.

Second, while escalations are commonly taken to refer only to the means of conducting a conflict, they also refer to other aspects of conflict behavior, including ends and agents (Rubin et al., 1994). The latter is particularly relevant. Pressure on a party in conflict often leads to the psychological reaction of worsening the image of the opponent, a natural tendency that is often decried as lessening the chances of reconciliation but that has the functional feature of justifying resistance. Thus, the conditions that are designed to produce the ripe moment tend to produce its opposite, as a natural reaction.

Third, particular types of adversaries are especially prone to reinforcing behavior. Parties thinking as true believers are unlikely to be led to
compromise by increased pain; instead, pain is likely to justify renewed
struggle (Hoffer, 1951). Justified struggles call for greater sacrifices, which
absorb increased pain. The cycle is functional and self-protecting. The
first party increases its resistance as pressure and pain increase, so that
pain strengthens determination. To this type of reaction it is the release of
pain or an admission of pain on the other side that justifies relaxation;
when the opponent admits the error of its ways, the true believer can
claim the vindication of its efforts, which permits a management of the
conflict (Moses, 1996).

The fourth level anchors the true believer in a particular culture.
There are no independent nontautological characteristics available to
identify cultures hospitable to true believers, and since the behavioral
type and the general culture tend to coexist rather than one preceding the
other, the predictive possibilities are slim. True-believer cultures are those
hospitable to high commitment, either in escatalogical or ideological
terms, where there are additional external rewards to hanging tough and
where higher goals or values are thereby enhanced. There have been
some attempts to relate such cultures to nonnegotiatory mindsets, as in
Nicolson's (1960) "warriors" and Snyder and Diesing's (1977) hard-liners
and irrational types, the former explicitly referring to Nazi Germany and
the latter implicitly to Communists, among others.

In the current era, cases of resistant reactions to hurting stalemates
come particularly from the Middle East, from Iran during the hostage
negotiations (Moses, 1996) to Iraq during the second Gulf War. In the
hostage negotiations the established wisdom is that negotiations were not
possible as long as holding the hostages was worth more to Iran than
releasing them and therefore not until the parliamentary election of 1980
(Christopher et al., 1985). However, new research and interpretations
also show that negotiations were not possible as long as the United States
was seen as exerting pressure on Iran, since pressure was seen as the
opposite of contrition and an arrangement was not possible as long as the
United States had not learned the lesson of its evil ways and turned from
them. Thus, while the United States was operating under the logic of the
hurting stalemate, Iran was following the logic of the justifying pain.
Negotiations came when the two different "lines" crossed each other.

In the second Gulf War, even though neither side was interested in
negotiation, the same class of logic obtained. The United States thought
that increasing pressure and threat of catastrophe would bring Iraq to
heel, but the higher the pressure the more justification it provided to Iraq
to raise its threshold of resistance. If there were any chance of negotiation
in the conflict, it was earlier rather than later (Jentleson, 1995); each turn

of pressure raised the level of acceptance correspondingly, rather than rising toward a constant threshold where the possibility of negotiation could be found. The very act of holding out against mounting pressure from the Great Satan was a religious and nationalistic act of heroism, itself worthy of being called a victory: lying down on the railroad tracks before the oncoming locomotive was a glorious gesture, highly meritorious in itself regardless of the consequences. It showed not only the high ideals and selflessness of the defender but also the inhumanity and ruthlessness of the opponent. Hurting stalemates in such cultures are meaningless, since breaking down and agreeing to negotiate are a denial of the very ideals that inspired the resistance in the first place. Of course, it takes two to make a mutually hurting stalemate, and American lack of interest in negotiation at any time can raise questions about the cultural approach.

In sum, there is a resistant reaction, which, whether stemming from perseverance, agent escalation, true belief, or ideological cultures, means that the mechanism of the hurting stalemate in certain conditions may be its own undoing. The more an MHS is sought, the more it may be resisted as a sign of a conflict unripe for resolution. Identifying the phenonenon is not always simple. Since part of the resistant reaction phenomenon is a normal response to pressure and since the hurting stalemate is a perceptual event, initial resistance is to be expected. A true-believer reaction and an ideological culture can generally be identified by their context and language. Probably most difficult to sort out is the agent escalation, since its very nature is to escalate to vilifying generalizations the reasons for opposing the adversary.

The remedy is less clear and certainly less straightforward. One could hardly advise: in cost-benefit cultures, create a hurting stalemate as a ripe moment; in true-believer cultures, exhibit contrition as a ripe moment. That is, however, what happened in the Pueblo incident between the United States and North Korea, an incident cited more frequently as an aberration than a model. In the two Gulf cases, the two American presidents' strategies were diametrically opposite, but Carter's success in negotiation may be more attributable to the additional factor of the change in value of the hostages than to any difference in approach to ripeness. At the same time, Carter continually held out negotiations as an option and finally succeeded, whereas Bush continually ruled out negotiations as an option (and he too succeeded, in his terms!). The ultimate lesson is probably no more startling than the notion of a ripe moment itself: negotiations with true believers take longer to come about because ripe moments are harder to find. But in the end, if time and patience are available, true believers (or their followers) must eat too, so that pain can be treated as a universal human feeling, with various antidotes and painkillers available to deaden or delay its effects.

Problems: Compelling Opportunities

The other drawback about the notion of a hurting stalemate is its dependence on conflict. Odd and banal as that may sound, its implications are sobering. It means, on the one hand, that preemptive conflict resolution and preventive diplomacy are unpromising, since ripeness is hard to achieve so far ahead. On the other hand, it means that to ripen a conflict one must raise the level of conflict until a stalemate is reached and then further until it begins to hurt—and even then work toward a perception of an impending catastrophe as well. The ripe moment becomes the godchild of brinkmanship.

At the same time, another limitation to the theory—seemingly unrelated to the above—is that it addresses only the opening of negotiations, as noted at the outset and often missed by the critics. Now that the theory of ripeness is available to explain the initiation of negotiation, people would like to see a theory that explains the successful conclusion of negotiations once opened. Can ripeness be extended in some way to cover the entire process, or does successful conclusion of negotiations require a different explanatory logic?

Practitioners and students of conflict management would like to think that there could be a more positive prelude to negotiation and can even point to a few cases of negotiations, mediated or direct, that opened or came to closure without the push of a mutually hurting stalemate but through the pull of an attractive outcome. Although examples are rare, as explained by prospect theory, one case is the opening of the Madrid peace process on the Middle East in 1992 (Baker and de Frank, 1995); another may be boundary disputes that are overcome by the prospects of mutual development in the region. But the mechanisms are still unclear in part because the cases are so few. As in other ripe moments these occasions provided an opportunity for improvement but from a tiring rather than a painful deadlock (Mitchell, 1995; Zartman, 1995a). In some views the attraction lies in a possibility of winning (paradoxically a shared perception) more cheaply than by conflict or else a possibility of sharing power that did not exist before (Mitchell, 1995). In other views, enticement comes in the form of a new ingredient, provided by a persistent mediator and more than simply an apparent way out, and that new ingredient is the chance for improved relations with the mediating third party (Touval and Zartman, 1985; Saunders, 1991). In other instances the opportunity for a settlement grows more attractive because the issue of the conflict becomes *depassé*, no longer justifying bad relations with the other party or the mediator that it imposed. Such openings might be termed mutually enticing opportunities (MEOs), admittedly a title not as catchy as MHS and a concept not as well researched (or practiced). Few examples have been found in reality.

But an MEO is important in the broader negotiation process and has its place in extending ripeness theory. As indicated, ripeness theory refers to the decision to negotiate; it does not guarantee any results. At most it can be extended into the negotiations themselves by indicating that the perception of ripeness must continue during negotiations if the parties are not to reevaluate their positions and drop out, in the revived hopes of being able to find a unilateral solution through escalation. But negotiations completed under the shadow—or the push—of an MHS alone are likely to be unstable and unlikely to lead to a more enduring settlement. A negative shadow can begin the process but cannot provide for the change of mentalities to reconciliation. As Ohlson (1998), Pruitt (1997), and Pruitt and Olczak (1995) have pointed out, that is the function of the MEO.

While an MHS is the necessary and insufficient condition for negotiations to begin, during the process the negotiators must provide the prospects for a more attractive future to pull them out of their conflict. The push factor has to be replaced by a pull factor, in the terms of a formula for settlement and prospects of reconciliation that the negotiating parties design during negotiations (see Figure 6.2). Here the substantive aspect of negotiation in analysis and practice pulls ahead of the procedural approach: the way out takes over from the hurting stalemate. The seeds of the pull factor begin with the way out that the parties vaguely perceive as part of the initial ripeness, but this general sense of possibility needs to be developed and fleshed out to be the vehicle for an agreement. When an MEO is not developed in the negotiations, the negotiations remain trun-

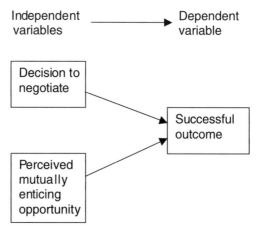

FIGURE 6.2 Conditions for a successful outcome of negotiations.

cated and unstable, even if a conflict management agreement to suspend violence is reached, as in the 1984 Lusaka agreement or the 1994 Karabakh cease-fire (Zartman, 1985/1989; Mooradian and Druckman, 1999). At this point the substantive literature on negotiation referred to at the beginning finds its place, which can be shown in a proposition: Proposition 6: *The perception of a mutually enticing opportunity is a necessary but not a sufficient condition for the continuation of negotiations to the successful conclusion of a conflict.*

Implications: Positioning and Ripening

Crocker (1992:471) states very forcefully (in boldface in the original) that "the absence of 'ripeness' does not tell us to walk away and do nothing. Rather, it helps us to identify obstacles and suggests ways of handling them and managing the problem until resolution becomes possible." Crocker's own experience indicates, first and above all, the importance of being present and available to the contestants while waiting for the moment to ripen so as to be able to seize it when it occurs. Thus, two policies are indicated when the moment is not ripe: positioning and ripening.

Strategies of positioning and ripening are adjuncts to ripeness theory, but they are very important to the practitioner. As such they are not theoretically tight but rather suggestive. To begin with, Crocker (1992; see also Haass, 1990, and Goulding, 1997) lists a number of important insights for positioning:

- Give the parties some fresh ideas to shake them up.
- Keep new ideas loose and flexible and avoid getting bogged down early in details.
- Establish basic principles to form building blocks of a settlement.
- Become an indispensable channel for negotiation.
- Establish an acceptable mechanism for negotiation and an appropriate format for registering an agreement.

Other strategies include preliminary explorations of items identified with prenegotiations (Stein, 1994):

- Identify the parties to be involved in the settlement.
- Identify the issues to be resolved, and separate out issues that are not resolvable in the conflict.
- Air alternatives to the current conflict course.
- Establish bridges between the parties.

- Clarify costs and risks involved in seeking a settlement.
- Establish requitement, the sense that each party will reciprocate the other's concessions.
- Assure support for a settlement policy within each party's domestic constituency.

Ripening can also be the subject of creative diplomacy. Since the theory (Proposition 3) indicates that ripeness results from objective indicators plus persuasion, these are the two elements that need attention in ripening. If some objective elements are present, persuasion is the obvious diplomatic element, serving to bring out the perception of both a stalemate and pain. Such was the message of Henry Kissinger in the Sinai withdrawal negotiations (Golan, 1976) and of Crocker in the Angolan negotiations (Crocker, 1992), among many others, emphasizing the absence of real alternatives (stalemate) and the high cost of the current conflict course (pain).

If there is no objective indicator to which to refer, ripening may involve a much more active engagement of the mediator, moving that role from communication and formulation to manipulation (Zartman and Touval, 1997; Touval, 1999; Rothchild, 1997). As a manipulator the mediator either increases the size of the stakes, attracting the parties to share in a pot that otherwise would have been too small, or limits the actions of the parties in conflict, providing objective elements for the stalemate. Such actions are delicate and dangerous since they threaten the neutrality and hence the usefulness of the mediator, but on occasion they may be deemed necessary. The NATO bombing of Serb positions in Bosnia in 1995 to create a hurting stalemate, or the American arming of Israel during the October war in 1973 or of Morocco (after two years of moratorium) in 1981 to keep those parties in the conflict, among many others, are typical examples of the mediator acting as a manipulator to bring about a stalemate. (Kissinger's action to increase the size of the pot during the second Sinai disengagement through U.S. aid is an example of the first type of manipulation.)

Finally, using ripeness as the independent variable, practitioners need to use all of their skills and apply all concepts of negotiation and mediation to take advantage of that necessary but insufficient condition in order to turn it into a successful peace-making process. Here the various notions of "readiness" already indicated are useful but not exclusively so. The study and practice of negotiation are so complex that both analysts and practitioners should be on guard against any single-factor theory or approach.

CONCLUSION

The investigation into ripeness and the attempt to turn an intuitive notion into an analytical concept was undertaken with the aim of producing a useful tool for practitioners as well as analysts. Parsimony, explicitness, and precision are particularly important not only in developing common terms and meanings so that the object can be discussed and used (i.e., in specifying the intuitive) but also in bringing out hidden implications and refocusing inquiry on refinements and new areas uncovered by a precision of the concept (i.e., in uncovering the counterintuitive). If the limitations on a concept are bigger than the concept itself, one should start looking elsewhere. But limitations become particularly interesting when they open up the possibilities and alternatives for better analysis and better practice. It is in that hope that this presentation will open fruitful discussions and applications of the use of hurting stalemates and the creation of compelling opportunities.

There is room for further research all along the ripening process. More work needs to be done on ways in which unripe situations can be turned ripe by third parties so that negotiations and mediation can begin, and, of course, the mainstream of negotiation research on how to take advantage of ripe moments by bringing the parties to a mutually satisfactory agreement needs to be continued. The proposed refinements need operationalization and testing. The relationship between objective and subjective components of stalemate needs better understanding, as does ex ante measurement and evaluation of the ripening process, of the MHS itself, and of the escalation process leading to it (Mooradian and Druckman, 1999; Zartman and Aurik, 1991; Faure and Zartman, forthcoming). It would indeed be desirable if there were "another side to the moon," that is, if an MEO could be theoretically developed and practically exploited as the other entry door to negotiation; most people engaged in the study and practice of negotiation would be pleased to see the MHS demoted to only one of two necessary (even if not sufficient) conditions for the initiation of negotiation.

ACKNOWLEDGMENTS

I am grateful to Chester Crocker, Daniel Druckman, Alexander George, James Goodby, Timothy Sisk, Stephen Stedman, Paul Stern, and an unidentified reader for their input in preparing this paper.

NOTES

[1]One could also identify a third school that focuses on relationships between the parties rather than either the substance or the procedure of the issues in conflict. See, for example, Lederach (1997), Sampson (1997), and Kelman (1997).

[2]Timing can refer to many things other than costs and benefits, including domestic political schedules, generational socialization, and attitudinal maturation. For an excellent analysis based on the first, see Quandt (1986); on the second, see Samuels et al. (1977). These are perfectly valid approaches, but ultimately they can be reduced to cost/benefits, calculated or affected by different referents. This is not to deny their separate value but simply to justify the conceptual focus used here.

[3]The same logic has been identified in regard to domestic elite settlements, produced by costly and inconclusive conflict: "Precisely because no single faction has been a clear winner and all factions have more nearly been losers, elites are disposed to compromise if at all possible" (Burton and Higley, 1987:298).

REFERENCES

Aggestam, Karin, and Jönson, Christer
  1997   (Un)ending conflict. *Millennium* XXXVI(3):771-794.
Arrow, Kenneth
  1963   *Social Choice and Individual Values.* New Haven, Conn.: Yale University Press.
Baker, James, and de Frank, Thomas M.
  1995   *The Politics of Diplomacy.* New York: Putnam.
Bazerman, Max, Magliozi, T., and Neale, M.A.
  1985   The acquisition of an integrative response in a competitive market. *Organizational Behavior and Human Performance* 34:294-313.
Brams, Steven J.
  1985   *Superpower Games: Applying Game Theory to Superpower Conflict.* New Haven, CT: Yale University Press.
  1990   *Negotiation Games.* New York: Routledge.
  1994   *Theory of Moves.* Cambridge: Cambridge University Press.
Brams, Steven J., and Taylor, Alan D.
  1996   *Fair Division.* Cambridge: Cambridge University Press.
Burton, Michael, and Higley, John
  1987   Elite settlements. *American Sociological Review* LII(2):295-307.
Campbell, John
  1976   *Successful Negotiation: Trieste.* Princeton, N.J.: Princeton University Press.
Christopher, Warren, et al.
  1985   *American Hostages in Iran.* New Haven, Conn.: Yale University Press.
Crocker, Chester A.
  1992   *High Noon in Southern Africa.* New York: Norton.
Crocker, Chester A., Hampson, Fen Osler, and Aall, Pamela, eds.
  1999   *Herding Cats: The Management of Complex International Mediation.* Washington, D.C.: United States Institute of Peace.
Deng, Francis
  1995   Negotiating a hidden agenda: Sudan's conflict of identities. In *Elusive Peace: Negotiating an End to Civil Wars,* I. William Zartman, ed. Washington, D.C.: The Brookings Institution.
de Soto, Alvaro
  1999   Multiparty mediation: El Salvador. In *Herding Cats: The Management of Complex International Mediation,* Chester Crocker, Fen Osler Hampson, and Pamela Aall, eds. Washington, D.C.: United States Institute of Peace.
Druckman, Daniel, and Green, Justin
  1995   Playing two games. In *Elusive Peace: Negotiating an End to Civil Wars,* I. William Zartman, ed. Washington, D.C.: The Brookings Institution.

Faure, Guy Olivier, and Zartman, I. William, eds.
Forth-   *Escalation and Negotiation.* Laxenburg: International Institute of Applied Systems
coming   Analysis.
Fisher, Roger, and Ury, William
1991   *Getting to Yes.* New York: Bantam.
Forrester, J.W.
1961   *Industrial Dynamics.* New York: Wiley.
Golan, Matti
1976   *The Secret Conversations of Henry Kissinger.* New York: Bantam.
Goldstein, Joshua
1998   The game of chicken in international relations: An underappreciated model. Unpublished paper, School of International Service, American University, Washington, D.C.
Goulding, Marrack
1997   *Enhancing the United Nations' Effectiveness in Peace and Security.* New York: United
Nations.
Goodby, James
1996   When war won out: Bosnian peace plans before Dayton. *International Negotiation*
1(3):501-523.
Haass, Richard
1990   *Conflicts Unending.* New Haven, Conn.: Yale University Press.
Hampson, Fen Osler
1996   *Nurturing Peace.* Washington, D.C.: United States Institute of Peace.
Hoffer, Eric
1951   *The True Believer.* New York: Harper.
Holbrooke, Richard
1998   *To End a War.* New York: Random House.
Hopmann, P. Terrence
1997   *The Negotiation Process and the Resolution of International Conflicts.* Columbia:
University of South Carolina.
Ikle, Fred Charles
1964   *How Nations Negotiate.* New York: Harper & Row.
Jentleson, Bruce
1995   *With Friends like These.* New York: Norton.
Kahneman, Daniel, and Tversky, Amos
1979   Prospect theory: An analysis of decisions under risk. *Econometrica* IIIL(3):263-291.
Kelman, Herbert
1997   Social psychological dimension in international conflict. In *Peacemaking in International Conflict,* I. William Zartman and I. Lewis Rasmussen, eds. Washington,
D.C.: United States Institute of Peace.
Kissinger, Henry
1974   *New York Times.* October 12.
Kleiboer, Marieke
1994   Ripeness at conflict: A fruitful notion? *Journal of Peace Research* XXXI(1):109-116.
1997   *International Mediation.* Boulder, Colo.: Lynne Rienner.
Kleiboer, Marieke, and 't Hart, Paul
1995   Time to talk? *Cooperation & Conflict* XXX(4):307-348.
Kriesberg, Louis, and Thorson, Stuart, eds.
1991   *Timing the De-escalation of International Conflicts.* Syracuse, N.Y.: Syracuse University Press.

Lachow, Irving
    1993   The metastable peace. In *The Limited Partnership*, James Goodby, ed. Oxford: Stockholm International Peace Research Institute.

Lax, David, and Sebenius, James
    1986   *The Manager as Negotiator.* New York: Free Press.

Lederach, John Paul
    1997   *Building Peace.* Washington, D.C.: United States Institute of Peace.

Licklider, Roy
    1995   The consequences of negotiated settlement in civil wars. *American Political Science Review* LXXXIX(3):681-690.

Lieberfield, Daniel
    1999a   Conflict 'ripeness' revisited: The South African and Israeli/Palestinian cases. *Negotiation Journal* XV(1):63-82.
    1999b   *Talking with the Enemy: Negotiation and Threat Perception in South Africa and Israel/Palestine.* New York: Praeger.

Maundi, Mohammed, Khadiagala, Gilbert, Nuemah, Kwaku, Touval, Saadia, and Zartman, I. William
    2000   *Entry and Access in Mediation.* Washington, D.C.: United States Institute of Peace.

Mitchell, Christopher
    1995   Cutting losses. Working Paper 9, Institute for Conflict Analysis and Resolution, George Mason University, Fairfax, Va.

Mooradian, Moorad, and Druckman, Daniel
    1999   Hurting stalemate or mediation? The conflict over Nagorno-Karabakh, 1990-95. *Journal of Peace Research* XXXVI(6):709-727.

Moses, Russell Leigh
    1996   *Freeing the Hostages.* Pittsburgh: University of Pittsburgh Press.

Nicholson, M.
    1989   *Formal Theories in International Relations.* Cambridge: Cambridge University Press.

Nicolson, Harold
    1960   *Diplomacy.* Oxford: Oxford University Press.

Norlen, Tove
    1995   *A Study of the Ripe Moment for Conflict Resolution and Its Applicability to Two Periods in the Israeli-Palestinian Conflict.* Uppsala: Uppsala University Political Science.

Nye, Joseph, and Smith, Roger, eds.
    1992   *After the Storm.* Lanham, Md.: Madison Books.

Ohlson, Thomas
    1998   *Power Politics and Peace Politics.* Uppsala: University of Uppsala, Department of Peace and Conflict Research.

Ohlson, Thomas, and Stedman, Stephen John
    1994   *The New Is Not Yet Born.* Washington, D.C.: The Brookings Institution.

Olson, Mancur
    1965   *The Logic of Collective Action.* Cambridge, Mass.: Harvard University Press.

Ottaway, Marina
    1995   Eritrea and Ethiopia: Negotiations in a transitional conflict. In *Elusive Peace: Negotiating an End to Civil Wars*, I. William Zartman, ed. Washington, D.C.: The Brookings Institution.

Pillar, Paul
    1983   *Negotiating Peace.* Princeton, N.J.: Princeton University Press.

Pruitt, Dean G.
    1981   *Negotiating Behavior.* New York: Academic.
    1997   Ripeness theory and the Oslo talks. *International Negotiation* II(2):237-250.

Pruitt, Dean G., and Carnevale, Peter
1993   *Negotiation in Social Conflict.* Pacific Grove, Calif.: Brooks/Cole.
Pruitt, Dean G., and Olczak, Paul V.
1995   Approaches to resolving seemingly intractable conflict. In *Conflict, Cooperation and Justice*, Barbara Bunker and Jeffrey Rubin, eds. San Francisco: Jossey-Bass.
Quandt, William B.
1986   *Camp David.* Washington, D.C.: The Brookings Institution.
Raiffa, Howard
1982   *The Art and Science of Negotiation.* Cambridge, Mass.: Harvard University Press.
Rothchild, Donald
1997   *Managing Ethnic Conflict in Africa.* Washington, D.C.: The Brookings Institution.
Rubin, Jeffrey Z., Pruitt, Dean G., and Kim, Sung Hee
1994   *Social Conflict.* New York: McGraw-Hill.
Salla, Michael
1997   Creating the "ripe moment" in the east Timor conflict. *Journal of Peace Research* XXXIV(4):449-466.
Sambanis, Nicholas
 In press Conflict resolution ripeness and spoiler problems in Cyprus. *Journal of Peace Research.*
Sampson, Cynthia
1997   Religion and peacebuilding. In *Peacemaking in International Conflict*, I. William Zartman and I. Lewis Rasmussen, eds. Washington, D.C.: United States Institute of Peace.
Samuels, Richard, et al.
1977   *Political Generations and Political Development.* Boston: Lexington.
Sandefur, J.T.
1990   *Discrete Dynamical Systems.* Oxford: Clarendon Press.
Saunders, Harold
1991   Guidelines B. Unpublished manuscript, Kettering Foundation, Washington, D.C.
Sen, Amartya
1970   *Collective Choice and Social Welfare.* San Francisco: Holden-Day.
Shultz, George
1988   This is the plan. *New York Times*, March 18.
Sisk, Timothy
1995   *Democratization in South Africa: The Elusive Social Contract.* Princeton, N.J.: Princeton University Press.
Snyder, Glenn, and Diesing, Paul.
1977   *Conflict Among Nations.* Princeton, N.J.: Princeton University Press.
Spector, Bertram I.
1998   Negotiation Readiness in the Development Context: Adding Capacity to Ripeness. Paper presented to the International Studies Association, Minneapolis, March.
Stedman, Stephen John
1991   *Peacemaking in Civil War.* Boulder, Colo.: Lynne Rienner.
1997   Spoiler problems in peace processes. *International Security* 22(2):5-53.
Stein, Janice, ed.
1994   *Getting to the Table.* Baltimore: The Johns Hopkins University Press.
Stein, Janice, and Pauly, Louis, eds.
1992   *Choosing to Cooperate: How States Avoid Loss.* Baltimore: The Johns Hopkins University Press.

Taisier, Ali, and Matthews, Robert O., eds.
   1999   *Civil Wars in Africa: Roots and Resolution*. Montreal: McGill-Queens University Press.
Touval, Saadia
   1982   *The Peace Brokers*. Princeton, N.J.: Princeton University Press.
   1996   Coercive mediation on the road to Dayton. *International Negotiation* I(3):547-570.
   1999   Mediators' Leverage. Paper prepared for Committee on International Conflict Resolution, National Research Council.
Touval, Saadia, and Zartman, I. William, eds.
   1985   *International Mediation in Theory and Practice*. Boulder, Colo.: Westview.
Walter, Barbara F.
   1997   The critical barrier to civil war settlement. *International Organization* LI(3):335-365.
Walton, Robert, and McKersie, Richard
   1965   *A Behavioral Theory of Labor Negotiations*. New York: McGraw-Hill.
Young, Oran, ed.
   1975   *Bargaining*. Urbana: University of Illinois Press.
Zartman, I. William
   1983   The strategy of preventive diplomacy in third world conflicts. In *Managing US-Soviet Rivalry*, Alexander George, ed. Boulder, Colo.: Westview.
   1986   Ripening conflict, ripe moment, formula and mediation. In *Perspectives on Negotiation*, Diane BenDahmane and John McDonald, eds. Washington, D.C.: U.S. Government Printing Office.
   1985/   *Ripe for Resolution*. New York: Oxford University Press.
   1989
Zartman, I. William, ed.
   1995a *Elusive Peace: Negotiating an End to Civil Wars*. Washington, D.C.: The Brookings Institution.
Zartman, I. William
   1995b Negotiations to End Conflict in South Africa. In *Elusive Peace: Negotiating an End to Civil Wars*, I. William Zartman, ed. Washington, D.C.: The Brookings Institution.
Zartman, I. William, and Aurik, Johannes
   1991   Power strategies in de-escalation. In *Timing the De-escalation of International Conflicts*, Louis Kriesberg and Stuart Thorson, eds. Syracuse, N.Y.: Syracuse University Press.
Zartman, I. William, and Berman, Maureen
   1982   *The Practical Negotiator*. New Haven, Conn.: Yale University Press.
Zartman, I. William, and Rasmussen, J. Lewis, eds.
   1997   *Peacemaking in International Conflict*. Washington, D.C.: United States Institute of Peace.
Zartman, I. William, and Touval, Saadia
   1997   International mediation in the post-Cold War era. In *Managing Global Chaos*, Chester Crocker, Fen Osler Hampson, and Pamela Aall, eds. Washington, D.C.: United States Institute of Peace.

7

Interactive Conflict Resolution: A View for Policy Makers on Making and Building Peace

Harold H. Saunders,

with contributions by
Louise Diamond, Herbert C. Kelman, John Marks,
Joseph V. Montville, and Vamık Volkan

Editors' Note: *Chapters 7 and 8 address a particular approach to conflict resolution, most often called interactive conflict resolution, from the distinct viewpoints of a practitioner (Chapter 7) and a scholar (Chapter 8). In Chapter 7, Harold Saunders and his collaborators provide an informative introduction that will be valuable to those unfamiliar with the approach and a set of conclusions based on his many years of experience with international conflict resolution. In Chapter 8, Nadim Rouhana examines international conflict resolution from an analytical standpoint, discussing what would be necessary for a systematic and scientific evaluation of its effectiveness. There is a difference in the perspectives of the two chapters: practitioners want handy judgments about the probable usefulness of international conflict resolution, while scholars are more patient about waiting for the evidence. From the perspective of this volume, case material and practitioners' judgments, such as are presented in Chapter 7, are important inputs to the kind of social scientific analysis described in Chapter 8. Social scientific methods can be used profitably to evaluate the effects of interventions and to better inform practitioners about the conditions favorable for their success.*

Policy making today must start from the recognition that relation ships between countries and groups are a political process of con tinuous interaction between whole bodies politic—not just what governments and leaders do to each other. Many of the deep-rooted human conflicts that seize our attention today demonstrate that significant dimensions of these conflicts are beyond the reach of governments. The list of examples is long, well known, and compelling. Many deep-rooted human conflicts are partly beyond the reach of governments because they are not ready for diplomacy, formal mediation, or negotiation. People do not negotiate about their identities, historic grievances, dignity, hopes, or fears.

We will not have an adequate conceptual framework for making or evaluating policy or operations either by government or by citizens outside government until we recognize that peace is not made by governments alone. Important as government is, ultimately peaceful relationships are built by people.

There will continue to be some things that only officials can do—such as negotiate, ratify, fund, and enforce binding agreements—but there are some things that only citizens can do—such as change human relationships and reconnect the severed sinews necessary to bridge divides in a functional society. We all know that peace accords—milestones that they are—do not by themselves make peace; only whole human beings in whole bodies politic can build peaceful relationships.

Consider what happens in a community, country, or region torn by conflict. A functioning society includes a range of interactions that span the natural differences that characterize any developed society. When conflict breaks out, people break those ties as they retreat within the safety of their combatant group. A mediator comes and helps reach an agreement to end violence. Then, too often, the mediator leaves, giving little attention that the agreement may not be sustainable until the severed sinews of a healthy society are restored. Or if a government does recognize the need to help with "reconstruction," that task is too often left for aid offices; those at the top of government who gave high-level political support for the mediator go on to other things, leaving those who are rebuilding torn societies to the mercies of those who initiated the conflict in the first place.[1]

It is time to recognize at the highest levels that citizens outside government now have a well-developed systematic approach to peace making—their counterpart to the mediation, negotiation, and diplomacy of governments. Policy for ending deep-rooted human conflict will not be realistic unless policy makers think in terms of a multilevel peace process that embraces both official and public peace-making efforts. A comprehensive peace process will work in the civil societies where citizens form the associations they need to build the practices and institutions of peace as well as in official negotiating rooms. It is time for citizens inside and outside government to work together to bring to peace making all that each has to offer. Policy at the highest levels must embrace all levels in the multilevel peace process—not just focus on negotiation and leave reconnecting the torn ligaments of society to functional agencies.

For three decades now a modest but increasing number of citizens outside government have been developing processes of nonofficial dialogue, analysis, and more recently common citizen action that enable citizens to act systematically to change conflictual relationships. In this paper that process is called "interactive conflict resolution." In the context of a comprehensive multilevel peace process, defining and naming this process give it at last a dignity, seriousness, and systematic character as the citizens' peace process. It deserves attention comparable to the study and recognition given over more than three centuries to the traditional instruments of statecraft. This methodology provides citizens with the capacity to conduct the public as contrasted to the official tracks of the peace process.

Although the impact of these unofficial efforts is sometimes difficult to assess precisely, policy makers ignore the potential of this complementary resource at the risk of failing to engage with a significant force for peaceful change. If governments and citizens could learn to work in complementary ways, the resources available for building peaceful societies would be infinitely increased. The purpose of this paper is to give policy makers a first-hand look at how interactive conflict resolution works.

THE MULTILEVEL PEACE PROCESS

As we flew on Secretary of State Henry Kissinger's shuttle aircraft around the Arab-Israeli arena after the October 1973 war, we began calling what we were doing the "negotiating process." It seemed a good name for what we were doing at the beginning. Kissinger openly stated that the strategy was to mediate one partial agreement after another with the expectation that a series of interim disengagement agreements could establish momentum and credibility. As people saw agreements carefully negotiated and implemented, they might support their governments in going further. That cumulative experience could gradually change the patterns of interaction, the perceptions, and the limits in relationships between Israel and its neighbors and eventually the relationships themselves.

After the first disengagement agreement between Egypt and Israel in January 1974, the prospect of a follow-on effort to achieve a comparable agreement between Israel and Syria created a political environment in which Saudi Arabia felt able to lift the oil embargo that had been imposed during the war. President Richard Nixon's visit to the Middle East after the Israel-Syria disengagement agreement in May generated a further sense of the possibility of movement toward peace. In recognition of the interaction between our mediation and the larger political environment, we began using the phrase "the peace process."

That process continued through a second Egyptian-Israeli interim agreement in 1975, the Camp David accords in 1978, the Egyptian-Israeli peace treaty in 1979, and the beginning of negotiations on the Israeli-Palestinian relationship. A high point in that process was Egyptian President Anwar al-Sadat's visit to Israel in November 1977. His purpose was not to advance the negotiations as such, but recognizing the deep distrust of the Israeli people for their Arab neighbors, he went to Israel to demonstrate that peace with a major Arab country was possible. His act changed the perceptions of the Israeli people and created a political environment in which they gave their government permission to try peace.

After I left government in 1981, I described that official peace process as "a series of mediated and negotiated agreements embedded in a larger political process." It was in that larger process that relationships changed—albeit glacially. I also remember thinking and later writing that, "until political leaders acted to change the political environment, the mediators and negotiators did not have a chance." As I have since learned, that political environment is populated by citizens who alone have the capacity to change human relationships.

During the 1970s we in the government paid only minimal attention to a slowly burgeoning series of workshops between Arabs and Israelis outside government—and between American and Soviet citizens on the subject of the Soviet-U.S. relationship as it affected and was influenced by the Arab-Israeli peace process. We focused on the official peace process. But as the official process led the way, this unofficial process—which I now call the "public peace process"—was building its foundations, methods, and experience. Launched by a small number of scholar-practitioners, those meetings were never ends in themselves. They always served as laboratories for refining a methodology for probing systematically and learning how to change those conflictual relationships. Alongside this growing number of systematic dialogues, countless interactions took place among Israelis and Palestinians in many walks of life.

In the 1980s the seminars, workshops, symposia, and dialogues proliferated. Although I have no proof, I would hypothesize that these countless interactions over two decades deserved a significant share of the credit when Israeli Prime Minister Yitzhak Rabin and Palestine Liberation Organization (PLO) Chairman Yasser Arafat shook hands on the White House lawn in 1993. I would further observe in another arena that many of the speeches and articles that cumulatively came to be called the "new political thinking" in Moscow during the Gorbachev period were produced by participants in the Dartmouth Conference—the longest continuous bilateral dialogue between American and Soviet citizens—and a handful of other such dialogues.[2]

In the Israeli-Palestinian context some would point to the credit earned by the nonofficial group that met in Oslo with Norwegian moderators and eventually negotiated an Israeli-Palestinian agreement on principles that were adopted by Israeli and Palestinian authorities. Nothing should be said to take any credit away from that small group or their Norwegian sponsors and mediators. But in a sense they were unique—a quasi-official process in which political authorities, in the end, endorsed and adopted their work.

One could point to a variety of roles played by citizens outside government in other peace processes—Franco-German rapprochement after World War II, Soviet-U.S., Sino-U.S., Guatemalan, Salvadoran, intra-Estonian, Armenian-Azerbaijani, Tajikistani, Indian-Pakistani-Kashmiri, Northern Irish, South African. My purpose here is not to detail these other examples. My purpose is to state forcefully that the concept of the peace process will not be complete until the potential contribution of citizens outside government is recognized and included. It will not be brought into play with full power unless it is seen at the highest levels as operating at both the official and the unofficial or public levels.

Having stated my thesis, I move now to describe how the unofficial or public peace process works. If official policy makers are to take into account the capacities of the public peace process to complement what governments do, officials need to understand that process in practical terms—what it is and is not, how it works, what it can and cannot do, and how in a complementary relationship with government it can contribute to progress in ways that governments often cannot.

INTERACTIVE CONFLICT RESOLUTION: WHAT IS IT?

Interactive conflict resolution is a well-defined and systematic approach used in small unofficial meetings of persons in tension or violent conflict to stimulate their talk together about the problems that divide the groups they identify with and the relationships that underlie those problems. Increasingly, practitioners see this approach at its best when it is a continuing process sustained over time, although one-time meetings can be fruitful in appropriate circumstances.

The approach is distinguished most clearly by its differences from formal mediation and negotiation. The talk is different. It is wider ranging. Participants speak only for themselves—not under instruction from government or other political authority. They are free to explore a broad range of ideas that they come to believe—as a result of listening to each other—are important. Often these are ideas that underlie or reach beyond present relationships. As participants exchange ideas, the talk is increasingly characterized by its interactive quality—that is, they gradually learn to talk, think, and work *together* on problems and relationships of importance to all in the group rather than only exchanging formal positions on agreed agenda items.

This is not to say that negotiators never engage in such talk. One of the major advantages of the setting at Camp David was the opportunity for walks and talks on the trails as well as informal exchanges over meals. But while good negotiation is often characterized by its thoughtful problem-solving approach, at the end of the day representatives must be just that—delegates whose talk is limited by the positions and agendas of the authority that sent them to the table. They must go back to the task of writing an agreement that can stand up under the legal and political tests of ratification in their bodies politic. Officials have the authority and duty to negotiate binding agreements; citizens outside government have the opportunity and responsibility to change perspectives and conflictual relationships.

The approach is different. Rather than focusing primarily on agenda issues and the need to write an agreement, participants explore their overall relationship. They examine their own human needs in relation to the needs of the other group. While participants in unofficial dialogue reflect the experience, feelings, and views of their own communities, their purpose in dialogue is to absorb the other party's perspective—not to force their own. Participants put themselves, to the extent possible, in the minds of the adversary to understand what he or she needs in order to change the relationship. Rather than defending their own interests alone, they may gain respect for the others' experience, feelings, and needs. They may experience change in themselves that can seem to bring them closer to the adversary. In a negotiation each side must claim to have defended its group's interests even where compromise has been necessary.

The product is different. Rather than aiming to produce a written agreement, the purpose is to generate insight, refocus perspective, redefine problems. Rather than seeking solutions, the hope is to shape new frameworks within which to tackle problems, change attitudes, alter relationships. When government policies hit a deadend, officials reach out for "ideas in the air" put there by groups with the freedom to think together outside established bounds.

Confusion about interactive conflict resolution arises because of the different functions it serves in different circumstances or because of the different styles of moderators. Different activities are placed under this umbrella—some properly and some perhaps not. Which deserve to be called "interactive conflict resolution"? For instance, participants are sometimes close to government and address an agenda close to the governmental agenda. They often talk like the governmental experts they are close to or were before retirement, and they think of their goal mainly as influencing government. Sometimes such groups are referred to as working on "track two"[3] alongside a first governmental track.

At the other end of the spectrum are groups that explicitly focus on changing the underlying dynamics of the relationships that cause conflict or on creating new networks of relationships. They give much more weight to understanding the psychology of the interaction than to finding technical solutions to technically defined problems. They seek changes in attitudes and relationships rather than policies. Some observers would reserve the term "interactive conflict resolution" for these latter groups.

My own inclination is not to be too precious in drawing lines. The main line is between official and unofficial. When we are dealing with whole human beings from whole bodies politic in conflict, there will normally be two items on the agenda simultaneously in unofficial dialogue. Of course, participants will talk about the concrete issues and actions that, at least on the surface, put them and their authorities at odds with each other. But their talk will quickly reveal the deep-rooted human causes of the conflict—blame for hurt, grievance over injustice, anger from humiliation.

My feeling is that the practice of interactive conflict resolution must reflect the approach defined in detail below. It is a well-defined systematic approach. But its practice is an art, not a science. The art—and like creative politics or diplomacy, it is an art—is revealed in the capacity to draw out human ability to talk about what is on their minds in a way that induces mutual comprehension and opens the door to talking, thinking, and working together differently to solve problems out of mutual need and interest. If a group can move that far, participants will learn within themselves what is involved in changing conflictual relationships. The guiding principles laid out below represent the parameters and the inspiration for this work.

One point of similarity between formal mediation and negotiation and interactive conflict resolution leads to understanding the value of their differences. Both work in a larger political context—often in the same political context. Both will reflect and be affected by developments in that larger context. But that larger context will also determine what instrument is most appropriate at a particular moment in a particular situation. For instance, experience in the Israeli-Palestinian context and in the early civil war period in Tajikistan demonstrates that interactive conflict resolution was the only instrument that those involved found they could use to pave the way for formal negotiation. At a certain point, negotiation was essential. During negotiation those practicing interactive conflict resolution were often able to introduce perspectives to break impasses, and they alone had the energy to look beyond the negotiation to the changes in relationships that are critical in turning a peace agreement into genuine peace.

On a spectrum from official negotiation through the various forms that interactive conflict resolution takes, it may be accurate to say that the latter becomes increasingly useful when the subject is taboo on official agendas, when the real subject is the relationship or when formal contacts are politically impossible. It seems to happen that, as official capacity diminishes, interactive conflict resolution becomes more effective.

One other definitional issue needs to be dealt with—the role of a third party in the process. One of the leading academic definitions of interactive conflict resolution reads "small group, problem-solving discussions between unofficial representatives of identity groups or states engaged in destructive conflict *that are facilitated by an impartial third party of social scientist-practitioners* [emphasis added]."⁴ As often happens, the definition depends partly on the experience and needs of the definer. That is understandable.

A scholar striving out of conviction to build legitimacy in an academic setting for study and practice of interactive conflict resolution has to define in rigorous social science terms both the field and the questions for research. He or she will also need to evaluate by social science standards the effectiveness and ethical behavior where the lives and resources of others are at stake. In this case one can understand the felt need to define the work in terms of expert third-party control.

For two reasons I find pinning the definition of this work partially on a third-party role too limiting. First, three leading examples have never depended on a third party. The Dartmouth Conference—the longest continuous bilateral dialogue between American and Soviet/Russian citizens, which began in 1960—and the Sino-U.S. dialogue begun in 1986 by the American Studies Institute of the Chinese Academy of Social Sciences and the Kettering Foundation as well as a dialogue begun by the National Committee on U.S.-China Relations have always been cochaired by senior participants from each group. Second, in my view the future of this work as a broadly used instrument in a changing bodies politic lies in the proliferation of such groups, whether between groups in Bosnia or in black-white or interethnic dialogue in American cities. That proliferation cannot be limited by a requirement that trained social scientists conduct the sessions.

This paper urges policy makers to join forces on appropriate occasions with those engaged in interactive conflict resolution. That encouragement is based on my conviction that this work can be placed in the hands of responsible and wise citizens, properly prepared. When citizens start talking, communities must have the flexibility to organize as their needs require while still taking advantage of the insights that have emerged from ongoing work by scholar-practitioners in interactive conflict resolution. Governments—not just academic departments—can judge their work on its merits within an overall peace process. This would inevitably sacrifice some professional expertise, but my experience suggests that such compromise is necessary and acceptable if interactive conflict resolution is to move beyond a small group of scholar-practitioners into wider public usage.

Perhaps another colleague has offered a useful way of thinking about this definitional point when he suggested, in writing about mediation, that we think of mediation as a process of many functions rather than in terms of a person.[5] When asked who performed the third-party role at the Dartmouth Conference, I responded that institutions on both sides were the conveners, sometimes other institutions were additional funders, and the comoderators of each group (highly educated and experienced but neither acting as a social scientist) were the stewards of the process in collaboration with participants—setting the agenda, enforcing ground rules, crystallizing insights from dialogue, reporting to governments as appropriate.

I repeat, however, that interactive conflict resolution is a well-defined systematic approach. Those who deserve to be called practitioners of this art must take seriously the body of literature and the experience that define this approach. To lay that out is the purpose of the next section.

INTERACTIVE CONFLICT RESOLUTION: PRINCIPLES AND PROCESS

No two unofficial processes are exactly alike. They differ in emphasis, approach, and specific goals. They use approaches ranging from academic seminar-style talk on over to a psychoanalytically driven process. But most of them have a number of important characteristics in common. First, all start with ground rules describing a mode of talk—genuine dialogue and analysis—that differs from the usual confrontational debates and arguments of the political arena or the adversarial proceedings of the courts, as well as from many of the exchanges around the negotiating table:

• Participants will interact civilly, listen actively to each other with attention and respect, not interrupt, and allow each to present her/his views fully.
• Speakers will observe time limits to allow genuine and balanced dialogue.

- Participants will speak from their hearts as well as their minds. Because they need to speak about the feelings and relationships behind specific problems, feelings will be expressed and heard with mutual respect.
- Participants will respond as directly and as fully as possible to points made and questions asked. Each will make a real effort to put her/himself in others' shoes and learn to speak with sensitivity for their views and feelings.
- Participants will try to learn from these expressions of others' views and feelings to increase the complexity of their thinking about the other side and the relationship.

Second, as suggested above, the focus and purpose are quite different from those in formal negotiation where adversaries work from precisely defined interests and positions toward a written agreement on specified material problems.

- A purpose in interactive conflict resolution is to probe the relationships that underlie a conflict and work on changing them. As noted above, there will always be two items in the agenda—not just the concrete problems that negotiators deal with but also the underlying feelings and interactions that cause those problems and must be changed if they are to be resolved.
- Unlike credentialed negotiators, dialogue participants do not formally represent organizations or groups. No one has the authority to negotiate.
- When such groups relate to negotiations, they often focus on obstacles that underlie negotiations, or they think beyond negotiations to political processes that will be necessary to implement and sustain the decisions that emerge from agreements. Unofficial dialogues can pave the way for negotiations, address the problems that block progress, and work in the larger society where peace will actually be made. Sometimes they make a direct contribution.
- The group itself becomes a microcosm of the conflict. Participants confront issues, experience change in their own relationships, and begin to understand how such change could be projected into the larger body politic.
- Because relationships change slowly, it is best if participants and conveners can commit themselves to meet regularly over a period of months. Most workshops involving international groups last three to five days at intervals of several months. Communities in the United States are beginning to experiment with monthly meetings of at least four to five hours in each meeting. The duration of the series should be open ended.

Third, dialogue groups normally preserve the confidentiality of their exchanges until they reach a point where they are ready to take their ideas into the public arena. They usually agree that nobody in the dialogue will be quoted outside the meeting room and that no one will speak publicly about the substantive discussion in the dialogue unless all agree. While the meetings are not secret, the approach is a quiet one.

Fourth, each group is chaired by a moderator, comoderators, or a panel of moderators—often by third-party moderators but sometimes by individuals from each side who accept responsibility to work together to protect the character of the dialogue and to advance the agenda and the relationship. The unique character of each group will suggest particular qualities in the moderator(s), but the qualities that seem essential underscore the focus of the process on the human dimension of the conflict:

- sensitivity to the human dimension of problems—what participants as human beings really need, why people hurt and feel victimized, why people may be understandably angry and intransigent—and the ability to relate to participants on that level rather than treating them as trainees to be instructed;
- commitment to the overall purpose of reconciliation between groups that have real grievances against each other;
- sensitivity to the cultural uniqueness of the groups involved;
- the ability to convey genuine caring and commitment at a person-to-person level and ability to gain respect from participants as a caring person and as a professional;
- realistic expectations for the pace at which people can change;
- some depth of experience with related problems and the ability to conceptualize that experience so as to draw on it in a particular group;
- the ability to help people see common elements in their experiences and views;
- a sense of political process—the ability to see the whole picture, keep a destination in sight, and not take sides; and
- the ability to help participants organize their thoughts.

A word of perspective on this process. The person(s) chosen as moderator(s) may have played roles in other settings, but the following must be noted:

- This is not like moderating a community policy discussion. This process is sustained over a longer period of time. Participants focus not just on problems but—even more importantly—also on the relationship issues that cause them. In focusing on changing relationships, the moderator will need to welcome expressions of emotion within reason and try to help the group learn from them. The moderator will share the experience of the dialogue, not be neutrally detached.

- This is not mediation. While many of a mediator's abilities may be helpful in this process, a mediator is usually asked to help participants reach a substantive agreement about one defined problem or complex of problems. Interactive conflict resolution involves the full range of problems that affect the relationships involved. Its purpose is to change relationships so that participants can deal with whatever problems arise.
- This is not negotiation. People in deep-rooted human conflict believe they have little to negotiate—at least initially. Their purpose is different, although their analysis and experience together may help pave the way for negotiation.
- The moderator does not act as a teacher or trainer. This is neither an academic conference or a skills-building exercise, although participants may learn a lot from how a moderator conducts her/himself, poses questions, draws on broader experiences or analytical concepts, expresses concern, and demonstrates respect and sincerity. At most the moderator should share experiences as an equal.

Whatever the exact approach, these experiences in dialogue and analysis tend to evolve through a progression of stages. This statement is a conceptualization of many experiences—not just my own and not as a theoretical proposition. Some other practitioners concur that it reflects their experience in broad terms. All would emphasize that the stages are not rigid but that they are a useful way of analyzing the progress of a group, the work it is capable of doing, and what its next tasks are.

- First, there is a period when potential participants decide whether to reach out to the adversary. It is a period of overcoming genuine fear and disgust of meeting and talking with the enemy. For a third party this involves decisions on shaping a group and recruiting worthy participants.
- Second, when a group sits down together, participants inevitably spend a lot of time presenting their case or "downloading" their picture of the relationship, their grievances with the other party, and their fears and positions. They are "mapping" the relevant relationships by pouring out the issues of concern to them and their sense of who is responsible for problems and for wrongs committed. Often, the two parties are unable to look each other in the eye but speak mainly to the third party. Anger is often expressed. As talk proceeds, it is essential that the group gradually move into an analytical mode together to establish a base for working on problems together.
- Third, at the end of the period of "mapping" in which a list of

issues may be generated, the participants will decide implicitly or explicitly that one or two problems deserve their in-depth priority attention. They begin to dig more deeply into one problem, using it as the vehicle for probing the underlying dynamics of their relationship. Each side will try to understand the other's needs. After they have worked for some time in this mode, they will begin to think analytically about where their relationship is going in this area if nothing is done to change it. As they think about those prospects, they often come to a sense that they must consider how the situation might be changed.

• Fourth is a stage when the participants talk about the obstacles to moving in the direction they have chosen, steps that could be taken to overcome those obstacles, who might take those steps, and how those steps might be arranged in a practical process of political interaction that would have the possibility of changing the political environment and their relationships.

• Fifth, participants must ask what they might do outside the dialogue room. They do not often decide to work together as a group. They often decide to take what they have learned individually into their own walks of life. Sometimes they have ideas they would like to pursue to the point of action.

I do not argue that every dialogue follows exactly this pattern or that this is the only way of identifying the stages in the progression. My point, which I believe is broadly accepted, is that our understanding of interactive conflict resolution becomes more systematic if we can analyze its progression. Understanding the function of each stage also facilitates seeing its contribution to the open-ended political process that it attempts to influence. Conceptualizing it as a political process itself enables us to apply the process in very different situations.

Finally, one must recognize that any process of interactive conflict resolution takes place in an evolving social and political context. It reflects and can affect the unfolding dynamics of a conflict. One of the points quickly learned by those who think in terms of stages of a process is the importance of the time between meetings. An ongoing group will process together developments between meetings and will often state in some form their thoughts on the direction of those developments and on changing that direction. Just as participants interact with each other, the process interacts with the world around it.

EVALUATING INTERACTIVE CONFLICT RESOLUTION

A degree of skepticism about the significance of interactive conflict resolution continues to characterize the response of some policy makers to this work. In its most benign form: "It really doesn't do any harm and may even do some good, but the bottom line is that it doesn't make much difference." Thoughtfully: "People outside government don't have the authority to negotiate or the knowledge of the issues under negotiation; they can mislead parties in a negotiation." More directly: "Give me some proof of what they can accomplish." More caustically: "Do-gooders without knowledge of policy issues and stakes can do serious damage by meddling in work that belongs to professionals."

There is some wisdom in those concerns, but there is also wisdom in asking what the real obstacles to peace are. Are they only issues in formal negotiation or also relationships that block political approval or full implementation of negotiated agreements? Skeptics can find reason for their views, and practitioners of interactive conflict resolution can judge with justification that professional negotiators have not always demonstrated the capacity to make peace by their own efforts alone. This gives all of us serious interest in the question: How does one evaluate this work?

My starting point, as I have said, is that neither governments nor practitioners in interactive conflict resolution will have an adequate base for evaluation until they enlarge their framework for peace making and peace building. Governments need to fully embrace citizens who change conflictual relationships and build the practices and institutions of peaceful society. Citizens outside government need to add to their theories of conflict prevention and resolution thinking now evolving about the politics of building peaceful societies.

As with the definition of interactive conflict resolution, how one evaluates work such as this depends very much on the needs of the evaluator. Academicians and some funders, including government offices, have come to rely heavily on evaluation techniques designed by social scientists. Unfortunately, many of those evaluations do not tell policy makers what they need to know, and they often speak in a language not meaningful to policy makers. Governments and some academics tend to think of success as negotiating agreement. One must respect that different groups legitimately need responses to different questions and may find different frameworks consistent with the contexts within which they work.

In "Interactive Conflict Resolution: Theoretical and Methodological Issues in Conducting Research and Evaluation" (Chapter 8), Nadim Rouhana provides a social scientist's approach to evaluation. He helps break down this work into its components so that we can think more precisely about our methods, objectives, and achievements. His purpose is frankly stated: "To increase confidence in this approach to practice, establish its relevance for policy makers, and enhance its legitimacy as an academic field of study and research, interactive conflict resolution should be held to the same standards of scrutiny as other established fields. . . .

Theory-building efforts and research activity can also be channels for mutual enrichment among scholars from international relations, political science, social psychology, sociology, and other disciplines."

Although his first concern is primarily academic, Rouhana poses questions of concern to anyone using this approach: Does learning take place within a group? Is that learning retained by participants outside the group? Do they use it in political discourse and behavior? Perhaps most importantly, what impact does using new learning have on the dynamics of the conflict? Obviously, anything that social science researchers can say on these and the other important questions Rouhana raises will be useful to all.

We need to remember, however, that the policy maker's first concern is different from the academic's interest in establishing the legitimacy of an academic field: Will this add to our overall practical capacity in making and building peace? At the end of the day, both social scientists and policy makers are interested in whether an approach is effective in producing desired results.

The policy maker, however, starts from a point that differs in three significant ways from the scholar's starting point. First, a policy maker, as a consequence of developing a course of action, has a more exact idea of what a desirable practical result is and of what the steps toward that result are. Second, her or his main interest is in changing a situation, not evaluating the usefulness of one tool or another. Third, direct engagement in carrying out a strategy gives a policy maker a personal feel for whether a particular activity is supportive or destructive, which the scholar necessarily lacks.

In the idea of a multilevel peace process, the policy maker has a framework that is appropriate both to policy making and judging the contribution of any effort to deal with conflict. Its primary focus is changing a situation. Change can be seen, although the exact degree of credit for change may be as murky for the policy maker as for the scholar. The difference in the two points of focus is captured in a remark often attributed to Bernard Baruch: "We know it works in practice; I wonder whether it will work in theory."

Policy makers, like scholars, have a choice in establishing a framework for making and judging policy. For instance, they can focus on the official peace process—that is, on mediating an agreement to end violence. Or they can decide to work within a larger framework for peace making and peace building in which negotiating one agreement is just a stepping stone to work in societal change.

The multilevel peace process proposed in this paper provides a large framework that embraces both official and unofficial resources. A comprehensive policy-making process in such a framework will reflect thinking about three questions that encompass the whole political context in which the conflict must be dealt with:

- First, what is the problem? This is a period of diagnosis. Policy makers work within an analytical framework to probe (1) the causes of conflict, (2) the relationships underlying it, (3) its dynamics, (4) the main actors, and (5) the cultural and societal contexts. Policy makers have a choice between basing their analysis only on government intelligence and diplomatic reporting and reaching out to the analyses of groups outside government with intimate direct experience in the conflict that may not be available to government in certain circumstances. The criterion for evaluation is simply whether a particular source adds a perspective in defining the problem or adds to knowledge.
- Second, why do I really care and, given my interests, what must I try to do? How and how much one's own interests are hurt will determine the large strategic or operational framework within which policy makers decide how in broad terms they will tackle a conflict. Policy makers will have a choice between working toward an official agreement to end a specific conflict and broadening their strategy to include unofficial efforts to create conditions for changes in relationships and building the institutions of peace. The realism of a strategy will depend on knowing what others' interests are and how intensely they are felt. What can others add to my depth of understanding about where the real obstacles to change are? What can others contribute to building the relationships of a peaceful society?
- Third, what do I have to work with and what can I realistically try to do? In designing a tactical framework—a possible course of action—policy makers will identify targets and points of intervention, a method, purpose, and the way in which an action would contribute to overall movement toward peace. Policy makers have a choice between using only government resources and including nongovernmental resources in their action plan as well. They can judge what reaching beyond would add. As they enter the less well-charted terrain of building the practices and institutions that sustain peace they can ask unofficial groups to experiment with different approaches to produce models for replication.

If policy makers choose to include nongovernmental actors in their strategy and tactics, they will have their own criteria for judging what and how well a particular group can contribute. The simple criterion will be more widely defined than the scholar's: Can this group and its way of working enlarge overall capacity in ways that will help achieve what we need to achieve? Policy makers' achievements will ultimately be submitted to public judgment.

One other point needs to be made: it may be that the maturing of the field of interactive conflict resolution shifts the research questions. In the early days of interactive conflict resolution, it was appropriate to ask whether learning took place in single meetings or whether one could demonstrate that participants learned to talk differently or to work together. Today, a series of meetings is more common, and when, for instance, a group in Tajikistan (see below) produces and publishes 10 joint memoranda in 20 meetings, the answers to those questions are obvious. The tougher question is what the contribution to the overall peace process is; because it is difficult in any complex situation to assign a percentage of responsibility for an outcome, perhaps the policy maker's question—does this add to overall capacity?—is good enough.

SNAPSHOTS OF INTERACTIVE CONFLICT RESOLUTION

Since the purpose of this paper is to illustrate clearly how these dialogue groups work, I asked five colleagues each to respond to the following requests: (1) provide a first-person brief background on your work in this area, (2) describe an illustratively important moment or moments in that work that make(s) vivid what can happen in these dialogue rooms and workshops, and (3) reflect on how what has come out of those rooms has interacted with larger peace processes. The disadvantage of this approach is that it does not always provide a sense of how a group works through successive stages over time; the advantage is that it shows concretely what can happen and what the product may be.

The difference among these experiences makes an important point: in a multilevel peace process, rarely is one actor likely to make the decisive move; change will result from the cumulative interaction of many actors, sometimes at quite different levels. The issue is not whether a group "made peace"; even peace treaties do not "make peace" without the work of people changing and building new institutions and relationships. The issue is whether a group addresses an important problem, what insights it contributes, or what relationships it strengthens.

The differences also exemplify the variety of potential uses of this approach and take us back to the question: What is interactive conflict resolution and what does not "qualify"? Six experiences are described below:

• A small group of Israelis and Palestinians in the early 1980s gained insight into what gives legitimacy to negotiating partners in each body politic: "There's no one to talk to and, if there is, he or she is probably marginal." It would take the accumulation of many such experiences and other events over a decade to change conventional wisdom on this point, but it changed.

• A group of political leaders from opposing parties in Northern Ireland took advantage of meeting in a rare safe setting at a fruitful moment to crystallize together a bill of rights for Northern Ireland. It was as much the development of one more vehicle for broadening common ground both in negotiations and for a just society as it was a contribution to negotiation. But this group had the opportunity to take its document into the negotiations.

• An ambitious effort planned to last 15 years or more is establishing and proliferating dialogue groups across lines rarely crossed in the Middle East, creating sinews for new relationships in a deeply divided region.

• More than 20 meetings over six years from the midst of civil war in Tajikistan into the postpeace agreement phase have created "a mind at work in the middle of a country making itself." Absorbing and responding to the unfolding problems of their new country between meetings, participants defined their framework as a multilevel peace process. They took insights from the dialogue into their work, which has ranged from participation in negotiation and the quasi-official National Reconciliation Commission to founding both the Tajikistan Center for Citizenship Education promoting citizens' dialogue across regional barriers and a new Public Committee for Democratic Development to work on four tracks to embed practices of dialogue in Tajikistan civil society.

• A series of "psychopolitical dialogues" in newly independent Estonia brought together native Estonians and Russian speakers who thought they were targeted for expulsion after the Soviet collapse. Dialogue among influential citizens in both groups brought to the surface psychological obstacles blocking development of a peaceful working relationship. The work ultimately enabled small groups in three communities to design their own projects to demonstrate for wider replication practical ways in which the two national groups could work together locally, reducing tensions and improving the chances of living peacefully together.

• In Greek and Turkish Cyprus a program of training workshops in the skills of conflict resolution—first in each community and then together—rather than dialogue has gradually built a foundation for a growing network of relationships and dialogues across the line between the two communities. As in other places, training in conflict resolution skills has provided the occasion for bringing people together, but once they are together dialogue begins.

These cases illustrate the technical problem of defining interactive conflict resolution. In each case the exact approach varies with the moderator, the objective, and the situation. Even the vehicle varied. The last case in which training is used to bring adversaries together may not qualify for inclusion by precise definition, but starting by explicitly teaching a different way of relating has led in demonstrable ways to problem-solving interaction. Even in those cases in which government policy was a principal target, one could trace the impact in other parts of the political spectrum. Each is part of an ongoing and cumulative political process.

Each story below is told in the practitioner's own words for the sake of authenticity. The Tajik story is mine. I have signaled return to my own voice as this paper's author with the word "Comment." I will in those comments try to put the program described in larger context and reflect on the question of evaluation.

Israeli-Palestinian

For some 25 years, writes Herbert C. Kelman, professor of social ethics at Harvard University, my colleagues and I have been bringing together politically influential Israelis and Palestinians in an unofficial, private, confidential setting for direct noncommittal communication. These meetings—which we call problem-solving workshops—are designed to enable the parties to explore each other's perspective and, through a joint process of creative problem solving, to generate new ideas for mutually satisfactory solutions to their conflict. The ultimate goal of the enterprise is to transfer the insights and ideas gained from these interactions into the political debate and the decision-making processes in the two societies.

Until 1990 the workshops were all self-contained events. In 1990, Nadim Rouhana and I organized our first continuing workshop, in which the same group of highly influential Israelis and Palestinians met periodically over a three-year period. Since 1994, we have convened a Joint Working Group on Israeli-Palestinian Relations as an ongoing effort to explore options and reframe issues for negotiations on the final status of the Palestinian territories and the Israeli-Palestinian relationship. Our work has contributed to the peace process primarily through the development of the individuals, the ideas, and the political atmosphere required for productive negotiation.

One of the central issues on which discussions have focused from the beginning has been the availability of a credible negotiating partner on the other side—a question that reflected the dominant view in both societies that there was no one to talk to on the other side and nothing to talk about. Despite the Oslo accord of 1993, in which the Israeli government for the first time accepted the PLO as its negotiating partner and which fostered the growth of working trust between the two sides, the question of the existence of a negotiating partner reemerged with the election of

Benjamin Netanyahu. It arises whenever there is a setback in the peace process occasioned by rhetorical statements, unilateral actions, or acts of violence on one or both sides. By now, however, significant segments of the two political communities are persuaded that they have counterparts in the mainstream of the other side who, like themselves, are committed to a negotiated settlement of the conflict. Problem-solving workshops and similar Israeli-Palestinian encounters—within the context, of course, of evolving political and strategic realities—contributed to this change and thus helped pave the way for the Oslo accord.

In the 1970s and 1980s, workshop participants—even though they came with an interest in exploring the possibilities of a negotiated solution—were generally skeptical about finding serious negotiating partners on the other side. Much of the time was spent on testing the sincerity of the participants on the other side—their genuine commitment to peace. Once participants were persuaded of the sincerity of their counterparts, a new question arose: Whom do these people represent? Do they speak for a sizable, influential element on their side, or are they marginal within their own community? To be convinced of the availability of a credible negotiating partner, each side had to learn not only that there were people on the other side who were genuinely interested in finding a peaceful solution, but also that these people represented a significant, influential part of the mainstream of their own society.

At one workshop in the early 1980s this learning process was particularly prominent. After a day or so of mutual testing, the participants on the two sides seemed to be convinced that their counterparts were not posturing—that they were serious and sincere in their search for a negotiated solution. On the second day, during a discussion of the fundamental needs of each side that would have to be met if a solution was to be acceptable, the Palestinians stated that the PLO had to be accepted as the legitimate representative of the Palestinian people. After the two sets of needs had been described, the third party presented a summary of what it understood to be the basic needs expressed by each party. In summarizing the Palestinian needs, we formulated the Palestinians' remarks about the PLO in more general terms, reflecting what we thought was the underlying need that they were expressing: the need to be able to choose their own leadership and have its legitimacy accepted. The Palestinians, however, pointed out that our summary did not fully capture their needs because it made no explicit mention of the PLO. In insisting on this point, they were signaling to the Israelis both the central role of the PLO and their own identification with it.

The next day in a discussion of possible ways to overcome the constraints against negotiations, the Palestinians remarked that there would be no problem in getting to the table and reaching agreement if they were dealing with non-Zionist Israelis like the ones in the room. At that point the Israeli participants said that the Palestinians had misunderstood them. They insisted that they were loyal Zionists, enumerated their Zionist credentials, and linked their search for a peaceful solution to their commitment to Zionism. Thus, the Israelis clearly identified themselves with the political mainstream of their own society, as the Palestinians had done the day before.

What the two sides learned from these exchanges was that the members of the other party, whose sincerity they had tested and come to trust over the course of the workshop, were part of the mainstream in their community who fully identified with its national movement and ideology. These exchanges, in the context of the workshop as a whole, allowed them to draw a lesson with major implications for a potential peace process: negotiations between mainstream members of the conflicting communities—between Israeli Zionists and Palestinian nationalists identified with the PLO—are not only *necessary* if peace is to be achieved, but also *possible* because significant segments of each community had concluded that peace was in their own best interest.

Through the cumulative effect of direct interactions between politically involved and often influential Israelis and Palestinians in our workshops and other contacts, this understanding gradually entered significant strata of the political cultures of both societies. Meaningful negotiations would be impossible without the belief that there are credible negotiating partners on the other side who are sincere in the search for a peaceful outcome and able to mobilize the support of their constituencies. This belief—though not universally accepted and subject to fluctuation with every setback in the peace process—has now become part of conventional wisdom, but it took many years of mutual learning before it achieved that status.

Comment

This workshop was one of some two dozen over two decades that generated an "alumni/alumnae" body of 300 to 400, many of whom later assumed significant positions. Even that impressive group is only part of a numberless series of dialogues and other such interactions. One could study the roles of those who participated. Or one could trace the evolution of ideas in both bodies politic about the basic issues in the relationship; that is a different level of investigation than any proposed that I know of.

On a more practical point, I have judged the cumulative value of such dialogues as so significant that in beginning the Inter-Tajik Dialogue in 1993 I explicitly stated a strategy of trying to proliferate dialogues as a vehicle for offering citizens an experience in a way of relating that is consistent with the practices of peace and democracy. While one often cannot demonstrate exactly how ideas emerge from the shadows of dialogue to currency in a body politic, experience suggests that it is fair to say that repeated experiences of this kind can generate "ideas in the air" that change perspectives, both in government and outside. It can also model a different way of acting in society.

Northern Ireland

In December 1991, writes Joseph V. Montville, director of the Preventive Diplomacy Program at the Center for Strategic and International Studies in Washington, D.C., there was an unprecedented, if limited, breakthrough in the negotiation history of the Catholic and Protestant constitutional political parties of Northern Ireland. In a two and one-half-day unofficial track-two diplomacy problem-solving workshop organized by Harvard's Center for Psychology and Social Change and cosponsored by the Iowa Peace Institute, senior representatives of the Protestant Ulster Unionist Party (UUP) and the Democratic Unionist Party (DUP) agreed with counterparts from the Catholic Social Democratic and Labor Party (SDLP) on the desirability of a bill of rights for Northern Ireland. Representatives of the nonsectarian Alliance Party and the Workers' Party also joined the consensus.

In an example of track-two success being directly ratified in a track-one process, three of the participants returned to the official constitutional talks in Belfast, joined a subcommittee on the bill of rights issue and reported out an agreement on the desirability of a bill of rights for Northern Ireland. Since British policy on Northern Ireland was to accept whatever political arrangements a majority agreed to, Sir Patrick Mayhew, secretary of state for Northern Ireland, announced in 1992 the UK government's agreement in principle to such a bill of rights.

As one of the principal leaders of the UUP wrote to the track-two organizers, "You will be pleased to know that we achieved agreement on the first phase of a Bill of Rights for Northern Ireland. . . . I was personally involved on the Sub-Committee which dealt with the Bill of Rights as was [X] of the SDLP and [Y] of the DUP, and we were able to use our 'Iowa experience' to good effect." The assumption was that the agreement would be folded into the final constitutional arrangements. Nevertheless, the bill of rights agreement, in principle literally for a major change in the unwritten British constitution, *but in one region of the country*, was a distinct achievement.

From my own personal perspective, acknowledging many other influences, this accomplishment was partly the fruit of more than 10 years of work on Northern Ireland. Years of seminars at the U.S. State Department and Foreign Service Institute, a conference on Northern Ireland at Airlie House in Virginia, collaborative work with Cooperation North in the Irish Republic and Northern Ireland, and ultimately the founding of the Irish Peace Institute codirected by Limerick University in the republic and Ulster University in Northern Ireland formed the basis for success in Des Moines in 1991. This earlier activity was essential to help clarify issues and identify partners for a track-two strategy.

One of the most important of those early experiences was hearing Professor Paul Arthur lecture at an Irish Peace Institute meeting at Magee College of the Londonderry campus of Ulster University. He was brilliant and insightful on the dynamics of the Northern Ireland conflict, and he came to be the linchpin to the success of my track-two work. A Catholic from Londonderry, Arthur had gradually won the trust of senior Protestant party leaders in Northern Ireland. He arranged the introductions and attended the individual meetings with politicians in which the Des Moines invitations were explained, issued, and accepted. And he continued to be the source of tough-minded counsel up to, during, and after the Des Moines meeting. The knowledge, credibility, wisdom, and collaboration of such a person are incomparable assets to a track-two effort.

The official and public purpose of the Des Moines seminar was to provide an opportunity for the politicians to hear constitutional experts from other Commonwealth countries talk about their experiences with bill of rights provisions. Through ensuing discussions about the possible elements of a bill of rights for Northern Ireland, the politicians would discuss basic human rights for the majority and minority to ensure equality under the law. But careful facilitation opened the technical discussions over a draft bill of rights into more profound consideration of underlying psychological issues related to human needs and human rights.

While the process began in the workshop, it flowered during the "corridor time" that is so important to learning and trust building in track-two diplomacy. In Des Moines the corridor was actually a hospitality suite in the hotel where the Protestant and Catholic politicians stayed up talking into the early hours of the morning. The effect of this informal interaction became apparent in the comments of several politicians at the end of the meeting that the process was useful both educationally and as an opportunity for extended contacts among political persons.

A Catholic said it was a "sad commentary" on politics at home that "the most constructive work I have been able to do in politics has been at Airlie House, Grenoble, and Des Moines. I have had many more hours of meetings at Stormont (Government House Belfast) but far fewer hours of personal contact with my political colleagues. Track two is very helpful in working toward ultimate track-one success." A Protestant said, "the only chance I have to see [my Catholic colleague] is at track-two events. On no occasion at home can I find out what the other fellow needs—how to develop confidence builders for his, and my, constituencies. Because of the difficulties in Northern Ireland, I have always valued track two. It is now all the more useful as a precursor to a formal talks process."

Track-two work is vulnerable to many exigencies. In Northern Ireland schedules for official negotiations complicated planning for track-two meetings. Upcoming election campaigns are especially big obstacles. Nevertheless, insights gained in track two can become permanent investments in reconciliation processes. For example, one of the Protestant politicians most transformed by track-two trust building with his Catholic opposite numbers was promoted in March 1997 to a senior cultural/political office in his community.

Comment

This is a clear example of a literal track-two exercise providing space for those involved in official negotiations and politics to step away from those official responsibilities to consolidate ideas that seem ready to jell. Participants came together with a specific possibility in mind, and they did what was hoped for. But that achievement was deeply rooted in relationships and processes from prior experiences.

It is also an example of how limited official conversation can be in a tense political atmosphere where hard-line colleagues make wide-ranging conversation impossible and how space provided by a meeting like this frees individuals to speak more freely. It illustrates how a practical issue—in this case a bill of rights—will naturally lead to discussing deeper issues and experiencing potential relationships. Finally, it reveals how each path on which a practitioner works represents a cumulative complex of interactions whose implications one can never fully know.

Middle East

In early 1991 before the official Middle East peace process was regenerated in Madrid, writes John Marks, president of Search for Common Ground in Washington, D.C., we at Search established the Initiative for Peace and Cooperation in the Middle East. The goal was to set up an unofficial multitrack process that could complement, supplement, and, on occasion, anticipate official negotiations.

The original organizing metaphor for the Initiative was the Conference on Security and Cooperation in Europe (CSCE, now the Organization for Security and Cooperation in Europe). We used the CSCE model both to conceptualize what we planned to do and to convince others the project was workable. As CSCE had done in Europe, largely through official channels, we wanted to create a whole web of unofficial relationships across the Middle East, connecting the region by bringing together a wide variety of groups—retired generals, human rights activists, business executives, editors, conflict resolution specialists. Not only did we want the groups to engage in dialogue, we also planned for them to take on joint action projects. We even planned to encourage regional cooperation by publishing a quarterly newsletter to chronicle it, including examples organized by us, as well as by others across the region. We were not thinking of only organizing one or two conferences. We knew that CSCE had existed for about 15 years before East-West relations turned around. We anticipated our process would probably take at least as long.

After initial funding was secured,[6] the next step was to convene a meeting of what we called the Core Working Group—a gathering of innovative thinkers and doers. These Arabs, Israelis, Turks, and Iranians were to be at the heart of the process. We scheduled the first meeting for three days in Rome in September 1991.

We wanted to establish a forum in which the Middle Easterners would meet, not as adversaries but as colleagues who would work together on shared problems. We realized that the structure and the process of the meeting were likely to be as important as the substance of what was discussed, and we knew that we wanted to avoid, as much as possible, the win-lose polemical approach so common to the Middle East. Indeed, we were convinced that for the region to move toward peace it had to move toward nonadversarial, win-win ways of resolving its problems and that our meetings needed to approximate that model. In other words—to paraphrase Marshall McLuhan—the medium would become the message.

In the abstract it seemed like a wonderful idea. What we did not know at the beginning was: Would the initiative actually work? Would high-level unofficial Middle Easterners actually get involved—and stay involved?

We knew the meetings had to be exciting and productive. To achieve the desired results, we believed, expert assistance was needed—not only substantively but in running meetings and designing process. Members of our organization had experience with professional facilitation, particularly as it applied to organizational development and personal growth. We knew how corporations, on occasion, use facilitators to manage difficult meetings and strategic planning sessions. We also understood that professional facilitation, as distinct from having a senior person act as chair, is not a usual component of international gatherings. However, we thought that the singular quality of our vision for the initiative called for a new approach. We decided to bring in a culturally sensitive facilitator both to chair the proceedings and to consult on how to structure the overall process. We enlisted Marc Sarkady, a corporate consultant in the organizational development field who volunteered to work with us.

At the Rome meeting, participants were initially mystified about the role of the facilitator, but they quickly caught on. They came to see him as the guardian of a level playing field, particularly among Arabs and Israelis. When there was a breakdown in a meeting or when something was not understood or even when someone's body language indicated unhappiness, the facilitator spent considerable time setting things right. He explained concepts such as *active listening*, and participants started paying attention. At the end of the meeting, several attendees noted that they had never been at a meeting at which so much was accomplished, and they requested that future sessions include training in facilitation—which was subsequently done.

There were two unique aspects to the meetings. First, we included right-wing Israelis. Most other meetings of Arabs and Israelis had included dovish Israelis who reflected a limited perspective. One of the more memorable moments came when a hard-line Israeli reserve general was involved in a heated exchange, and a Lebanese participant walked over and put his arm around his new Israeli friend. Second, Jordanians and Arabs from the Gulf sat together with Israelis (and talked amiably in the corridors and over meals). While this has since become commonplace, it was revolutionary at the time.

The meetings were intense. Unlike most Middle Eastern meetings that participants had attended, people arrived on time, paid attention, and asked for longer sessions. There was remarkable frankness, a willingness to work through obstacles, a determination to try new ideas, and a commitment to results. Participants achieved sufficient bonding that they became a working group with shared aims. In the end they endorsed the overall concept of the initiative and agreed on a number of specific things, ranging from adopting a set of operating principles to forming a series of working groups.

There were wonderful moments. For example, the Israelis and Gulf Arabs discovered together that they shared some common ground: how to make sure that the U.S. government kept its promises. There was another instance after participants broke down into working groups and then returned to plenary. The civil society group recommended that the group, which included Arabs and Israelis, launch a campaign on certain basic human rights issues, preventing torture and protecting human rights activists. Arab and Israeli members of the civil society group agreed on common language and a common program of public action. However, the core group had earlier agreed to operate by consensus, so civil society participants needed agreement from the plenary group before moving forward. When they reported back, there were two initial dissenters—one retired Egyptian general and one Israeli general. Both used the same reasoning. They wanted everyone to understand that they opposed human rights abuses, but they thought that if the initiative got involved in human rights the region's governments would oppose all of its activities. Then a Kuwaiti who had recently been tortured by Iraqi captors declared with quiet passion that, if the initiative could not even take a stand against torture, he was not interested in being involved. He was supported by others, including an Israeli human rights activist. In the end the generals relented. They did not want to jeopardize the initiative as a whole and particularly its security working group. Other participants later noted that this was the first time they had seen Israelis and Arabs arguing on both sides of an issue—a breakthrough on its own terms.

Now, almost six years later, we are still building on the groundwork laid at that first meeting. The Lebanese who put his arm around the Israeli general has become one of Yasser Arafat's key advisers on the peace process. One of the right-wing Israelis played a similar role for Benjamin Netanyahu. Good personal friends because of the initiative and steeped in the *common ground approach*, these two men are in almost constant touch. Several years ago that same Israeli collaborated with a retired Jordanian general who also was an initiative regular to set up the first meeting between Netanyahu and the Jordanian ruling family.

There have been scores of meetings, workshops, trainings, and other gatherings since the first meeting in Rome, and the initiative continues to produce a range of achievements. Among others, it has sponsored unofficial talks between Israelis and Syrians on the Golan Heights for 18 months, which laid out a basis for an eventual settlement if and when that time should come; facilitated Swedish government sponsorship of unofficial *final status* talks held by key Palestinians and Israelis; sponsored jointly authored Israeli-Jordanian, Israeli-Palestinian, and Israeli-Lebanese papers on security issues that reached unofficial agreements, well before official talks reached fruition; sponsored the Middle East's only meetings and joint action projects for Arab, Israeli, Iranian, and Turkish human rights activists; established conflict resolution programs in Gaza, the West Bank, Lebanon, Egypt, and Jordan to teach mediation, negotiation, and problem solving; and regularly convened the Middle East's top editors and television executives to encourage support of the peace process and development of joint projects.

Comment

Like the peace process, this project is itself an open-ended political process. Obviously, careful attention has been given to establishing the practice of interactive thinking, talking, and working, but that work in the meetings themselves has been complemented on occasion by establishment of training programs in conflict resolution for broader audiences. Above all this broad effort to introduce a culture of interactive conflict resolution in a number of arenas is an example of how an open-ended process can begin on a highly professional level without the managers being able to honestly say exactly what their objectives are because those objectives are most realistically shaped by the participants.

Tajikistan

The Inter-Tajik Dialogue was formed in 1993 by a team of three Americans, including myself, and three Russians who had been working together since 1981 in the Dartmouth Conference Regional Conflicts Task Force. I have cochaired that task force since the beginning, first with a Soviet (Yevgeny Primakov) and now a Russian colleague (Gennady Chufrin). The "Inter-Tajik Dialogue Within the Framework of the Dartmouth Conference," as participants came to call themselves, has operated within the conceptual framework of the five-stage process described above.[7] As of July 2000, it had met 28 times .

The strategy explicitly stated in the first grant proposals was to see whether we could create a group from within the civil war that would develop the capacity to design a peace process for their country. We would create the space and help set the tone and the course of dialogue. They would define, pursue, and adjust the agenda. The question was what capacities for peace making and peace building such a group could develop and put into play. Our assumption was that such a group could play a significant role in developing a peace process where there was none, but at the outset we could be no more specific about our objectives. By definition the specific objectives would have to grow out of the dialogue.

The dialogue's experience in its first year reflected the role that unofficial dialogue can have in an environment where no official peace process has yet begun. (This could also be said of the Israeli-Palestinian meetings in the 1970s and 1980s.) In effect, governments stand back to see whether it is possible for two conflicting groups to work together. When the dialogue began, Tajikistan had been in the grips of a vicious civil war since the second year of its post-Soviet independence. Between 25,000 and 200,000 are said to have died, and one out of every seven Tajikistanis had fled from the towns and villages where they lived.

Toward the end of the dialogue's third meeting (August 1993), one participant said, "What we really have to work on is how to start negotiations between the government and the opposition on creating conditions for return of the refugees to their homes." Having identified this as a problem they needed to probe, they could not at that moment bring themselves to talk about assurances that each side would have to offer the other to make negotiation possible—government assurances for the safety of opposition leaders and opposition assurances that they would not use the negotiations to embarrass or undermine the government.

In the period between that third meeting and the next, participants reflected deeply on this problem and came to the fourth meeting in November 1993—just after Russian president Yeltsin's shelling of the White House—for a highly substantive discussion of the problem. One of the main obstacles to negotiation, participants said, was that the opposition was geographically dispersed and ideologically diffuse. "Who would come to the table?" asked progovernment participants. "How could we find you if we wanted to invite you? How would we deal with those who have blood on their hands?" While solutions were offered in the meeting, the real response to this problem came a month later when opposition leaders met in Tehran, adopted a common platform, and established an opposition coordinating center in Moscow. Two participants in the dialogue were signatories of the document, and four became members of the center's steering group. Did the dialogue produce that outcome? Presumably not by itself, but individuals informed in the dialogue participated.

At the fifth meeting in January 1994 those who had been in Tehran presented and explained the opposition's platform. Progovernment participants quizzed them mercilessly for two days. The opposition participants handled themselves tactfully and substantively. At the end of the meeting the progovernment participants said, "We will report this to our government. We think the basis for a negotiation exists."

Meanwhile, a United Nations (UN) emissary had been attempting to begin negotiations and won the agreement of the government three weeks after that meeting. Before negotiations began in April, participants of their sixth meeting wrote their first joint paper, "Memorandum on a Negotiating Process in Tajikistan."

Did the dialogue produce the negotiations? We cannot make that claim because we know that in any public decision many inputs are involved. Did participants in the dialogue play a role? Yes. Was it a significant role? The man who was foreign minister when the government decided to begin negotiations says the fact that the two adversaries could work together in the dialogue group through five meetings helped persuade skeptics that negotiation was possible.

Three years later in June 1997 a capstone peace agreement emerged from the UN-mediated negotiations. During those three years three dialogue participants were delegates in the official negotiations—one con-

tinuously. The peace agreement included a number of ideas that participants had developed in seven additional joint memoranda, all of which
were circulated to the negotiating teams, the UN mediator, UN headquarters, and the U.S. government. Again, it is impossible to know exactly
what role those memoranda played except to say that they put ideas "into
the air." It is probably accurate to say that those memoranda contain the
most coherent cumulative statement of the philosophy behind the multilevel peace process in Tajikistan. To mark the twentieth meeting of the
dialogue, participants published their first 10 joint memoranda in December 1997 in Tajiki, Russian, and English.[8]

With the beginning of negotiations in April 1994, the dialogue turned
its attention to thinking through a political process of national reconciliation for Tajikistan. On several occasions the mechanisms considered
proved useful in breaking impasses in the negotiations. One was reflected in the peace accord's establishment of a Commission on National
Reconciliation to oversee implementation of the peace accord through
four subcommissions. One dialogue member became chair of one sub-
commission and another became vice-chair of a second; two other participants became members of the commission. Another idea was acceptance
of establishing a transitional period in which changes in political relationships would take place.

Perhaps more significant, the attention of dialogue participants to a
political process of national reconciliation brought them to focus on steps
for bridging the dividing lines in the society opened up by the civil war.
They wrote one joint memo on the multilevel peace process and the need
for involving Tajikistani society at all levels. Two participants started
their own nongovernmental organizations. With the signing of the peace
accords, they identified their new goal as "identifying the obstacles to
democracy and civil society and ways of overcoming them." A first step
has been an effort to engage Tajikistani citizens across deeply divisive
regional lines in dialogues on the new political rules being shaped by
the National Reconciliation Commission. That has been the work of the
Tajikistan Center for Citizenship Education, formed by one dialogue
participant, and the Public Committee for Democratic Development.

Since the third year of the dialogue, university-based participants
asked the managing team to help them develop courses in conflict resolution and building civil society at five universities. Two workshops have
been held for some three dozen university professors and administrators,
a collection of readings mostly from U.S. literature was translated into
Russian, articles have been written in Tajikistan, and courses are being
taught. This is perhaps the best opportunity to embed the philosophy
reflected in the work of the dialogue in the structure of Tajikistani
education.

Comment

First, as with the Middle East initiative described above, the strategy behind the Inter-Tajik Dialogue was to see whether a group could be created from within a conflict to produce constructive results—in this case, developing the capacity to design a peace process for the country. That is quite different from an outside group going to a troubled area to mediate a peace agreement. It has been very much an open-ended process, with participants redefining their focus as the process of national construction unfolded.

Second, in terms of the five-stage process, we have learned that a well-established group will fall into a pattern of returning regularly to the second or third stage of the five-stage process to define or redefine the problem they need to work on in light of changing circumstances. They work through their deliberations, regularly producing a joint memo from each meeting.

Estonia

The approach of Vamık Volkan, founding director of the Center for the Study of Mind and Human Interaction (CSMHI) of the University of Virginia's School of Medicine, is unique in using a psychoanalytic lens to examine the deeper human dimensions of conflict. With colleagues at CSMHI, he writes, a methodology has been developed that aims to reduce ethnic tensions through unofficial psychopolitical processes as well as community and democracy-building activities.

We have come to call our approach the "Tree Model," for visual presentation and growth symbolism. The methodology begins with a psychopolitical diagnosis of the tree's "roots." Psychopolitical diagnosis does not replace a political assessment but rather adds to it through in-depth, psychoanalytically informed interviews that detect shared and often hidden perceptions, expectations, and fears. The interviewers seek to understand how psychological factors may interfere with making and carrying out rational decisions. Well beyond insights on an individual level, the ultimate goal of a psychopolitical diagnosis is to identify societal processes between groups that were initiated by trauma and conflict. It, too, conceives of itself as working through stages.

During the diagnostic period, key individuals from each side of the conflict are selected to participate in a series of psychopolitical dialogues that form the tree's "trunk." Again, these gatherings are called psychopolitical since they deal with both realistic political issues and emotional poisons. For example, in most conflicts the memory of a past trauma ("chosen trauma") becomes reactivated, and the expectations and feelings about the enemy of the past become condensed and focused on the enemy of the present; in a sense a time collapse occurs. One of the aims of the psychopolitical dialogue series is to create a time expansion that decontaminates past influences from current issues, allowing for realistic discussions.

Psychopolitical dialogue is a process. Once decontaminated of past influences, the participants themselves are able to make appropriate and helpful suggestions as to how to proceed, and more rational adaptive solutions begin to emerge. The point is to encourage absorption of insights learned in the dialogue series into actual political processes. A subgroup of the dialogue participants then evolves into a contact group (part of the tree's trunk) that becomes CSMHI's local partner in carrying out the dissemination of dialogue insights, community-building activities, and democratization initiatives. These actions and initiatives may be models of coexistence between communal groups in conflict, political work on actual peace processes, or the preventive "inoculation" against prejudices among children. These actions are the tree's "branches" that symbolize and promote positive growth.

Since April 1994, CSMHI has assembled an interdisciplinary team— two years in collaboration with the Carter Presidential Center—to conduct psychopolitical dialogues aimed at reducing ethnic tension in Estonia.

Through centuries of domination by other powers, most recently the brief but devastating Nazi occupation and the half-century incorporation into the Soviet Union after a short two decades of independence between the two world wars, the Estonians have maintained their identity remarkably well. Having regained their independence at the end of the Soviet period, they faced the challenge of consolidating their identity while a quarter of their population consisted of Russians mostly left behind by the Soviet withdrawal.

Those Russians had come to Estonia in waves over four centuries. They included the "old believers" who were escaping division in the Russian Church, those who fled the Communist Revolution, and a sequence of groups that came with the Soviet occupiers and stayed or were born of Soviet parents serving in Estonia. Their lives turned upside down with the end of Soviet rule. First, they faced the humiliation of falling from a position of political and cultural domination where they had forced Estonians to adopt the Russian language and had only rarely learned Estonian themselves. Next they faced understandably deep resentment from Estonians who had suffered the Soviet occupation, and they feared that the Estonians were determined to drive them out into a Russia that could not house or support them. To gain any chance of status, they would have to meet a stiff and sometimes erratically administered requirement to learn the Estonian language. When the dialogues began, tension was high between the two groups and Russia was threatening the use of its troops, which had not fully withdrawn, to protect Russians in Estonia.

The center's strategy was to use the dialogues to bring together prominent individuals from the two communities as well as from Russia into a space where they could begin to know each other and where the American team could help them examine the dynamics of their relationships. The objective was to gradually reduce the poisonous emotions between the groups and to spread new insights from the dialogue into the body politic. Through several of its participants, the dialogue was in close communication with the Estonian President's Round Table on Ethnic Minorities. Through the efforts of other participants who were community leaders and members of parliament, other international groups and countless Estonians, tensions were gradually diminished.

In each of the dialogues the participants were encouraged to share experiences that revealed their feelings about each other. Although subjects of discussion ranged from political to human, the most insightful moments came when exchanges enabled participants to bring to the surface their deepest emotions and mental constructs of their own identities as well as those of the other side. These discussions were supplemented by visits together to various "hot spots"—places such as cemeteries and former Soviet bases that evoked high emotion.

One Estonian told the following story:

> Let me tell you what is "integration" [the integration of Estonians and Russian speakers in Estonia]. When I was four years old, my family and some Soviet officers were "integrated." In our apartment we were forced to live in one room so that the Soviet officers could live in all of the other rooms. Furthermore, the new inhabitants of our home did not even bother to learn Estonian to communicate with us but wanted us to learn Russian and adopt the Russian culture. They brought their wives and children also, but they would not learn Estonian either.

Against that background, the dialogue work groups discussed the possible integration or assimilation of Russians in Estonia. Assimilation would mean an influx of more "enemy blood" that could weaken Estonian identity. "If more Russian blood mixes with our own, we would not stay as Estonian as we are now. We will be contaminated." Integration could also corrupt Estonian identity because Estonians perceived Russians as more "aggressive"—they would alter the Estonian way of life and make it more Russian. In a discussion of integrating Russian and Estonian children in kindergarten, Estonians recounted that they had heard of situations in which the "aggressiveness" of even a few Russian children in an Estonian class would result in all the children behaving in a "Russian" way and in Estonian children learning Russian on the playground instead of Russian children learning Estonian.

During a tour of Paldiski, a former Soviet naval base now mostly shut down with only a few Soviet soldiers guarding a nuclear reactor, we took aboard our bus an Estonian history teacher as a "guide." The once proud base looked like a huge garbage dump. When two Russian military officers in civilian clothes offered to come on the bus to give a briefing on the base, the Estonians said they were not welcome, since Estonia was independent and the base was now Estonian.

As we toured the base the Estonian historian listed one after another the historical grievances of Estonia, while the Russian dialogue participants on the bus listed "facts" supporting their "superiority" and previous "protection" of the "ungrateful" Estonians. I could sense an underlying feeling of humiliation and rage among the Russians, and I increasingly perceived the messy physical condition of Paldiski as a concrete symbol of relations between the antagonists. While on the surface the issue of Paldiski centered around who should be responsible for cleaning up the base, I saw a "hidden transcript" among the Russians present that I could translate as: "Since we Russians, the sons and daughters of a large and powerful country, are forced to dismantle our military might and retreat from Paldiski, we will leave behind our waste and hope that you ungrateful Estonians drown in it. At least we will force you to clean up our mess."

Meanwhile, I also heard in the Estonians' remarks a subtext beneath their position of being in no hurry to clean up the mess themselves, though they similarly claimed that they presently lacked the funds to do so. Comments from the Estonians reflected both their wish to elicit sympathy from the American group for their victimization under Soviet rule and their unconscious resistance to change their identity as victims. As long as Paldiski remained a dump, the Estonians had a concrete symbol of the suffering and injustice they felt they were subjected to by the USSR.

In 1996 the dialogues spun off three projects in communities where both groups lived in about equal numbers. These projects were designed to help citizens form their own joint nongovernmental organizations to improve relationships. One was built around a group of elementary school teachers who were organizing classes in Estonian for Russian children. Another was formed in a vandalized former Soviet army base where the remaining residents were almost without hope. They have organized community work projects, built a community center, and staged festivities aimed at improving self-esteem. The third focused on a fishing and agricultural community around the country's largest lake that had lost its Russian market. They began with small projects with the objective of gradually developing the recreational and touristic potential of the region.

Comment

More than any of the other examples, this one embodies the combined insights of psychoanalysts, historians, diplomats, and others practiced in work with citizens. With insights piled one on another and discussed among the Estonians and Russians, some of the tensions became more manageable. It is not that officials made policy to deal with these perceptions and misperceptions or the dynamics of relationships. The hope is that encouraging the creation of public spaces where systematic interaction brings them to the surface can provide opportunities for citizens to change relationships. These are opportunities that citizens outside government are much more likely to develop and work with than are citizens in government. Beyond this broader objective the three concrete projects are already being studied by other communities for replication.

Cyprus

Our work in Cyprus since 1991, writes Louise Diamond, president of the Institute of Multi-Track Diplomacy (IMTD) in Washington, D.C., has been a training-based systems approach to interactive conflict resolution. As such it has attempted to strengthen local capacity among Greek and Turkish Cypriots for facilitating their own intergroup dialogue, rapprochement, and cooperative action. It has also sought to enhance the culture and quality of discourse on the island as its inhabitants seek peaceful ways to manage their relationships, locally and regionally.

Although by 1991 there were several problem-solving workshops and other efforts at bicommunal dialogue,[9] contact in Cyprus between Turkish and Greek Cypriots was sporadic and uncommon, involving a small number of individuals and entailing significant personal and political risk. Our work was designed to grow organically, with separate meetings on each side of the UN buffer zone for nearly two years, in order to build trust with us as a third party and with the concepts and skills of the conflict resolution approach.

These meetings began as "getting to know each other" discussions with interested individuals and moved gradually to public presentations and then to short conflict resolution workshops as local partners expressed interest in learning more. The training was offered in response to a direct request to "put the tools of conflict resolution in our hands, so we can solve our own problems within and between the two communities."[10]

By 1993 the two sides expressed a strong interest in moving to bicommunal training activity, and the first major program of that nature was held in Oxford, England, in August, sponsored by the IMTD and the National Training Laboratory's Institute for Applied Behavioral Science. By 1994 the Fulbright Commission on Cyprus with funding from the U.S. Agency for International Development had adopted conflict resolution programs as a major initiative, and IMTD joined with the Conflict Management Group to form the Cyprus Consortium, which has since run nearly two dozen such workshops and related programs under Fulbright and other auspices. Several points are worth noting.

First, the initiative has achieved as much as it has partly because of an unusual degree of synergy among various players. The Fulbright Commission, backed consistently by the U.S. Embassy in Cyprus, brought in a series of full-time residential Fulbright scholars, who have provided the day-to-day, on-the-ground support and expansion of the program over the years. Other international players have been able to build on the increasing acceptability of such bicommunal programs to sponsor their own workshops in conflict resolution and other topics. The result of these overlapping initiatives has been a strong multifaceted bicommunal movement strongly supported by the international community with a committed core group and ever-growing numbers of local participants.

A second critical factor relates to the multitrack nature of the consortium's program and of the larger movement. The training events have been both generally and specifically targeted. People from many professions and walks of life have been included, and specific programs were offered to public policy leaders from political parties, the news media, and business; educators; journalists; students; and grass-roots groups. Thus, the skills, concepts, and new ideas coming out of these programs have been made available to a broad cross-section of the fabric of society on both sides in Cyprus.

The third significant element of the consortium's program has been the development of a strong and sustainable internal capacity for furthering the work. Three programs for training trainers have provided advanced training, mentoring, and supervised professional development to over 50 local trainers. These people are creating and managing their own bicommunal groups and projects, which now number close to 30, involving over 2,000 individuals on something of a regular basis.

The training workshops themselves, although each unique in form and content, combine skill-building and dialogue processes. In many cases these programs are the first time ever (or in decades) that the participants have had the opportunity to meet someone from the other community. Our basic format for the programs follows a five-stage conceptual framework that is generally consistent with the process that Saunders describes as his five stages of a public peace process.

1. We begin with *source*, exploring motivation and purpose for participating. This is the testing or trust-building phase.

2. We move to *quest*, where we explore individual and collective hopes and vision.

3. What Saunders refers to as "mapping the relationship" we address in a section about the *test*. Here the participants probe deeply into the interests, experiences, needs, and issues behind their positions, speaking freely about their concerns and feelings and hearing the same from the other side.

4. This almost inevitably leads to what we call the *shift*, where participants, as they gain new information and new perspectives about themselves, the "other," and the overall situation in Cyprus, find themselves experiencing a change of heart and mind about the relationship.

5. Finally, we address the *renewal* stage in which there is some examination of the opportunities and obstacles to moving forward and consideration of possible action, individually and collectively.

We have found that progressing through these general stages structures the program so as to allow for safe and progressive exploration of the authenticity of the experience of all parties and of the nature of the relationship among and between them. Since these explorations are coupled with skill building, the means for advancing the inquiry both inside and beyond the training room become conscious and available to all. The training workshops also include most of the elements associated by Saunders with an interactive conflict resolution process. They operate on a basis of collectively generated ground rules much like those described earlier in this paper.

Since it is difficult to determine the effect of any one of these workshops on the official policy-making process, we can report on the overall impact, as we can best understand it. There is both a cumulative and an expansive aspect to this—cumulative in that many participants move through several programs, advancing their skills and commitment, and expansive in that participants return home and share what they have learned with family, friends, organizations, and the public (through television, radio, seminars, workshops, lectures). Some specific outcomes that we can notice are as follows:

• Concepts and ideas from the training programs, including previously unmentionable or "taboo" topics, now appear in daily public discourse and even political campaigns.

• Bicommunal interaction has become normative, now involving thousands of people.

• Significant numbers of people in official and influential positions in both communities have participated in this training, thus spreading its effects into the top leadership strata and also providing a base of contact and trust between counterparts from each side.

• Many of the methodologies introduced in the workshops are being used in each community in various political and institutional settings.

• Communication between the different factions in each community has improved as new friendships and trust relationships have evolved across party lines.

• Bicommunal activities have mushroomed in quantity and scope.

• The people involved in these activities refer to themselves as a social movement.

• This movement is generating opposition, which suggests that those elements attached to the status quo or to a rigid view that allows for little exploration of creative ideas are feeling a significant threat to their entrenched positions.

• Specialized groups are exploring current and "day after" cooperative activities (e.g., lawyers, women, university students, psychologists, academics, private citizens, educators, business leaders).

• There has been significant development of conflict resolution as a human resource at home and abroad, with a number of participants going on to M.A. and Ph.D. programs in the field and with many participants being invited to share their expertise at international conferences and events involving other deeply rooted conflicts.

If one example could be used to demonstrate the effect of this work, it would be the events of August-October 1996. In August demonstrations by Greek Cypriot motorcyclists and responses by the Turkish side led to the well-publicized killing of two Greek Cypriot citizens in clashes in the UN buffer zone. In the aftermath of these events the political tension in Cyprus heightened dramatically. Talk of war was heard on the streets. All bicommunal contact was stopped.

In that climate the key actors in the peace-building movement were emotionally devastated and deeply discouraged. They were concerned that everything they had worked for was going down the drain and wondered how they should respond. They had been planning a special bicommunal fair for late September but assumed they would have to cancel it. However, the bicommunal Trainers' Group, with the assistance of then Fulbright scholar Benjamin Broome, undertook to turn things around. With patient person-to-person contact and invitations issued by the international community and diplomatic missions, the group managed to convene 300 people for a bicommunal reception in late September.

Coming less that two months after such a highly emotional and tragic reminder of the ongoing hostilities and potential for violence, this event proved a major rallying point for the forces of rapprochement, especially in the international community. The UN had decided to cancel its annual celebration day in October but was spurred to proceed by the success of the September meeting. In a new level of partnership and cooperation the Trainers' Group agreed to work with the UN to find the people for that event. Using its own citizens' network and building on the pool of trust, goodwill, and credibility generated by its work over the years, the group managed to convene 2,500 people—the largest such bicommunal event ever despite the August events. Following its achievement, other countries besides the United States and the European Union (EU) recognized the importance of such a movement, and the number of programs and sponsors swelled.

From that time until December 1997 the bicommunal movement entered a new phase. Cross visits became common, with people returning to visit their previous homes on the other side of the so-called Green Line that divides the Greek and Turkish areas, thus advancing the process of mourning and healing beyond the hardened formal political positions on both sides. Bicommunal groups continued to multiply in number and sectoral diversity. A new Fulbright Commission building was erected in the UN buffer zone to handle the increased demand for space for meetings. More specialized Fulbright scholars were hired. A new group of trainers was developed to manage the growing requests for groups. Contacts between Greek and Turkish Cypriot peace builders and their counterparts in other conflict situations (e.g., Northern Ireland, Israel-Palestine, South Africa) increased dramatically.

Then in December 1997 bicommunal activity was cut off following the Luxembourg decision by the EU regarding the accession of Cyprus to the EU and the relegation of Turkey to the third-tier "waiting room" for EU membership. Although subject to the changing political winds in Cyprus and the region, the momentum and presence of this movement are now, the consortium believes, so integrated into the Cyprus landscape after more than seven years as to be irreversible. The very existence of bicommunal programs and contact has itself become one of the political issues in each community and between the two sides and the various international and third-party actors who support this work as a matter of policy. A growing human infrastructure exists, providing momentum for peace building from the bottom up and offering an informal individual, group, and institutional capacity for sustaining a viable peace process should there be a nonviolent political settlement. In short, the training-based interactive conflict resolution program has grown into a significant social and political factor whose ultimate role in the peace process of Cyprus is still unfolding.

Comment

By the strict definition cited earlier, this training-based program might well not technically qualify as interactive conflict resolution. (That would probably also be true of some of the joint activities generated by Search for Common Ground's Middle East Initiative.) On the other hand, a number of organizations in the international community on Cyprus have recognized its achievement. And it does teach, if not formally conduct, a systematic process of bringing people together in dialogue. I have included this experience here to suggest the need for flexibility in policy making and in academic recognition that this kind of work may be defined more by the nature and quality of interaction than by the format of the meetings.

WHAT HAVE WE LEARNED?
THE CHALLENGES OF CUMULATIVE EXPERIENCE

First, the experience of 30 years has produced a significant track record for interactive conflict resolution. A growing body of literature on theory, practice, and case studies[11] justifies saying that interactive conflict resolution is a systematic, well-thought-through approach. The experiences described above and others like them demonstrate that it is widely tested and available for use in a variety of conflict situations. Such experiences cannot be dismissed out of hand.

Second, interactive conflict resolution is by definition directed at the work citizens outside government can do within the multilevel peace process. While I would not exclude its usefulness in any arena, it is increasingly fruitful as one moves across the political spectrum from those quasi-official situations—those in which the primary task is to develop analysis of conflict not available to government, provide a channel of communication where none exists, or find a particular solution to a problem in negotiation—on over toward those situations where the main task is to analyze the dynamics of relationships and design ways to work in the body politic to change them.

Third, the contribution of interactive conflict resolution increases as the capacities of government diminish. In other words, interactive conflict resolution can help fill a serious gap in the multilevel peace process— the gap left by state-centered thinking about peace processes. This gap, which is only beginning to be recognized, is the space where citizens outside government can work to change the relationships that must be changed if peace is to be sustained. Government desperately needs this addition to peace making and peace building.

Fourth, the experiences described above demonstrate that projects that "work" create a well-designed opportunity for individuals within conflict to develop the capacity to take responsibility for setting their own courses and for applying what they learn in their own ways. As their capacities increase, their incentive increases, because their sense of possibility increases. These are not just nice social gatherings or educational experiences—useful as they might be. Participants can define tasks and know when they have accomplished those tasks.

Fifth, the people whose lives are at stake will be the most authentic judges of the value of the approach to them. They will demonstrate that value by investing themselves in it, using it, and developing it. That must be regarded as significant evidence of its usefulness. Policy makers will judge what they do for its contribution to the multilevel peace process. In the larger political context the question for research is how what they do contributes to the unfolding of peace—to how societies change.

Sixth, policy makers are likely to have a more precise sense of specific objectives within the multilevel peace process than practitioners of interactive conflict resolution. If they have designed specific courses of action for a multilevel peace process, they will have concrete views about what needs to be done. They can see whether what needs to be done is being done. Practitioners of interactive conflict resolution can only know that secondhand unless they develop their own designs for the multilevel peace process.

Seventh, one of the reasons both officials and practitioners outside government have been imprecise about the specific relationship between actions and their contribution to peace is that both have worked in too narrow a framework. As I said earlier, most thinking about conflict resolution inside government and outside has focused on the official peace process; most conflict resolution theory has not focused on what needs to happen in civil society to make, build, and sustain peace. There will not be an adequate theory of conflict prevention, management, and resolution until it includes ways in which citizens change conflictual relationships and build the practices and institutions of living together peacefully. When the framework is larger, as in the framework of the multilevel peace process, evaluation will be less frustrating.

Eighth, in reaching judgments about how such work contributes to peace making and peace building, we must probably reach beyond the methods of present social science. We must accept the fact that in complex political situations exact cause and effect or the precise contribution of ideas may be unknowable in any measurable terms. How ideas emerge from the shadows to center stage and the role they play in changing the course of events may belong more to the history of ideas than to social science research methods. How citizens become engaged may be better understood by citizen activists.

INTERNATIONAL CONFLICT RESOLUTION: A VIEW FOR POLICY MAKERS

Ninth, policy makers could extend the reach of peace making and peace building by consciously seeking complementary ways of bringing both governmental and unofficial work under the same conceptual umbrella at the highest levels. They would accept a framework such as the multilevel peace process as theirs.

One vehicle for doing this was tried in the Tajikistani context. The Kettering Foundation brought together in Washington on three occasions representatives of nongovernmental organizations (NGOs) working in Tajikistan to develop a rolling draft of an experimental paper titled "Framework for an NGO Strategy for Tajikistan." The proposition was that, if each organization added capacity to make its project partly a vehicle for helping local people expand their confidence and capacity to manage their own organizations, the NGOs could—in addition to their primary humanitarian work—contribute to building the postconflict structures of peace on a local level. The results of the effort were passed on to the office of the UN High Commissioner for Refugees (UNHCR) in Tajikistan, which coordinated NGO activities, but UNHCR's mission ended shortly thereafter. But there are numerous ways that citizens inside and outside government could coordinate their approaches.

My point is that this work needs to be included in the policy framework at the highest levels—not be consigned to the bureaucratic level in functional agencies, though that is where it must eventually be managed. High-level policy makers must demonstrate that this work is important to them.

Tenth, one of the greatest challenges today is no longer how to conduct productive dialogues—an obvious challenge in the first years of the work—but how to move ideas from the dialogue room into practice over a wider field. This challenge will not be fully met only by closer collaboration between those who conduct the official and public peace processes; an even greater challenge is building an active citizenry and engaging it. The particular question is how to spread the experience of interactive conflict resolution that teaches people a different way of thinking, talking, and working together. One approach is to try to proliferate dialogue groups in conflicted bodies politic, much as happened over 20 years in the Israeli-Palestinian arena. An even more ambitious approach is to make this mode of interaction a regular part of the educational experience in school and college.

Underlying each of these challenges is the task of learning how to take fullest advantage of both the official and the public peace processes and the opportunities in their working together. It is to generate groups in conflicted communities that can become "minds at work" in the middle of communities making and building peace. Such groups can play leading roles in changing communities, able to absorb problems and events and respond to them on a continuing basis. Such is the task of making and building peace.

NOTES

[1]This perspective is more fully developed by Harold H. Saunders in *A Public Peace Process: Sustained Dialogue to Transform Racial and Ethnic Conflicts* (New York: St. Martin's Press, 1999).

[2]In addition to the Dartmouth Conference, which began in 1960, the United Nations associations of the United States and the USSR held a continuing series of meetings as did elements of the John F. Kennedy School of Government at Harvard University.

[3]The term "track two" was coined in an article by William D. Davidson and Joseph V. Montville, "Foreign Policy According to Freud," *Foreign Policy*, no. 45 (Winter 1981-1982), pp. 145-157. With track one as governmental policy, "track-two diplomacy is unofficial, nonstructured interaction."

[4]Ronald J. Fisher, *Interactive Conflict Resolution* (Syracuse, N.Y.: Syracuse University Press, 1997), p. 8.

[5]Christopher Mitchell, "The Progress and Stages of Mediation: Two Sudanese Cases," in David Smock, ed., *Making War and Waging Peace: Foreign Intervention in Africa* (Washington, D.C.: United States Institute of Peace, 1993), especially pp. 139-160.

[6]Initial funding was provided by the W. Alton Jones Foundation and the John D. and Catherine T. MacArthur Foundation.

[7]The five-stage process was first described in a publication by Gennady I. Chufrin and Harold H. Saunders, "A Public Peace Process," *Negotiation Journal*, vol. 9, no. 2 (April 1993), pp. 155-178. It is more fully described by Saunders in *A Public Peace Process*, op. cit.

[8]Gennady Chufrin, Ashurboi Imomov, and Harold H. Saunders, eds., *Memoranda and Appeals of the Inter-Tajik Dialogue Within the Framework of the Dartmouth Conference (1993-1997)* (Moscow: Russian Center for Strategic Research and International Studies, 1997).

[9]Such events were offered by Leonard Doob, John Burton, Herbert Kelman, Christopher Mitchell, and Ronald Fisher, among others.

[10]This request was made first by a Greek Cypriot man who had been involved in several previous bicommunal efforts. Throughout the early period of this work (1991-1993), this request was repeated by a growing core group of individuals who became the first Bi-communal Steering Committee. The request gradually became articulated as a desire to become "catalysts for change in Cyprus."

[11]Fisher, *Interactive Conflict Resolution*, op. cit., provides an excellent overview of these three decades of experience. Janice Gross Stein and Alan Alexandroff in "The Future of Canada Is Our Business: Citizen Engagement in Conflict Resolution," an unpublished paper written in 1996 for the C. D. Howe Institute, describe the field in relation to problems surrounding the threat of Canada's fragmentation.

8

Interactive Conflict Resolution: Issues in Theory, Methodology, and Evaluation

Nadim N. Rouhana

ollowing Fisher (1997), I use the term *interactive conflict resolution* to denote[1] "small group, problem-solving discussions between unofficial representatives of identity groups or states engaged in destructive conflict that are facilitated by [an] impartial third party of social scientist-practitioners" (p. 8). More broadly, interactive conflict resolution also refers to a field of study and practice that includes similar activities, the rationale for carrying them out, their short-term objectives, and their long-term impact on the dynamics of conflict.[2] I use the term problem-solving workshop—the main intervention tool of interactive conflict resolution—to refer to the specific activities carried out by third parties in the small group meetings between participants from societies in conflict.

Interactive conflict resolution's general goals are defined in terms of contribution—the nature and size of which are unclear—to the resolution of international conflict, particularly to ethnonational conflicts between identity groups. It is naive and misleading to consider interactive conflict resolution an alternative to the existing diplomatic and other means of conflict resolution. It is best conceived as a set of methods and activities that can be used by unofficial trained third parties in parallel to—not in lieu of—official efforts. As such, interactive conflict resolution faces a host of core theoretical and methodological questions. As an emerging field, in parallel to the expansion in practice and training, questions are raised about theories of conflict resolution that guide practice, methodologies used in research, and evaluation of interventions' impact on the macrodynamics of conflict.[3] To increase confidence in this approach to practice, establish its relevance for policy makers, and enhance its legitimacy as an academic field of study and research, interactive conflict resolution should be held to the same standards of scrutiny as other established fields.

This scrutiny will be expressed in three areas. First, programmatic attention should be focused on theory building that could guide the practice of interactive conflict resolution activities in the field; these activities should be anchored in theories of conflict and conflict resolution that delineate theory-guided goals for unofficial intervention in ethnonational conflict and variables that influence the achievement of these goals. Second, research efforts are needed to examine theory-driven hypotheses or to help theory-building efforts. This will require the development of methodologies for empirical testing of theoretical connections, practice-related hypotheses, impact of the intervention on conflict dynamics, the usefulness of various intervention tools to practitioners, and the comparative effectiveness of various approaches. Based on the accumulation of theoretically guided empirical evidence, the field can establish taxonomies of practice—descriptions of what methods work, in what type of conflicts, at what stage of conflict, and under what conditions. Finally, programs need to be developed that provide training in intervention techniques that are explicitly based on theoretical foundations and guided by research findings. The dynamic relationship among all three elements should help in strengthening the academic foundations of interactive conflict resolution and guide the practice carried out by its practitioners. It should also help provide a coherent basis for developing guidelines or standards of professional accountability.

Theory-building efforts and research activity can also be channels for mutual enrichment among scholars from international relations, political science, social psychology, sociology, and other disciplines. Increasing the relevance of practice based on this approach can open essentially needed channels of dialogue with policy makers and practitioners of other approaches. The inherent interdisciplinary nature of the field can provide scholars with a wealth of available theories and methodologies to draw on in the theory-building effort and in designing methodologies for empirical research.

In this paper I focus on what needs to be done to increase confidence in the interventions that practitioners of interactive conflict resolution advance and to enhance the field's relevance to policy makers and academic study with special emphasis on two issues. The first is the need to formulate, and to develop methodologies to examine, theoretical connections among current intervention techniques, microobjectives in the problem-solving workshop, and macrogoals of changing the dynamics of conflict. The second is to more explicitly conceptualize the long-term impact of interactive conflict resolution and possible ways for assessing specific effects, even though their direct measurement may be infeasible and their impact may be slow acting. In this context I note the inherent cognitive and motivational factors that increase the likelihood of overestimating the impact of interactive conflict resolution as well as ways to guard against such inclination; I also propose ways to increase the real impact of unofficial intervention—that is, the impact on the dynamics of the conflict on the ground.

METHODS AND OBJECTIVES IN INTERACTIVE CONFLICT RESOLUTION

The discussion in this section focuses on the three components of interactive conflict resolution and the relationships among them. These components are (1) the methods and activities that compose the problem-solving workshop, (2) the microobjectives of the problem-solving workshop in the contained setting of small group discussions, and (3) the macrogoals of interactive problem solving in terms of its impact on the relationship between the societies in conflict. The two main theoretical paths between these components are (1) the links between the methods and the microobjectives and (2) the links between the microobjectives, if achieved, and the macrogoals. Perhaps the most important conceptual task for interactive conflict resolution is to delineate the theoretical relationships between the intervention method that a practitioner uses, the microobjectives of the intervention effort, and how these objectives could contribute to macrogoals of conflict resolution. In this section I describe the three components and the two theoretical paths that should connect them (see Figure 8.1).

Deconstructing the Problem-Solving Workshop: Methods and Activities

The package of activities that the problem-solving workshop is composed of should be described and deconstructed to its basic elements. This would include a description of the agenda the third party designs for the workshop, the content of the discussions that take place between participants, the level of interaction among participants promoted by the third party, and the type of intervention the third party employs. A full description of intervention methodology should also include the rationale for and process of participants' selection and recruitment, the practical aspects of holding the problem-solving workshop, and assembling the third party.

Selection of the participants and the third party and some practical issues related to preparation for and conducting of the problem-solving workshop have been described elsewhere by some scholar-practitioners (e.g., Burton, 1987; Kelman, 1992; Mitchell and Banks, 1996; Rouhana and

**Activities Within the
Problem-Solving Workshop**

**Microobjectives of the
Problem-Solving Workshop**

**Macrogoals of the
Problem-Solving Workshop**

Examples of Activities

- Sensitivity training
- Training in negotiating
  techniques
- Training in conflict resolution
- Mutual examination of political
  needs
- Learning about political concerns
  and constraints
- Brainstorming about new
  political ideas
- Brainstorming about new
  solutions
- Writing joint concept papers

Examples of Objectives

- Increasing differentiation of the
  other side
- Improving interpersonal
  relationships
- Changing the enemy image
- Communicating political
  needs
- Reducing mutual stereotypes
- Arriving at deeper understanding
  of psychological conflict
- Reaching mutual understanding
  of political ideas
- Involving potential future leaders
  in interactive conflict resolution
- Producing joint concept papers

Examples of Goals

- Changing societal beliefs about
  the adversary
- Disseminating new ideas to the
  public
- Influencing decision makers
- Creating a sense of possibility
- Reconciliation
- Changing the climate of conflict
- Creating or increasing trust
  between parties
- Transforming the relationship
  between parties
- Changing the dynamics of the
  conflict

How intervention leads to the stated
(micro-) objectives

How microobjectives lead to macrogoals
of influencing the conflict dynamics

FIGURE 8.1 Three major components of interactive conflict resolution and the theoretical paths between them.

Kelman, 1994). But from the limited description given in the literature of the actual activities that take place in unofficial intervention efforts the problem-solving workshop became a kind of an umbrella rubric under which activities that differ in fundamental ways are included and levels of interactions among participants that are qualitatively different are promoted by various third parties. One way to understand the differences is to look at the levels of interaction in the problem-solving workshop that facilitators promote. Surveying the literature I found three broadly defined levels of interaction that I described elsewhere: intrapsychic, interpersonal, and intergroup (Rouhana, 1998).

On the intrapsychic level the workshop participants deal with their feelings about the other side and with intrapsychic conflicts in the form of anxieties, ambivalence, and threats to one's self-image. Issues such as healing of past psychological wounds and forgiveness of the other side as preconditions for reconciliation can take a central part in the discussion. Participants' awareness of their own unconscious intrapsychic conflicts regarding these and other conflict-related issues and their dealing with intense feelings toward the other side are also central to the group discussion.[4]

On the interpersonal level, interactions between participants focus on the "here and now" in the context of generalizations, stereotypes about the other group and group members, possible misperceptions of the other side, and attributional errors about the other's causes of behavior. Sensitivity training to avoid inadvertently hurting the other's feelings and training in human communications skills across the conflict divide are central components of the group discussion.[5] Although the group discussion of stereotypes and misperceptions has clear implications for intergroup relations, when the interpersonal level of analysis is applied, the interaction in the small group and its analysis are focused on the individuals themselves.

On the intergroup level, participants examine the dynamics of the conflict between the two societies and the collective needs and concerns that have to be met for a satisfactory political solution to emerge. Reference to the here and now of intergroup dynamics is only relevant to the extent that it helps participants understand the dynamics between the two societies at large. Taking the political realities into account, the thrust of the discussion is joint thinking about how to resolve the conflict between the two societies, with the specifics determined by the stage of the conflict. Improved communications, increased sensitivity, and mutual trust are not ends in themselves but are means to achieving a political goal: productive interaction about the intersocietal conflict issues that the participants are examining.[6]

The three levels of analysis are conceptually distinct and could indeed be addressed independently. In practice, too, the three levels are distinguishable, although it is quite possible, for example, that the inter-personal level might be intermingled with the intrapsychic level of inter-action. Or in unofficial interventions that focus on the political intergroup level, while some references to interpersonal interactions might occur, they would not be encouraged except insofar as their use enhanced dis-cussion at the intergroup level. For example, while the classical problem-solving workshop is designed to engage participants at the intergroup level, issues of interpersonal communications (group stereotypes, attribu-tions about the other side's behavior, and sensitivity to language used by each side) often get interlaced in the discussion but only as they contrib-ute to analysis of the conflict at the group level. Indeed, when participants expect the workshop to focus on political analysis of the conflict, they might find interventions that do not maintain the same level of analysis improper and may express their dislike for such interventions.[7]

In addition to the fact that problem-solving workshops can be de-signed to foster different levels of analysis, there is considerable variabil-ity in what practitioners actually do and to what extent what they do is similar. For example, it is not clear what tools are used, how active and directive the third party is, what the agenda is that the third party pre-pares, or even what participants are invited to do. Yet some general description of the role of the third party is provided by some scholar-practitioners.[8] For example, third parties can prioritize different levels of analysis even in the same workshop design. While Rouhana and Kelman (1994) emphasize the intergroup level focusing on structural political is-sues, d'Estree and Babbit (1998), working in the same framework, empha-size the importance of personal experiences and self-disclosure, emotional expressions, and the ability to recognize relational issues in interpersonal interactions in the problem-solving workshop. It is also possible that some practitioners use more than one level of analysis in the same problem-solving workshop and a combination of various activities such as prob-lem solving, negotiation simulation,[9] and lecturing (Gutlove et al., 1992).

Thus, one item on the conceptual and research agenda is to demystify the package called the problem-solving workshop by simply describing what it consists of in as much detail as possible. There should be enough elements described that other practitioners or scholars can recompose the problem-solving workshop for purposes of research, replication, or use. Whatever analogy is used to help describe the group dynamics in the problem-solving workshop—for example, mediation, negotiation, thera-peutic process, or any small group dynamics—scholars and practitioners should be able to specify a more concrete set of activities that are transfer-able to other practitioners and replicable in other similar contexts by oth-ers.[10] Practitioners should also be able to present some analysis of the dynamics that take place among the participants and the role of the third party in directing these processes (e.g., Rothman, 1992; Rouhana, 1995b; Saunders and Slim, 1994).

Defining the Microobjectives of the Problem-Solving Workshop

The problem-solving workshop is the means of unofficial intervention that the third party uses with the implicit or explicit goal of introducing change in the dynamics of a conflict. The participants are the third party's conduits to the desired change. So far, within the broad problem-solving workshop methodology, the target of change and the conduit of intervention in the conflict are assumed to be the participants' views (not the third party's) and some assumed activities that they can potentially undertake. Thus, on the microlevel the immediate objective of the intervention is some change in the way participants view the conflictual relationship and the future relationship with their adversary, and perhaps some activities the participants can undertake (by design or not by design), that can bring about some change on the macrolevel, that is, in the dynamics of the conflict on the ground. Therefore, practitioners should be able to define the intervention's (micro-) objectives in terms of what changes they want the problem-solving workshop to bring about in the participants and what activities, if at all, they want the participants to undertake. In other words, if the problem-solving workshop is conceptualized (and defined as precisely as possible) as the independent variable (or more realistically a set of independent variables), practitioners should be able to define and describe their dependent variables and formulate a set of hypotheses about the relationship between the independent and dependent variables. Practitioners should be able to explain what changes they expect in the participants and/or what outcomes they want the workshops to achieve.

The dependent variables, or the objectives of many unofficial intervention activities, when extracted from published reports fall into four categories: psychological, such as forgiving the other and achieving psychological healing; interpersonal, such as reducing mutual stereotypes, attitudinal changes, improving interpersonal relationships, and establishing personal relationships across the divide of the conflict; political, such as changing participants' views about the conflict through mutual learning about the other side's political needs and political constraints and having participants create new ideas for solving particular problems between the two sides; and educational, such as training participants in conflict resolution logic and tools or integrative negotiation strategies. Not surprisingly, the first three sets of objectives are related to the three levels of interaction between participants that various problem-solving workshops promote, as described above.

Defining the Macrogoals of the Problem-Solving Workshop

The third major component of interactive conflict resolution is the goal or set of macrogoals that the unofficial intervention activity is intended to achieve. Problem-solving workshops are designed to influence the dynamics of conflict, even if in minor ways. Putting aside, for the moment, the difficulties of validating such influence, interactive conflict resolution should at least be able to articulate the goals of unofficial activity in terms of the intended impact on conflict dynamics on the ground.

Surprisingly, the goals of the problem-solving workshop are most often left undescribed. Except for the original work of Burton and his colleagues (Burton, 1986; Mitchell, 1981), in which the goals were defined as reaching a solution to the conflict and relaying it to decision makers (who, in that model, would have designated the workshop participants), most other approaches leave the goals undefined or most general. Thus, conflict resolution, or the more modest goal of contribution to the resolution of conflict and changing the dynamics of conflict on the ground, are frequently stated as the goal of unofficial activities. When it comes to the details of contribution, its nature, what exactly in the dynamics of the conflict on the ground is expected to change and through what mechanisms, or the estimated strength of such contribution, most unofficial interventions have little to say.

Without clearly predesignated expected outcomes and reasonably established means (both theoretical and empirical) to explain how these outcomes could be achieved, unofficial intervention is doomed to the status of double marginality: it will neither be taken seriously by policy makers and practitioners of the official diplomatic track nor will it succeed to become established as an academic discipline. It is to the theoretical paths that unofficial interventions need to establish between intervention and outcomes that I turn next.

Theoretical Path 1: How the Intervention Leads to the Stated (Micro-) Objectives

Practitioners and scholars of various approaches need to formulate the linkages between the particular methods they use and the objectives they define for their unofficial intervention. How, for example, would the chosen levels of interaction among participants and the intervention and facilitation of the third party lead to a stated set of objectives? Or, if the objective is to sensitize people to negotiation strategies or to expose them to conflict resolution methodologies, how, at least theoretically, could these "dependent variables" be traced to the particular activities in the problem-solving workshop? Thus, for example, training participants in negotiation methods could be described as one class of independent variables in certain problem-solving workshops (see, e.g., Gutlove et al., 1992, and Diamond, Chapter 7, this volume). Similarly, if one of the objectives were to get participants to think jointly of new ways to resolve a particular conflict-related issue, it would be necessary to show which activities and methods in the problem-solving workshop lead to such an objective. If healing and forgiveness are the objectives, practitioners will need to specify the tools and methods they use in order to achieve those ends.

An explicit theoretical connection of activities in the first component, the problem-solving workshop itself, to the set of dependent variables specified in the second component will help researchers in this field amass a set of testable hypotheses each of which can be examined by using the appropriate research design and methodology.[11] Consistent with conventional scientific practice, the connection between the dependent and independent variables will have to be anchored in theoretical grounds, thus encouraging researchers to critically examine and/or develop appropriate theories for supporting these connections and to use theories and scientific findings from adjacent fields. This scientific effort will enrich the field both methodologically and theoretically.

Relating the variables in the first and second components and explicitly stating theoretical hypotheses that connect the two present a major part of a research agenda that researchers and scholars in conflict resolution, from different disciplines, should pursue in order to begin establishing an empirically demonstrated set of theoretical and empirical connections between the methods they use and the objectives they seek. Establishing such connections would provide practitioners with tested tools for practice and training and would bolster confidence in interactive conflict resolution intervention, not as a handful of artful techniques or a magic set but as a set of methods that are theoretically founded and empirically validated. These connections lend themselves to a variety of research methods that are described below.

Theoretical Path 2: How the Microobjectives Lead to Macrogoals of Influencing the Conflict Dynamics

Perhaps the most difficult task that scholars and practitioners of interactive conflict resolution face is demonstrating how the objective they designate for their problem-solving workshop, if attained, can lead to the change in conflict dynamics they seek to achieve—in other words, how the variables in the second component of interactive conflict resolution are connected to variables in the third set. For intervention in history it is difficult to achieve a level of clarity in explaining social and political change as mandated by standard models of social science, especially because relationships of cause and effect are hard to demonstrate as

Saunders (Chapter 7) argues and for other reasons elaborated on by Stern and Druckman (Chapter 2). Yet this difficulty should not become an excuse for dismissing the question or the propriety of the social science framework within which the question is raised.[12] At a minimum, scholars and practitioners have to explicate the theoretical or conceptual relationships between the two sets of variables and produce a set of hypotheses on how the objectives of their problem-solving workshop can affect the dynamics of conflict. While demonstrating such connections empirically is not always attainable, producing clear theoretical connections is a minimum requirement without which the whole field of interactive conflict resolution risks becoming an empty exercise with little theoretical foundation and scientific value. It is also important, when possible, to produce indicators that can be used by scholar-practitioners to help evaluate these connections, such as the extent to which a connection is anchored in a solid theoretical foundation, empirical finding, or even common sense. Even if the hypothetical connections are not demonstrable by standard empirical research, their theoretical value could be judged by other scholar-practitioners.

Scholar-practitioners should be able to present their own theoretical connections depending on their disciplinary training, insights, or experience. When stated in the form of testable hypotheses, such hypotheses should, to the extent possible, be subjected to empirical tests. If that is not possible, other scholar-practitioners and policy makers will be in a position to evaluate these connections; offer their own analyses to support them, modify them, or challenge them; and decide for themselves whether interactive conflict resolution is a worthy effort.

A number of examples can serve to explain this point. As mentioned above, some interventions include elements geared toward training participants in the methodology of negotiation, and other interventions seem to include elements of "training" in various methods of conflict resolution. Others focus on improved communication, promoting understanding, establishing and/or strengthening interpersonal relationships, and lowering tension, anger, fear, or misunderstanding by humanizing the "face of the enemy" and giving people direct personal experience with one another (see, e.g., Diamond and McDonald, 1991). Similarly, Montville (1986, 1990) calls for more emphasis on psychological analysis, such as the examination of victimhood, mourning, and forgiveness. It would be necessary for any theory of conflict resolution to delineate the connections between these objectives (if met) and the goal of contributing to conflict resolution between parties on the ground, articulated in most specific theoretical terms. It will be left to other scholar-practitioners to evaluate (empirically and/or theoretically) whether achieving the objectives contributes to conflict resolution in the delineated ways.

To explain this last point, consider, for example, the problem-solving workshop that has been conducted for many years by Kelman and his colleagues on a one-time basis (Kelman and Cohen, 1976; Kelman, 1992) and later by Kelman and Rouhana on a continuing basis (Rouhana and Kelman, 1994). The objectives of the one-time workshops were defined in terms of having the participants understand the political needs and constraints under which each party operates. A major objective of the continuing workshops was defined in terms of jointly creating new ideas based on the needs of both parties and to have these ideas disseminated by the participants to upper-echelon leaders and constituencies; the goals were defined in terms of interjecting new political insights, acceptable to the mainstreams of both societies, into the political discourse of both parties. However, the potential impact of such goals on the dynamics of conflict is left unevaluated. Whether some of the ideas are really disseminated remains to be shown and to what extent they leave a discernable impact on the dynamics of conflict, even if they are, must be further explained. Kelman (1995) argues that the problem-solving activities he carried out over the years have contributed to the Oslo accords, which some consider as a breakthrough in Israeli-Palestinian relations, through three mechanisms: "development of *cadres* prepared to carry out productive negotiation; the sharing of information and the formulation of new ideas that provided important *substantive input* into the negotiation; and the fostering of *a political atmosphere* that made the parties open to a new relationship" (p. 21, italics in source). Although there is no clear empirical evidence to support these claims, once the theoretical connection is hypothesized, it will be up to practitioners (as well as participants) to decide whether the objective designated by an approach is valuable and whether the theoretical connection with the political goal delineated by the scholar-practitioners is sufficiently valid to be worthy of their effort.

Explaining why achieving the objectives of the problem-solving workshop is important depends, to a large extent, on one's theory of conflict. Given the range of conflict theories developed in various disciplines and the varying levels of analysis used to explain the development and perpetuation of international and ethnonational conflicts (see, e.g., Levy, 1989; Singer, 1969), it is imperative not only to articulate the goals of a problem-solving workshop design but also to anchor the goals in these or other theories of conflict. This task is achieved by identifying the theory's key causal variables and explaining how the workshop's objectives affect these variables and, accordingly, the dynamics of the social or political conflict.

Whatever the theory of conflict, the goals of intervention depend to a large extent on the stage of conflict and perhaps the type of conflict under consideration. One can divide the stages of conflict into three broad categories: prenegotiation, negotiation, and postnegotiation. The goals of interventions, and accordingly the objectives of the problem-solving workshop and the type of participants to be selected, depend, to a large extent, on the stage of conflict. There is no one problem-solving workshop that applies to all conflicts, at all stages, and for all goals. A major question that the research agenda should answer is that of which methods work, in what type of conflicts, at what stage of conflict, and under what conditions. A theory-driven taxonomy of interventions is needed to answer such a question (Rouhana and Korper, 1999).[13]

ASCERTAINING THAT INTERACTIVE CONFLICT RESOLUTION ATTAINS ITS MICROOBJECTIVES

As described above, one way to conceive of the political contribution of the problem-solving workshop to participants is the opportunity it provides for acquiring new ways of analyzing the conflict. This is achieved by learning about the dynamics of the conflict as perceived by the other side, their collective needs and fears, their political constraints, and the social and political dynamics that drive the conflict. This learning is a prerequisite for joint problem solving to take place in the workshop, for new ideas to be jointly generated by the participants, and for these ideas to be disseminated to the public with conviction. Thus, if the problem-solving workshop is to achieve its declared microobjectives, participants should leave the meeting with important learning about the other side, the range and depth of which depend on the exact objectives of the method and the success of the particular intervention effort.

For the change in the participants and the generation of new ideas to make any impact beyond the contained setting of the workshop, two additional objectives must be achieved: (1) the learning and the new ideas should be retained beyond the workshop setting and (2) the learning should also be used and the new ideas disseminated.

In summary, for interactive conflict resolution to achieve its microobjectives, three conditions are required: (1) participants should leave the meetings with new learning, (2) they should retain the learning when they return to the conflict arena, and (3) they should use it in their political discourse and behavior.

Does Learning Take Place?

Learning about the other side can be conceived in terms of increased differentiation of the other side's politics and society, increased cognitive complexity about its political needs and concerns, and increased human-ization. This learning lays the groundwork for joint problem solving and joint generation of new options.

Differentiation

The homogeneous perception of the outgroup, even in the absence of conflict, is a well-established cognitive mechanism in the perception of others (Linville et al., 1986). Such homogeneity is typically exacerbated in conflict conditions, which promote psychological processes that essentialize and homogenize the other. Increased differentiation of the other side and expanded familiarity with the range of political thought and social forces are immediate achievements of problem-solving workshops. In many cases participants learn about the diversity of the other party's political thinking, social forces, political structures, and the range of political perceptions and analyses of the other side.

The unique strength of this learning process is that it takes place first hand, directly from the other side, without the mediation of experts from one's own party. The interactive aspect adds to the powerful impact that this learning might have on the participants. Having participants who are motivated to learn about the other and have the capacity to process com-plex (political) information provides two essential conditions for serious analysis of information (or what is known in social psychology as the central route to information analysis; see Petty and Cacioppo, 1986; Kressel et al., 1994).

Given the unique character of this learning process, its political func-tion should not be underestimated, particularly for the party with less available resources to study the other. But even for the party that has resources, learning about the other side through the other's own eyes is of unique value.

Cognitive Complexity

In addition to differentiation of the other side, participants learn about the vital political needs, political constraints, and political fears and con-cerns of the other. The dynamics of conflict and the nature of its discourse limit the opportunity for the needs, concerns, and constraints of the other side to be fairly presented to one's own group. Awareness of one's own needs and constraints often engulfs the political cognition of partisans in such conflicts.

Exposition to the other side's needs in the careful process of a prob-lem-solving workshop, which often have the mutual understanding of vital human needs on the top of the agenda, introduces participants to new and important political data. Based on familiarity with the other's needs, it is possible that participants' cognitive complexity (Tetlock, 1984, 1986; Tetlock et al., 1984) will increase when thinking about the problem that faces both sides. Participants may then recognize the needs of the other group and perhaps try to incorporate them in their analysis of the conflict and their thinking about possible and desirable solutions. These changes can promote integrative approaches to reaching an agreement.

Humanization

Learning about the other side in the ways described above can contribute to a process of humanizing the other side by recognizing its human political needs and the forces that operate in its society. In addition, the interpersonal contacts that take place in the setting of a problem-solving workshop increase the likelihood of this process. Many workshop participants, however, choose to participate in these activities after having already engaged in the process of humanizing the enemy long before their participation.

Generating New Options

If the learning described above takes place, it might be possible for participants to generate new ideas and options to approach the conflict. According to Needs Theory (Burton, 1990), for example, ethnonational conflicts are over basic human needs. Therefore, in order for an agreement to stand a chance of acceptability by two groups in conflict, it will have to respond to the basic human needs of both groups, such as security, equity, and recognition. Mutual learning facilitates the generation of such agreements. The goal of intervention will be, correspondingly, to disseminate new ideas and insights (or even agreements) that reflect the basic human needs of both sides. Depending on the stage of conflict, the problem-solving workshop will be designed to generate such ideas and insights and to introduce them into the political discourse.

Interactive conflict resolution does not provide empirical evidence that the objectives described above are achieved, although the literature provides some anecdotal evidence. Conceptualizing the objectives is only the first step in the scientific inquiry into whether interactive conflict resolution attains its microobjectives. Theoretically based hypotheses should be developed to link interactive conflict resolution activities that various methodologies use with the objectives, and empirical research should provide the means of examining these hypotheses. These issues are examined below in the section on research and methodology.

Is Learning Maintained Outside the Contained Setting of the Problem-Solving Workshop?

The impact of a problem-solving workshop on the dynamics of conflict is assumed to be achieved through the impact of the participants on others. For participants to influence others, they should maintain the learning they acquire in the workshop and use it over time (in unspecified ways to be examined below) to influence the dynamics of the conflict between their communities.

Before examining how the learning is used, it would be important to determine whether changes in views last beyond the contained setting of the meetings. The idea is to examine whether the learning that is expected to take place generalizes from the insulated climate of the meetings out into the reality of conflict when participants go back to their home environments and, perhaps, whether they use their learning to analyze new events in ways they would not have done without the workshop experience.

It is certainly possible that deep insights that participants gain in a problem-solving workshop will last and be used in the analysis of new conflict-related events and that therefore participants will incorporate what they learned into their political discourse. However, it is also possible that a process of "unlearning" might take place when participants return to their natural conflict setting and are reexposed to continuing conflict-related incidents without the advantage of having them explained from the other's point of view—a major benefit of the problem-solving workshop. It is not at all clear that insights gained about the other side's ways of viewing events can generalize to the analysis of new conflict-related events, nor is it clear that participants have the motivation to do so. The dynamics of protracted conflict (see Rouhana and Bar-Tal, 1998) provide a psychological climate that is not conducive to maintaining such new insights. Conflict dynamics promote both cognitive (such as selective perception) and motivational processes (such as the motivation to see oneself in a positive light) that help perpetuate the conflict or even escalate it (Jervis, 1976; Rubin et al., 1994; White, 1984) and that therefore make it difficult to maintain such learning. Furthermore, conflict-related events that dominate the national agenda, and which are analyzed constantly from one point of view, provide ample opportunity for unlearning whatever insights the problem-solving workshop provided.

Indeed, our work gives a strong basis for believing that the process of learning that takes place in a problem-solving workshop does go through at least some unlearning outside the workshop and that some relearning is often needed if participants meet again for another workshop. For example, in the continuing workshop that brought together a

number of high-ranking Israeli and Palestinian participants for a number of years (Rouhana and Kelman, 1994; Kelman, 1997) and the joint
Israeli-Palestinian Working Group on Israeli-Palestinian Relations in
which a group of Israelis and Palestinians have been meeting periodically for more than three years, there were signs in each meeting that
insights gained in previous meetings could not always be used by participants to analyze new events, particularly when the relationship on
the ground witnesses intense mutual negative interactions.

In summary, learning retention cannot be taken for granted in a conflict climate. It can be examined in a number of ways in the context of a
continuing and evolving conflict as described below.

Do Participants Use Learning in Their Political Discourse and Behavior?

For the problem-solving workshop to have political impact the participants must use the learning they gained in their political behavior.
They should share some of their learning with others in their communities. Potentially, and depending on their access and influence, participants can share their new learning with decision makers and political
leaders, or they can share it by writing, giving speeches or interviews to
the news media, or in other interactions with members of their own group.
To what extent participants share these educational outcomes with others
is a question that research on interactive conflict resolution should try to
answer. In some approaches a major criterion for recruiting participants
is their ability to disseminate learning through a variety of means (such as
heads of think tanks, senior journalists, leaders of grass-roots organizations, former high-ranking officials, senior academics, and so forth).

Indeed, for some intervention methods the dissemination of learning
is central to the rationale of the problem-solving workshop. For example,
in Kelman's (1979, 1986) work and Rouhana and Kelman's (1994) work,
the selection of participants is central to the unofficial intervention effort
precisely because participants are selected who occupy positions from
which they can disseminate some of the new ideas they are expected to
develop in the workshop and to decision makers and bodies politic.

It is quite possible that workshop participants do share some ideas
with both leaders and publics in their communities. Indeed, there is good
reason to believe that participants, particularly high-ranking people who
work together on a continuing basis, will share some ideas with others in
their communities. However, it is also possible that the conflict climate—
which is often charged with emotions against the other and is less permis-
sive of expressing empathetic views toward the adversary—deters participants from expressing their new learning in public or sharing it with

others. The conflict climate helps create a set of social norms that do not favor expressing conciliatory views or engaging in conciliatory actions and establishes contingencies of reward and punishment for deviating from these social norms. Many participants will be hesitant to speak in a way that shows understanding for their adversary for various reasons, not the least of which is being accused of siding with the enemy, betraying their community's cause, becoming marginalized, or being delegitimized. Thus, even if participants retain the new learning and decide to share it with others, they might modify the way they present their insights in order to make them acceptable to others in the conflict climate, but in the process of both "packaging" the new insights and adding qualifications the insights lose much of their potential effectiveness.[14] Because of these conflicting pressures on participants regarding dissemination of learning, the issue of using new learning should be a priority in the research agenda. Participants' public political discourse can provide valuable research material in this regard.

DOES INTERACTIVE CONFLICT RESOLUTION ATTAIN ITS MACROGOALS?

While examining the objectives of the problem-solving workshop seems at least conceptually to be a forthright task whose achievement depends on the appropriate use of standard social science methodologies, examination of the macrogoals faces a number of major challenges. First, there is the lack of conceptual clarity as to the nature of the expected impacts and how they follow from the objectives of the problem-solving workshop. These objectives are defined in terms of changes in the participants that the scholar-practitioner would like to achieve, but the larger goals of the intervention relate to changes in the conflict dynamics that are often not clearly delineated by the scholar-practitioner, except in most general terms, and whose theoretical connections to the objectives of the problem-solving workshop are left uncharted.

Second, the goals of interactive conflict resolution are often confused with official diplomatic intervention goals that are defined more sharply in terms of bringing parties to the negotiation table, ceasing hostilities, or reaching agreements, depending on the stage of conflict. Unrealistic goals and unsubstantiated claims by scholar-practitioners only exacerbate this confusion and increase the likelihood that the same yardstick used in official intervention will be applied to evaluate unofficial intervention. Third, even if the theoretical connections between objectives and goals are delineated and the desired changes in the conflict dynamics are defined, examination of their achievement is most difficult because the expected impact on the dynamics of conflict between ethnonational communities is too diffused to be assessed using standard research methodology or a traditional evaluation framework.

It is against these three challenges—lack of clarity about goals, the absence of theoretical connections between objectives of the problem-solving workshop and the desired effects on the conflict, and the evaluation of impact in terms of demonstrable achievements—that questions about the utility of interactive conflict resolution have been raised by some diplomats and scholars.[15]

As a beginning to responding to the first of these challenges, the goals of the problem-solving workshop should be defined depending on the stage of conflict, the nature of the conflict, and the particular dynamics of the conflict. With regard to conflict stage, in most general terms, before negotiations between the parties begin, the goals could be defined in terms of creating visions of peace that are acceptable to both communities and that can support dynamics for bringing parties to the negotiation table. In a negotiation stage the goals could be defined in terms of contributing to the achievement of an equitable agreement that can lead to just and stable peaceful relations between the two sides; and in a postagreement stage the goals could be defined in terms of supporting dynamics that can sustain peaceful relations. But the goals are also inextricably related to the theory of ethnonational conflict that one works with. Once the conflict stage and the conflict theory are incorporated into the goals of intervention, objectives that are theoretically guided to lead to these goals can be designed and participants who can help in achieving these goals can be selected.

These are broad definitions that will have to be fine-tuned. For example, as progress from one stage of conflict to another is nonlinear, in a negotiation stage the conflict could go through a number of phases: progress, stalemate, regression, progress, and so forth. Similarly, in a prenegotiation stage the conflict could be in a phase of complete absence of legitimized contact between political elites or in a phase where contact is legitimized but not formal. Because the goals differ at different stages, the relationship of goals to these substage fluctuations would need to be examined more closely.[16]

Once the goals are defined, the question becomes one of whether the microobjectives, even if achieved, lead to the foreseen impact. In other words, even if the ideas were successfully developed in the workshop and new insights were learned, and if these ideas and insights were retained, used, and successfully disseminated (i.e., the best-case scenario), are the macrogoals achieved, and how can the impact of learning and generating new ideas be measured? The effect of the participants' learning on the dynamics of conflict is far from linear, nor is it the same for all participants in a given workshop. But it can be hypothesized that if participants share some of their learned differentiation, complexity, and humanization, this learning will have similar effects on some audiences as it had on them. For example, it is possible that some learning that takes place in one problem-solving workshop will be shared when it is publicly or privately used by a participant (knowingly or unknowingly) in analyzing new conflict-related events. Or if participants share their learning in the form of new beliefs or new information about the other side, this may contribute to changing recipients' attitudes toward their adversary or about the desirable form of relationship with the adversary. Social-psychological research offers empirical evidence about the importance of changing beliefs and of gaining new information for changing attitudes (Ajzen and Fishbein, 1980). Changed beliefs and attitudes can contribute to a public climate that is more receptive to political agreements with an adversary.

Do new ideas have a chance of being accepted by the publics and the elites? To what extent do they influence the dynamics of the conflict interaction and through what mechanisms? Answers to these questions lie in the complex nature of the process of social change, which defies the linear thinking of the standard social research methodologies.[17] Accordingly, interactive conflict resolution could have a slow but dynamic and potentially important impact through a number of effects that characterize social change but that are hard or even impossible to measure.

CONCEPTUALIZING THE IMPACT OF INTERACTIVE CONFLICT RESOLUTION: PLAUSIBLE EFFECTS[18]

The impact of interactive conflict resolution should not be conceived against the goals determined by official diplomacy, such as reaching agreements between adversaries. Hoffman (1995) suggests that an unofficial intervention should be viewed as one initiative in a wider context of ongoing processes in which the effects of various efforts are dynamically interconnected. Similarly, Kelman (1992) argues that the objectives of unofficial intervention are different than those of formal international mediation. It contributes to creating an environment "that makes conflicting parties more ready to enter into negotiations, to bring the negotiations to a satisfactory conclusion, and to transform the relationship in the wake of a political agreement" (p. 69).

The impact should be conceived in terms of more complex and dynamic processes that reflect certain desired changes in a larger process of change in the conflictual relationship between the two societies. Impact in this context is not only unquantifiable using standard "hard-nosed" methodologies but also hard to conceptualize. But even if it is impossible to demonstrate definitively most of the effects that are hypothesized to constitute the ultimate impact of interactive conflict resolution, the analytical task of conceptualizing these effects and of anchoring them in theory is not irrelevant.[19] To the contrary, given the empirical difficulties, the theoretical delineation of plausible effects of the problem-solving workshop are essential in order to give the scholar-practitioner a handle on the theoretical evaluation of such efforts. Furthermore, although largely unmeasurable, some methodologies can be used to study the nature of some of these effects and even to assess their occurrence.[20]

The Exploratory Function

The contained and controlled climate of the problem-solving workshop allows for examination of how acceptable the ideas of one side are to participants from the other side—a function that becomes an integral part of the workshop activity and the effect of which is hard to measure or even identify. Throughout the process but particularly in the stage of joint thinking, participants present suggestions to deal with difficult conflict-related problems. By using the interactive process, participants learn that some of their ideas might fail to respond to or may even thwart vital political needs of the other side and what they need to do (including modifying their ideas) to make them acceptable or at least politically possible. They can examine the sources of objection and explore means to overcome the objection.

The exploratory function is important because participants themselves learn new insights about how the other side thinks about these issues. It is also important because it is possible that some participants can informally examine some of these ideas with policy makers. In a prenegotiation stage, when direct contact between the parties is not available, the problem-solving workshop can, in principle, fulfill a different exploratory function: it is possible that participants in prior coordination with policy makers can use the context of the problem-solving workshop to probe the acceptability of some ideas to the other side.[21]

Participants can also probe ideas that they develop in the problem-solving workshop with other politically influential colleagues and examine with them the political value and viability of these ideas. In a continuing workshop participants will be able to bring back the evaluation of others in their community and continue an iterative probation process that can improve further the ideas they examined earlier.

The Innovation Function

Once participants formulate new ideas acceptable to both sides, they can be instrumental in introducing those ideas to the political discourse in their political communities. They can share ideas with policy makers and political elites through their participation in seminars, professional and journalistic writings, speeches, and so forth. The potential for these ideas to be accepted by the respective publics is always in question, yet three factors may increase the likelihood of their acceptability. First, the ideas are presented by the participants themselves, who are usually credible members of their respective societies—and credibility of the source has been demonstrated to be an important factor in persuasion (Hovland and Weiss, 1951). Second, participants can present the ideas with some authority because they can say that they know from their own contacts with participants on the side that these ideas are acceptable to many people from the other society. This adds to the authority of the source and the credibility of the ideas. Third, participants can explain that the ideas are based on the political needs and concerns of both sides, which strengthens the rationale for adopting the ideas and for seeing greater possibility that any formal agreements linked to those ideas has the potential to contribute to an enduring peace.

Until now there has been only anecdotal evidence of these innovation mechanisms, such as the observation that participants engage in dissemination of ideas to various publics, including higher echelons of political elites. They often present the ideas and say that they are acceptable to the other side and quote their own experience (within the ground rules of confidentiality, i.e., nonattribution to specific individuals in the workshops).

The Legitimization Effect

The problem-solving workshop can have an important indirect effect, depending on the stage of conflict, by legitimizing problem-solving activities between adversaries.[22] The mere existence of the activity can, therefore, under some circumstances be a contribution. For example, in a prenegotiation stage a problem-solving workshop can contribute to a political climate that legitimizes meetings between adversaries. Often contacts are not legitimate, or even legal, for one side and sometimes for both sides.

Prior to the peace process between Israel and the Palestinians, Israel rejected the idea of negotiating with the Palestine Liberation Organization (PLO) and for Israelis to meet with the PLO representative was a violation of Israeli law. At the same time Palestinians sought recognition of the PLO by Israel. In meetings between high-ranking Israelis and Palestinians (Rouhana and Kelman, 1994), Palestinian participation was conditioned by having the explicit approval of the PLO and having a PLO member as a participant. For the Palestinians, whose position at the time called for direct negotiation between Israel and the PLO, such participation provided political gain. For many years left-wing Israelis had been meeting with PLO representatives, thereby giving some legitimacy to talking to the PLO. But the participation of high-ranking mainstream Israelis increased the legitimacy effect. Indeed, the PLO representative met within the context of a problem-solving workshop with Israeli Knesset members, a former ambassador, and a future minister in the Israeli cabinet. Although confidential, the meetings were not secret and it was the responsibility of the participants to get the political clearance they needed and to report about the meetings to policy makers. Once open channels of negotiation between Israel and the PLO were established, the participation of a PLO representative was no longer a political condition for Palestinian participation.

The legitimizing effect works by gradually accustoming the public to these kinds of meetings and by increasing the political options for the parties, so that if negotiation with the other side is to be held officially the unofficial meetings would have contributed by preparing the public for such possibilities and reducing the intensity of opposition.

The Accumulation Effect

Interactive conflict resolution can contribute to changing the dynamics of conflict by gradually accumulating public opinion in favor of negotiation or a negotiated agreement. Conflict has the powerful impact of unifying societies at a time of open confrontation with the enemy. But when the possibility of negotiating with the enemy emerges, deep division in the society may surface.

One effect that interactive conflict resolution can have on the dynamics of conflict is to bolster the forces that favor negotiation. The "dialogue industry" that mushroomed between Israelis and Palestinians before the Oslo process may have strengthened the hands of the Israeli government in pursuing open negotiation with the PLO. Political and intellectual elites from the Israeli left and the Labor Party, who by then had participated in the hundreds of meetings organized over many years in many parts of the world (particularly by European institutions), introduced to some segments of the Israeli and Palestinian elites a new way to view the other side. Perhaps the accumulation of so many participants tipped the balance in a divided society in favor of negotiation. This repertoire of support could have made it possible for the Israeli government to make the daring step of negotiating with the PLO at a time when its strategic interests favored such a step. There is no evidence to support the argument that these meetings themselves pushed the Israeli government to take these steps. Strategic considerations related to the continued confrontation with the Palestinians on the ground and the weakening of the PLO in the aftermath of the Gulf War, as well as international changes after the fall of the Soviet Union and the emergence of the United States as the hegemonic power in the area, together played a major role in moving the

Israeli government to consider such an option. But once the possibility emerged for negotiations with the PLO, the potential contribution of the accumulated repertoire of support was there to be taken advantage of.

Although the move toward the Israeli-Palestinian negotiation could provide a good example of this potential effect, it should be noted that this conflict, for a variety of reasons beyond the scope of this paper, received unprecedented attention in many international circles. The European Community, in particular, has been involved in a steady effort to organize meetings between Israelis and Palestinians (which continue until now in different forms), a phenomenon that many in the region call the dialogue industry. It is not clear whether other conflicts could have received the same level of attention and resources to make such an effect potentially possible.

The Clarification Effect

The in-depth analysis of political issues that the interactive conflict resolution makes possible, particularly when workshops between the same participants are held on an ongoing basis, gives participants (and third parties) good understanding of what is possible and what is not in the existing structure of power relations. It shows the boundaries of agreement between the two sides and the margins of disagreement. It can also provide participants with an understanding, based on comprehension of the other side's political needs, of the contours of agreements that are acceptable to the other side and the extent of possible concessions.

When discussions get specific and participants focus on conflict-related issues in detail, the problem-solving workshop can help define more precisely the zones of agreements and disagreements on each issue. Problem-solving workshops can try to bridge the gap between the two sides and therefore demonstrate the extent to which problem solving can reduce differences between the parties as well as the areas that cannot be bridged.

Such analysis provides an important understanding of the conflict issues. The joint analysis has the potential to provide the parties, particularly the third party, with valuable insights about the general shape of an agreement that would be agreeable to both sides. The dissemination of such analysis can introduce into the public debate valuable information and joint insights that can be examined, improved, or modified. It can also give formal negotiators on both sides useful information about what the areas of disagreement are on important conflict issues and what tradeoffs are possible. These insights can be even better used to increase the potential impact of interactive conflict resolution.

The Preparatory Effect

The accumulated effect of interactive conflict resolution activities can increase the mutual familiarity with the other side in many areas: political concerns, social and political structure, sensitivities to language, and so forth. A broad understanding of these issues can become most useful when an official process of negotiation starts. Interactive conflict resolution could contribute to a political culture of the political elite that is familiar with the other. This familiarity can help establish a smoother negotiation process. It is even possible that people who participate in a problem-solving workshop will take part in policy-making decisions or in think tanks involved in producing policy recommendations about managing conflict or negotiation with the other side. In this case familiarity with the other side's political landscape can be a major asset in contributing to better understanding.[23]

Continued meetings between participants create a network of communication, albeit limited, across the divide that participants use in their various activities. Thus, participants can and do call on each other for participation in conferences, meetings, and journalistic interviews. These networks can become a useful preparatory infrastructure for future structural cooperation between the parties after an agreement is achieved.

The Latency Effect

The problem-solving workshop is designed with the idea of providing participants from both sides equal power at the meetings themselves. This is reflected in the methodology of considering the political needs of each side equally when thinking about new ideas for resolving the conflict. However, the power equality in the problem-solving workshop cannot ignore the power relations on the ground. The ideas developed in the workshop, therefore, while not reflective of the power asymmetry on the ground, cannot ignore it either. Many ideas developed in such a context could be used as the foundation for equitable agreements, but on the ground they are not usually acceptable to the party that has more power because they do not fully reflect the power asymmetry in its favor.

However, this is not to say that these ideas have no use at all. In addition to their educational value, once they enter the political discourse about the conflict these ideas have the potential to maintain a latent effect, even if they are initially dismissed. They can become useful for either party when the structural power between the two parties changes for whatever reason (military balance, demographic change, external pressure, or change in leadership). The changed power relations can become the proper context for ideas developed in interactive conflict resolution to be available in the right time—an investment that pays off. This is why Alexander George (personal communication, 1997) calls this potential contribution of interactive conflict resolution a capital investment in political ideas. The unique value of these ideas, which increases the chances of payoff, is their foundation in both sides' political needs and their development by participants from both sides in a context that is less bound by power relations than the negotiation context. However, as the investment analogy suggests, the return could be nil, or the ideas may eventually be lost if too much time passes without any progress.

The latency effect of ideas developed in the problem-solving workshop can become relevant for both decision makers and publics. Not only could changes in the structure of power relations render new ideas more relevant but also the climate of the conflict such as a hurting stalemate, or its opposite, improved climates, brought about by internal or regional changes. Dismissed, for example, in the context of open violence or gross power asymmetry, these ideas can become more acceptable in the context of negotiation or as a basis for negotiation.

The value of the investment is very hard to measure. But it is clear that one can think of numerous circumstances under which such an investment will be wasted. However, it is also possible to think of political circumstances that can make use of such ideas and that will need ideas to be available for use to advance relations between conflicting parties. The circumstances that control the value of the investment fall completely outside the contained limits of the problem-solving workshop.

RESEARCH AND METHODOLOGICAL ISSUES

Mapping the theoretical connections between intervention methods, objectives, and goals serves not only to clarify theoretical assumptions but also to guide the research agenda. By the nature of the theoretical paths outlined above, the research agenda will require multiple methodologies that social scientists can use, depending on the question they ask: survey research, interviews, archival research, discourse analysis, limited ethnographic studies, and controlled laboratory and field experiments. Indeed, the interdisciplinary nature of the field could be utilized effectively if the proper disciplinary research methods are tailored to the various questions that scholars and practitioners from different fields raise.

Attaining and Retaining the Desirable Change

The field of conflict resolution, as practiced, does not actually have a broad range of techniques to offer the scholar-practitioner. Because the problem-solving workshop is the single most important format that the field of interactive conflict resolution has developed, it is the focus of the research agenda. Therefore, the first theoretical path outlined above, that which connects the elements of the problem-solving workshop to the various objectives it is designed to achieve, becomes a major item on the research agenda.

It cannot be assumed that any "package" of the potential elements that can compose the problem-solving workshop will achieve the objectives designated by the scholar-practitioner. Even the most simple goals, such as achieving change in stereotypical attitudes, cannot be taken for granted or assumed to occur just by bringing parties in conflict into contact with each other. Nor should it be assumed that any activity of contact between adversaries is better than no activity, a widely held assumption in the field. Indeed, the social-psychological research points to strict conditions under which contact between members of adversarial groups should take place if attitudinal change is to be achieved—such as equal status of the participants, institutional support by both sides in terms of lending social legitimacy for such contacts, common goals for all participants, and interdependency between the two sides (Amir, 1976; Hewstone and Brown, 1986; Stephan, 1985). Furthermore, it is not clear that problem-solving workshops geared toward a goal of changing stereotypes are of use to all parties at all times, regardless, for example, of the power asymmetry between the parties (Rouhana and Korper, 1997). Similarly, the history of reported meetings between adversaries indicates that sometimes the opposite of the desired goals could occur, as critics of Doob's intervention in Northern Ireland claim. (See report about the intervention and the ensuing controversy in Doob and Foltz, 1973, 1974; Boehringer et al., 1974; Alvey et al., 1974).

The refinement of intervention tools and the establishment of a repertoire of activities to be used in the problem-solving workshop require empirical examination of the elements in the problem-solving workshop and the methods of third-party facilitation that lead to the intended outcomes. By using experimental research methods it will be possible to examine hypotheses connecting some elements of the workshop package of activities with intended outcomes, to compare various methods of intervention, and to test and compare the effectiveness of various third-party intervention techniques (for a similar approach to negotiation, see Druckman, 1993).

There are, however, serious limitations to the possibility of using experimental methods when conducting real-life intervention in ethnonational conflict for practical reasons (such as using control groups) and ethical considerations (such as using the participants for experimental purposes). From a practical point of view, in order to carry out an experimental study it would be necessary to compare the experimental group—

the group that participates in the problem-solving workshop—with a control group (or a number of control groups) that does not receive the same intervention or that receives no intervention at all. It would also be necessary to have the participants in the experimental and the control groups drawn randomly from a broad pool of potential participants and then randomly assigned to the experimental and the control groups and for the third-party facilitators to be kept in the dark as to the purpose of the study. In addition, research tools such as questionnaires before and after the intervention can constitute a serious intrusion into the intervention process that raises awareness about the questions of concern to the researcher; furthermore, many participants will resent the idea of being used as experimental subjects. The intrusion also introduces a sense of artificiality into the intervention, which itself reduces the likelihood that the intervention will contribute either to the participants or to the larger goals of conflict resolution.

There are also serious ethical considerations against using experimental designs, such as assigning participants to control groups, using participants as subjects, and the inevitable deception involved in keeping the goals of the experiment from participants. In addition, there might be a violation of confidentiality—as all information about the workshops will become a public record—which many problem-solving workshop organizers see as essential to the process.

Although interactive conflict resolution is not inherently conducive to experimental studies, such studies are not impossible to conduct. For example, simulated conflict situations can be used with student populations (as done, for example, by Druckman et al., 1988), as is the case with other experimental designs in social sciences in the academic context. A second approach would be to conduct field experiments with high school and university students on real-life conflicts and interventions, such as using field studies in the tradition of Sherif's (1967) classical conflict studies. It would also be possible to conduct studies using quasi-experimental designs (Campbell and Stanley, 1963; Stern and Kalof, 1996) that employ unobtrusive measures or measures that are minimally intrusive to the intervention process (such as observing and recording the extent of social interaction between participants from opposite sides).[24] Both the field experiments and the quasi-experimental studies in the context of real social and political conflicts are essential for attaining the external validity that laboratory and survey studies lack. More effort is needed to validate the effects that the laboratory studies demonstrate in the natural settings of conflict.

For each of the ways described above, consider the following hypothetical example. Think of the independent variable as the primary activity carried out by the third party in a problem-solving workshop. Compare the following four classes of activities: (1) facilitating the presentation of the political needs of each party, (2) sensitivity training, (3) examination of issues of forgiveness, and (4) training in principled negotiation. Design an intervention for each activity that takes two sessions of one and one-half hours each. Consider a list of possible objectives as dependent variables: cognitive complexity in thinking about the conflict, acceptability of the other side's political needs, changes in stereotypes about the other, willingness for reconciliation, and ability to reach an integrative agreement. It is possible to design experimental studies to examine the effectiveness of the various interventions in achieving the designated goals and in comparing which of the interventions is more effective in achieving which outcomes. It is also possible to examine more directed hypotheses based on theoretical foundations, such as that mutual examination of political needs will increase cognitive complexity more than sensitivity training. Such a hypothesis could be anchored in the social-psychological research on cognitive complexity (Tetlock, 1984, 1986; Tetlock et al., 1984).

Experimental and quasi-experimental designs allow for the examination of hypotheses that are generated by and anchored in the social-psychological literature, theories of negotiation, and theories of conflict resolution. The studies could be fine-tuned to examine hypotheses about learning that takes place in problem-solving workshops and changes in participants' attitudes and cognitive styles, to compare the effectiveness of different methods in reaching agreements (Cross and Rosenthal, 1999), to examine questions about third-party perceived neutrality and bias (Arad and Carnavale, 1994), to identify which third-party interventions are most useful to achieve the designated objective, and so forth.

Carrying out research by using simulations and field studies, although tedious and resource intensive, should provide scholar-practitioners with empirically validated findings about useful methods, activities, and third-party techniques. Like experimentation in many other social issues, these studies will no doubt raise some ethical questions; similarly, studies based on simulated conflict raise questions about external validity. External validity is also an issue for field research insofar as any study is limited in space, time, setting, and so forth. Similarly, there is a problem of sampling in terms of defining the universe of situations of which the simulation or field experiment is representative. (For further discussion of these and other problems in the context of international conflict resolution, see Chapter 2 by Stern and Druckman). But these are not insurmountable problems, as one can benefit from the long tradition of experimental studies in the social sciences.

Although experimental studies can be applied in a straightforward way to examine hypotheses in this theoretical path, other techniques also can be used. When records of meetings are available for examination, qualitative techniques can be used to examine some hypotheses in this path—for example, that participants show new learning or that participants get involved in joint problem solving. Similarly, in-depth analysis of meetings transcripts, videotapes, or audiotapes and interviews with participants could help answer relevant questions of interest.

Take, for example, the issue of retained learning. Interviews held with participants at various times after the problem-solving workshop can provide introspective data on this issue. Participants might point to incidents that either make them strengthen or weaken their learning and can share their experience of whether it was difficult to maintain their new learning. The disadvantage of such interviews is that they can only tap into change processes of which the participant is aware. Many changes in a person's views, attitudes, and even behavior can take place without full awareness (Langer, 1989). Analysis of participants' writings and speeches can also help in examining the retention of new learning and its use in interpreting related political events.

In other cases, when ethical and practical problems can be surmounted, additional research methods can be used. For example, when workshop participants are students who agree to participate in research efforts, it is possible to use quasi-experimental designs to examine learning retention. Bargal and Bar (1992) compared scores of attitudinal changes in Arab and Jewish high school student workshop participants with students who had not participated in the workshops. The findings compiled for five separate years from 1984 to 1988 showed that in some years change took place in "favorable" directions and in other years in "unfavorable" directions. The authors concluded from the fluctuations in change that attitudinal changes might be more closely related to major political events constantly taking place in the conflict area than to workshop participation. Bargal and Bar concluded that their "questionnaires do not seem to capture the full range and depth of change that has occurred among workshop participants" (p. 151) and recommend qualitative methods to examine change.

The question of retention of new learning in a nonconducive conflictual environment can be studied, in theory, with other methodologies. Social scientists can use other experimental designs, as discussed above, to examine the extent of learning retention in conflict settings and to test variables that increase or decrease the likelihood of retention in such climates.

Assessing the Impact of the Conceptualized Effects

Another major item on the research agenda is the second theoretical path—that which connects the microobjectives of the problem-solving workshop with the goals of changing the dynamics of conflict on the ground. I have suggested conceptualizing the theoretical connections as effects whose impacts cannot be precisely measured. Although mostly unmeasurable, it is important to estimate the overall impact of these effects on the dynamics of conflict. After all, given the absence of hard evidence, many scholars and practitioners will make their own judgments about the value of interactive conflict resolution based on some assessment of the hypothesized impact. Scholars and practitioners should identify ways to provide their audiences with as much information as possible to make such a judgment.

Many methods, including interviews with participants, can be used to examine in what circumstances they shared insights from the problem-solving workshop with either decision makers or publics and whether they expressed some of their learning in writing. In coordination with participants, some discourse analysis could be used in which participants' writing and speeches could be analyzed to test hypotheses related to the use of new learning by participants in their political discourse. In one research project I am attempting to assess the extent to which participants in the workshops that Kelman and I have been holding over the past eight years have shared some of the views they learned in the problem-solving workshop with either decision makers or publics.

Participants should be able to help us understand how they used the learning they gained in the problem-solving workshop and how they evaluate these contributions. It is possible that participants will be biased evaluators of the impact and that some may fall prey to cognitive dissonance effects (Aronson, 1969) in the sense that they might justify the effort of their participation by overestimating the impact of the intervention. However, participants might be able to provide valuable information and instances of sharing and disseminating insights and of the estimated impact of such activities. They can provide leads to other people to interview and might be able to enrich our thinking on how to conceptualize the impact. Participants can help us evaluate each of the effects outlined above.

Unfortunately, the difficulty of measuring the effects described above and of estimating their combined impact generates additional obstacles beyond the obvious technical challenge posed to the whole field of conflict resolution. First, the difficulty can be used as an excuse for not studying these effects and for deemphasizing the importance of examining the theoretical connections between objectives and goals. Second, these difficulties can be used as an easy excuse for applying any intervention, presumably because effects are not measurable anyway and because some intervention is better than none. Third, in the absence of evidence, the door is open for overestimation of the impact by both practitioners and observers of problem-solving workshops.

However, the impossibility of applying more precise quantification methods to truly measure these effects does not mean that research on these effects is not at all possible. Innovative methods can be used to provide indirect estimation of some of these effects (such as examining the acceptability of new ideas developed in the problem-solving workshop to nonparticipants from both sides, or a participatory observation in meetings in which some of these ideas are presented in public, and so forth). An elaboration of such methods is beyond the scope of this paper.

WHY THE IMPACT OF INTERACTIVE CONFLICT RESOLUTION IS LIKELY TO BE OVERESTIMATED

Overestimation of the achievements of interactive conflict resolution by scholar-practitioners could be prompted by conscious and unconscious motivational and cognitive processes geared to present the outcome of interactive conflict resolution in its best light. On the motivational side, it is often the case that the professional and scholarly identity of practitioners becomes intertwined with such activities and that the funds and effort exerted will have to be justified. Yet one would expect that many practitioners are aware of these processes and perhaps try to combat them. But overestimation can also stem from complex cognitive processes that are harder to combat. Yet it is important to identify these processes and develop educational means to sensitize practitioners to them.

Deemphasizing the Reality of the Conflict on the Ground

The problem-solving workshop, as conducted by the scholar-practitioner, is a time-consuming effort that can bring together a small group of people for extended and controlled examination of a conflict. In some workshops the participants are influential in their own societies; in others they are not. For most participants this is one of many conflict-related activities. For many third parties, however, this could be a primary activity in relation to this conflict. This different grounding in the experience of the conflict could lead to cognitive divergence in the way the conflict is perceived and how the value of the activity is judged. Participants return to their daily activities in which, by definition, the conflict is central— being involved in conflict-related events, active participation in meetings, informal discussions, and just living the conflict on the ground as members of their own groups. For the third party the problem-solving workshop is an important and engaging analytical exercise, but it provides a limited window on the conflict that can become confused with the conflict itself. There is the danger that for the third party the dynamics on the ground that steer the direction of the conflict gain secondary importance to the dynamics in the problem-solving workshop. This is, perhaps, why many third parties do not care to learn the details of the conflict, its history, or, most importantly, its recent developments on the ground and thus judge progress by relationships in the problem-solving workshop disregarding the relationship between the parties in reality.

Treating the Problem-Solving Workshop as the Conflict Reality

Because for third parties a problem-solving workshop is their window on the conflict and because they may confuse this window with the conflict on the ground, it seems likely that third parties will see the problem-solving workshop on center stage when assessing its impact on the conflict at large. For example, in describing the goals of unofficial intervention on a conflict's dynamics, there is a tendency to generalize from what takes place in the workshop to the relationship between the two nations in conflict at large. Thus, if the parties to a problem-solving workshop establish a sense of mutual trust, the impact of the workshop is sometimes reported as having achieved trust between the two sides and improving the political climate of the conflict or as having reduced tension between the parties. Such reporting disregards that the conflict in the workshop is not equivalent to the conflict itself and that a transfer of trust from the small group to the larger societies is not automatic.

Overemphasizing the Dynamics in the Problem-Solving Workshop

In many approaches there seems to be an underlying assumption that the problem between two ethnonational groups is in the way people solve problems (a cognitive problem) or in the way people interact (a relationship problem). Thus, if we can only address the cognitive obstacles and find a formula to solve the conflict or if we can improve mutual perceptions between the protagonists and lead to better relationships between them, the ethnonational conflict can be solved. This is often assumed regardless of what is happening on the ground in terms of realistic conflict over tangible resources, power relations and the related motivations of each side, societal dynamics, international dynamics, the nature of the conflict itself, and the role of ideologies. It is this analogical thinking that stands behind the problem-solving expertise, almost in complete disregard to regional expertise, and that is why some practitioners who are not familiar with the dynamics of a particular conflict are comfortable intervening in it.

Overestimating the Participants' Influence

In estimating the impact of any single problem-solving workshop, we should always remember the limited number of people who participate in a workshop against the richness, complexity, and dynamics of the conflict on the ground. As much as these people can learn in a problem-solving workshop and as influential as they might be, there are powerful forces at work to minimize the workshop's impact. If we consider the small number of participants in a workshop (four to eight from each side) as a sample of the population of participants, this sample is certainly insignificant given the thousands of potential participants on each side. Thus, there are by definition limited circles of influence.

It is possible that the impact of interactive conflict resolution altogether is viewed differently from different perspectives and even that participants from each side come to these activities for different reasons from each other and from those designated by the third parties. From a foreign stance (where the third party usually comes from) and from the conflict's grounds, the following important factors are seen differently: the powerfulness of the dynamics on the ground, the richness and complexity of the actors, the importance of power relations, the significance of participants given the huge number of potential participants who can also influence the public, the powerfulness of the conflict's climate on participants when they go back to their conflict areas, and the importance of the whole activity of the problem-solving workshop.

Thus, in estimating the impact of interactive conflict resolution it should be noted that, even if the long chain of variables work in the desired direction—the objectives of the problem-solving workshop are clearly designed and demonstrably achieved, the goals are articulated, the theoretical connections proposed above are delineated, and the new insights gained and ideas generated in the problem-solving workshop are disseminated—there are serious questions about the impact of the problem-solving workshop in its present form.

INCREASING THE VALUE AND AUGMENTING THE IMPACT OF INTERACTIVE CONFLICT RESOLUTION

Given the various nonlinear ways in which interactive conflict resolution can contribute to the resolution of ethnonational conflict, one can, on the one hand, argue the merits of the method, at least in its potential. But given the unmeasurable nature of these potential contributions, and the multiple conditions under which they occur, one can, on the other hand, argue that interactive conflict resolution, at least as currently practiced does not demonstrably contribute to conflict resolution. Indeed, it seems to be a matter of judgment (and sometimes faith) on the part of the scholar-practitioner to decide to invest in interactive conflict resolution. However, given the potential of the method, it would be a mistake to dismiss it before trying to provide the means for realizing its potential. Most importantly, we need to devise new means for increasing the impact of interventions, as well as a more careful delineation of variables that could be expected to influence the impact.

For example, the third party is a key component in interactive conflict resolution, but surprisingly its role in increasing the impact of this effort has generally been neglected. According to most models the role of the third party is facilitative, both in the structural sense of providing participants the specially designed setting for their controlled interaction and process-wise in the sense of facilitating the discussion, according to a set of ground rules and mostly in nondirective ways. However, even in this facilitative role the third party provides a key function in the design of the problem-solving workshop project and its outcome. Third parties can take on a more active role in increasing the impact of the problem-solving workshop, provided that the role itself is carefully coordinated with participants and is part and parcel of the design of the workshop of which the participants are fully informed.[25]

The current design of the problem-solving workshop emphasizes the learning process of both parties in the workshop but neglects the learning that the third party undergoes (see Fisher, 1972, for an exception). Interactive problem solving is a powerful educational tool, particularly for third parties with some regional expertise and an interest in substance (in addition to the process). As interactive conflict resolution is currently conceptualized, there is no clear place for the transfer of insights from the problem-solving workshop in any systematic way to the policy-making level among the parties in conflict or other important players depending on the conflict.[26] Insights from interactive conflict resolution can provide an original and valuable input to foreign policy. However, for such input of the problem-solving workshop to be possible the whole effort will have to be reconceptualized and the contract with participants revised. Future workshops will have broader societal impact if conceived of as a joint learning opportunity for both participants and third party, on whom equal responsibility rests for transfer of insights into the broader societal context.

The value of the problem-solving workshop as a laboratory for conflict analysis is also overlooked.[27] Indeed, the problem-solving workshop provides an ideal setting for a unique way to analyze a conflict with the participation of both sides in the analysis. The analysis itself could become a major contribution of the problem-solving workshop if it is articulated by the third party in full cooperation with the participants themselves. The deep understanding of the political needs of each party, their internal dynamics, their limitations and constraints and the views of the other party of these constraints, and the dynamics of conflict as displayed in the problem-solving workshop setting are all important material to get out to experts, the public, and decision makers in an evenhanded and responsible manner. This kind of analysis, even if it does not include agreed upon ideas for resolving the conflict, provides unique input that the dynamics of conflict usually preclude. The introduction of such input to the political discourse can be another way to influence, perhaps in a minor way, the dynamics of a conflict.

It is obvious that reconceptualizing interactive conflict resolution in this direction entails careful consideration of the inherent risks, difficulties, and costs of such changes. The design of the workshop, the ground rules, and the methods to be used will have to be reshaped according to newly defined goals. Nevertheless, such reconceptualization is crucial if the potential contribution of interactive conflict resolution is to be maximized.

SUMMARY AND CONCLUSION

Examining major theoretical and methodological issues in interactive conflict resolution might, at face value, appear to be an academic exercise anchored in a social sciences framework and detached from the more lofty goals of intervening in conflict, changing history, and reaching policy makers and decision makers who have no interest in the tedious details of theory and research. However, I argue that the way to achieve these lofty goals is to systematically examine interactive conflict resolution's practices, methodologies, rationale, and achievements and to develop theories of practice that guide interventions in history. Stern and Druckman's (Chapter 2) conclusion about international conflict resolution is equally applicable to interactive conflict resolution: "[T]he practical concern with how best to develop generic knowledge about what works in international conflict resolution leads to a perhaps surprising conclusion: there is a critical need to develop theory."

Developing theory is even more important for interactive conflict resolution given its status of double marginality: both within the academic disciplines and with the diplomatic practitioners, policy makers, and decision makers. Assessments of the state of the field range from full satisfaction with "a significant track record" for a "systematic, well-thought-through approach" (Saunders, Chapter 7), to dubiousness over demonstrated impact or even the potential to achieve impact (e.g., Bercovitch, 1992). As Saunders mentions in his chapter, many see interactive conflict resolution as a naive approach practiced by do-gooders. Others are cynical about the value of problem-solving workshops and other meetings arranged by interactive conflict resolution practitioners.

In this chapter I posit that there is an urgent need to scientifically examine interactive conflict resolution and evaluate its achievements by addressing central theoretical and methodological issues. The main question I try to answer is what can be done—theoretically and methodologically—to increase confidence in using this approach. This chapter delineates the existing methods and objectives of interactive conflict resolution. It then encourages practitioners to deconstruct the problem-solving workshop to its components and to relate their various methodologies to the objectives they want to achieve within the contained context of the problem-solving workshop. Bringing adversaries together and conducting dialogue works neither by magic nor an act of faith. Practitioners should be able to present their methods, the objectives they aim to achieve, and how their methods achieve the objectives. Intervention in history should not be discharged from scientific accountability. To the contrary, given the importance of such interventions, all efforts should be made to demonstrate how the objectives of problem-solving workshops are achieved. Social science theories and research methodologies can be beneficially used to achieve this goal.

Practitioners should also be able to define the macrogoals of their interventions and explain how their workshops were designed to accomplish or help achieve the macrogoals. In this regard, scholar-practitioners face the grievous problem that the effects of their intervention on the dynamics of the conflict are nonlinear and therefore do not lend themselves to standard social science methodology, are complex and perhaps unmeasurable, and are slow to become manifest (if at all). But these problems cannot absolve the scholar-practitioner from the responsibility to explain how he or she conceives the impact of the intervention to take place, even if such impact is slow and unmeasurable, and to delineate plausible ways in which intervention influences a conflict's dynamics. Theory building requires advancing theory-anchored hypotheses about how the impact is supposed to occur and in what time frame as well as some indicators for assessing this impact. Even if the hypotheses cannot be empirically tested, they can be judged by scholars, practitioners, and policy makers on the merits of their theoretical plausibility or common sense. Furthermore, new innovative methodologies could be applied to examine some of these hypotheses.

Theory building in this sense contributes not only to the academic disciplines or to persuading policy makers of the value of this work, it also contributes to interactive conflict resolution practitioners to becoming more persuaded (or perhaps less depending on the outcomes) of the value of this work and to students and a new generation of practitioners who want to critically examine the practice in this area. Perhaps most importantly, it helps parties in conflict—among many of whom one encounters skepticism and even cynicism—whether to invest their time and effort in these interventions.

This chapter presents a conceptualization of the impact of interactive conflict resolution on the dynamics of conflict through a number of possible effects. I propose these effects here as a way of demonstrating what I mean by the need for defining goals and developing theoretical ways of achieving the desired impact. I also examine the methodological difficulties and suggest some ways to assess them.

The theoretical suggestions, the conceptual model (as summarized in Figure 8.1), and the research questions (and some answers) presented here are all conceived of as steps that must be taken to increase confidence in interactive conflict resolution as a field of practice and scholarly research. This goal, which is related in part to the academic standing of the field, is inextricably related to increasing the effectiveness of interactive conflict resolution and establishing its relevance to policy makers and those interested in intervention in the dynamics of conflict.

NOTES

[1]In earlier papers I used the term unofficial intervention (to emphasize the distinction from official interventions in conflict), whose definition overlaps broadly with Fisher's definition of interactive conflict resolution (Rouhana, 1995a, 1998). In this paper the two terms are used interchangeably.

[2]For a description of the approach see Harold Saunders's chapter in this volume. Saunders points out that the requirement of a third party of social scientist-practitioners is too limiting. The dialogue could be chaired by members from each group, and the role of third parties cannot be restricted to trained social scientists.

[3]These questions earn additional importance as interactive conflict resolution seeks to become established as an academic field—as witnessed by the increasing number of scholars who study conflict analysis and resolution and the rising number of academic institutes and programs on conflict resolution.

[4]This level of analysis is often used by scholar-practitioners to various degrees. It is emphasized in the works of Volkan (1990, 1991), Montville (1986, 1990), and (Moses, 1990). See an illustration of Volkan's approach in Saunders's chapter in this volume.

[5]Scholar-practitioners give this level of analysis various degrees of emphasis. It occupies a central role in the works of Doob (1970), Doob and Foltz (1973), and Lakin (1972). Lakin applied his approach to meetings between Arab and Jewish citizens in Israel. Doob and his colleagues used a similar approach in unofficial intervention efforts in the dispute between Ethiopia, Kenya, and Somalia, as well as the Northern Ireland conflict.

[6]The political level of analysis is lumped with the intergroup level of analysis, although conceptually they can be differentiated (see Rouhana and Korper, 1999). Burton and his colleagues introduced this level of analysis to unofficial intervention, first as "controlled communication" and later as "problem-solving" (Burton, 1986, 1987). Based on Burton's work, the problem-solving workshop was consequently developed, modified, and practiced by many others over the past three decades. Thus, Kelman and colleagues developed the "interactional problem-solving" approach (Kelman and Cohen, 1976; Kelman, 1979; Cohen et al., 1977). Azar, working closely with Burton, developed the "problem-solving

forums" (Azar, 1990); Fisher introduced the third-party consultation model (1972, 1980, 1983); Saunders and later Saunders and Slim applied a similar, although independent, model based on Saunders's unique and rich experience in both official and unofficial processes (Saunders, 1985; Chufrin and Saunders, 1993); Kelman and Rouhana developed the "continuing workshop" model (Rouhana and Kelman, 1994, Kelman, 1997; Rouhana, 1995b); and Rothman applied an intergroup level of analysis in his workshops (Rothman, 1997). For a comprehensive review of the various models and their applications, see Fisher (1997).

[7]Participants might even express resentment to "psychological interventions" and consider them a breach of the ground rules on the part of the third party. Indeed, Rouhana and Korper call for the level of analysis to be part of the contract between the third party and the participants. Participants should be informed, among other things, of the level of analysis and type of discussion they should expect to carry out in the workshop. See Rouhana and Korper (1996).

[8]For example, Rothman (1992, 1997) describes a method in which the third party actively leads the participants through preset stages: adversarial framing, reflexive reframing, inventing integrative solutions, and agenda setting. From excerpts of transcripts provided by Rothman (1992), it seems that the third party combines active facilitating and some simultaneous training. Saunders and Slim (1994) present five phases through which a sustained dialogue proceeds, implying that it captures a natural progress of such activities. Rouhana (1995b), presenting the third-party approach in the problem-solving workshop with Kelman, describes a model that takes into consideration both the inherent dynamics of a small group process and the agenda set by the third party. The third party steers the group through a set of phases by balancing the group's dynamics and the agenda.

[9]In a recent issue of *International Negotiation* edited by Ron Fisher (vol. 2, no. 3, 1997), the editor contends that training in negotiation and/or conflict resolution techniques can be considered an intervention only if it involves conflict analysis and dialogue and if it is jointly experienced by members of both parties. These conditions highlight the need that practitioners describe the activities they carry out in the problem-solving workshop. For an approach utilizing research findings in negotiation training programs, see Druckman and Robinson (1998).

[10]The analogy to the format of reports on studies in the social-psychological tradition should be considered. This format includes sufficient details for replicating the study in a different laboratory, under other circumstances, and by adding new independent variables or manipulating existing ones differently. An important advantage of this tradition is the accumulation of empirical knowledge.

[11]For example, Louise Diamond (in Saunders, Chapter 7) describes the connection between methods and outcomes in her intervention in Cyprus as follows: "The participants probe deeply into the interests, experiences, needs, and issues behind their positions, speaking freely about their concerns and feelings and hearing the same from the other side. This almost inevitably leads to what we call *shift*, where participants, as they gain new information and new perspective about themselves, the "other," and the overall situation in Cyprus, *find themselves experiencing a change of heart and mind about the relationship*" (emphasis added). Such a connection between intervention method and outcome in protracted social conflict cannot be taken at face value without further validation. It must, and can, be submitted to empirical testing.

[12]Saunders (Chapter 7), for example, argues that "in reaching judgment about how [interactive conflict resolution] contributes to peace making and peace building, we must probably reach beyond the methods of present social science. . . . How ideas emerge from the shadows to center stage and the role they play in changing the course of events may belong more to the history of ideas than to social science research methods."

[13]Rouhana and Korper (1999), who devised such a taxonomy, argue that it can also

help the scholar-practitioner deal with some of the major controversies in the field, such as: Should unofficial intervention encourage cooperation between adversaries in all stages of a conflict, or could such cooperation be used to legitimize power asymmetries? Should intervention be geared toward improving relationships at all stages of conflict? Can interventions harm relationships between protagonists? How important are interpersonal relationships in protracted ethnonational conflict? When is promoting reconciliation most useful? For example, whereas before negotiation and during open violence and mutual blame discussions of reconciliation could be futile and perhaps inappropriate, in a postsettlement stage there could be a major role for problem-solving workshops that focus on both interpersonal and intergroup reconciliation.

[14]In preparation for the referendum on the peace agreement in Northern Ireland, both Unionist and Republican leaders who supported the agreement campaigned with their constituencies. A Unionist leader reported a few days before the referendum: "I use the euphemism 'responsibility sharing'. It goes down a little better than 'power sharing'." See Maureen Dowd, "Center Holding," *The New York Times*, May 20, 1998.

[15]Bercovitch (1992), for example, articulated many of the criticisms and concluded that unofficial activities represent a model of mediation that is ineffective in dealing with ethnonational conflicts.

[16]Kriesberg (1991, 1992) demonstrates how during its life course a conflict goes through various nonlinear stages such as escalation, crisis, stalemate, or self-generating deescalation and argues that intervention should be based on conflict analysis that can determine the current stage. Despite the nonlinear nature of its evolution, transitions between stages of conflict often take the form of turning points—often identifiable by major stepping stones such as agreements or crises that could be critical periods for the transformation of the conflict and therefore for defining the goals of intervention accordingly.

[17]Perhaps, the sociological literature can guide conceptualizing the impact of interventions in the theoretical framework of social change.

[18]To focus the discussion I limit the following section to problem-solving workshops that use the intergroup/political level of analysis and, in particular, those based on basic human needs theory.

[19]For a social-psychological approach that draws a nexus between psychological processes and political processes in regional politics, see Druckman (1980).

[20]Some of the effects described below are overlapping. The distinctions made here between similar effects are helpful for conceptualizing the impact, but there is no assumption that they take place in the same distinct manner in reality.

[21]This function of the problem-solving workshop is not without risks and disadvantages. For one, the positive or negative reaction by the other side to a floated idea could be taken by a participant to mean that the official level on the other side is willing to accept or reject it as the case may be. Thus, despite the emphasis on the unofficial function of the meetings, it is not inconceivable that some participants generalize from the response they receive from nonofficials to the views of officials. Second, the function could be exploited by some participants for negotiation gains in the sense that they can learn what is the minimum their party should offer for the other side to accept.

[22]If the type of contact is not tailored to the stage of conflict on the ground, this contribution of the problem-solving workshop can easily backfire, as discussed in Doob's intervention in Northern Ireland (Doob and Foltz, 1973, 1974; Boehringer et al., 1974; Alvey et al., 1974). Furthermore, this effect, precisely because it legitimizes contact between adversaries, can become controversial if its exact objectives and goals are not explained. For example, professional and other contacts between Israelis and other Arabs are opposed by many intellectuals and professional associations in the Arab world (including Egypt and Jordan, which have formal peace agreements with Israel). The central argument against

such contacts is that, in the absence of comprehensive peace they create a sense of normalcy in conditions that are not normal. The conditions that contribute to the lack of normalcy must be changed, not the impression. Therefore, these contacts are perceived as being part and parcel of an image management by Israel called "normalization," and the opposition movement is, accordingly, called "antinormalization."

[23]A striking example of the effect of familiarity is the difference between the political culture of the Labor and Likud governments in Israel in relation to the Israeli-Palestinian conflict and Palestinian society. Before the peace process, some of the Labor negotiators had met Palestinians, including open supporters of the PLO, in academic and private settings. Likud members had consistently declined such opportunities.

[24]So far very little research has been conducted to assess the effectiveness of the problem-solving workshop in achieving attitudinal change, and even when such research was conducted it was not always clear which activity in the workshop was designed to lead to what change in attitudes. For example, Gutlove et al. (1992) provide some raw data from workshops they held in Yugoslavia to demonstrate conflict resolution techniques. Post-workshop data provided by participants showed that the workshops had a "limited impact upon the way people feel about their own role in the conflict and the role of their adversary" (p. 12). In answering the question "Do you feel differently about any aspect of the conflict now?," the average of each of three groups did not reach the midpoint of the scale from low (zero) to high (seven).

[25]Consider the following components that the third party takes a leading role in implementing: selection of participants, setting the agenda, setting the ground rules, choosing the level of analysis, and the initial design of the end product, all of which are components that should be part of a clear contract between the third party and the participants (Rouhana and Korper, 1996).

[26]In a recent problem-solving workshop in the series of workshops of the Joint Working Group in Israeli-Palestinian Relations, cochaired by Herbert Kelman and Nadim Rouhana, participants suggested that a document on general principles to guide the relationship between Israel and the Palestinians should be shared with American policy makers, in addition to Israeli and Palestinian policy makers. Many argued that sharing it with American policy makers is even more important than with parties themselves.

[27]Refraining from using the problem-solving workshop as an analytical tool is probably rooted in the legitimate ethical concern about "using" participants for analytical or educational purposes. I make the suggestion to take advantage of the analytical value in a way that gives participants full charge of the use of the analytical material, rather than having them being used as subjects who can demonstrate to others the dynamics of conflict.

REFERENCES

Ajzen, I., and Fishbein, M.
   1980   *Understanding attitudes and predicting social behavior.* Englewood Cliffs, N.J.: Prentice-Hall.
Alvey, D.I., Bunker, B., Doob, L.W., et al.
   1974   Rationale, research, and role relations in the Stirling Workshop. *Journal of Conflict Resolution,* 18:276-284.
Amir, Y.
   1976   The role of intergroup contact in change of prejudice and ethnic relations. In P. Katz (Ed.), *Toward the elimination of racism.* New York: Pergamon.
Arad, S., and Carnavale, P.
   1994   Partisanship effects in judgments of fairness and trust in third parties in Palestinian-Israeli conflict. *Journal of Conflict Resolution,* 38:423-451.

Aronson, E.
1969 The theory of cognitive dissonance: A current perspective. Pp. 1-34 in L. Berkowitz (Ed.), *Advances in experimental social psychology* (vol. 4). New York: Academic Press.

Azar, E.E.
1990 *The management of protracted social conflict: Theory and cases.* Hampshire, England: Dartmouth Publishing.

Bargal, D., and Bar, H.
1992 A Lewinian approach to intergroup workshops for Arab-Palestinian and Jewish youth. *Journal of Social Issues,* 48(2):139-154.

Bercovitch, J.
1992 The structure and diversity of mediation in international relations. In J. Bercovitch and J. Rubin (Eds.), *Mediation in international relations: Multiple approaches to conflict management.* New York: St. Martin's Press.

Boehringer, G.H., Zeruolis, V., Bayley, J., et al.
1974 Stirling: The destructive application of group techniques to a conflict. *Journal of Conflict Resolution,* 18:257-275.

Burton, J.W.
1986 The history of international conflict resolution. In E.E. Azar and J.W. Burton (Eds.), *International conflict resolution: Theory and practice.* Brighton: Wheatsheaf.

Burton, J.W.
1987 *Resolving deep-rooted conflict: A handbook.* Lanham, Md.: University Press of America.
1990 *Conflict: Resolution and prevention.* New York: St. Martin's Press.

Campbell, D.T., and Stanley, J.C.
1963 *Experimental and quasi-experimental design for research.* Chicago: Rand-McNally.

Chufrin, G.I., and Saunders, H.H.
1993 A public peace process. *Negotiation Journal,* 9:155-177.

Cohen, S., Kelman, H., Miller, F., and Smith, B.
1977 Evolving intergroup techniques for conflict resolution: An Israeli-Palestinian pilot workshop. *Journal of Social Issues,* 33(1):165-188.

Cross, S., and Rosenthal, R.
1999 Three models of conflict resolution: Effects on intergroup expectancies and attitudes. *Journal of Social Issues,* 55(3):561-580.

D'Estree, T.P., and Babbit, E.
1998 Women and the art of peacemaking: Data from Israeli-Palestinian problem-solving workshops. *Political Psychology,* 19:185-209.

Diamond, L. and McDonald, J.
1991 Multi-track diplomacy: A systems quide and analysis. Grinnell: Iowa Peace Institute.

Doob, L., ed.
1970 *Resolving conflict in Africa.* New Haven, Conn.: Yale University Press.

Doob, L., and Foltz, W.J.
1973 The Belfast Workshop. *Journal of Conflict Resolution,* 17(3):489-512.
1974 The impact of a workshop upon grass root leaders in Belfast. *Journal of Conflict Resolution,* 18:237-256.

Druckman, D.
1980 Social-psychological factors in regional politics. In W.J. Weld and G. Boyd (Eds.), *Comparative regional systems.* New York: Pergamon.
1993 The situational levers of negotiating flexibility. *Journal of Conflict Resolution,* 37:236-276.

Druckman, D., Broome, B., and Korper, S.
  1988   Value differences and conflict resolution. *Journal of Conflict Resolution*, 32(3):489-510.
Druckman, D., and Robinson, V.
  1998   From research to application: Utilizing research in negotiation training programs. *International Negotiation*, 3:7-38.
Fisher, R.J.
  1972   Third party consultation: A method for the study and resolution of conflict. *Journal of Conflict Resolution*, 16:67-94.
  1980   A third party consultation workshop on the India-Pakistan conflict. *Journal of Social Psychology*, 112:191-206.
  1983   Third party consultation as a method of intergroup conflict resolution: A review of studies. *Journal of Conflict Resolution*, 27(2):301-334.
  1997   *Interactive conflict resolution.* Syracuse, N.Y.: Syracuse University Press.
Gutlove, P., Babbit, E., Jones, L., and Montville, J.
  1992   *Towards a sustainable peace in the Balkans: A report on a pilot effort to introduce conflict resolution theories and techniques.* Cambridge, Mass.: The Balkans Peace Project.
Hewstone, M., and Brown, R.
  1986   Contact is not enough: An intergroup perspective on the 'contact hypothesis.' Pp. 1-44 in M. Hewstone and R. Brown (Eds.), *Contact and conflict in intergroup encounters.* Oxford: Basil Blackwell.
Hoffman, M.
  1995   Defining and evaluating success: Facilitative problem-solving workshop in an interconnected context. *Paradigms: The Kent Journal of International Relations*, 9(2):150-167.
Hovland, C.I., and Weiss, W.
  1951   The influence of source credibility on communication effectiveness. *Public Opinion Quarterly*, 15:635-650.
Jervis, R.
  1976   *Perceptions and misperceptions in international politics.* Princeton, N.J.: Princeton University Press.
Kelman, H.C.
  1979   An interactional approach to conflict resolution and its application to Israeli-Palestinian relations. *International Interactions*, 6:99-122.
  1986   Interactive problem-solving: A social-psychology conflict resolution. In W. Klassen (Ed.), *Dialogue toward interfaith understanding.* Tantur/Jerusalem: Ecumenical Institute for Theological Research.
  1992   Informal mediation by the scholar-practitioner. Pp. 64-96 in J. Bercovitch and J.Z. Rubin (Eds.), *Mediation in international relations: Multiple approaches to conflict management.* New York: St. Martin's Press.
  1995   Contributions of an unofficial conflict resolution effort to the Israeli-Palestinian breakthrough. *Negotiation Journal*, 11:19-27.
  1997   Group processes in the resolution of international conflict. *American Psychologist*, 52:212-220.
Kelman, H.C., and Cohen, S.P.
  1976   The problem solving workshop: A social-psychological contribution to the resolution of international conflicts. *Journal of Peace Research*, 13:79-90.
Kressel, K., Frontera, E.A., Forlenza, S., Butler, F., and Fish, L.
  1994   The settlement orientation vs. the problem-solving style in custody mediation. *Journal of Social Issues*, 50(1):67-84.

Kriesberg, L.
1991   Timing conditions, strategies, and errors. In L. Kriesberg and S.T. Thorson (Eds.), *Timing the de-escalation of international conflicts*. Syracuse, N.Y.: Syracuse University Press.
1992   *International conflict resolution: The US-USSR and Middle East cases*. New Haven, Conn.: Yale University Press.
Lakin, M.
1972   *Interpersonal encounter: Theory and practice in sensitivity training*. New York: McGraw-Hill.
Langer, E.J.
1989   *Mindfulness*. Reading, Mass.: Addison-Wesley.
Levy, J.
1989   The causes of war: A review of theories and evidence. Pp. 209-333 in P.E. Tetlock, J.L. Husbands, R. Jervis, P.C. Stern, and C. Tilly (Eds.), *Behavior, society, and nuclear war*. Oxford: Oxford University Press.
Linville, P.W., Salovy, P., and Fischer, G.W.
1986   Stereotyping and perceived distribution of social characteristics: An application to ingroup-outgroup perception. Pp. 165-208 in J.F. Dovidio and S.L. Gartner (Eds.), *Prejudice, discrimination, and racism*. Orlando, Fla.: Academic Press.
Mitchell, C.
1981   *Peacemaking and the consultants' role*. Westhead, U.K.: Grower.
1993   Problem solving exercises and theories of conflict resolution. In D.J. Sandole and H. van der Merwe (Eds.), *Conflict resolution: Theory and practice*. Manchester: Manchester University Press.
Mitchell, C., and Banks, M.
1996   *Handbook of conflict resolution*. London: Pinter.
Montville, J.V.
1986   Psychoanalytic enlightenment and the greening of diplomacy. An address to the American Psychiatric Association, New York, December.
1990   The psychological roots of ethnic and sectarian terrorism. Pp. 163-180 in V.D. Volkan, D.A. Julius, and J.V. Montville (Eds.), *The psychodynamics of international relationships, Volume I: Concepts and theories*. Lexington, Mass.: Lexington Books.
Moses, R.
1990   On dehumanizing the enemy. In V.D. Volkan, D.A. Julius, and J.V. Montville (Eds.), *The psychodynamics of international relationships, Volume I*. Lexington, Mass.: Lexington Books.
Petty, R.E., and Cacioppo, J.T.
1986   *Communication and persuasion: Central and peripheral routes to attitude change*. New York: Springer-Verlag.
Rothman, J.
1992   *From confrontation to cooperation: Resolving ethnic and regional conflict*. Newbury Park, Calif.: Sage.
1997   *Resolving identity-based conflict*. San Francisco: Jossey-Bass.
Rouhana, N.N.
1995a   Unofficial third party intervention in international conflict: Between legitimacy and disarray. *Negotiation Journal*, 11(3):255-271.
1995b   The dynamics of joint thinking between adversaries in international conflict: Phases of the continuing problem solving workshop. *Political Psychology*, 16(2): 321-345.
1998   Unofficial intervention: Potential contribution to resolving ethnonational conflicts. Pp. 111-132 in J. Melissen (Ed.), *Innovations in diplomatic practice*. Basingstoke: MacMillan.

Rouhana, N.N., and Bar-Tal, D.
1998   Psychological dynamics of ethnonational conflict: The Israeli-Palestinian case. *American Psychologist*, 53:761-770.
Rouhana, N.N., and Kelman, H.C.
1994   Promoting joint thinking in international conflict: An Israeli Palestinian continuing workshop. *Journal of Social Issues*, 50(1):157-178.
Rouhana, N.N., and Korper, S.H.
1996   Dealing with dilemmas posed by power asymmetry in intergroup conflict. *Negotiation Journal*, 12:353-366.
1997   Power asymmetry and goals of unofficial third party intervention in protracted social conflict. *Peace and Conflict: Journal of Peace Psychology*, 3:1-17.
1999   The who, what, and when of interactive conflict resolution: A taxonomy of intervention design in ethnonational conflicts. Unpublished manuscript.
Rubin, J.Z., Pruitt, D.G., and Kim, S.
1994   *Social conflict: Escalation, stalemate, and settlement* (2d ed.). New York: McGraw-Hill.
Saunders, H.H.
1985   *The other walls: The politics of the Arab-Israeli peace process.* Washington, D.C.: American Enterprise Institute for Public Policy Research.
Saunders, H.H., and Slim, R.
1994   Dialogue to change conflictual relationships. *Higher Education Exchange,* pp. 43-56.
Sherif, M.
1967   *Group conflict and cooperation.* London: Routledge & Kegan Paul.
Singer, J.D.
1969   The levels-of-analysis problem in international relations. In J.N. Rosenau (Ed.), *International politics and foreign policy.* New York: Free Press.
Stephan, W.G.
1985   In G. Lindzey and E. Aronson (Eds.), *Handbook of social psychology: volume II,* New York: Random House.
Stern, P.C., and Kalof, L.
1996   *Evaluating social science research* (2d ed.). New York: Oxford University Press.
Tetlock, P.E.
1984   Cognitive style and political belief systems in the British House of Commons. *Journal of Personality and Social Psychology,* 46:365-375.
1986   A value pluralism model of ideological reasoning. *Journal of Personality and Social Psychology,* 50:819-827.
Tetlock, P.E., Hannum, K. and Micheletti, P.
1984   Stability and change in senatorial debate: Testing the cognitive versus rhetorical style hypotheses. *Journal of Personality and Social Psychology,* 46:621-631.
Volkan, V.D.
1990   Working conclusions. In V.D. Volkan, J.V. Montville, and D.A. Julius (Eds.), *The psychodynamics of international relationships.* Lexington, Mass.: Lexington Books.
1991   Psychological processes in unofficial diplomacy meetings. Pp. 93-120 in *The psychodynamics of international relationships, volume II: Unofficial diplomacy at work.* Lexington, Mass.: Lexington Books.
White, R.
1984   *Fearful warriors: Psychological profile of U.S.-Soviet relations.* New York: The Free Press.

9

Past Truths, Present Dangers: The Role of Official Truth Seeking in Conflict Resolution and Prevention

Priscilla B. Hayner

The subjects of transitional justice and historical memory have received increasing attention in recent years, as many countries representing a wide range of political contexts and transitional circumstances have confronted the legacy of widespread abuses by a prior regime or armed opposition group.[1] States have turned to a range of transitional mechanisms in an effort to confront past crimes, hoping to achieve some measure of accountability, advance national reconciliation, and secure necessary institutional reforms to prevent future human rights abuses or the return to violence. The various mechanisms that have been used include prosecuting perpetrators in national and international courts; lustration or purges of those affiliated with a previous authoritarian government; the imposition of other noncriminal sanctions; material or nonmaterial compensation for victims; and official truth seeking, usually in the form of temporary investigative bodies that have acquired the generic name of "truth commissions."[2]

Each of these transitional measures serves different (although sometimes overlapping) ends, and each has its strengths as well as its limitations. The decision to undertake one of these approaches over others will be determined by a wide variety of factors. These various mechanisms are not mutually exclusive, however, and there can be a positive interplay between the different structures or processes put in place. A number of states have attempted to prosecute perpetrators while also creating a truth commission, for example, sometimes using a truth commission to collect evidence for later prosecutions. Some truth commissions have been tasked with designing a follow-up reparations program.

To date, these accountability mechanisms have been studied and advanced primarily by those with an interest in combating human rights abuses and responding to abuses of the past. However, these various mechanisms are typically turned to at the point of transition out of a period of violent conflict or authoritarian rule, sometimes following a bitter civil war. During a negotiated transition, the means and manner by which accountability will be addressed are usually discussed directly at the negotiating table. This paper looks more closely at the role of one of these mechanisms—that of officially sanctioned truth investigations—in the resolution and prevention of violent conflict. After an introduction to the use of truth commissions in the past, their function, purpose, and limitations and their relationship to other transitional accountability mechanisms, this paper proposes three ways in which truth commissions may contribute to halting or preventing violent conflict. It then proposes how the "success" of truth commissions might be evaluated and the outside factors that influence their strength and effectiveness. The paper concludes by suggesting unanswered questions and areas of research in need of focused attention.

THE EMERGENCE OF TRUTH COMMISSIONS
AS A TRANSITIONAL TOOL

At the point of transition following a brutal and repressive regime, a state and its people are left with a legacy of violence, bitterness, and pain and often many hundreds or thousands of perpetrators who deserve prosecution and punishment for their crimes. But successful prosecutions after a period of massive atrocities have been limited, as underresourced and sometimes politically compromised judicial systems struggle to confront such widespread and politically contentious crimes. Given limited options for confronting past atrocities, and with an eye toward the need for healing and reforms, many new governments have turned to mechanisms outside the judicial system to confront horrific crimes of a prior regime. The increasing attraction to official truth seeking as a transitional tool is partly a result of the limited reach of judicial-oriented approaches to accountability. As truth commissions have been more widely used and studied, however, it has become clear that they fill a very different role from judicial inquiries and trials. Truth commissions, defined as official, temporary mechanisms that are established to investigate a pattern of past human rights abuses or violations of international humanitarian law, are tasked with investigating, reporting, and recommending reforms, and in the process serve to formally acknowledge past wrongs that were silenced and denied.

Truth commissions have no prosecutorial powers (and only the South African truth commission had the power to grant amnesty), although a few to date have chosen to name perpetrators in their reports, in part to instill at least a sense of public and moral accountability. But while a truth commission cannot impart judicial decisions or punishment for wrongdoers, their strengths are in those very areas that fall outside the parameters or capabilities of a court. While trials are aimed at achieving individual criminal accountability, truth commissions are focused on describing patterns of crimes over a period of time, recommending policies to prevent the repetition of such abuses, and proposing measures to formally recognize or make reparations for past wrongs. Trials are narrowly focused: they typically do not investigate the social or political factors that led to the violence or the internal structure of abusive forces, such as death squads or the intelligence branch of the armed forces, all of which might be the focus of a truth commission. While some trials help shed light on overall patterns of human rights violations or may engage the public more broadly in confronting and reevaluating its past, this is generally not their focus or intent. Courts do not submit policy recommendations or suggestions for political, military, or judicial reforms. Finally, while the records of a trial may be public, judicial opinions are generally not widely distributed or widely read, as is the intention of truth commission reports.

A truth commission should be distinguished from a government human rights office set up to watch over current human rights abuses and also from nongovernmental projects documenting past abuses. Likewise, these truth-seeking bodies should be distinguished from international tribunals, such as the International Criminal Tribunal for the Former Yugoslavia and the International Criminal Tribunal for Rwanda, both created by the United Nations (UN), or the permanent International Criminal Court that may soon be established. These international tribunals are also designed to respond to abuses by the state, but they function with the purpose and powers of a court.

Truth commissions differ as well from other mechanisms that have been used in recent years to confront past human rights crimes after a political transition from authoritarian rule. Several East European countries have turned to a policy of lustration, which removes persons who worked with the prior government or intelligence service from employment in the public sector. These lustration policies generally have relied on information in the files of the former intelligence service. But because some of these files may contain incorrect information and because of the limited rights of appeal and due process that have been granted, lustration has been criticized by international observers.[3] This strategy also requires that detailed files were kept by the previous government (and not destroyed in the transition), that the new authorities have access to them, and that the new government has the political power to sustain a policy of discharging civil servants, factors that would not be present in most postauthoritarian transitional states outside Eastern Europe.

Other approaches to documenting past rights crimes include investigation and reporting by a specially appointed rapporteur of the UN or by a national or international nongovernmental organization. These two approaches do not depend on governmental sponsorship of an inquiry (although a UN rapporteur must receive a formal invitation from the government before visiting a country for a special investigation), but they are also unlikely to have access to extensive official documentation. While they may overlap to some degree, all of these various mechanisms or approaches to confronting past human rights abuses have different aims, powers, and outcomes and complement rather than replace each other.

Transitional truth-seeking bodies became much more common in the 1990s and only in the past few years have taken on the generic name of *truth commissions*. Each of the 20-odd truth commissions to date has been unique, with considerable differences in the form, structure, and mandate used to carry out their work. Not all, in fact, are formally called truth commissions: in Guatemala, for example, there was a Historical Clarification Commission created under the UN-negotiated peace accords; Argentina set up a National Commission on the Disappearance of Persons; and in some countries these bodies are called Commissions of Inquiry (see Table 9.1). All of these commissions share certain common elements and are created for similar purposes. Truth commission is now a term of art that refers to a fairly specific kind of investigatory commission, identified by four common characteristics. First, a truth commission focuses on the *past*. Second, it investigates not a singular event but the record of abuses over a period of time (often highlighting a few cases to demonstrate and describe patterns). Third, a truth commission is a temporary body, concluding with the submission of a final report that is intended to be made public. Finally, a truth commission is somehow officially sanctioned by the government (and by the armed opposition where appropriate). This official sanction allows the commission greater access to information and greater security to undertake sensitive investigations and increases the likelihood that its conclusions and recommendations will be given serious consideration.

Differences between commissions should be expected, as each country must shape a process out of its own historical, political, and cultural context. Unlike courts, which generally stand as permanent bodies and about which there are many international norms regarding their appropriate structure, components, and powers, and minimal standards under which their proceedings should be undertaken, there are many aspects of truth commissions that will vary from country to country and about which there are no established standards. Some are given subpoena powers or

TABLE 9.1 Truth Commissions to Date (in chronological order)

Country	Name of Truth Commission	Title of report (Publication Date)	Date of Commission	Dates Covered	Empowered by
Uganda	Commission of Inquiry into the Disappearance of People in Uganda Since the 25th January, 1971	Report of the Commission of Inquiry into the Disappearance of People in Uganda Since the 25th January, 1971 (1975)	1974	1971-1974	President
Bolivia	Comisión Nacional de Investigación de Desaparecidos (National Commission of Inquiry into Disappearances)	Did not complete report	1982-1984	1967-1982	President
Argentina	Comisión Nacional para la Desaparición de Personas (National Commission on the Disappearance of Persons) ("The Sábato Commission" or "CONADEP")	Nunca Más (Never Again) (1985)	1983-1984	1976-1983	President
Uruguay	Comisión Investigadora sobre la Situación de Personas Desaparecidas y Hechos que la Motivaron (Investigative Commission on the Situation of "Disappeared" People and Its Causes)	Informe Final de la Comisión Investigadora sobre la Situación de Personas Desaparecidas y Hechos que la Motivaron (Final Report of the Investigative Commission on the Situation of the "Disappeared" People and Its Causes) (1985)	1985	1973-1982	Parliament

Zimbabwe	Commission of Inquiry	Report kept confidential	1985	1983	President
Uganda	Commission of Inquiry into Violations of Human Rights	The Report of the Commission of Inquiry into Violations of Human Rights: Findings, Conclusions, and Recommendations (Oct. 1994)	1986-1995	Dec. 1962-Jan. 1986	President
Chile	Comisión Nacional para la Verdad y Reconciliación (National Commission on Truth and Reconciliation) ("The Rettig Commission")	Informe de la Comisión de la Verdad y Reconciliación (Report of the National Commission on Truth and Reconciliation) (1991)	1990-1991	Sept. 11, 1973-March 11, 1990	President
Chad	Commission d'Enquête sur les Crimes et Détournements Commis par l'Ex-Président Habré, ses co-Auteurs et/ou Complices (Commission of Inquiry on the Crimes and Misappropriations Committed by the Ex-President Habré, his Accomplices and/or Accessories)	Rapport de la Commission (Report of the Commission) (May 7, 1992)	1991-1992	1982-1990	President

TABLE 9.1 Continued

Country	Name of Truth Commission	Title of report (Publication Date)	Date of Commission	Dates Covered	Empowered by
South Africa (ANC)	Commission of Enquiry into Complaints by Former African National Congress Prisoners and Detainees ("The Skweyiya Commission")	Report of the Commission of Enquiry into Complaints by Former African National Congress Prisoners and Detainees (Oct. 1992)	1992	1979-1991	African National Congress
Germany	Enquete Kommission Aufarbeitung von Geschichte und Folgen der SED-Diktatur in Deutschland (Study Commission for the Assessment of History and Consequences of the SED Dictatorship in Germany)	Bericht der Enquete-Kommission "Aufarbeitung von Geschichte und Folgen der SED-Diktatur in Deutschland" (June 1994)	1992-1994	1949-1989	Parliament
El Salvador	Comisión de la Verdad Para El Salvador (Commission on the Truth for El Salvador)	De la Locura a la Esperanza (From Madness to Hope) (March 1993)	1992-1993	Jan. 1980-July 1991	United Nations-moderated peace accord
South Africa (ANC)	Commission of Enquiry into Certain Allegations of Cruelty and Human Rights Abuse Against ANC Prisoners and Detainees by ANC Members ("The Motsuenyane Commission")	Report of the Commission of Enquiry into Certain Allegations of Cruelty and Human Rights Abuse Against ANC Prisoners and Detainees by ANC Members (Aug. 20, 1993)	1993	1979-1991	African National Congress

Sri Lanka	Commissions of Inquiry into the Involuntary Removal or Disappearance of Persons (three geographically distinct commissions)[a]	Final Reports of the Commissions of Inquiry into the Involuntary Removal or Disappearance of Persons (three distinct final reports, plus eight interim reports from each commission) (Sept. 1997)	Nov. 1994-Sept. 1997	Jan. 1, 1988-Nov. 13, 1994	President
Haiti	National Commission for Truth and Justice	Si M Pa Rele (If I Don't Cry Out) (Feb. 1996)	April 1995-Feb. 1996	1991-1994	President
Burundi	International Commission of Inquiry	Report never released publicly	1995-1996	Oct. 21, 1993-Aug. 28, 1995	United Nations Security Council
South Africa	Truth and Reconciliation Commission	Truth and Reconciliation Commission of South Africa Report (Oct. 1998)	Dec. 1995-2000[b]	1960-1994	Parliament
Ecuador	Truth and Justice Commission	Did not complete report	Sept. 1996-Feb. 1997	1979-1996	President

346

TABLE 9.1 Continued

Country	Name of Truth Commission	Title of report (Publication Date)	Date of Commission	Dates Covered	Empowered by
Guatemala	Comisión para el Esclarecimiento Histórico (Commission for Historical Clarification) (Formal name: Commission to Clarify Past Human Rights Violations and Acts of Violence that Have Caused the Guatemalan People to Suffer)	Guatemala: Memory of Silence (February, 1999)	Aug. 1997- Feb. 1999	1960-1996	United Nations-moderated peace accord

[a]In Sri Lanka there were three geographically distinct commissions that operated simultaneously and with identical mandates: Commission of Inquiry into the Involuntary Removal or Disappearance of Persons in the Western, Southern and Sabaragamuwa Provinces; Commission of Inquiry into the Involuntary Removal or Disappearance of Persons in the Northern and Eastern Provinces; and Commission of Inquiry into the Involuntary Removal or Disappearance of Persons in the Central, North Western, North Central and Uva Provinces. When these three commissions ended, a follow-up body was formed to close the outstanding cases, called the Presidential Commission of Inquiry into Involuntary Removals and Disappearances.

[b]Although the South African Truth and Reconciliation Commission submitted its main report in 1998, the commission continued to operate, with fewer staff and only a few commissioners operationally involved, into 2000, with an expected completion date in late 2000. This extra time was necessary for the Amnesty Committee to process all applications and has also allowed reparations policies to be put in place and victims' lists to be finalized.

even strong search and seizure powers and hold public hearings in front of television cameras or covered live on national radio (such as in South Africa or in the 1986 commission in Uganda). Others hold all investigations and interviews of victims and witnesses behind closed doors, may not have the power to compel witnesses to testify, and release information to the public only through a final report (such has been true of all such commissions in Latin America). Commission mandates also differ on the types of abuses to be investigated, perhaps including acts by the armed opposition as well as government forces, for example (as in Chile, El Salvador, or South Africa), or are limited to certain specific practices such as disappearances (as in Argentina and Sri Lanka). Such variations are a natural reflection of the variations between countries and their distinct political contexts, political cultures, histories, and needs.

Truth commissions can play a critical role in a transition. Some past commissions have been notable successes: their investigations have been welcomed by survivors of the violence and by human rights advocates alike; their reports have been widely read; their summaries of facts have been considered conclusive and fair. Such commissions are often referred to as serving a "cathartic" effect in society and as fulfilling the important step of formally acknowledging a long-silenced past. But not all truth commissions have been so successful. Some have been significantly limited from a full and fair accounting of the past—limited by mandate, by political constraints or restricted access to information, or by a basic lack of resources and have reported only a narrow slice of the truth.

Truth commissions have been multiplying rapidly around the world and have gained increasing attention in recent years.[4] Although there have been about 20 such bodies in the past 25 years, many have received little international attention—such as those in Chad, Sri Lanka, and Uganda—despite considerable interest from the press and public on a national level as the inquiries were under way. The few that have received considerable international attention have helped define the field and shape the truth commissions that followed elsewhere—particularly the Commission on the Disappeared in Argentina, which ended in 1984; the Chilean National Commission on Truth and Reconciliation, completed in 1991; the United Nations Commission on the Truth for El Salvador, which finished in 1993; the Truth and Reconciliation Commission in South Africa, which released its report in October 1998; and the Guatemalan Historical Clarification Commission, which completed its report in early 1999. Only since the early 1990s have countries begun to look closely at the experiences of previous truth commissions before designing their own. For example, South Africa crafted its Truth and Reconciliation Commission after studying the truth commissions that preceded it, particularly in Latin America. Those who crafted the legislation for the South African commission were particularly conscious of the blanket amnesties awarded in many Latin American countries and the failure of most truth commissions to gain the cooperation of perpetrators in their search for the truth. These reflections contributed to the crafting of the truth-for-amnesty formulation in which perpetrators who disclose all they know about politically motivated crimes during the apartheid era are granted amnesty for those crimes. Table 9.1 provides an overview of the truth commissions that have existed to date.

There are a number of other examples of official inquiries into past human rights violations that fill many functions of a truth commission but that for various reasons do not fully qualify as a truth commission by the definition used here. For example, some of these inquiries have been undertaken at the initiative of a permanent governmental human rights office, created to monitor present-day human rights matters but that began to look into the past after receiving complaints. The important initiatives of the Human Rights and Equal Opportunity Commission in Australia, which in 1997 reported on a long-term state policy of forcibly removing Aboriginal children from their families,[5] and of the National Commissioner for the Protection of Human Rights in Honduras, which in 1994 reported on 179 people who disappeared in the 1980s and early 1990s, are examples of such projects. This Honduran national commissioner received no assistance from authorities during his inquiry into disappeared persons, and he continued to call for a full truth commission even as he published his own report documenting extensive abuses.[6]

A broad official truth-telling exercise might also take place as an extension of a judicial inquiry. In Ethiopia the Special Prosecutor's Office (SPO) intended to thoroughly document the broad pattern of abuses under the Mengistu regime in the course of preparations for trials of hundreds of accused perpetrators and to publish a truth commission-like report. For several years it maintained an extensive computerized system and dozens of staff members to cull names and incriminating details from the extensive documentation that was left behind as the Mengistu regime crumbled. While the SPO continues to rely on this documentation in its strategy to show a broad pattern of events pointing to an overall policy of genocide under Mengistu, ultimately the plan for a truth report was dropped as it turned its attention to prosecutions alone.

There are other important differences that distinguish these ad hoc inquiries from formal truth commissions. In contrast to truth commissions, these ad hoc investigations generally do not work under a written mandate, which would define what period and exactly what acts are to be investigated, under what investigative powers, and by what deadline it must finish. These projects may operate without a budget for inquiries into the past and are thus forced to divert funds from other responsibilities of the office or raise funding independently, sometimes from private foundations. Because a truth commission is created by authorities with the explicit purpose of investigating past human rights abuses and making this history known through a final report, it carries an air of explicit state acknowledgment of a silenced past, which many of these ad hoc projects lack. But these alternative approaches should not be automatically discounted. Indeed, some of these quasi-truth commissions have been more effective in bringing the past to light and in engaging the larger population in the need to confront a silenced past than some formal truth commissions. Examples of these quasi-truth commissions are listed in Table 9.2.

There are also important examples of nongovernmental projects that have documented the patterns and practices of abuses of a prior regime, usually sponsored by national human rights organizations or churches. Despite some limitations to such private investigations, particularly restricted access to government information, these unofficial projects have sometimes produced remarkable results. In Brazil, for example, a team of investigators was able to secretly photocopy all of the official court papers that documented prisoners' complaints of abuse. Working quietly and with the support of the archbishop of São Paulo and the World Council of Churches, the team produced *Brasil: Nunca Mais*, a report analyzing the military regime's torture practices over a 15-year time period, based entirely on official records.[7] In Uruguay the nongovernmental Servicio Paz y Justicia (SERPAJ) published *Uruguay: Nunca Más*, which is far stronger than the report resulting from the parliamentary inquiry, which was given a significantly limited mandate.[8] The Human Rights Office of the archbishop of Guatemala undertook an extensive project to document decades of abuses and massacres in advance of the official truth commission there, hoping to both complement and strengthen the commission's work.[9] In Russia the nongovernmental organization Memorial was set up in 1987 around the question of accountability and fact finding over past events. Its staff has collected extensive archives on state abuses back to 1917 and published several books with lists of victims' names and analysis of state policies of repression.[10]

In Latin America the truth has often been a first and fundamental demand as repressive regimes or bitter civil wars have come to an end. As one of the first acts of the new civilian government, Argentina crafted the first truth commission that was to attract significant international attention. Over nine months, beginning in late 1983, the National Commission on the Disappeared documented close to 9,000 disappearances of people that took place under military rule from 1976 to 1983 (though even the commission understood this was not an inclusive total; the real number of people who disappeared is estimated to be 15,000 to 30,000). With

TABLE 9.2 Quasi-Truth Commissions—Alternative Forms of Official or Semiofficial Inquiry into the Past

Country	Name of Investigative Body	Title of Report (Publication Date)	Date of Inquiry	Dates Covered	Description of Investigative Body
Rwanda	International Commission of Investigation on Human Rights Violations in Rwanda Since October 1, 1990	Report of the International Commission of Investigation on Human Rights Violations in Rwanda Since October 1, 1990 (March 1993)	1993	Oct. 1990-1993	Sponsored by four international nongovernmental organizations; granted quasi-official status
Ethiopia	Office of the Special Prosecutor	Prosecutions ongoing; plans for overall "truth" report have been dropped	1993-present	1974-1991	Special prosecutor focused on crimes of prior regime
Honduras	National Commissioner for the Protection of Human Rights in Honduras	Los Hechos Hablan por sí Mismos: Informe Preliminor sobre los Desaparecidos en Honduras 1980-1993 (The Facts Speak for Themselves: Preliminary Report on the Disappeared in Honduras 1980-1993) (Jan. 1994)	1993	1980-1993	Government human rights ombudsman: inquiry into disappeared persons taken at his own initiative

United States	Advisory Committee on Human Radiation Experiments[a]	Report of the Advisory Committee on Human Radiation Experiments (1995)	Jan. 1994-1995	1944-1974	Established by U.S. energy secretary to inquire into radiation experiments on unknowing patients and prisoners
Australia	Human Rights and Equal Opportunity Commission	Bringing Them Home: Report of the National Inquiry into the Separation of Aboriginal and Torres Strait Islander Children from Their Families (May 1997)	1996-1997	1910-1975	Special inquiry undertaken by permanent government human rights monitoring body
Northern Ireland	Northern Ireland Victims Commissioner	We Will Remember Them (April 1998)	Nov. 1997-April 1998	1967-1997	Special one-person commission established by British Secretary of State for Northern Ireland

[a]In fact, this U.S. commission of inquiry into radiation experiments fits closely into the definition of a truth commission but seems to be of a different nature. All of the truth commissions listed above took place at the point of and as part of a political transition, and most focused on grave violations of human rights affecting great numbers of people, and reflecting statewide policies of violence and abuse. This inquiry and the other inquiry like it on the syphilis experiments in Tuskegee (and perhaps the inquiry into the internment of Japanese Americans during World War II) represent what we might call mini truth commissions. Calling a body a truth commission is helpful for classification terms, but a clear and precise definition of what is included in this classification is still in the process of being fine-tuned.

the assistance of survivors of detention and torture, the commission surveyed over 300 former torture centers, primarily in police and military installations. The commission's report, *Nunca Más*, is one of the bestselling books ever in Argentina and is still sold in kiosks in the streets of Buenos Aires.[11] Perhaps most importantly in the eyes of Argentineans, the commission's files were handed directly to prosecutors, providing the backbone of evidence and a pool of witnesses for the successful high-level trials that followed.[12]

When the dictatorship of Augusto Pinochet ended in Chile seven years later and after the government of Patricio Aylwin concluded that it could not overturn the Pinochet-installed amnesty that prevented prosecution and punishment for the great majority of crimes, Chile also turned to official truth seeking to confront acts over the prior 17 years by state forces or the armed opposition. Chile's years of repression resulted in greater numbers of survivors of torture and fewer executions and disappearances compared to Argentina, but the National Commission on Truth and Reconciliation was restricted from documenting cases of torture unless the torture resulted in death. Instead, it focused on close to 3,000 cases of disappearances and killings and a number of political kidnappings and only described practices of torture in general terms. As a result, the extensive reparations policies that were put in place by a follow-up commission did not reach torture survivors, who constituted the majority of the victims. But the commission's formal acknowledgment of state responsibility for disappearances and abuses, including an emotional plea of apology by President Aylwin at the time he released the report, was a critical turning point in gaining respect for victims and advancing public understanding of the country's past.

Shortly after the Chilean report was released in 1991, the parties in the peace talks in El Salvador agreed to a Commission on the Truth, to be appointed and administered by the UN, to investigate abuses on both sides of the country's 12-year civil war. Due to political polarization and continued insecurity and fear about reporting human rights crimes, the commission would have only international commissioners and staff, in sharp contrast to the truth inquiries that preceded it elsewhere. The commission's report, released in a UN ceremony in 1993, was criticized on some grounds, particularly for an imbalance in identifying which sectors of the armed left were implicated in abuses and for failing to address who was behind the country's death squads. But the commission's naming of dozens of high-level perpetrators and its strong and detailed policy recommendations helped force the retirement of abusive officers and eventually push through important judicial reforms. The political leadership, however, was not ready to accept, acknowledge, or apologize. The high command of the armed forces openly rejected the report as biased and unfair, and the government passed a sweeping amnesty law just five days after the commission report was published.

The Truth and Reconciliation Commission in South Africa has brought a whole new level of interest to the subject of healing through confronting past pain, reconciling through admitting wrongs, and washing even the worst of past crimes in the public view of television cameras and public audiences. The commission was established in 1995 through national legislation after over a year and a half of public debate and input from all political parties and many sectors of civil society. It was given two and a half years to collect information about gross human rights violations by state bodies or the armed opposition between 1960 and 1994, to hold public hearings, and to publish a report with recommendations for reparations and reform. Over 20,000 victims came forward to give testimony, some 2,000 in public hearings. In addition, the commission held a number of thematically focused hearings to examine the role of the churches, the medical establishment, the legal sector, the business community, and other institutions in passively or actively contributing to the human rights violations of the past. With the use of a strong subpoena power, the ability to grant amnesty to perpetrators who confessed their crimes, and with many high-level political leaders appearing before it, the commission was in the center of the news almost daily.

Truth commissions are often proposed in part to serve a cathartic effect for victims and society at large. There is much anecdotal evidence to support the claim that some victims are greatly served by the opportunity to tell their stories and to have their suffering formally acknowledged. But it should not be assumed that truth always leads to healing. For many victims and survivors, healing will require access to longer-term structures for psychological and emotional support, either community based or through more formal health care services. Likewise, it has yet to be proven that reconciliation will always be advanced from confronting the pains of past conflicts. Healing and reconciliation are both long-term processes that go far beyond the capacity of any one short-term commission. But given the scarcity of transitional mechanisms and the limited resources to pour into peace-making projects, many national leaders pin high hopes on the ability of truth commissions to carry a country down the path of reconciliation, healing, and peace, and many couch their support for such a commission in those terms.

Clearly, some skepticism about the inherent healing qualities of truth commissions is deserved. Many questions remain that demand greater study and exploration. But this skepticism should be tempered by indications of quite positive contributions from national truth seeking in some circumstances. For example, I have spoken with many victims who say that only by learning the full truth about their past horror can they ever begin to heal. Only by remembering, telling their story, and learning the full details about what happened and who was responsible are they able to begin to put the past behind them. In South Africa many survivors told me that they could only forgive their perpetrators if they were told the full truth; almost incomprehensibly, hearing even the most gruesome details of the torture and murder of a loved one somehow brought them some peace.

When is a truth commission an appropriate mechanism to help prevent, resolve, or at least mitigate violent conflict? Not all countries will choose to institute official truth seeking. Because of political constraints and resistance from those in power or because of the nature of a conflict, cultural factors (such as indigenously rooted community-based mechanisms to address past conflicts and pain), or because of an urgent priority around rebuilding after a devastating and exhausting war, some countries may decide against any form of truth body.[13] Each situation must be evaluated independently, and this decision should always, ultimately, be made by the country itself. Outsiders can offer suggestions and comparative experience from other countries and can and should support those civil society actors and victims communities that may push for an accounting, but the international community should not impose or be perceived as imposing the decision to undertake such an exercise. Even if the international community were able to do so, the results of such an exercise would likely be disappointing, as national ownership would be lacking and cooperation with the commission may be minimal. Past experience suggests, however, that a truth commission is especially appropriate or advisable to the extent that one or more of the following three conditions or circumstances exist (in many countries a combination of these three indications may be found, though one is likely to be more prominent):

- *A silenced or denied past,* where there is an all-encompassing silence around past events and where it seems unsafe to talk about past abuses.
- *A contested past,* where two or more contradictory versions of the past vie for acceptance. In El Salvador fervent denials of abuses from the Salvadoran government, together with their backers in the U.S. government, fundamentally skewed the truth about major massacres during that country's 12-year civil war. Only with the submission of the truth commission's report were some of these lies put to rest.
- *An unknown or undocumented past,* where much information is not known or where certain sectors of society are unaware of the details of the dark side of their country's recent history. In South Africa the truth commission documented practices that were unknown to a good number of whites in the country, such as widespread practices of torture

against political opponents in police stations. It is often only by capturing verbal testimony from victims that this past can be documented and preserved.

In many countries issues around past abuses continue to bubble to the surface in the public or political arena long after a democratic transition, with or without a truth commission. The experiences of Uganda, El Salvador, Argentina, Chile, Haiti, Sri Lanka, and elsewhere have made it clear that the conclusion of a commission does not end the interests in and tensions around past conflicts; rather, they have generally opened the space for the public to confront a previously taboo subject. In most of these countries, even many years after a democratic transition, there remains a demand for further attention to the atrocities of the past, and these interests continue to affect the politics of the present for years into the future. In Chile, for example, a follow-up commission called the National Corporation for Reparation and Reconciliation was established to investigate cases left unresolved by the truth commission and to put a reparations policy into place. Years later the arrest of General Augusto Pinochet in London, on an extradition request from Spain, resulted in intense attention being refocused on the years of Pinochet's rule and the still contentious issues of responsibility and national recovery. In Argentina, 15 years after the end of military rule, nongovernmental victims organizations, particularly the Madres de la Plaza de Mayo and other groups representing family members of the people who had disappeared, continue to hold regular public protests and push for judicial action, further investigations into the location of those missing, and reparations for those illegally imprisoned or for families of people who disappeared or were killed.

Confronting, recording, understanding, and recovering from a brutal national past of dictatorship or civil war can be a process of many years, decades, or generations. It is not a process that can be closed in one or two years, the typical tenure of a truth commission. Thus, while a truth commission can fill the important role of bringing official acknowledgment to past state crimes, documenting previously denied events, and outlining needed reforms, its work should be seen as one part of a much broader process. Rather than closing the subject of the past, a successful truth commission should open up the issue to facilitate a more free and public discussion and help spark a longer-term process of national healing and reconciliation.

Truth commissions might be categorized according to various overarching and defining characteristics, such as the following three means of classification, which are useful in recognizing the different forms that truth commissions take:

- *Sponsorship.* A commission may be created through an *international* body, such as the UN (as in El Salvador and Guatemala) or may result from a *national* initiative of a president or parliament (as in Haiti, Chile, Argentina, and South Africa).
- *International or national membership and staff.* Likewise, a commission may be staffed entirely with nationals and be appointed with national commissioners (as in Chile and Argentina); it might employ and be appointed with only nonnationals (as in El Salvador); or it may use a mixed model of both national and international staff members and commissioners (as in Haiti and Guatemala).
- *Public hearings or confidential inquiries.* Those commissions that hold public hearings (South Africa, Uganda II, Germany) are able to engage the attention and interest of the public much more than those that hold all investigations and take all testimony behind closed doors (such as all Latin American commissions to date).

But while these categories are descriptively accurate, they are not necessarily prescriptively useful, since the experience of commissions to date does not argue that any one type (national versus international, UN versus presidential or parliamentary, etc.) is inherently better than another. A more useful typology of past commissions might focus instead on some of the more specific qualities of each commission that reflect its real capacities and contextual constraints. Table 9.3 summarizes the critical qualities of truth commissions and notes what is the ideal in most circumstances (the outside factors that affect a commission are addressed further below).

TRUTH COMMISSIONS AND THE PREVENTION OR RESOLUTION OF VIOLENT CONFLICTS

The study of truth commissions has been framed to date around the issue of accountability for past human rights abuses and violations of international humanitarian law and an interest in the prevention of such abuses in the future.[14] Little focused attention has been given to the interplay between truth seeking and the resolution or prevention of violent conflict per se.[15] A distinction is in order: human rights abuses and violations of humanitarian law often include violence, including violent and illegal arrests, torture and abuse in police stations and prisons, the disappearance or killing of activists or other political suspects, large-scale massacres, or harassment of minority communities. These are generally unilateral forms of repression against all too often unarmed opponents of a regime. Most of this type of violence is relatively covert, neither carried out in public spaces nor in competition between armed groups. Some of these practices, such as torture and police abuse, may continue long after a formal transition to peace or democracy. While recognizing the urgency of combating such unilateral state violence against individuals and the need to build protections for the respect of basic human rights and the rule of law in the future, those matters can be distinguished from the challenge of resolving or preventing overt violence between armed groups. How a truth commission might play a role in helping to resolve or prevent such overt violent conflict remains largely unaddressed, even while these bodies are often discussed in the course of formal negotiations for peace.

Before proposing the potential peace-making qualities of official truth seeking, it must first be recognized that by its very nature an exercise in digging up the crimes of powerful perpetrators—who often maintain considerable de jure or de facto power during the course of a transition—is almost by definition an exercise that will create conflict. The point of seeking the truth is that it has been intentionally well hidden, often silenced through force, and usually remains hotly contested. The full truth is likely to be a threat to those who were in power—those same persons whose cooperation is critical to reaching or maintaining peace. In a politically unstable period when these perpetrators are angling to maintain some measure of power and keep themselves out of jail, it is also virtually a given that a serious truth-seeking exercise will be met with threats aimed at curtailing the inquiry. Usually, these threats, including bomb scares and death threats, are targeted at the commission itself, though to date none of the serious threats have been carried out. In at least one case there was a threat or rumor of a military coup if the truth commission went too far.[16] It is also very common for victims to fear retaliation if they give testimony to the commission, especially if they name their assailants.

In addition, there is sometimes reason to fear that a strong truth commission report could spark revenge violence from victims and survivors or exacerbate tensions between ethnic or other groups that are already fragile. In Haiti the National Commission on Truth and Justice decided not to name perpetrators in its report in part because of concerns that those named could become victims of street justice, especially given the degree of general frustration and anger in the lack of prosecutions in court.[17] In Zimbabwe some have worried that releasing a long-closed human rights report could spark further conflict between groups. In Burundi, where the Commission of Inquiry's report was finished on the day of a military coup, the UN explicitly chose not to release the report publicly because of concerns that it could further inflame violence. Even in South Africa, the national organization representing victims and survivors, Khulumani, warned that many of the thousands of victims that it worked with were intensely frustrated, and they expected there might be

TABLE 9.3 Qualities or Characteristics of Truth Commissions: What Works Best?

	Large/ Strong/ Broad	→			Small/ Weak/ Narrow	Comments
Budget	>$35 million South Africa	*$5-$35 million Guatemala	$1-$5 million Chile, El Salvador	$500,000-$1 million Uganda II	<$500,000 Chad, ANC (I and II)	
Size of staff	*>200 South Africa, Guatemala	*101-200 Haiti	57-100 Argentina, Chile	11-50 El Salvador, Uganda II	1-10	
Length of commission	>3 years Uganda II	2-3 years South Africa, Sri Lanka	*1-2 years Guatemala	Nine months to 1 year Argentina, Chile, Haiti	<9 months El Salvador	Commission should always be given a deadline, even if extendable
Mandate: period of time to be investigated	>30 years South Africa Guatemala	15-29 years Chile	10-14 years El Salvador	5-9 years Argentina	<5 years Haiti	Must be determined by circumstances

Mandate: powers of investigation (subpoena, search and seizure, witness protection)	*Strong: South Africa		Some powers: Sri Lanka, El Salvador, Uganda II	Few powers: Chile, Argentina	Few powers: Argentina, Chile, Haiti, Guatemala	
Mandate: powers of reporting (name perpetrators, make mandatory recommendations)	*Very strong: El Salvador	Strong: South Africa	Some powers: Sri Lanka	Much excluded: Chile	Clear restrictions: Guatemala, Haiti	
Mandate: breadth of investigation	*Very broad: El Salvador, Chad, Guatemala	*Some abuses excluded: South Africa	Sri Lanka		Narrow focus: Argentina	Sometimes necessary and appropriate to narrow mandate
Mandate: what parties to be investigated	Complex conflict of three parties or more: South Africa		Two sides of conflict: El Salvador, Guatemala, Chile		One side only: Argentina, Chad, Haiti, ANC I and II	Must be determined by individual cases

* Ideal in most circumstances.

some violence against known perpetrators after the Truth and Reconciliation Commission finished its work.[18]

These examples suggest that a strong truth commission report can spark violence if it is not backed up by reasonable and fair institutional responses to gross and widespread human rights crimes. This is most likely to be true where there is intense frustration with the lack of justice, little outlook for change, and no sign of remorse, apology, or even symbolic reparation from former perpetrators and beneficiaries of the abusive rule. This is hardly an argument to weaken truth accounts, however, as it may also be true that a very weak truth report could increase tensions. Where victims have no doubt about the widespread abuses they suffered, a weak or compromised report could meet an angry response from organized victims' communities, especially if the account is seen as an intentional effort to rewrite history or whitewash the truth. While there are no clear examples of this occurring, it is easy to imagine such a situation in countries where a sense of history plays a powerful role in politics and nationalism.

In Rwanda a prominent international inquiry in 1993 revealed the extent of abuses perpetrated by government forces against Tutsis across the country. While this commission was created as a result of an agreement between the government and rebels calling for such an inquiry, the government showed no serious intention of curtailing its anti-Tutsi and inflammatory rhetoric. The commission's hard-hitting report, which named the president of Rwanda and other senior officials as playing a direct part in the atrocities, caused an uproar in the policy-making circles of Europe, especially in those countries that were then actively supporting the Rwandan government. The Belgium government recalled its ambassador for consultation, and France pulled its troops back from regions where fighting was ongoing. The commission's report was the first widely distributed report to clearly spell out the abusive practices of the Rwandan forces. While it had a short-term impact on international policy and made it difficult for the international community to claim ignorance of the severity of the situation as the 1994 genocide began, this knowledge did not produce the international political will to step in to prevent the unfolding tragedy. Where national or international will is lacking, knowing the truth alone is insufficient to halt further atrocities.

Some truth commissions begin their work even while political violence continues. While a truth commission is usually part of a peace agreement or other formal transition, sometimes certain regions continue to see fighting, perhaps as part of a separate conflict (as in the fighting in northern Sri Lanka that continued even while the disappearances commission proceeded with its work). This situation places constraints on a commission's work, in some cases making information collection difficult in certain regions of a country and raising questions about the impact of an inquiry on the ongoing violence. While a solid inquiry could perhaps play a positive role in bringing the conflict to a close, it is also possible that speaking the truth in the context of continuing battles could further inflame tensions (such as in KwaZulu Natal, South Africa, as described below). Ongoing overt violence or the threat of violence has sometimes dampened enthusiasm for digging up truths and hampered investigations. Because of a fear of retaliation, victims who live in the same community as their former perpetrators may hesitate to tell their stories, especially if those persons are still armed. For example, many victims in Haiti and Guatemala gave testimony to their respective commissions even while expressing fear of possible repercussions for doing so.[19]

In some countries the resolution of intercommunal violence may be so fragile that communities resist national efforts to dig into exactly what took place. In the eastern South African region of KwaZulu Natal, for example, intercommunity violence has continued long after the end of apartheid and the transition to democracy.[20] In recent years some communities have patched together local peace agreements and established "peace committees," which have ended the vicious cycles of violence and allowed refugees who fled the violence to return home. The idea of pointing out those who were responsible for previous killings was widely considered by villagers as certain to spark another round of violence, and thus they had little interest in a visit by the Truth and Reconciliation Commission.[21] Because of continuing violence throughout the region, some of the commission's public hearings that took place in KwaZulu Natal were sparsely attended.[22]

Given the clear threat of greater conflict and potential violence resulting from a serious inquiry into past abuses, it is ironic that truth commissions have come to be seen as a peace-making tool. But the fact that they have is a testament to the power of a silenced and forbidden history, the great demand from victims to know the full truth behind their suffering, and a widespread perception that such a history, if left unaddressed, could be an even greater source of conflict for years to come. Official truth seeking into past abuses will never by itself be enough to end or prevent the reoccurrence of violent conflict, but it can be a central piece of a peace-making strategy. A truth commission is likely to affect conflict resolution and prevention in three distinct ways. First, when official truth seeking is agreed to as part of a peace accord between warring parties, it may be seen as a concrete and positive initiative that can serve as an incentive for reaching peace. Second, a commission may help prevent the return of violence by confronting and defusing tensions around past conflict. And third, a truth report helps outline the needed reforms of state institutions so that conflicts can be mediated nonviolently and disenfranchised groups might be better represented in the political sphere.

Halting Ongoing Violent Conflict:
Addressing the Past at the Negotiating Table

When a war ends in a negotiated peace, mechanisms to address past human rights abuses and violations of international humanitarian law are likely to be addressed at the negotiating table. A truth commission may be proposed by the moderator, as took place in El Salvador, or might be pushed by one of the parties. But the idea of an official inquiry into past abuses is usually an attractive entity to at least one of the negotiating parties and may thus serve as an incentive to agreeing to a final peace accord.

UN-moderated peace talks led to an end to the civil wars in both El Salvador and Guatemala; the resulting peace accords committed the parties to institutional and policy reforms and set out the structure of new state entities. Among these agreements were the terms for a Commission on the Truth in El Salvador and a Historical Clarification Commission in Guatemala. Both of these commissions represented the central transitional mechanism for addressing past abuses, and reaching agreement on the powers of these commissions was a critical point in the respective negotiations.

Because of the intense passion around these issues, negotiations for a truth commission are usually very difficult. There is often a struggle between those who want a strong and in-depth inquiry and those who want to limit its terms. As there is an increasing understanding in recent years of the potential powers and constraints that can be written into a commission's terms of reference, negotiating parties and outside advocates can be expected to press hard to shape a commission's mandate to fit their interests, and the parties may be put under considerable pressure by their various constituencies. Former perpetrators may insist on favorable terms to any truth body before agreeing to leave power, such as a prohibition on naming the persons who carried out atrocities.

When a truth commission was discussed for Guatemala in 1994, there was serious pressure from civil society organizations on the parties and the UN negotiators. The agreement that was signed in Oslo, Norway, in June 1994 included a number of limitations on the commission that human rights and popular organizations in Guatemala considered unacceptable (their most serious concerns were that the commission was prohibited from "individualizing responsibility," was given only one year to complete its work, and was restricted from having any "judicial aim or effect").[23] While there had been several previous accords on other matters and a number of issues yet to be negotiated before arriving at a final peace accord, the agreement for the Historical Clarification Commission was by far the most contentious. The disappointment and protests from these groups after the accord was signed, and their intense pressure on the armed opposition that agreed to the accord, came close to derailing the peace talks altogether.

In other countries there have been negotiated peace agreements that have not included either the creation of a truth commission or any other measure to address past crimes. In Mozambique, for example, the government and armed opposition insisted on one unwritten but fairly explicit condition before even sitting down for talks on the terms of peace: that the issue of past abuses would not be addressed at the negotiating table. Almost no one has raised the issue since, as there is a wide perception that digging into the past might spark further violence. In Cambodia, as well, the issue of past abuses—including the 1 million to 2 million people killed by the Khmer Rouge in the late 1970s—was only obliquely referred to in the 1991 Paris agreements, which set the stage for a democratic transition, stating that "the policies and practices of the past shall never be allowed to return."[24] But the parties to the agreements, many of whom were closely connected to past abusive forces, had no interest in a thorough truth-seeking process.[25] Some discussion of a truth commission has arisen in recent years but has not gained momentum in the country.[26]

Thus, we are left with the paradox that the proposition of inquiring into the truth about past horrors may intensify conflict and risk violence, at least in the short term. It will sometimes be wholly rejected for fear of these repercussions. But where it is used, it is usually presented as an incentive to reaching peace and as a means for building a foundation for peaceful coexistence between former enemies in the future. Which of these seemingly contradictory dynamics develops around any particular set of negotiations will be determined by a number of real or perceived conditions: (1) What are the interests of the parties to the peace talks or those with the power to influence such talks? Are they served by truth seeking, or would they feel threatened by such investigations? (How powerful and vocal is civil society, and what are its interests, for example?) (2) Is there a widespread perception that violence would increase or could be resparked by such investigations, especially if perpetrators are identified? (3) Are there other community-based or indigenous mechanisms that may fill the demand for a reckoning with the past (such as firmly rooted traditional cleansing ceremonies prominent in Mozambique), which may reduce the felt need for a national-level initiative? The answers to these questions will help to determine the role that a proposal for truth seeking will play during the course of negotiations toward peace.

To the degree that a truth commission is an inducement to reach a peace settlement, the commission's work will of course not be taken up until after the agreement is reached, and thus the peace agreement will be affected more by the idea of and commitment to truth revealing rather than by the actual quality of the commission's work or report. However, it is generally possible to gauge the seriousness with which a commission will be able to undertake its task by the mandate and powers it is given, and these factors will usually affect the negotiations. The intensity of protest over the Guatemalan truth commission accord, for example, as described above, shows the delicacy of those negotiations, the danger of misreading the popular demand, and the importance of carefully considering the terms of any agreement for a truth commission.

Preventing Future Violence: Defusing Conflicts Over the Past

A denied and silenced past is likely to lead to simmering conflict, especially where former victims or survivors feel unheard and uncompensated. Even in countries such as South Africa, with the relative freedom to speak out and to approach the courts for legal recourse, there would surely be much more tension around the legacy of apartheid if the country had not instituted a strong and very public truth commission. While all complaints certainly have not been resolved by the commission, it has opened the space for demands and tensions to be aired and has explicitly recognized the pain and loss of victims on all sides of the violence.

Reconciliation is the stated goal of many transitional initiatives, and none more so than truth commissions. But despite often being stated as an aim in a truth-seeking exercise, what is intended by "reconciliation" is rarely spelled out. It is often unclear, for example, whether those hoping to find reconciliation through truth are referring to reconciliation on the national level among political leaders and the elite or a local and individual reconciliation between perpetrators and those who have been harmed, which may require a very different kind of truth process. Conceptions of reconciliation differ widely, including nonlethal coexistence; healing, forgiveness, and acceptance of one's former enemies, sometimes based on religious grounds; the narrative incorporation of contradictory events or stories; or the harmonization of contradictory world views.[27] For purposes of maintaining peace between groups, the simplest form of reconciliation—that of establishing ground on which conflicting groups can coexist side by side in a peaceful manner—should be the first priority.

Leaving aside these basic questions of how reconciliation is defined, which will not be explored further here, it is nonetheless reasonable to assume that understandings and conceptions of past conflicts will help shape future relationships and, as a corollary, that fundamentally different understandings of recent history and events can prevent former opponents from moving beyond the conflicts of old. Elsewhere I have proposed that reconciliation can be measured by the answers to three basic questions: How is the past dealt with in the public sphere? Are relationships between former opponents based on the present or the past? Finally, is there one version of the past or many?[28] Countries that carry competing versions of history are apt to see tensions simmer around these disagreements, which may then merge with fundamental conceptions of community or ethnic identity and nationalism. There are obvious examples today of the calamities that can result from using history—and the need to protect and avenge one's own understanding of history—to justify violence against opponents (the former Yugoslavia and the Middle East are but two examples). While a truth commission cannot be expected to resolve all historical misconceptions or even to win the support of all communities or parties it is directed to, past experience makes clear that a solid investigation and public report immediately after the cessation of conflict can virtually remove "the past" as a point of major conflict between political opponents, especially where abuses on both sides are investigated. Members of a commission, or those who originally craft its terms, should keep in mind these goals when weighing the question of how long the commission should continue its work before concluding its report. There is always a tension between the desire to undertake an extensive and in-depth investigation—and the need to do so in order to produce credible results—and the importance of finishing more quickly in order to contribute to the spirit of the political transition and to support the concrete reforms that may follow.

On the other hand, deeply rooted reconciliation may require acknowledgment and even sincere apology by those representing former perpetrators. Some commissions' reports have been rejected by the armed forces under investigation or have met with silence. Unfortunately, resistance to the truth will all too often continue, and serious efforts by former perpetrators to reach out to their victims or their families are rare. Some recent commissions have begun to address this problem in the course of their work, but much more serious and creative thinking is needed on how official truth seeking can consciously be used to initiate a wider process of community- and national-level reconciliation.

In addition to agreeing on basic history and a process of acknowledgment or apology from wrongdoers, reconciliation can be advanced through a process that airs differences between perpetrator or victim or where there are indigenous procedures in place to cleanse perpetrators of their wrongs and welcome them back into society, as exists in some African cultures. Ultimately, however, reconciliation is most likely where there were preexisting ties between the parties before the rift or conflict took place. Where racial, ethnic, or deep political or class differences separate victims and perpetrators, or separate two or more groups emerging from war, and where there was no genuine connection or understanding between these groups before the conflict started, the idea of any deep "reconciliation" developing from a truth-telling process is probably impractical. In contrast, in those societies where conflicting groups or individuals are connected by family, community, or ethnic ties, for example, a natural forgiveness and reconciliation might take place quickly. Experiences in South Africa (where some former black perpetrators have been forgiven and welcomed back into their home communities), Mozambique, and Sierra Leone (where, in both countries, children abducted into the war sometimes fought against their brothers on the opposing side) show this clearly to be true. Thus, a truth commission can facilitate a process that is supportive of reconciliation between opponents, but such reconciliation will also depend on other factors and existing circumstances that are largely outside a commission's control.

In stark contrast to South Africa and Chile, it should be noted that some truth commissions have held no presumption of promoting or achieving reconciliation as part of their work. The commissions on forcibly removed and disappeared persons in Sri Lanka, for example, which finished their reports in late 1997, used no rhetoric about reconciliation; they saw their task as documenting who had disappeared and recommending which families should receive reparations.[29] To suggest individual reconciliation would have been unreasonable, since virtually no perpetrators in Sri Lanka have stepped forward to express regret or even acknowledge their responsibility. Instead, the commissions called for legal justice and forwarded the names of the accused to prosecutors for further action.

Outlining Reforms to Mitigate Conflicts and Protect Human Rights

Beyond simply describing the past, truth commissions usually dedicate a portion of their reports to propose institutional and policy reforms to help prevent abuses in the future. Some commissions have included a full and detailed outline of specific reforms across many sectors of government. These have included changes needed in the judiciary, armed forces, police, and political sector; the need to prosecute perpetrators or purge them from active military or police duty; the promotion of a national human rights culture through educational and other programs; and the need to commit to international human rights norms through the ratification of international rights instruments. Other recommendations have included reparations for survivors and memorials for those killed, reconciliation initiatives, and follow-up measures to further investigate those matters not closed by the current commission. Where relevant, a report may make explicit reference to the urgency of stopping ongoing abusive practices, but the emphasis is usually on long-term institutional protections in order to prevent a slide back to the dark days of repression.

Many of these recommended reforms are relevant here, pertaining directly or indirectly to conflict prevention. For example, these reforms may lead to increased political representation of disenfranchised groups; more fair and transparent political competition in an appropriately structured electoral system; the halting of any ongoing harassment of groups or individuals of particular political, ethnic, or regional affiliation; or the enactment of compensation and other measures to assist those injured and to lessen the anger over previous wrongs. Reforms that pertain to the reduction of violent conflict might be grouped into two types. First are those that aim to strengthen structures and laws that protect against abuses or to respond to abuses when they take place, including changes in the police or armed forces or in systems to hold accountable and punish those responsible for past abuses. These reforms are clearly intended to act as a deterrent to future abuses and discriminatory practices, including those patterns that may feed into broader intergroup conflict. A second kind of reform are those that create or strengthen institutional structures to facilitate democratic conflict management, reduce the marginalization of any one group, and advance a sense of justice and equal participation by all groups in society. These may pertain to changes in the electoral system or institutional structures to give minorities or other under-represented groups a voice. Other papers in this volume address the conflict reduction aspects of these kinds of mechanisms in some detail.

Clearly, strong and useful recommendations are most likely to result from a strong and thoughtful truth commission, one with sufficient staff resources and expertise to think through the implications of its findings and to craft relevant recommendations in response. A commission that structures its work to allow it to investigate and better understand prominent patterns of past abuses and the causes and consequences of past policies and practices will be much better suited to suggest broad changes, compared to commissions that focus the bulk of their energies on individual case investigations. In addition, many past commissions have turned to the recommendations for reform suggested previously by foreign donor agencies, intergovernmental agencies, nongovernmental organizations, or independent scholars. The most conducive environment in which to expect strong recommendations flowing from a truth commission is where considerable attention and thought have already been given to designing solutions to the country's difficult problems—in fully understanding the weaknesses of the judiciary, for example, or in thinking through how elections could be better structured to bring in all minority parties—thus laying the groundwork for the commission to reiterate or build on this foundation. Finally, in designing new recommendations a commission will greatly benefit from reaching out to experts and interested parties for ideas and assistance.

Despite the best of intentions, however, most commissions can only make recommendations, leaving implementation to the initiative of the state president or legislature. Many countries have seen solid commission recommendations that go largely unimplemented. To date, only the truth commission in El Salvador had the power to make mandatory recommendations, per its mandate spelled out in the peace accord. Even there implementation of many of the reforms required significant pressure from the international community (and even under such pressure some of that commission's recommendations still were not implemented). Elsewhere, the momentum of a political transition and pressure from nongovernmental organizations and the international community can help push through reforms, but ultimately the most important factor is the existence of national political interest and the will to make changes, at least for the vast majority of recommendations that are usually directed at governmental actors. Without the political will, such recommendations are not likely to be put in place. Those designing future commissions should give careful thought to how they might empower the concluding recommendations of a commission so that they are more likely to be given serious consideration and the most appropriate or urgent recommendations are fulfilled.

GAUGING SUCCESS

There can be a wide range of expectations regarding a truth commission, and when observers and critics begin to evaluate the degree to which a commission was a "success," it is sometimes not clear which set of expectations they are responding to. Although these expectations are usually not clearly articulated, they will shape reaction to a commission's work and will define how it is judged. It is appropriate for the success of a truth commission to be evaluated on a number of different levels. Perhaps most importantly, the members of a truth commission should themselves consider these wide-ranging goals when outlining their work plan and methodology. In addition, these differing goals should be considered by the government or international agency that sponsors or facilitates the creation of the commission, nongovernmental advocacy groups pressing for improvements in a commission's work, international donor agencies

that may provide it with financial assistance, as well as researchers studying these bodies from a more academic perspective. The three general
areas that should be considered—that of *process, product,* and *impact* of the
commission—suggest a number of questions:

- *Process*
—Positive process for victims and survivors: Did the commission
reach out to all victims to invite them to give testimony? Did it include
psychologically supportive procedures or services for traumatized victims? Did the commission offer a witness protection program?
    —Encouraging broad public understanding of the past: Did the com-
mission hold public hearings? (Not all commissions are able to hold
public hearings, but where they are possible such hearings will engage
the public much more in the commission process.) Was the commission
perceived to be unbiased and fair?
    —Broad participation in search for truth: Did the commission invite
the participation of all sectors of society, such as churches, the armed
forces, former civilian leaders, nongovernmental organizations, and others? Did the commission gain the cooperation of former perpetrators or
others that are affiliated with abusive forces in its investigations?
- *Product*
—Quality of the report: Is the report accurate, accessible in style,
unbiased, and reasonably complete? Does it fairly represent the evidence
and the victims' testimony collected by the commission? Are there appropriate and specific recommendations outlined for reforms and other
measures to deal with the past?
    —How much truth is revealed? Are some important or representa-
tive cases resolved? Does the report fairly describe patterns of abuses?
Does it outline institutional and/or individual responsibility? (Not all
commissions will name perpetrators, but those that do will generally be
judged to be stronger and more powerful than those that do not.)
- *Postcommission impact*
—Healing and reconciliation at the individual and community levels:
Has the tension and conflict over the past been reduced? Is there now less
fear in speaking about the past? Has community or individual healing
been advanced? Have state officials or those representing former armed
opposition groups acknowledged and apologized for past abuses? Have
perpetrators themselves apologized for their wrongs? Has the report
been widely distributed? Is memory kept alive in the long term? Did the
commission spark broader and longer-term processes for communities to
address the past?
    —Prevention of future abuses and reparations for past wrongs at the
policy level: Have the recommendations of the commission been imple-

mented? Have prosecutions resulted or been strengthened as a result of the commission's report? Are reparations offered to victims?

This paper does not evaluate every truth commission according to each of these criteria, but a review of past experience leads to a number of basic conclusions. First, it is clear that most commissions have understood their primary responsibility to lie in their *product* and have thus structured their work around the investigation and resolution of key cases and the production of a final report. Questions of how the truth-seeking *process* might impact on society, especially how the commission's work might be structured to advance national-, community-, or individual-level reconciliation or healing, have usually not been seriously considered by past truth commissions as they designed their work plans (South Africa stands as the major exception). Meanwhile, the longer-term *impact* of a commission's work, especially in the implementation of its recommendations, lies largely outside the commission's control, since much of this will be determined by actions and decisions taken by others after the commission has closed its doors. Nevertheless, many critics have judged the success of past truth commissions in part by developments that do or do not take place long after the commissions have ended. While this is a fair, indeed an important, means of evaluation, political realities and outside actors should be recognized for the failure or success of a commission's long-term impact, as much as the work of the commission itself.

A commission's contribution to conflict resolution and prevention will be determined primarily by the criteria for evaluation listed earlier under *process* and *impact*. A commission report sets the stage for reforms through its recommendations, and an unbiased and far-reaching report can best encourage further societywide processes confronting past crimes. But the real effect on conflict reduction will be in how the process of truth seeking is undertaken, how and whether the recommendations are implemented, how public actors and participants in past violent conflict respond to the process and the report, and what other efforts follow that institute a longer-term process for grappling with this history.

Factors Influencing the Strength and
Success of a Truth Commission

There are a number of factors that together determine a truth commission's strength and success. Most of these factors are elements that a commission itself cannot control, such as the degree of governmental political backing it receives (which will determine the commission's access to official documentation and the cooperation of officials in assisting its inquiries), the degree of operational independence it is granted, the level of resources it is given to undertake its work, and the written mandate that defines its powers and investigatory focus. The strength and success of past commissions were most influenced by the following (this list excludes some important internal factors that are largely determined by management decisions, such as the quality of the staff and the commission's methodology for investigation and information management):

- *Domestic political will.* A strong commission depends on political backing and operational independence from authorities as well as access to official documentation in its investigations. Additionally, the impact of a truth commission will be greatest where civilian authorities hold the power to implement recommended reforms and have the political interest to do so and the willingness to accept and acknowledge the commission's conclusions and make its information broadly available to the public.
- *Role of perpetrators.* In some countries, perpetrators of old continue to hold significant power and are able to restrict a commission's mandate and powers. In addition, they may continue to justify their past wrongs and refuse to cooperate with investigations. The strongest commissions operate in circumstances where the power of former perpetrators has been significantly weakened and where perpetrators have clear incentives to acknowledge and apologize for past wrongs.
- *Role of civil society.* A strong and organized civil society is often critical to the creation of a strong commission, as human rights and victims' groups push for a strong mandate. In addition, the files from human rights monitoring groups, turned over to a truth commission when it begins its work, can help map out the patterns and concentration of abuses and help target investigations. In some countries, experienced staff from human rights groups have been recruited to staff commissions, providing the backbone of expertise and investigative experience. During the course of a truth commission's work, advocacy groups can play an important role in pushing to improve the reach or substance of the commission's work, and a range of civil society groups may be in a position to evaluate a commission's contributions both during its tenure and after its completion.
- *International role.* In some cases the international community may play an important role in the creation of a truth commission, in providing information and funding for the commission, and in pressing for implementation of its recommendations.
- *Available resources.* Some commissions have operated on very restricted budgets, several even running out of funds during the course of their work and spending considerable time on fund raising from international sources. Ideally, in order to avoid any appearance of inappropriate influence, all funds should be available or committed at the start of a

commission's work, especially when they come from the government that will be a target of investigation.

• *Mandate of a commission.* Many of the basic limitations and powers of a commission will be spelled out in its written mandate (usually a presidential decree, legislative act, or peace accord), which generally includes exactly what acts or events are to be investigated, over what period of time, and whether the commission has any powers such as an enforceable subpoena or witness protection capacity.

• *Composition of a commission.* Who the members of a truth commission are will ultimately have the greatest effect on the actual work of the commission, as they must shape out of whole cloth its procedures, priorities, methodology, work plan, and ultimately its final report.

• *Political climate.* A commission can have the greatest effect where there has been a loss of support for the old regime on both the popular and the elite levels, where there is a lack of polarization between sectors differently affected by the violence, and where the level of fear from reporting past abuses has lessened.

Each of these factors influences the success of a commission not only during its work but also before it begins (in the design of its mandate and in the preparatory stage) and after it ends (in implementing its recommendations and responding to, making use of, and distributing its report). How the influence of these factors changes through these different stages is outlined in Table 9.4.

Interim Indicators

If one ultimate goal of a conflict resolution exercise is to prevent further violence in the future, it would be useful to be able to point to markers along the way that might indicate whether violent conflict was more or less likely to develop. Interim indicators can also influence policy by suggesting what positive developments should be encouraged and what signs of potential problems should be addressed. The time frame in which these indicators should be watched will depend on each case. It would be important to gauge these indicators immediately after the cessation of violence and then immediately after a truth commission has finished its report. But since it is common for communities to hold on to their history (especially their grievances of wrongdoing) for many generations, some of the indicators listed here would be useful almost indefinitely or as long as there is a threat of conflict arising in part as a response to past events.

The kinds of indicators that should be watched are discussed below. While these indicators point to the potential for conflict based on how and whether the past is addressed, whether such conflict turns violent depends on a whole host of factors separate from the question of truth seeking. Most importantly, this depends on whether there are actors present in the political mix whose interests are served through violence and who have the means to turn their grievances into violent action. In Bosnia, Rwanda, and elsewhere "the past," mixed with an exaggerated fear of the future, has very much been used as a tool by which to shape public opinion and rally followers into brutalities. Elsewhere, armed opposition groups have pointed to past injustices and abusive policies to win popular support.

But if neither armed resistance, a military coup, or intergroup fighting is likely, even severe frustrations and unacknowledged pain may not lead to political violence. For example, according to Table 9.5, Chile shows the potential for conflict around issues of the past. When questions around the legacy of the Pinochet regime arise in Chile, it is with much conflict—including police violence against demonstrators at least twice in 1998, for example—but serious political violence in the form of a civil war, armed opposition, or military coup is considered extremely unlikely.

Likewise, an analysis of the implementation of reforms and institutional protections could be done to gauge whether conflicts can be addressed fairly through legal means and whether groups that may have previously turned to violence are now given a fair voice in the political process.

CONCLUSION

The field of truth seeking as an official transitional mechanism is still relatively new. As more and more states begin to turn to truth commissions or similar bodies as a means to address a difficult past, researchers and academics are just beginning to understand the complexity of questions and difficulties around this subject matter and to grapple with it seriously. The primary limitations in this field to date are as follow: (1) Most who have written on the subject have in-depth experience pertaining to only one country or one region, and may not always be in a position to cull lessons from these experiences that are applicable in very different contexts and regions. This field is best served by a broadly comparative approach. (2) Most of the articles to date that analyze any one truth commission in depth have been written by participants in the commission—a commissioner or senior staff person. While these articles have been extremely valuable, there may always be a potential for bias or blind spots when a comission's activities are recorded by participant-observers. This in part is a reflection of the parallel problems that (3) most commissions have not been monitored closely by an outsider while the commissions

TABLE 9.4 How Strong and Effective a Truth Commission? Influencing Factors Over Time

Factors	Precommission	During Commission	Postcommission
Domestic political will	Political interest in strong inquiry	Political backing for commission's work; respect for commission's independence; access to official documentation	Political interest and investment in implementation of commission's recommendations; symbolic acts of contrition
Role of perpetrators	Power of perpetrators in shaping or limiting inquiry	Willingness of perpetrators to cooperate with commission	Willingness to acknowledge or apologize for wrongs done
Role of civil society	Civil society and victims' role in lobbying for a strong inquiry	Contacts, case files, and assistance from civil society	Lobbying for implementation of recommendations and broad distribution and use of report
International role	International pressure, as necessary, for a fair and strong inquiry	Funding for commission; declassification of foreign government information to assist in commission's investigations	Pressure for implementation of commission's recommendations

Available resources	Resources available for preparation and planning	Commission's financial resources; expertise and experience of commissioners and staff	Resources for implementation of recommendations, including reparations policy
Mandate of commission	Is a preparation period stipulated before commission begins?	What powers and limitations in commission's investigations; how much time to complete work?	Are recommendations mandatory? What happens to commission's archives?
Composition of commission	Transparent appointment procedure?[a]	Perceived to be unbiased, knowledgeable, and trustworthy?	—
Political climate	Broad public and political support for reckoning with past	Level of fear and protection for victims and witnesses to speak out	Public interest and political space for broad discussion of report

[a]In fact, with the exception of South Africa and to some degree Guatemala, most truth commissions to date have not been appointed through a transparent procedure and with public input. Most are appointed at the sole discretion of the president or parliament or in consultation with parties to a peace accord. In South Africa the commission resulted from a months-long selection process that collected public nominations and culminated in public hearings to interview the final candidates. A transparent appointment procedure should be encouraged for future commissions.

TABLE 9.5 Is the Past Likely to Be a Source of Future Conflict? A Few Indicators[a]

Indicators	Tensions Reduced; Violence Over the Past Unlikely	Tension Over the Past Likely to Remain	More Serious Tension; Potential for Future Violence if Unresolved
How is a truth commission's report used?	Broad distribution of commission's report (or summary) and extensive media and public discussion of conclusions and recommendations (South Africa)	Report released but not broadly available; little public discussion (El Salvador, Chile)	Report kept sealed; discussion of past discouraged (Zimbabwe)
Government attitude and policy: acknowledgment of wrongs?	Formal acknowledgment and apology on behalf of the state (Chile)	Prefer silence on the topic (Argentina-Menem)	Denial and disinformation about past conflict (Rwanda, 1993)
Perpetrators' response to truth commission's report	Willingness of perpetrators to accept and apologize for wrongs and to contribute to symbolic reparations to victims (some in South Africa and Mozambique)	Silence about past wrongs (Argentina until 1995)	Continued denial of or justification for past abuses (Chile, El Salvador, Serbia, Sri Lanka)

Are victims formally recognized?	Memorial built in honor of victims; days of remembrance honored; individual or symbolic reparations for victims	Disagreements about who and what should be remembered; lack of political interest in honoring victims	Unwillingness to acknowledge victims or continued denial that there were unjustified victims; memorials remain in place that honor abusive forces
How is history taught in schools?	Use of truth report in schools; fair and balanced treatment of subject	Silence about the past; recent conflict not integrated into teaching (El Salvador, Chile)	Different versions of the past are taught in different schools and to different communities (Bosnia)
Societal consensus about past wrongs?	Apparent societal consensus that abuses were wrong (South Africa, Argentina)	Lack of consensus but silence on the matter (Chile until 1998)	Lack of consensus and open conflict based partly on different conceptions of past violence (Rwanda, Bosnia)

[a]This table includes examples of countries where there both have and have not been truth commissions.

were under way, and some commissions severely restrict access by outsiders for confidentiality reasons. In addition, (4) truth commissions to date have been studied and described largely on an anecdotal and impressionistic level, with little scientific rigor or theoretical modeling that may propose generic lessons for future cases.

There is much room for more thorough and in-depth studies of these processes. The needs are many, but include the following:

• *Case studies.* A thorough and lengthy write-up of key cases would be useful for scholars and practitioners alike. Very little of this has been done.

• *Comparative and theoretical research,* including monitoring ongoing truth-seeking processes and those now in development. Some questions that call for attention include the following:

—When will conflict around the past turn to *violent* conflict around the past? What serves as a spark to long-held grievances? What role do memory and history play in the ongoing conflicts of today (Sri Lanka, Cyprus, Middle East, Kosovo, etc.)?

—The cases examined here are all conflicts that took place within national borders (although sometimes with the help of outsiders, like U.S. funding and arms for Central American and Southern Cone militaries, or with violence that spilled over borders, such as the South African attacks against activists exiled abroad). Is there a role for official truth seeking following international wars or conflicts? How might such bodies be created and by whom would they be overseen? The Israeli-Palestinian conflict may eventually approach the subject of the past and would need to consider new models that take into account the different perceptions of history across the political and national divides.

—What is the range of alternate forms of truth seeking (here labeled quasi-truth commissions) and in what circumstances are they most appropriate?

—What will be the relationship between the future International Criminal Court and national truth commissions, especially around legal questions of sharing evidence, confidentiality of investigations, and the use of witnesses?[30]

—What kind of international guidelines might be proposed, both to assist those designing future truth commissions and to hold commissions to reasonably high standards? In drafting such guidelines, attention should be given to the elements of evaluation outlined earlier (process, product, and impact).

—What are the real psychological and emotional impacts on victims and witnesses of truth inquiries, and how can the healing effect be strengthened? How do these effects compare with the impacts of victims' participation in judicial inquiries?

- *Historical research*
—What does history tell us about the legacy of unaddressed pain and unacknowledged events? What can we learn from France after World War II, Spain after Franco, the Armenian genocide early in this century, Native Americans throughout the Americas, and other uncommissioned but unforgotten periods of authoritarian rule or brutality? Why in some cases was there no demand for truth seeking, while in other cases the wounds of the past remain open?

The most useful contribution of a truth commission is to open, rather than close, a difficult period of history. Ideally, it should lead to other processes or institutions, such as memorials, museums, new educational curricula, and perhaps other commissions of inquiry or reparations bodies, all of which may better integrate a silenced and conflicted past into a respectful and peaceful memory. How these national pains are best addressed and how a society and its political life will be affected by this legacy will differ in every country. But as new and creative approaches to building peaceful relations are explored and developed further, the question of how to best respond to the full texture of past conflicts will continue to demand attention.

NOTES

[1]The field of "transitional justice" is in rapid development, although writers and commentators have used the term in different ways. Some have focused primarily on newly democratized states or those recently emerging from civil war. Others have inferred a broader sense of responding to a widespread practice of human rights crimes or violations of humanitarian law, including those that may have taken place under a democratic government or those that may have taken place many years before. In some cases, fully democratic and nontransitional countries grapple with these very same issues (as in specific events or practices that have taken place in the United States, or in European states that today are still grappling with the legacy of World War II).

[2]For an overview of the transitional justice approaches available and experiences in a number of transitional countries, see Neil J. Kritz, ed., *Transitional Justice: How Emerging Democracies Reckon with Former Regimes*, Vols. I-III (Washington, D.C.: United States Institute of Peace Press, 1995).

[3]See Herman Schwartz, "Lustration in Eastern Europe," *Parker School of East European Law*, vol. 1, no. 2 (1994), pp. 141-171.

[4]For a more detailed treatment of the subject of truth commissions, including descriptions of over 20 commissions to date, see Priscilla B. Hayner, *Unspeakable Truths: Confronting State Terror and Atrocity*. (New York and London: Routledge, 2000).

[5]This Australian policy, which between 1910 and the early 1970s forcibly removed as many as 100,000 Aboriginal children from their homes, was based on the racist notion that mainstreaming Aboriginal children into white society would be to their benefit. This government inquiry concluded that the policy was "genocidal" and urged reparations and apology. See the report of this goverment inquiry, *Bringing Them Home: Report of the Na-*

380 PAST TRUTHS, PRESENT DANGERS: THE ROLE OF OFFICIAL TRUTH SEEKING

tional Inquiry into the Separation of Aboriginal and Torres Strait Islander Children from Their Families (Sydney: Human Rights and Equal Opportunity Commission, 1997).

6Leo Valladares, National Commissioner for the Protection of Human Rights in Honduras, in conversation with the author, October 1995.

7 *Brasil: Nunca Maís* (Rio de Janeiro: Editora Vozes Ltda., 1985). For a description of the Brazilian project, see Lawrence Weschler, *A Miracle, A Universe: Settling Accounts with Torturers* (New York: Penguin, 1990; reprint with postscript, Chicago: University of Chicago Press). Because the Brazil project was carried out secretly, church backing not only provided financial support but also lent legitimacy to the published report.

8Servicio Paz y Justicia, *Uruguay: Nunca Más: Informe Sobre la Violación a los Derechos Humanos (1972-1985)*, 1989. The parliamentary commission was mandated to investigate disappearances only, which missed the great majority of abuses in the country (illegal imprisonment and torture).

9The Archbishop of Guatemala's Office of Human Rights project resulted in a four-volume final report, published in 1998. See *Guatemala: Nunca Más*, vols. I-IV (Guatemala City: Oficina de Derechos Humanos del Arzobispado de Guatemala, 1998). A summary of the report has been published in English as *Guatemala: Never Again!* (Maryknoll, N.Y.: Orbis Books, 1999).

10See, for example, *Links: Historical Almanac, Volume I* (Moscow: Progress Phoenix, 1991) and *List of Executed People: Volume I: Donskoi Cemetery 1934-1943* (Moscow: Memorial, 1993), both in Russian. For a description of Memorial's activities, see "Making Rights Real: Two Human Rights Groups Assist Russian Reforms," *Ford Foundation Report*, Summer 1993, pp. 10-15, or Nanci Adler, *Victims of Soviet Terror: The Story of the Memorial Movement* (New York: Praeger, 1993).

11National Commission on the Disappeared, *Nunca Más: Informe de la Comisión Nacional Sobre la Desaparición de Personas* (Buenos Aires: Editorial Universitaria de Buenos Aires, 1984), or, in English, *Nunca Más: The Report of the Argentine National Commission on the Disappeared* (New York: Farrar Straus Giroux, 1986).

12A number of high-level members of the military junta were convicted and jailed based in part on files from the commission on disappeared persons. But trials in Argentina were limited by pseudo-amnesty laws that prevented the prosecution of many perpetrators. Those who were convicted and imprisoned were freed several years later under a presidential pardon.

13The author has looked into the question of why some states may prefer to leave the past alone in her book, *Unspeakable Truths: Confronting State Terror and Atrocity* (New York and London: Routledge, 2000), Ch. 12.

14Human rights abuses generally refer to abuses by the state against an individual and in some cases also to abuses by armed opposition groups, such as when they control territory. Violations of international humanitarian law refer to crimes against the laws of war as articulated in the Geneva Conventions of 1949, committed by either government or opposition forces.

15While little serious research has been dedicated to this question, two recent important studies—by the Carnegie Commission on Preventing Deadly Conflict and by the Aspen Institute's Justice and Society Program—have identified official truth seeking as a central component to be considered in peace-making endeavors. See Carnegie Commission on Preventing Deadly Conflict, *Preventing Deadly Conflict: Executive Summary of the Final Report* (New York: Carnegie Corporation, 1997, p. 27), and Alice H. Henkin, ed., *Honoring Human Rights: From Peace to Justice: Recommendations to the International Community* (Washington, D.C.: The Aspen Institute, 1998, pp. 17-19, 35-37).

16A coup was threatened in El Salvador if the Commission on the Truth named perpetrators. The commission proceeded to publish names, but the coup threat was not carried out (though a sweeping amnesty was passed immediately, perhaps to pacify the armed forces).

[17]The Haitian commission suggested that trials ensue first and that their list of persons responsible for crimes might be made public at a later date.

[18]Interviews by author with staff of Khulumani, September 1997, Johannesburg, South Africa.

[19]Interviews by author with commission staff in Haiti (December 1996) and Guatemala (May 1998).

[20]The intercommunity violence of KwaZulu Natal has roots in the struggle against apartheid; the Inkatha Freedom Party was funded and armed by the apartheid state to attack supporters of the African National Congress.

[21]Based on the author's interviews in Isipingo, South Africa, including members of the Nsimbini KwaNkonka Local Peace Committee, September 1996.

[22]The Truth and Reconciliation Commission was well aware of these tensions and tried to choose its hearing locations partly in response to these localized dynamics.

[23]See the "Agreement on the Establishment of the Commission to Clarify Past Human Rights Violations and Acts of Violence that Have Caused the Guatemalan Population to Suffer," United Nations Document A/48/954/S/1994/751, Annex II. Once under way, the commission's period of work was extended to 18 months.

[24]"Agreement on a Comprehensive Political Settlement of the Cambodian Conflict," signed in Paris on October 23, 1991, Article 15.

[25]See Stephen P. Marks, "Forgetting 'The Policies and Practices of the Past': Impunity in Cambodia," *Fletcher Forum of World Affairs*, vol. 18, no. 2 (Summer/Fall 1994).

[26]A UN-commissioned Group of Experts recommended in early 1999 that a truth commission be considered in Cambodia, suggesting especially the need for discussion and due consideration by Cambodians themselves on the question. See "Report of the Group of Experts for Cambodia Established Pursuant to General Assembly Resolution 52/135," United Nations Document A/53/850/S/1999/231, pp. 52-54. For a discussion of recent developments and debates around truth seeking and justice in Cambodia, see Brad Adams, "Snatching Defeat from the Jaws of Victory?," *Phnom Penh Post*, January 23, 1999; Balakrishnan Rajagopal, "The Pragmatics of Prosecuting the Khmer Rouge," *Phnom Penh Post*, January 8-21, 1999; and Stephen P. Marks, "Elusive Justice for the Victims of the Khmer Rouge," *Journal of International Affairs*, vol. 52, no. 2 (Spring 1999), pp. 691-718.

[27]For further discussion of these different conceptions of reconciliation, see Susan Dwyer, "Reconciliation for Realists"; David Crocker, "Reckoning with Past Wrongs: A Normative Framework"; and David Little, "A Different Kind of Justice: Dealing with Human Rights Violations in Transitional Societies," all appearing in *Ethics and International Affairs*, vol. 13 (1999). See also Donald W. Shriver, Jr., *An Ethic for Enemies: Forgiveness in Politics* (New York: Oxford University Press, 1995); Kader Asmal, Louise Asmal, and Ronald Suresh Roberts, *Reconciliation Through Truth: A Reckoning of Apartheid's Criminal Governance* (Cape Town: David Philip Publishers, 1996).

[28]For a full exploration into this concept of reconciliation, see Priscilla B. Hayner, "In Pursuit of Justice and Reconciliation: Contributions of Truth Telling," in *Comparative Peace Processes in Latin America*, Cynthia J. Arnson, ed. (Washington, D.C.: Woodrow Wilson Center Press and Stanford CA: Stanford University Press, 1999), pp. 363-383.

[29]Interview by the author with Manouri Muttetuwegama, chair of the Commission of Inquiry into the Involuntary Removals and Disappearances of Persons in the Western, Southern, and Sabaragamuwa Provinces of Sri Lanka, on September 18, 1998, in Brighton, England.

[30]The question of the relationship between the future International Criminal Court and national truth commissions has been raised in discussions of a truth commission for

Bosnia. The chief prosecutor and president of the International Criminal Tribunal for the Former Yugoslavia strongly opposed the idea of a truth commission, seeing such an inquiry as likely to damage the tribunal's prosecution efforts. Others disagree with this view, seeing a truth commission as potentially advantageous in helping to gather information and material for later use by the tribunal. All agree, however, that these issues raise many questions that are likely to arise in the operations of the permanent International Criminal Court. For further exploration of this issue, see Priscilla B. Hayner, *Unspeakable Truths*, Ch. 13.

10

New Challenges to Conflict Resolution: Humanitarian Nongovernmental Organizations in Complex Emergencies

Janice Gross Stein

In an emergent global politics the definition of conflict that is interna tionally relevant has burst through the constraints of sovereignty. It is not surprising that ethnic conflict that spills across borders and secessionist movements that wish to reconfigure existing states should be the subject of global concern. These conflicts either threaten existing state borders or flow over them and are logically included in established con- cepts of international conflict. What is new are the scope and intensity of global attention to the actions of a state against its own citizens, when these actions violate international norms, and to the violent actions of one group against another group even when the violence does not spill over state borders.

Within this expanded definition of international conflict, new types of dilemmas are emerging that present unprecedented challenges to conflict resolution. The shape of these new challenges is only beginning to be defined as established institutions and new players work to adapt and develop strategies of conflict resolution. Conflict resolution here refers to efforts to prevent or mitigate violence resulting from inter- group or interstate conflict as well as efforts to reduce underlying dis- agreements (see Chapter 1, this volume). Here I look at the challenges faced by those who are seeking to mitigate violence within the context of complex humanitarian emergencies. These emergencies arise from violence inflicted by one group against another within the confines of a state, from the capture of state institutions by one group, or by the collapse of these institutions and the failure of governance. These kinds of problems have created recurrent challenges for international conflict resolution in the past decade.

These new challenges have developed in a context of disengagement by the major powers from all but areas of core interest. After the intervention in Somalia, the United States as well as most of the other big powers have generally been unwilling to commit forces to mitigate violence and prevent humanitarian disasters. NATO's unprecedented intervention in Kosovo—its attack against a sovereign state for violence committed against its own citizens—may well be the exception that proves the more general rule: the intervention took place in Europe, at the core of NATO's mandate. As the great powers disengage from all but areas of core interests, international institutions are increasingly hobbled as willing troop contributors to emergency forces become ever scarcer. And not only are the great powers less willing to provide security, they are disengaging as well from the provision of emergency assistance to those who are deliberately targeted and victimized by violence. Assistance and relief to the victims of violence are also being privatized.

It is in this context of disengagement and privatization that international nongovernmental organizations (NGOs) face new responsibilities in far more complex and dangerous situations than before. NGOs are playing a growing role, directly and indirectly, in international conflict resolution only in part because they can make good use of some of the less traditional, integrative strategies of conflict resolution. More importantly, states are increasingly less willing to run the risks created by strategies to mitigate violence. The humanitarian NGOs are at the forefront of those that confront most directly the consequences of great power disengagement and privatization in the complex humanitarian emergencies that are now considered legitimately as part of international conflict. This paper focuses on the challenges facing humanitarian NGOs as the paradigmatic case that best exemplifies the new set of challenges to international conflict resolution.

I first analyze the dimensions of complex humanitarian emergencies and explore how these emergencies create new challenges for conflict resolution, with special attention to the global factors that make these challenges more acute. I identify the challenges that humanitarian NGOs face and their implications for processes of conflict resolution. I then assess the troubling evidence that, on occasion, humanitarian NGOs have inadvertently contributed to the escalation of violence rather than conflict resolution. I review what NGOs have done to address the challenges and then examine three possible strategies, some of them counterintuitive, which could contribute to the mitigation of violence and promote conflict resolution. In the final section I assess how relevant these challenges and strategies are to other organizations and institutions seeking to mitigate violence and resolve conflicts.

COMPLEX HUMANITARIAN EMERGENCIES AND THE NEW CHALLENGES

In the past several years humanitarian NGOs have increasingly found themselves facing a set of powerful and largely unprecedented choices. This challenge is best exemplified in the humanitarian work that was done with Rwandan refugees in eastern Zaire in the aftermath of the genocide and the victory of the Rwanda Patriotic Front in 1994. Agencies charged with running refugee camps, using the most tested and progressive methods of camp management, nevertheless found themselves by the autumn employing mass murderers and war criminals as local staff. The perpetrators of the genocide had reimposed authority over hundreds of thousands of refugees under the supervision of the United Nations (UN) and humanitarian NGOs and were organizing to use the camps as a springboard to attack the government of Rwanda. Humanitarian assets were being used to fuel rather than resolve conflict. A more perverse outcome from the perspective of humanitarian NGOs is difficult to imagine.

The perversion cannot be explained exclusively or even largely by NGO practices. Certainly, practices were flawed at times, but in this case better practices would not have prevented the militias from organizing the camps. The roots of the unanticipated and negative consequences of assistance are found in the attributes of complex humanitarian emergencies and in the global conditions that intensify the challenges created by these emergencies: the growing international security vacuum and the privatization of international assistance.[1]

Complex Humanitarian Emergencies

I define a complex humanitarian emergency as a multidimensional humanitarian crisis created by interlinked political, military, and social factors most often arising from violent internal wars that in turn frequently are the result of state failures. It almost always involves some combination of mass population movements, severe food insecurity, macroeconomic collapse, and acute human rights violations up to and including genocidal projects. These kinds of emergencies have tripled in the past decade, affecting millions of people.[2]

The root causes of these complex emergencies grow from failures of development, the weaknesses of the state and the withering of its capacity, or the capture of the state apparatus by organized fragments of the population. In the violence that develops, social control over elements of the population is a key strategic objective of internal war, with civilians as a principal target, rather than a byproduct of other military activity.[3] Many of these internal wars that are fought for control over resources become cyclical and self-perpetuating, as violence generates profit for those who use it most effectively.

State failure can refer to a lack of capacity on the part of state institutions to secure territory, enforce authority, or maintain a monopoly on coercive violence.[4] The state cannot secure the basic rights of citizens, fails to provide fundamental protection, and becomes unable to fulfill essential international legal responsibilities. As the authority and capacity of the state weaken, it may invite attack from disaffected segments of the population who can mobilize resources. In response, a weakening state may attack its own population in an effort to reassert authority, or the state may collapse or implode.[5] The Somali bombing of sections of northern Somalia is an example of the former, while the flight of Siyaad Barre from Somalia is an example of failure through collapse.

Alternatively, segments of the population can capture even a relatively strong state for parochial purposes and use instruments of the state to attack segments of the population. The militant Hutu militias, motivated by their strong opposition to a negotiated power-sharing agreement, itself the result of a major international effort at conflict resolution, captured the state in Rwanda in April 1994 and launched a genocidal massacre of Tutsis and moderate Hutus.

It is in this context that humanitarian organizations attempt to provide emergency assistance and, increasingly, to mitigate the violence. Humanitarianism occurs when the political system is in crisis or has failed; humanitarians act to relieve the human suffering that is the consequence of political failure.[6] The essence of humanitarianism has been its neutrality and universality, its refusal to choose one distress over another.[7] Not only those NGOs that deliver relief assistance but also those working explicitly to facilitate conflict resolution seek to promote human welfare among distressed populations. The imperative is for action, to save lives.[8] This categorical imperative creates the political legitimacy for action in humanitarian emergencies.[9] Humanitarian action is designed for the short term, for limited groups, for limited objectives, until legitimately constituted authority can assume its obligations.

Humanitarian action in a complex humanitarian emergency, however, occurs in a context very different from the natural earthquakes and disasters that are familiar terrain to NGO personnel. Increasingly, NGOs are struggling to provide relief and assistance under conditions of civil war, often brutal civil war. In the insurgencies and counterinsurgencies characteristic of modern civil wars, human populations are both the principal targets and the shields. They are not the unanticipated consequences of military strategy, as they are in major conventional battles, but rather its principal targets. The aim of much contemporary military strategy in civil wars is to make the civilian population hostage and, if possible, to prevent or undo the effects of emergency relief and the protection of civilians.

In the internecine struggle for dominance in Somalia and Sierra Leone, and even more so in the openly genocidal landscapes of Rwanda and Burundi, strategies of insurgency and counterinsurgency warfare seek political control over civilian populations, inflict costs on those populations, at times force their movements en masse, and in some cases systematically kill large numbers for political or military ends. Civilian casualties are not counted as "collateral damage" but as measures of strategic gain. In Somalia and Sierra Leone, militias and army units alike looted communities, destroyed available resources, engaged in scorched-earth tactics against the local infrastructure, and attacked civilian populations. All over Central Africa in the 1990s insurgency campaigns were fought behind the shields of population groups.

The human costs that nongovernmental agencies address are not incidental to the conflict; rather, they are its essential currency. Civilians, and those humanitarian NGOs that would protect them, become the objects of military action. They and their resources stand not apart from but directly on the battlefield. Becoming part of the battle challenges all of the fundamental precepts of humanitarian action and creates qualitatively new challenges for conflict resolution.

Disengagement by the Major Powers and the Consequent Security Vacuum

The challenge to NGOs of engagement where civilians are deliberately targeted is made far more difficult by the repeated unwillingness or incapacity of the major powers to act through the UN Security Council, regional organizations, or through other appropriate instruments, to provide security first for endangered civilians and then for NGO personnel who are in the field offering protection. Somalia was the exception at one stage of its emergency, but so negative were the experiences of the UN and particularly the U.S. "military humanitarian" missions in Somalia, and so limited the strategic goals in comparison to the apparent costs, that Somalia set a "Mogadishu line" of active engagement that the U.S. and other Western forces were thereafter unwilling to cross in the African context. The great exception was the NATO engagement in Kosovo, in the heartland of Europe, when the abuse of a population by its government was transparent; even then, military involvement came only after a decade of experience with the abusive government. Almost everywhere else the nongovernmental sector has found itself working in a political/ security vacuum created by a decline of interest on the part of the major powers. It is the absence of an adequate security envelope, I argue, that creates many of the observed negative externalities of assistance and relief and creates unprecedented challenges for conflict resolution.

Even levels of support far less demanding than military engagement to provide security for beleaguered populations are dropping. The substantial increase in what the humanitarian community calls the "internally displaced" is telling; it reflects an increasing inability of populations in distress to seek asylum across borders and become officially recognized "refugees" with access to the political and humanitarian rights of refugees.[10] The growth in the numbers of internally displaced persons reflects the growing tendency for the international community to disengage politically and economically from these conflicts, to attempt to contain their effects, and to ensure that the costs are "internalized" in the affected communities.[11] This strategy of containment gives relief priority over protection of the basic rights of displaced populations.[12] Containment also constrains and limits available strategies of conflict resolution.

The Privatization of International Assistance

As the major powers become more unwilling to engage directly or through the UN, they are channeling ever-larger shares of their assistance through NGOs. Their funding to NGOs has increased even as their spending on bilateral emergency assistance programs has diminished.[13] In 1996, for example, more aid to Africa was channeled through NGOs than through official development assistance programs. Of course, Western government aid agencies are still the largest source of resources, but in complex emergencies in particular NGOs are increasingly the principal conduit of assistance and so face an ever-larger share of the challenges that complex emergencies generate for humanitarians.[14] The major powers are increasingly privatizing their assistance programs.[15] They expect—unrealistically—that the community of NGOs can fill the security vacuum left by inaction on the part of states.[16] International institutions have also vastly increased the proportion of their funding for emergency assistance that is channeled through NGOs; the European Commission, for example, raised its funding for NGOs from zero to 40 percent, with a corresponding reduction in bilateral emergency aid from 95 to 6 percent between 1976 and 1990.

The growing importance of NGOs as international actors is a function both of the privatization of assistance and the withdrawal of states and international organizations from the field. Increasingly, it is NGO personnel who are providing relief and assistance to the victims of conflict in the space vacated by states and international institutions. These NGOs, with a long-standing commitment to a humanitarian ethic, now find themselves in the eye of the storm. Particularly since the end of the Cold War, NGOs have become more prominent—and more controversial—especially in the complex humanitarian emergencies that arise from local conflicts.[17] For several of the worst months of the Somali famine in 1991, for example, a handful of NGOs and the ICRC were the only international presence in the country providing relief and assistance. In Sierra Leone, NGOs provided relief in parts of the country declared off limits by the UN. In Rwanda/Zaire the flood of refugees in the autumn of 1994 was met by NGOs, working without an official UN presence. In Burundi, where military activity kept the UN out of important regions of the country, NGOs were again at the front line in the delivery of humanitarian relief assistance.[18]

As governments have retreated and assistance has been privatized, the responsibilities of humanitarian NGOs to channel aid directly to vulnerable populations has grown. As their responsibilities—and power—have grown, NGOs have become targets of opportunity for both the local governments that are losing power and the militias that seek to control resources, to finance their own activities and to bleed the government. NGOs consequently become "targets at best and enemies at worst," similar to the civilian populations they seek to help.[19] In 1998, for the first time in the history of the UN, casualties among humanitarian workers exceeded those of military peacekeeping missions.[20]

Increasingly, the large NGOs specializing in traditional development assistance and relief have adopted components of a conflict resolution agenda in their emergency programming. Action Aid, for example, has explicitly designed programs for internally displaced persons around principles of reconciliation. CARE Canada is running a theater program for young people in Sarajevo that is explicitly designed to promote reconciliation. This represents a significant departure for most of the large NGOs and one that is likely to represent a growing trend in their activities, as political backing and funding for these kinds of conflict resolution activities increase. Conflict prevention and resolution are now squarely on the NGO agenda.

Here I focus on the role of the large humanitarian NGOs in the context of a complex humanitarian emergency that grows out of violent conflict, in order to examine some of the central challenges of contemporary conflict resolution. Analysis of the challenges facing humanitarian NGOs highlights attributes of violent conflicts in the current system: most importantly, the growing security vacuum that is creating painful choices for NGOs and impeding effective conflict resolution. Before examining these interrelated challenges that have important implications for conflict resolution, especially for the mitigation of violence, I briefly describe the cases and the evidence I use in my analysis.

EVIDENCE AND CASE SELECTION[21]

This study draws on three principal case studies as well as ongoing tracking of other complex humanitarian operations in Africa. Somalia, Rwanda, and Sierra Leone are three of the best-known cases where political violence led to a large-scale humanitarian disaster that required a multidimensional response. They are the principal case studies.[22] Liberia and Burundi share some of these characteristics and have been the location of important humanitarian programs; eastern Zaire was the site of a multifaceted response to a complex emergency and the focus of some of the most vociferous debates about strategies of conflict resolution. These three cases have been tracked as important checks on evidence drawn from the principal cases.

The cases were chosen at different points along the "crisis" time line: Sierra Leone, at the time a case of incipient state failure; Rwanda/Zaire, an ongoing crisis; and Somalia, a postemergency in the aftermath of large-scale intervention. This variation in time line permits some consideration of competing theoretical propositions against different bodies of evidence. Restriction of the cases to Africa was deliberate. Once the Cold War ended, the attention Africa received from the major powers dropped precipitously. As the major powers withdrew and economic failure and violence increased, and in some cases states collapsed, development and humanitarian NGOs significantly increased their presence.

THE CRITICS: HUMANITARIANISM AS AN
OBSTACLE TO CONFLICT RESOLUTION

Drawing on the experience of humanitarian intervention in complex emergencies in Africa in the past several years, critics have concluded that the relief effort can jeopardize conflict resolution and, at worst, prolong and even fuel war and conflict through the diversion of assistance. They identify several interrelated ways in which the unintended consequences of humanitarian assistance can impede conflict resolution.

When Humanitarian Relief Fuels War and
Conflict Through Asset Transfer[23]

The evidence is strong, though not determining, that in recent complex humanitarian emergencies the assistance that NGOs have provided to endangered populations has at times become the fuel for continued and renewed warfare.[24] In Somalia, for example, food was extraordinarily scarce as a result of drought and civil conflict and, consequently, its absolute value rose to unprecedented levels. Its high price, in the context of economic collapse, mass unemployment, and a dramatic drop in family income, increased the relative value of food. Therefore, food brought into Somalia through the relief effort was plundered by merchants, by organized gangs of young men profiteering from the black market, and by militia leaders who used the wealth that the food brought to buy weapons and the loyalty of followers.[25] In Rwanda and Sierra Leone, as well as Somalia and Sudan, assistance has been "taxed" or stolen to fuel processes of conflict escalation rather than promote conflict resolution.

Resources channeled into Somalia by UN agencies and NGOs became part of a complex economy of warfare between rival militias and clans. Theft of those resources by militias was common. Equally significant was the ability of militias, in the absence of a security envelope for the local population and NGO personnel, to use force and the threat of force to compel NGOs to hire some of the same forces to guard relief supplies and convoys that were the source of the humanitarian crisis.[26] In so doing, the NGOs legitimated those who were preying on local populations.[27]

In Sierra Leone and Liberia conflict analysts and medical NGOs learned that they could plan by following the pattern of UN food deliveries: when food was distributed to a village or displaced-persons camp, the militias would quickly attack to steal the relief supplies, killing dozens of villagers as they did so. In Sudan, food, agricultural tools, and livestock were transferred from weaker to strong groups through restrictions on the passage of food aid by government forces and militias. In Somalia as well as Sudan, this transfer of assets was integrated into a parallel black economy controlled at the highest political levels.[28] The one supported the other.

UN and NGO resources in eastern Zaire were subject to political control and taxation by the forces that perpetrated the Rwandan genocide of 1994. Less by theft and diversion than by controlling the distribution of relief supplies and the flow of information, Rwanda's *genocidaires* turned UN-managed and NGO-operated refugee camps into political and resource bases for continued and renewed genocidal warfare, in both Zaire and western Rwanda.[29] When the post-1994 Rwandan regime sought to break the *genocidaires'* control of the camps, civilian refugees became moving shields between two armies. Relief supplies and the NGO presence were used to lure starving refugees out of hiding in the forests of Zaire, and these refugees were then slaughtered by the tens of thousands. At the extreme, NGOs were transformed from sources of protection into resources for destruction.

The diversion of humanitarian assets by warring parties, at the same time they are targeting civilians, is the most serious challenge that NGOs face. If the assistance that humanitarian NGOs provide is significant in perpetuating and fueling the processes of violence, humanitarian assistance can be a serious obstacle to the resolution of conflict. To the extent that humanitarian NGOs are inadvertently perpetuating the cycle of violence that is making populations vulnerable, they and those they seek to help are trapped in a vicious process. Yet to abandon populations at risk to predators is an almost unthinkable choice.

How can these painful choices be eased? Some suggest that better local knowledge would help NGOs avoid some of the traps that became obvious only in hindsight. It is almost universally acknowledged that NGOs need a higher degree of knowledge of the societies in which they work—their cultures, histories, and languages—if they are to be effective in mitigating violence, in conflict resolution, and in reconstruction in the wake of violence. In Somalia and Rwanda, for example, few NGOs had long-standing experience in the country, few were fluent in the local language, few appreciated the social and cultural norms, and few were experienced in working at the grass roots.[30] Of the large number of expatriate NGO staff in Rwanda in 1994, only a handful were conversant in Kinyarwanda. Knowledge of local parties, their networks, and their purposes and strategies is a necessary but far from sufficient condition to minimize some of the negative consequences of relief assistance that prolong rather than resolve conflicts. NGOs must find far better ways of giving voice to the people they wish to help.

Closely related, humanitarians need better skills in conflict resolution. In Somalia traditional systems of authority, which did not depend on violence and could have attempted to resolve the conflict, continued to exist even after the violence erupted. A peace-building initiative sponsored by an NGO at the local level was successful because it drew on these customary Somali conflict management practices.[31] The relief effort, in contrast, helped to cripple the traditional systems because it did not channel assistance through traditional structures but strengthened the militia forces that relied on violence.[32] NGO personnel certainly needed far greater knowledge of the local systems of conflict management and the importance of elders as authoritative voices in society. One experienced analyst is deeply pessimistic, however, that any strategy of conflict resolution could have succeeded in Somalia, given the structural constraints created by the collapse of the state and the complex emergency.[33]

The violence is perpetuated as well, critics continue, because humanitarian organizations have reluctantly acceded to the constraining conditions imposed by governments and militias to gain access to populations at risk.[34] In complex humanitarian emergencies, NGOs indeed have experienced enormous difficulties in gaining access to populations vulnerable to violence.[35] These difficulties are deliberately created by warring parties that exploit the vulnerability of civilian populations for political or military purposes.[36] NGOs find themselves constantly renegotiating access and facing new designations of previously consented space as off limits. Variants of these negotiations have occurred in Sudan, Angola, Ethiopia, Bosnia, and Rwanda. The warring parties in turn frequently use negotiated access agreements to build international credibility. At the extreme this leads to the perverse outcome that the more killing that is done the more NGOs respond with additional resources.[37]

NGOs have attempted to address the issue of secure access to areas controlled by hostile forces through the negotiation of ground rules. Ground rules to notify faction leaders of the movement of aid convoys have been established to ensure that groups lower down in the chain of command do not compromise the protection of humanitarian assistance. In southern Sudan, for example, Operation Lifeline Sudan negotiated ground rules in the wake of the murder of three expatriate workers and a journalist.

Ground rules provide at best a limited and partial solution to the problem of access. In southern Sudan diversion of assistance remains very high. In Liberia and Rwanda the Department of Humanitarian Affairs attempted to negotiate ground rules but did not succeed. With no good choices, NGOs have consented tacitly to unilateral changes in access and so empower belligerents who impose conditions that clearly violate international humanitarian law.

When Humanitarian Assistance Interferes with the Social Contract

Critics level a deep structural challenge as well. They allege that political accountability, through contractual arrangements, is the critical constraint on government violence against civilians, an important component of complex humanitarian emergencies. Third-party humanitarian assistance, they maintain, interferes directly with the formation of social and political contracts in Africa that are essential to restrain violence.[38] Analysis of the political and economic purposes of those who prey on their own civilian populations does not suggest, however, that the perpetrators are likely candidates for accountable governments. The authoritarian quality of many governments, the absence of institutions that can meaningfully hold leaders accountable, and the high levels of corruption make contractual constraints unlikely as a near-term solution to complex emergencies and violent conflicts. Acknowledging these obstacles, optimistic analysts estimate that it will take at least a decade for political contracts to form; others are even more pessimistic.[39]

No matter how bumpy and slow the trajectory, humanitarians must contribute directly and indirectly to the seeding of this accountability if the vulnerable populations they seek to help are ever to be given voice. At best, however, the evidence suggests that empowerment and accountability will be painfully slow processes. Political contracts cannot provide a near-term solution to violent conflict and humanitarian emergencies. Until they do, if they do, the complex emergency continues and the third party and the local humanitarian challenges intensify.[40]

When Humanitarian NGOs Are Manipulated by States that Seek to Contain Violence Without Direct Engagement

Critics insist that NGOs are being substituted for effective action by the major powers and exploited as a cover for their absence.[41] As I argued earlier, there is indeed a growing international indifference to humanitarian crises. Governments have privatized their assistance policies and adopted strategies of containment.[42] They are increasingly resistant to accepting refugees and unwilling to grant asylum as mandated by the international refugee regime, even as they are less inclined to intervene politically or militarily to protect populations at risk.

It is far from apparent, however, that humanitarian assistance is the cause of disengagement by the major powers. It is rather the consequence of the withdrawal by the big powers once southern societies were no longer a theater of competition in the Cold War. Here too, as in the analysis of accountability of political leaders, the alternative is not clear. Were NGOs not present, there is no evidence that states and international organizations would return as providers of security and assistance. The one is not fungible for the others.

When Humanitarian Assistance Unintentionally Disempowers Those in Society Who Are Important for Reconstruction

Critics of classical humanitarian relief insisted that it had negative consequences for development, removed initiative and responsibility from local parties, empowered "expatriates" rather than community leaders, and undermined the local economy.[43] In response to those criticisms some NGOs have shifted their emphasis to a new paradigm of "developmentalist" models of relief, usually called the "relief to development and democracy (RDD) continuum." To avoid creating a culture of dependency and to move a population toward peace as quickly as possible, some analysts insist that relief and development should and can occur simultaneously, even while violence is ongoing.[44] The purpose is to create alternative livelihoods for those associated with war and a criminalized economy and thereby reduce the attractiveness of violence as a career.[45]

Developmentalist strategies of conflict resolution posit a quick end to the complex emergency and a return to stability where peaceful development is possible. The fundamental elements of the strategy are local partnerships based on capacity building and the empowerment of local communities as the choosers and managers of strategies of postwar reconstruction. The approach is multifunctional and loosely structured, and on the continuum the boundary between relief and peace building blurs and indeed virtually disappears.[46]

Local partnerships and community empowerment should be central elements of any process of conflict resolution. Vulnerable communities must be given voice if predators are to be constrained in any way and a sustainable process of conflict resolution is to begin. Ironically, however, the emphasis on more "participatory" emergency relief led more or less directly to the greatest crisis of conscience and credibility in the nongovernmental sector. In eastern Zaire where aid agencies were setting up camps for the influx of thousands from Rwanda, they used the latest techniques of camp management involving, among others, "refugee self-management." The goal is to use indigenous leadership in refugee populations to govern themselves. In this case, however, the leadership cadres were precisely those who had engineered the genocide and then the forced mass migration. The painful choices that resulted stretched over two years, with no obvious solution.

This new model that blurs emergency assistance with postwar reconstruction also ignores the scope of the violence and the extent of the emergency that make an early return to "stability" extremely unlikely. In some cases—Liberia and Somalia—the emergency has continued for a decade or more. In other cases—Rwanda and Sudan—the premature declaration of an end to the emergency to fit with the new agenda is belied by the continuing, indeed, escalating violence in the country.

In Rwanda the governing expectation for planning in 1996 was gradual but progressive rehabilitation and development. There were positive trends: return of the refugees, restoration of some basic government services, and limited economic improvement. By December 1997, however, 50 percent of Rwanda was again considered "insecure" and the number of internally displaced persons was increasing rather than diminishing.[47] The emergency had not ended; it had ebbed briefly before intensifying again. The expectation of stability proved wholly unrealistic in the context of intensifying violence. Similarly, in Sudan, despite ongoing hostilities, an end to the emergency was declared. The government subsequently permitted NGOs to register only for development and rehabilitation, despite the growing numbers of people in desperate need of emergency relief.[48] The premature end to the emergency served the political purposes of a regime that was oppressing vulnerable populations.

The RDD approach also creates pressure to reclassify emergencies so that the multifunctional approach can begin to work. Premature relabeling has led to the "normalizing" of emergencies and the raising of thresholds of civilian violence before an emergency can be declared.[49] More generically, developmentalist approaches to relief seriously underestimate the difficulty of implementing reconstruction and peace-building programs in the context of the acute violence and extreme insecurity that are characteristic of protracted humanitarian emergencies. They do so in part because they ignore the politics of those who benefit from the prolonged emergency. I return to this point later.

There is little systematic evidence, moreover, to sustain the argument that relief generally displaces the reconstruction of war-torn societies. It may well do so under certain conditions, but we do not know enough to differentiate the conditions under which relief does block postwar reconstruction. Given the limited amount of relief that is provided and the relatively short duration of most, though not all, large relief operations, it seems unlikely that relief would be an attractive option compared to the alternative coping strategies usually available to subsistence populations. It is more likely that acute violence disrupts these coping strategies, and vulnerable populations have no choice but relief assistance.[50]

It is worth noting the risk in a tight linkage between emergency assistance as a process and conflict resolution as an outcome. Conflict resolution and good governance, when they succeed, are the result of complex processes as yet poorly mapped and understood. It is unreasonable to expect emergency assistance to achieve conflict resolution; indeed, such an expectation is virtually certain to be unmet and, when it is unmet, to lead to the inappropriate politicization of aid as publics and governments become cynical.[51] Cautious modesty far better reflects the available evidence and the political environment of complex humanitarian emergencies.

When Humanitarian Aid Emphasizes Reconstruction at the Expense of Accountability

When there is attention to reconstruction, it is largely focused on restoring services and rebuilding economies, not on the political accountability that is central to a reformed political system. At times the governments that created the economic and social disruption are invited to partner in processes of reconstruction. Humanitarian relief, in part because of its commitment to impartiality and neutrality, avoids dealing with the political ambitions and past actions of predators.[52] This criticism of NGOs that deliver relief assistance, which is apt on its terms, applies equally, however, to the conflict resolution NGOs when they work in complex humanitarian emergencies. Reconstruction of any kind assumes a benign rather than a predator state or militia that systematically targets civilian populations for economic or political ends. Yet it is often precisely those who originally created the massive disruption who are subsequently invited to participate, first in reconstruction and finally in conflict resolution.

Critics disagree radically on the appropriate solutions to these challenges of conflict resolution, postwar reconstruction, and peace building. Some urge that relief assistance be radically restructured or even eliminated. There is agreement among radical critics that conflict can be resolved only through a long process of creating a vibrant civil society that can demand and contract for good governance, but there is considerable difference of opinion about how civil society can best be promoted. Some urge the virtual exclusion of third-party humanitarians, so that governments and populations have no alternative but to create contracts; at the other extreme, some urge a high level of partnering between "progressive" northern and southern NGOs to force governments to be accountable.[53] Assistance would be made conditional on good governance and respect for human rights.

I have already examined the real and serious obstacles to the development of binding contractual relationships as near-term strategies to mitigate violence. In the fragmented politics of those marginalized by the global economy, some claim that even evolutionary processes toward political accountability are delusional.[54] Society is fragmented, politicized, and incorporated into black or gray predatory economies, where "nonentitlements" accrue from raiding, illicit drug trade, extortion, and diversion of assets.[55] In this context the model of a civil society separate from a centralized state does not fit; there simply is no civil society to strengthen. One pessimistic analyst of "postmodern violence" concludes that "war and famine do not stand out from normal social relations; they are simply a 'deepening' of exploitative processes."[56] The same kind of contextual challenges would confront those northern NGOs that partner with their southern counterparts to demand that local militias and predators be held accountable.[57]

The overarching critique—that emergency assistance inadvertently prolongs violence and retards conflict resolution—is important. From this inadvertent but negative consequence flows many of the related challenges that critics have identified. It is important to note, however, that not only relief but also many other economic activities fuel and sustain violence. The importance of relief is likely to vary by context: in eastern Zaire relief assistance was a critical resource to militia leaders, while in other cases the drug trade, smuggling, and thriving gray and black economies were far more important generators of resources to predators. No study systematically investigates the proportionality of effects on war, yet only careful empirical analysis can resolve the question of the proportional impact of humanitarian aid on the prolongation of violence and specify the conditions when negative externalities are likely to be greatest.

ADDRESSING THE CHALLENGE

There are no easy or obvious solutions to the fundamental challenges that humanitarian NGOs face as they seek to both help populations preyed on by governments or militias and help reduce the violence and resolve the conflict so that vulnerable populations will no longer be systematically targeted. Indeed, analysis of the structure and context of complex humanitarian emergencies offers little grounds for optimism about a quick end to violence. Accumulated experience in attempting to manage these emergencies and resolve the internal conflicts of the past decade is no more encouraging. For humanitarians the challenges are likely to persist and intensify.

Two conclusions are clear from the analysis. First, complex humanitarian emergencies of the kind we have seen in the past decade in Africa are likely to continue, and not only in Africa, well into the future. Second, NGOs committed to humanitarian values will continue to engage on behalf of vulnerable populations. Disengagement is not an option for humanitarian NGOs, even if it is for states. If anything, given the privatization of assistance and the retreat of the UN, NGOs will play an even larger role than they have in the past.[58]

Minimizing the Negative Consequences of Aid on Protracted Violence

The central challenge from the perspective of conflict resolution is to find ways of minimizing the negative externalities of assistance as aid flows to the most vulnerable populations. NGOs are looking for ways to prevent the transfer of assets to warring parties, so that their work does not fuel the cycle of war. Humanitarian NGOs must constantly evaluate their practices to assess whether alternatives exist that would minimize the negative consequences of their work in the context of a complex emergency. In the past five years there has been considerable progress in exploring alternative ways of mitigating the contribution of emergency assistance to violence.[59] I consider only a few of a large number of strategies that have been tried and programs that have been put in place in the past several years.

Paying explicit attention to the diversion of food aid to warring parties, NGOs have begun to distinguish types of food aid by their market

value. They ask how "lootable" their assistance is. In Somalia, for example, rice was extraordinarily attractive to looters while sorghum evoked
little interest. When a food convoy organized by CARE was attacked
along the Jubba River in Somalia, the thieves left without stealing anything when they discovered that the trucks carried sorghum.[60] Blended
foods, generally less tasty, are less attractive, and foods that can be stored
for extended periods of time can be hidden from predators. The ICRC, for
example, moved to cooked food to reduce the interests of looters. Careful
monitoring, important on its own as NGOs seek to become transparent
and accountable, was remarkably successful in Rwanda and Angola in
reducing diversion.[61] Similarly, seeds can be selected so that they are less
attractive to looters: those that are easily stored, that match local habits of
consumption, and that displaced populations can take with them as they
move to different locales are less likely to be diverted.

The Office of Foreign Disaster Assistance, of the U.S. Agency for International Development, tried an innovative strategy of "monetizing"
food that was delivered to Somalia. Insofar as food had become a medium
of exchange, flooding the country with food would depreciate its attractiveness and diminish the incentive for looting.[62] Selling cereals as well as
cooking oil to merchants would permit people to buy food with their
limited incomes as the price of food declined. The monetization strategy
was also designed to force onto the markets all of the food hoarded by
organized criminals and warlords. Monetization did affect market prices
by 1993 and produced enough currency to fund significant rehabilitation
and reconstruction. It did not succeed, however, in reducing diversion;
the drop in food prices drove the warlords to "tax" at higher levels. Only
after military intervention did monetization accelerate and break the hold
of the warlords.

NGOs are also trying to increase the ratio of nonfood to food aid
within the constraints imposed by a complex emergency. There is much
greater emphasis on supporting sustainable livelihoods—distribution of
fishing nets where fish are available; vaccination programs against mea-
sles, a perennial killer of children in complex emergencies; and portable
educational materials so that schools can continue even as populations
are forced to move. None of this is easily "lootable" material that can fuel
a wartime economy.

NGOs have also recognized how the economic side effects of their
operations can contribute to a wartime economy. Collaboration among
NGOs, difficult as it is, to standardize physical costs can drastically reduce the negative externalities of assistance. In Baidoa, for example, all
agencies collaborated to reduce the costs of vehicles. In Rwanda, Save the
Children (U.K.) organized some NGOs to standardize the prices of hous-
ing and transport. In Goma the UN High Commissioner for Refugees

(UNHCR) and the NGOs cooperated to put a ceiling on labor costs; salaries were immediately reduced by 50 percent.[63]

Proposals have also been developed to share information, coordinate and plan better, improve institutional memory, and increase area expertise so that NGO personnel can learn quickly about local politics and structures. Since the genocide and mass exodus from Rwanda in 1994, some NGOs have consciously begun to develop their capacity to collect information about and analyze political and security developments that might have an important impact on diversion of aid and, more generally, on operations. Médecins Sans Frontières (MSF) has an ongoing global country watch; Action Aid has created an office called Emergency Response and Information Collection (ERIC) for the Great Lakes Region; and many NGOs feed into and from the UN's Department of Humanitarian Affairs Integrated Regional Information Network for the Great Lakes and for West Africa. UNICEF has created a global Rapid Response Team and CARE is examining how it can pre-position experienced staff in areas where populations seem particularly at risk. NGOs recognize that they need good operational knowledge of differentiation along identity and class lines if they are to succeed in minimizing the diversion of aid to warring parties.[64]

Political Options in a Politicized Environment

Strategies to minimize diversion, alone or together, can reduce the scope and severity but never completely eliminate the transfer of assets to warriors and other negative externalities of emergency assistance. Analysis of these cases suggests that the more complex the conflict, the more chaotic the security markets, and the more traumatized the social order, the more important an adequate security envelope is for effective delivery of humanitarian assistance. For humanitarians working in complex emergencies, painful choices will continue to arise as long as the UN or regional organizations are unable to provide security as a public good and the major powers continue to disengage and privatize assistance as a substitute for political action.

NATO's intervention in the humanitarian emergency in Kosovo in 1999 may be the beginning of a reversal of the pattern of major power disengagement. The military action was precedent setting: NATO used force against a sovereign state that was systematically abusing its own population. It is difficult to extrapolate from this one intervention in NATO's core area of interest, however, to a more general pattern of reengagement, particularly in Africa. Even in Europe some officials in NATO regard the "successful" operation as a high-risk, never-to-be-repeated action. There is no solid evidence that the supply of security as a public good is likely to increase. Until it does, the range of choices for humanitarian NGOs will frequently be narrow, and at the extreme there will be no "good" strategies of conflict resolution. Some analysts are even more pessimistic: one concludes that "there is literally no space for conflict resolution or development activities when deep insecurity prevails."[65]

In the camps in eastern Zaire in 1994 and 1995, for example, there was considerable resource transfer, misappropriation, taxation, and theft by militias. Here, the *genocidaires* unquestionably drew their main political support from the physical presence of the humanitarian effort; the humanitarian presence provided an economic base from which they and, most importantly, their key strategic resource—Rwandan civilians—could live. The critical and agonizing issue for NGOs was whether to stay and fuel the capacity of the *genocidaires* to make war or leave and abandon the civilian population that the militia had targeted and exploited. The choices were cruel and stark, not amenable to any technical solution available then or now. NGO personnel may not be able to choose to do no harm, if by doing nothing they abandon civilian populations at risk, deprive them of their voice, and violate their humanitarian ethics.[66] In the face of those who are determined to do harm to civilians, NGOs may well be forced to choose the option that does the least harm. To make that choice, humanitarian NGOs must situate their work in its larger political context. In this context three strategies are worth considering.

First, humanitarians must acknowledge that their actions in a complex emergency can have profound political consequences. Even as they insist on the imperative of legitimate authorities assuming responsibility, they must explicitly analyze the political consequences of their strategies to mitigate violence—relief delivery, refugee protection, election monitoring, postwar reconstruction, peace building—and plan for those consequences.[67]

NGOs traditionally have insisted, and many still do, that only strict adherence to principles of neutrality and consent of the parties can insulate relief assistance from political and military agendas.[68] Neutrality, it is argued, contributes to the amelioration of violence and conflict resolution by effectively inducing UN agencies and governments to provide assistance, by deterring violence through the capacity to witness by their presence on the ground and their access to the media, and by their capacity to mediate among the warring parties.[69] I, and others, allege that the context of relief assistance has changed so radically that apolitical neutrality is a useful fiction but no longer a viable option. As the president of MSF's International Council argued in Oslo when he accepted the Nobel Peace

Prize on behalf of MSF, "the humanitarian act is the most apolitical of all acts, but if its actions and its morality are taken seriously, it has the most profound of political implications."[70]

Neutrality is appropriate in a neutral environment, but the environments of complex emergencies are generally predatory rather than neutral. As Weiss argues, the fact that humanitarian space cannot be opened or sustained by humanitarians alone suggests the clear benefit of thinking politically and coordinating with diplomatic and military institutions.[71] If the political purposes of those who target civilian populations are ignored, NGOs will miss the inherently political nature of the relief they deliver to those targeted populations and miscalculate the politics of protecting those they seek to help.

NGOs in increasing numbers have consultative status at the UN and are invited to participate in policy discussions.[72] If they are to be effective in shaping policies to mitigate violence, they need to improve their analytical capacities to be more effective at the policy table. NGOs will have to begin as well to invest time and resources in long-term policy research and development. National donors, governments, and the UN system all devote considerable effort to policy analysis and development. For the nongovernmental sector to be able to contribute effectively, it must begin to do likewise.

NGOs must also improve their capacity to monitor the consequences of their actions on a scale of "perverse outcomes" so that they can properly assess the consequences of their strategic choices. I discuss this challenge later when I examine the potential of "diagnostics" to improve policy monitoring and evaluation. NGOs need as well to enhance the knowledge and skills required for effective negotiation with implementing partners, other NGOs in the regions in which they are working, and with potentially predatory forces so as to define appropriate conditions for engagement.

It will also be important to develop a sophisticated understanding of the political economy of the humanitarian assistance "marketplace" in which NGOs are embedded if they hope to influence the critical set of contractual relationships with the UN and donor institutions that can severely constrain strategic choices. A little-understood dimension of the international humanitarian system is the economic relationship between NGOs and their institutional funders. In a complex emergency, NGOs function as contractors and implementers on behalf of multilateral agencies. This relationship resembles an oligopoly: many sellers and very few and, at times, only one buyer. In the humanitarian marketplace the buyers are national and multilateral aid organizations, and the sellers are the NGOs. Without an implementing contract from one of the UN agencies, it is unlikely that an NGO will be able to deliver relief. During a typical complex emergency, a humanitarian NGO can obtain the necessary funds from one of at most six agencies in the UN family and normally the agency of the national government where the NGO resides. Often the national agency will provide funding only after one of the UN agencies has committed itself.

The dependence of an NGO is even greater than this structure suggests. UN agencies often behave as monopolies: the World Food Program (WFP) manages food from donor countries, the UNHCR is charged with caring for refugees, and the World Health Organization is responsible for health. Because both NGOs and UN agencies tend to specialize, most NGOs are consequently quite limited in their contracting options. For example, an NGO with food logistics expertise generally has one potential partner, the WFP. Any NGO with refugee camp management experience must as a general rule contract with the UNHCR. At the national level, governments have an inherent monopoly over domestic funds devoted to international assistance.[73]

This economic structure conforms broadly to what economic theory would suggest: the contracting UN agencies have fixed nonnegotiable rates, penalty clauses, payment schedules, and reporting requirements and are able to enforce compliance by an individual NGO seeking a contract in the broader field of available NGOs. As a practical matter, while the UN can no longer do without NGOs in general, it can do without any particular NGO. These conditions often constrain the strategic choices that an individual NGO can make and limit its capacity to act politically.

If NGOs are to assess the impact of emergency assistance in an arena of civilian conflict and make effective political choices to reduce any negative externalities and mitigate violence, they will have to act collectively to establish new guiding principles that will reduce the inflexibility of current funding arrangements with the UN. An individual NGO cannot be effective politically by acting alone. This collective-action problem is a recurrent and generic challenge for the humanitarian community.

The second strategy worth considering is for NGOs to urge the UN secretary-general to provide security from private markets when public security for humanitarian operations is unavailable. This analysis suggests that the more complex a conflict is, the more chaotic are the security markets. Yet the more traumatized the social order is, the more important is an adequate security envelope for effective delivery of humanitarian assistance.[74] Complex emergencies feed on themselves, enfeebling and even wiping away legitimate security resources, spreading chaos and violence, and generating the need for even greater security resources from outside. The cycle can only be broken if security is again supplied as a public good, ideally by the major powers acting through international institutions or by members of regional organizations acting collectively. This analysis suggests, however, that the prospects of repairing the shredded security envelope in which humanitarian NGOs currently operate are not promising.

The major powers that are critical to authorization of a UN force are likely to consider most of the humanitarian emergencies as "discretionary" and, consequently, be unwilling to commit forces, directly or through the UN, to a crisis that humanitarians consider urgent. The falling budget for UN peacekeeping speaks loudly. Given the demographic and social forces that reinforce the aversion to casualties in postindustrial states, this caution can only become more pronounced over time. The Mogadishu line became at the close of the 1990s a military and political firebreak that, other than in exceptional circumstances, major powers outside the region seem increasingly unwilling to cross.

UN Under Secretary-General for Humanitarian Affairs Sergio Vieira de Mello, in observing the general lack of willingness of members of the UN to provide security forces for humanitarian operations, noted that states are not at all "averse to letting humanitarian staff go where they dare not send their . . . invariably better equipped, better trained and better protected [troops]." He proposed the creation of "regional humanitarian security teams" trained and equipped to support humanitarian personnel on short notice; teams would be drawn from "selected troops from a variety of nations in the region concerned."[75] This proposal is consistent with the so-called regional or subregional approach to conflict resolution in which the responsibility for peacekeeping and security rests with the countries closest to the problem.

In the wake of the terrible failure first to prevent and then to stop the genocide in Rwanda, the United States, Britain, and France supported the African Crisis Response Initiative, a project to help train and equip a standby rapid-reaction peacekeeping force; this has yet to be put to the test.[76] By far the most extensive trial of regional peacekeeping has been the eight-year-long deployment of a multinational force or "monitoring group" (the Economic Community Monitoring Group, or ECOMOG) first in Liberia and more recently in Sierra Leone by the Economic Community of West African States (ECOWAS). The record of ECOMOG has been mixed, but no more so than UN and NATO forces deployed elsewhere.[77]

African peacekeeping and peace-enforcing efforts have been effective in providing a security envelope where they have been deployed, but the overall pattern is nevertheless not encouraging. Forces have been infrequently deployed and the choices as to where and when to intervene have been essentially arbitrary. There is also growing concern at the UN about compliance with international standards in regional operations that the UN authorizes. The UN secretary-general recently urged the UN Security Council to confirm that regional organizations have the capacity to carry out operations consistent with international norms and standards and to put in place mechanisms to monitor regional peacekeeping forces operating under the authority of the UN.[78]

When security is scarce as a public good, the security of NGO personnel in the field is, as I have noted, not surprisingly increasingly at risk. There are, however, very limited arrangements currently in place through the UN to promote their security, even when they are contracted to the UN. Within the UN, the United Nations Security Coordinator (UNSECOORD) coordinates, plans, and implements safety programs and acts as the nexus for interagency cooperation on security issues, exclusive of peacekeeping forces.[79] These arrangements are restricted to personnel engaged in operations specifically authorized by the Security Council or the General Assembly.[80] In a memorandum of understanding circulated in early 1997, NGOs that are implementing partners of agencies in the UN may request to be included in UN security arrangements; to do so they must agree to pay their share of the costs and abide by UN security guidelines. These arrangements are restricted to expatriate staff of NGOs that are implementing partners and to those employees directly engaged in fulfilling the contract; they do not include local staff, or even all expatriate staff, much less extend to vulnerable populations.[81] It is not surprising that NGOs objected to the loss of autonomy, the inequities, and the cost. Here donors could be helpful: they could emphasize as a priority and fund security costs as part of their envelopes for humanitarian assistance, and they could also press for a long-overdue review of the role of UNSECOORD. Even if more inclusive agreements were to be negotiated with the UN, they would not address the fundamental challenge of the deep insecurity of the vulnerable populations that humanitarians seek to help.

When security is not being provided as a public good, as it frequently is not in a complex humanitarian emergency, NGOs should reluctantly consider urging the UN secretary-general to draw on private resources to provide security. The absence of international public security forces, and the lack of effective and legitimate alternatives, empowered the militias of Somalia, eastern Zaire, Sierra Leone, and Liberia to terrible effect. It is only when security is absent that humanitarian assistance prolongs rather than mitigates violence. Under these circumstances and only under these circumstances, the UN might consider hiring paid volunteer professionally trained security personnel, employed without regard to national origin and beholden to their employer rather than to any single government, to secure the delivery of emergency assistance. This concept was seriously considered in Rwanda in late 1994, and some official UN circles appear to be exploring the concept as well.[82]

The primary purpose of private security guards would not be to protect NGO personnel but to avoid the need to hire local providers from among belligerents to protect convoys of relief assistance. In eastern Zaire, for example, after months of inaction, two battalions of Zairean troops were hired to maintain security in Rwandan camps under UNHCR authority. The presence of the troops significantly improved law and order in the camps and diminished the authority of the militias among the refugees.[83] Even then the Zairean troops were not impartial in the broader conflict in Rwanda nor were they mandated to deal with the central issue of separating refugees from militia leaders. At the very least, private security personnel from outside the region would not fuel the local war economy or sustain those who preyed on local populations.

This kind of proposal will not be well received in the humanitarian community, and many would consider it infeasible. For both practical and normative reasons, NGOs undoubtedly would prefer to avoid such a solution. There are already indications, however, that the hiring of security guards from the private sector is acceptable under specific conditions in the humanitarian community. The ICRC prohibits the hiring of local armed escorts for relief convoys but acknowledges that the hiring of guards to combat crime and provide security for personnel may be necessary if there is no other option. When armed guards are necessary, the ICRC recommends that they be hired from "an established security firm or the police rather than the army."[84] A report recently submitted to the European Commission proposed that donors could field security units to protect humanitarian work, either from national resources or "through funding specialist third parties."[85] It is worth considering whether the hiring of security guards from specialized third parties is an appropriate strategy not only to combat crime but also to mitigate the violence that flows inadvertently from current policies. Private providers of security working under the authority of the UN may be the least harmful response to both the privatization of assistance and the absence of security as a public good.[86]

A third strategy to consider is that of conditionality and exit. Finally, and only as a desperate last resort, NGOs must be prepared to consider seriously the option of temporary withdrawal when assistance intended for humanitarian purposes is being diverted into renewed cycles of conflict. Withdrawal during an emergency flies in the face of the most fundamental humanitarian commitment and impulse to protect lives at risk: NGOs cannot justify the loss of access and witness. Withdrawal of the humanitarian presence, I argue, should be only the last in a staged series of options, and even then it has negative consequences because those who are watching and reporting to the outside world will no longer be there, even as a mild deterrent and as a witness. Yet only if humanitarian actors are willing to suspend delivery and withdraw presence when their assistance is forming part of a cycle of violence can they regain sufficient leverage to retain or recapture control over the delivery and management of relief supplies and reconvert their presence into protection. When other options are exhausted, NGOs must be willing to take the necessary organizational steps to ensure that they are not part of the problems they are committed to alleviating. Strategic withdrawal can also send crucial signals to future would-be perpetrators of violence hoping to use relief resources for their own purposes.[87]

To argue that NGOs must consider withdrawing if assets are being diverted to fuel a wartime economy raises difficult operational, strategic, and ethical questions.[88] Can NGOs withdraw in the midst of an emergency? In the past, humanitarians have withdrawn largely when their staff was harmed or at risk—the ICRC from Burundi and Chechnya, Caritas from Burundi—or when necessary infrastructure was destroyed—CARE from Mogadishu.

Withdrawal as a strategic choice is rare, but humanitarian NGOs have very occasionally made this choice. In eastern Zaire in November 1994, 15 NGOs withdrew from Mugunga camp in the Goma region in the face of attempts by militias to assert political control over the camps. The decision was made in response to untenable security conditions and unacceptable ethical compromises but also to increase pressure on the international community to respond to the security dilemma. At the same time, in a controversial decision the Economic Community Humanitarian Office (ECHO) decided to stop all funding for NGOs serving the internally displaced camps in Rwanda, hoping to create a "push" for people to return to their homes. The impact of the withdrawal was unclear, since agencies with independent funding that considered continued assistance a humanitarian imperative remained in the camps.[89]

In the autumn of 1998, even though it was the first humanitarian organization to gain access to the population in North Korea three years earlier, MSF explicitly chose to withdraw when its leaders concluded that assistance could not be delivered independently of state authorities and that assistance was being used by North Korean leaders to sustain the system that created the vulnerability and starvation among millions. Again, in November 1999, MSF withdrew from refugee camps in Burundi when MSF concluded that it was helping the government sustain the camps. Not surprisingly, the withdrawal was strongly criticized by other humanitarian groups that have continued to deliver assistance. The dilemmas of the humanitarian organizations were sharpened by the withdrawal of staff members of the WFP after two UN staffers were executed in southeastern Burundi. As a result, those NGOs that remained have taken on some of the responsibilities of the departed UN staff. In a somewhat different context, in 1996, after all NGOs were evacuated from Liberia to surrounding countries because fighting had destroyed the local infrastructure, for the first time NGOs organized to "coordinate the resumption of NGO-implemented humanitarian assistance."[90]

An important constraint on strategic withdrawal to mitigate violence is the oligopolist structure of contractual relationships with donor agencies that I have detailed. Inflexible funding arrangements create incentives for NGOs to continue relief operations even when security deteriorates. Fixed schedules and penalty clauses can work against a decision to make assistance conditional insofar as the NGO violates the contract either by politically motivated withdrawal or by allowing waiting time for compellent strategies to work. Instead of an obstacle, agency contracts could create incentives for relief conditional on appropriate behavior toward vulnerable populations. Contracts could include incentives to assist in the monitoring and reporting on abuse of vulnerable populations and require regular reporting of agreed-upon indicators of diversion of assistance. They could also eliminate the penalties for failure to deliver and for changes in the types of assistance delivered when these changes are a response to deteriorating security and increased diversion of assistance. Contracts should also explicitly commit UN agencies to continue funding their NGO partners even when they withdraw or evacuate their staff temporarily because of deteriorating security, as long as that withdrawal occurs within defined parameters and in accordance with agreed-upon principles. If NGOs are unable to pay their staff when they are pulled out because assistance is fueling violence, perverse incentives will work to keep staff members in the field.

A more formidable constraint is the generic difficulty of collective action. A unilateral withdrawal by one NGO, no matter how large, is unlikely to be effective in constraining the behavior of predators. Even the collective withdrawal from Mugunga had only limited impact; the NGOs that withdrew continued to provide relief in other camps, and the flow of resources into Mugunga continued.

At least two conditions are necessary if a strategic withdrawal by NGOs is to have any impact. First, there must be coordination among the principal NGOs that are providing assistance to act in concert. This kind of decision will not be reached easily; many NGOs continue to believe that withdrawal violates the fundamental humanitarian ethic, that it is tantamount to abandoning the most vulnerable, that it will provoke looting and violence, that it furthers the lamentable processes of privatization of assistance and disengagement by major powers, and that the politics of withdrawal compromise humanitarian neutrality and impartiality. The most serious criticism leveled at a strategy of political withdrawal is that it is ineffective. In the aftermath of the cessation of humanitarian aid to Rwandan refugees, violence and war increased, and several hundred thousand people died; the Great Lakes region became more violent after international humanitarian assistance was withdrawn.[91]

This intense debate among humanitarians may limit the possibilities of coordination to arrangements between those who leave and those who stay so that there can be both public statement and quiet assistance.[92] Within the limits of the possible, consulting the recipients of assistance— rather than the predatory leadership—as to whether agencies should remain silent or protest abuses even if they lose their access would empower local populations, enhance accountability, and make it easier for NGOs to reach a collective decision.[93]

Second, a withdrawal should be accompanied by a clearly stated set of conditions for return—an end to diversion of relief, unobstructed access to vulnerable populations, and/or cooperation in the registration of refugees or displaced persons. There are cases where conditionality has succeeded. In response to looting of cars in eastern Equatoria, four NGOs and agencies collaborated to make continuing assistance conditional on safety on the roads, as an essential component of the larger principle of unfettered secure access. The Sudanese People's Liberation Army was concerned enough about the consequences of a cessation of aid that it made certain that the raiding of vehicles stopped.[94] A consortium of NGOs working in southern Sudan insisted on independent access and monitoring as conditions of continued assistance. Only if withdrawal is coordinated and strategic, if the conditions NGOs set can be met by the targets, can concerted withdrawal have any impact whatsoever on the behavior of a predatory government or militia.

Developing Diagnostics

If humanitarian NGOs are to consider withdrawal as a strategy to influence warring parties and reluctant major powers and participate effectively at national and global policy tables, above all they need the analytical capacity to assess the severity of the negative consequences of their aid and a set of diagnostics they can collectively use to judge that they may be doing relatively more harm than good. I have already addressed the importance of developing the analytical capabilities of NGOs so that they can enhance their contribution to policy debates. Development of diagnostics ideally flows from an enhanced analytical capability among NGOs. I suggest three such diagnostics as a first cut.

There is, of course, significant variation within complex humanitarian emergencies, and the diagnostics will be sensitive to differences in underlying conditions. Two such underlying conditions have been plausibly suggested. The likelihood of negative externalities of assistance depends in part on the degree of coherence among militias and their capacity to organize effectively; when it is very high, as in Rwanda, diversion is more likely than when coherence is low, as in Sierra Leone. The coherence of militias in turn depends in part on the shape of export markets. When primary commodities dominate exports, militias can generate revenues from the taxation of these commodities, either directly by imposing levies or by demanding contributions in kind and then exporting through extra-legal marketing channels. It is far easier to market generic products illegally than to disguise the origins of branded products.[95] Under these conditions, militias are likely to do well in civil war and to seek to prolong the violence.

The political taxation of relief is an obvious diagnostic indicator that aid is being diverted. Initially, diversion can be difficult to assess since theft and hijacking can be high but not part of a pattern of systematic political diversion. The better informed NGO personnel are about local political and military organizations, about ethnic and religious fault lines, and about local social, economic, and political structures the more easily they will be able to distinguish simple theft from systematic diversion. Systematic political diversion that is not reduced by the strategies considered earlier should trigger consideration of coordinated political strategies to mitigate the violence.

A second warning light is the unwillingness of local authorities to cooperate with the UN and NGOs to register recipients of relief assistance, especially in refugee or displaced-persons camps, and to make available lists of the registrants. Failure to cooperate in registration suggests that local authorities are seeking to supplant or subvert existing distribution mechanisms in order to divert relief assistance. If local authorities are willing to use force to monopolize control over a registration process, there is a very high likelihood that aid will subsequently become a resource for violent conflict.

Third, negotiation of access to populations at risk often provides predatory governments and militias with the opportunity to impose inequitable political conditions, which privilege some vulnerable populations at the expense of others. Especially when access is obstructed after consent has been obtained, relief is being used as an instrument to assert control over local populations for political purposes. The government of Mobutu Sese Seko repeatedly denied access to large groups of refugees and displaced persons. Access is central to protection, support, and witness.

These three diagnostics are suggestive of the kind of indicators NGOs might agree to use collectively. No set of indicators performs entirely satisfactorily, but agreement among NGOs on several diagnostics on a trial basis, to be tested in the field and refined and then benchmarked in time, would significantly enhance the analytical capability of NGOs, their capacity to monitor the political consequences of their actions, their ability to coordinate and reduce collective-action problems, and their collective capacity to act politically to reduce violence.

CONCLUSION

Wittingly and unwittingly, humanitarian NGOs have become important participants in conflict resolution as assistance has been privatized and security has become a very scarce public good in many parts of the world. In large part because of the failure of the wider international community to provide security as a public good, humanitarians increasingly find themselves confronting painful choices. In complex humanitarian emergencies, where security is absent, some of the assistance NGOs provide has gone to those who prey on the vulnerable and has prolonged and even fueled the cycle of violence. Rather than contributing to conflict resolution, humanitarians have inadvertently contributed to conflict escalation.

The painful choices that NGOs face is most acute for but not unique to humanitarians. International financial institutions, the family of UN agencies, and regional organizations are grappling with the same kinds of painful options, although not often with front-line personnel on the ground. They and humanitarian NGOs all suffer from the disappearance of security as a public good and, to a greater or lesser degree, require a security envelope to help resolve conflicts, reconstruct war-torn societies, and build peace. Without a minimal security envelope, the assets they commit to conflict resolution and peace building can be diverted to fuel rather than break a cycle of violence. Those who do well out of war have every incentive to perpetuate the violence and to continue to prey on those who have no protection.

I have argued that these painful choices have grown out of the disengagement of the major powers, the privatization of assistance, and the complexity of contemporary emergencies. Humanitarian emergencies are triggered by the failure of states or their capture by one group that uses the instruments of the state against another and the violent economic and social disruptions that follow as societies break apart and refugees spill across borders. A recent study concluded that humanitarian emergencies constitute the most serious contemporary threat to security and that they are likely to continue into the foreseeable future.[96]

The strategies of conflict resolution that I have identified as appropriate for humanitarian NGOs are no panacea even for the humanitarian community. On the contrary, each raises deep ethical, political, and strategic problems. Collectively, they underline the continuing importance of states, regional organizations, and global institutions, the traditional providers of security as a public good. When security is scarce—or absent—no strategy of conflict resolution, postwar reconstruction, or peace building is likely to succeed.

NOTES

[1]See Michael Brown, ed., *The International Dimensions of Internal Conflict* (Cambridge, Mass.: MIT, 1996).

[2]From the early 1980s to the mid-1990s, the number of humanitarian crises increased from an average of 20 to 25 per year to approximately 65 per year. Emergencies occurred most frequently in Africa and then Asia but were also prevalent in the former Soviet Union, Latin America, and the Caribbean. The International Committee of the Red Cross (ICRC) has estimated that the number of people affected by these emergencies is increasing by about 10 million annually. Simultaneously, humanitarian assistance increased from $845 million in 1989 to $7.1 billion in 1995. See *The Wave of Emergencies of the Last Decade: Causes, Extent, Predictability, and Response* (Helsinki and Oxford: World Institute for Development Economics Research, International Development Centre, 1999).

[3]The targeting of civilian populations in war is not new. In Stalinist Russia, in Nazi Germany and occupied Europe, and in China during the Cultural Revolution, to cite only the best-known cases, civilians were deliberately targeted to catastrophic effect. What are different are the transparency of the violence and the access of humanitarian organizations. The principal humanitarian organization operating in all three of these periods, the Red Cross, was effectively excluded, and civilian deaths occurred mostly unobserved and with a few notable exceptions, largely unhindered. Today, humanitarian organizations have unprecedented access, in part through the technical assets of major powers, in part through the people NGOs have on the ground, and in part because of the weakness of the collapsing states and their inability to limit access to their populations.

[4]See Daniel C. Esty, Jack A. Goldstone, Ted Robert Gurr, Barbara Harff, Marc Levy, Geoffrey D. Dabelko, Pamela T. Surko, and Alan N. Unger, "State Failure Task Force Report: Phase II Findings," in *Environmental Change and Security Report*, 5(1999):49-72. State failure is operationally defined more broadly as revolutionary wars, ethnic wars, regime transformation, and genocide and politicide. The critical discriminators between stable states and state failures were infant mortality rates, as an indicator of quality of life, trade openness, and level of democracy. Partial democracies are far more vulnerable to state failure than either full democracies or autocracies.

[5]See I. William Zartman, *Collapsed States: The Disintegration and Restoration of Legitimate Authority* (Boulder, Colo.: Lynne Rienner, 1995). Collapse is a severe reduction in capacity, authority, security, identity, institutions, and, at times, territory, so that institutions effectively cease to function. It can be understood as the most severe form of state failure. Analysis of collapse requires assessment of who wins and who loses from the collapse of the state and the void that is created.

[6]James Orbinski, "The 1999 Nobel Peace Prize Speech," delivered in Oslo, Norway, 10 December 1999, on behalf of Médecins Sans Frontières.

[7]Bernard Kouchner, *Le malheur des autres (The Misfortunes of Others)* (Paris: Odile Jacob, 1993); Dylan Hendrickson, "Humanitarian Action in Protracted Crises: The New Relief Agenda and Its Limits," *Network Paper*, 25 (London: Overseas Development Institute Refugee Research Network, 1998); and Philippe Delmas, *The Rosy Future of War* (New York: Free Press, 1997), p. 201.

[8]Interviews, CARE personnel, Goma, April 1995. See also Joelle Tanguy and Fiona Terry, "Humanitarian Responsibility and Committed Action," *Ethics & International Affairs*, 13(1999):29-34.

[9]As Delmas observes: "Humanitarianism is non-governmental by nature, not by default. Its legitimacy derives from the distress of each and not from the interests of the collectivity, as the States' actions do. Humanitarian action is not a policy; it is a spiritual need" (*The Rosy Future of War*, p. 203).

[10]In 1991 the UNHCR was responsible for 17 million refugees; by 1995 the number had risen to 27.4 million. This increase, however, masks a qualitative change: the number of refugees who cross international borders and are granted asylum in another state has declined in the past decade. In 1998 the UNHCR estimated the number of refugees at 13.2 million, while the representative of the secretary-general for internally displaced persons estimates their number at 2 million to 25 million. The increases in UNHCR numbers are internally displaced and war-affected populations in their own home countries and people outside their home countries who have not been granted asylum. See UNHCR, *The State of the World's Refugees 1995: In Search of Solutions* and *The State of the World's Refugees 1997-1998* (Oxford: Oxford University Press for the United Nations High Commissioner for Refugees, 1995 and 1999); *Report of the Secretary-General to the Security Council on the Protection of Civilians in Armed Conflict* (New York: United Nations, 1999); Mark Duffield, "NGO Relief in War Zones: Toward an Analysis of the New Aid Paradigm," in *Beyond UN Subcontracting: Task Sharing with Regional Security Arrangements and Service-Providing NGOs*, Thomas G. Weiss, ed. (New York: St. Martin's Press, 1998), pp. 139-159, 143; and Myron Weiner, "The Clash of Norms: Dilemmas in Refugee Policies," *Journal of Refugee Studies*, 11(1998):1-21.

[11]Mark Bradbury, "Complex Humanitarian Emergencies," working paper for CARE Canada, Ottawa, 1998.

[12]Duffield, "NGO Relief in War Zones."

[13]The United States, for example, spent $1.3 billion on development aid to Africa in 1994; in 1997 spending was reduced to $700 million.

[14]This phenomenon is one part of a wider structural change in the international relief system. NGOs have proliferated in concert with decisions by donors to disburse official development aid through NGOs rather than governments. From 1980 to 1993 the number of NGOs in the north that focused on development almost doubled. The Organization for Economic Cooperation and Development recorded a rise in northern-development NGOs between 1980 and 1993 from 1,600 to 2,970. The Commission on Global Governance recorded 28,900 international NGOs in 1995.

[15]For an analysis of the privatization process in Britain, see "NGOs—Humanitarian Cure or Curse?," *Department of Humanitarian Affairs (DHA) News*, No. 14, May/June 1995. For a discussion of the "privatizing" of world politics or the provision of public goods financed with public resources but carried out by private organizations, see Steven R. Smith and Michael Lipsky, *Non-profits for Hire: The Welfare State in the Age of Contracting* (Cambridge, Mass.: Harvard University Press, 1993), and Leon Gordenker and Thomas G. Weiss, "Pluralizing Global Governance: Analytical Approaches and Dimensions," in *NGOs, the UN, and Global Governance* (Boulder, Colo.: Lynne Rienner, 1996), pp. 17-47.

[16]See John Borton, Emery Brusset, and Alistair Hallam, "Humanitarian Aid and Its Effects," Study #3, *Joint Evaluation of Emergency Assistance in Rwanda* (Copenhagen: Danish International Development Assistance, 1996). This theme was reinforced by Sue Lautze, Bruce D. Jones, and Marc Duffield in *Strategic Humanitarian Coordination in the Great Lakes Region 1996-1997* (New York: Office for the Coordination of Humanitarian Affairs, 1998).

[17]The significant transfer of resources from intergovernmental organizations to NGOs may weaken the capacity of international institutions to develop public policy. See Isebill V. Gruhn, "NGOs in Partnership with the UN: A New Fix on a New Problem for African Development," *Global Society: Journal of Interdisciplinary International Relations*, 11(1997):325-337.

[18]Not only have the numbers and responsibilities of NGOs increased, but new kinds of NGOs have developed. A decade ago it was largely NGOs with religious affiliations that

focused explicitly on mediation and conflict resolution, using integrative problem-solving strategies. Now, secular NGOs that specialize in conflict prevention and resolution and operate independently of states and the UN are active in the field. International Alert and the International Crisis Group, two of the best-known among these new NGOs, have played an important role, for example, in Sierra Leone. Engaged in such activities as negotiating hostage releases, supporting local NGOs committed to peace building and conflict resolution, advising parties to the conflict, and helping to facilitate political negotiations, the conflict resolution NGOs are an important part of the international political landscape. At times they complement and at times they compete with the traditional diplomatic efforts of the UN, regional organizations, or individual states. Their work is the subject of some controversy. Critics allege that through their work they have legitimated parties that have engaged in terrorist actions and killing and undermined the work of UN officials charged with negotiating on behalf of the UN Secretary-General. See E. Voutira and S.A. Whishaw Brown, *Conflict Resolution: A Review of Some Non-governmental Practices—A Cautionary Tale* (Oxford: Refugee Studies Programme, Queen Elizabeth House, 1995). These criticisms cannot be evaluated without a systematic and comprehensive evaluation of the range of initiatives undertaken by the specialized NGOs. See Janice Gross Stein, "The Resolution of Identity Conflict: The Role of Non-governmental Organizations," in *International Nongovernmental Organizations and Conflict Resolution*, Shibley Telhami, ed. (Ithaca, N.Y.: Cornell University Press, forthcoming).

[19]Barry Brown and Christopher Brown, "Complex Emergencies: The Institutional Impasse," *Third World Quarterly*, 20(February 1999):207-221.

[20]Judith Miller, "U.N.'s Workers Become Targets in Angry Lands," *New York Times*, 19 September 1999, p. A1. In 1998, 20 UN civilian workers were killed in Sudan, Uganda, Georgia, Tajikistan, Burundi, and Afghanistan. These figures do not include humanitarian personnel who were not on contract with one of the UN agencies.

[21]This research was done as part of a larger project of CARE Canada and the Program on Negotiation and Conflict Management at the University of Toronto on humanitarian NGOs in complex emergencies. The project produced working papers on Somalia by Bruce Jones, on Rwanda by Bruce Jones, on Sierra Leone by Ian Smillie, and on NGOs by Mark Bradbury. See also Bruce Jones and Janice Gross Stein, "NGOs and Early Warning: The Case of Rwanda," *Synergies in Early Warning* (New York: Columbia International Affairs Online, Columbia University Press, 1999). For the final report of the project, see Michael Bryans, Bruce Jones, and Janice Gross Stein, "Mean Times: Humanitarian Action in Complex Political Emergencies— Stark Choices, Cruel Dilemmas," *Coming to Terms* (Toronto: Program on Negotiation and Conflict Management, 1999).

[22]In the three principal cases the activities of NGOs were tracked and personnel in the field at the time were asked to identify the principal obstacles to a more effective contribution to the delivery of assistance and conflict resolution. The focus on personnel in the field was driven very much by the nature of NGO relief and development work: labor-intensive activities employing field staffs in often remote areas; focusing on the lowest level of organization (village, family); refugee camp management (including food, medical, and social services); community-based health, agriculture, and microenterprise; and primary education. Examination of processes and attitudes at a microlevel fills an important gap in the analysis of complex emergencies.

[23]Mark Duffield, "NGOs, Disaster Relief, and Asset Transfer in the Horn: Political Survival in a Permanent Emergency," *Development and Change*, 24(1993):131-157.

[24]A recent study by the Overseas Development Institute in the United Kingdom argues that the role of humanitarian assistance in fueling war has been slight. See *The State of the International Humanitarian System* (London: Overseas Development Institute, March 1998), p. 3.

[25]Andrew S. Natsios, "Humanitarian Relief Intervention in Somalia: The Economics of

Chaos," in *Learning from Somalia: The Lessons of Armed Humanitarian Intervention*, Walter Clarke and Jeffrey Herbst, eds. (Boulder, Colo.: Westview Press, 1997), pp. 77-95, 82-83.

[26]See Clarke and Herbst, *Learning from Somalia*, and John Prendergast, *Crisis Response: Humanitarian Band-Aids in Sudan and Somalia* (London: Pluto Press, 1997).

[27]Mary Anderson, *Do No Harm: Supporting Local Capacities for Peace Through Aid* (Cambridge, Mass.: Local Capacities for Peace Project, The Collaborative for Development Action, 1996).

[28]Duffield, "NGOs, Disaster Relief, and Asset Transfer," p. 137.

[29]Mark Duffield, "The Political Economy of Internal War: Asset Transfer, Complex Emergencies, and International Aid," pp. 209-221 in *War and Hunger: Rethinking International Responses to Complex Emergencies*, Joanna Macrae and Anthony Zvi, eds. (London: Zed Books, 1994).

[30]Peter Shiras, "Humanitarian Emergencies and the Role of NGOs," pp. 106-117 in *After Rwanda: The Coordination of United Nations' Humanitarian Assistance*, James Whitman and David Pocock, eds. (New York: St. Martin's Press, 1996).

[31]Kenneth Menkhaus, "International Peacebuilding and the Dynamics of Local and National Reconciliation in Somalia," pp. 42-63 in *Learning from Somalia: The Lessons of Armed Humanitarian Intervention*, Walter Clarke and Jeffrey Herbst, eds. (Boulder, Colo.: Westview Press, 1997).

[32]Natsios, "Humanitarian Relief Intervention," pp. 85-86.

[33]Menkhaus, "International Peacebuilding."

[34]Cindy Collins, "Humanitarian Action: The Crises and the Critics," paper prepared for the Office for the Coordination of Humanitarian Affairs, February 1998.

[35]*Report of the Secretary-General to the Security Council on the Protection of Civilians in Armed Conflict* (New York: United Nations, 1999).

[36]Ibid.

[37]John Prendergast, *Frontline Diplomacy: Humanitarian Aid and Conflict in Africa* (London: Lynne Rienner, 1996), pp. 63-64.

[38]This criticism has been leveled most tellingly in the context of the analysis of famines. It is not natural disasters or economic collapse that creates starvation and mass migration; alone they are insufficient. Rather, famine is the result of systematic violence, deployed for political purposes, and designed to destroy coping mechanisms and survival strategies. Amartya Sen, in his seminal work *Poverty and Famines: An Essay on Entitlement and Deprivation* (Oxford: Clarendon Press, 1981), demonstrated that subsistence farmers in Africa use a set of "coping mechanisms"—migrating for wage labor, selling assets—designed primarily not to avoid hunger but rather to maintain such critical assets as seed, tools, and oxen. Famine becomes an instrument of violence by governments that deliberately target these assets so that civilians become vulnerable to famine.

The argument has been made that relief assistance does not address the causes of famine and may indeed exacerbate its severity by making political leaders less accountable to their constituencies that are necessary for the next planting. See Mark Duffield, *War and Famine in Africa* (Oxford: OXFAM Research Paper 5, OXFAM Publications, 1991); David Keen, *The Benefits of Famine: A Political Economy of Famine and Relief in Southwestern Sudan, 1983-1989* (Princeton, N.J.: Princeton University Press, 1994); William DeMars, "Mercy Without Illusion: Humanitarian Action in Conflict," *Mershon International Studies Review*, 40(April 1996):81-89; and Alexander de Waal, *Famine Crimes: Politics and the Disaster Relief Industry in Africa* (Bloomington: Indiana University Press, 1998). When assistance is distributed in rural areas, governments in central areas are able to avoid the political responsibility incumbent on any government to feed its own populations. John Prendergast, *Crisis Response: Humanitarian Band-Aids in Sudan and Somalia* and *Frontline Diplomacy: Humanitarian Aid and Conflict in Africa* (London: Lynne Rienner, 1996). In Sudan, for example, relief made the authorities less accountable to their civilian populations. Critics find it easier to diagnose the politically motivated violence of famine than to suggest strategies that can alleviate the hunger that is its consequence. They suggest that rural areas must be empowered politically so that they can forge ties with a center that becomes accountable. Logically elegant, such a strategy ignores the context of acute insecurity created by the predatory violence that is so critical to the diagnosis.

[39]De Waal, *Famine Crimes,* and Mark Duffield, *Post-modern Conflict, Aid Policy, and Humanitarian Conditionality* (London: Department for International Development, Emergency Aid Department, 1997).

[40]An attempt to shift responsibility to African NGOs for humanitarian relief will, in the immediate future, encounter serious problems of capacity. It has been estimated that even without responsibility for emergency relief there is a shortage of trained African personnel—between 25 and 200 percent are needed above present capacity—to meet current needs in education, health care, and physical infrastructure. Cindy Collins, "Humanitarian Action," p. 9. This incapacity dictates a serious investment in capacity building even as it cautions against a rapid transfer of all responsibility for humanitarian assistance. Clearly, such a transfer would overwhelm the existing system.

[41]Hendrickson, "Humanitarian Action in Protracted Crises."

[42]Duffield, "NGO Relief in War Zones," makes a compelling argument that Western governments are seeking to contain the consequences of globalization—poverty and social exclusion—by privatizing assistance to keep these consequences offshore. See also Mark Duffield, "Symphony of the Damned: Racial Discourse, Complex Political Emergencies and Humanitarian Aid," *Disasters,* 20(1996):173-193.

[43]De Waal, *Famine Crimes,* and *Famine that Kills: Darfur, Sudan, 1984-1985* (Oxford: Clarendon Press, 1989).

[44]M. Buchanan-Smith and S. Maxwell, "Linking Relief and Development: An Introduction and Overview," *Institute of Development Studies Bulletin,* 25(1994):2-16.

[45]For a related analysis of those who benefit from prolonging civil war, see Paul Collier, "Doing Well Out of War," paper prepared for the Conference on Economic Agendas in Civil Wars, London, 1999.

[46]Mark Duffield, "Symphony of the Damned," and Buchanan-Smith and Maxwell, "Linking Relief and Development." Duffield argues that within this new paradigm earlier concepts of social convergence have been replaced by the provision of sustainable "welfare safety nets" by private agencies. See Duffield, "NGO Relief in War Zones," p. 142.

[47]Joanna Macrae and Mark Bradbury, *Aid in the Twilight Zone: A Critical Analysis of Humanitarian-Development Aid Linkages in Situations of Chronic Instability* (London: Overseas Development Institute/Humanitarianism and War Project, 1998).

[48]Sue Lautze and John Hammock, *Coping with Crisis, Coping with Aid: Capacity Building, Coping Mechanisms and Dependency, Linking Relief and Development* (New York: UN Department of Humanitarian Affairs, December 1996), p. 27.

[49]Duffield, "NGO Relief in War Zones."

[50]In a major attempt to assess the impact of assistance, the authors conclude that "it is hardly possible to gain comprehensive knowledge of the impact of aid." Jerker Carlsson, Gunnar Koehlin, and Anders Ekbom, *The Political Economy of Evaluation: International Aid Agencies and the Effectiveness of Aid* (London: Macmillan Press, 1994), p. 203. Theirs is a cautionary tale of asserting the impact of relief assistance on development.

[51]Thomas G. Weiss, "Principles, Politics, and Humanitarian Action," *Ethics & International Affairs,* 13(1999):1-22, 18.

[52]Duffield, "NGO Relief in War Zones," and David Keen, "Organized Chaos: Not the New World We Ordered," *The World Today,* 52(January 1996):14-17, and *The Benefits of Famine.*

[53]De Waal, *Famine Crimes,* and Prendergast, *Frontline Diplomacy,* pp. 92-110.

[54]See Duffield, *Post-modern Conflict.*

[55]F. Stewart and U. Fitzgerald develop the concept of "non-entitlement" to encompass the acquisition of commodities by breaking the law. "Introduction: Assessing the Economic Costs of War," paper prepared for the Queen Elizabeth House Project on Institutions and Development, Oxford, October 1998.

[56]Keen, *The Benefits of Famine,* p. 12.

[57]Alan F. Fowler, "Authentic NGO Partnerships in the New Policy Agenda for International Aid: Dead End or Light Ahead?," *Development and Change,* 29(1998):137-159.

[58]*Preventing Deadly Conflict,* Final Report of the Carnegie Commission on Preventing Deadly Conflict (New York: Carnegie Corporation of New York, 1997), pp. 105-127.

[59]There is a significant difference between evaluation of past experience and the development of proposals for improved performance, on the one hand, and the adoption of these practices by the UN and humanitarian NGOs. Particularly at the UN, learning has been erratic and slow. Larry Minear, "Learning to Learn," paper prepared for the *Seminar on Lessons Learned on Humanitarian Coordination,* Stockholm, April 1998.

[60]Natsios, "Humanitarian Relief Intervention in Somalia," p. 87.

[61]One agency delivering large amounts of food to Rwanda increased its monitoring rapidly after the emergency erupted in 1994. A representative of the agency explained: "We went from 120 tons/month diversion to five tons/month within Rwanda between July 1993 and January 1994. We did it through monitoring. It's monotonous, boring, but critical in cutting down mismanagement." Cited in Prendergast, *Frontline Diplomacy,* p. 84.

[62]Natsios, "Humanitarian Intervention in Somalia," pp. 86-93. The UN field staff of the WFP and the UN Development Program opposed monetization because they thought it would be abusive to sell food in the context of a complex emergency. The proposal to monetize was endorsed by CARE and the International Rescue Committee.

[63]Prendergast, *Frontline Diplomacy,* p. 83. He observes that UN agencies have far greater difficulty controlling overheads and rarely standardize to reduce the costs of purchasing equipment.

[64]NGOs have also worked together to define more carefully the responsibilities of emergency aid and to refine the ethics of humanitarian action. International humanitarian agencies have adopted standards of performance and codes of conduct: the Code of Conduct for the International Red Cross Movement and NGOs in Disaster Relief; the elaboration of a set of technical standards in the field of water and food aid delivery by the Steering Committee for Humanitarian Response (SCHR); the development of principles and best practices for the recruitment and management of relief workers by "People in Aid" in the United Kingdom; and the development by the SCHR and InterAction, through the SPHERE Project, of a "claimants" charter defining beneficiary rights. Joanna Macrae, "Humanitarian Ethics Versus Humanitarian Impulse," in ECHO report on Dublin, NGO forum, op. cit.

[65]Weiss, "Principles, Politics, and Humanitarian Action," p. 19.

[66]Anderson, *Do No Harm.*

[67]For a strong argument of this kind, see Weiss, "Principles, Politics, and Humanitarian Action." See also *Development Assistance as a Means of Conflict Prevention* (Oslo: Norwegian Institute of International Affairs, 1998). For a rejoinder insisting on the continuing importance of neutrality, see Joelle Tanguy and Fiona Terry, "Humanitarian Responsibility and Committed Action," *Ethics & International Affairs,* 13(1999):29-35. See also Orbinski, "The 1999 Nobel Peace Prize Speech," where the president of the MSF International Council argues that "ours is not to displace the responsibility of the state. . . . Ours is not to allow a humanitarian alibi to mask the state responsibility to ensure justice and security."

[68]David Keen and Ken Wilson, "Engaging with Violence: A Reassessment of Relief in Wartime," pp. 50-69 in *War and Hunger: Rethinking International Responses to Complex Emergencies,* Joanna Macrae and Anthony Zwi, eds. (London: Zed Books, 1994).

69Nicholas Berry, *War and the Red Cross: The Unspoken Mission* (New York: St. Martin's Press, 1997).

70Orbinski, "The 1999 Nobel Prize Speech."

71Weiss, "Principles, Politics, and Humanitarian Action," p. 21.

72Forty-one NGOs were granted consultative status to the UN in 1948, 377 by 1968, and more than 1,200 by 1997. John Stremlau, *People in Peril: Human Rights, Humanitarian Action, and Preventing Deadly Conflict* (New York: Carnegie Corporation, 1998).

73There are some circumstances in which the monopolistic forces are less powerful. Anecdotal evidence indicates that in the United States the number of effective funding "windows" available at the U.S. Agency for International Development and its relatively decentralized structure combined with the large volume of funding tend to mitigate the agency's monopoly power. In addition, some NGOs—CARE International, for example— have developed their own multilateral structures that create opportunities for field operations to access multiple national donors.

74Natsios, "Humanitarian Relief Intervention in Somalia," p. 93.

75*DHA News*, December 1997, no. 23, pp. 5, 7-8.

76Council for a Livable World, *Project on Peacekeeping and the United Nations*, prospectus, www.clw.org/pub/clw/un/acri.html.

77The lead African state in ECOMOG, Nigeria dominated the force that was seen by other Africans as serving regional hegemonic interests. The UN exercised virtually no control over the force once it had authorized its operations through a Security Council resolution. See Edwin M. Smith and Thomas G. Weiss, "UN Task-Sharing: Towards or Away from Global Governance," *Third World Quarterly*, February 1997; Michèle Griffen, "Retrenchment, Reform and Regionalization: Trends in UN Peace Support Measures," *International Peacekeeping*, Summer 1999, pp. 21-25; Stremlau, *People in Peril: Human Rights, Humanitarian Action, and Preventing Deadly Conflict*, pp. 57-58; Sylvester Ekundayo Rowe, "ECOMOG—A Model for African Peace-keeping," *African Law Today*, October 1998; and Colin Scott, with Larry Minear and Thomas G. Weiss, *Humanitarian Action and Security in Liberia*, Occasional Paper #20 (Providence, R.I.: Thomas J. Watson Jr. Institute for International Studies, 1995).

78*Report of the Secretary-General to the Security Council on the Protection of Civilians in Armed Conflict* (New York: United Nations, Office of the Secretary-General), p. 34.

79UNSECOORD also helps agencies identify field security officers, and a designated official, usually a senior official from a UN agency, reports to UNSECOORD in New York. *Security of Relief Workers and Humanitarian Space*, Background Document to the Commission Working Paper (European Commission, ECHO, April 1999).

80The Convention on the Safety of United Nations and Associated Personnel of 1994 entered into force on January 15, 1999. The UN secretary-general has recommended the addition of a protocol to the convention that would extend the scope of legal protection to all UN and associated personnel. *Report of the Secretary-General to the Security Council on the Protection of Civilians in Armed Conflict*, pp. 3, 10.

81*Security of Relief Workers and Humanitarian Space*, pp. 14-15.

82In the fall of 1994 the UN received a proposal from a British company to provide training and support to Zaire's army in order to wrest control of the camps from the militias. The idea received support from one permanent member of the UN Security Council, but other members rejected the idea on the basis of cost and principle: using a private company to fulfill an international public responsibility was wrong. None of the states rejecting the proposal on principle subsequently offered troops and resources when requested by the secretary-general.

83Prendergast, *Frontline Diplomacy*, p. 66.

[84]ICRC, "Working Paper on Armed Protection of Humanitarian Assistance," Council of Delegates, Geneva, 1-2 December 1995, and ICRC, "Seminar on the Security of Humanitarian Personnel in the Field for Non-governmental Organizations," Graduate Institute for International Studies, Geneva, 5 December 1997.

[85]*Security of Relief Workers in Humanitarian Space*, p. 19.

[86]The "privatization of security" for humanitarian purposes is part of a broader and deeper trend in contemporary global politics. Governments and international organizations are subcontracting to private organizations the training and staffing of international observer missions, police forces, and even military forces. See Janice Gross Stein, "The Privatization of Security in Global Space," *International Studies Review*, Summer 2000, forthcoming.

[87]For a similar argument, see Weiss, "Principles, Politics, and Humanitarian Action," p. 21.

[88]Many NGOs reject any conditionality of humanitarian assistance at all. As Tanguy and Fierry of MSF argue, "although the provision of aid in conflict is *implicitly* political, the possibility of constructing humanitarian space is jeopardized by tying aid to conflict resolution initiatives. The use of aid as a carrot to bring about peace destroys all notions of giving aid according to needs and without discrimination" ("Humanitarian Responsibility and Committed Action," p. 33).

[89]The head of one of the agencies that remained explained: "Total withdrawal would provoke chaos, looting, and violence." Cutting off water, he continued, could create an epidemic within days. Cited by Prendergast, *Frontline Diplomacy*, pp. 139-140.

[90]CARE Canada internal memorandum, record of Liberia-NGO Steering Committee teleconference, June 19, 1996.

[91]Nicholas Stockton, "In Defence of Humanitarianism," paper presented to the *Disasters Emergency Committee Seminar*, London, 1998.

[92]Médecins sans Frontières withdrew from Goma, objecting publicly to political conditions in the camps, but other humanitarian NGOs stayed to provide assistance. Prendergast, *Frontline Diplomacy*, p. 138.

[93]Ian Levine argues that the humanitarian community has not been very successful in identifying the best interests of those living under the control of groups whose respect for human rights is nonexistent. See "Promoting Humanitarian Principles: The Southern Sudan Experience," Overseas Development Institute Refugee Research Network Paper 21, May 1997, p. 24, and James Darcy, "Human Rights and International Legal Standards: What Do Relief Workers Need to Know?," Overseas Development Institute Refugee Research Network Paper 19, February 1997.

[94]The four were Save the Children (U.K.), the WFP, Sudan Medical Care, and Diocese of Torit that assisted in animal health. Prendergast, *Frontline Diplomacy*, p. 140.

[95]Collier, "Doing Well Out of War"; David Keen, *The Economic Functions of Violence in Civil Wars* (Oxford: Oxford University Press, 1998); and Francois Jean and Jean-Christophe Rufin, *Economies des Guerres Civiles* (Paris: Hachette Pluriel, 1996).

[96]*The Wave of Emergencies of the Last Decade.*

11

Electoral Systems and Conflict in Divided Societies

Ben Reilly and Andrew Reynolds[1]

T his work examines whether the choice of an electoral system in a culturally plural society can affect the potential for future violent conflict. We find that it can, but that there is no single electoral system that is likely to be best for all divided societies. We distinguish four basic strategies of electoral system design. The optimal choice for peacefully managing conflict depends on several identifiable factors specific to the country, including the way and degree to which ethnicity is politicized, the intensity of conflict, and the demographic and geographic distribution of ethnic groups. In addition, the electoral system that is most appropriate for initially ending internal conflict may not be the best one for longer-term conflict management. In short, while electoral systems can be powerful levers for shaping the content and practice of politics in divided societies, their design is highly sensitive to context. Consideration of the relationship between these variables and the operation of different electoral systems enables the development of contingent generalizations that can assist policy makers in the field of electoral system design.

INTRODUCTION

Several fundamental assumptions that underlie the thinking of many Western policy specialists are called into question by the evidence assembled here concerning the relationship between conflict and elections. The first assumption, derived from Western experience, is that "free and fair elections" are the most appropriate way both to avoid and to manage

420

acute internal conflict in other countries. The second assumption, which goes hand in hand with the first, is the implicit approval of "winner take all" models of both government and election and disapproval of arrangements that emphasize power sharing and cooperation. The third, again derived from Western experience, is that the types of electoral systems used in the West can be successfully transplanted to the developing world. A final assumption is that stable democracies need to be based on a system of individual rights rather than group rights. This work, to varying degrees, calls all of these assumptions into question.

The multicountry evidence cited here offers some insights about how to diagnose a country's situation for the purpose of selecting an electoral system that can help that country address its communal conflicts peacefully. Realistic diagnosis of key social-structural issues is a necessary precondition to designing a successful system. In practice, there is little evidence of such diagnosis at work in the historical record. Moreover, the choice of an electoral system involves tradeoffs among a number of desirable attributes. Thus, the role of local actors, who can draw both on international experience and on their knowledge of domestic conditions and priorities, is key.

Institutions, Conflict Management, and Democracy

The study of political institutions is integral to the study of democratization because institutions constitute and sustain democracies:[2] as Scarritt and Mozaffar succinctly summarize, "to craft democracies is to craft institutions" (1996:3). Perhaps most important for newly democratizing countries is the way that institutions shape the choices available to political actors. Koelble notes that this emphasis on "rules, structures, codes, and organizational norms" is based upon Weber's view of organizations as constructs designed to distribute rewards and sanctions and to establish guidelines for acceptable types of behavior (1995:233). March and Olsen argue that "constitutions, laws, contracts, and customary rules of politics make many potential actions or considerations illegitimate or unnoticed; some alternatives are excluded from the agenda before politics begins, but these constraints are not imposed full-blown by an external social system; they develop within the context of political institutions" (1984:740). In his important 1991 book *Democracy and the Market*, Adam Przeworski develops a concept of democracy as "rule open-endedness or organized uncertainty . . . and the less the uncertainty over potential outcomes the lower the incentive for groups to organize institutionally" (1991:13). Thus his influential conclusion, central to the spirit of this paper, was a recognition that democratic government, rather than oligarchy or authoritarianism, presented by far the best prospects for managing deep societal divisions, and that democracy itself operates as a system for *managing* and *processing* rather than resolving conflict.[3]

In their preface to *Politics in Developing Countries*, Larry Diamond, Juan Linz, and Seymour Martin Lipset argue that institutions influence political stability in four important respects:

(i) Because they structure behavior into stable, predictable, and recurrent patterns, institutionalized systems are less volatile and more enduring, and so are institutionalized democracies.

(ii) Regardless of how they perform economically, democracies that have more coherent and effective political institutions will be more likely to perform well politically in maintaining not only political order but also a rule of law, thus ensuring civil liberties, checking the abuse of power, and providing meaningful representation, competition, choice, and accountability.

(iii) Over the long run well-institutionalized democracies are also more likely to produce workable, sustainable, and effective economic and social policies because they have more effective and stable structures for representing interests and they are more likely to produce working congressional majorities or coalitions that can adopt and sustain policies.

Lastly, (iv) democracies that have capable, coherent democratic institutions are better able to limit military involvement in politics and assert civilian control over the military (1995:33).

Institutions and Democratization in the Developing World

While accepting that throughout the developing world the societal constraints on democracy are considerable, such constraints still leave room for conscious political strategies which may further or hamper successful democratization. As a result, institutions work not just at the margins, but are central to the structuring of stability, particularly in ethnically heterogeneous societies. Scarritt and Mozaffar push the critical role of institutions even further by arguing that distinct institutional arrangements not only distinguish democracies, but also invest governments with different abilities to manage conflicts, and thus that the survival of third-wave democracies under extremely adverse conditions often hinges on these institutional differences (1996:3).

Institutional design takes on an enhanced role in newly democratizing and divided societies because, in the absence of other structures, politics becomes the primary mode of communication between divergent social forces. In any society, groups (collections of individuals who identify some sort of mutual bond) talk to each other—sometimes about resolving distributive conflicts, sometimes about planning for the national future, and often about more mundane issues of everyday concern. In the pluralist democracies of the West, there are a variety of channels of communication open through which to carry on these conversations. Individuals from different cultures and perspectives can communicate with each other through the institutions of civil society via the press, social and sporting clubs, residence associations, church groups, labor unions, and so on.[4]

In fledgling democracies, however, where society is more deeply divided along ethnic, regional, or religious lines, political institutions take on even greater importance. They become the most prominent, and often the only, channel of communication between disparate groups. Such societies do not yet have the mixed institutions which characterize a broad civil society. Sporting, social, and religious groups are rigidly segregated, and various peoples do not live together, play together, or really talk to each other. Similarly, many new democracies do not yet have a vigorous free press where groups can talk. This holds true in the West as well, where different media outlets speak to different social groups or classes, and where cities are often segregated along racial, ethnic, and economic lines; but divided societies in the developing world often represent the extreme of the continuum, and that is why political institutions exist as the primary channel of communication.

Because political institutions fulfill this role as the preeminent method of communication, they must facilitate communication channels between groups who need to talk. If they exclude people from coming to the table, then their conflicts can only be solved through force, not through negotiation and mutual accommodation. Further, those doing the talking, the representatives, must be just that—representative. To be able to make promises and then deliver on them, each political representative needs to be accountable to his or her constituency to the highest degree possible through institutional rules. The extent to which institutional rules place a premium on the representational roles of such figures, or rather seek to break down the overall salience of ethnicity by forcing them to transcend their status as representatives of only one group or another, is central to the scholarly debate about political institutions in deeply divided societies.

The Validity of Constitutional Engineering

There is little dispute that institutions *matter*, but there is much greater dispute regarding how much one can (or would wish to) engineer political outcomes through the choice of institutional structures. In this regard there exists an important distinction between an *institutional choice* approach and those who seek institutional innovation through *constitutional engineering* to mitigate conflict within divided societies. Sisk notes that "there has been an implicit assumption by scholars of comparative politics who specialize in divided societies that such political conflict can be potentially ameliorated if only such societies would adopt certain types of democratic institutions, that is, through 'political engineering'" (1995:5). Indeed, Horowitz proposes that "whatever their preferences, it remains true that a severely divided society needs a heavy dose—on the engineering analogy, even a redundant dose—of institutions laden with incentives to accommodation" (1991:280-281). Similarly, Sartori argues that "the organization of the state requires more than any other organization to be kept on course by a structure of rewards and punishments, of 'good' inducements and scary deterrents" (1994:203).

However, Sisk runs counter to Horowitz, Lijphart, Sartori, and others in arguing that constitutional engineering should not be the primary focus of research: "most scholarship about democracy in divided societies centers too much on examining the best outcomes, as opposed to looking at the ways these outcomes evolve through bargaining processes" (1995: 18). Indeed, Elster supports Sisk with the view that "it is impossible to predict with certainty or even qualified probability the consequences of a major constitutional change" (1988:304). Elster and Sisk remain in the minority on this question, given that most comparative political scientists would be happy to predict with "qualified probability" the results of a shift in electoral law or democratic system. As Sartori correctly notes, if we follow Elster's somewhat defeatist logic, then "the practical implication of the inability of predicting is the inability of reforming" (1994:200). There seems little reason to give up the potential power of institutions for conflict resolution if we are confident of some degree of predictive ability when it comes to institutional consequences.

Ultimately, there is a temporal dimension to both constitutional design and the politics of institutional choice. Political actors in a fledgling democracy may choose certain structures (rationally) because they maximize their gain in the short term. Thus, negotiators may not alight upon more inclusive structures recommended by political scientists posing as constitutional engineers. However, the promise of constitutional engineering rests on the assumption that long-term sociopolitical stability is the nation's overarching goal; and the institutions needed to facilitate that goal may not be the same as those which provide maximum short-term gain to the negotiating actors in the transitional period. Thus, *institutional choice* and *constitutional engineering* are, in practice, compatible approaches. One seeks to understand what drives short-term bargains, while the other seeks to offer more long-term solutions with the benefit of comparative cross-national evidence. The task of the constitutional engineer is not only to find which institutional package will most likely ensure democratic consolidation, but also to persuade those domestic politicians making the decisions that they should choose long-term stability over short-term gain.

Electoral Engineering and Conflict Management

The set of democratic institutions a nation adopts is thus integral to the long-term prospects of any new regime as they structure the rules of the game of political competition. Within the range of democratic institutions, many scholars have argued that there is no more important choice than which electoral system is to be used. Electoral systems have long been recognized as one of the most important institutional mechanisms for shaping the nature of political competition, first, because they are, to quote one electoral authority, "the most specific manipulable instrument of politics"[5]—that is, they can be purposively designed to achieve particular outcomes—and second, because they structure the arena of political competition, including the party system; offer incentives to behave in certain ways; and reward those who respond to these incentives with electoral success. The great potential of electoral system design for influencing political behavior is thus that it can reward particular types of behavior and place constraints on others. This is why electoral system design has been seized upon by many scholars (Lijphart, 1977, 1994; Sartori, 1968; Taagepera and Shugart, 1989; Horowitz, 1985, 1991) as one of the chief levers of constitutional engineering to be used in mitigating conflict within divided societies. As Lijphart notes, "if one wants to change the nature of a particular democracy, the electoral system is likely to be the most suitable and effective instrument for doing so" (1995a:412). Nevertheless, the fact that electoral system design has not proved to be a panacea for the vagaries of communal conflict in many places has shed some doubt upon the primacy that electoral systems are given as "tools of conflict management." What we attempt to do in this paper is assess the cumulative evidence of the relationship between electoral systems and intrasocietal conflict, and determine under what conditions electoral systems have the most influence on outcomes.

An electoral system is designed to do three main jobs. First, it translates the votes cast into seats won in a legislative chamber. The system may give more weight to proportionality between votes cast and seats won, or it may funnel the votes (however fragmented among parties) into a parliament which contains two large parties representing polarized views. Second, electoral systems act as the conduit through which the people can hold their elected representatives accountable. Third, different electoral systems serve to structure the boundaries of "acceptable" political discourse in different ways, and give incentives for those competing for power to couch their appeals to the electorate in distinct ways. In terms of deeply ethnically divided societies, for example, where ethnicity represents a fundamental political cleavage, particular electoral systems can reward candidates and parties who act in a cooperative, accommodatory manner to rival groups; or they can punish these candidates and instead reward those who appeal only to their own ethnic group. However, the "spin" which an electoral system gives to the system is ultimately contextual and will depend on the specific cleavages and divisions within any given society.

That said, it is important not to overestimate the power of elections and electoral systems to resolve deep-rooted enmities and bring conflictual groups into a stable and institutionalized political system which processes conflict through democratic rather than violent means. Some analysts have argued that while established democracies have evolved structures which process disputes in ways that successfully avoid "conflict," newly democratizing states are considerably more likely to experience civil or national violence (see Mansfield and Snyder, 1995). The argument that competitive multiparty elections actually exacerbate ethnic polarism has been marshaled by a number of African leaders (for example, Yoweri Museveni in Uganda and Daniel arap Moi in Kenya) in defense of their hostility to multiparty democracy. And it is true to say that "elections, as competitions among individuals, parties, and their ideas are inherently just that: competitive. Elections are, and are meant to be, polarizing; they seek to highlight social choices" (Reynolds and Sisk, 1998:18). Elections may be "the defining moment," but while some founding elections have forwarded the twin causes of democratization and conflict resolution, such as South Africa and Mozambique, others have gone seriously awry, such as Angola and Burundi.

While it is important not to overemphasize the importance or influence of political institutions (and particularly of electoral systems) as factors influencing democratic transitions, it is more common when dealing with developing countries that the reverse is true: scholars and policy makers alike have typically given too much attention to social forces and not enough to the careful crafting of appropriate democratic institutions by which those forces can be expressed. As Larry Diamond has argued, "the single most important and urgent factor in the consolidation of democracy is not civil society but political institutionalization."[6] To survive, democracies in developing countries need above all "robust political institutions" such as secure executives and effective legislatures composed of coherent, broadly based parties encouraged by aggregative electoral institutions.[7] We thus return to the underlying premise of constitutional engineering as it relates to electoral system design: while it is true that elections are merely one cog in the wheel of a much broader framework of institutional arrangements, sociohistorical pressures, and strategic actor behaviors, at the same time electoral systems are an indispensable and integral part of this broader framework. One electoral system might nurture accommodatory tendencies which already exist, while another may make it far more rational for ethnic entrepreneurs to base their appeals on exclusionary notions of ethnochauvinism.

What the collective evidence from elections held in divided societies does seem to suggest is that an appropriately crafted electoral system can do some good in nurturing accommodative tendencies, but the implementation of an inappropriate system can do severe harm to the trajectory of conflict resolution and democratization in a plural state (see Reilly, 1997a; Reynolds and Sisk, 1998). Given this, is it possible to outline criteria that one might use to judge the success or failure of any given electoral system design? In light of the multicausal nature of institutions, democracy, and political behavior, it would be foolhardy to say with absolute certainty that a particular electoral system was solely, or even primarily, responsible for a change—for better or worse—in ethnic relations in a divided society. Nevertheless, with the benefit of a holistic view of a nation's democratization process, it is possible to highlight instances where the electoral system itself appears to have encouraged accommodation, and those where it played a part in exaggerating the incentives for ethnic polarization. We hope that the typologies and analytical tools introduced in this paper as part of a contingent theory of electoral system design may help future research elucidate such electoral system effects.

Our Knowledge to Date

To date, our academic knowledge of electoral systems and their consequences has been predominantly based upon the more generic and abstract study of electoral systems as decision-making rules, structuring games played by faceless "rational actors" in environments which are often devoid of historical, socioeconomic, and cultural context. A comprehensive body of work exists which points to the mathematical effects of various systems on party systems, proportionality, and government formation (see, for example, Farrell, 1997; Grofman and Lijphart, 1986; Lijphart and Grofman, 1984; Lijphart, 1994; Rae, 1967; and Taagepera and Shugart, 1989). This is not to deride those very important works—and the discipline as a whole—rather it reflects the fact that much less work has been carried out on the subject of electoral systems, democratization, and conflict resolution. In addition, the majority of work on electoral systems to date has both exhibited a strong bias toward the study of established democracies in the West, and has been mostly country specific. This paper seeks to give a fillip to the increasingly important and more truly comparative study of how electoral systems can be crafted to improve the lot of divided societies.

Historically, Huntington has identified three periods in which each contained a "wave" of transitions of states from nondemocracy to multi-party competition (Huntington, 1991). Each wave saw the crafting of new constitutions for a new order, and electoral systems were regularly the most controversial and debated aspect of the new institutions. Huntington's "first wave" takes in the period from 1828 to 1926 when the United States, Great Britain, Australia, Canada, New Zealand, and a number of smaller European states began to evolve degrees of multiparty competition and "democratic" institutional structures. The debates over electoral systems (especially in Scandinavia and continental Europe) during this first wave of democratization mirrored many of the debates that new democracies are experiencing in the 1990s—the perceived tradeoffs between "accountability" and "representativeness," between a close geographical link between elector and representative and proportionality for parties in parliament (see Carstairs, 1980). Huntington's second wave encompasses the post-second world war period through the decolonization decades of the 1950s and early 1960s. This wave saw many states either inherit or receive electoral systems designed and promoted by outside powers. West Germany, Austria, Japan, and Korea are examples of such "external imposition" by Allied powers in the postwar period, while virtually all the fleetingly democratic postcolonial nation states of Africa and Asia inherited direct transplants of the electoral and constitutional systems of their colonial masters.

Finally, the "third wave" of democratization, which began with the overthrow of the Salazar dictatorship in Portugal in 1974 and continues on to this day, gives us a wealth of case study material when it comes to assessing electoral system design in new democracies and those societies divided by cultural or social hostilities. In 1997, Reynolds and Reilly found only seven countries (out of 212 independent states and related territories) which did not hold direct elections for their legislatures, and of those 98 were classified as "free" on the basis of political rights and civil liberties in the 1995-1996 Freedom House *Freedom in the World* (Reynolds and Reilly, 1997). Therefore, we can be confident that a considerable range of comparative material is available for a study of how electoral systems influence democratization and stability in divided societies. This is even more so if we are mindful not to ignore the important lessons of nineteenth-century emerging democracies such as the British dominions (Canada, Australia, South Africa, New Zealand), with their divisions between and within "settler" and "indigenous" groups, or the multiethnic societies of continental Europe (Belgium, Austria-Hungary, Switzerland, the Netherlands, and Luxembourg), which fulfilled many of the classic elements of "plural" or "divided" societies at the turn of the century. In both groups, electoral system design was seen as a means of dealing with divisions and, particularly in the European examples, as a tool of accommodation building between potentially hostile religious or linguistic groups.

DEVELOPING AN ANALYTICAL FRAMEWORK FOR A
CONTINGENT THEORY OF ELECTORAL SYSTEM DESIGN

Consultants on electoral system design rightly shy away from the "one-size-fits-all" approach of recommending one system for all contexts. Indeed, when asked to identify their "favorite" or "best" system, constitutional experts will say "it depends" and the dependents are more often than not variables such as: What does the society look like? How is it divided? Do ethnic or communal divides dovetail with voting behavior? Do different groups live geographically intermixed or segregated? What is the country's political history? Is it an established democracy, a transitional democracy, or a redemocratizing state? What are the broader constitutional arrangements that the legislature is working within?

Historically, the process of electoral system design has tended to occur on a fragmented case-by-case basis, which has led to the inevitable and continual reinvention of the wheel because of limited comparative information. In this paper, we seek to develop an analytical framework upon which a contingent theory of electoral system design may be built. When assessing the appropriateness of any given electoral system for a divided society, three variables become particularly salient:

(1) knowledge of *the nature of societal division* is paramount (i.e., the nature of group identity, the intensity of conflict, the nature of the dispute, and the spatial distribution of conflictual groups);

(2) the nature of the *political system* (i.e., the nature of the state, the party system, and the overall constitutional framework); and

(3) the *process* which led to the adoption of the electoral system (i.e., was the system inherited from a colonial power, was it consciously designed, was it externally imposed, or did it emerge through a process of evolution and unintended consequences?).

In the following section we describe these three key variables and then operationalize them in the Conclusion.

Nature of Societal Division

The Nature of Group Identity

As noted earlier, appropriate constitutional design is ultimately contextual and rests on the nuances of a nation's unique social cleavages. The nature of division within a society is revealed in part by the extent to which ethnicity correlates with party support and voting behavior. And that factor will often determine whether institutional engineering is able to dissipate ethnic conflicts or merely contain them. There are two dimensions to *the nature of group identity*: one deals with foundations (i.e., whether the society divided along racial, ethnic, ethnonationalistic, religious, regional, linguistic, etc., lines), while the second deals with how rigid and entrenched such divisions are. Scholarship on the latter subject has developed a continuum with the rigidity of received identity (i.e., primordialism) on one side and the malleability of constructed social identities (i.e., constructivist or instrumentalist) on the other (see Shils, 1957; Geertz, 1973; Young, 1976; Anderson, 1991; Newman, 1991; Esman, 1994).

Clearly, if ethnic allegiances are indeed primordial, and therefore rigid, then a specific type of power sharing, based on an electoral system which primarily recognizes and accommodates interests based on ascriptive communal traits rather than individual ideological ones, is needed to manage competing claims for scarce resources. If ethnic identities and voting behaviors are fixed, then there is no space for institutional incentives aimed at promoting accommodatory strategies to work. Nevertheless, while it is true that in almost all multiethnic societies there are indeed correlations between voting behavior and ethnicity, the causation is far more complex. It is far from clear that primordial ethnicity, the knee-jerk reaction to vote for "your group's party" regardless of other factors, is the chief explanation of these correlations. More often than not ethnicity has become a proxy for other things, a semiartificial construct which has its roots in community but has been twisted out of all recognition. This is what Robert Price calls the antagonistic "politics of communalism"— ethnicity which has been politicized and exploited to serve entrepreneurial ends (1995).

In practice, virtually every example of politicized ethnic conflict exhibits claims based on a combination of both "primordial" historical associations and "instrumentalized" opportunistic adaptations.[8] In the case of Sierra Leone, for example, Kandeh (1992) has shown that dominant local elites, masquerading as "cultural politicians," shaped and mobilized ethnicity to serve their interests. In Uganda, President Museveni has used the "fear of tribalism" as an excuse to avoid multipartism. Nevertheless, in both the colonial and postcolonial "one-party state" eras, strategies to control and carve up the Ugandan state were based upon the hostile mobilization of ethnic and religious identities. Malawi acts as a counterfactual to the primordial ethnicity thesis and offers an example of how political affiliations play out differently when incentive structures are altered. In the multiparty elections of 1994, a history of colonial rule, missionary activity, and Hastings Banda's "Chewa-ization" of national culture combined together to plant the seeds of conflictual regionalism which both dovetailed with, and cut across, preconceived ethnic boundaries. The south voted for the United Democratic Front of Bakili Muluzi, the Center for the Malawi Congress Party of Banda, and the north for the

Alliance for Democracy led by Chakufwa Chihana. But voting patterns depended more upon region than ethnicity. Kaspin notes that "not only did non-Tumbuka in the north vote for AFORD, and non-Yao in the south vote for the UDF, but non-Tumbuka and non-Yao groups divided by regional borders tended to support the opposition candidates of their own region" (1995:614).[9]

If ethnic conflict is not predetermined, or is more often a proxy for other interests, then incentives can be laid for other cleavages to emerge as ethnic divides becomes less salient. In South Africa, for example, the rules of the game encouraged parties to appeal across ethnic boundaries. As Price (1995) notes, South Africa has been remarkably free of ethnic conflict in the postapartheid period, bearing in mind its history of repressive racial laws. Challenging conventional wisdom, he argues that "the South African case is important for the contemporary study of ethnicity in politics precisely because it is an ethnically heterogeneous society *without* significant ethnic conflict." The election of April 1994 also lent credence to the claim that the inclusive institutional incentives of the interim constitution helped make politicized ethnicity far less salient. All parties (bar the Afrikaner Freedom Front and the National Party in the Western Cape) strived to appeal across ethnic divides, and the African National Congress (ANC), National Party (NP), Inkatha Freedom Party (IFP), DP, and PAC presented multiethnic and multiracial lists of parliamentary candidates. In a 1994 postelection survey, Robert Mattes (1995) of the Institute for Democracy in South Africa found only 3 percent of voters claimed to have based their political affiliations on ethnic identity.[10]

Intensity of Conflict

A second variable in terms of the nature of any given conflict and its susceptibility to electoral engineering is simply the intensity and depth of hostility between the competing groups. It is worth remembering that, although academic and international attention is naturally drawn to extreme cases, most ethnic conflicts do *not* degenerate into all-out civil war (Fearon and Laitin, 1996). While few societies are entirely free from multiethnic antagonism, most are able to manage to maintain a degree of mutual accommodation sufficient to avoid state collapse. There are numerous examples of quite deeply divided states in which the various groups maintain frosty but essentially civil relations between one another despite a considerable degree of mutual antipathy—such as the relations between Malays, Chinese, and Indians in Malaysia. There are other cases (e.g., Sri Lanka) where what appeared to be a relatively benign interethnic environment and less pronounced racial cleavages nonetheless broke down into violent armed conflict, but where democratic government has nonetheless been the rule more than the exception. And then, of course, there are the cases of utter breakdown in relations and the "ethnic cleansing" of one group by another, typified most recently and horribly by Bosnia.

The significance of these examples is that each of these states is deeply divided, but the different intensity of the conflict means that different electoral "levers" would need to be considered in each case. Malaysia has been able to use a majoritarian electoral system which utilizes a degree of "vote pooling" and power sharing to manage relations between the major ethnic groups—a successful strategy in terms of managing ethnic relations there, but possible only because Chinese voters are prepared, under the right circumstances, to vote for Malay candidates and vice versa. By contrast, under the "open-list" proportional representation (PR) system used for parliamentary elections in Sri Lanka, research has found that Sinhalese voters will, if given the chance, deliberately move Tamil candidates placed in a winnable position on a party list to a lower position—a factor which may well have occurred in South Africa as well, had not the electoral system used been a "closed" list, which allowed major parties such as the ANC and the NP to place ethnic minorities and women high on their party list. But even in Sri Lanka, the electoral system for presidential elections allows Tamils and other minorities to indicate who their least-disliked Sinhalese candidate is—a system which has seen the election of ethnic moderates to the position of president at every election to date (Reilly, 1997b).

Contrast this with a case like Bosnia, where relations between ethnic groups are so deeply hostile that it is almost inconceivable that electors of one group would be prepared to vote for others under any circumstances. There, the 1996 transitional elections were contested overwhelmingly by ethnically based parties, with minimal contact between competing parties, and with any accommodation between groups having to take place *after* the election—in negotiations between ethnic elites representing the various groups—rather than before. The problem with such an approach is that it assumes that elites themselves are willing to behave moderately to their opponents, when much of the evidence from places like Bosnia tends directly to contradict such an assumption. We will return to this problem, which bedevils elite-centered strategies for conflict management, later in this paper.

The Nature of the Dispute

Electoral system design is not merely contingent upon the basis and intensity of social cleavages but also, to some extent, upon the nature of the dispute, which is manifested from cultural differences. The classic issue of dispute, is the issue of group rights and status in a "multiethnic democracy," that is, a system characterized both by democratic decision-making institutions and by the presence of two or more ethnic groups, defined as a group of people who see themselves as a distinct cultural community; who often share a common language, religion, kinship, and/ or physical characteristics (such as skin color); and who tend to harbor negative and hostile feelings toward members of other groups.[11] The majority of this paper deals with this fundamental cleavage of ethnicity.

Other types of disputes often dovetail with ethnic ones, however. If the issue that divides groups is resource based, for example, then the way in which the national parliament is elected has particular importance as disputes are managed through central government allocation of resources to various regions and peoples. In this case, an electoral system which facilitated a broadly inclusive parliament might be more successful than one which exaggerated majoritarian tendencies or ethnic, regional, or other cleavages. This requirement would still hold true if the dispute was primarily cultural (i.e., revolved around the protection of minority languages and culturally specific schooling), but other institutional mechanisms, such as cultural autonomy and minority vetoes, would be at least as influential in alleviating conflict. The range of mechanisms available to conflicting parties is thus likely to include questions of parliamentary rules, power-sharing arrangements, language policies, and various forms of devolution and autonomy (see Harris and Reilly, 1998).

Lastly, disputes over territory often require innovative institutional arrangements which go well beyond the positive spins that electoral systems can create. In Spain and Canada, asymmetrical arrangements for, respectively, the Basque and Quebec regions, have been used to try and dampen calls for secession, while federalism has been promoted as an institution of conflict management in countries as diverse as Germany, Nigeria, South Africa, and Switzerland. All of these arrangements have a direct impact upon the choice of an appropriate electoral system. An example is the distinction in federal systems between lower "representative" chambers of parliament and upper "deliberative" ones, which create very different types of demands on politicians and thus require different electoral system choices to work effectively.

Spatial Distribution of Conflictual Groups

A final consideration when looking at different electoral options concerns the spatial distribution of ethnic groups, and particularly their relative size, number, and degree of geographic concentration or dispersion. For one thing, it is often the case that the geographic distribution of conflicting groups is also related to the intensity of conflict between them. The frequent intergroup contact facilitated by geographical intermixture may increase the levels of mutual hostility, but it is also likely to act as a moderating force against the most extreme manifestations of ethnic conflict.[12] Familiarity may breed contempt, but it also usually breeds a certain degree of acceptance. Intermixed groups are thus less likely to be in a state of all-out civil war than those that are territorially separated from one another.

Furthermore, intermixing gives rise to different ethnic agendas and desires. Territorial claims and self-determination rallying cries are more difficult to invoke when groups are widely dispersed and intermixed with each other. In such situations, group mobilization around issues such as civil or group rights and economic access is likely to be more prevalent.[13] Conversely, however, territorial separation is sometimes the only way to manage the most extreme types of ethnic conflict, which usually involves consideration of some type of formal territorial devolution of power or autonomy. In the extreme case of "ethnic cleansing" in Bosnia, areas which previously featured highly intermixed populations of Serbs, Croats, and Muslims are now predominantly monoethnic.

Another scenario is where the distribution of ethnic groups is such that some types of electoral system are naturally precluded. This is a function not of group size so much as the geographic concentration or dispersion of different communities. Any electoral strategy for conflict management needs to be tailored to the realities of political geography. Territorial prescriptions for federalism or other types of devolution of power will usually be a prominent concern, as will issues of group autonomy. Indigenous and/or tribal groups tend to display a particularly strong tendency toward geographical concentration. African minorities, for example, have been found to be more highly concentrated in single contiguous geographical areas than minorities in other regions, which means that many electoral constituencies and informal local power bases will be controlled by a single ethnopolitical group (Scarritt, 1993). This has considerable implications for electoral engineers: it means that any system of election that relies on single-member electoral districts will likely produce "ethnic fiefdoms" at the local level. Minority representation and/or power sharing under these conditions would probably require some form of multimember district system and proportional representation.

Contrast this with the highly intermixed patterns of ethnic settlement found as a result of colonial settlement or labor importation and the vast Chinese and Indian diasporas found in some Asia-Pacific (e.g., Singapore, Fiji, Malaysia) and Caribbean (Guyana, Trinidad and Tobago) countries, in which members of various ethnic groups tend to be much more widely intermixed and, consequently, have more day-to-day contact. Here, ethnic identities are often mitigated by other cross-cutting cleavages, and even small single-member districts are likely to be ethnically heteroge-neous, so that electoral systems which encourage parties to seek the sup-port of different ethnic groups may well work to break down interethnic antagonisms and promote the development of broad, multiethnic parties. This situation requires a very different set of electoral procedures.

A final type of social structure involves extreme ethnic *multiplicity*, typically based upon the presence of many small, competing tribal groups—an unusual composition in Western states, but common in some areas of central Africa and the South Pacific—which typically requires strong local representation to function effectively. In the extreme case of Papua New Guinea, for example, there are several thousand competing clan groups speaking over 800 distinct languages (see Reilly, 1998a). Any attempt at proportional representation in such a case would be almost impossible, as it would require a parliament of several thousand mem-bers (and, because parties are either weak or nonexistent in almost all such cases, the usual party-based systems of proportional representation would be particularly inappropriate). This dramatically curtails the range of options available to electoral engineers.

Nature of Political System

Institutional prescriptions for electoral engineering also need to be mindful of the different political dynamics that distinguish transitional democracies from established ones. Transitional democracies, particular-ly those moving from a deep-rooted conflict situation, typically have a greater need for inclusiveness and a lower threshold for the robust rheto-ric of adversarial politics than their established counterparts. Similarly, the stable political environments of most Western countries, where two or three main parties can often reasonably expect regular periods in office via alternation of power or shifting governing coalitions, are very differ-ent from the type of zero-sum politics which so often characterizes di-vided societies. This is one of the reasons that "winner-take-all" electoral systems have so often been identified as a contributor to the breakdown of democracy in the developing world: such systems tend to lock out minorities from parliamentary representation and, in situations of ethni-cally based parties, can easily lead to the total dominance of one ethnic group over all others. Democracy, under these circumstances, can quickly become a situation of permanent inclusion and exclusion, a zero-sum game, with frightening results.

Electoral laws also affect the size and development of political par-ties. At least since Duverger, the conventional wisdom among electoral scholars has been that majoritarian electoral rules encourage the forma-tion of a two-party system (and, by extension, one-party government), while proportional representation leads to a multiparty system (and coalition government). While there remains general agreement that majority systems tend to restrict the range of legislative representation and PR systems encourage it, the conventional wisdom of a causal relationship between an electoral system and a party system is increasingly looking out of date. In recent years, first-past-the-post (FPTP) has facilitated the fragmentation of the party system in established democracies such as Canada and India, while PR has seen the election of what look likely to be dominant single-party regimes in Namibia, South Africa, and elsewhere.

Just as electoral systems affect the formation of party systems, so party systems themselves have a major impact upon the shape of electoral laws. It is one of the basic precepts of political science that politicians and parties will make choices about institutions such as electoral systems that they think will benefit themselves. Different types of party systems will thus tend to produce different electoral system choices. The best-known example of this is the adoption of PR in continental Europe in the early 1900s. The expansion of the franchise and the rise of powerful new social forces, such as the labor movement, prompted the adoption of systems of PR which would both reflect and restrain these changes in society (Rokkan, 1970). More recent transitions have underlined this "rational actor" model of electoral system choice. Thus, threatened incumbent regimes in Ukraine and Chile adopted systems which they thought would maximize their electoral prospects: a two-round runoff system which overrepresents the former communists in the Ukraine (Birch, 1997), and a unusual form of PR in two-member districts which was calculated to overrepresent the second-place party in Chile (Barczak, 1997). An interesting exception which proves the validity of this rule was the ANC's support for a PR system for South Africa's first postapartheid elections. Retention of the existing FPTP system would almost undoubtedly have seen the overrepresentation of the ANC, as the most popular party, but it would also have led to problems of minority exclusion and uncertainty. The ANC made a rational decision that its long-term interest would be better served by a system which enabled it to control its nominated candidates and bring possibly destabilizing electoral elements "into the tent" rather than giving them a reason to attack the system itself.

Lastly, the efficacy of electoral system design needs to be seen in juxtaposition to the broader constitutional framework of the state. This paper concentrates on elections that constitute legislatures. The impact of the electoral system on the membership and dynamics of that body will always be significant, but the electoral system's impact upon political accommodation and democratization more generally is tied to the amount of power held by the legislature and that body's relationship to other political institutions. The importance of electoral system engineering is heightened in centralized, unicameral parliamentary systems, and is maximized when the legislature is then constitutionally obliged to produce an oversized executive cabinet of national unity drawn from all significant parties that gain parliamentary representation.

Similarly, the efficacy of electoral system design is incrementally diminished as power is eroded away from the parliament. Thus, constitutional structures which diffuse and separate powers will distract attention from elections to the legislature and will require the constitutional designer to focus on the interrelationships between executives and legislatures, between upper and lower houses of parliament, and between national and regional and local governments. This is not to diminish the importance of electoral systems for these other institutions (for example, presidencies or federal legislatures); rather, it highlights the fact that constitutional engineering becomes increasingly complex as power is devolved away from the center. Each of the following institutional components of the state may fragment the focal points of political power and thus diminish the significance of electoral system design on the overall political climate: (1) a directly elected president, (2) a bicameral parliament with a balance of power between the two houses, and (3) a degree of federalism and/or regional asymmetrical arrangements. Similarly, greater centralization of power in the hands of one figure, such as a president, raises the electoral stakes. Thus, some analysts have attributed the failure of democracy in Angola in 1992 to the combination of a strong presidential system with a run-off electoral system, which pitted the leaders of two competing armed factions in a head-to-head struggle that only one could win, thus almost guaranteeing that the "loser" would resume hostilities (Reid, 1993).

THE WORLD OF ELECTORAL SYSTEMS

There are countless electoral system variations, but essentially they can be split into 11 main systems which fall into three broad families. The most common way to look at electoral systems is to group them by how closely they translate national votes won into parliamentary seats won; that is, how *proportional* they are. To do this, one needs to look at both the vote-seat relationship and the level of wasted votes.[14] If we take the proportionality principle into account, along with some other considerations such as how many members are elected from each district and how many votes the elector has, we are left with the family structure illustrated in Figure 11.1.

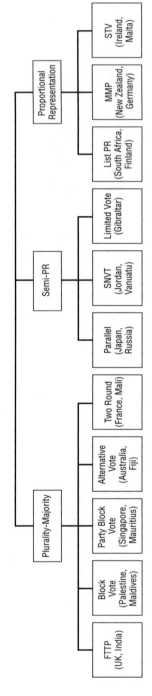

FIGURE 11.1 The world of electroal systems.

Plurality-Majority Systems

These comprise three plurality systems—first past the post, the block vote, and the party block vote—and two majority systems, the alternative vote and the two-round system.

1. *First-Past-the-Post (FPTP)* is the world's most commonly used system. Contests are held in single-member districts, and the winner is the candidate with the most votes, but not necessarily an absolute majority of the votes. FPTP is supported primarily on the grounds of simplicity, and its tendency to produce representatives beholden to defined geographic areas. Countries that use this system include the United Kingdom, the United States, India, Canada, and most countries that were once part of the British Empire.

2. The *Block Vote (BV)* is the application of FPTP in multi- rather than single-member districts. Voters have as many votes as there are seats to be filled, and the highest-polling candidates fill the positions regardless of the percentage of the vote they actually achieve. This system is used in some parts of Asia and the Middle East.

3. The *Party Block Vote (PBV)* operates in multimember districts and requires voters to choose between party lists of candidates rather than individuals. The party which wins the most votes takes all the seats in the district, and its entire list of candidates is duly elected. Variations on this system can be used to balance ethnic representation, as is the case in Singapore (discussed in more detail later).

4. Under the *Alternative Vote (AV)* system, electors rank the candidates in order of choice, marking a "1" for their favorite candidate, "2" for their second choice, "3" for their third choice, and so on. The system thus enables voters to express their preferences between candidates, rather than simply their first choice. If no candidate has over 50 percent of first preferences, lower-order preference votes are transferred until a majority winner emerges. This system is used in Australia and some other South Pacific countries.

5. The *Two-Round System (TRS)* has two rounds of voting, often a week or a fortnight apart. The first round is the same as a normal FPTP election. If a candidate receives an absolute majority of the vote, then he or she is elected outright, with no need for a second ballot. If, however, no candidate has received an absolute majority, then a second round of voting is conducted, and the winner of this round is declared elected. This system is widely used in France, former French colonies, and some parts of the former Soviet Union.

Semiproportional Systems

Semi-PR systems are those which inherently translate votes cast into seats won in a way that falls somewhere in between the proportionality of PR systems and the majoritarianism of plurality-majority systems. The three semi-PR electoral systems used for legislative elections are the single nontransferable vote (SNTV), parallel (or mixed) systems, and the limited vote (LV).

6. In *SNTV Systems*, each elector has one vote, but there are several seats in the district to be filled, and the candidates with the highest number of votes fill these positions. This means that in a four-member district, for example, one would on average need only just over 20 percent of the vote to be elected. This system is used today only in Jordan and Vanuatu, but is most often associated with Japan, which used SNTV until 1993.

7. *Parallel Systems* use both PR lists and single-member districts running side by side (hence the term parallel). Part of the parliament is elected by proportional representation, part by some type of plurality or majority method. Parallel systems have been widely adopted by new democracies in the 1990s, perhaps because, on the face of it, they appear to combine the benefits of PR lists with single-member district representation. Today, parallel systems are used in Russia, Japan, South Korea, Thailand, and the Philippines, among others.

8. The *Limited Vote (LV)*, used in Gibraltar, the Spanish upper house, and in many U.S. local government elections, usually gives voters one less vote than there are seats to be filled. In its Spanish and U.K. manifestations, the limited vote shared many of the properties of the block vote, but Lijphart, Pintor, and Stone (1986) argue that because it facilitates minority representation it should be referred to as a semiproportional system.

Proportional Representation Systems

All proportional representation (PR) systems aim to reduce the disparity between a party's share of national votes and its share of parliamentary seats. For example, if a major party wins 40 percent of the votes, it should also win around 40 percent of the seats, and a minor party with 10 percent of the votes should similarly gain 10 percent of the seats. For many new democracies, particularly those that face deep divisions, the inclusion of all significant groups in the parliament can be an important condition for democratic consolidation. Outcomes based on consensus building and power sharing usually include a PR system.

Criticisms of PR are twofold: that it gives rise to coalition governments, with disadvantages such as party system fragmentation and government instability, and that PR produces a weak linkage between a representative and her or his geographical electorate. And since voters are expected to vote for parties rather than individuals or groups of individuals, it is a difficult system to operate in societies that have embryonic or loose party structures.

9. *List PR Systems* are the most common type of PR. Most forms of list PR are held in large, multimember districts that maximize proportionality. List PR requires each party to present a list of candidates to the electorate. Electors vote for a party rather than a candidate, and parties receive seats in proportion to their overall share of the national vote. Winning candidates are taken from the lists in order of their respective positions. This system is widely used in continental Europe, Latin America, and southern Africa.

10. *Mixed Member Proportional* (MMP) *Systems*, as used in Germany, New Zealand, Bolivia, Italy, Mexico, Venezuela, and Hungary, attempt to combine the positive attributes of both majoritarian and PR electoral systems. A proportion of the parliament (roughly half in the cases of Germany, New Zealand, Bolivia, and Venezuela) is elected by plurality-majority methods, usually from single-member districts, while the remainder is constituted by PR lists. The PR seats are used to compensate for any disproportionality produced by the district seat results. Single-member districts also ensure that voters have some geographical representation.

11. The *Single Transferable Vote* (STV) uses multimember districts, where voters rank candidates in order of preference on the ballot paper in the same manner as AV. After all first-preference votes are tallied, a "quota" of votes is established, which a candidate must achieve to be elected. Any candidate who has more first preferences than the quota is immediately elected. If no one has achieved the quota, the candidate with the lowest number of first preferences is eliminated, and their second preferences are redistributed among remaining candidates. And the surplus votes of elected candidates (i.e., those votes above the quota) are redistributed according to the second preferences on the ballot papers until all seats for the constituency are filled. This system is well established in Ireland and Malta.

THE IMPORTANCE OF THE PROCESS WHICH LED TO THE CHOICE OF ELECTORAL SYSTEM

Although the choice of electoral system is one of the most important institutional decisions for any democracy, it is relatively unusual in historical terms for electoral systems to be consciously and deliberately chosen. Often, the choice of electoral system is essentially accidental: the result of an unusual combination of circumstances, of a passing trend, or of a quirk of history. The impacts of colonialism and the effects of influential neighbors are often especially strong. Yet in almost all cases, a particular electoral system choice has a profound effect on the future political life of the country concerned. Electoral systems, once chosen, tend to remain fairly constant, as political interests quickly congeal around and respond to the incentives for election presented by the system.

If it is rare that electoral systems are deliberately chosen, it is rarer still that they are carefully designed for the particular historical and social conditions present in a given country. This is particularly the case for new democracies. Any new democracy must choose (or inherit) an electoral system to elect its parliament. But such decisions are often taken within one of two circumstances. Either political actors lack basic knowledge and information, and the choices and consequences of different electoral systems are not fully recognized or, conversely, political actors do have knowledge of electoral system consequences and thus promote designs which they perceive will maximize their own advantage (see Taagepera, 1998). In both of these scenarios, the choices that are made are sometimes not the best ones for the long-term political health of the country concerned; at times, they can have disastrous consequences for a country's democratic prospects.

The way in which an electoral system is chosen can thus be as important and enlightening as the choice itself. There are four ways in which most electoral systems are adopted: via colonial inheritance, through conscious design, by external imposition, and by accident. We will now deal with each of these processes in turn.

Colonial Inheritance

Inheriting an electoral system from colonial times is perhaps the most common way through which democratizing societies come to use a particular system. For example, out of 53 former British colonies and members of the Commonwealth of Nations, a full 37 (or 70 percent) use classic first-past-the-post systems inherited from Westminster. Eleven of the 27 Francophone territories use the French two-round system, while the majority of the remaining 16 countries use list PR, a system used by the French on and off since 1945 for parliamentary elections, and widely for municipal elections. Fifteen out of the 17 Spanish-speaking countries and territories use PR (as does Spain), while Guatemala and Ecuador use list PR as part of their parallel systems. Finally, all six Lusophone countries use list PR, as in Portugal. This pattern even extends to the former Soviet Republics of the Commonwealth of Independent States (CIS): eight of these states use the two-round system in some form (see Reynolds and Reilly, 1997).

Colonial inheritance of an electoral system is perhaps the *least* likely way to ensure that the institution is appropriate to a country's needs, as the begetting colonial power was usually very different socially and culturally from the society colonized. And even where the colonizer sought to stamp much of its political ethos on the occupied land, it rarely succeeded in obliterating indigenous power relations and traditional modes of political discourse. It is therefore not surprising that the colonial inheritance of Westminster systems has been cited as an impediment to stability in a number of developing countries, for example, in the Caribbean (Lewis, 1965), Nigeria (see Diamond, 1995, and Laitin, 1986), and Malawi (see Reynolds, 1995). Similarly, Mali's use of the French two-round system has been questioned by Vengroff (1994), Indonesia's Dutch-inherited list PR system has been cited as restricting that country's political development (MacBeth, 1998), and Jordan and Palestine's use of the British-inspired block vote has also led to problems (Reynolds and Elklit, 1997).

Conscious Design

The deliberate design of electoral systems to achieve certain preconceived outcomes is not a new phenomenon, although its incidence has waxed and waned over this century. Enthusiasm for electoral engineering appears to correspond, logically enough, to successive "waves" of democratization (Huntington, 1991). Huntington's first wave, from 1828 until 1926, saw several examples of deliberate electoral engineering that are now well-established electoral institutions. The alternative vote system introduced for federal elections in Australia in 1918, for example, was intended to mitigate the problems of conservative forces "splitting" their vote in the face of a rising Labor Party. It did exactly that (Reilly, 1997b). At Irish independence in 1922, both the indigenous political elite and the departing British favored the single transferable vote due to its inherent fairness and protection of Protestant and Unionist minorities (Gallagher, 1997). The adoption of list PR systems in continental Europe occurred first in the most culturally diverse societies, such as Belgium and Switzerland, as a means of ensuring balanced interethnic representation (Rokkan, 1970). All of these cases represented examples of conscious institutional engineering utilizing what were, at the time, new electoral systems in fledgling and divided democracies.

The short second wave of democratization in the decolonization decades after the second world war also saw the electoral system used as a lever for influencing the future politics of new democracies. Most of the second wave, however, featured less in the way of deliberate design and more in the way of colonial transfer. Thus, ethnically plural states in Africa and fragile independent nations in Asia inherited British first-past-the-post or French two-round systems; and in nearly all cases these inappropriate models, transplanted directly from colonial Western powers, contributed to an early "reverse wave" of democracy.

The "third wave" of democracy has seen a new appreciation of the necessity for and utility of well-crafted electoral systems as a key constitutional choice for new democracies. In recent years, transitions to democracy in Hungary, Bolivia, South Africa, Korea, Taiwan, Fiji, and elsewhere have all been accompanied by extensive discussion and debate about the merits of particular electoral system designs. A parallel process has taken place in established democracies, with Italy, Japan, and New Zealand all changing their electoral systems in the 1990s. In most cases, these choices are based on negotiations between political elites, but in some countries (e.g., Italy and New Zealand) public plebiscites have been held to determine the voters' choice on this most fundamental of electoral questions.

External Imposition

A small number of electoral systems were more consciously designed and imposed on nation states by external powers. Two of the most vivid examples of this phenomenon occurred in West Germany after the second world war, and in Namibia in the late 1980s.

In postwar Germany, both the departing British forces and the German parties were anxious to introduce a system which would avoid the damaging party proliferation and destabilization of the Weimar years,[15] and to incorporate the Anglo tradition of constituency representation because of unease with the 1919-1933 closed-list electoral system, which denied voters a choice between candidates as well as parties (Farrell, 1997:87-88). During 1946, elections in the French and American zones of occupation were held under the previous Weimar electoral system. But in the British zone a compromise was adopted which allowed electors to vote for constituency members with a number of list PR seats reserved to compensate for any disproportionality that arose from the districts. Thus, the mixed-member proportional (MMP) system, which has since been emulated by a number of other countries, was born. This mixed system was adopted for all parliamentary elections in 1949, but it was not until 1953 that two separate votes were introduced, one for the constituency member, and another based on the Länder, which ultimately determined the party composition of the Bundestag. The imposition of a 5 percent national threshold for party list representation helped focus the party system around three major groupings after 1949 (the Social Democrats, Christian Democrats, and Free Democrats), although in all 12 parties gained representation in those first postwar national elections.

The rationale for a national list PR system in Namibia came initially from the United Nations, which urged as early as 1982 that any future nonracial electoral system ensure that political parties managing to gain substantial support in the election be rewarded with fair representation. The option of discarding the incumbent first-past-the-post electoral system (the whites-only system operating in what was the colony of South West Africa) and moving to PR was proposed by Pik Botha, then South African foreign minister. South Africa had previously, but unsuccessfully, pressed for separate voters' rolls (à la Zimbabwe 1980-1985), which would have ensured the overrepresentation of whites in the new Constituent Assembly. After expressions of unease that South Africa was promoting PR solely in order to fractionalize the assembly, the UN Institute for Namibia advised all political parties interested in a stable independence government "to reject any PR system that tends to fractionalize party representation" (see Cliffe et al., 1994:116). But this advice remained unheeded, and the option of a threshold for representation (one of the chief mechanisms for reducing the number of parties in a list PR system) was never put forward by the UN or made an issue by any of the political parties. For the first elections in 1989, the South West African People's Organization (SWAPO) expressed a preference for keeping the single-member district system, no doubt reasonably expecting (as the dominant party) to be advantaged by such winner-take-all constituencies. However, when the Constituent Assembly met for the first time in November 1989, and each parliamentary party presented its draft constitution, SWAPO gave in on the issue of PR—apparently as a concession to the minority parties for which they hoped to gain reciprocal concessions on matters of more importance.

Accidental Adoption/Evolution

Although this paper concentrates on the possibilities of deliberate "electoral engineering," it is worth remembering that most electoral systems are *not* deliberately chosen. Often, choices are made through a kaleidoscope of accidents and miscommunications leading to a multitude of unintended consequences.

Accidental choices are not necessarily poor ones; in fact, sometimes they can be surprisingly appropriate. One example of this was the highly ethnically fragmented democracy of Papua New Guinea, which inherited the alternative vote (see below) from its colonial master, Australia, for its first three elections in the 1960s and 1970s. Because this system required voters to list candidates preferentially on the ballot paper, elections encouraged a spectrum of alliances and vote trading between competing candidates and different communal groups, with candidates attempting to win not just first preferences but second and third preference votes as well. This led to cooperative campaigning tactics, moderate positions, and the early development of political parties. When this system was changed, political behavior became more exclusionary and less accommodatory, and the nascent party system quickly unraveled (Reilly, 1997a).

With the benefit of hindsight, Papua New Guinea thus appears to have been the fortuitous recipient of a possibly uniquely appropriate electoral system for its social structure. Most accidental or evolutionary choices are, however, more likely to lead to less fortuitous unintended consequences—particularly for the actors who designed them. For example, when Jordan reformed its electoral system in 1993, on the personal initiative of King Hussein, it had the effect of increasing minority representation but also facilitating the election of Islamic fundamentalists to the legislature (Reynolds and Elklit, 1997). Many fledgling democracies in the 1950s and 1960s adopted copies of the British system, despite consistent misgivings from Westminster that it was "of doubtful value as an export to tropical colonies, to primitive societies in Africa and to complex societies in India."[16] The sorry history of many such choices has underlined the importance of designing electoral and constitutional rules for the specific conditions of the country at hand, rather than blithely assuming that the same "off-the-shelf" constitutional design will work identically in different social, political, and economic circumstances.

ELECTORAL SYSTEMS AND CONFLICT MANAGEMENT

The comparative experience suggests that four specific systems are particularly suitable for divided societies. These are usually recommended as part of overall constitutional engineering packages, in which the electoral system is one element. Some constitutional engineering packages emphasize inclusiveness and proportionality; others emphasize moderation and accommodation. The four major choices in this regard are (1) *consociationalism* (based, in part, on list proportional representation); (2) *centripetalism* (based, in part, on the vote-pooling potential of the alternative vote); (3) *integrative consensualism* (based, in part, on the single transferable vote), and (4) a construct not previously mentioned, which we call *explicitism*, which explicitly recognizes communal groups and gives them institutional representation, which in theory can be based on almost any electoral system, but in practice is usually based on the block vote (e.g., in Mauritius, Lebanon, and Singapore).

Consociationalism

One of the most discussed prescriptions for plural (segmented) societies remains that of *consociationalism*, a term first used by Althusius and rescued from obscurity by Lijphart in the late 1960s. Consociationalism entails a power-sharing agreement within government, brokered between clearly defined segments of society which may be joined by citizenship but divided by ethnicity, religion, and language. Examples of consociational societies include Belgium, the Netherlands, Austria, and Switzerland. Cyprus and Lebanon are cited as countries which had, but no longer have, a consociational ethos (Lijphart, 1977). The mechanics of consociationalism can be distilled into four basic elements which must be present to make the constitution worthy of the consociational name. They are: (1) executive power sharing among the representatives of all significant groups (*a grand coalition in the cabinet*); (2) a high degree of internal autonomy for groups that wish to have it (*constitutionally entrenched segmental autonomy*); (3) proportional representation (through list PR) and proportional allocation of civil service positions and public funds (*proportionality*); and (4) a minority veto on the most vital issues (*a mutual veto for parties in the executive*) (Lijphart, 1977:25).

These arrangements encourage government to become an inclu-sive multiethnic coalition, in contrast to the adversarial nature of a Westminster winner-take-all democracy. Consociationalism rests on the premise that in bitterly divided societies the stakes are too high for politics to be conducted as a zero-sum game. Also, the risks of governmental collapse and state instability are too great for parties to view the executive branch of government as a prize to be won or lost. The fact that grand coalitions exist in Westminster democracies at times of particular crisis further supports the consociational claim.[17]

Arguments in Favor

Consociationalism is particularly reliant on a PR electoral system to provide a broadly representative legislature upon which the other tenets of minority security can be based. Lijphart clearly expresses a preference for using party list forms of PR rather than STV, or by implication open-list PR systems and mixed systems which give the voter multiple votes. In a discussion of the proposals for South Africa he noted that STV might indeed be superior for reasonably homogeneous societies, but "for plural societies list PR is clearly the better method" because it: (1) allows for higher district magnitude—thus increasing proportionality, (2) is less vulnerable to gerrymandering, and (3) is simpler (than STV) for the voters and vote counters and thus will be less open to suspicion.[18]

In many respects, the strongest arguments for PR derive from the way in which the system avoids the anomalous results of plurality-majority systems and facilitates a more representative legislature. For many new democracies, particularly those which face deep societal divisions, the inclusion of all significant groups in the parliament can be a near-essential condition for democratic consolidation. Failing to ensure that both minorities and majorities have a stake in these nascent political systems can have catastrophic consequences. Recent transitional elections in Chile (1989), Namibia (1989), Nicaragua (1990), Cambodia (1993), South Africa (1994), Mozambique (1994), and Bosnia (1996) all used a form of regional or national list PR for their founding elections, and some scholars have identified the choice of a proportional rather than a majoritarian system as being a key component of their successful transitions to democracy (Lijphart, 1977; Reynolds, 1995). By bringing minorities into the process and fairly representing all significant political parties in the new legislature, regardless of the extent or distribution of their support base, PR has been seen as being an integral element of creating an inclusive and legitimate postauthoritarian regime.

More specifically, PR systems in general are praised because of the way in which they: (1) faithfully translate votes cast into seats won, and thus avoid some of the more destabilizing and "unfair" results thrown up by plurality-majority electoral systems; (2) give rise to very few wasted votes; (3) facilitate minority parties' access to representation; (4) encourage parties to present inclusive and socially diverse lists of candidates; (5) make it more likely that the representatives of minority cultures/ groups are elected;[19] (6) make it more likely that women are elected;[20] (7) restrict the growth of "regional fiefdoms";[21] and (8) make power sharing between parties and interest groups more visible.

Arguments Against

While large-scale PR appears to be an effective instrument for smoothing the path of democratic transition, it may be less effective at promoting democratic *consolidation*. Developing countries in particular which have made the transition to democracy under list PR rules have increasingly found that the large, multimember districts required to achieve proportional results also create considerable difficulties in terms of political accountability and responsiveness between elected politicians and voters. Democratic consolidation requires the establishment of a meaningful relationship between the citizen and the state, and many new democracies—particularly those in agrarian societies (Barkan, 1995)—have much higher demands for constituency service at the local level than they do for representation of all shades of ideological opinion in the legislature. It is therefore increasingly being argued in South Africa, Indonesia, Cambodia, and elsewhere that the choice of a permanent electoral system should encourage a high degree of *geographic accountability*, by having members of parliament who represent small, territorially defined districts and servicing the needs of their constituency, in order to establish a meaningful relationship between the rulers and the ruled. While this does not preclude all PR systems—there are a number of ways of combining single-member districts with proportional outcomes—it does rule out the national list PR systems often favored by consociationalists.

In terms of electoral system choice, the major critique of list PR systems is thus that they fail to provide any link between a member and his or her electorate, hence lessening the "geographic accountability" between the two. But there are other critiques of list PR in divided societies that center on the ease with which ethnic leaders can be elected exclusively by members of their own group, thus replicating (rather than breaking down) social divisions in the legislature. The experience of list PR in post-Dayton Bosnia is a good example of how proportionality alone will not encourage accommodation. In Bosnia, groups are represented in parliament in proportion to their numbers in the community as a whole, but because parties can rely exclusively on the votes of members of their own community for their electoral success, there is little incentive for them to behave accommodatively on ethnic issues. In fact, the incentives work in the other direction. As it is easy to mobilize support by playing the "ethnic card," major parties in Bosnia have every incentive to emphasize ethnic issues and sectarian appeals. Bosnia's 1996 elections were effectively an ethnic census, with electors voting along ethnic lines and each of the major nationalist parties gaining support almost exclusively from their own ethnic group (see Reilly, 1998b).

More generally, consociationalism rests on several key assumptions that may not always be viable in divided societies. The most important of these is the assumption that ethnic leaders will be more moderate on key sectarian issues than their supporters. While this may hold true in some cases, it appears to be untrue as a generalized proposition about the relationship between ethnic elites and policy positions on ethnic issues. In fact, some studies have argued the opposite: leaderships of ethnic parties are often the ones who have the most to gain by maintaining ethnocentric politics.[22] Furthermore, the ability of leaders to compromise on issues may be extremely limited: "It has been shown repeatedly that leadership leeway is very narrow on issues of ethnic power in severely divided societies. Compromisers can readily be replaced by extremists on their flank" (Horowitz, 1997:439). The lack of a mechanism to encourage accommodation means that consociational prescriptions rely, sometimes unwisely, on enlightened political leadership and preparedness to compromise to achieve accommodatory outcomes.

Conclusion

The underlying ethos of consociationalism stresses that while there is joint decision making over common interests, regarding a cultural minority's area of exclusive domain the minority should be autonomous. This requires a clear definition of groups and group rights, which has led to the criticism that consociationalism may well perpetuate divisions rather than alleviate them. Indeed, Lijphart argues that "it is in the nature of consociational democracy, at least initially, to make plural societies more thoroughly plural. Its approach is not to abolish or weaken segmental cleavages but to recognize them explicitly and to turn the segments into constructive elements of a stable democracy" (1977:42).

Consociationalism is probably best seen as a stop-gap measure, the lesser of two evils which keeps the lid on the pressure cooker of a divided society that is about to blow and perhaps manages to turn down the heat just a little. Perhaps the most powerful criticism is that, by entrenching segments and defining all politics in those divisive terms, one actually postpones or even obstructs the breakdown of segmental barriers.[23] Indeed, some of the favorable conditions that Lijphart quotes for consociationalism seem to guard against it withering away. The way in which power sharing requires geographically concentrated groups who have autonomy, not only in regional affairs, may ultimately increase the segmental divides. The tension remains: How does one recognize segmental groups, while at the same time attempt to diminish their importance? An even greater danger exists of imposing *ethnically aware* consociational structures on societies where political segments are not clearly or primarily defined along the lines of ethnicity. Nagata argues that in some cases, "the depth of segmental cleavages frequently follows rather than precedes consociational arrangements, thus creating instead of solving problems of pluralism" (1979:506).

The great value of consociationalism is that it offers powerful conflict-resolving solutions to those divided societies which show no hope of generating such interethnic political accommodation. It is the solution when all else fails. But if consociational structures are entrenched in plural societies which do show potential for the withering away of ethnic voting, then the very institutions designed to alleviate tensions may merely entrench the perception that all politics must be ethnic politics. Consociationalism provides few incentives for political entrepreneurs to appeal for support beyond their own ethnic bases.

Centripetalism

An alternative electoral path to accommodation in deeply divided societies is what we (following Sisk, 1995) call "centripetalism": institutions and policies which encourage cooperation and centrist policies, and which counter extremism and conflict behavior. Centripetalism focuses on the electoral system as the chief agent of interethnic accommodation because of the incentives for election that such systems provide. Centripetalists argue that the use of particular electoral rules which encourage politicians to campaign for the votes of members of rival groups, via "vote pooling" and "preference swapping" can induce interethnic bargaining and promote accommodative behavior. At the core of this approach, as developed by Donald Horowitz (1985, 1990, 1991), is the need "to make politicians reciprocally dependent on the votes of members of groups other than their own."[24]

The most reliable way of achieving this aim, according to proponents of the centripetal approach, is to offer sufficient electoral incentives for campaigning politicians to court voter support from other groups. In deeply divided societies, this can be very difficult to achieve. Under conditions of purely ascriptive ethnic identity and hostility, for example, almost nothing will convince a member of one ethnic group to cast his or her vote for a member of a rival group. However, some electoral systems such as the alternative vote (AV) permit (or even require) voters to declare not only their first choice of candidate on a ballot, but also their second, third, and subsequent choices amongst all candidates standing. This feature presents candidates who wish to maximize their electoral prospects with a strong incentive to try and attract the second preferences of voters from other groups (the assumption being that the first choice of voters will usually be a candidate from their own group). An alternative strategy is for major parties contesting FPTP elections in heterogeneous districts to nominate members of different ethnic groups as their chosen candidates in different districts. In Malaysia, for example, Chinese voters will help elect Muslim candidates in some seats, while Muslims will help elect Chinese in others.

Arguments in Favor

The argument for the integrative effects of AV is premised on the assumption that politicians are rational actors who will do what needs to be done to gain election. Under AV, "what needs to be done" varies considerably depending on the makeup of the electorate. The optimal scenario is a case where no candidate can be assured of an outright majority of support, so that the role of second and later preferences becomes crucial to attracting an overall majority. Those candidates who successfully "pool" both their own first preferences and the second preferences of others will be more successful than those who fail to attract any second-order support. To attract such second-order support, candidates need to attract the support of groups other than their own, and this is usually achieved by their moving to the center on policy issues to attract floating voters, or by successfully accommodating "fringe" issues into their broader policy. There is a long history of both these types of behavior in Australian elections, the only established democracy to use AV. There is also widespread agreement that AV has facilitated coalition arrangements in Australia, such as that between the Liberal and National parties, and that it works to the advantage of center candidates and parties, encouraging moderate policy positions and a search for the "middle ground" (see Reilly, 1997b).

In cases of deeply divided societies, however, policy-based cleavages are usually considerably less salient than ethnic or linguistic identities. But the incentives for election under AV rules can still operate in the same manner: candidates will do what they need to do to gain election. Where a candidate needs the support of other ethnic groups to gain election, there is a powerful incentive for him or her to reach out to these groups in search of their second preferences. The more groups present in a given constituency, the more likely it is that meaningful vote pooling will take place. To build support from other groups, candidates must behave moderately and accommodatively toward them. In ethnically divided societies, this means that electoral incentives can promote policy concessions: even small minorities have a value in terms of where their preferences are directed, as small numbers of votes could always be the difference between victory and defeat for major candidates.

The only time that these theories have been properly tested has been in preindependence Papua New Guinea (PNG), which held elections in 1964, 1968, and 1972 under AV rules. Analysis of the relationship in PNG between political behavior and the electoral system provides significant evidence that accommodative vote-pooling behavior *was* encouraged by the incentives presented by AV, and further significant evidence that behavior became markedly less accommodative when AV was replaced by FPTP, under which the incentives for electoral victory are markedly different. Under AV, vote pooling took place in three primary ways, all of which were predicated on the assumption that most voters would invariably give their first preference to their own clan or "home" candidate. The most common and successful method of vote pooling was for a candidate who had a limited "home" support base to campaign widely for second-level support among rival groups. This required a range of techniques, such as translating campaign speeches and traveling widely throughout an electorate, with the essential request being not for a first-preference vote but for a second preference. This enabled electors to cast their primary vote for their ascriptive candidate—an essential element in cases of ascriptive ethnic identity—but also to indicate their second choice if their ascriptive candidate was not elected. For this strategy to succeed, candidates needed to be able to sell themselves as the "second-best" choice, which meant, in general, someone who would look after all groups, not just his own. A second strategy for victory under AV was for candidates with significant existing support bases to reach out to selected allies for secondary support. Traditional tribal contacts and allegiances, for example, could be utilized to create majority victors. This similarly necessitated a commitment to behave positively toward that group if elected. In one seat at the 1972 elections, for example, tribal leaders of previously hostile groups made deals with each other for preference support. The winning candidate forged particularly close connections with a traditional ally tribe via "intensive ties of ceremonial exchange," urged his supporters to cast their preferences for a member of a hostile rival tribe as well as for himself, and consequently received a generous proportion of that opponent's second preferences to win the seat. A third strategy, increasingly common by the time of the third AV election in 1972, was for groups and candidates to form mutual alliances, sometimes campaigning together and urging voters to cast reciprocal preferences for one or the other. This similarly necessitated a strong cooperative approach to electoral competition (Reilly, 1998a).

The central appeal of the integrated approach is thus that it produces *incentives* for accommodative behavior—via the search for secondary support—rather than relying on *constraints* (such as minority vetoes) against hostility. A second virtue is that it relies on popular rather than elite activity: campaigning politicians and their supporters are directly rewarded by moderation and can directly expect to reap what they sow. Candidates who are elected will be dependent on the votes of groups other than their own for their parliamentary positions, and can be expected to serve the needs of these groups as well as their own ethnic group if they are to establish their positions and gain reelection. A system similar to AV has been used to elect the Sri Lankan president since 1978, and some observers have argued that this has led to increasing recognition of minority Tamil and Muslim interests by the major Sinhalese parties (de Silva, 1994; Reilly, 1997b). AV was also recommended for elections to postapartheid South Africa (Horowitz, 1991) and was recently chosen as the basis of a new, nonracial constitution in Fiji as the best way of encouraging the development of peaceful multiethnic politics in that deeply divided society (Constitution Review Commission, 1996). Other arguments for AV include its use of small single-member electorates, thus guaranteeing geographic accountability, and the fact that it guarantees that victorious candidates will be supported by an absolute majority of the electorate.

Arguments Against

Critics of the centripetal approach have focused on four themes. The first is that there are no examples of successful centripetalism in practice (Sisk, 1996; Lijphart, 1995a) and that, "although vote pooling is theoretically compelling, there is simply insufficient empirical evidence at the level of national politics to support claims that subsequent preference voting can lead to accommodative outcomes."[25] In fact, there is a considerable range of evidence from PNG, Australia, Sri Lanka, and elsewhere which demonstrates centripetalism in action, although much of this material remains relatively obscure (see Reilly, 1998a). Other objections to AV are more substantial. The first is that, because AV is a majoritarian system, it results in highly disproportional electoral results and minority exclusion, especially when compared to PR systems (Lijphart, 1991; Reynolds, 1995). There is some truth in this, although many of these arguments focus less on standard single-member AV than on the multimember AV system proposed by Horowitz (1991), which did indeed produce dangerously disproportional results when used in the Australian senate between the wars (Reilly and Maley, 1999; Lijphart, 1997). Research indicates that single-member AV is actually among the *least* disproportional of majoritarian systems, although it is clearly less proportional than PR systems (Reilly, 1997a; but see Lijphart, 1997, for a reply). A second criticism argues that AV actually acts in practice much like other majoritarian electoral systems such as TRS and FPTP, and consequently that there is no more incentive to compromise under AV than under these systems (Lijphart, 1991). Again, the evidence from PNG in particular tends to undermine this argument, as the political behavior at both the elite and the mass levels became markedly less accommodatory when the electoral system changed from AV to FPTP (Reilly, 1997a).

The third criticism is that AV would fail to encourage integrative behavior in some regions because of the demographic distribution of ethnic groups (Reynolds, 1995). This last criticism is the most significant. In many ethnically divided countries, members of the same ethnic group tend to cluster together, which means that the relatively small, single-member districts which are a feature of AV would, in these cases, result in constituencies which are ethnically homogeneous rather than heterogeneous. Where one candidate is confident of achieving an absolute majority of first preferences due to the domination of his or her own ethnic group in an area, they need only focus on maximizing their own vote share from their own supporters in order to win the seat. This means that the vote pooling between different ethnic groups which is a precondition for the accommodative influences of AV would not, in fact, occur. Most regions of Latin America and southern Africa, for example, feature geographically concentrated ethnic groups.[26] For this reason, it is likely that AV will work best either in cases of extreme ethnic fragmentation (such as that found in some areas of the South Pacific and Central Africa) or, alternatively, the more common scenario of a few large ethnic groups which are widely dispersed and intermixed (e.g., Malaysia, Lebanon, Singapore, Fiji, Mauritius, Trinidad and Tobago). Both of these social structures, which appear to be particularly common in the Asia-Pacific region, would result in ethnically heterogeneous electoral districts and thus, under AV rules, strong incentives toward accommodative preference-swapping deals (see Reilly, 1998a).

Conclusion

The arguments for and against centripetalism are a good example of the contextual nature of electoral system design, and how proponents of different approaches run the risk of talking past each other. There is strong evidence that AV has worked or will work well in some types of social setting (PNG, Fiji, and other intermixed areas) but poorly in some others (e.g., ethnically concentrated states in southern Africa). AV also requires a reasonable degree of literacy to be utilized effectively, and because it operates in single-member districts it can often produce results that are disproportional when compared to PR systems. These are drawbacks, but they are mitigated by the strength of incentives toward centripetal politics that AV appears to encourage. The experiences of AV in PNG, Sri Lanka, and in Australia all suggest that it does encourage moderate, centrist politics and enables diverse interests to be aggregated. In the right type of social setting, it can provide significant incentives for accommodatory and cooperative politics, and deserves more consideration as an attractive model of electoral system design, particularly for ethnically intermixed states, than it has received to date.

Integrative Consensualism

In many ways the theory of *integrative consensualism* (as advocated by Reynolds, 1996) attempts to build on the philosophies underpinning both consociationalism and centripetalism, by retaining the key consociational planks of mandatory executive power sharing and a PR electoral system, but utilizing the centripetal electoral system incentives of STV rather than rigid list PR. Indeed, one of the two most important institutional planks of integrative consensualism is the STV electoral system (the other being the rejection of institutions which entrench ethnic or cultural political blocks within the party system).

There are important differences, both theoretically and practically,

between consociationalism and an integrative consensualism. Both types
contain power-sharing provisions but are based upon different structures
and objectives and, most importantly, rest on different premises. As noted
earlier, consociationalism rests on the premise that society is deeply divided along ethnic lines, what Robert Price calls "politicized ethnicity,"
segmented into a number of nonconversing and antagonistic cultural
groups (Price, 1995). Voting affiliation is primarily driven by such ascriptive identities. While there are strong arguments in favor of consociationalism for ethnically polarized societies, other types of societies may be
able to manage sociopolitical conflicts with consensus-oriented systems
in which some of the institutional mechanisms of consociation are practiced, but not all of them are institutionalized. Such consensus systems
rest on the premise that society is conflictual and may indeed be divided,
but those divisions and voting behavior are not primarily motivated by
ascriptive identities. Other cleavages, along the lines of class, wealth, regionalism, and clan, may be more salient.

Arguments in Favor

Institutionally, *integrative consensus* democracy prescribes STV in order to encourage cross-cutting ethnic cleavages, while at the same time
ensuring the fair representation and inclusion of minorities in decision
making. The argument is that if the institutional incentives embedded
within integrative consensual democracy work as hypothesized, they will
allow the space for and, indeed, provide incentives for, the growth of
multiethnic political parties, but they will not guarantee that such parties
flourish. It follows, therefore, that integrative consensus democracy is
only an option in plural societies which show signs that ethnicity need not
endure as the sole driving force of politics. If voters are never likely to
look outside of their ascriptive identity to vote for nonethnic parties, then
elections will never be anything more than *ethnic* or *racial censuses*, and
integrative consensualism is redundant. In a society where politics is determined entirely by primordial affiliations, consociationalism may be the
only viable option.

Interestingly, the rationale of integrative consensus shares much with
the logic of centripetalism, but its institutional prescriptions are at variance with those prescribed by Horowitz and Reilly and are likely to produce different results. Chiefly, integrative consensualism rests on the principles of proportionality and coalition government, while it is more likely
that elections under centripetalism would produce nonproportional parliaments and single-party executives. Reynolds argues that, in a plural
society which is ripe for consensus government, members of an ethnic
group may indeed be more likely to vote for a certain political party, but

it is not clear that they do so out of a knee-jerk desire to vote as a communal block for candidates of a similar skin color. Where there is doubt about what drives voting behavior, and the intuition that the electorate is more sophisticated than an ethnic census explanation would give them credit for, then there is space for constitutional mechanisms which encourage crosscutting cleavages. The goal of integrative consensus strategies is to proliferate such incentives, while at the same time retaining the benefits of inclusionary government (i.e., proportional representation through STV, grand coalition cabinets, and a variety of access points to political power).

While the consociational and integrative consensus types share a number of traits (indeed they are both forms of power sharing or consensual democracy), such as proportionality, federalism, bicameralism, and minority vetoes, they differ in the institutional mechanisms they utilize to facilitate such traits. One of the key differences is the choice of electoral system. While consociationalism is nearly always based on a list PR system, integrative consensualism requires the use of the single transferable vote to encourage party appeals beyond defined ethnic boundaries. Under this system, segments of opinion would be represented proportionately in the legislature, but there would be a great incentive for political elites to appeal to the members of other segments, given that second preferences on the ballot paper are of prime importance. Lakeman argues that under STV "political considerations can gradually assume more importance and racial ones less, without the elector ever being faced with a conflict of loyalties" (1974:136).

Arguments Against

Advocates of majoritarianism see the dangers of immobilism and paralysis just as inherent in consensual government as in consociationalism (due to the mandated oversized coalition governments). Proponents of both consociationalism and centripetalism have also criticized consensualism's electoral recommendations. Lijphart argues that STV is better suited to homogenous societies than plural ones (Lijphart, 1990:11), while Horowitz objects to STV on the grounds that the threshold for winning a seat in a multimember STV district is too low to ensure that incentives for vote pooling influence party campaign strategies (1991:191).

It is true that, with one important exception, the use of STV in divided societies to date has been limited, inconclusive, and generally not supportive of integral consensual theories. Until the 1998 "Good Friday" peace agreement in Northern Ireland, only two ethnically divided states had utilized STV in "one-off" national elections: Northern Ireland in 1973 (and again in 1982) and Estonia in 1990. In both cases, little vote pooling took place. In elections to the abortive Northern Ireland assembly, parties neither campaigned for nor received votes across the Protestant-Catholic divide, in part "because the chances of winning an extra seat by adding a few votes from the other community were much less than the chances of losing votes by appearing 'soft' on key sectarian issues."[27] In Estonia, which is similarly divided between the majority indigenous Estonian (60 percent) community and a minority (35 percent) immigrant Russian one, STV was used for the first national independence elections in 1990 before being replaced with list PR. Again, ethnicity appeared to be the dominant factor in voter choice at these elections, with little evidence of cross-ethnic voting.[28]

Conclusion

Just as there are few cases of the use of STV in divided societies, to date there have been no full-blown examples of the integrative typology in the real world. Perhaps the bundle of constitutional arrangements which come closest to the typology are the newly constructed arrangements for self-government and multistate consultation in Northern Ireland that were adopted and passed by referendum (in both the north and south) in May 1998. The Northern Irish Assembly elected in July 1998 consists of 108 parliamentarians elected by STV in 17 multimember districts. The size of the constituencies, already small in population, means that a candidate will only need 2,000-3,000 votes to be elected. Other integrative consensus arrangements include obligatory power sharing in the executive (the first prime minister will come from the largest community, while the deputy will come from the minority community), proportional power sharing at all levels of government and in the special commissions set up to deal with particularly culturally contentious issues, and a minority veto over legislation deemed to be relevant to communal interests. However, these institutional mechanisms owe just as much to the theory of consociationalism and the designation of ethnic groups. Voters will self-identify themselves as Catholic/Nationalist or Protestant/Unionist, and offices will be shared upon that basis rather than simple party strength. Therefore, while the Northern Irish peace agreement instituted (or reinstituted) an electoral system aimed to encourage the development of crosscutting ethnic voting behavior (as integrative consensus democracy would applaud), it mitigated these benefits by entrenching the single aspect of consociationalism which most solidifies ethnic identification (i.e., rewards, the trappings and offices of power, are allocated on the basis of groups rather than party strength per se).

Explicit Recognition of Communal Groups

A final approach to elections and conflict is to recognize explicitly the overwhelming importance of group identity in the political process, and to mandate this in the electoral law so that ethnic representation and the ratio of different ethnic groups in the legislature is fixed. There have been four distinct approaches which reflect this thinking: the use of communal electoral rolls; the presence of reserved seats for ethnic, linguistic, or other minorities; the use of ethnically mixed or mandated candidate lists; and the use of "best loser" seats to balance ethnic representation in the legislature. Each of these will be described below.

Communal Rolls

The most straightforward way of explicitly recognizing the importance of ethnicity is to utilize a system of communal representation. Seats are not only divided on a communal basis, but the entire system of parliamentary representation is similarly based on communal considerations. This usually means that each defined "community" has its own electoral roll and elects only members of its "own group" to Parliament.

Communal roll arrangements have often been used to cement a privileged position for certain minorities. Colonial India, for example, had separate electorates for Christians, Anglo-Saxons, Sikhs, and non-Brahmans. Burma's 1937 constitution reserved 40 of the House of Representative's 132 seats for Karens, Indians, Chinese, Anglo-Indians, and Europeans. Rhodesia/Zimbabwe maintained separate electoral rolls for "white" electors until independence, and (as part of the constitutional settlement) for seven years after. Cyprus continues to use communal roll arrangements to distinguish between Greek and Turkish communities, but the 24 seats set aside for Turkish Cypriots, who have boycotted Parliament since 1963, remain unfilled. But in most countries, most communal systems were abandoned after it became increasingly clear that communal electorates, while guaranteeing group representation, often had the perverse effect of undermining the path of accommodation between different groups as there were no incentives for political intermixing between communities. The issue of how to define a member of a particular group, and how to distribute electorates fairly between them, was also strewn with pitfalls.

Today, the only democracies which continue to use communal representation are Fiji and (for Maori only) New Zealand. Fiji has maintained a system of communal rolls for its indigenous, Indian, and "general" (i.e., European and Chinese) voters since independence in 1970. Until 1987, electors could vote not only for their own communal candidates but for some "national" candidates as well, a system known as "cross-voting." The military coup in 1987 led to the abolition of this provision and the entrenchment of an indigenous Fijian majority in the legislature. A constitutional review completed in 1996 recommended a "gradual but decisive" move away from communal politics toward genuine multiethnic competition (Constitution Review Commission, 1996). But the 1997 constitution, as enacted, did not make a decisive break with communalism, and two-thirds of all seats continue to be elected on a communal basis. Among established democracies, the one predominant example of a communal roll system left is the optional separate roll for Maori voters in New Zealand. Maori electors can choose to be on either the national electoral roll or a specific Maori roll, which elects five Maori MPs to Parliament. The results of New Zealand's first PR elections in 1996 could be said to have weakened the rationale for the communal system, however. Twice as many Maori MPs were elected from the general rolls as from the specific Maori roll.

Reserved Seats

Reserved seats are one way of ensuring the representation of specific minority groups in parliament. Countries as diverse as Jordan (Christians and Circassians), India (scheduled tribes and castes), Pakistan (non-Muslim minorities), Colombia ("black communities"), Croatia (Hungarian, Italian, Czech, Slovak, Ruthenian, Ukrainian, German, and Austrian minorities), Slovenia (Hungarians and Italians), Taiwan (aboriginal community), Western Samoa (nonindigenous minorities), Niger (Tuareg), and the Palestinian Authority (Christians and Samaritans) reserve parliamentary seats for identifiable ethnic or religious minorities. Representatives from these reserved seats are usually elected in much the same manner as other members of parliament, but are often elected by members of the particular minority community designated in the electoral law.

Instead of formally reserved seats, regions can be overrepresented to facilitate the increased representation of minority groups. In essence this is the case in the United Kingdom, where Scotland and Wales have more MPs in the British House of Commons than they would be entitled to if population size were the only criterion. The same is true in the mountainous regions of Nepal. Electoral boundaries can also be manipulated to serve this purpose. The Voting Rights Act in the United States has in the past allowed the government to draw weird and wonderful districts with the sole purpose of creating majority black, Latino, or Asian American districts. This might be called "affirmative gerrymandering." While it is often deemed to be a normative good to represent small communities of interest, the manipulation of any electoral system to protect minority representation is rarely uncontroversial. It has often been argued that it is a better strategy to design structures which give rise to a representative parliament naturally rather than mandate the representation of members who may be viewed as "token" parliamentarians who have representation but often do not have genuine influence. Quota seats may also breed resentment on the behalf of majority populations and increase mistrust between various minority groups.

Ethnically Mixed Lists

Some countries use variations on a block vote to ensure balanced ethnic representation, as it enables parties to present ethnically diverse lists of candidates for election. In Lebanon, for example, election is dependent, at a practical level, on being part of a mixed list. In most cases, candidates must compete for election against other members of their own group. Electors choosing between party lists must thus make their choice on the basis of criteria other than ethnicity. In Singapore, most MPs are elected from multimember districts known as group representative constituencies, which each return between three and six members from a single list of party or individual candidates. Of the candidates on each party or group list, at least one must be a member of the Malay, Indian, or some other minority community. Voters choose between these various lists of candidates with a single vote.

The advantages of such a system is that it is simple to use, encourages strong parties, and allows for parties to put up mixed slates of candidates in order to facilitate minority representation. However, a critical flaw is the production of "supermajoritarian" results, where one party can win almost all of the seats with a simple majority of the votes. In the Singaporean elections of 1991, for example, a 61 percent vote for the ruling People's Action Party gave it 95 percent of all seats in parliament, while in 1982 and 1995 the Mauritian elections saw a parliament with no opposition at all. To counter this possibility, the Lebanese constitution predetermines the ethnic composition of the entire parliament, and of key positions such as the president and the prime minister as well.

Best Loser

A final mechanism sometimes used in conjunction with the block vote is to assign seats to the "best loser" from a specified community. In Mauritius, for example, four best loser seats are allocated to the highest polling candidates of underrepresented ethnic groups in order to balance ethnic representation. Recently, however, there has been a strong movement in favor of the abolition of such seats, which are seen as representing the last vestiges of communalism in Mauritian politics (Mathur, 1997). Singapore also uses best loser seats for opposition candidates in some circumstances, as does Ecuador where, if the party which takes second-place wins half the votes of the first party, it is rewarded with a seat. However, neither of these cases utilizes the specific ethnic determination which characterizes the use of this mechanism in Mauritius.

Conclusion

The main argument in favor of all four explicitist approaches above is that they try to defuse ethnicity as a political issue, and to encourage the growth of other, competing cleavages, by making the recognition of ethnicity explicit in the electoral law. Yet because of this, they each suffer from the same fundamental drawback: each requires some official recognition and determination of group identity. Someone, somewhere, has to be able to determine who is and is not an Indian, a black, a scheduled caste member, and so on. A second major drawback is that such approaches assume that ethnic identities are immutable and enduring, and thus can contribute to the solidification of ethnic politics rather than its break-down. Moreover, all the systems outlined above suffer from a distinct lack of flexibility: changes in the proportions of ethnic groups present in the community are not reflected in the legislature, which is effectively frozen in time from whenever the original determinations of group pro-portions were made. In Lebanon until 1990, for example, the ratio of parliamentary seats was fixed at six Christian for every five Muslim, which became a major issue of contention as the Muslim population grew more rapidly than the Christian one, and was consequently amended to a one-to-one ratio under the Taif Accords. While there may be some ex-tremely deeply divided societies which demand such approaches (Leba-non appears to be one, and Bosnia may turn out to be another), in general most multiethnic societies need political institutions which help to break down the salience of ethnicity rather than predetermining it as the basis of electoral competition.

CONCLUSIONS

Divided societies, like Tolstoy's unhappy families, tend to be divided in different ways. This may seem like a simple or even simplistic state-ment, but it is surprising how often "one size fits all" conflict-managing packages are recommended for divided societies, usually by foreign "ex-perts," without sufficient understanding of the structure of the conflict itself. As our earlier discussion of the typologies of conflict attempts to make clear, there are many variables in terms of the nature of a political conflict which will directly influence the optimum electoral system prescriptions. Table 11.1 presents a summary of the four electoral system options for conflict mediation outlined in the previous section, and the major examples of their application in divided societies around the world.

Having outlined and summarized these four major options, the following tables represent a first attempt to categorize some of these issues which need to be considered when attempting to implement one or another approach. While it is clear that constitutional choices such as electoral systems can have a substantive impact on the moderation or exacerbation of a conflict (indeed, for the "electoral engineering" approach typified by this paper, this is a fundamental precept), for policy makers the choice of electoral system is almost always dependent upon the nature of the conflict and of the society in question. In other words, the choice of appropriate electoral system is usually seen first and foremost as a response to a preexisting set of circumstances, which may then go on to affect the nature of those circumstances. For this reason, the following matrixes treat the choice of electoral system as the *dependent* variable, and the nature of the conflict as the *independent* variable, for the purposes of our analysis.

In the following tables, we look at the relationship between social structure, the nature of the conflict, and electoral system choice in order to determine whether there are any observed regularities that appear to influence or determine these choices. The systems we concentrate upon, as integral parts of the four "engineering packages" we identified in the section on Electoral Systems and Conflict Management, are: list proportional representation (e.g., Belgium, Switzerland, and postapartheid South Africa), the alternative vote (e.g., Papua New Guinea, 1964-1975, and Fiji since 1997), the single transferable vote (e.g., Estonia in 1990, and Northern Ireland), and explicitist strategies such as separate communal voting rolls and mixed lists (e.g., Singapore, Lebanon, and Mauritius).

Nature of Group Identity

As noted earlier, it is appropriate to see the intensity of an individual's identification with any given group, and the nature of overall social group identity, as running along a continuum. Some conflictual identities are clearly more rigid than others, and a broad rule for electoral system design might be that the more rigid communal identification is, the higher the premium that should be placed on institutions which will represent "groups" in close approximation to their power and size. As identities become increasingly fluid and malleable, the more space there may be for

TABLE 11.1 The Characteristics of System Choices Types

Type	List PR (Consociationalism)	AV (Centripetalism)	STV (Consensualism)	Communal Rolls, Party Block Vote (Explicitism)
Ethos	Proportional representation elections which lead to an inclusive legislature which includes all significant groups. Under a full consociational package, each group is represented in the cabinet in proportion to its electoral support, and minority interests are protected through segmental autonomy and mutual vetoes.	Majority system with in-built incentives for interethnic party appeals. To maximize electoral prospects, parties need to cultivate the second-preference votes from groups other than their own. There is a *centripetal* spin to the system where elites are encouraged to gravitate to the moderate multiethnic center. In ethnically mixed districts, majority threshold leads to strong incentives to gain support from other groups.	The electoral system delivers proportional results but also encourages politicians to appeal to the votes of members from other groups via secondary preferences. This can result in inclusive power sharing between all significant political forces, but also in incentives for politicians to reach out to other groups for preference support.	The system explicitly recognizes communal groups to give them (relatively fixed) institutional representation. Competition for power between ethnic groups is defused because the ratio of ethnic groups is fixed in advance. Electors must therefore make their voting choice on the basis of criteria other than ethnicity.
Examples	Switzerland; The Netherlands; South Africa, 1994 (partially)	Papua New Guinea, 1964-1975, Fiji, 1997- (partially)	Estonia, 1990; Northern Ireland, 1998- (partially)	Lebanon, Singapore, Mauritius (partially)

electoral rules which encourage multiethnic voting coalitions and the representation of minority interests by candidates who may not be from that
minority.

As Table 11.2 illustrates, large-district closed-list PR systems have
often been used in societies where communal identity has been perceived
to be hostile and rigid (e.g., South Africa, Bosnia, and Cyprus), while
preference voting has been chosen for societies where identity was seen to
be more fluid or at least open to cooperation with others (e.g., Fiji, Papua
New Guinea). The exception to this rule has been the use of STV for
various elections in Northern Ireland, which is clearly a deeply divided
society and where interethnic vote transfers have not historically been a
factor in conflict management (see Elliott, 1992). Finally, explicitist strategies are used in both high-intensity (Lebanon, Fiji) and low-intensity
(Mauritius, New Zealand) conflicts, but it is instructive to note that in the
latter two countries, where ethnic issues have become less sensitive, support for communal strategies has correspondingly declined.

Intensity of Conflict

There has been an ongoing debate among scholars of ethnic conflict
as to the applicability of the various electoral engineering options to different levels of intensity of a conflict. On the one hand, advocates of
consociationalism and list PR point to its use as a successful conflict management tool in the divided societies of Western Europe, such as Belgium,
the Netherlands, and Switzerland—societies which have become less
conflictual over the course of this century (Lijphart, 1977). On the other
hand, advocates of centripetal approaches point to the general failure of
consociationalism in the developing world, arguing that it is precisely the
low level of conflicts in the divided societies of Western European cases
which accounts for consociationalism's success there (Horowitz, 1985).

In the earlier discussion of the relationship between the intensity of a
conflict and the most appropriate electoral system, we suggested that
centripetal and consensual approaches based on AV or STV elections are
likely to work best where there is a degree of fluidity to ethnic identities
and lower levels of ethnic conflict, while approaches in which ethnicity
was more explicitly recognized (consociationalism and explicitism) may
be more appropriate for the more intense conflicts. If we look at actual
cases of electoral system choice in multiethnic societies (see Table 11.3),
then it does appear that, outside the developed West, examples of conflict
mitigation packages based on list PR elections are concentrated at the
high-intensity ends of the scale (e.g., Bosnia, South Africa, Cyprus), while
centripetalism has been applied to societies divided with more moderate
intensity (Papua New Guinea from 1964 to 1975 and most recently Fiji,

TABLE 11.2 Electoral System Choice and the Nature of Group Identity

Nature of Group Identity	List PR (Consociationalism)	AV (Centripetalism)	STV (Consensualism)	Communal Rolls, Party Block Vote (Explicitism)
Rigid	Bosnia, 1996; Cyprus	Fiji, 1997	Northern Ireland, 1973, 1997	Lebanon; Fiji, 1997 (communal rolls)
Intermediate	South Africa, Switzerland	Papua New Guinea, 1964-1975	Estonia, 1990	New Zealand (Maori seats)
Fluid	The Netherlands	Australia	—	Mauritius

TABLE 11.3 Intensity of Conflict and Electoral System Choice

Intensity of Conflict	List PR (Consociationalism)	AV (Centripetalism)	STV (Consensualism)	Communal Rolls, Party Block Vote (Explicitism)
Low	Belgium, Switzerland, Spain	Australia	—	New Zealand (Maori seats), Mauritius
Moderate	Israel	PNG, 1964-1975	Estonia, 1990	Singapore
High	South Africa, Guyana	Fiji	—	India (scheduled castes), Fiji
Extreme	Bosnia, Cyprus, Sri Lanka	—	Northern Ireland	Lebanon

467

which appears in the list twice, as its new constitution makes use of both a centripetal electoral system—AV in heterogeneous constituencies—and the explicitist device of communal-roll seats). "Extreme"-intensity conflicts are classified as having occurred in those societies in which civil wars have been fought around issues of ethnicity and identity, such as Bosnia, Northern Ireland, Lebanon, and Sri Lanka.

Size, Number, and Distribution of Ethnic Groups

Possibly the most important contextual differences between the various systems become apparent when we examine the *size, number,* and *distribution* of ethnic groups. As explained earlier, centripetal approaches based on AV are likely to work best with a low to medium number of geographically intermixed groups, or with a very high number of geographically concentrated groups. Both of these social structures result in heterogeneous electoral districts, as does our "part concentrated, part intermixed" category, where larger districts utilizing STV should also be sufficiently heterogeneous for vote pooling to take place in many areas. Ethnic groups which are organized "semigeographically," such as Hispanic and Asian minorities in the United States, can also be represented via "the ethnic gerrymandering of amoeba-like districts" (Jenkins, 1994).

If we compare this with the situation where groups are geographically *concentrated,* then list PR systems are likely to be a more appropriate choice, as they do not rely on a geographically intermixed ethnic structure to work effectively and are capable of maintaining highly proportional results as the numbers of competing groups increase. Lijphart himself identifies the geographic concentration of ethnic groups as being a "favorable condition" for consociational democracy (Lijphart, 1985). A highly segregated social structure is also often an indicator of a more intense interethnic hostility. In the former Yugoslavia, for example, "ethnic cleansing" in the 1991-1995 war dramatically increased ethnic homogeneity in many regions. It is no surprise, then, that countries with a few large, geographically concentrated groups (Belgium, Switzerland, South Africa, much of post-Dayton Bosnia) have typically chosen PR electoral systems, while countries with more intermixed populations were more likely to choose mixed or majoritarian models (pre-war Yugoslavia, India, Trinidad and Tobago, Fiji). It is interesting to note that the other model associated with more intense conflict, ethnically defined lists under a party block vote, has always been used in situations where ethnic groups are geographically interspersed (e.g., Lebanon, Singapore) rather than concentrated, as it enables candidate lists to be structured in such a way as to replicate the social structures of particular districts (such as in Lebanon).

Prescriptions for electoral engineering are thus heavily dependent on questions of social structure and, in particular, group demography. Clearly, we need to look more carefully at the *type* of ethnic division within a particular country or region. According to Lijphart, the optimal number of "segments" for a consociational approach to work is three or four, and conditions become progressively less favorable as more segments (i.e., groups) are added.[29] The centripetal approach, by contrast, requires a degree of proliferation of ethnic groups (or, at least, ethnic parties) to present the essential preconditions for vote pooling to take place, and its chances for success will typically improve as the number of segments increases (Reilly, 1998a). The converse is also true: centripetal systems like AV are likely to result in majoritarian monoethnic dominance when applied in situations of group concentration, while list PR has had the effect of reinforcing ethnic parties when applied to intermixed societies like Guyana and Suriname.

Another factor is the relative size of ethnic groups: consociationalism favors groups of roughly equal size (although "bicommunal systems," in which two groups of approximately equal sizes coexist, can present one of the most confrontationalist formulas of all);[30] while for centripetalism the crucial variable is the combination of size with the geographic concentration or dispersion of ethnic groups. In cases of group concentration, only highly fractionalized social structures can still exhibit the necessary degree of district-level heterogeneity to make centripetalism an effective strategy. In many cases, however, indigenous and/or tribal groups tend to display a strong tendency toward geographical concentration, but are not sufficiently fragmented to create heterogeneous districts. African minorities, for example, have been found to be more highly concentrated in single contiguous geographical areas than minorities in other regions, which means that many electoral constituencies and informal local power bases are dominated by a single ethnopolitical group (Scarritt, 1993). This has considerable implications for electoral engineers: it means that any system of election that relies on single-member electoral districts will likely produce "ethnic fiefdoms" at the local level. Minority representation and/or power sharing under these conditions would probably require some form of multimember district system such as proportional representation.

Contrast this with the highly intermixed patterns of ethnic settlement found as a result of colonial settlement, labor importation, and diaspora populations found in some Asia-Pacific (e.g., Singapore, Fiji, Malaysia) and Caribbean (Guyana, Suriname, Trinidad and Tobago) countries, in which members of various ethnic groups tend to be much more widely intermixed. Under such circumstances, many electoral districts are likely to be ethnically heterogeneous, so centripetal electoral strategies which make broad-based support a precondition for victory may well work to break down interethnic antagonisms and promote the development of broad, multiethnic parties. On such prosaic details rest much weightier prescriptions for the success or failure of consociational and centripetal approaches to the management of ethnic conflict.

Transitional Versus Consolidated Democracies

A final approach to electoral system choice is to ask whether the state in question is a transitional democracy, an established democracy, or a failed democracy. This gives us a quite different typology (Table 11.4). For one thing, almost all of the "extreme"-intensity conflicts from Table 11.3—Bosnia, Sri Lanka, Northern Ireland, and Lebanon—suffered a breakdown in democracy under the specified system, which serves as a sobering reminder of the limits of constitutional engineering. Second, there is a clear regional concentration of electoral system choices: virtually all the countries of continental Europe, whether ethnically divided or not, use list PR systems (which are also common in Latin America and Southern Africa); AV systems are found exclusively in the South Pacific (Australia, preindependence PNG, post-1997 Fiji, and Nauru); STV is used exclusively in countries which have had some colonial relationship with Britain (Ireland, both north and south; Malta; and in various jurisdictions in Australia); while explicitism is a strategy which, outside New Zealand, appears to be the near-exclusive preserve of the developing world (Fiji, Lebanon, Mauritius, India, etc.).

In a forthcoming work, Arend Lijphart identifies nine countries which can be classified as being both *established democracies* and *plural societies*: Belgium, Canada, India, Israel, Mauritius, Papua New Guinea, Spain, Switzerland, and Trinidad and Tobago (Lijphart, forthcoming). Again, the breakdown of these is illuminating: most established democracy examples of list PR elections for divided societies have taken place in relatively small industrialized countries, while all the examples of centripetalism and explicitism are in the developing world (Papua New Guinea, India, and Mauritius). No divided society in an established democracy outside the West uses PR, although PR has been a common choice in transitional democracies in Africa in recent years.

The final variable that may prove illuminating is whether breakdowns of democracy have occurred more or less under a particular system choice. As Table 11.4 suggests, advocates of different approaches can point to democratic successes and failures among divided societies. It is also the case, however, that countries such as Fiji, Lebanon, Northern Ireland, Sri Lanka, and others have persisted with (or reintroduced in modified form) the same electoral system design in place when democracy broke down. As discussed earlier, however, the bulk of new democracies in the post-

TABLE 11.4 Nature of State and Electoral System Choice

Nature of Democracy	List PR (Consociationalism)	AV (Centripetalism)	STV (Consensualism)	Communal Rolls, Party Block Vote (Explicitism)
Transitional democracy	South Africa, 1994-; Bosnia, 1996	Fiji, 1997-	Estonia, 1990	Lebanon, 1990-; Fiji, 1997-
Established democracy	Belgium, Spain, Switzerland	Australia; PNG, 1964-1975	—	Mauritius, India
Democratic failure	Sri Lanka, 1983; Suriname, 1980; Guyana, 1980	—	Northern Ireland, 1973	Lebanon, 1975; Fiji, 1987

war period simply adopted the electoral systems of their former colonists, evidencing equally unsatisfactory results across both majoritarian and proportional systems.

Conclusion

If the foregoing section suggests more randomness than regularity, it is still possible to isolate several factors that appear to be crucial when choosing between different models of electoral system design. First, the *intensity* of conflict does appear to have had an impact on the choice of electoral system for many divided societies. Specifically, the experience to date suggests that centripetal methods have been adopted in cases of more moderate conflicts and/or more fluid group identities, while list PR has tended to be adopted for transitional elections in more intensely conflictual situations. This fits with our earlier theoretical speculation that systems which require a degree of bargaining and cross-ethnic voting may be less realistic in extremely divided societies—where interethnic bargains, if any, may have to be made by elites alone—than in cases where there is a degree of fluidity to ethnic identities. This is why a system which combines elements of both approaches—such as STV—may well offer an attractive "middle road" position, combining as it does some incentives for vote pooling with reasonably good proportionality. Unfortunately, the use of STV in divided societies has been extremely limited and inconclusive to date. Nonetheless, there is some encouraging evidence from Northern Ireland's 1998 elections, where STV formed part of a wider prescription for power sharing between the Catholic and Protestant populations, that STV served to advantage the proagreement, nonsectarian center (Wilder, 1998).

The experience of systems in which ethnicity is explicitly recognized in the electoral system is somewhat contradictory. Both Lebanon and Fiji have suffered democratic breakdowns under such systems, but both have chosen to reintroduce elements of communalism in their new constitutions. It may well be that the value of such approaches lies in their ability to contain and manage a deep ethnic conflict until new cleavages arise to take their place. The experience of Mauritius is instructive in this regard: now that ethnicity is no longer a core political issue, the communal elements of the Mauritian electoral system, via ethnically designated "best loser" seats, are seen as a relic of times past (Mathur, 1997).

In terms of the four major electoral options for managing multiethnic conflicts, all have been successfully used in some divided societies, and all have suffered democratic failure at various points in time as well. But the respective needs of transitional versus consolidated democracies are often quite different. Put simply, the most important factor for democratic

TABLE 11.5 Ideal Qualities of Electoral Institutions for Transitional and
Consolidated Democracies

Transitional Democracy	Consolidated Democracy
• Inclusive • Simple for voters to understand • Fairness in results (proportionality) • Minimizes areas of conflict • Simple to run • Transparent • "Grand" or "oversized" coalition governments	• Accountable • Enables voters to express more sophisticated range of choice • Ability to "throw the rascals out" • Responsive to electorate • Promotes sense of "ownership" of political process among voters • "Minimal winning" coalitions or single-party governments

transition in electoral terms is usually a system that maximizes inclusiveness, is clearly fair to all parties, and presents minimal areas for potential preelection conflicts (such as the drawing of electoral boundaries)—goals that are usually best maximized by some form of regional or national list PR and which can lead to the election of a "grand" or "oversized" coalition government.

By contrast, the priorities of a consolidated democracy may be more concerned with crafting a system which gives rise to minimal winning coalition or single-party governments, is accountable in both geographic and policy terms, and allows the voters to "throw out" a government if it does not perform to their satisfaction—goals that are enhanced by a system based, at least to some extent, upon small geographically defined electoral districts that do not entrench oversized coalition governments. South Africa, which successfully conducted its transitional 1994 election using a national-list PR system and a mandated "Government of National Unity," has moved away from power-sharing measures and may change to some form of constituency-based PR system for its next elections in 2004. The differences between the needs of transitional and consolidated democracies are represented diagramatically at Table 11.5.

ADVICE FOR POLICY MAKERS

There is no perfect electoral system, and no "right" way to approach the subject of electoral system design. The major criteria for designing electoral systems for all societies, not just divided ones, are sometimes in conflict with each other or even mutually exclusive. Devices that increase proportionality, such as increasing the number of seats to be elected in each district, may lessen other desirable characteristics, such as promoting geographic accountability between the electorate and the parliament. The electoral system designer must therefore go through a careful process of prioritizing which criteria are most important to the particular political context before moving on to assess which system will do the best job. For example, an ethnically divided state in Central Africa might want above all to avoid excluding minority ethnic groups from representation in order to promote the legitimacy of the electoral process and avoid the perception that the electoral system is unfair. In contrast, while these issues would remain important, a fledgling democracy in a multiethnic state in Eastern Europe might have different priorities—for example, to ensure that a government could efficiently enact legislation without fear of gridlock and that voters are able to remove discredited leaders if they so wish. How to prioritize among such competing criteria can only be the domain of the domestic actors involved in the constitutional design process.

Two levels of tension exist in the choice of electoral system options for divided societies. The first concerns those systems which place a premium on *representation* of minority groups (list PR and ethnically defined lists) compared to those which try to emphasize minority *influence* (AV and STV). As Horowitz has noted, "measures that will guarantee representation to a given ethnic or racial group may not foster the inclusion of that group's interest more broadly in the political process" (1991:165). The best option, of course, is to have both: representation of all significant groups, but in such a way as to maximize their influence and involvement in the policy-making process. This goal is best achieved by building both devices to achieve proportionality and incentives for interethnic accommodation into the electoral system itself. However, these goals are not always mutually compatible.

A second level of tension exists between those systems which rely on elite accommodation (especially list PR) and those which rely on the electorate at large for moderation (AV and STV). Where elites are likely to be more moderate than the electorate, then list PR enables the major parties to include candidates from various groups on their ticket. Where the electorate itself is the major engine of moderation, then AV and other systems which encourage vote pooling are likely to result in the election of more moderate leaders and more accommodative policies. When neither group is likely to display moderation, then ethnically mandated lists may need to be considered, as this provides the best way of "defusing" the salience of ethnicity as an electoral issue.

It should also be remembered that, although conflict management packages based on consociationalism, centripetalism, consensualism, and explicitism do represent alternative approaches, they are not mutually exclusive. In fact, creative constitutional engineering that utilizes appropriate levers from a number of divergent approaches may well offer the

optimum strategy in some cases. A good example of this is the 1997 constitutional settlement in Fiji. In 1987 Fiji experienced an armed coup on
the part of the indigenous Fijian armed forces against an elected government dominated by Indo-Fijians, which resulted in the formulation of a
racially weighted constitution which discriminated against Fiji's Indian
population. After years of international condemnation and economic decline, a new constitution specifically designed to promote peaceful, multiethnic government was promulgated. This constitution mandated a centripetal approach to electoral competition (via the alternative vote), but
also included provisions borrowed from consociationalism (mandated
power sharing) and, more controversially, from explicitism (a partial continuation of the system of communal representation for Fijian, Indian,
and "general" electors). The new constitution is thus a structure in which
a high, or even a redundant, level of institutional levers for conflict management has been deliberately built into the system.

   While Fiji's constitution makers saw fit to make communal representation part of this new system, in general the comparative evidence to
date suggests that *explicitist* approaches—ethnically mandated lists, communal rolls, racial gerrymandering, and the like—may serve artificially to
sustain ethnic divisions in the political process rather than mitigating
them. For this reason, we would counsel against their use in all but the
most extreme cases of ethnic division. We would also recommend against
systems that are overtly majoritarian in their operation: namely, the block
vote and the two-round system. It is remarkable to note how many fledgling democracies in Africa, Asia, and the former Soviet Union use one or
the other of these systems, considering their propensity to produce undesirable results. Both tend to reduce minority representation, and are thus
unsurprisingly associated with authoritarian or other "unfree" regimes
(Reynolds and Reilly, 1997:22). In addition, the block vote typically leads
to single-party domination of parliaments and the elimination of opposition elements, while two-round systems place considerable strain on a
state's electoral apparatus by having to run elections twice within a short
space of time. The continuation of such systems points to the basic problem of inertia in any electoral reform.

   Too often, constitutional drafters simply choose the electoral system
they know best (often, in new democracies, the system of the former
colonial power if there was one) rather than investigating the most appropriate alternatives. This does not mean we would necessarily advocate
wholesale changes to existing electoral systems. In fact, the comparative
experience of electoral reform to date suggests that moderate reforms that
build on those things in an existing system which work well are often a
better option than jumping to a completely new and unfamiliar system.
What we do know is that there are several approaches to designing elec-

toral systems for divided societies and that there is no single choice that is likely to be best in all cases. The optimal choice depends on several identifiable factors specific to each country, including its political history, the way and degree to which ethnicity is politicized, the intensity of conflict, and the demographic and geographic distribution of ethnic groups. While the combination of such variables in a given country gives us some useful pointers about electoral system design, it also can place considerable constraints upon constitutional engineers. The choice of electoral systems is always politically sensitive and always constrained by political considerations. Constitutional engineers in practice usually have limited room for maneuver. Nonetheless, despite such constraints, appropriate (and inappropriate) electoral system choices are powerful levers of democratic engineering, which inevitably have a marked influence on the future conduct of electoral politics.

NOTES

[1]Ben Reilly is a senior programme officer at the International Institute for Democracy and Electoral Assistance based in Stockholm, Sweden. Andrew Reynolds is an assistant professor in the Department of Government and International Studies at the University of Notre Dame, USA.

[2]See March and Olsen, 1984:747, and Koelble, 1995:232.

[3]See Prezworski, 1991:10-14.

[4]See also Putnam, 1993.

[5]Sartori, 1968:273.

[6]Diamond, 1996:238.

[7]Diamond, 1996:239.

[8]Esman, 1994:14.

[9]Crawford Young also notes that the Ghanaian elections of 1996 were another example of substantial nonethnic block voting. Only the Ewe community could be categorized as "ethnic voters."

[10]Crawford Young, however, argues that "95 percent of whites voted for the NP, the IFP drew its votes heavily from Zulu, and the Colored vote was importantly shaped by the communal insecurities and concerns of that group."

[11]Lijphart, 1995b:853.

[12]In many African states, urbanization has led to ethnic intermixing. Mines and plantations are also more likely to have multiethnic work forces and thus communities.

[13]We are indebted to Crawford Young for pointing this out.

[14]For example, South Africa used a classically proportional electoral system for its first democratic elections of 1994, and with 62.65 percent of the popular vote the African National Congress (ANC) won 63 percent of the national seats. The electoral system was highly proportional, and the number of wasted votes (i.e., those which were cast for parties who did not win seats in the assembly) was only 0.8 percent of the total (see Reynolds, 1994). However, under some circumstances nonproportional electoral systems (such as FPTP) can accidentally give rise to relatively proportional overall results. This was the case in a third southern African country, Malawi, in 1994. In that election the leading party, the United Democratic Front, won 48 percent of the seats with 46 percent of the votes, the Malawian Congress Party won 32 percent of the seats with 34 percent of the votes, and the

Alliance for Democracy won 20 percent of the seats with 19 percent of the votes. The overall level of proportionality was high, but the clue that this was not inherently a proportional system, and so cannot be categorized as such, was that the wasted votes still amounted to almost one-quarter of all votes cast.

[15]It must be noted, however, that the party system fragmentation of 1919-1933 was not a direct result of the PR system adopted from post-Great War Germany as party fragmentation was equally high and problematic under the pre-1919 two-round German electoral system. As Lakeman notes, the number of parties in the Reichstag in 1912 was 21, while during Hitler's rise to power in the early 1930s the party system had coalesced to four or five major blocks (Lakeman, 1974:209).

[16]Madden, 1980:20.

[17]Most notably in times of war, as in Britain, and times of internal upheaval, as in West Germany in the 1970s.

[18]Lijphart, 1990:11.

[19]For example, the South African National Assembly elected in 1994 was 52 percent black (11 percent Zulu, the rest of Xhosa, Sotho, Venda, Tswana, Pedi, Swazi, Shangaan, and Ndebele extraction), 32 percent white (one-third English, two-thirds Afrikaans), 7 percent colored and 8 percent Indian. And the Namibian parliament is similarly diverse, with representatives from the Ovambo, Damara, Herero, Nama, Baster, and white (English- and German-speaking) communities (see Reynolds, 1995).

[20]See Rule and Zimmerman, 1994, and the Inter-Parliamentary Union, 1993.

[21]See Reynolds, 1996.

[22]See Horowitz, 1991:140-141.

[23]Connors argues that in South Africa consociationalism "rather than mitigating ethnic conflict, could only wittingly or unwittingly provide a basis for ethnic mobilization by providing segmental leaders with a permanent platform" (1996:426).

[24]Horowitz, 1990:471.

[25]Sisk, 1996:62.

[26]Scarritt, 1993:256

[27]Rose, 1976:78.

[28]See Taagepera, 1990.

[29]Lijphart, 1977:56.

[30]See Milne, 1982.

REFERENCES

Anderson, Benedict
  1991   *Imagined Communities: Reflections on the Origin and Spread of Nationalism*. London: Verso.
Barczak, Monica
  1997   "Electoral Rules, Responsiveness, and Party Systems: Comparing Chile and Ecuador." Paper delivered at 1997 Annual Meeting of the American Political Science Association, Washington, D.C., August 28-31, 1997.
Barkan, Joel D.
  1995   "Elections in Agrarian Societies." *Journal of Democracy* 6:106-116.
Birch, Sarah
  1997   "Ukraine: The Perils of Majoritarianism in a New Democracy." Pp. 48-50 in Andrew Reynolds and Ben Reilly, eds. *The International IDEA Handbook of Electoral System Design*, Stockholm: International Institute for Democracy and Electoral Assistance.

Carstairs, Andrew M.
  1980   *A Short History of Electoral Systems in Western Europe.* London: George, Allen and Unwin.
Cliffe, Lionel, with Ray Bush, Jenny Lindsay, Brian Mokopakgosi, Donna Pankhurst, and Balefi Tsie
  1994.   *The Transition to Independence in Namibia.* Boulder: Lynne Rienner.
Connors, Michael Kelly
  1996   "The Eclipse of Consociationalism in South Africa's Democratic Transition." *Democratization* 3:420-434.
Constitution Review Commission
  1996   *The Fiji Islands: Towards a United Future.* Parliamentary Paper No. 34 of 1996. Suva: Parliament of Fiji.
Diamond, Larry
  1995   "Nigeria: The Uncivil Society and the Descent into Praetorianism." In *Politics in Developing Countries: Comparing Experiences with Democracy*, Larry Diamond, Juan Linz, and S.M. Lipset, eds. Boulder: Lynne Rienner.
  1996   "Towards Democratic Consolidation." Pp. 227-240 in *The Global Resurgence of Democracy*, Larry Diamond and Marc F. Plattner, eds. Baltimore and London: Johns Hopkins University Press.
Diamond, Larry, Juan Linz, and S.M. Lipset, eds
  1995   *Politics in Developing Countries: Comparing Experiences with Democracy.* Boulder: Lynne Rienner
de Silva, K.M
  1994   *Ethnic Diversity and Public Policies: Electoral Systems.* Geneva: UNRISD.
Elliott, Sydney
  1992   "Voting Systems and Political Parties in Northern Ireland." Pp. 76-93 in *Northern Ireland: Politics and the Constitution*, Brigid Hadfield, ed. Bristol, U.K.: Open University Press.
Elster, Jon
  1988.   "Arguments for Constitutional Choice: Reflections on the Transition to Socialism." In *Constitutionalism and Democracy*, Jon Elster and Rune Slagstad, eds. Cambridge: Cambridge University Press.
Elster, Jon, and Rune Slagstad, eds.
  1988   *Constitutionalism and Democracy.* Cambridge: Cambridge University Press.
Esman, M.
  1994   *Ethnic Politics.* Ithaca and London: Cornell University Press.
Farrell, David M.
  1997   *Comparing Electoral Systems.* London: Prentice Hall/Harvester Wheatsheaf.
Fearon, James D., and David D. Laitin
  1996   "Explaining Interethnic Cooperation." *American Political Science Review* 90:715-735.
Gallagher, Michael
  1997   "Ireland: The Archetypal Single Transferable Vote System." Pp. 85-87 in *The International IDEA Handbook of Electoral System Design*, Andrew Reynolds and Ben Reilly, eds. Stockholm: International Institute for Democracy and Electoral Assistance.
Geertz, Clifford
  1973   *The Interpretation of Cultures.* New York: Basic Books.
Grofman, Bernard, and Arend Lijphart, eds.
  1986   *Electoral Laws and Their Political Consequences.* New York: Agathon Press.
Harris, Peter, and Ben Reilly, eds.
  1998   *Democracy and Deep-Rooted Conflict: Options for Negotiators.* Stockholm: International IDEA.

Horowitz, Donald L.
  1985   *Ethnic Groups in Conflict.* Berkeley: University of California Press.
  1990   "Making Moderation Pay: The Comparative Politics of Ethnic Conflict Manage-
         ment." Pp. 451-475 in *Conflict and Peacemaking in Multiethnic Societies,* Joseph V.
         Montville, ed. New York: Lexington Books.
  1991   *A Democratic South Africa? Constitutional Engineering in a Divided Society.* Berkeley:
         University of California Press.
  1997   "Self-Determination: Politics, Philosophy, and Law." Pp. 421-463 in *Ethnicity and
         Group Rights,* I. Shapiro and W. Kymlicka, eds. New York and London: New York
         University Press.
Huntington, Samuel P.
  1991   *The Third Wave: Democratization in the Late Twentieth Century.* Norman: University
         of Oklahoma Press.
Inter-Parliamentary Union
  1993   *Electoral Systems: A World-wide Comparative Study.* Geneva: Inter-Parliamentary
         Union.
Jenkins, Laura D.
  1994   *Ethnic Accommodation Through Electoral Systems.* Geneva: UNRISD.
Kandeh, Jimmy D.
  1992   "Politicization of Ethnic Identities in Sierra Leone." *African Studies Review* 35:81-
         99.
Kaspin, Deborah
  1995   "The Politics of Ethnicity in Malawi's Democratic Transition." *Journal of Modern
         African Studies* 33:595-620.
Koelble, Thomas
  1995   "The New Institutionalism in Political Science and Sociology." *Comparative Poli-
         tics* 27:231-243.
Laitin, David
  1986   *Hegemony and Culture: Politics and Religious Change Among the Yoruba.* Chicago:
         University of Chicago Press.
Lakeman, Enid
  1974   *How Democracies Vote.* London: Faber and Faber.
Lewis, W. Arthur
  1965   *Politics in West Africa.* London: George Allen and Unwin.
Lijphart, Arend
  1977   *Democracy in Plural Societies: A Comparative Exploration.* New Haven: Yale Univer-
         sity Press.
  1985   *Power Sharing in South Africa.* Policy Papers in International Affairs No. 24. Insti-
         tute of International Studies, University of California, Berkeley.
  1990   "Electoral Systems, Party Systems and Conflict Management in Segmented Soci-
         eties." Pp. 2-13 in *Critical Choices for South Africa: An Agenda for the 1990s,* R.A.
         Schreirer, ed. Cape Town: Oxford University Press.
  1991   "The Alternative Vote: A Realistic Alternative for South Africa?" *Politikon* 18:91-
         101.
  1994   *Electoral Systems and Party Systems: A Study of Twenty-Seven Democracies, 1945-
         1990.* New York: Oxford University Press.
  1995a "Electoral Systems." Pp. 412-422 in *The Encyclopedia of Democracy,* S.M. Lipset.
         Washington, D.C.: Congressional Quarterly Press.
  1995b "Multiethnic Democracy." Pp. 853-865 in *The Encyclopedia of Democracy,* S.M.
         Lipset, ed. Washington, D.C.: Congressional Quarterly Press.

1997   "Disproportionality Under Alternative Voting: The Crucial—and Puzzling—Case of the Australian Senate Elections, 1919-1946." *Acta Politica* 32:9-24.
Forth-   *Patterns of Democracy: Government Forms and Performance in Thirty-Six Countries.*
coming New Haven: Yale University Press.
Lijphart, Arend, and Bernard Grofman, eds.
1984   *Choosing an Electoral System: Issues and Alternatives.* New York: Praeger.
Lijphart, Arend, Rafael Lopez Pintor, and Yasunori Stone
1986   "The Limited Vote and the Single Nontransferable Vote: Lessons from the Japanese and Spanish Examples." Pp. 154-169 in *Electoral Laws and Their Political Consequences*, B. Grofman and A. Lijphart, eds. New York: Agathon Press.
MacBeth, John
1998   "Dawn of a New Age." *Far Eastern Economic Review* (17 September):24-28.
Madden, A.F
1980   "'Not for export': The Westminster Model of Government and British Colonial Practice." In *The First British Commonwealth: Essays in Honour of Nicholas Mansergh*, N. Hillmer and P. Wigley, eds. London: Frank Cass.
Mansfield, Edward D., and Jack Snyder
1995   "Democratization and War." *Foreign Affairs* 74:79-97.
March, James, and Johan Olsen
1984   "The New Institutionalism: Organizational Factors in Political Life." *American Political Science Review* 78:734-749.
Mathur, Raj
1997   "Parliamentary Representation of Minority Communities: The Mauritian Experience." *Africa Today* 44:61-77.
Mattes, Robert B
1995   *The Election Book: Judgement and Choice in South Africa's 1994 Elections.* Cape Town: IDASA Public Information Centre.
Milne, R.S
1982   *Politics in Ethnically Bipolar States.* Vancouver: University of British Columbia Press.
Nagata, Judith
1979   "Review of Lijphart's *Democracy in Plural Societies*." *International Journal* 34:505-506.
Newman, Saul
1991   "Does Modernization Breed Ethnic Political Conflict?" *World Politics* 43:451-478.
Price, Robert M
1995   "Civic Versus Ethnic: Ethnicity and Political Community in Post-Apartheid South Africa." Unpublished paper.
Przeworski, A
1991   *Democracy and the Market: Political and Economic Reforms in Eastern Europe and Latin America.* Cambridge: Cambridge University Press.
Putnam, Robert D., with Robert Leonardi and Raffaella Y. Nanetti
1993   *Making Democracy Work: Civic Traditions in Modern Italy.* Princeton: Princeton University Press.
Rae, Douglas W.
1967   *The Political Consequences of Electoral Laws.* New Haven: Yale University Press.
Reid, Ann
1993   "Conflict Resolution in Africa: Lessons from Angola." INR Foreign Affairs Brief. Washington, D.C.: U.S. Department of State.

Reilly, Ben
    1997a "The Alternative Vote and Ethnic Accommodation: New Evidence from Papua
           New Guinea." *Electoral Studies* 16:1-11.
    1997b "Preferential Voting and Political Engineering: A Comparative Study." *Journal of
           Commonwealth and Comparative Studies* 35:1-19.
    1998a "Constitutional Engineering in Divided Societies: Papua New Guinea in Com-
           parative Perspective." Ph.D. dissertation, Australian National University, Can-
           berra.
    1998b "With No Melting Pot, a Recipe for Failure in Bosnia." *International Herald Tri-
           bune*, 12-13 September, p. 6.
Reilly, Ben, and Michael Maley
    1999   "The Single Transferable Vote and the Alternative Vote Compared." In *STV in
           Comparative Perspective*, Shaun Bowler and Bernard Grofman, eds. Ann Arbor:
           University of Michigan Press.
Reynolds, Andrew, ed
    1994   *Election '94: South Africa—An Analysis of the Results, Campaigns, and Future Pros-
           pects.* New York: St. Martin's Press.
Reynolds, Andrew
    1995   "The Case for Proportionality." *Journal of Democracy* 6:117-124.
    1996   "Electoral Systems and Democratic Consolidation in Southern Africa." Ph.D. dis-
           sertation, University of California at San Diego.
Reynolds, Andrew, and Ben Reilly
    1997   *The International IDEA Handbook of Electoral System Design*. Stockholm: Interna-
           tional Institute for Democracy and Electoral Assistance.
Reynolds, Andrew, and Jørgen Elklit
    1997   "Jordan: Electoral System Design in the Arab World." In *The International IDEA
           Handbook of Electoral System Design*, Andrew Reynolds and Ben Reilly, eds. Stock-
           holm: International Institute for Democracy and Electoral Assistance.
Reynolds, Andrew, and Timothy D. Sisk
    1998   "Elections, Electoral Systems, and Conflict Management." In *Elections and Conflict
           Resolution in Africa*, Timothy Sisk and Andrew Reynolds, eds. Washington, D.C.:
           United States Institute of Peace Press.
Rokkan, Stein
    1970   *Citizens, Elections, Parties: Approaches to the Comparative Study of the Processes of
           Development.* Oslo: Universitetsforlaget.
Rose, Richard
    1976   *Northern Ireland: A Time of Choice.* Washington, D.C.: American Enterprise Insti-
           tute.
Rule, Wilma, and Joseph Zimmerman, eds.
    1994   *Electoral Systems in Comparative Perspective: Their Impact on Women and Minorities.*
           Westport, Conn.: Greenwood.
Sartori, Giovanni
    1968   "Political Development and Political Engineering." *Public Policy* 17:261-298.
    1994   *Comparative Constitutional Engineering: An Inquiry Into Structures, Incentives, and
           Outcomes.* New York: Columbia University Press.
Scarritt, James R.
    1993   "Communal Conflict and Contention for Power in Africa South of the Sahara." In
           Minorities at Risk, T.R. Gurr, ed. Washington, D.C.: United States Institute of Peace
           Press.

Scarritt, James R., and Shaheen Mozaffar
    1996   "The Potential for Sustainable Democracy in Africa." Paper presented at the International Studies Association, San Diego, April 19, 1996.
Shils, Edward
    1957   "Primordial, Personal, Sacred, and Civil Ties." *British Journal of Sociology* 8:130-145.
Sisk, Timothy D.
    1995   *Democratization in South Africa: The Elusive Social Contract.* Princeton: Princeton University Press.
    1996   *Power Sharing and International Mediation in Ethnic Conflicts.* Washington, D.C.: United States Institute of Peace Press.
Taagepera, Rein
    1990   "The Baltic States." *Electoral Studies* 9:303-311.
    1998   "How Electoral Systems Matter for Democratization." *Democratization* 5(3):68-91.
Taagepera, Rein, and Matthew S. Shugart
    1989   *Seats and Votes: The Effects and Determinants of Electoral Systems.* New Haven: Yale University Press.
Vengroff, Richard
    1994   "The Impact of Electoral System on the Transition to Democracy in Africa: The Case of Mali." *Electoral Studies* 13:29-37.
Wilder, Paul
    1998   "A Pluralist Parliament for a Pluralist People? The New Northern Ireland Assembly Elections, 25 June 1998." *Representation* 35:97-105.
Young, Crawford
    1976   *The Politics of Cultural Pluralism.* Madison: University of Wisconsin Press.

12

Autonomy as a Strategy for Diffusing Conflict

Yash Ghai

In recent years several conflicts, especially ethnic ones, have centered on demands for, and resistance to, autonomy. Equally, several conflicts have been resolved by the concession of autonomy. In some instances the form of dispute has been transformed by an offer of autonomy. In other cases an agreement in principle to consider autonomy has been sufficient to get the parties to the negotiating forum. The international community, particularly regional European organizations and the Organization for Security and Cooperation in Europe (OSCE), have attached particular importance to autonomy as a conflict management device and have brought pressure on governments to concede, and on minorities to accept, autonomy as a suitable compromise. The use of autonomous or federal arrangements for dealing with ethnic conflicts is a relatively new development, although federalism was instituted in Canada as early as 1867 to manage tensions between the Anglophone and Francophone communities (Watts, 2000) and autonomy arrangements mediated the relationship between Russia and its possession of the Duchy of Finland at an even earlier period (Rae, 1997).

AUTONOMY AS A CONFLICT-RESOLVING DEVICE

Those who are concerned with the settlement of internal conflicts must explore the potential of autonomy. We need to pay attention to this device because disaffected groups frequently ask for it, it is central to negotiations over many present conflicts, and it may be emerging as an entitlement under international law to groups in certain circumstances. Sometimes autonomy may not be sufficient to satisfy the aspirations of groups; they may want to settle for nothing less than separation (as happened in the East Timor referendum). At other times separation, rather than autonomy, may be the first choice of a group, but it is willing to opt for autonomy, realizing that independence is not realistic (as with the Tibetans or the earlier position of the East Timorese, before President Habibe's surprise offer of separation). Other factors may also change options, such as persistent refusal to consider effective autonomy (as in Sri Lanka in the late 1970s and early 1980s) or intensification of the oppression of the group (as of the Tamils in Sri Lanka and the Albanians in Kosovo).

Because of the relative newness of the device, the variety of forms it can take, and the different historical and political contexts in which it has operated, there is inadequate knowledge of autonomy, even among those who demand it, to form a secure basis for negotiations, policy, and implementation. The growing interest in autonomy and successful (and unsuccessful) examples of its use as well as skepticism of and resistance to it suggest the need for further research to enable a more productive and realistic use of autonomy to bring parties to the negotiating table, provide a framework for negotiations, indicate when such negotiations or their outcomes are likely to be successful, and highlight processes and institutions that are likely to promote and sustain a settlement. In a modest way this is the aim of this paper.

Autonomy Defined

Autonomy is a device to allow ethnic or other groups that claim a distinct identity to exercise direct control over affairs of special concern to them while allowing the larger entity to exercise those powers that cover common interests. Autonomy can be granted under different legal forms. There is no uniform use of terms for the different kinds of arrangements for autonomy (for useful discussions, see Elazar, 1987; Watts, 1994a). I use autonomy as a generic term. Specialized terms are used to designate particular types of arrangements. The best known is federalism, in which all regions enjoy equal powers and have an identical relationship to the central government. Traditionally, federalism has not been used as a way to solve problems of ethnic diversity, although two old federations, Switzerland and Canada, were adopted in part to accommodate ethnic diversity. Classical federalism, in which all regions have equal powers, may not be sufficiently sensitive to the peculiar cultural and other needs of a particular community, which may require a greater measure of self-government. Federal systems in which one or more regions are vested with special powers not granted to other provinces are known as asymmetrical (Stevens, 1977; Watts, 1994b; Agranoff, 1994; Boase, 1994; Brown-John, 1994). Most multiethnic federations are in fact asymmetrical, starting with Canada and Switzerland; other examples are India, Spain, Russia, and Malaysia. Federations in which some provinces are more populous or have more resources than others have also been described as asymmetrical (Tarlton, 1965), but this is not the way I use the term here.

The federal model may be regarded as unnecessary if the need is to accommodate only one or two minority groups. In these situations, special powers may be devolved only to a part of the country where the minority constitutes a majority; these powers are exercised by regional institutions. Normally, very significant powers are devolved and the region, unlike in a federation, plays relatively little role in national government and institutions. This kind of autonomy is referred to as regional autonomy (Heintze, 1998) or federacy (Stevens, 1977; Elazar, 1987). By its nature this kind of regional autonomy is asymmetrical. Examples of autonomous regions include the Åland Islands (Finland), South Tyrol (Italy), Kosovo (the former Yugoslavia), Cordillera and Mindanao (the Philippines), Puerto Rico (United States), Zanzibar (Tanzania), Hong Kong and Macao (China), Greenland and Faroes (Denmark), New Caledonia (France), and Scotland (U.K.).

Both federalism and regional autonomy are characterized by constitutional entrenchment of autonomy. When territorial devolution of powers is not constitutionally protected or not sufficiently protected, the arrangements are sometimes referred to as regionalism (where central powers and institutions remain dominant, as in Italy) or decentralization (which is frequently a form of administrative transfer of powers, as in France). Local government can also be an effective way to give certain powers to a group since the geographical scale of local government is small and the prospects of its inhabitants being ethnically homogeneous are better. Some federations now constitutionally protect local government as a third tier of government for this very reason (Nigeria and Spain; but constitutional protection was rejected in India). When a federal-type state enters into economicopolitical regional arrangements like the European Union (EU), a third constitutional tier appears (such as in Spain, Finland, and Germany).

Reserves are a special instance of spatial organization of government first used by European settlers in America to isolate and dominate indigenous peoples and subsequently adopted in Australia, Africa, and parts of Asia. The apartheid policy of Bantustans was a modern version. However, in recent years the aspirations and historical claims of indigenous peoples have been recognized through the transformation of reserves into self-governing areas, particularly in Canada and the Philippines, although the extent to which they can opt out of national laws, which may be necessary for the preservation of their political and cultural practices, is variable.

A new but uneven element in the spatial organization of government is the emergence of international regional organizations in which national sovereignty has been traded for a share in participation and decision making in these organizations. Common policies over larger and larger matters are determined by the organization, so that a measure of control of the affairs of a national region has been transferred from national to supranational authority. The consequences are that the diminution of the salience of national sovereignty opens up possibilities of new arrangements between the state and its regions, the state feeling less threatened by regions in a multilayered structure of policy making and administration and the region more willing to accept national sovereignty, which may be the key to its participation in the wider arrangements. This trend is most developed in the EU (with its developing concept of the Europe of Regions; Bullain, 1998), where it is helping to moderate tensions between states and border regions previously intent on secession, as in Spain and Belgium (and which has facilitated the interesting spatial arrangements for policy, administration, and consultation in the two parts of Ireland, each under separate sovereignty, which underlie the new peace settlement). However, it might have different implications for Quebec, which through Ottawa has been drawn into closer economic relations with the United States and Mexico and may feel able to be an independent member of the North American trading area. Attempts to provide for unified Nordic arrangements for the Saami people (including a substantial element of autonomy), regardless of the sovereignty they live under, are another instance of similar kind (Hannum, 1990).

Nonterritorial Autonomy

A major limitation of territorial devolution of power is that it is restricted to circumstances where there is a regional concentration of an ethnic group. Sometimes attempts are made to transcend this limitation by corporate autonomy, whereby an ethnic group is given forms of collective rights. There are different forms and uses of corporate autonomy. Rights or entitlements protected under such autonomy can be personal, cultural, or political. At one end is corporate autonomy or, more accurately, corporate identity as the basis of wide-ranging rights, as exemplified by the independence constitution of Cyprus (1970), which had set out in detail the role of the Greek and Turkish communities in government and administration, provided for separate seats and electoral rolls, fixed the proportion of ministries, and established communal vetoes to protect specific interests, separate municipal councils, and so forth. Contemporary examples include the Constitution of Bosnia-Herzegovina, which combines more traditional federalism with corporate shares in power and communal vetoes. A more limited version is the application to members of a community of its personal or religious laws (covering marriage and family and occasionally land, particularly for tribal communities; see Ghai, 1998b; for its application in Israel, see Edelman, 1994; for a historical account of its use in Europe, see Eide, 1998). Sometimes group autonomy takes the shape of communal representation, whereby a person's candidacy and voting are based on a communal electoral roll, as in Bosnia, Fiji, and proposed for Kosovo. These forms of autonomies were significant features of old and modern empires. Modern examples include provisions in the constitutions or laws of Estonia, Hungary, Slovenia, and the Russian Federation (Eide, 1998). More central reliance on group autonomy through cultural councils is found in the developing constitutional dispensation of Belgium. In 1970 separate councils were established for Dutch-, French-, and German-language speakers with competence over aspects of cultural and educational matters; their competence was considerably extended in the 1980s (Peeters, 1994; Murphy, 1995). Personal or communal autonomy is not directly dealt with in this paper for reasons of space (but it is also my view that communal autonomy is unsuitable for modern economic and social life, with its multiple and cross-cutting identities, an integrated economy, and democratic politics). However, in some new constitutions group autonomy is related to, or is part of a package of, federal or other devices for the protection of ethnic communities, frequently in consociatialist arrangements (such as in Belgium, Bosnia-Herzogovina, and the Fiji Islands) and are briefly examined here (see Chapter 11, on how electoral systems can promote consociationalism).

These different legal and political forms of autonomy cannot always be easily distinguished and frequently shade off into others. Spain is increasingly analyzed in federal and not just regional terms. Papua New Guinea, although officially a decentralized state, has marked federal features (Ghai and Regan, 2000). The choice of labels is not important for purposes of negotiations, and some deliberate fudging may indeed be beneficial, especially if the constitution seems to prohibit some options (as in China, Sri Lanka, and Spain where a unitary state is mandated) or where there is particular sensitivity about sovereignty (as in China). Labels often refer to legal status—matters such as the degree of entrenchment and the method of division of subjects/powers, which may not always be a true guide to the scope of autonomy. Even when it is possible to be specific about the labels, a legal form may not exist to the exclusion of other forms. Thus, Canada has both symmetrical (for the most part) and asymmetrical federalism (for Quebec), federacy or regional autonomy for aboriginals, and group council for Metis. Similar diversity is found in India. It is important to avoid seeing these devices as alternatives or exclusive; contemporary variations in diversity, in terms of numbers, identity, and resources, in a single state, requiring differential responses, may benefit from a combination of devices.

The developments regarding federalism and autonomy outlined above have greatly increased the flexibility in devising arrangements for forms of self-government to suit widely varying circumstances and contingencies. Added to these broad categories of self-government are the variations in detailed arrangements in each category, such as in the division of powers between different layers of government, structures of government, the relationship between these structures at different levels, and the distribution of financial and other resources. While this flexibility is important in the negotiation process and facilitates compromises, there is the danger that it may lead to complex arrangements and systems, producing a lack of cohesion and the difficulties of governability. When negotiations enter a difficult phase, there is the temptation to devise some fancy scheme that may produce a temporary consensus that is hard to operationalize; thus, there is a conflict between immediate and long-term interests. Federal or autonomy arrangements are inherently hard to operate, requiring both high administrative capacity and political skills, and the embroidery on classical systems that tough negotiations may lead to would undermine long-term prospects of settlement by their sheer weight or complexity. Good examples of this experience would be the regional arrangements in Kenya's independence constitution (Ghai and McAuslan, 1970), Papua New Guinea's system of provincial government established in 1976 (Ghai and Regan, 1992), and even Spain's autonomous communities (Conversi, 2000); the lack of resources is likely to render large parts of Ethiopia's complex and complicated constitution of 1994 largely negatory (Paul, 2000).

The definitions I have adopted concentrate on divisions of powers and corresponding institutions. It is frequently said that autonomy is also, perhaps more fundamentally, a process. It is also said that federalism connotes attitudes, a spirit of mutual respect, and tolerance (Elazar, 1987). These are undoubtedly important points, but I believe that in a comparative study of this kind the more neutral definition in terms of powers and institutions serves our interests better. However, specific arrangements cannot be understood without a consideration of process and values, and I use these in my account of factors that influence the success or failure of autonomy.

Autonomy and State Structures

These developments in autonomy regimes have significantly changed the nature and organization of states. Therein lies both the positive and the negative aspects of autonomy. The positive aspect is that it helps in restructuring the state to accommodate cultural and ethnic diversity. It is often assumed that conflicts can be prevented or mediated by restructuring the state and official policies by, for example, redistribution through affirmative policies, recognition of personal laws and other forms of pluralism, fairer electoral laws, and forms of power sharing. The negative aspect is that majority groups (and others with a vested interest in a more centralized state) resist modification to the state structure. Most contemporary conflicts are not about territory but about its political organization. They center on the role of the state in society; control over the state provides access to economic power, the state being the major means for reproduction of capital. The state is the most powerful organization in most countries, even when it is not very effective in implementing policy. Consequently, there is strong competition for control over the apparatus of the state.

The dominant model of the state derives largely from Western liberal theory. It relies heavily on the concept of citizenship, defining an individual's relationship to the state and to other individuals, on the basis of equality (Tully, 1995; Parekh, 1993; Walker, 1997). There is also a sharp distinction between public and private spheres, although the public sphere is infused with the values and idiom of the majority and can be alienating for minorities. The exercise of power in the Western state is based on majoritarianism, and it is partly for this reason that there has been considerable resistance to multiethnic federations and asymmetry. Federations in liberal societies are meant to reflect principles of equality (symmetry) and common values (Glazer, 1977). The danger of excesses that majoritarianism may give rise to is frequently tempered by mechanisms of accountability, conventions of tolerance, and a regime of human rights. The danger is also mitigated by varying degrees of homogeneity, with many common bonds among the people acting to discourage the oppression of others. When transplanted to places with significant heterogeneity, the model rapidly lost the elements of accountability, tolerance, and rights and assumed an authoritarian, or at least an exclusionary, form. Even in the land of its origin, the model has come under attack as its population has become more diverse culturally, religiously, and ethnically, and the consciousness of these and other differences has sharpened (Tully, 1995; Kymlicka, 1989; Taylor, 1994).

THE LEGAL BASES FOR AUTONOMY

A discussion of the legal bases of autonomy is useful both in providing a sense of how the idea of autonomy has developed in recent decades, the forms of entitlements and legitimacy they offer negotiating parties, and the status of the resulting system of autonomy. Legal bases are relevant to the possibilities of intervention by the international community in a dispute and its role in supervising and guaranteeing the outcome. The presence or absence of an entitlement in either international or national law to autonomy, as well as provisions limiting its scope, can play an important role in the conduct of negotiations and the relative bargaining position of parties, especially when there is international or third-party mediation. Despite increasing adoption of autonomy, its legal basis is unclear (Hannum, 1990; Thornberry, 1998). In principle, the case for autonomy rests on three principal sources: minority rights; indigenous peoples' rights; and, more controversially, the right to self-determination.

Minorities

When the United Nations (UN) began work on an international regime of rights, it emphasized individual rights and carefully avoided giving rights, particularly political rights, to groups. There are trends now, however, toward a greater recognition of cultural and ethnic bases of autonomy. Article 27 of the International Covenant of Civil and Political Rights (ICCPR), until recently the principal UN provision on minorities, was drafted to exclude collective rights and was narrowly interpreted. But in recent years the UN Human Rights Committee (which supervises implementation of the covenant) has adopted interpretations of Article 27 that recognize that a measure of autonomy and group rights may be necessary for the protection of the cultural rights of minorities. Efforts have also been made by that committee and others to interpret the right to self-determination to mean, where relevant, internal autonomy rather than secession. This broader approach is reflected in a UN Declaration on the Rights of Minorities adopted by the General Assembly in 1992. Unlike the ICCPR, it places positive obligations on the state to protect the identity of minorities and encourage "conditions for the promotion of that identity" (Article 1). It does not go so far as to require autonomy for minorities, but it lays the foundation for it by recognizing community rights and the importance of identity.

Several initiatives have been taken in Europe, through the OSCE, the Council of Europe, and the EU to promote the concept of autonomy, although its impact so far is restricted to Europe. This is manifested both in formal declarations and interventions to solve ethnic conflicts in Europe (such as in the Dayton Accord over Bosnia-Herzogivina or the Rambouilet proposals for Kosovo). Article 35 of the Copenhagen Declaration on Human Dimension of the Conference on Security and Cooperation in Europe (CSCE) recognizes "appropriate local or autonomous administration as one of the possible means" for the promotion of the "ethnic, cultural, linguistic, and religious identity of certain minorities." The principal instrument of the Council of Europe is the Framework Convention for the Protection of National Minorities (1994), which protects various rights of minorities, obliges the state to facilitate the enjoyment of these rights, and recognizes many rights of identity. There is no proclamation of a right to autonomy, but the exercise of some of these rights implies a measure of autonomy. The Copenhagen Declaration and statements of principle by the Council of Europe, although not strictly binding, have been used by the OSCE High Commissioner for Minorities and other mediating bodies as a basis for compromise between contending forces and have thus influenced practice in which autonomy has been a key constituent (Bloed, 1995; Packer, 1998; Thornberry, 1998, Hopmann, Chapter 14, this volume; see also OSCE High Commissioner for Minorities, 1999).

The European Community has also used conformity with the Copenhagen Declaration as a precondition for the recognition of new states in Europe. The ability of existing states (which is relatively unregulated by international law) to confer recognition on entities, especially breakaway states, can be a powerful weapon to influence their constitutional structure. When various republics within the Federations of Yugoslavia and the Soviet Union were breaking away, the European Community issued a Declaration on the Guidelines on the Recognition of New States in Eastern Europe and in the Soviet Union (December 16, 1991), although it was not applied in all cases. Among the conditions a candidate had to satisfy before it would be recognized was that its constitution contained "guarantees for the rights of ethnic and national groups and minorities in accordance with the commitments subscribed to in the framework of the CSCE" (European Community, 1991:1487). Entities requesting recognition were asked to submit evidence that their constitutions conformed to the guidelines; recognition was granted only if the evidence satisfied a European Community constitutional tribunal set up for this purpose (Rich, 1993; Weller, 1992; Rady, 1996). Similar principles have been used for admission to the Council of Europe and the EU.

Indigenous Peoples

The Convention on Indigenous Peoples, adopted in 1991 and representing a reversal of paternalistic and assimilationist approaches followed in the 1959 convention, recognized the "aspirations of these [indigenous] peoples to exercise control over their own institutions, ways of life and economic development and to maintain and develop their identities, languages and religions, within the framework of the States in which they live." Their cultural and religious values, institutions, and forms of traditional social control are to be preserved (Article 4). The system of land ownership and the rules for the transmission of land rights are to be protected (Articles 14 and 17). The Draft UN Declaration on the Rights of Indigenous Peoples (submitted by the UN Sub-commission on Minorities, August 1994) goes even further and proclaims their right to self-determination, under which they may "freely determine their political status and freely pursue their economic, social and cultural development" (Article 3). The principle of self-determination gives them the "right to autonomy or self-government in matters relating to their internal and local affairs," which include social, cultural, and economic activities and the right to control the entry of nonmembers (Article 31). It recognizes their collective rights (Article 7) and the right to maintain and strengthen their distinct political, economic, social, and cultural characteristics (Article 4). These ideas have already formed the basis of negotiations between indigenous peoples and the states in which they live, giving recognition not only to their land rights (as in Australia and New Zealand) but also to forms of autonomy (as in Canada), although Asian and African governments deny the existence of indigenous peoples in their states and the instruments have had little impact there (Brölmann and Zieck, 1993; Stavenhagen, 1998; Alfredson, 1998; Kingsbury, 1999). Indigenous people, particularly in North America, also base their claims on other legal bases: (a) their "inherent sovereignty," which predates colonization, and (b) treaties with incoming powers (for what has been called "treaty federalism," see Henderson, 1994).

Self-Determination

The broadest source of autonomy is self-determination, in itself a difficult and controversial concept but one that has increasingly been analyzed in terms of the internal democratic organization of a state rather than in terms of secession or independence. The marked bias of the international community of states against the use of self-determination, other than for classical colonies, is well known (Franck, 1993). The UN General Assembly resolved many years ago that autonomy is a manifestation of self-determination. The greater involvement of the UN or consortia of states in the settlement of internal conflicts has also helped to develop the concept of self-determination as implying autonomy in appropriate circumstances, such as in Bosnia, Eastern Europe, and Kosovo (Rosas, 1993; Franck, 1993; Higgins, 1993). However, the birth of new states following the collapse of the communist order in the Soviet Union, Eastern Europe, and the Balkans, has removed some taboo against secession, and the international community seems to be inching toward some consensus that extreme oppression of a group may justify secession. This position has served to strengthen the internal aspect of self-determination, for a state can defeat the claim of separation if it can demonstrate that it respects the political and cultural rights of minorities. A further, and far-reaching, gloss has been placed on this doctrine by the Canadian Supreme Court, which decided in 1999 that Quebec has no right under either the Canadian Constitution or international law to unilateral secession but that, if Quebec were to decide on secession through a referendum, Ottawa and other provinces would have to negotiate with Quebec on future constitutional arrangements (2 SCR 217, 1998). However, these rules or understandings are not accepted everywhere, and they are unlikely to persuade leaders in Africa or Asia.

Such a view of self-determination has some support in certain national constitutions, indicating no more than a trend at this stage. Often constitutional provisions for autonomy are adopted during periods of social and political transformation, when an autocratic regime is overthrown (when there is considerable legitimacy for autonomy), or when a crisis is reached in minority-majority conflicts, or when there is intense international pressure (in which case legitimacy is granted rather grudgingly). Propelled by these factors, a number of constitutions now recognize some entitlement to self-government, such as the Philippines in relation to two provinces, one for indigenous people and the other for a religious minority; Spain, which guarantees autonomy to three regions and invites others to negotiate with the center for autonomy; Papua New Guinea, which authorizes provinces to negotiate with the central government for substantial devolution of power; Fiji, which recognizes the right of indigenous people to their own administration at the local level; and recently Ethiopia, which gives its "nations, nationalities, and peoples" the right to seek wide-ranging powers as states within a federation and guarantees them even the right to secession. The Russian Constitution of 1993, in the wake of the breakup of the Soviet Union, provides for extensive autonomy to its constituent parts, whether republics or autonomous areas (Agnew, 1995; Lynn and Novikov, 1997; Smith, 1996). Chinese constitution entrenches the rights of ethnic minorities to substantial self-government, although in practice the dominance of the Communist Party negates their autonomy (Ghai, 2000). In other instances the constitution authorizes but does not require the establishment of autonomous areas, with China again an interesting example (Article 31), in order to provide a constitutional basis for "one country, two systems" for the reunification of Hong Kong, Macau, and Taiwan. On the other hand, it should also be noted that some constitutions prohibit or restrict the scope of autonomy by requiring that the state be unitary or some similar expression; such a provision has retarded the acceptance or implementation of meaningful devolution in, for example, Sri Lanka, Papua New Guinea, and China.

PROS AND CONS OF AUTONOMY: AN OVERVIEW OF
EXPERIENCE AND SOME ARGUMENTS

The record of the success of autonomy to resolve or manage ethnic conflicts is mixed. There are many instances when its use has defused tensions, reorganized the state, and provided the basis for the existence of ethnic groups. There are also numerous occasions when autonomy has been unacceptable to a party in conflict, either the central government or the ethnic group. There are examples of the abrupt withdrawal of autonomy because the central government rejects pluralism or considers that its continued operation is a threat to state integrity through secession (as in southern Sudan and Kosovo).

There are several other attractions of autonomy. Autonomy can comprise a wide variety of arrangements regarding structure and powers. The flexibility of the federal device in terms of the division of powers and the structure of institutions enables various kinds of accommodations to be made; it is more hospitable to compromises than other kinds of minority protection. It can also allow for a gradually increasing transfer of powers. As far as minorities are concerned, it ensures them a measure of state power—executive, legislative, and fiscal powers, not merely parliamentary representation, which offers little prospect of a share in policy making or distribution of resources. It ensures better prospects for preserving their culture (language, religion, etc.) and resisting state homogenizing policies and practices. It is a device to control local physical and natural resources. The problem of natural and other resources is not so easily resolved, but state control over national revenue enables other regions to be compensated in other ways to maintain a measure of equity necessary for national unity. From the viewpoint of the central authorities, such arrangements may forestall or terminate demands for secession.

Autonomy has been used for different purposes. Most importantly, it has been used for long-term accommodation of linguistic or ethnic diversity. The first important example of federalism for this purpose was the division of Canada into the two provinces of the largely Anglophonic Ontario and Francophone Quebec in 1867. Although the Canadian federation has now come under pressure due to secessionist claims in Quebec, the federal solution provided a satisfactory basis for the accommodation of Francophonie for over a hundred years (Watts, 2000). Federalism was adopted by India on independence, largely for administrative reasons, and it was not until 1956 that the federation was transformed to serve as a device to accommodate linguistic diversity. Controversies over linguistic policies and demands for the linguistic reorganization of states led to a great deal of violence and threatened India's unity (Harrison, 1960). It is widely recognized that this reorganization brought considerable stability to India (Gupta, 1975), even if it has required further reorganizations of state boundaries. In Nigeria it was the federal device, as reorganized after the Biafara war, that helped maintain the country's unity and provide security to most of its ethnic communities. A striking example of the successful use of federal-type autonomy is Spain after Franco's death (Heywood, 1995; Moreno, 1994; Conversi, 2000). Various cultural and linguistic communities or nations in Spain, prominently the Catalans and the Basque, resisting centralization of the state started in the late nineteenth century, had been seeking separation through violence. The 1978 constitution recognized these historical and other communities and guaranteed them autonomy.

An outstanding example of the successful use of regional autonomy is Åland, where a predominantly Swedish-speaking population under Finnish sovereignty has enjoyed a large measure of cultural and political autonomy since 1921. Åland had been administered by Sweden as part of Finland; when Russia acquired Finland, Åland went with it. On the grant of independence to Finland in 1917, the inhabitants of Åland demanded reunification with Sweden, which backed their claims. The dispute was referred to the newly established League of Nations, which recommended that Åland remain under Finnish sovereignty but with a high degree of autonomy, under international guarantee, designed to protect the linguistic, cultural, and property rights of Ålanders. Over time Åland has come to value its autonomy as well as its links with Finland (Hannikainen, 1997).

Åland's experience has been a model of regional autonomy and inspired arrangements for the autonomy of Greenland and Faroes under Danish sovereignty. Other examples of regional autonomy include the Italian South Tyrol, for the protection of cultural and political rights of its substantial German-speaking population, the Atlantic Coast of Nicaragua for the protection of its indigenous people, and Chittagong Tract Hills in Bangladesh. Its imaginative use by China for the reunification of Hong Kong and Macau helped to resolve differences between China on the one hand and the United Kingdom and Portugal on the other; but its potential for the resolution of the Taiwan question has yet to be tested (Ghai, 1997, 1998a, 2000). The agreement by Israel to grant autonomy to Palestinians brought most hostilities to an end and set a promising stage for negotiations on self-government and eventual statehood. In the Philippines Muslim secessionist activity in Mindanao, lasting for a quarter of a century, has abated due to an agreement in 1996 between the Moro National Liberation Front and the government (Stankovitch, 1999). There are many lesser-known examples from the South Pacific where autonomy helped bring disputes to some settlement (prominently the 1975 differences between Papua New Guinea and Bougainville and the Francophone claims in Vanuatu; Ghai, 1996). The use of regional autonomy in the wake of the collapse of the Soviet Union and the former Yugoslavia has been well documented.

Autonomy often facilitates a compromise as it is a midpoint of competing claims—that of a separate statehood/sovereignty and a unitary state. Autonomy can provide the basis for a long-term resolution because it can fudge the thorny issue of sovereignty, which has been so troublesome in several conflicts. Self-government and self-determination can be accommodated within the confines of autonomy (with substantial devolution of powers and the paraphernalia of statehood such as a flag, postal stamps, and even an anthem) while retaining intact the boundaries of the state.

Autonomy has also been used as a transitional or interim device to postpone the more difficult issue of the ultimate resolution of a dispute or conflict to provide a cooling-off period to examine other alternatives. Autonomy can serve this purpose because both parties can reserve their position, although it is hard for the government then to offer anything less. The relations of autonomy may provide a better basis for negotiating the ultimate resolution by generating trust and a framework for discussions. This was envisaged as an essential purpose of the Israeli-Palestinian agreement for autonomy for Gaza and the West Bank. While the course of subsequent negotiations has not been smooth, the concession of autonomy undoubtedly eased tensions and helped the longer-term process of finding a definitive status for a Palestinian state. In Hong Kong autonomy is also seen as transitional—it is guaranteed only for 50 years. But unlike Palestine, the ultimate destination is full integration into China, the transitional period facilitating political and psychological adjustments. The conflict between the indigenous people of New Caledonia and the French government and French settlers on the future status of New Caledonia has also been overcome through an agreement that gives the colony wide-ranging autonomy and postpones the final decision that is to be reached through a referendum. The Bougainville separatists proposed a similar method to the Papua New Guinea government in November 1999. In these situations the expectation of governments is that the experience of autonomy in which the local group is able to determine most matters of concern to it may counsel against separation, especially as it is possible to increase autonomy during further negotiations.

Third, the offer to consider autonomy has served to bring hostilities to an end. Bougainville was persuaded to bring its rebellion to an end by the Papua New Guinea government in early 1976 by the offer to consider significant autonomy or other options. Truces in many other conflicts have been made for similar reasons (including such difficult customers as the Tamil Tigers, the southern Sudanese, and secessionists in Catalonia and the Basque Country). The promise or grant of autonomy can transform the nature of dispute—from territorial claims to the nature of government, as in Åland, Mindanao, and New Caledonia.

Autonomy has enabled a region to exercise substantial self-government without assuming all functions of state or losing the benefits of metropolitan nationality (as with associated states such as the Cook Islands, which opted for a link with New Zealand after decolonization but assumed most functions of self-government). On the other hand, autonomy has also been used when a region of a state does not want to join a bigger union (e.g., in Greenland and Faroes when Denmark joined EU; and special provisions could be negotiated for Åland when Finland joined the EU because of its preexisting autonomy).

Autonomy has been used as a complement to other conflict-resolving devices or packages. Various forms of autonomy (personal, corporate, or territorial) have been linked to consociationalism, which has been gaining popularity in recent years, as in Bosnia, Belgium, and Fiji.

Territorial autonomy can increase the political integration of ethnic groups with the rest of the country by accentuating intragroup differences and leading to the fragmentation of previously monolithic ethnic parties. The proliferation of parties enables coalitions of similarly situated ethnic parties (Nigeria, India) across the state. Local problems that might otherwise have created a national crisis are dealt with by the locality itself. Territorial asymmetrical arrangements encourage demands for similar arrangements by other groups (India, Nigeria, Papua New Guinea, China). The proliferation of these arrangements increases the prospects of national unity as it diffuses state power and enables central authorities to balance regional interests with national interests.

Autonomy arrangements also contribute to constitutionalism in that they divide power. The guarantees for autonomy and the modalities for their enforcement emphasis the rule of law and the roles of independent institutions. The operation of the arrangements, particularly those parts governing the relationship between the center and the region, being dependent on discussions, mutual respect, and compromise, frequently serve to strengthen these qualities. They help break up the hegemony of the dominant group and give the minority some influence at the center, depending on the precise institutional arrangements, and integrates it in the state. This justification is offered by current Ethiopian leaders who were instrumental in adopting the most ethnic-oriented constitution of recent decades, which gives any "nationality" or "people" the right to a federal state or secession (Paul, 2000; Tronvoll, 2000).

A particular advantage of territorial autonomy, being based on the territorial principle, is that it enables ethnic problems to be solved without entrenching ethnicity. However, some forms of autonomy may indeed entrench ethnicity, as with reservations or tribal areas where cultural dimensions and the need to preserve the identity of the group may serve to sharpen boundaries against outsiders.

Objections to Autonomy

Despite the theoretical and practical advantages of autonomy, there has been considerable resistance to it by governments. It has proved impossible to muster enough political support for significant autonomy in Sri Lanka despite years of negotiations and waves of violence. The Sudanese government has strenuously resisted autonomy for southern Sudan. In the South African postapartheid constitutional negotiations, the majority party was able to evade autonomy and was strongly backed by whites and the Zulu-dominated Inkatha Party, although a form of regionalism was conceded (Klug, 2000). Even when autonomy is established, it may be repealed by the government; examples of this abound. Federalism, established only upon independence in Indonesia, was abolished shortly thereafter. Likewise, regionalism, as part of independence packages, was repealed in Uganda and Kenya soon after independence; Ethiopia swallowed Eriteria in 1962, although it was united with Ethiopia under UN auspices through a highly autonomous relationship in 1952; and the elaborate Cyprus independent constitution that created federalism based on group rather than territorial principles was short lived. China did not long honor its promises of autonomy to Tibet, nor did Sudan to its southern province. The union between Malaya and Singapore on federal principles was soon terminated, effectively by mutual agreement. In some cases where the facade of autonomy has been preserved, the reality of pluralism and diversity has not, as in Malaysia or communist federations (Ghai, 1998b). Many federations or autonomous systems have suffered acute tensions or crises (Pakistan, Nigeria, and even such a well-established federation as Canada). We have seen in recent years the disintegration of federations into a multiplicity of states—the secession of Bangladesh from Pakistan, the breakup of Czechoslovakia, and the collapse of the Soviet Union and Yugoslavia. In many contemporary conflicts a settlement on autonomy has eluded negotiators for long periods or at all, as in the Philippines or over Kosovo, or one party has escalated its demands beyond autonomy (Sudan and Sri Lanka are obvious examples). The UN has had a singular lack of success in persuading the Cypriot Greeks and Turks to try cohabitation again, this time in the form of a territorial federation, facilitated now by the transfers of population following the breakdown of the republic. In the eyes of many policy makers and scholars, autonomy has been truly discredited.

Various reasons for resisting or for objections to autonomy can be identified. Some of them relate to resistance to autonomy by those who have a vested interest in a more centralized regime; others relate to its inadequacies (and are more directly relevant to us). For a long time autonomy was seen to undermine the process of nation and state building that underlay much modernization theory—and with the ambitions of nationalist leaders. Autonomy is resisted because it is feared that it would consolidate ethnic solidarity and divisiveness or entrench what might be a passing fad in this volatile age of identity. The concept of autonomy upsets long-held views of the sacredness of territory and the unity of the motherland. From a more narrow ethnic view, which sees the state as a way of consolidating the domination of one group, the reorganization of the state and the reallocation of resources entailed in autonomy is unacceptable. Sometimes, as in postapartheid South African constitutional negotiations, there may be suspicions about the real motive in the claim for autonomy. The claim may be merely a way of perpetuating the group's privileged position and refusal to share resources with less developed areas; similar motives were ascribed to white settlers who lobbied for regionalism in Kenya at its independence. Secessionist groups or those demanding internal autonomy are frequently accused of greed and unwillingness to share their resources with others, as in Katanga, Biafra, and Bougainville. Even if persuaded of the value of autonomy, leaders of the majority community may be reluctant to concede it, fearing the loss of electoral support among its own community (a problem that has bedeviled Sri Lanka). They may not have the confidence that they would be able to implement the autonomy agreement especially if it requires an amendment to the constitution, a referendum, or even merely new legislation.

Government leaders fear that autonomy would inhibit the performance of key state functions. Autonomy may jeopardize economic and administrative efficiency due to the complexity and duplication of administrative institutions. Autonomy inevitably adds to the costs of government (even if there are in fact efficiency gains, as much theory of decentralization claims). Autonomy may also affect the operation of the economy, especially as there may be regional taxes and restrictions on the mobility of labor or preferences for local capital. Autonomy may retard the state's function of redistribution of resources and thus place in jeopardy the very legitimacy of autonomy.

Another objection to territorially based solutions is that a complete identity of ethnicity and territory is impossible without a infinite fragmentation of the state (and even not then since some groups are dispersed throughout the state). The discrimination against groups that do not qualify for or are not granted autonomy may be unfair. There is another way in which certain groups may be treated unfairly. Ethnically based autonomy will create new minorities, and the position of these minorities will be worse than in a nonethnic state since they may be subjected to discrimination or have to acknowledge the symbols and cultures of the group enjoying the autonomy (the partition of Ireland in 1921 produced minorities on both sides of the border; the more substantial Catholic minority in Northern Ireland was then subjected to institutionalized discrimination). One has only to examine the position of minorities in the Soviet republics with their titular dominant groups or of blacks in apartheid South Africa who were deprived of South African citizenship because they were deemed to belong to territorial homelands outside that state to see the force of this argument. These kinds of discrimination may trigger demands for autonomy by the new minorities and lead to further fragmentation of the state. Connected with the preceding point is the fear that, if autonomy can be justified on ethnic grounds, the rules justifying the grant of autonomy (identity, a sense of discrimination/injustice) may encourage the mobilization of other communities along ethnic lines, indeed to manufacture ethnic communities.

There may also be anxiety that the fundamental values of the state may be compromised by the recognition through autonomy of different cultural or religious values or that these differences will work against the smooth operation of autonomous systems. A classic although simplified case of this was the civil war in the United States (when Abraham Lincoln justified the stance of the northern states by saying that "this country cannot endure permanently half slave and half free"). In more modern times this was one (although not the fundamental) reason for the rejection of a federal solution to the Jewish-Arab problem in Palestine under mandate or UN schemes (O'Brien, 1986). The Muslim League in colonial India rejected a federal solution for Muslims for the same reason, and it has been claimed that an Ethiopian-Eritrean federation was impossible for the same reason (Tekle, 1991). The position of the French in Quebec is not dissimilar. Some of the problems that arise in Hong Kong, and are likely to arise in a more acute form in Taiwan if it is unified with the Peoples Republic of China, are due to very different values and practices in mainland China. Indeed, Taiwan's position on reunification is that it cannot take place unless the mainland starts to respect human rights and practice democracy.

A specific objection to autonomy regimes comes from those who espouse an individual-oriented view of human rights. Autonomy frequently relies on group rights (such as that of indigenous peoples or in the Quebecois version), and group rights involve discrimination against both those inside and outside the group. But even those who are less committed to an individualist conception of rights have problems with some kinds of autonomy systems. Steiner (1991), valuing the diversity and richness of ethnic groups, has cautioned against autonomy regimes that hermetically divide one community from another. He writes: "Rights given ethnic minorities by human rights law to internal self-determination through autonomy regimes could amount to authorisation to them to exclude 'others'. . . . Enforced ethnic separation both inhibits intercourse among groups, and creative development within the isolated communities themselves. It impoverishes cultures and peoples" (pp. 1551-1554). Some autonomy regimes have indeed raised these difficulties, but in most states fundamental rights are protected against regional violations (Spain, India, United States).

Finally, and perhaps more fundamentally, there are widely shared fears that autonomy will be merely a springboard to secession. This is seen to be a serious problem when the group demanding autonomy is related and contiguous to a neighboring kin state (as with Indian reluctance about autonomy in Kashmir, Sri Lankan resistance to autonomy for northern Tamils, and the fear in Kuala Lumpur that Malaysian Borneo states may get too close to Indonesia). Autonomy granted to a minority in its "homeland" may in turn create new minorities (as with Muslims in northeastern Sri Lanka, which the Tamil Tigers want under their control, or Christians in Mindanao).

The mixed picture of success and the denial of autonomy suggests that it is difficult to say a priori that autonomy is an effective device. It is necessary to examine circumstances in which autonomy is likely to be negotiated and in which it is likely to be successful and the consequences of the denial of autonomy. I examine the experiences of autonomy with a view to providing some hypotheses for answering these questions. I do not necessarily assess all of the arguments for and against autonomy outlined above; instead, I focus on the feasibility and utility of autonomy from the standards of the concept and criteria of success, which is elaborated on in the next section.

CRITERIA FOR JUDGING THE SUCCESS OF AUTONOMY

Ethnicity raises complex problems of social harmony, identity, security, and equity, while autonomy itself seeks to balance various, sometimes conflicting, considerations. Success must be judged with reference to the purposes of autonomy, the primary purpose being to ensure a significant measure of self-government to a group, acknowledge its identity, promote diversity, and facilitate harmonious, or at least conflict-free relations, with other communities and the central government. The motivating factor is to bring a dispute to an end and to maintain the unity of the state. These goals frequently override other objectives of national policy, such as an efficient or fair allocation of resources, integrated economic planning, and the equal rights of all. Even within these overriding goals there may be different priorities. When a civil war is raging, attention is focused on bringing the killing to an end, rather than the long-term consequences of the settlement. It is also useful to refer to the process by which future differences are resolved; fairness and justice are also important. As Young (1998:5) has stated: "Conflict—class, interest, and ethnic— is a natural aspect of social existence; the heart of the matter is that it be conducted by civil process, by equitable rules, through dialogue and bargaining, in a framework facilitating cooperation and reconciliation."

The criteria for judging success, within these overall goals, will depend on the circumstances of the case. Gurr and Khosla (forthcoming) propose two criteria in the case of armed conflict. First, do the arrangements lead to some degree of accommodation between the interests of the parties? Each party must attain some of its objectives over the dispute. They say that in the case of communal challengers this usually means some mix of recognition, participation in governance, and material benefits; in the case of states it usually means an end to armed resistance by communal rebels and acceptance of the state's authority. The second criterion is a substantial and sustained shift away from armed conflict (a short-term shift being one that lasts less than one year). A related but more specific criterion is the durability of autonomy (Nordquist, 1998). According to Nordquist, a solution is likely to be durable, that is, an operative political solution, when it reflects and meets the needs and interests of the parties. He proposes a qualitative way of measuring durability based on a combination of two factors. A high level of durability is one in which the conflict has subsided militarily after the initiation of the autonomy *and* the autonomy has continued to exist on the basis of an operative political document after at least one constitutional change of government/head of government in the central state. A low level of durability is one in which one of these conditions is missing. As Nordquist makes clear, this is not a test of longevity, although the time factor does enter into it.

A key criterion is the manner in which the concession of autonomy transforms the previous situation. When the previous situation is marked by bloody battles, peace or the cessation of fighting itself is success. When there are differences of opinion that threaten the constitutional and political system, as in Canada, a test is whether negotiations on autonomy or alternative arrangements help to overcome extreme positions and produce a framework for a solution. Indeed, in some circumstances autonomy that ultimately leads to separation may be a good solution, as in the disintegration of empires, where there may be no credible moral, political, or economic reasons for continuation of common sovereignty.

But the success of an autonomy arrangement must also be judged by its long-term consequences. Does it lead to an improvement of ethnic relations, rehabilitation of rebels and their participation in national affairs, settlement of emerging problems through dialogue rather than the use of force, and ultimately the strengthening of national unity? Does an autonomy arrangement lead to fragmentation of the political community, with the carving of separate political spaces and the provision of mutual vetoes, based on the assumption of persistent hostilities?

It is necessary to notice some methodological problems in assessing the effectiveness of autonomy. How are we to assess the usefulness of autonomy when autonomy is abolished soon after its inauguration, as in the Sudan, Kenya, Uganda, and Ethiopia-Eriteria? On what basis can we say that the problems faced by these countries stem from that abolition? Another difficulty is that different parties have different expectations from autonomy arrangements, precluding a common measure of performance. There are frequently diverse objectives of autonomy, so that there may be a tradeoff between them. Even regarding ethnicity there are different objectives—those of separate coexistence and integration; autonomy may enhance the former at the expense of the latter. It is hard to isolate the effect of autonomy on ethnic groups from other factors that influence ethnic relations.

The end of tensions or hostilities through autonomy does not mean that tensions will not resurface. Autonomy is not purely instrumental, acting on social and political forces. It is a set of institutions and arrangements as well as process. Similar provisions have produced quite different results in different countries. Just by providing a framework for interethnic relations and negotiations, autonomy affects and shapes these relations. They may fashion new forms of identity or reinforce old ones. They may enhance or decrease the capacity of particular groups to extract resources from the state. They may provide new forms of contention and dispute. They may reduce the salience of specific problems and issues (e.g., by making them intra- rather than intercommunal). These remarks illustrate no more than that ethnic situations do not stand still and need constant readjustments. They also demonstrate that the reason for and the impact of these arrangements must be understood in specific historical and national contexts. Moreover, autonomy comes in different forms. These factors also make generalizations on the adoption or utility of these arrangements problematic. For these reasons it is necessary to avoid judging success in dichotomous terms but to locate it along a spectrum, "like a balance sheet" in Young's expression (1998:5).

EXPERIENCES OF AUTONOMY: PROPOSITIONS

From the above analysis it is evident that autonomy arrangements, appropriately arrived at and operated, can defuse and make more peaceful identity-based conflicts in states. The classical literature on federalism and autonomy is of limited utility, being based on different assumptions to those of multiethnic federalism or regional autonomy. As the analysis in this paper shows, multiethnic federations are different from other federations in their aims, structures, and operations. Moreover, while many nonethnic federations are the result of aggregation, that is, of independent and separate states or territorial units coming together, ethnic federations or regional autonomy are frequently achieved through disaggregation, that is, by devolution from the central government. The dynamics of these two methods are different; for example, in the former there is a stronger sense of the previous sovereignty of the territorial units, with the result that central powers are likely to be more limited than in the latter and there is likely to be stronger constitutional provisions for their autonomy. Aggregation tends to provide the possibility of compact and contractual federalism and so gives some kind of a moral status to the joining communities. Disaggregation tends to end up with a strong center; Jay (1989:221) says that "the very existence of an operational central heart made it difficult to contemplate a new 'bargain' or 'social contract' between the nationalities which might reconstruct the nature of center-periphery relations." Likewise, the dynamics of federalism, whether asymmetrical or not, are different from those of regional autonomy, where historically there has been a greater tolerance for diversity.

In the propositions discussed below I try to indicate the circumstances in which the grant of autonomy is feasible, the structuring of arrangements that may enhance the prospects of its success, and the social and political consequences of autonomy arrangements. The propositions do not of course fit neatly into these categories. Nor can they do more than provide a guide to policy; it is necessary to examine them in the specific context of actual conflict and its history. I pay particular attention to two factors that have dominated discussions on autonomy—the viability of asymmetrical arrangements and the tendency of autonomy toward secession.

Propositions About Circumstances When the Concession of Autonomy Is Likely

The prospects of establishing autonomy arrangements are strongest when the state undergoes a regime change. The establishment of autonomy involves a major reorganization of the state. Those who enjoy positions of power in the apparatus of the state are unlikely to give up their control of power willingly. They may of course be compelled to renegotiate the structure of the state if irresistible or strong pressures build up for reform or their own position becomes weaker (as when autonomy was provided for southern Sudan).

Times of regime change provide opportunities for autonomy for a variety of reasons. Those who are in charge of the transition may have been opposed to the previous centralized system. The framers of the 1994 Ethiopian Constitution had fought against the centralization of both Emperor Selassie and his communist successors, which had denied recognition to the ethnic diversity of the Ethiopian people and thus stifled them (Nahum, 1997). The end of an old regime may usher in a new balance of forces that may necessitate or facilitate restructuring of the state (as in Spain). The new or aspiring leaders may need to find allies, to be secured by the promise of autonomy (as with the rise of the communist regimes in the Soviet Union and China; Connor, 1984; Mackerras, 1994). After the collapse of the Soviet Union, Russia tried to maintain its territorial integrity by promising autonomy to its constituent parts (Smith, 1996; Lynn and Novikov, 1997). The Philippines conceded the principle of autonomy for the indigenous people and the southern Muslims after the overthrow of Marcos both because autonomy was more consistent with notions of people power and because the new regime needed to consolidate its hold on power.

The weakness of a new regime may be seized on by groups wanting secession or autonomy by pushing their demands. There was considerable optimism in East Timor in 1998 that the crisis of the Indonesian state would facilitate its independence or at least a high degree of autonomy. Similarly, Tibetan leaders considered that the end of the Cultural Revolution was propitious for its own autonomy and for a time the prospects looked promising. However, experience does not suggest that a change in regime will always lead to autonomy when a group is demanding it.

Change in a regime has commonly come with the independence of a state (largely with decolonization), which provides an opportunity for a fresh look at the apparatus of the state and a structure to accommodate new social and political forces. Imperial rule produced many multiethnic colonies; centralized rule established during colonial rule was unacceptable to many communities upon independence. A large number of autonomy arrangements were established upon independence (e.g., India, Nigeria, Ghana, Kenya, Uganda, Papua New Guinea, Vanuatu, and Indonesia). The end of British sovereignty over Hong Kong was facilitated by extensive autonomy under Chinese sovereignty. Sometimes autonomy is established following a compromise among local groups; sometimes it is forced by the colonial power. The latter has been more common. It is less likely to ensure the successful implementation of autonomy because the majority resents the imposition (as in Cyprus). For that reason few autonomy regimes in Africa have survived for any length of time after independence.

Autonomy arrangements are likely to be established if the international community becomes involved in conflict resolution. At both the international and the regional levels there has been considerable support for autonomy, as reflected in emerging international norms. The increasing involvement of the international community in national conflicts has facilitated the application of these norms to the settlement of conflicts. The League of Nations showed a particular preference for autonomy, and a number of treaties for minority protection were based on autonomy, of which Åland's autonomy survives to this day. Contemporary examples include Bosnia Herzogovina, the Rambouillet proposals for Kosovo, Crimea, Palestine, and the continuing involvement of the UN in a search for a federal solution in Cyprus. The Organisation of Islamic States brought considerable pressure on the Philippine Muslims to accept autonomy; in Sri Lanka the Indian government intervened to secure autonomy for the Tamils; and the UN oversaw the development of autonomy proposals for East Timor. It is not surprising that the international community, consisting of states, is reluctant to see the dismemberment of states; autonomy seems a suitable compromise. Pressures to accept autonomy are facilitated by the willingness of the international community to guarantee it and to provide material and other incentives (such as for the EU and the OSCE to offer greater integration into the European system).

However, once autonomy is established, the international community is less willing to provide continuing support. It is reluctant to make long-term commitments, particularly as they involve continuing intervention in the affairs of a state and are likely to require police or military maneuvers and considerable sums of money. Yet international involvement for a substantial period of time is frequently necessary as strong-arm tactics may have been required to impose autonomy. The Cyprus independence settlement broke down because the United Kingdom, Greece, and Turkey were not willing to abide by the guarantees they had given, and India withdrew from its participation in the Sri Lankan scheme for autonomy because of pressure on its military. However, the EU and NATO now appear to accept that they are in Bosnia and Kosovo for the long haul.

Autonomy arrangements are most likely to succeed in states that have established traditions of democracy and the rule of law. Of autonomy arrangements in liberal societies, communist states, and third world states, most successful examples are in liberal societies (Ghai, 1998a). The record is worst in communist states, where provisions for autonomy for areas dominated by a titular nationality were negated by the overall control of the Communist Party, with little commitment to pluralism. The record in the third world is mixed, with some successful examples but also some spectacular failures. The reason that liberal societies have the best record is that they have established traditions of democracy and the rule of law. On the whole, pluralism is valued and there is respect for cultural and religious differences. Autonomy arrangements require give and take; they depend on frequent negotiations for adjustments of relationships or the implementation of law. Elected representatives at the center and regions enjoy the support of their people and are respected as such. The law provides the framework for relations between the center and regions and defines the powers of the respective governments. Disputes on the meaning of the law are resolved ultimately by the courts, whose decisions must be respected by all parties concerned. These conclusions are borne out by Nordquist's (1998) research, who found a strong relationship between the level of democracy at the center and the durability of autonomy. He concluded that democratic countries were most hospitable to autonomy and that Europe was the most successful region in the practice of autonomy.

Autonomy has a better chance of success if the autonomous area is small, has limited resources, and is marginal to the state. A state finds it easier to accommodate the aspirations of small communities for autonomy. Small communities may not be strong enough to pose the threat of secession. Autonomy may not involve a substantial reorganization of the state. Indeed, it may involve hardly any reorganization, as forms of local government can be used for their self-government. The impact of small communities or the territories they inhabit on the larger political or economic system is often negligible. Typically, these autonomies also exist on the geographical peripheries of the state—another factor that might minimize their impact on the state. Some of the most successful autonomies fall into this category: Åland, Faroes, and Greenland (Denmark); Azores and Madeira (Portugal); the Channel Islands (Britain); Saami (various Nordic states); and Corsica (France). The form that this kind of autonomy takes is often that of regional autonomy or federacy.

These uncontroversial autonomies can be compared with, for example, the autonomies of Buganda and southern Sudan. Both of these regions were central to the politics of their states. Buganda was also physically central. Both had rich resources that were then or are potentially of great significance to the economic well-being and development of the state. In neither case could the authority of the central government be effectively consolidated as long as these autonomous areas were not brought under a greater measure of national hegemony. The experiences of the autonomy of Bougainville in Papua New Guinea serve to remind us that an island, although geographically separated from the other parts of Papua New Guinea and containing only a small proportion of the national population, can be caught up in the maelstrom of national politics if it is rich in resources. The mineral wealth of Bougainville meant that national politics would always impact on policies of the island and that there would be serious limits on its autonomy. The larger territories that had happier experiences with autonomy, as in Spain, have nevertheless profound impact on national policies and institutions, and the negotiation and establishment of autonomy have been difficult and complex.

Autonomy is easier to concede and is likely to succeed when there is no dispute about sovereignty. Autonomy has been a cause of great contention because it is associated with assertions of or qualifications on state sovereignty. Autonomy becomes less problematic if it can be disassociated from sovereignty. China's official position is that it would be prepared to discuss autonomy for Tibet if the Dalai Lama acknowledged that Tibet was an inalienable part of China. China was able to accept autonomy for Hong Kong in part because its leaders realized that it was inconceivable that the residents would ever try to secede. Franco's followers were prepared to discuss regional autonomy in Spain only when agreement was reached on what is now Article 2 of the 1978 constitution: "The Constitution is based on the indissoluble unity of the Spanish Nation, the common and indivisible country of all Spaniards." In some countries preemptive steps are taken against the concession of large measures of autonomy by declaring the unitary nature of the state or the inalienability of the legislative supremacy of the national parliament (e.g., Sri Lanka and Papua New Guinea, respectively).

Autonomy is easier either because the autonomists are not claiming independence or because the national government is not concerned with maintaining sovereignty. The classic example of the latter situation is the attitude of a metropolitan state to its associated states. The decolonization of the Cook Islands and Niue was accomplished by their transformation as associated states of New Zealand. The Cook Islands enjoy a considerable amount of autonomy; over the years their autonomy has increased, under encouragement from New Zealand. New Zealand would not be upset if the Cook Islands wanted to break off the association. In fact, links to that sovereignty are more important to the Cook Islands for they entitle Cook Islanders the right to enter and reside in New Zealand (and derivatively Australia). Relations between Åland and Finland are relaxed and cordial because Finland is not now overly concerned with the maintenance of its sovereignty over Åland, whereas the Ålanders see significant benefits from their connection with Finland. Italy was able to contemplate significant autonomy for South Tyrol with a substantial majority of Austro-Germans once the proportion of Italian-speaking residents had increased (principally with its merger with Trentino). The autonomy of linguistic provinces in India, which have no separatist ambitions, has been much less problematic than in Kashmir, whose status has been more controversial. Regional autonomy in Sri Lanka has become difficult because of the secessionist claims of the Tamil Tigers. It also reflects a situation in which autonomy is rejected by its potential beneficiaries precisely because the acceptance of autonomy is seen to compromise their grander design of independence.

The success of autonomy negotiations may therefore depend on diffusing, fragmenting, or fudging sovereignty. One method lies in the use of terminology; *federation* may imply splitting sovereignty, and so the labels *devolution, autonomy,* or *decentralization* can be used to obscure the extent of autonomy (as in Spain or Papua New Guinea). The Ethiopian constitution finesses sovereignty by declaring that all sovereignty lies among its many diverse "Nations, Nationalities and Peoples." This approach was foreshadowed in the 1974 Yugoslav constitution that defined the units of the federation as "states based on the sovereignty of the people" (a provision that also held the federation hostage to the "people" of the different republics). In a more practical way the sovereignty of Northern Ireland has been fudged through a kind of condominium arrangement. Jay (1989) had anticipated the Good Friday agreement when he said that an opening lay in recognizing Northern Ireland's location at the interstices of two sovereign powers, a border area for which both might assume responsibility, focusing on federalism not as a constitutional process but as a broad process of building institutional links across exclusive areas of sovereignty.

The reverse side of the coin is to make autonomy acceptable to the recipients by attaching the indicia of sovereignty to it—in the form, for example, of regional flags, distinct passports, regional stamps, and grand titles like republics and premiers.

Autonomy is more likely to be negotiated and to succeed if there are several ethnic groups rather than two. Autonomy arrangements that bring together two communities have a poor record. They are, to start with, hard to negotiate. Negotiations between the Cypriot Greeks and Turks for a federation have led nowhere after more than 20 years. Autonomy discussions in Sri Lanka have been bedeviled by the Sinhala-Tamil polarity. The problem in Cyprus is that the Greeks want a strong center and the Turks want strong regions; the former would enhance the role of the Greek community in the affairs of Cyprus, and the latter would grant greater autonomy to the Turks. Similar dialetics have obstructed agreement in Sri

Lanka, and the government has effectively subordinated the present devolution arrangements to its policy objectives. The collapse of the Czechoslovakian federation occurred due to similar differences as to its role; the Slovaks, as a minority, wanted a weak center with Slovakia as the main arena of its activities, while the Czechs saw the federal authorities as the main avenue of policy and administration (Pithart, 1994). The collapse of the Ethiopia-Eriterian and Pakistan federations is attributed to the desire of the Ethiopian emperor and the West Pakistanis to use federal institutions to rule Eriteria and what is now Bangladesh, respectively. (If the need is to accommodate one or two small geographically based minorities, regional autonomy rather than federalism may be a better solution.)

Even when agreement may be forthcoming, the federation may be hard to operate when there are basically two communities (or when, as in Canada now, the founding assumption of the federation of two communities has been outlived). Biracial federations with about equal-sized communities have larger possibilities of conflict and limited scope for tradeoffs. When the communities are unequal, the federal arrangements become merely a form for supplication by the smaller community to the larger—in patent negation of the federal principle (as the Francophones in Canada often claim). Tripolarity, while an improvement, is still fraught with problems, as in the original Nigerian federation (Watts, 1994a). A larger number of groups allows for flexibility in arrangements and the establishment of a certain kind of balance and has the capacity to diffuse what are essentially bilateral disputes. A bigger constellation of interests have a stake in the success of the federal arrangements and the clout to achieve this (well demonstrated by the Indian experience, where there are numerous linguistic, religious, and regional groups, although the Papua New Guinea-Bougainville experience shows that multipolarity cannot always diffuse bilateral problems).

Consequently, ways should be found to transform bipolarity into multipolarity. Nigeria achieved multipolarity (and some equality among the new regions) by dividing existing regions, particularly the dominant north, into several regions. Papua New Guinea based its regions neither on the Papua New Guinea divide nor the highland-coastal-island divide but on the more numerous districts. Spain achieved multipolarity by extending the offer of autonomy to communities defined as "nonhistoric" and Sri Lanka tried to make autonomy more palatable to the Sinhala by dividing the Sinhala-dominated area into districts and generalizing autonomy. Belgium has tried to overcome bipolarity by a combination of regional and cultural councils, providing some cross-cutting cleavages.

Multipolarity is helpful if all territorial units are to be equal partners. Sometimes multipolarity cannot be achieved in this way. Canada has become multipolar in recent years, with the claims of the aboriginals and recent immigrants but has served merely to complicate Canada's problems. If multipolarity leads to differential or competing claims, implying asymmetry, negotiating agreement on autonomy can be very difficult (see below).

   Autonomy is more likely to be conceded and to succeed in being conceded and in operation where it is not explicitly based on ethnicity. Ethnically based claims to autonomy provoke resentment among the majority community. For that reason it is harder to persuade the majority community to concede it. Autonomies based on ethnicity may also be harder to operate, for if the autonomous regions are separated by ethnic differences, there may be more antagonism than cooperation. The relative success of autonomy in Switzerland, India, and until recently in Canada is explained on the basis of cross-cutting identities. In Switzerland, for example, there are three principal languages (German, French, and Italian) and one subsidiary (Romansch), of which the dominant one is German, being spoken by 65 percent of the people, followed by the French, with nearly 44 percent. It also has two major religions (Catholics constitute just over 47 percent of the population and Protestants just over 44 percent). In addition, the communities that make up the country have strong local traditions and loyalties, fostered by the topography. Although each of the cantons has a majority of one or other linguistic communities, there is no direct relationship between territory and religion or between religion and language. This provides for a measure of flexibility without detracting from the distinctive linguistic orientation of a canton. Autonomy in Indian federalism is based primarily on language, but different linguistic groups have many cross-cutting identities in religion, caste, and traditions. The current problems in Canada perhaps spring from an exclusive emphasis on one criterion at the expense of cross-cutting identities that would reduce its salience. From the Francophones' point of view, the emergence of claims based on other ethnicities might well turn out to be a blessing, allowing for a more balanced federation, but it is not perceived in this way by them.
   Many modern autonomy systems are based on ethnicity, for even in territories with mixed populations, ethnicity is reintroduced through consociatialist arrangements (as in Bosnia and Kosovo). Such arrangements bring in all the complicated rules of consociatialism, like separate electorates and blocking mechanisms, which put an enormous strain on autonomy.

Propositions About Actions that Can Increase the Likelihood that an Autonomy Arrangement Will Succeed

Autonomy arrangements that have been negotiated in a democratic and participatory way have better chances of success than those that in effect are imposed. The process of negotiating autonomy affects its success. Many systems of autonomy that were established in the dying days of colonialism were imposed rather than negotiated—the price that nationalist leaders had to pay for independence. Those leaders resented the systems of autonomy and took early opportunities to dismantle them. In most instances, members of the groups for whose benefit autonomies were established had little understanding of the mechanisms. At best the arrangements were interelite bargains. Some contemporary settlements may suffer from the same difficulties—agreements produced in the hothouses of hegemonic powers.

Participatory and negotiated settlements are more likely to have dealt with pressing problems, avoiding the superficiality of settlements produced under heavy external pressure. They are likely to represent a balance of interests. The parties have a stake in their success. The least successful of India's autonomies is Kashmir, which was not negotiated but provided for in response to a complex international situation, with Kashmiris not having been involved, and the other Indians resenting what they regard as unfair privileges for Kashmir. A negotiated settlement may also convince the party sceptical of autonomy of its value; for example, in Nicaragua the Sandistas were impressed, during negotiations, with the advantages of autonomy for peace and unity that modified their class-based analysis of political organizations (Gabriel, 1996). Negotiated settlements may also help develop understandings among contesting parties, facilitating the implementation of autonomy.

Participation, however, is not a *sine non quo* of success. Ålanders were not only not involved in the negotiations for their autonomy but were initially opposed to it (as representing a lesser degree of recognition than they wanted). However, subsequent changes to the system of autonomy involved their full participation, and now Ålanders have a strong sense of ownership of autonomy. Hong Kong's autonomy also owes little to the participation of its residents, being an agreement between the incoming and departing sovereigns. However, Hong Kong's autonomy is valued greatly by its residents because they realize that the alternative would be complete assimilation into the Chinese political and economic system. Contemporary examples of autonomy, like Bosnia-Herzegovina, Crimea, and the NATO proposal for Kosovo, have been secured under considerable external pressure and negotiated at best through elites, not the people.

The last statement raises the question of the role of referenda or plebiscites on autonomy—on which there seems to be no standard practice. The peace proposals in Northern Ireland, the autonomy arrangements for Scotland and Wales, the various constitutional accords in Canada, and the choice between autonomy and independence in New Caledonia and East Timor have been put to the people. On the other hand, there were no referenda in Bosnia, Sri Lanka, Papua New Guinea, or Mindanao. It is hard to generalize about the role of the referendum. First, there are technical problems to overcome—the form of choice put to the people and who votes in such referenda (e.g., all of the people or only those in the proposed autonomy area). The Canadian experience of recent decades shows the destabilizing effect of referenda, although arrangements that do not enjoy popular support may also be hard to implement. If there is substantial public support for autonomy, a referendum can consolidate the agreement and isolate politicians who may be opposed to it (as in Northern Ireland). But equally, a referendum, under the influence of extremists, may thwart an agreement that has been carefully negotiated to satisfy different, including minority, groups when unpopular concessions may have been necessary. Sometimes political leaders are ahead of the people; at times they are behind. This consideration affects the role of the referendum.

Systems that provide for consultation and mechanisms for renegotiation are more likely to succeed. In any system of devolution of power there are likely to be disputes about the proper relationship between different levels of government. Modern systems are more cooperative than coordinate; that is, they require or facilitate cooperation between different levels. In such instances it is extremely important to have mechanisms through which cooperation can be pursued and disputes resolved. Ultimately, as shown below, these disputes may have to be resolved by the judiciary, but it is sensible to try to resolve them by political means first. Some disputes are unsuitable for judicial resolution and are best dealt with through political settlements. A spirit of consultation and good-faith negotiations are vital for autonomy systems. Both are also vital to a democratic system, a point on which the Canadian Supreme Court placed a particular emphasis in its August 1998 decision on whether Quebec had a right to secede from Canada (2 SCR 217, 1998). Indeed, Canada has pursued this strategy for several years now in its search for a constitutional settlement that would satisfy the aspirations of the Francophones and First Nations—and a host of other special interests. They have not solved all of the problems (see criticisms by Russell, 1993) but have kept Canada from falling apart and have lent to the participants a sense of common enterprise. Switzerland's success is often attributed to habits of consultations and negotiations. The integrity of India as a state can also be attributed to the willingness to negotiate differences: so often when a region has been on the brink of breaking away, negotiations have been initiated and disaster averted.

As the Canadian Supreme Court has pointed out, it is important that negotiations be conducted in good faith. If they are not, negotiations can be counterproductive. This point is well illustrated by the experience of Papua New Guinea. The relevant constitutional instruments provided for various mechanisms for consultation and mediation, particularly important as they also provided for the phased transfer of powers to the provinces. Meetings were indeed held regularly, but the central government regularly disregarded agreements reached or recommendations made. This created great resentment in the provinces, particularly in the eastern island provinces, including Bougainville (Ghai and Regan, 1992).

The South African experience shows the importance of negotiating seriously claims of autonomy and in that process to changed perspectives of the parties. In January 1994 the South African legislature adopted a new constitution that was negotiated between various political groups, principally the African National Congress and the National Party. The Inkatha Freedom Party (largely Zulu) and some white groups stayed out of the settlement that had produced the 1994 constitution, until the principle of provincial autonomy and provision for a Volkstaat Council to pursue further proposals for self-government were accepted. This recognition by itself defused ethnic tensions and enabled subsequent agreement on a system of regionalism in which the provincial authorities participate in national law making (Klug, 2000).

Successful arrangements are likely to have built in flexibility to deal with an evolving situation. Ethnic relations/situations are both fluid and dynamic. They are affected by changing economic circumstances, international developments, changing expectations of groups, and manipulation of ethnic sentiments by political or religious leaders. Solutions that may have been acceptable at one time may no longer be acceptable at a later date. Also, not all groups desire the same solutions; some groups may want greater autonomy than would satisfy other groups. It is therefore useful to have arrangements for autonomy that can respond to changing situations.

Classical federations provided for one model for its constituents. Changes in their relationship with the center required constitutional amendments. India has created several new states since independence, but they have to fit into one model (with a major exception for Kashmir and minor exceptions for a few other states). In recent years, however, constitutional arrangements have provided considerable flexibility. Spain and Papua New Guinea essentially set up a framework for negotiations for autonomy. Provinces desiring autonomy can request it, subject to procedures in the province to ensure that the request has the support of the majority of its people. There is also flexibility about the powers that a province may acquire; a province can make requests from a menu of powers but must satisfy certain tests before it can get more than a pre-scribed minimum. Powers can be phased in over a period of time, as the province demonstrates its ability to take on additional responsibilities. The arrangements under the Charlottetown Accord in Canada would have provided for negotiations by various groups for their autonomy or rights.

While this flexibility (and the habits of negotiations it generates) has positive consequences, it is not without its critics. From the point of view of a group wanting autonomy, there is an advantage in getting what it wants in one go; there are critical moments in history when the group is in a strong negotiating position, such as when it is willing to end a revolt or there are international pressures on the central government. If the prov-ince does not capitalize on that moment, it may be unable to secure trans-fers of further power. This is very much the experience in Papua New Guinea; no province has been able to secure further powers than were conceded upon the establishment of autonomy.

There are other reasons as well that militate against flexibility. Too much time can be spent on negotiations. Negotiations can become acri-monious. The center can drag its feet or impose additional preconditions for transfers of new powers. This was the experience in Spain; it seemed at one point as if the whole scheme might collapse. Negotiations require good faith on the side of all parties. But if this good faith is forthcoming, there is much to be said for flexibility.

An independent dispute settlement mechanism is essential to long-term op-eration. Autonomy is based on constitutional and legal provisions. The enforcement of these provisions through what we might call the principle of legality, is essential to the maintenance of autonomy. Disputes can and do arise as to the scope and meaning of provisions. The persistence of autonomy depends crucially on how these disputes are resolved. The most common form for this is judicial; courts are traditionally concerned with solving constitutional disputes. They are qualified for this task be-cause of their well-established independence and competence and the rules of due process that ensure a fair hearing of all parties. Courts also enjoy considerable public respect and are thus well placed to provide authoritative and binding decisions.

Courts provide protection for a party with limited or no political clout (compare tiny Åland with the Finnish state). Papua New Guinea provided a limited and residual role for courts in intergovernmental rela-tions. But the political processes it envisaged did not produce harmony or progress because the center had little interest in autonomy. When the existing autonomy was invaded by the center, it was the judiciary that came to the assistance of provinces, although courts have not already supported provincial autonomy (Ghai and Regan, 1992). In India the more recent interventionist stand of the judiciary has helped curb the arbitrary suspension of regional governments by the national government. Experience in Spain has been somewhat similar; a key decision of the Constitutional Court was necessary to overcome legislative and bureaucratic obstacles to constitutionally guaranteed autonomy. In South Africa the Constitutional Court has played a valuable role in adjudicating disputes between the center and the provinces and in maintaining a balance between them. In the former Yugoslavia, the only communist federation to provide for a constitutional court, the court was unable to stem the disintegration despite its rulings on legislative and administrative competence of state institutions geared to the maintenance of the federation—political forces were firmly in control by then. In Hong Kong the absence of secure guarantees of autonomy that can be enforced through independent courts is a major weakness. The final powers of interpretation vested in the Standing Committee of the National People's Congress, a political body under the control of the Communist Party, have effectively negated the autonomy.

It is not necessary, and indeed may not be desirable, that courts should be the first port of call when a dispute arises. A political settlement of disputes can strengthen autonomy (and the consensus on autonomy) more effectively than a court decision. Also, there are some kinds of disputes (e.g., regarding the allocation of funds or forms of intergovernmental cooperations) that cannot be regulated through rules; a bargaining and negotiating process is more suitable. Unfortunately, experience shows that this process cannot always be relied on, for the center may disregard representations of weak regions. Therefore, the ultimate authority of courts should be provided. Judicial decisions need not curb political bargaining; their function is to maintain constitutional parameters and when necessary provide authoritative rulings to break political deadlocks (as the Canadian Supreme Court has tried to do, in contrast with the more authoritarian style of its predecessor, the Privy Council). A balance between political and judicial processes is necessary to ensure the successful operation of autonomy.

A careful design of institutional structures is essential for the success of autonomy. On the whole, international and regional norms say little about the content and structure of autonomy (although the OSCE has produced some guidelines), and there is inadequate knowledge of various technical points in the drafting of autonomy arrangements. There is frequently such pressure for agreement on broad political principles that institutional details are paid insufficient attention. It is not possible here to expand on what would be useful structures; instead I draw attention to some key considerations. The system for settlement of disputes and the procedures for flexibility and ongoing negotiations have already been discussed.

Autonomy arrangements should be properly guaranteed. Sometimes they can be guaranteed through treaties; experience has shown, though, that these are seldom effective. They should be entrenched in the domestic constitutional order. This is common for federalism but not always for regional autonomy. It is best to entrench autonomy in such a way that the consent of the region is necessary for change.

In federations by disaggregation and in regional autonomy, provision is often made for the center to issue directives to the regional government in specified areas. The central government also has the power to suspend regional government for prescribed reasons. These provisions can sour center-regional relations and limit the exercise of regional autonomy. Such provisions should be avoided if possible; where they are considered necessary, adequate safeguards against the abuse of the power of suspension should be inscribed in the law.

Democratic structures are necessary for the exercise and protection of autonomy. Democratic politics in the region both compel regional leaders to protect autonomy and empower them to do so. The failure of autonomy in the former Yugoslavia is often explained by the absence of democratic politics (Malesevic, 2000). The weakening of autonomy in Hong Kong is the result of having a China-appointed executive and a nondemocratic legislature (Ghai, 1997, 1998).

Agreement on autonomy is easier if guarantees of the rights of minorities, which are created by autonomy arrangements, can be secured. In Canada provision was made from the very beginning of the federation for provincial minorities to appeal to the center against discrimination, but this power was seldom used and is unlikely to be used now. Considerable attention has been paid to devices for regional protection of minorities. Most constitutions now include bills of rights that preclude discrimination and other forms of oppression. Local government structures and powers can be entrenched (as in Nigeria). There can be special representation for minorities on local councils; this is often linked to forms of power sharing (as in Sri Lanka). There can be cultural councils for minorities, as in Estonia and Hungary. The most elaborate schemes have been established in Bosnia and Herzogovina and in the proposals for Kosovo, inspired by Lijphartian consociatialism. China provides autonomy whenever there is a concentration of a minority, so that in autonomous regions there may be autonomous townships controlled by minorities.

Of particular importance in ethnic autonomy is the method for the division of legislative and executive competence. There are different methods of division, depending on whether or not relations between the center and regions are seen as cooperative. Cooperative federalism, in which governments at different levels coordinate policies, is more fashionable now given the complexity of economic and social life, but for ethnic autonomy there may be considerable desire for separate policy making, so that regional autonomy for cultural and other policies can be exercised without regard to central directions of legislative powers. It is important to avoid divisions and institutional arrangements that rely heavily on cooperation. It is easier to provide for separate policy making in regional rather than federal autonomy.

Propositions About the Social and Political Consequences of Autonomy Arrangements

Asymmetric arrangements are a characteristic feature of ethnic autonomy, but they tend toward symmetry. A major factor that distinguishes ethnic autonomy from classical federations is its asymmetrical features. Just as in liberal theory all individuals must be treated equally, so must regions in a federation. This approach is not very constructive when autonomy is used to acknowledge and manage ethnic differences. Asymmetry acknowledges the unevenness of diversities. It opens up additional possibilities of awarding recognition to specific groups whose needs or capacities may be different from other groups, such as indigenous peoples whose traditional culture is central to their way of life or a minority linguistic group (both are present in Canada). Examples of asymmetry abound; China has at least four types of autonomy (economic zones, metropolitan cities, ethnic minorities, and special administrative regions) responding to different imperatives (Ghai, 2000). So has India, with its "standard" provinces, special arrangements for Kashmir, and provinces in the northeast, tribal areas, and union territories, each enjoying a different relationship with the center.

Asymmetry arises in various ways. Regional autonomy is, by definition, asymmetrical. Sometimes the constitution enables a region to negotiate with the center for autonomy and establishes a menu from which powers may be devolved (Spain, Papua New Guinea, Russia). This can result in only some regions having autonomy and those with autonomy having different degrees of autonomy. A region may be free to legislate on a list of powers, in default of which central laws apply; some regions may make more use of this facility than others. Regions may be endowed with the power of determining their own structures for the exercise of autonomy, leading to differences in constitutional arrangements. National laws may apply differentially for other reasons, the outstanding example being the "notwithstanding" clause in Canada that enables a province to opt out of most provisions of the Charter of Rights under prescribed conditions and another provision that limits the application of the charter in aboriginal areas by the supremacy of treaties between indigenous groups and the Crown. Asymmetry can also be used as a general technique for opting out of a scheme or for a phased entry to full membership, as has happened frequently with the EU. Other forms of asymmetry include special representation for a region at the center (Quebec's entitlements to seats in the Senate and the Supreme Court) or special voting power given to the region at the center (double voting or vetoes). On a corporate basis, asymmetry arises out of the application of special bodies of laws, including personal laws. Residents of a region may have special rights, at least in the region, that are not available to other citizens (as in the concept of a permanent resident of the Hong Kong Special Administrative Region; Ghai, 2000). Asymmetry enables different degrees of assimilation or integration into the state. In these ways asymmetry opens up possibilities of accommodating the special concerns of a group or region. Questions about the feasibility of negotiating and sustaining asymmetry are therefore fundamental to the design and operation of ethnic autonomy. The viability of the Russian federation depends on the acceptance and successful operation of asymmetry; 88 units have different relationships with Moscow.

In recent decades there has been increasing use of asymmetry, although its feasibility was noted by Mill as early as 1861 (Mill, 1972). Perhaps it is not surprising that asymmetry has also become controversial; concerns about it have, for example, prevented a satisfactory resolution of Canada's constitutional problems. It is in Canada that the issue has been most extensively debated, in politics as well as academia. Canadian academics have argued that differences over asymmetry may be the undoing of ethnic or multinational federations. Milne (1994:159) noted an "overwhelmingly" hostile attitude toward proposals for asymmetry in Canada (see also Kymlicka, 1998a, 1998b). There is resentment in India toward the privileged position of Kashmir (Kashyap, 1990), although it has not emerged as a major political issue, perhaps because of Indo-Pakistani conflict over Kashmir. It is said that President Habibe offered independence to East Timor because he was afraid that the UN proposals for autonomy would set a precedent for other provinces of Indonesia and that it would be politically difficult to restrict the high degree of substantive and institutional autonomy to East Timor.

One objection to asymmetry is that it is administratively and politically difficult to manage. The center has to deal with regions with varying degrees of devolution and different institutional structures. This can pose problems in states as well developed as Spain; it can be a nightmare in states with less efficient bureaucracies or politicians not given to political compromises (as in Papua New Guinea and Ethiopia). A consultancy firm that advised Papua New Guinea on the implementation of decentralization, expected to be asymmetrical under negotiated constitutional provisions, recommended the equal devolution of powers to all provinces, regardless of their capacity or willingness to assume these powers. If this proposal avoided one bureaucratic nightmare, it created another—poorly equipped provinces struggling to carry out new responsibilities, which they neither understood or wanted. The result was continuing domination by central bureaucrats and a not inconsiderable degree of inefficiency (Ghai and Regan, 1992).

But the political problems with asymmetry are even more decisive. I have already referred to the difficulty of conceding autonomy on a purely ethnic basis. The difficulty is greater if only one or two groups are to enjoy autonomy. If the national government is inclined to support autonomy, it may have to generalize conditions for the granting of autonomy. In Papua New Guinea in 1976, negotiations for autonomy were conducted between the national government and representatives of Bougainville. The assumption was that the arrangements under negotiations were for Bougainville only, and in fact Bougainville leaders insisted that only their province was to be entitled to them (to recognize their distinctiveness). However, the government realized that parliamentary support for these arrangements could not be guaranteed unless all provinces were given similar options. Similar developments took place in Spain, where all provinces or groupings of provinces were given roughly the same options as the "historic territories." Increasingly, Spain takes on the appearance of a federation and a symmetrical one at that. The devolution to provincial councils in Sri Lanka followed a similar trajectory, diluting the special claims of Tamils to autonomy. Asymmetry has come under considerable attack in Canada. In Britain, following autonomies for Scotland and Wales, there is agitation for officially defined English regions. The tendency toward symmetry is, however, not universal; sometimes there may be a recognition of the historical claims of a community or the clear distinctiveness, and vulnerability, of its culture (as in Greenland, Faroes, Åland, Corsica, and Cordilleras). Sometimes a community may desire a greater measure of political integration than asymmetry would permit; for example, the Swedish-speaking community on the Finnish mainland rejected the offer of an Åland type of autonomy.

Asymmetry is particularly controversial when the region benefiting from it wants equal or even superior representation in central institutions. Logically, the region should not participate in decisions at the national level on areas that are within its autonomy, for then it would be making decisions for other regions, especially when the votes of its representatives hold the balance. When there is substantial asymmetrical autonomy, the moral or political right of the representatives of an autonomous region to count toward a parliamentary majority and thus determine the formation of the central government group can be questioned. Claims might be made by the rest of the country that representatives from that region should be excluded from holding ministries whose portfolios cover areas within asymmetrical autonomy or indeed that the number of ministries given to them should be severely restricted. If there is equal representation for the autonomous region, other provinces would resent it; if the representation is less favorable, the region would tend to look inward, political parties would tend to become regional and the region's integration with the state would weaken.

The conversion of asymmetry into symmetry is not necessarily against the interests of the original claimants of autonomy. They would cease to be the object of envy and resentment. A greater number of beneficiaries would produce a more balanced state. It would also increase the capacity of regions to negotiate with the center and extract higher benefits. But for many groups the exact amount of devolved power is less important than they alone should enjoy some special powers, as a way to mark their status. If the powers they have are generalized, they increase their own demands for more, leading not only to a higher level of general devolution than is desirable or desired but also pushing the special groups toward confederal solutions. They regard asymmetry as a proper recognition of their "distinctive society" status (to use the Canadian parlance). This conflict, rather than bureaucratic problems of managing institutional diversity, is the real problem besetting asymmetry. Kymlicka (1998a, 1989b) has pointed to a number of problems about asymmetry in Canada that may make it unsustainable. If a group insists on asymmetry and others do not concede it, the stalemate may result in attempts at secession (as some Quebecois are threatening). On the other hand, the concession of asymmetry merely encourages the demand for further powers and emboldens the group, having already won and operating with a large measure of autonomy, to go to the logical next step, that of separate statehood. It is said that Chamberlain considered the asymmetrical home rule proposals for Ireland to have such a potential for the breakup of the British Empire that he even contemplated a symmetrically constituted British federation (Jay, 1989).

The future feasibility and viability of multiethnic autonomy thus depend greatly on how asymmetry is negotiated. While the utility of asymmetry may be acknowledged, political and bureaucratic difficulties may limit its application. On the other hand, it must be noted that outside Canada the difficulties are more theoretical than practical. The Indian experience and that of other federations shows that groups claiming or enjoying autonomy do not see themselves as nations alienated from others. They are strongly bonded to the wider nation and their representatives, through regional or national parties, and play a full part in national institutions. But equally one must not underestimate the ability of politicians to erect these theoretical difficulties into real barriers to asymmetrical autonomy.

Autonomy does not promote secession; true autonomy prevents it. I have already discussed examples where the concession of autonomy has reconciled ethnic minorities to the state and diluted the appeal of secession. The concession of autonomy reduces the level of the stridency of minorities and the consciousness of their ethnic identity. Such concession strengthens the hands of the moderates in the ethnic group. Equally the denial or removal of autonomy aggravates ethnic discontent and sentiments of separatism and enables those least interested in a peaceful solution to exploit the sense of grievance of the group. Nevertheless, it is widely believed that territorial autonomy will lead to secession and that corporate autonomy will impede national integration.

Autonomy increases the resources and strengthens the identities of regional minorities, frequently justifying a claim of secession under the principles of self-determination. Moreover, Kymlicka (1989) argues, the members of one ethnic group are indifferent to the rights and interests of the other groups and are unwilling to make sacrifices for them, particularly since they do not expect reciprocity (Kymlicka, 1989). He considers that multinational federations are inflexible and prone to deadlocks and instability, particularly in the ways that boundaries are drawn or powers divided. Kymlicka draws attention to what he claims is a paradox—that the more the federation is successful in promoting the interest of national minorities, "the more it will strengthen the sense that these minorities are a separate people with inherent rights of self-government, whose participation in the larger country is conditional and revocable" (p. 140).

In practice the situation is quite different. Few instances of the granting of autonomy have led to secession. What it has led to is a demand by other groups for similar treatment, leading to a kind of dispersal of authority. What this often does is strengthen national unity; the Indian and Papua New Guinean experiences with their linguistic communities are evidence. Secession frequently arises when autonomy is denied or abolished.

In discussing secession it may be important to make a distinction between federations by aggregation and disaggregation. In the first case the federation is based on mutual consent and voluntariness, and it is on the whole forwarding looking. It is in the second case that there is a particular worry about secession, as federal arrangements are often a concession to overwhelming pressures or threats (it is interesting that of the examples of voluntary federalism, as in Canada and Switzerland, the attempted secession by a province or canton is unlikely to be resisted militarily by the others).

Instances of secession or attempted secession from a federation reveal on closer investigation that they are not the logical result of autonomy. If we take first the case of Bangladesh's breakaway from Pakistan, it is clear that the central authorities in Islamabad had in fact refused to treat East Pakistan as an equal partner (despite its larger population) (Young, 1976; Ahmed, 1991). It tried to impose Urdu upon a Bengali-speaking people; banned the broadcast of the songs of the leading Bengali poet, Tagore; drained off economic resources to the West; discriminated against Bengalis in state services (particularly in the armed forces); and in the end denied its major party, the Awami League, the fruits of its electoral victory. So East Pakistan not only ruled the country as a unitary state but also discriminated heavily against a part of it. The crisis was precipitated by the refusal of the center to accept Mujib Rahman's proposals for a genuine and equal federation.

The breakups of the federations in the USSR and Yugoslavia were also the result of the failure to implement a genuine federation. This is less true of Yugoslavia; the federation there had tried to bring together people who had a long history of enmity but provided relatively little opportunities for the development of a real Yugoslavian identity. Both federations relied heavily on the Communist Party to hold them together, preventing an organic unity. Also the central authorities used ethnicities in opportunistic ways, not calculated to promote good inter-ethnic relations. In any case the situations in the USSR and Yugoslavia are more correctly analyzed less as secessions than as implosions of the federations. Perhaps less so in Yugoslavia, the separation of constituent parts followed rather than caused the breakdown of the central authorities. The breakup of Czechoslovakia is different. It was consensual (at least elite consensual) and therefore not secession. It does not appear to have been connected with the nature and operation of the federation, for this was negated by the dominance of the Communist Party. After the "velvet" revolution, there appears to have been a vague feeling on the part of each community that it was getting less than the other from the federation and that it would be better off without the other (Musil, 1995; Seroka, 1994). But fundamentally, the federation became a prey to the general salience of ethnicity elsewhere in the wake of the collapse of communist regimes.

I turn finally to Papua New Guinea, where parts of Bougainville are in rebellion and want secession. The settlement of 1976, which established a wide-ranging decentralization, solved the problems of Bougainville. An elected provincial government was established, responsible to an elected local assembly. With its human and physical resources, it quickly built an enviable reputation for efficiency and was assessed by various enquiries as the most effective and accountable of provincial governments. Regular elections were held, and its leaders played a full role in national politics. The troubles of 1989 had a common source—the inequitable distribution of income from the copper mine—but this time it was not a provincial-wide protest but had its origins in disputes among the community that owned the land on which the mine was located and concerned the internal distribution of royalties (Ghai and Regan, 2000). The local democratic forces to which autonomy gave rise were as much the victims of the anger and violence of the rebels as the central authorities. The granting of autonomy to Bougainville had helped to strengthen its links to the rest of the country, for it eliminated some genuine grievances and established a democratic order internally connected to the national system. There is little doubt that without the 1977 autonomy the rebellion of 1989 would have garnered more support in Bougainville—so autonomy prevented rather than promoted secession.

These case studies point to the need to distinguish secession from the termination of a federation. There may be little to mourn in the second case; it suggests that ethnic communities have decided, mutually, to lead separate lives. Autonomy is important for ethnicity because it represents a compromise, a balance between those who want a tight unitary system of government and those who may prefer separation. It loses that function if the wish to separate is mutual and the separation is achieved without strife or recrimination.

CONCLUSION

The question of autonomy is central to many conflicts today. Autonomy can play an important constructive role in mediating relations between different communities in multiethnic states. It can defuse conflicts. It is a particularly appropriate mechanism for the protection and promotion of culture and the values of a community, but it is not an easy device to operate. Great political and technical skills are required to structure and make it work. Given the difficulties of managing multiethnic states, autonomy is a valuable option, notwithstanding its own difficulties.

But autonomy can also be fragmenting, pigeon-holing and dividing communities. Sometimes in an attempt to preserve the integuments of a state, autonomy is so structured that it is difficult to find the common ground on which communities can find a moral or political basis for coexistence. Autonomy, particularly federal autonomy, is built around the notion that the people of a state are best served through a balance between the common and the particular. If the emphasis is so much on the particular, separation may be the better option, notwithstanding the proliferation of states. The secret of autonomy is the recognition of the common; certainly it seems to be the condition for its success. Perhaps about 30 years ago too much emphasis was placed on the common, and for this reason autonomy was narrow and contingent. Today we may be placing too much emphasis on the particular. It may be necessary to consider devices that stress common bonds and construct institutions that hold people together, as Nigeria did with the principles to federalize the center in the 1979 constitution, as in election of a president, the composition of the federal executive, or the registration of parties, to promote broad interregional support, to counter the tendency toward disassociating that comes with disaggregating ethnic autonomy (Kirke-Green, 1983). Autonomy should be chosen not because of some notion of preserving sovereignty but in order to enable different groups to live together, to define a common public space.

REFERENCES

Agnew, John
    1995   Postscript: Federalism in the post-Cold War era. In *Federalism: The Multiethnic Challenge*, Graham Smith, ed. London: Longman.
Agranoff, Robert
    1994   Asymmetrical and symmetrical federalism in Spain: An examination of intergovernmental policy. In *Evaluating Federal Systems*, Bertus de Villiers, ed. Cape Town: Juta.
Ahmed, Moudad
    1991   *Bangladesh: Constitutional Quest for Autonomy*. Dhaka: University Press Ltd.
Alfredson, Gudmunder
    1998   Indigenous peoples and autonomy. In *Autonomy: Applications and Implications*, Markku Suksi, ed. The Hague: Kluwer.
Bloed, A.
    1995   The OCSE and the issue of national minorities. In *Universal Minority Rights*, A. Phillips and A. Rosas, eds. Abo: Abo Akademi University Press.
Boase, Joan Price
    1994   Faces of asymmetry: German and Canadian federalism. In *Evaluating Federal Systems*, Bertus de Villiers, ed. Cape Town: Juta.
Brölmann, C.M., and M.Y.A. Zieck
    1993   Indigenous peoples. In *Peoples and Minorities in International Law*, Catherine Brölmann, René Lefeber, and Marjoleine Zieck, eds. Dordrecht: M. Nijhoff.
Brown-John, Lloyd
    1994   Asymmetrical federalism: Keeping Canada together? In *Evaluating Federal Systems*, Bertus de Villiers, ed. Cape Town: Juta.
Bullain, Inigo
    1998   Autonomy and the European Union. In *Autonomy: Applications and Implications*, Markku Suski, ed. The Hague: Kluwer.
Connor, Walker
    1984   *The National Question in Marxist-Leninist Theory and Strategy*. Princeton: Princeton University Press.

Conversi, Daniele
  2000   Autonomous communities and the ethnic settlement in Spain. In *Ethnicity and Autonomy: Negotiating Competing Claims*, Yash Ghai, ed. Cambridge: Cambridge University Press.
Edelman, Martin
  1994   *Courts, Politics and Culture in Israel*. Charlottesville: University of Virginia Press.
Eide, Asbjorn
  1998   Cultural autonomy: Concept, content, history and role in world order. In *Autonomy: Applications and Implications*, Markku Suski, ed. The Hague: Kluwer.
Elazar, Daniel
  1987   *Exploring Federalism*. Tuscaloosa: University of Alabama Press.
European Community.
  1991   Declaration on the "Guidelines on the Recognition of New States in Eastern Europe and in the Soviet Union." 31 International Legal Materials 1486. Brussels: European Community.
Franck, T.M.
  1993   Postmodern tribalism and the right to secession. In *Peoples and Minorities in International Law*, Catherine Brölmann, René Lefeber, and Marjoleine Zieck, eds. Dordrecht: M. Nijhoff.
Gabriel, John
  1996   UNO . . . What happened to autonomy? Politics and ethnicity on Nicaragua's Atlantic Coast. *Ethnic and Racial Studies* 19(1):158-184.
Ghai, Yash
  1996   Reflections on self-determination in the South Pacific. In *Self-Determination: International Perspectives*, Donald Clark and Robert Williamson, eds. Basingstoke: Macmillan Press.
  1997   *The New Constitutional Order of Hong Kong: The Resumption of Chinese Sovereignty and the Basic Law*. Hong Kong: HKU Press.
  1998a Autonomy with Chinese characteristics: The case of Hong Kong. *Pacifica Review* 10(1):7-22.
  1998b Decentralisation and the accommodation of ethnic diversity. In *Ethnic Diversity and Public Policy: A Comparative Inquiry*, Crawford Young, ed. Basingstoke: Macmillan.
  2000   Ethnicity and autonomy: A framework for analysis. In *Ethnicity and Autonomy: Negotiating Competing Claims in Multi-ethnic States*, Yash Ghai, ed. Cambridge: Cambridge University Press.
Ghai, Yash, and Patrick McAuslan
  1970   *Public Law and Political Change in Kenya*. Nairobi: Oxford University Press.
Ghai, Yash, and Anthony Regan
  1992   *The Law, Politics and Administration of Decentralisation in Papua New Guinea*. Waigani: National Research Institute.
  2000   Bougainville and dialectics of ethnicity, autonomy and separation. In *Ethnicity and Autonomy: Negotiating Competing Claims in Multi-Ethnic States*, Yash Ghai, ed. Cambridge: Cambridge University Press
Glazer, Nathan
  1977   Federalism and ethnicity: The experiences of the United States. *Publius: The Journal of Federalism* 7(4):71-89.
Gupta, Jyotirindra Das
  1975   Ethnicity, language demands, and national development in India. In *Ethnicity: Theory and Experience*, Nathan Glazer and Daniel Moynihan, eds. Cambridge, Mass.: Harvard University Press.

Gurr, Ted Robert, and Deepa Khosla
Forth- Domestic and transnational strategies for managing separatist conflicts: Four
coming Asian cases. In *Contemporary Conflicts: The Anticipation, Avoidance and Termination of Inter-Group Violence*, Hayward Alker, T.R. Gurr, and Kumar Rupesinghe, eds.
Hannikainen, Lauri
1997 The international legal basis of the autonomy and Swedish character of the Åland Islands. In *Autonomy and Demilitarisation in International Law: The Åland Islands in a Changing Europe*, Lauri Hannikainen and Frank Horn, eds. The Hague: Kluwer.
Hannum, Hurst
1990 *Autonomy, Sovereignty, and Self-Determination: The Accommodation of Conflicting Rights*. Philadelphia: University of Philadephia Press.
Harrison, Selig
1960 *India: The Most Dangerous Decades*. Madras: Oxford University Press.
Heintze, Hans-Joachim
1998 On the legal understanding of autonomy. In *Autonomy: Applications and Implications*, Markku Suski, ed. The Hague: Kluwer.
Henderson, James (sákéj) Youngblood
1994 Empowering treaty federalism. *Saskatchewan Law Review* 58:241-329.
Heywood, Paul
1995 *The Government and Politics of Spain*. Basingtoke: Macmillan.
Higgins, R.
1993 Postmodern tribalism and the right to secession, comments. In *Peoples and Minorities in International Law*, Catherine Brölmann, René Lefeber, and Marjoleine Zieck, eds. Dordrecht: M. Nijhoff.
Jay, Richard
1989 Nationalism, federalism and Ireland. In *Federalism and Nationalism*, Murray Forsyth, ed. New York: St. Martin's Press.
Kashyap, Anirban
1990 *Disintegration and Constitution*. New Delhi: Lancer Books.
Kingsbury, Benedict
1999 The applicability of the international legal concept of indigenous peoples in Asia. In *The East Asian Challenge for Human Rights*, Joanne Bauer and Daniel Bell, eds. Cambridge: Cambridge University Press.
Kirk-Greene, A.H.M.
1983 Ethnic engineering and the federal character of Nigeria: Boon of contentment or bone of contention? *Ethnic and Racial Studies* 6(4):457-476.
Klug, Heinz
2000 How the center holds: Managing claims for regional and ethnic autonomy in a democratic South Africa. In *Ethnicity and Autonomy: Negotiating Competing Claims in Multi-ethnic States*, Yash Ghai, ed. Cambridge: Cambridge University Press.
Kymlicka, Will
1989 *Liberalism, Community and Culture*. Oxford: Clarendon Press.
1998a Is federalism a viable alternative to secession? In *Theories of Secession*, Percy B Lehning, ed. London: Routledge.
1998b *Finding Our Way: Rethinking Ethnocultural Relations in Canada*. Toronto: Oxford University Press.
Lynn, Nicholas J., and Akexei V. Novikov
1997 Refederalizing Russia: Debates on the idea of federalism in Russia. *Publius* 27(2): 187-203.

Mackerras, Colin
  1994   China's Minorities: Integration and Modernization in the Twentieth Century. Hong
          Kong: Oxford University Press.
Malesevic, Sinisa
  2000   Ethnicity and federalism in communist Yugoslavia and its successor states. In
          Ethnicity and Autonomy: Negotiating Competing Claims in Multi-ethnic States, Yash
          Ghai, ed. Cambridge: Cambridge University Press.
Mill, J.S.
  1972   Utilitarianism, On Liberty and Considerations on Representative Government. London:
          Dent.
Milne, David
  1994   Exposed to the glare: Constitutional camouflage and the fate of Canada's federa-
          tion. In Seeking a New Canadian Partnership: Asymmetrical and Confederal Options, F.
          Leslie Seidle, ed. Ottawa: Institute for Research on Public Policy.
Moreno, Luis
  1994   Ethno-territorial concurrence and imperfect federalism in Spain. In Evaluating
          Federal Systems, Bertus de Villiers, ed. Cape Town: Juta.
Murphy, Alexander
  1995   Belgium's regional divergence: Along the road to federation. In Federalism: The
          Multiethnic Challenge, Graham Smith, ed. London: Longman.
Musil, Jiri
  1995   The End of Czechoslovakia, Jiri Musil, ed. Budapest: Central European University
          Press.
Nahum, Fasil
  1997   Constitution for a Nation of Nations: The Ethiopian Prospect. Lawrenceville, N.J.: Red
          Sea Press.
Nordquist, Kjell-Ake
  1998   Autonomy as a conflict-resolving mechanism—An overview. In Autonomy: Appli-
          cations and Implications, Markku Suksi, ed. The Hague: Kluwer.
O'Brien, Conor Cruise
  1986   The Siege: The Saga of Israel and Zionism. New York: Simon and Schuster.
OSCE High Commissioner for Minorities
  1999   The Lund Recommendations on the Effective Participation of National Minorities in
          Public Life. The Hague: Foundation on Inter-ethnic Relations. Also available at
          http://www.osce.org/indexese.htm.
Packer, John
  1998   Autonomy within the OSCE: The case of Crimea. In Autonomy: Applications and
          Implications, Markku Suksi, ed. The Hague: Kluwer.
Parekh, Bhiku
  1993   The cultural particularity of liberal democracy. In Prospects for Democracy: North,
          South, East and West, David Held, ed. Cambridge: Polity Press.
Paul, James
  2000   Ethnicity and the new constitutional orders of Ethiopia and Eriteria. In Ethnicity
          and Autonomy: Negotiating Competing Claims in Multi-ethnic States, Yash Ghai, ed.
          Cambridge: Cambridge University Press.
Peeters, Patrick
  1994   Federalism: A comparative perspective—Belgium transforms from a unitary to a
          federal state. In Evaluating Federal Systems, Bertus de Villiers, ed. Cape Town:
          Juta.

Pithart, Petr
  1994   Czechoslovakia: The loss of the old partnership. In *Seeking a New Canadian Part-
          nership: Asymmetrical and Confederal Options*, F. Leslie Seidle, ed. Ottawa: Institute
          for Research on Public Policy.
Rady, Martyn
  1996   Self-determination and the dissolution of Yugoslavia. *Ethnic and Racial Studies*
          19(2):379-389.
Rae, Kenneth
  1997   *Conflict and Compromise in Multilingual Societies*. Waterloo, Ontario: Wilfred
          Laurier University Press.
Rich, Roland
  1993   Recognition of states: The collapse of Yugoslavia and the Soviet Union. *European
          Journal of International Law* 4:36-65.
Rosas, A.
  1993   Internal self-determination. In *Modern Law of Self-Determination*, C. Tomuschat,
          ed. Dordrecht: Martinus Nihoff.
Russell, Peter
  1993   *Constitutional Odyssey: Can Canadians Become a Sovereign People?* Toronto: Uni-
          versity of Toronto Press.
Seroka, Jim
  1994   The dissolution of federalism in East and Central Europe. In *Evaluating Federal
          Systems*, Bertus de Villiers, ed. Cape Town: Juta.
Smith, Graham
  1996   Russia, ethnoregionalism and the politics of federation. *Ethnic and Racial Studies*
          19(2)391-410.
Stankovich, Mara, ed.
  1999   *Accord: Compromising on Autonomy, Mindanao in Transition*. London: Conciliation
          Resources.
Stavenhagen, Rodolfo
  1998   Indigenous peoples: Emerging international actors. In *Ethnic Diversity and Public
          Policy: A Comparative Inquiry*, Crawford Young, ed. Basingstoke: Macmillan.
Steiner, Henry
  1991   Ideals and counter-ideals in the struggle over autonomy regimes for minorities.
          Notre Dame Law Review 66(5):1539-1568.
Stevens, R. Michael
  1977   Asymmetrical federalism: The federal principle and the survival of the small re-
          public. *Publius: The Journal of Federalism* 7(4):117-203.
Tarlton, C.
  1965   Symmetry and asymmetry as elements of federalism: A theoretical speculation.
          The Journal of Politics 27:861-874.
Taylor, Charles
  1994   The politics of recognition. In *Multiculturalism*, Amy Gutman, ed. Princeton, N.J.:
          Princeton University Press.
Tekle, Amare
  1991   Another Ethiopian-Eritrean federation?—an Eritrean view. *World Today* 47:47-50.
Thornberry, Patrick
  1998   Images of autonomy and individual and collective rights in international instru-
          ments on the rights of minorities. In *Indigenous Peoples and Autonomy*, Marrku
          Suksi, ed. The Hague: Kluwer.

Tronvoll, Kjetil
  2000   *Ethiopia: The National Question*. London: Minority Rights Group.
Tully, James
  1995   *Strange Multiplicity: Constitutionalism in an Age of Diversity*. Cambridge: Cambridge
          University Press.
Walker, Graham
  1997   The idea of nonliberal constitutionalism. In *Ethnicity and Group Rights*, I. Shapiro
          and W. Kymlicka, eds. New York: NYU Press.
Watts, Ronald
  1994a   Contemporary views on federalism. In *Evaluating Federal Systems*, Bertus de Villiers,
          ed. Cape Town: Juta.
  1994b   Discussant's comments. In *Seeking a New Canadian Partnership: Asymmetrical and
          Confederal Options*, F. Leslie Seidle, ed. Ottawa: Institute for Research on Public
          Policy.
  2000   Federalism and diversity in Canada. In *Ethnicity and Autonomy: Negotiating Com-
          peting Claims in Multi-ethnic States*, Yash Ghai, ed. Cambridge: Cambridge Uni-
          versity Press.
Weller, Marc
  1992   The international response to the dissolution of the Socialist federal Republic of
          Yugoslavia. *American Journal of International Law* 86:569-607.
Young, Crawford
  1976   *The Politics of Cultural Pluralism*. Madison: University of Wisconsin Press.
  1998   Ethnic diversity and public policy: An overview. In *Ethnic Diversity and Public
          Policy: A Comparative Inquiry*, Crawford Young, ed. Basingstoke: Macmillan.

13

Language Conflict and Violence: The Straw that Strengthens the Camel's Back

David D. Laitin

Tower of Babel in a single country—in which groups of people speak radically different languages—is all too often portrayed as incendiary. Selig Harrison wrote ominously about the "dangerous decades" that India would face because of its conflicts over language.[1] Popular representations of language conflicts in Belgium, Quebec, and Catalonia suggest that cultural issues of this sort unleash irrational passions, leading otherwise sober people away from the realm of civic engagement. And the unjust underpinnings of language laws are often said, even by the combatants themselves, to induce violent rebellion. In late 1999, for example, the leader of the Kurdish rebels in Turkey, Abdullah Ocalan, referred to the restrictions on the Kurdish language as the principal motivating factor for the war against Turkish rule. He told the judges:

> These kinds of laws give birth to rebellion and anarchy. . . . The most important of these is the language ban. It provokes this revolt. The way to resolve this problem is to develop Kurdish as a normal language for private conversation and broadcasting.[2]

That language conflict is one manifestation of a genre of uncivil politics is a principal theme in the iconic "The Integrative Revolution" by Clifford Geertz, where language was included with a set of other "primordial" attachments that were seen as threats to civil society. "When we speak of communalism in India," Geertz wrote:

> we refer to religious contrasts; when we speak of it in Malaya, we are mainly concerned with racial ones, and in the Congo with tribal ones. But the grouping under a common rubric is not simply adventitious; the

phenomena referred to are in some way similar. Regionalism has been the main theme in Indonesian disaffection, differences in custom in Moroccan. The Tamil minority in Ceylon is set off from the Sinhalese majority by religion, language, race, region, and social custom; the Shiite minority in Iraq is set off from the dominant Sunnis virtually by an intra-Islamic sectarian difference alone. Pan-national movements in Africa are largely based on race, in Kurdistan, on tribalism; in Laos, the Shan States, and Thailand, on language. Yet all these phenomena, too, are in some sense of a piece. They form a definable field of investigation.[3]

Language difference is perceived here as one of those symbolic cultural realms in which conflict can all too easily leave the realm of politics and become a threat to peace. In this paper I present powerful evidence to the contrary. Language conflict is not of a piece with religious or other forms of cultural conflict; it has its own particular dynamic. Furthermore, conflict over language is not a prescription for violence. In fact, under certain potentially incendiary conditions, language conflict can help to contain violence.

The empirical source of my challenge to the conventional wisdom is the Minorities at Risk (MAR) database developed by Ted Gurr, which analyzes the status and conflicts of 268 politically active communal groups in 148 different countries. Among the 449 original variables included in the dataset, there are assessments of cultural, economic, and political differences between minority and dominant groups; group grievances and organizational strength; transnational support of minority goals; polity characteristics; and protest, communal violence, and rebellion.[4] In the analysis that follows, rebellion of minority groups against the state is the dependent variable. Linguistic differences between minority and dominant groups as well as grievances of minority groups over state language policies are the independent variables.

In the second section of this paper I review the standard theory linking modernization to language conflict, suggesting why conflicts over language issues become incendiary. In the third section I explore the MAR database. The findings are stunning:

• The greater the language difference between the language of the minority group and that of the dominant group, the *lower* is the probability of violence.
• Language grievances held by the minority regarding the official language of the state or the medium of instruction in state schools are not associated with group violence, but there is a weak *negative* relationship between language grievances and rebellion.
• Language grievances are strongly associated with increased levels

of political protest, suggesting that the remedy for these grievances is more likely to be sought in the political realm rather than by guerrilla action.

• Language grievances when compounded by religious grievances (which are a reasonable predictor of rebellion) strongly and significantly *reduce* the magnitude of rebellion. In this sense when language and religious grievances are cumulative, language grievances lower the probability of large-scale violence. Language grievances are, therefore, straws that appear to strengthen the camel's back.

In the fourth section I formalize an "official language game" and then speculate on why the relationship between language grievance and group violence is not positive. Central mechanisms have to do with the ability of the state to commit to compromises and the inability of minority language entrepreneurs to solve collective-action problems. A theoretical sketch shows why language grievances (as opposed to, say, religious grievances) tend to redirect conflict from the military to the political/bureaucratic realm. In the fifth section I discuss specific cases—India and Sri Lanka—to show that the statistical and theoretical analyses compel us to see oft-told national histories in new ways. Then I present new data on language policies and their associations with violent conflict and suggest the relevance of my findings for public policy. Policies that are equitable may not, the data show, have equally beneficial consequences in terms of reducing the probability of ethnic violence. To be sure, international intervention may be called for if the implementers of unfair language policies use minority protest as an invitation for all-out war against the minority group, but the unfair language policies themselves are not a threat to peace. I conclude that those interested in peace should encourage the open expression of language grievances and the subsequent political bargaining over the official language and the language of education.

THE RELATIONSHIP OF LANGUAGE TO POLITICAL CONFLICT

In the premodern era language was not politicized. As Ernest Gellner has masterfully demonstrated, in preindustrial times for most people the language of official state business was of no concern.[5] Many states with considerable ethnic (especially linguistic) heterogeneity within their boundaries legislated official languages of state business without inducing the ire of their populations. This was no different from establishing a basic law of the state, of establishing uniform weights and measures, and other standardizing practices that Max Weber called "rationalization."[6] Furthermore, these states induced (over much longer periods) the vast majority of the population living within their territories to adopt the state language as their own, often with objections from the church but rarely with strong popular protest.[7] This is part of what is today called "nation building." It was so painless (compared to relations with other states or religious issues) that many political scientists writing in the 1960s erroneously coded early developers as having "natural" boundaries, linking nation and state. Within-state heterogeneity may have been substantial, but the language rationalization aspect of nation building was relatively benign.

Take, for example, the infamous (to contemporary Catalans) Decree of the New Foundation, issued by King Philip V of Spain in 1716. Among other articles in a decree that sought to transform Spain from a decentralized kingdom to one based more on Bourbon principles, it required that all legal papers submitted to the king's court be written in Spanish. Late nineteenth- and twentieth-century Catalan nationalists point to this decree as signaling the death of the Catalan nation. Yet historical reality reveals a quite different picture. A large database of royal court submissions in Spain from the midseventeenth through the mideighteenth centuries shows that Philip V was demanding a practice that had already become normal a quarter century earlier. In the 1660s, when most petitions brought to the king's attention were requests for payment in recompense for quartering the king's troops in the war in the Pyrenees against France that ended in 1659, Catalan petitioners hired notaries to translate their requests into Spanish. By the 1680s virtually all such documents were routinely produced in Spanish. It is no wonder that at the time of the New Foundation's issuance there was hardly a murmur from Catalonia about the burdens that would be imposed on Catalans by having to communicate with the political center in Spanish.[8] Although revival movements in Catalonia (as well as Basque Country and Galicia) politicized language in nineteenth- and twentieth-century Spain, it is historically remarkable how painless rationalization was; and even though nation building was never a full success in Spain,[9] by the twentieth century virtually all Spanish citizens were fluent in Spanish.

It is for states that consolidated rule in the modern era that language rationalization became a grave political problem. The source of the problem is in large part due to the fact that, as Gellner has highlighted, in the modern age social mobility and economic success have been dependent on literacy. Thus, clerks replaced peasants as the backbone of modern economies in the industrial age. Furthermore, as states got into the business of providing education, the language of state business became a much broader concern for far more people than when states were not providing such services to individual citizens. Under modern conditions, people have become quite sensitive to the language of state business, and if it is not their own they feel alienated from the state. They feel as well a sense of unfair competition for jobs that are more easily garnered by those whose mother tongue is the state language. Indeed, the classic case of the unraveling of the Habsburg Empire, where peasants from non-German-speaking areas who became urban migrants were most receptive to pleas for the official recognition of their languages, fits this theory to a T.[10]

Postcolonial states that emerged after World War II, committed to the provision of public education and social welfare, were heavily constrained from following the path of Philip V and other earlier rationalizers. Newly elected political leaders were handed bureaucracies with a vested interest in continued reliance on colonial languages, as fluency in these languages differentiated the high-paid civil servants from their poorly paid brethren in the countryside. Furthermore, these same national leaders were held under suspicion by leaders from regions in which distinct languages were spoken. To impose one indigenous language on all groups would surely threaten the incumbency of any would-be rationalizer. Yet the goals of many postcolonial leaders included superseding the colonial language with an indigenous one. This difficult problem of choosing an official language (used for public administration and as a medium of instruction in schools), under conditions in which greater access to the official language translates into higher prospects for social mobility, has led many analysts to link language conflict with the potentiality of inducing ethnic violence. Nevertheless, their blunt theory is unable to make specific predictions about levels or types of conflict.

THE ROUTE FROM ETHNIC CONFLICT TO ETHNIC VIOLENCE

As I indicated in the Introduction, the standard literature on ethnic conflict often conflates all forms of ethnic contestation as a form of zero-sum intractable conflict, all with equally high potentialities for engendering violence. The leading theories provide a basis for understanding why language gets politicized in the modern era, but links to violent conflict are weakly theorized. In this section, relying on MAR data (supplemented with new variables), I show that language conflict does not translate inexorably into a higher probability of ethnic violence. The dependent variable for this section is REBELLION.[11] The scale goes from 0 (no rebellion) through 4 (small-scale guerrilla activity) and up to 7 (protracted civil war). The question I ask is whether language difference, language grievance, or language grievance in association with other factors helps explain the values on REBELLION. To address this question I provide evidence from analysis of the MAR database that supports the four findings announced in the Introduction.

Language Difference and Violence

The independent variable describing the level of language difference is LANGSIM. Here I consider the hypothesis that linguistic distance between people living in the same country is a source of tension and that therefore people with different languages cannot easily live together in the same political unit. The MAR database lends some support to this thesis, but its coding on linguistic distance is invalid.[12] Recognizing the failures of the MAR indicator to assess linguistic distance, James D. Fearon and I took the world classification of languages, produced by *Ethnologue*,[13] a society of linguists interested in producing versions of the Bible in all languages of the world. *Ethnologue* linguists rely on linguistic trees, classifying languages by structure, with branch points for language family (e.g., Indo-European from Afro-Asiatic), language groups, and even sub-dialects. LANGSIM has three values depending on whether the language of the minority is the same as the language of the dominant group, the language is different but of the same family of languages (the initial branching point in the *Ethnologue* codings), or the language is of a different family.[14]

Linguistic difference alone between the dominant and minority groups in a country is not a predictor of intergroup violence. If we correlate LANGSIM with REBELLION, in fact, the trend is opposite what Gurr's data show and what would be predicted from a theory that cultural difference promotes conflict. In a bivariate relationship between rebellion and linguistic similarity, the correlation is positive (.1359, significant at $p = .03$). Table 13.1 illustrates this relationship through the comparison of mean scores on REBELLION (here the maximum rebellion scores from 1945 through 1995). In the table we see that the mean score for rebellion is lowest when the groups are from a different language family and highest when the two groups share the same language. Thus, without introducing controls, *the data show that greater linguistic similarity raises the probability of violence.*

Examination of the list of cases in each of LANGSIM's categories helps show why an important cultural difference such as language does

TABLE 13.1 Language Similarity and Rebellion (1945-1995):
Comparison of Mean Scores on REBELLION

LANGSIM	Mean Value of Rebellion	Number of Cases
Entire population	2.49	244
1. Different family	2.06	111
2. Same family	2.62	93
3. Same language	3.40	40

not provoke violent group conflicts. On the one hand, there are many cases where there are vast differences in language but where the conditions do not permit large-scale rebellion. One type includes postindustrial settlers who moved into urban areas and had no territorial base in which to mobilize for military action against the state. These groups differed greatly linguistically from the dominant groups that controlled the state. Another category contains groups living in states ruled by "settler" populations whose language is different from any of the autochthonous groups—their state-building activities achieved success in earlier eras, and they are less likely to face ethnic rebellions in the post-1945 period. Third, former slave groups, many of them classified as having Creole languages, are of a different language family from the dominant groups of their societies, yet they have not been in a position to radically oppose the state in the post-World War II period. Finally, some nomadic groups (the Romani) may well be subject to pogroms but do not have the resources to challenge the state through violent action. They too differ considerably linguistically from the dominant groups in the societies in which they live.

On the other hand, there are many indigenous populations (defined by Gurr as "conquered descendants of original inhabitants of a region who typically live in peripheral regions, practice subsistence agriculture or herding, and have cultures sharply distinct from dominant groups")[15] who speak languages in close proximity to their conquerors yet harbor long-standing grievances and have a rural base to rebel. Here, despite language similarity, we see a breeding ground for violent confrontation. Once we control for factors such as urban versus rural base of the minority population, language similarity will be shown to have no explanatory power. But presenting the bivariate correlations helps to undermine the oft-expressed opinion that cultural differences in and of themselves are prescriptions for violent confrontations, especially in an age of identity politics.

Language Grievances and Violence

The Gurr dataset has two variables measuring language grievance, each measured for two-year time periods (1990-1991, 1992-1993, 1994-1995). The first variable measures the level of demands by the minority to have its language given greater official status. The second variable measures the level of demands by the minority to have its language used as a medium of instruction in state schools. I constructed a composite variable, MAXLANG, which is the maximum value of grievance on either of the variables in any of the time periods. The bivariate relationship between MAXLANG and REBELLION is $-.055$. Not only is the relationship not significant in a positive direction, but the sign is the opposite of what the Gellnerian approach to modernization would have led us to expect.[16]

Perhaps language grievances *alone* are not a causal factor explaining group violence but in conjunction with other factors can raise its probability. To find out it is necessary to go beyond bivariate correlations and comparisons of means and examine these relationships through regression analysis. In the multiple regressions that follow, using a cross-sectional study of rebellion that I completed in collaboration with James Fearon,[17] I enter three control variables that have the greatest predictive power: namely, the log of gross domestic product (GDP) taken from 1960, the rate of GDP growth from 1960 to 1980, and a dummy variable I call RURBASE that indicates whether the group has had a long-term rural settlement in a specific region of the country.[18] With these controls the coefficient of MAXLANG is not always negative when regressed against REBELLION. But, as we will see, as I analyze Table 13.2, language grievances do not add to the straws on the camel's back, fostering violence.

The intuition behind the camel's back approach to ethnic violence is that language grievances alone are not a sufficient cause for rebellion but in conjunction with other factors can add to an atmosphere that induces rebellion. The specification listed in Table 13.2 examines this intuition. Besides the control variables, it includes a variable MAXRELGR, which is the maximum score of religious grievances expressed by the minority group in the first half-decade of the 1990s. It also includes a value taken from the polity database on the degree to which the country was democratic in 1989, called here DEMOCRACY. Finally, it includes an interaction term called LGxRG, which is the product of MAXRELGR and MAXLANG.[19]

TABLE 13.2 Rebellion and Cultural Grievances—Dependent Variable: REBELLION; Linear Regression: OLS

Independent Variable	Coefficient (*B*)	Standard Error
MAXLANG	.202	.167
MAXRELGR**	.418	.152
LGxRG*	−.200	.101
DEMOCRACY 1989	.062	.050
GDPCHANGE 1960-1980**	−.874	.249
RURBASE**	1.277	.396
LANGSIM	.125	.227
LOGGDP60**	−.682	.221
Constant**	6.249	1.63

$R^2 = .27105$.

* Significant at $p < .05$; ** Significant at $p < .01$

Several important relationships need to be elaborated from the analysis of Table 13.2. First, although the positive relationship of LANGSIM and REBELLION remains as in the bivariate analysis, the relationship is not significant at all once controls are added. Second, the relationship of MAXLANG and REBELLION is no longer a negative one, but that relationship as well is not statistically significant. Third, the relationship between MAXRELGR and REBELLION is significantly positive, suggesting that a one-point jump in MAXRELGR (on a four-point scale) raises the likely rebellion score by nearly half a point. The statistical effects of language grievance on rebellion are thus quite distinct from those of religious grievance on rebellion, a point I return to later. Fourth, the level of democracy has no significant relationship to the scale of REBELLION. I elaborate on this point later as well.

Fifth, and most significant for challenging the straw and camel's back intuition, is the strong negative relationship between the LGxRG interaction term and REBELLION. What this captures is a slope for MAXLANG that is marginally positive (.21) when there are no religious grievances at all (MAXRELGR = 0). Yet the slope of MAXLANG changes sign (to −.4) when there are high levels of religious grievance (MAXRELGR = 3).[20] One way to see this relationship is to compare the REBELLION mean score of 2.58 when MAXRELGR = 3 and MAXLANG = 0 to the mean score of 1.05 for REBELLION when MAXRELGR stays at 3 but MAXLANG = 3. Adding a powerful language grievance to a powerful religious grievance thereby *reduces* the REBELLION score by 1.53, a very powerful effect indeed.

Suppose (in a stylized portrait of Sudan) that a Muslim-dominated country where Arabic is the official language dominates over a Christian region whose people speak a variety of languages, but none of them have Arabic as their mother tongue. Further suppose that the majority imposes Shari'a (i.e., Muslim law) on the minority, activating regional entrepreneurs to use the churches as recruiting grounds for a rebellion, overcoming the logic of collective inaction. Finally, suppose that the majority adds fuel to the fire by imposing Arabic as the sole official language for schools throughout the country. (Because the dominant region already was relying on Arabic, there is no problem of implementation.) Now not only the priests but the schoolteachers are mobilized. But this additional mobilized group need not add fuel to the revolutionary fire, as Table 13.2 counterintuitively demonstrated. First, there will be an incentive for some southerners to learn Arabic and get prized jobs, without a school hierarchy policing their linguistic defection. Second, the aggrieved schoolteachers face a difficult choice: whether to fight in the guerrilla camps (with the anti-Shari'a forces) on the religious front or in the state bureaucracies on the linguistic front. To the extent that they can win delays and concessions on the latter front, the oppressive language laws may take some potential rebels out of the rebellion.

Not all cases of high religious and high language grievances are peaceful (Catholics in Northern Ireland, Sri Lankan Tamils in Sri Lanka, and Serbs in Croatia are members of this category), but most are quite peaceful (Russians in Uzbekistan, Indian Tamils in Sri Lanka, Germans in Kazakhstan, Malays in Singapore). If a score on REBELLION that is greater than three is taken as an indicator of large-scale ethnic war, under conditions of high language and religious grievances in only three out of 22 cases (14 percent) were there large-scale wars. For the entire sample of 267 cases, 65 (24 percent) were experiencing a high level of rebellion in the 1990s. The conjunction of both language and religious grievances yields a far lower probability of large-scale ethnic war than language alone. To sum up, although MAXLANG in isolation has no significant relationship to REBELLION, as an interaction term with MAXRELGR, language grievances reduce the potential for violence.

Language Grievances and Political Protest

Language grievances alone do not increase the probability of violence (but they appear to have some ameliorative effects), but this does not mean that grievances over language policy lead to political quiescence. In fact, the reverse is true. The MAR database has a separate six-point scale for level of political protest, going from "none reported" to "demonstrations of greater than 100,000 people." Table 13.3 contains the result of a regression equation that is precisely the same as in Table 13.2, except that here the dependent variable is PROTEST, the maximum degree of protest in the years 1990-1995. Here MAXLANG is powerfully and positively

TABLE 13.3 Protest and Cultural Grievances—Dependent Variable: PROTEST; Linear Regression: OLS

Independent Variable	Coefficient (B)	Standard Error
MAXLANG*	.284	.121
MAXRELGR	.061	.110
LGXRG	−.059	.074
DEMOCRACY 1989	.055	.036
GDPCHANGE 1960-1980	.144	.181
RURBASE**	.924	.288
LANGSIM	−.155	.165
LOGGDP60	.130	.161
Constant	.312	1.19

$R^2 = .177$.
* Significant at $p < .05$; ** Significant at $p < .01$

related to PROTEST, but this is not the case for MAXRELGR nor the interaction term of language and religious grievances (LGxRG). In a point I develop in the following section, language grievances seem to draw angry citizens into the realm of political protest but not into guerrilla armies.

Turning the Question on Its Head: Explaining the Modulating Effects of Linguistic Conflict

How to interpret the data so far? Language issues themselves do not cause group violence. In fact, language conflicts, under conditions where religious grievances are powerful, are associated with lower levels of ethnic violence than under conditions where religious grievances are weak. We might therefore turn the usual question on its head: Why does language conflict moderate ethnic violence?

HOW CAN A STRAW STRENGTHEN THE CAMEL'S BACK?

It is a stretch (not justified by the data) to claim that language griev-ances reduce violence; but since the bivariate relationship with REBEL-LION is negative (and in interaction with religious grievances it is sig-nificantly negative when regressed on REBELLION), it is useful to ask theoretically why the effect of language grievances on ethnic rebellion is not strongly positive and what ameliorative influence language griev-ance might have on ethnic relations. In this section I present a stylized model of an "official language" game. Traveling down its strategic steps will suggest three ameliorative mechanisms that reduce the probability of official language policy turning into violent intergroup conflict. The first centers on the potential subversion of the oppressive language laws by educated members of the dominant group, which makes it more difficult for a state to implement a new official language. The second centers on the general bureaucratic problem, even if there is substantial support from government and business elites in the dominant group, of changing language norms. These problems ironically enable the govern-ment to make credible commitments in bargaining with the discrimi-nated-against minority language groups. The third centers on the prob-lem of collective action that is faced when language entrepreneurs of the minority language groups seek to recruit warriors to fight on their behalf.

Consider the stylized "official language game" represented in Figure 13.1. Suppose a popular postcolonial government is being pressed by its ethnic constituency to pass language laws in favor of the dominant na-tional group. It can either accept the status quo (say, continued use of the

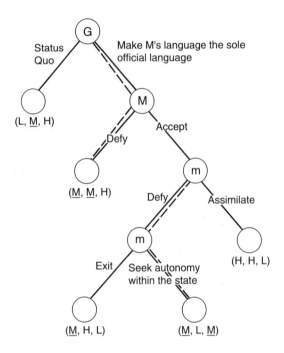

G = government
M = majority group
m = minority group
Values (G, M, m); H = high; M = medium; L = low
— — — — = equilibrium path

FIGURE 13.1 Official language game.

neutral colonial language) or make the majority group's language the
official language of the state. If the government does the latter, the leading bureaucratic and business elites among the majority must decide individually whether to subvert the law they had demanded or accept it and
begin operating in the new state language for their official duties. If they
accept the law, the burden is put on the minority population, which can
learn the newly official language (i.e., assimilate) or defy the government,
by either migrating out of the country or organizing politically for linguistic autonomy in the state.

The values for each outcome reckoned in Figure 13.1 are as follows.
The government would most prefer full acceptance and assimilation by
the minority (as this would be a rationalized state); it would least prefer
the status quo, as this would be a signal that it is unresponsive to its own

constituency. It is indifferent among the three other possible outcomes. The majority group would most prefer either assimilation (like its government) or minority exit (which would provide purity for the majority at a cost of a lower tax base for the government). It would least prefer minority autonomy, as this would assure protected jobs for the minority population. The majority would be indifferent between the status quo (where they can blame their government) and majority defiance of the government's language law (where they can blame each other). The minority would prefer the status quo or defiance by the majority, as either would assure it continued use of the colonial language in schools and in state administration. It would least prefer assimilation (as this would be costly and take generations) and exit (because this would uproot people from their homes). Autonomy for the minority would be better than assimilation but worse than the status quo.

Given this game structure and stipulated values for each player, through backward induction we can see that it would be rational for the government to make the majority language official. But the majority population, should it accept, would see the minority population defy and then seek autonomy. This path would yield the majority its worst outcome. If the majority defied, it could assure itself a medium return, and this dominates the expected return of acceptance. The unique equilibrium here is the officialization of the majority language while the majority population subverts and continues to rely on the colonial language.

This dynamic might be thought of as a game of "chicken," with Indian language policy being the prime example. The Indian constitution committed the federal government to the promotion of Hindi as the official language of interstate communication and state communication with the union government. To the extent that the federal government pressed for rapid achievement of this outcome, Indian politicians from non-Hindi-speaking states pretended total ignorance of Hindi and demanded greater regional autonomy. To the extent that the future was put off indefinitely, non-Hindi speakers accommodated themselves to the constitutional arrangement and tempered their autonomist desires. I described the outcome in these terms: "The Union authorities promote Hindi but deny that they will impose it; the people from non-Hindi zones learn Hindi but deny they can use it." To a considerable extent, that analysis is consistent with the official language equilibrium proposed here—with a Union commitment to Hindi coinciding with the continued use of English in virtually all official domains.[21]

This equilibrium may help explain the weak negative coefficient for language grievance regressed on rebellion. If rebellion occurs only when the minority seeks autonomy from the state, it will occur (only rarely) when the game has gone off the equilibrium path. Most cases of grievance occur on the equilibrium path after officialization of the majority language, while the *majority* is in the course of undermining its provisions. Only in cases of majority acceptance—when the majority is uncertain how the minority will respond—would language grievance have incendiary implications. Thus, this interpretation of the weakly negative coefficient: it is not that language grievances cause peace; it is that language grievances on the equilibrium path are less likely to be so threatening to any party as to make violence a rational response.

Besides the incentive for the backward-inducing majority to defect, two other mechanisms embedded in this game merit consideration. Consider first the burden on the elites in the majority (especially those in the civil service) in accepting the new language laws they claim publicly to have supported. Civil servants in general oppose the rationalization of heretofore unofficial, and partly in consequence low-status, languages because entrenched bureaucrats initially received their positions by taking examinations in the soon-to-be proscribed language. They will do all they can to make the switchover appear as technically difficult as possible, to delay the time when their special linguistic competence will have little value for promotion.

Therefore, one theoretical reason why language conflicts are associated with lower levels of violent conflict is that it is possible for the government in a language conflict to commit to a compromise without the minority fearing that the commitment hides a secret plan to overturn the status quo when conditions are more propitious for full-scale language rationalization.[22] The ability to credibly commit is largely due to the fact that a language shift takes generations, and it is impossible for a state to impose a new language of education, administration, or certification without a long lead time.[23] In Figure 13.1's game this means that the move to "accept" by the majority group is not a simple choice but a coordination dynamic among fellow majority-language speakers that might take a generation to complete. Thus, the breaking of a commitment by an emboldened rationalizing state would require myriad new regulations and teaching programs, consuming years of effort, thereby giving the affected linguistic regions a chance to mobilize in opposition. Language compromises—amenable to commitments—are therefore less incendiary than other types of center/periphery agreements (e.g., the commitment of a weak state that it would never disband a regional parliament).

A second theoretical reason why language conflicts are associated with lower levels of violent conflict has to do with collective-action problems faced by minority groups. Once a language-rationalization program is legislated in the modern era, minority-language entrepreneurs in the periphery of the state invariably get activated, and they usually join in alliance with their own poets, philologists, lexicographers, and international activists (often with financial support from UNESCO, the UN Educational, Scientific, and Cultural Organization) in order to save "their" languages from extinction due to the projected effects of a rationalization program. Language is so intimately connected to group identity that these entrepreneurs have little trouble articulating a powerful collective grievance if their language is threatened. But these very language entrepreneurs have a problem: although collective refusal to assimilate would be in everyone's interest, it would be individually rational for any particular member of the minority to assimilate.[24]

Because of the relative ease of linguistic "defection"—that is, the choice by some subset of the minority population to assimilate—it is much more difficult for language entrepreneurs (even if funded by emigrés and international organizations) to organize collectively against linguistic discrimination than it is for religious entrepreneurs to organize collectively against religious discrimination. To be sure, students and the educated unemployed who are not literate in the newly upgraded language will be gravely affected by language regulations in an immediate way, without the long lead time that would protect entrenched bureaucrats. Absent the chance for middle-class jobs, these youths are easily mobilized into militant opposition groups. The founding leader of the Liberation Tigers of Tamil Eelam (LTTE), as we shall see, is an example of such a reaction. But these youths, employment threatened through discrimination, may find many of their compatriots (or their younger siblings) developing competence in the state language and thereby decreasing the solidarity of a minority linguistic group in opposition to the state.

We now have a basis to distinguish the different coefficients for language and religious grievance. Compared to religion, language groups never have organizational hierarchies with powers to police members. In fact, language discrimination (because of the social reality of multilingualism) easily permits those who are discriminated against to invest in their children's expanded language repertoires, so that intergenerationally the linguistic discrimination they face will become attenuated. Religious organizations are much more attentive to bireligiosity and strongly sanction allegiance to more than one faith. Conversion often entails high costs in social status from within one's former religious group. As seen in Table 13.2, compared to religious grievance, under conditions of high ethnic potential for violence, language grievances are more conducive to peace than rebellion. This is not to say that religious grievances cannot be negotiated. After all, the European states after the Thirty Years' War in 1648 developed a formula for doing so. And evidence from southwestern Nigeria shows that religious differences can be depoliticized by state authority.[25] But my point here is that the organization of language groups in confrontation with state authority has greater organizational and strategic constraints than the organization of religious groups.

In sum, the official-language game, once specified, makes the relationship between oppressive language laws and violence weakly negative. The language game encompasses features that show how the commitment problem, and the difficulty faced by language entrepreneurs in punishing defectors, work to reduce the incentives for intergroup violence over language issues. Along with backward induction giving majority speakers incentives to defy language laws passed in their name, these additional strategic factors provide plausible reasons why language grievances do not add fuel to the ethnic fire.

COMPARATIVE SPECULATIONS

The statistical and theoretical expositions on the ameliorative effects of language oppression (compared to the expectations that one would find a strong positive coefficient) remain difficult to accept. But a perusal of well-known cases in the Organization for European Cooperation and Development (OECD) states on language conflict and its supposed disruptive influences on the integrity of the state—in Quebec, Norway, the Jura, Catalonia, and Belgium—gives an ex post obviousness to my claims. What is noteworthy about these cases is that none were linked in any way to significant guerrilla activity. Although many political analysts have treated these conflicts with exaggerated fears of what may come to pass if the program of the linguistic nationalists (as in Quebec) is fulfilled, combined with mockery at the passions that apparently tiny slights can raise (as in Belgium, with the fall of governments hanging on such slights), few have recognized that language conflicts in the West have been far more peaceful than the industrial conflicts of an earlier era. In comparison, the cases in the Western democratic states that have captured the greatest attention in regard to ethnically based violence are those of Northern Ireland and the Basque Country in Spain. In both of these cases, language issues (vis-à-vis the state) were not central to the violence.

In this section my argument is best developed not by examining the peaceful versus the violent conflicts in OECD states (as in the MAR database, all those conflicts are on a world standard quite peaceful) but rather by looking closely at two well-known cases (one where violence was predicted, the other where it occurred) to identify in the real world some of the mechanisms that were theoretically elaborated on earlier. By looking at some individual cases we can also capture elements of the theorized processes that are missed in cross-sectional analyses.

Language Policy in India and the Movement
for State Status in Andhra Pradesh

Upon independence, as indicated by Harrison's ominous prediction of violent confrontation (cited in the Introduction), India suffered from language heterogeneity. Yet slowly but inexorably, a peaceful equilibrium developed, in part a result of the chicken game described earlier. I have called this equilibrium a 3±1 language outcome. The colonial language maintains its status in the bureaucracy, in international business, and in higher education. Meanwhile, an indigenous lingua franca plays a supportive role as the national language, more important in popular culture (television, music, and movies) than in the corridors of political power. At the same time, regional leaders are able to consolidate local power by developing realms for state languages and a state-level civil service operating in each. Local services would thereby require literacy in the state language. Finally, minorities and migrants in any region have won protection from the center so that they can receive education and services in their own language. For many Indians seeking a wide range of mobility opportunities, therefore, trilingualism is normal: English, Hindi, and the state language. For Indians living in states where Hindi or English is the state language, only bilingualism (3–1) is required. For minorities in non-Hindi and non-English states, who themselves are not Hindi speakers, a fourth language (3+1) is required.

If this formula were to be fully institutionalized, all Indians would be able to communicate with one another, and individual multilingualism would allow for constantly changed language use depending on circumstance and interlocutor. In this section I first look at language grievances articulated by the Telugu speakers (who initially did not have a state of their own) in reaction to the emergence of government-supported state languages throughout the Indian federation. I then look more generally at the relatively peaceful consolidation of the 3±1 equilibrium in India as a whole.

Nationalist leaders in the Telugu-speaking areas of Madras, Hyderabad, and Mysore states at the time of Indian independence hoped to gain recognition for their homeland as a linguistically based state. For 30 years the Congress Party had been committed to the reorganization of India's states on the basis of language. But in the postindependence period two commissions reneged on this promise, contending that national integration, efficiency of administration, and protection of minorities all argued for the preservation of linguistically mixed states. The second commission (the so-called JVP Committee) left the door open a crack for a future Telugu-speaking state and helped induce a Gandhi-style movement of protest, culminating in 1952 in the death through fasting of Potti Sriramula. The Congress Party government was shocked, and a new state was granted in 1953.

The movement for Telugu autonomy, organized in the 1930s, was induced in part by the rabid nationalism and strong cultural revival of the Tamil speakers in the Madras presidency. This movement struck a positive chord among early nationalist leaders in Telengana, an economically backward region of Telugu speakers in Hyderabad State, and in their alliance with the Madras Telugus, a notion of "Vishalandhra" (Greater Andhra), recalling the greatness of the ancient Nizam kingdom, became a mobilizing idea. Linguistic unity prevailed and Andhra Pradesh became a state, though working out an official list of translations for standard Telugu was a bureaucratic nightmare.[26]

One of the greatest obstacles to the peaceful emergence of an Andhra state was intralinguistic (though Telengana Telugu is more heavily Urduized than the Telugu in Andhra) because of a popular sense in Telengana that Telenganas would lose out in job competition with the more highly educated Telugu speakers from Madras. Telengana leaders therefore got a "sons of the soil" agreement from Delhi protecting their right to government jobs in the Telengana region of Andhra Pradesh. Nonetheless, communal riots in 1969 and 1972 undermined the peace. Although dialect issues brought some tensions, and the much higher percentage of Muslims in Telengana raised the specter of religious conflict, the issues that sparked these agitations had to do with economic development funds, the use of revenue surpluses generated by Telengana local government, the purchasing of Telengana domicile certificates by Andhras (allowing them to get reserved jobs), and the composition of the state cabinet. Andhra leaders spread propaganda that all state jobs (as the capital, Hyderabad, was in Telengana) would go to Telenganas. The proximate cause of the 1969 agitation was the decision by the Andhra Pradesh High Court that the job reservation system did not apply to the state electricity board. But in 1972 when the Indian Supreme Court supported the Telenganas, the issue turned violent. From November through January (1973) there were six separate incidents, with separatists claiming more than 250 deaths caused by police shootings.[27] These incidents were far more disruptive than the one death associated with the movement to create a linguistic state in the first place. Intralinguistic agitation over job reservations was more violent than was interlinguistic agitation.[28]

The concession of statehood to Andhra induced yet a third language commission in India, the States Reorganization Commission, which now had to develop a revised long-term policy in regard to language and state boundaries. It faced demands and pressures from all over the country, but there was no violence. Once its recommendations were published, however, riots broke out in Bombay (as Marathis and Gujaratis each wanted their own state, with Bombay as the capital) in which 80 people were killed. In 1961 the States Reorganization Commission granted separate statehood to Nagaland, where Naga speakers would no longer be in the grip of Assamese-speaking leadership. This concession helped end a nasty war in the northeastern provinces of India. It also helped establish a linguistic criterion for statehood that, when minorities were given protection by the central government, consolidated the 3±1 equilibrium, an equilibrium that has been uncontested for more than 30 years.

Two leading students of Indian politics have remarked on the pluralist, democracy-enhancing, and violence-mitigating language policies that developed in the wake of the Andhra agitation. In Paul Brass's distinguished work on language and religion in north India, a basic set of rules concerning ethnic politics is outlined. Most important, Brass points out, as a result of the murderous secession of Pakistan, the Indian government does not entertain demands based on religious membership or demands for any form of secession. The government does not make concessions to any ethnic group, Brass further finds, if the result is unacceptable to a rival group. Finally, no concessions are made to an ethnic group unless it proves itself by being able to mobilize the masses in favor of its leaders' goals. What follows from this set of principles is that linguistic entrepreneurs who can successfully mobilize constituents, and who do so without raising the specter of secession from India or war with neighboring groups, get recognition and with that recognition comes a package of group rights and protected jobs.[29] The legitimacy of language claims made on behalf of groups has brought language demands into the realm of normal (nonviolent) political conflict.

Jyotirindra Das Gupta has also emphasized the pluralist and associational logic of the implicit rule legitimating language demands by disaffected groups. Although the bulk of his book considers the political implications of the constitutional stipulation that Hindi replace English as the all-India language (projected to occur in 1965), the final chapter addresses some broader questions concerning language, democracy, and violent conflict. With the reduced political power of the Hindi proponents in Congress after the 1962 elections, Das Gupta writes, Congress proposed an Official Languages Act in 1963 that would remove the requirement that English give way to Hindi for all administrative affairs by 1965. Though anti-Hindi forces from the south were dissatisfied (because of a loophole), the Hindi supporters in the administrative services began implementing the switchover to Hindi with all too much gusto. In Madras, where graduates were more successful than in any other state in gaining entrance to the prestigious Indian Administrative Service because of the excellent English instruction in state schools, students reacted with protests, which were repressed by the government. Two nationalist party leaders in Madras publicly burned themselves to death in protest against government repression. Agitation, claiming the lives of 66 people, continued for two months, until the government gave in to all student demands. Das Gupta judges that the deaths were caused not by language activism but rather by the police in repressing normal political protest.

Das Gupta recounts the language battles of the 1960s, including the Report of the Education Commission of 1966, which gave a much greater role to the state languages in higher education (leading in 1967 to a situation in which 35 universities allowed the regional language to be used in examinations, and in 15 universities, a majority of students opted for their regional language as the medium of lectures), and including as well the Official Language (Amendment) Bill of 1967, which legally entrenched English to stand with Hindi as the link languages between the union and the states. The give and take of normal democratic politics comes out quite clearly.

"Given the nature of the Indian language situation," Das Gupta concludes, "it is hard to imagine a more acceptable solution than this compromise," which in its specifics is summed up by the 3±1 formula. But for Das Gupta, not only was the outcome relatively peaceful and satisfying to all parties but the politics itself "offered a way to diversify the structure of the political movements through autonomous, modernized, interest associations." Forced to form coalitions to succeed politically, language associations, according to Das Gupta, have contributed to "the initiation of large numbers of people in organizational modes of participation," and language politics itself "has proved to be one of the most important positive democratic channels for pursuing political integration as well as political development."[30]

In terms of my theoretical argument, language politics in India have been subject to pluralistic bargaining (with no zero-sum nonnegotiable issues). Indeed, language issues quickly moved from the streets to the arenas of bureaucratic regulation, defusing their symbolic power. Unlike issues that escalate into warfare because both sides are unable to commit to their agreements, the Indian government (after some halting efforts) was able to commit to a continued reliance on English as long as the southern states wanted to communicate with the center in the colonial language; they did so by building into law civil service examination procedures that were self-enforcing in that senior civil servants (many from Madras) had an interest in their continuation.

Through all the protest, while the central government was giving assurances that Hindi would not replace English, more and more southerners, working in the north (and watching northern television sagas and movies), became well acquainted with Hindi. Because of increased knowledge of Hindi by southerners, it will surely be more difficult for anti-Hindi forces to mobilize a united front against future small moves to increase the realms of Hindi use. For all of these reasons, language politics in India were not the cause of the dangerous decades that Selig Harrison feared. Nor were they anticivil, as are all primordial ties, as Geertz foresaw. Rather, language in India has been an arena of conflict that is fought politically rather than militarily. And as the Telugu discussion emphasizes, the battles to overcome language grievances can be far less incendiary than those resulting from job reservation grievances (with language not a factor at all). The route to the 3±1 equilibrium in India was in no way guaranteed to avoid violence; but as I have argued, there are many attributes of language politics leading up to 3±1 or related equilibria that politicize rather than militarize ethnic conflict.[31]

Language-Based Violent Confrontations in Sri Lanka

In Sri Lanka, of course, the judgments of scholars lead to the opposite conclusion, namely, that language conflict can play into economic, religious, and territorial conflicts to exacerbate tensions, making violence more likely. Language-based conflict in Sri Lanka is certainly associated with the highest scales of ethnic violence. Indeed, all of the ingredients for such violence were in the stew by the mid-1950s. In my recodings of the MAR database, the Sri Lankan Tamils receive a RURBASE = 1, suggesting high potential for violence. The Tamils are ethnically distinct from the Sinhalese (but nothing close to the "racial" division often portrayed in the press)[32] and conceive of a distinct region of the island (the northeast) as part of a Tamil homeland. With this demographic situation, postcolonial Sri Lankan ethnic violence has the ethnic dimension suggested by the rationalization logic, with an apparent language motivation.

The violence in Sri Lanka has been egregious. In the MAR six-level scale (from acts of harassment to communal warfare), communal conflict involving the Sri Lanka Tamils was at level 5 (communal rioting) in the 1950s, went down to 4 (antigroup demonstrations) in the 1960s, went up to 5 in the 1970s, and achieved a 6 with the riots of the 1980s. In the 1990s the level was recorded at 5. As for rebellion, on a seven-point scale, going from the very lowest scores in the 1950s to 1970s, the score went to 7 in the 1980s, making the Tamil rebellion among the bloodiest of all ethnic wars in the post-World War II era.

The MAR violence scores cannot be accounted for by any notion of ancient hatreds. Sinhalese and Tamils had been living in peace with one another for centuries. To be sure, there were religious riots in 1883 (Buddhists versus Catholics) and much more violent ones in 1915 (Buddhists

versus recent Muslim migrants from southern India). These riots, however, had almost nothing to do with the so-called ethnic division between
Sinhalese and Tamils. Therefore, a contemporary explanation for ethnic
violence is in order, and language *appears* to have played a central role in
fostering the tragic postcolonial conflict between Tamils and Sinhalese.

In fact, the very first violent riot of the postcolonial period in 1956
followed directly from an intense battle over language policy. As a result,
Sri Lanka has become a paradigmatic case for illustrating the relationship
of language rationalization and ethnic war. The explanation follows the
logic of late state consolidation. Under British colonial rule, English was
the language of social mobility, and Sri Lankan Tamils (many taking advantage of missionary education), despite colonial restrictions putting
geographic and demographic constraints on Tamils and keeping them
from achieving as many coveted positions as they might have gotten by
merit alone, achieved excellent government positions and settled into
good middle-class lives in Colombo.

But with independence in 1948 there was increasing pressure by the
majority Sinhalese voters to limit the Tamil presence in high political and
bureaucratic circles. Here is where political Buddhism comes into the
picture. Leading Buddhist monks began to portray the Sinhalese as a
"beleaguered majority" at the hands of the Tamils. Part of their story was
the ideology of a new Buddhism in which "to be Buddhist is to be Aryan
Sinhalese by 'race' and 'language,' and to be Sinhalese by race gives the
right to exclude, perhaps even exterminate, other 'races' in Sri Lanka,
especially the Dravidians." Buddhism in Sri Lanka since the 1950s, in
Tambiah's judgment, has therefore centered on cults that emphasize the
Sinhalese people's distinction from the Tamil population. Political Buddhists deny the historical fact that many of the cults were of Hindu origin
incorporated into Buddhism and in the nineteenth century were jointly
worshiped by Tamils and Sinhalese.[33]

In the context of religious fanaticism and political independence, a
new coalition formed. On one side were the politicized Buddhists. On
the other side were the rural elites, teachers, indigenous doctors, trad-
ers, merchants, all educated in Sinhalese and opposed to the English-
speaking elites in the capital. They were exclusivist in their nationalism,
combining Buddhism, Sinhalese "people," and myths of their "Aryan
race." These politicized Buddhists and rural nationalist followers joined
to overturn the first government of the United Nationalist Party (UNP)
and brought to power S.W.R.D. Bandaranaike, the leader of the Sri Lanka
Freedom Party (SLFP). Shortly thereafter, in 1956, the Sinhala-Only Act
was passed with a promise that the society would be Sinhalized within
24 hours. In terms of Figure 13.1 this was the first move in the official-

language game, which made the majority language the sole official language of the state, supplanting English, the colonial language.

As the Parliament was voting on this Sinhala-Only Act, the Tamil-led Federal Party leaders (who got little support in 1952 but had much greater success in 1956 as its leaders in response to UNP promises spoke out for parity status of the Tamil language) successfully organized a work stoppage in Tamil-majority areas and a Gandhi-inspired sit-in in front of the House of Representatives in Colombo. A confrontation emerged between the protesters and the police; it eventually included bands of Sinhalese youths, who engaged in vandalism throughout Colombo. Only injuries resulted from these confrontations, but the sit-ins and the subsequent melee induced a second wave of violence in which there were more than 100 deaths in the Eastern Province where Tamils and Sinhalese lived intermingled.

Another round of riots in 1958 followed, despite a pact between Prime Minister Bandaranaike and S.J.V. Chelvanayagam, the leader of the Federal Party, that provided for official use of Tamil and creation of regional councils in Tamil-populated areas. UNP politicians opportunistically saw this as an opening for their return to power. They joined forces with the monks to decry the peace pact as a "betrayal of the Sinhalese" and staged provocative pilgrimages to mobilize support. With tensions already high and provoked by news that Tamils in the north had defaced National Transport buses painted with Sinhalese lettering, Sinhalese gangs in the south joined the fray and vandalized Tamil signs on retail establishments. Politicized monks pressed Bandaranaike to renounce the pact. A series of violent confrontations ensued. They continued for two weeks in a chain reaction, first to riots on the eastern coast linked to anger over population resettlement schemes, then to Sinhalese vandalism of Tamil property in the south, and finally to Tamil attacks on Sinhalese-minority communities in the north and east. Martial law was finally imposed.[34]

Relations between the Tamil and Sinhalese after 1958 teetered on the brink of civil war. A solution appeared to be in sight, however, when President Jayewardene won the election in 1977 with great support from the Indian Tamils. He recognized their Ceylon Workers' Congress, the union of plantation workers and had Tamil awarded the status of national language (though not the official language). He also negotiated with the Tamil United Liberation Front (TULF) for district councils in the regions. And he negotiated to lessen the impact of the educational "affirmative action" programs that favored Sinhalese youth. Yet in 1981 and (much worse) in 1983, large-scale violence erupted between Tamils and Sinhalese.

The 1983 violence had some important features that Tambiah empha-

sizes. It was the product of "organized mob" work: the rioters had detailed knowledge of Tamil homes through access to voter lists, and this
made their destruction quite specific. Systematic vandalism was aimed at
Tamil businesses and factories. Not only Sri Lankan Tamil interests were
targeted but "*all* Indian enterprises." The motivating idea was "that every
Indian is a Tamil and that every Tamil is a terrorist." The police and army
either actively participated or passively encouraged the rioting. Worse,
the president allowed the rioting to go on too long before declaring a state
of emergency. He asserted then that "the time has come to accede to the
clamor and the national respect of the Sinhalese people." He therefore
banned the TULF. Neither he nor his minister of security had a word of
sympathy for the condition of the Tamils. It is clear that they were playing
to the hard-line racists in the government and army. In Tambiah's assessment, "those who stood to gain [the] most were, firstly, middle-level
Sinhala entrepreneurs, businessmen, and white-collar workers, and sec-
ondly, the urban poor, mainly through looting." The result of this pogrom
was that 350 to 2,000 were killed and about 100,000 were made refugees.[35]

Tambiah's accounts of the bases of this violence are fair minded and
judicious. He elegantly weaves the language issue with the religious problems of the newly politicized Buddhists, the demographic challenges in
the Eastern Province, and the economic problems of job scarcity in a
postcolonial economy. One of his important insights emerged when he
asked why the riots, presumably caused by a language law, spread with
such ferocity to the rural areas, where social mobility and government
jobs were hardly the burning issues facing the peasants. The answer that
Tambiah provides is that in this area the government was resettling Sinhalese in such numbers as to make the Eastern Province into a Sinhalese-
majority area, with vast consequences for any future federal design.[36]
Fear of becoming a minority in their home region, rather than loss of civil
service opportunities, was surely a more important motivating force for
peasants. In no sense does Tambiah even suggest that the language issue
was a principal cause of the riots; rather, from his point of view it contributed to the layers of mistrust and threat that divided Sinhala and Tamil in
the postcolonial era.

Yet a few facts make one wonder if Tambiah's accounts hold together.
Why, if it were the Tamils who were most threatened by the language
policy, was most of the rioting in Colombo in both 1956 and 1958 initiated
by the Sinhalese, with virtually no Tamil violence aimed at Sinhalese until
1975?[37] Or, why did the most horrifyingly fatal riots (those in 1981 and
1983) and the formation of a full-scale rebellion occur after Tamil was
accorded nearly equal status in Sir Lankan law? Or, finally, why did the
language issue disappear from public debate in inverse proportion to the
level of escalation of violence on the island? The theory I presented ear-

lier, along with the comparative data on language conflict, suggests a different story from the one Tambiah and most of the objective observers of the Sri Lankan conflict tell. My alternative story line is that the language conflict was one of the factors that worked to ameliorate violence, but other factors outweighed the language issue to drive Sri Lanka into large-scale ethnic war. Let us now return to the language issue, with an eye toward its bureaucratization.

Bureaucratization of Language Policy in Sri Lanka

In 1833 a British commission recommended that English become the language of public proceedings in Ceylon, though it took a half century before a Sri Lankan actually qualified for high-level service. A new governing elite of English-speaking Sri Lankans was thereby created, only to be challenged by populist politicians campaigning in the 1940s under conditions of universal suffrage. In 1943-1944 the State Council adopted a motion introduced by J.R. Jayewardene to replace English by Sinhalese and Tamil (overcoming the original motion, which mentioned only Sinhalese).

It was only after three years of independence that the governor general put the whole language issue under the auspices of the ministry of finance and appointed an implementing commission for this motion. Five interim reports from 1951 through 1953 were issued before the final report came in October 1953, which essentially subverted the bill by claiming that the introduction of ill-developed languages such as Sinhalese and Tamil into official life was unrealistic. One hundred nine recommendations followed for a future introduction of the national languages into official life. Some of the commission's recommendations, such as the issuance of official terms (developed by "Official Terms Committees of Sinhala and Tamil," which by 1955 had indexed 43,000 Sinhala and 48,117 Tamil terms and phrases used in the public sector),[38] training in stenography and typing (as reading shorthand in Sinhalese turned out to be quite difficult and for which was published *A Guide to the Reading of Handwritten Documents* in 1955), and the organization of language schools for civil servants not competent to write either Sinhalese or Tamil, were already being addressed. To coordinate all of the implementing activities, the Official Languages Bureau was made a special unit of the ministry of finance. Annual reports of the bureau pointed to wide areas of progress, but in its begging for more funds, more personnel, more official terms in Sinhalese and Tamil, and more laws written in those languages, success seemed eons away.

In 1956 the government changed course and passed the Sinhala-Only Act. It was a brief act, just giving a few principles, with no official regulations. However threatening this act was to the Tamil community, it was not self-enforcing. A variety of subsequent government memoranda set out general guidelines. First, to keep the civil service operating, the cabinet determined that "old entrants" (those who were currently in the civil service) had joined the civil service "on the assumption that the language through which their duties have to be carried out will be English." Determining that "it does not appear to be fair . . . that an officer recruited in this way should be forced to adopt Sinhalese," the cabinet determined that English-speaking old entrants not only would not be fired but would never be forced to use Sinhalese to carry out their official duties, could not be subject to fines, and would be given cash bonuses for learning Sinhalese. Even "new entrants" would be able to take civil service examinations in English, but they would be required to learn Sinhalese in a three-year grace period. Gunasekera concludes from his analysis of the legal situation that "in effect, although the election pledge of [the] government was to make Sinhala the official language within 24 hours, the policies that were enunciated were quite inconsistent with that pledge."[39] What Gunasekera does not mention, however, is that the entire upper-level bureaucracy (including Sinhalese), in utter disregard for the spirit of the law, throughout this period relied almost solely on English.[40]

Partly in reaction to Tamil outrage and the subsequent riots, the government passed the Tamil Language (Special Provisions) Act No. 28 of 1958 (with no implementing legislation until 1966, when the UNP replaced the SLFP in the government), providing for the use of Tamil as a medium of instruction in schools and as a medium of examination for public service jobs. But better than Tamil resistance to the Sinhala language was popular indifference and bureaucratic inertia. Training classes in the official language were abandoned because of low attendance and lack of interest by both Sinhalese and Tamils. Meanwhile, the commissioner for official languages issued circular after circular demanding that government contractors develop a plan to switch over from English, that retirement schemes be worked out for non-Sinhala speakers still in the service, and that proficiency tests in Sinhala be standardized. The department operated in an environment that was almost unconnected to society. In one report the commissioner wistfully asked "whether the hoped-for objectives could be realized."[41] Subsequent circulars sought to round the square of a Sinhala-Only orientation tempered by the promotion of Tamil as a national language. An official "clarification" of the rules in 1969 provided (to simplify a gaggle of regulations whose relevant sections are reproduced in full by Gunasekera)[42] that Sinhala was a necessary language for all official matters but that in the Northern and Eastern provinces, where Tamil could be used for official purposes, a Tamil version must be attached. This new orientation led to utter stasis, and in 1970 the

SLFP (in coalition with two Marxist parties) regained state power with an ideology of returning to the principles of the 1956 Sinhala-Only Act.

The politics of language continued to zig-zag in the way of all pluralist conflicts. The 1972 constitution gave the 1969 clarifications the status of basic law. Yet in 1973 the Official Language Department was taken out of the hands of the ministry of finance and parceled out to a variety of ministries. The department itself fell into desuetude, and its offices were cleared out. In 1977 in a Sinhalese attempt to put flesh on the Sinhala-Only skeleton, a de facto quota system for Tamils was legislated; only 30 percent of university admissions would be based on merit, the rest on population categories. The 1978 constitution essentially gave parity to Sinhala, Tamil, and English (which had previously been *the* language of elite communication and most bureaucratic activity but without official recognition). Thus, the status of Sinhala was lowered (it was to be the official language but not the "one official language") and correspondingly the status of Tamil was raised (it became "an official language"). Both were given equal status as national languages, and all citizens had the right to a basic education in either. Each language was envisioned to be prominent in its own regions, but now with English as the link language between them, and a language that could be designated for higher education and courts of law.[43] Legal change easily outpaced sociolinguistic reality, and in 1978 an Official Language section was reconstituted, with the hope that coherence could be restored. In 1991 a new Official Language Commission was appointed, with wide theoretical powers. It again sought to develop policies and incentives that would make the official languages the principal means of official communication in their respective regions, but its impact on sociolinguistic reality can only be regarded as minimal. In Sri Lanka the ethnically charged politics of language had become the bureaucratically entrenched subversion of state language policy.

Toward a Reinterpretation Consistent with the Macrodata

There can be no doubt that the language issue provided a powerful symbolic rallying cry in 1956. The Sinhala-Only Act was more of a public humiliation than workable statute. The riots in Colombo were clearly the secondary consequence of the tensions that bedeviled the island in the weeks of debate leading up to the historic vote. The language act of 1956, and the subsequent riots, helped strengthen the Federal Party and made it exclusively Tamil. And the sources of the separatist movement, marked by the rise of the Liberation Tigers of Tamil Eelam (LTTE) in the mid-1970s, can be traced to a set of humiliations, one of which was the Sinhala-Only Act.[44]

The bureaucratic tale told above suggests that taken alone the language issue unleashed a powerful nonsymbolic dynamic. The need to make rules for the use of Sinhalese, and to make provisions for both non-Sinhalese and Sinhalese to use it in official domains, created a vast administrative task. The Department of Official Languages was beset with pressures from a variety of interests, and it required the work of many Tamils to write translations of official terms. Meanwhile, setting standards for Sinhala writing competence too high could backfire, as it could have jeopardized the tenure of many Sinhalese. Language politics, if implementation were to occur, moved into the realm of pluralistic give and take rather than symbolic pronouncement.

Furthermore, because of its inability to implement the Sinhala-Only Act in 24 hours, the government found itself able to commit to Tamils in the bureaucracy that they would not be out in the streets jobless by decree. The regulations for the fulfillment of Sinhala-Only gave assurances to Tamils in the civil service that their jobs and promotions were secure. This helped defuse the anxieties and anger of the Tamil elite. It might also help explain why there was never an alliance of northern autonomists in Jaffna with Tamil professionals in Colombo. The latter group preferred cosmopolitan life in Colombo or emigration to the West over migration to the Northern Province to give intellectual leadership to Tamil Eelam. In 1988, with the Indian government's intervention, a North Eastern Provincial Government was constituted, and during its honeymoon period it was able to recruit leading Tamil civil servants. But there is no indication in my sources that Tamil officials from the south were moving to Jaffna.[45]

It is not possible in this context to prove a counterfactual, but it seems at least plausible to argue that with the politicized Sinhala Buddhists in alliance with the rural Sinhalese elites there would easily have been induced pogroms against both Sri Lankan and Indian Tamils as both religious and economic threats. The populating of the Eastern Province with Sinhalese peasants going back to the colonial period continued to threaten the Tamils' hope for a majority in both the north and east of the island. Reduction in homeland space has been conducive to a national separatist movement, with or without a language issue. Meanwhile, in the arena of language politics, there was a considerable amount of political interaction between Sinhalese and Tamils, with common interests in the development of a reasonable language policy that served both communities' interests.

If the Tamils were willing to negotiate peacefully over language, we should ask, what explains the systematic refusal by Sinhalese to abjure violence in the 1970s and negotiate a fair language policy? This refusal to negotiate, in Tambiah's judgment, was a principal source of the violence.[46] The standard answer to this question is that the Sinhalese were themselves divided into two parties, representing different dynastic families. Each sought dominance by promising the same electoral base the job opportunities that would become theirs should the Tamils be excluded from the white-collar job market. Either party in power that sought reconciliation was challenged by the other party, waiting in the wings. To establish their anti-Tamil bona fides, leaders of both parties underwrote young thugs to victimize innocent Tamils.

Here we can say that the Sinhalese language policy of 1956 was an instrument of oppression. It is also the case that the job and university quotas based on language increased the number of disaffected youth who had no better alternatives than to join the guerrilla forces. But the economic downturn in the postcolonial period was a cause of the language laws in the first place and was sufficient to marginalize young men (both Sinhalese and Tamils) in the modern economy. More important, however, is that the language policy in itself drew many Tamils into the political arena, a point not recognized by all too many analysts looking for the mechanisms by which language policy pushed Sri Lanka into ethnic war.

Although I concede that the language issue sparked some of the early rioting by Tamils (and the defacing of some Sinhalese signs), a comparativist's perspective leads me to hold that over the past 40 years its impact has been more ameliorative than exacerbating. The critical piece of evidence, overlooked by several area experts, is that violence was not initiated by those who were aggrieved by an unfair language policy but rather by the group in whose interests the law was passed. The grievances themselves cannot therefore be held to motivate Sri Lankan interethnic violence. A closer look shows that many aggrieved Tamils were drawn by the language policy to bureaucratic insurgency and political protest, peacefully. *Here is an example where even the best and most informed case studies may be wrong on the very sign of an important independent variable.*

POLICY ANALYSIS

The thesis of this paper, even with the historical reinterpretations of India and Sri Lanka, is so counterintuitive as to leave any reader with a sense of deep skepticism. Many readers will have cases in mind where language decrees fomented popular demonstrations, which brought in the police and spilled over into violence. The Russification decrees in Poland in the 1870s, the promotion of Afrikaans in South Africa's township schools in 1976, and the law on language in Moldova in 1989 are all associated with riots and revolution by the oppressed. I submit, however, that a careful reconstruction of these cases, similar to what I have done with Sri Lanka, will give support to my thesis. In Poland the revolution against Tsarist Russia preceded the language decrees rather than resulted from them; in South Africa the riots in Soweto brought accommodation on the linguistic front, and the subsequent war was fueled by the denial of political rights to Africans; and in Moldova the law on language that was said to provoke the rebellion in Transdniester was indistinguishable from the language laws in the 13 other non-Russian republics, with none of the others bringing the Russian-speaking populations into armed conflict. The comparative speculations that have informed this section, however counterintuitive, should be sufficient to undermine the claim that language grievances are a spark that can all too easily set off incendiary ethnic wars. Good policy cannot ignore this finding.

In this section I analyze official language policies of states to see if there is a clue as to which policies are associated with the lowest levels of violence. To do so I coded all countries in the Gurr dataset on the basis of their language policies, in a variable I call LANGREGIME, short for Language Regime. There are five values for this variable, and they are characterized in the left column of Table 13.4. Examples of "1," where there is a single official language corresponding to the ethnic majority or dominant settler group, include English in the United States, German in Austria, Hungarian in Hungary, Malay in Malaysia, and Spanish in Argentina. Examples of "2," where there is a single (or sometimes a second) official language corresponding to a language not associated with a major ethnic group in the country, include Bahasa in Indonesia, French and English in Cameroon, and English in Kenya. This language is usually referred to as a lingua franca. Examples of "3," where both an indigenous language and a nonindigenous language are official, include English, Hindi and state languages in India, and Hebrew, English, and Arabic in Israel. The value "3"

TABLE 13.4 Language Regimes and Rebellion—Mean Scores for Rebellion (number of cases)

Language Regime	All Cases	Where RURBASE =1	Where RURBASE = 1 and Independent After 1944
All cases	1.68 (n = 218)	2.10 (n = 171)	2.51 (n = 95)
1. Rationalization	1.32 (n = 92)	1.74 (n = 68)	2.92 (n = 26)
2. Official lingua franca	1.60 (n = 45)	1.82 (n = 39)	1.86 (n = 36)
3. 3±1 language formula	2.88 (n = 41)	3.14 (n = 37)	2.78 (n = 32)
4. More than one domestic official language with no lingua franca	1.80 (n = 10)	2.25 (n = 8)	NA (n = 0)
5. Rationalization + recognition of regional language(s)	1.20 (n = 30)	1.89 (n = 19)	6.0 (n = 1)

NA = not applicable

corresponds broadly to the 3±1 model discussed in this paper. Examples of "4," where there is more than one official language corresponding to the leading ethnic groups of the country, include German, French, Italian, and Rhaeto-Romance in Switzerland and Pashto and Persian in Afghanistan. Examples of "5," where there is but one official language but with recognized regional languages, include cases such as Spanish with Catalan, Basque, and Galician in Spain and Arabic with Kurdish in Iraq.

I then compared in Table 13.4 the mean REBELLION scores for each policy, under all cases and under cases where RURBASE = 1. It is clear that the 3±1 model, however attractive it is from a welfare or identity point of view, is associated with higher levels of violence. This result should be taken with skepticism. For one thing, groups that have been successfully incorporated into states under the 3±1 formula (e.g., the Tamils, Gujaratis, Kannada speakers in India; the Romansch speakers in Switzerland) are not in the dataset, as they were not considered "at risk."[47] Second, minority violence could well have impelled states to accept such language regimes, which would explain the association but have the causal arrow in the wrong direction. Third, when a dummy for 3±1 is constructed and entered into the equation displayed in Table 13.2, although the coefficient is positive, it is not anywhere close to being significant.[48] Nonetheless, it would be foolhardy from the point of view of policy prescription to advertise this policy as a model for other states. Meanwhile, rationalization with concessions to minorities for regional languages (a policy increasingly apparent in Western democracies) has the lowest mean score for REBELLION in the entire sample, and perhaps this is a clue as to how best to handle language grievances when they become heavily politicized (although this is what Sri Lanka did eventually but unsuccessfully).

Finally, I examined only those minorities with a rural base and in accordance with Gellner's theory only from countries that entered into the community of states after 1944. These are the states most subject to problems establishing an official language, many having relied on the colonial language as the official language of modern government. From this set the mean score for REBELLION is 2.51. But for those with LANGREGIME = 3 (the set with India as paradigm), the mean score is higher at 2.78; those with LANGREGIME = 1 (rationalization) had a mean score of 2.68; meanwhile, for those with LANGREGIME = 2 (the set with Kenya as paradigm), the mean score is lowest at 1.86. (The Sri Lankan Tamils are the only case where LANGREGIME = 5.) This last column suggests that a single neutral lingua franca has been more peaceful than the indigenous-promoting multilingual schemes and more peaceful as well than the rationalization policies. A dummy for cases with a neutral lingua franca added to the specification for Table 13.2 has a negative coefficient (i.e., this language regime lowers the expected value for rebellion), but it is not significant.[49]

More interesting still is the comparison of the 32 cases where LANGREGIME = 3 (i.e., the 3±1 model) and examining whether the minority group living under such a language regime has its language recognized in the official language formula. The result is that groups whose languages are recognized (n = 17) have a mean REBELLION score of 3.6; those whose languages are not recognized (n = 15) have a mean score of 3.5. Thus, there is slightly more violence associated with recognition of a group's language in a multilingual scheme than in keeping the language group out of the scheme altogether. In those 32 cases only 7.3 percent of the groups had any recorded language grievance. Meanwhile, in the cases where there was acceptance of a lingua franca (i.e., where LANGREGIME = 2), 13.3 percent of the groups articulated language grievances. This means that bringing groups into the official language formula is not a prescription for peaceful ethnic relations and that fomenting language grievances (by ignoring a group's plea for official recognition of its language) is not a prescription for violence.[50]

SUMMARY AND CONCLUSION

The purpose of this paper was to explore the relationship between language-based political conflict and ethnic violence. The standard view in the literature is that language issues, especially when a nationalizing elite in control of a state in the modern period seeks to impose its language as the principal means of state business and social mobility, exacerbate ethnic tensions, with potential for ethnic violence. An analysis of the Gurr dataset does not support this standard view. Instead, the data support a view that language distance (between groups) and language grievances (by minorities) play no causal role in the emergence of rebellion. In fact, there is some support for the counter hypothesis, namely, that language grievances when expressed under conditions of religious tension tend to ameliorate violence. Theoretical considerations—having to do with the bureaucratization of language conflict, the ability of the state to make language commitments, and the difficult collective-action problems faced by minority-language entrepreneurs—help us make sense of the statistical findings. With the surprising statistical results and the new theoretical considerations brought to mind, a reexamination of two well-known cases of language politics—in India and Sri Lanka—gives added support to the data and the theory seeking to make sense of those data.

A necessary condition for violence to be averted, it should be emphasized, is that the state must be willing to bargain over demands articulated by language activists in society. In India the central government's unwillingness to provoke the Telugu speakers into unyielding opposition is key to the peaceful resolution of that conflict. Violent confrontations between Marathis and Gujaratis in Bombay, and between Nagas and Assamese in the northeast, were also defused in part because the central government went to the bargaining table and was willing to make concessions. In Sri Lanka the government's passage of the Tamil Language Acts of 1966, as well as the constitutional guarantees of 1972 and 1978, helped limit the range of the civil war mostly to the northeast of the island. My argument is not that even with government intransigence language conflicts will reduce the likelihood of large-scale violence; rather I believe that language conflicts allow for extensive and successful bargaining without making it seem as if either side is a traitor to its group's interests. But absent utter intransigence by government authorities, the hypothesized route from discriminatory language policy to ethnic civil war and state breakdown is not supported by the comparative data.

Willingness to bargain with minorities does not imply democracy. The MAR dataset includes 40 cases where DEMOCRACY was of low quality, MAXLANG was substantial, yet REBELLION did not reach a critical threshold. These include the Indian Tamils in Sri Lanka, the Taiwanese in Taiwan, the Berbers in Algeria, and the Roma in Croatia. There are also two cases with high levels of DEMOCRACY where MAXLANG was also substantial, yet REBELLION has been significant.[51] These include the Bodos in India and the Kurds in Turkey. Democratic institutions are neither necessary nor sufficient to ensure official-language bargaining. In fact, statistical evidence does not allow us to reject the hypothesis that democratic institutions play no role in ameliorating or exacerbating language-based conflict.

Even more surprising, there is no evidence that sensitive language policies are nostrums for ethnic arousals. For countries that received independence after World War II, bureaucracies usually operated with the colonial language. Leaders of many groups expressed firm desires to have their languages recognized as official and relied on as media of instruction in state schools. Yet the sensitive granting of these desires did not lower the likelihood of violent rebellion, and the failure to do so for some groups did not raise that likelihood. Grievances over language were expressed under all forms of policy; they were expressed regardless of whether the group's language was represented in multilingual official formulas. Yet when those grievances were expressed, the trend was not to enhance the chances of violence but (if anything) to reduce them.

The principal policy recommendation of this paper is that governments should be encouraged to allow groups to express language demands on the political stage. In fact, the Indian case shows that the payoff for peace is enhanced if the government rewards groups with a variety of concessions (e.g., jobs) for making language-based claims on the state. Essential as well is that the government must assure the minority groups that the dominant group will not take minority expression of language grievances as a pretext for genocide against them. In sum, governments must be willing to engage in political and bureaucratic conflicts over language issues. Meanwhile, the substance of any particular language framework has no bearing on peaceful outcomes.

This recommendation has special relevance for the newly independent states of the former Soviet Union. In 1989 all of these republics passed new language laws that reversed the tides, giving greater official status to the republican language vis-à-vis Russian. In some republics, after independence in 1991, these laws became more stringent still. In 1999 Anatol Lieven of the International Institute for Strategic Studies excoriated the Latvian parliament for its measures that, he claims, "would have virtually banished the Russian language from public life." Holding up the specter of Kosovo, he argued that because the proposed law embodied "gratuitous provocations" the West had a "special duty to help prevent such legislation." The argument of this paper is not that the Latvian legislation was fair minded. It was not. Rather, the argument is that the "special provocations" were more likely to drive the Russian-speaking population in Latvia to political action rather than guerrilla action. The international gendarmerie must distinguish those policies that are merely unfair from actions that plant the seeds of civil war. The analysis in this paper helps make that distinction.[52]

Policy makers—for states that face language conflict and for states that provide support for an international gendarmerie when ethnic conflict spills over into ethnic violence—should be made aware that language conflict, even if it is not threatening to states or democratic regimes, can be extremely dangerous for incumbents. Leaders of disaffected language groups have the skills and intellectual resources to mobilize constituencies that are outraged by current language policies. Incumbents on the unpopular side of a language conflict can be ruthlessly thrown out of office. But this does not mean that language conflict is dangerous to democratic governance or civil peace. In fact, language conflict, when not directly and brutally repressed by fearful incumbents, tends to be fought out in translation committees, school boards, and bureaucracies. If language entrepreneurs are given the chance to mobilize their constituencies, incumbents might lose their positions, but partisans of other languages are not likely to lose their lives.

To be sure, people have died while participating in language-based riots. But the data in this paper demonstrate that it is far more likely that language grievances will result in political protests than military action. Politics is the realm where intense conflicts can be resolved peacefully.

Policy analysts need to recognize that the politicization of language issues is not a danger signal for ethnic war. In fact, the politicization of language ameliorates the violent potential of religion-based conflict. To understand that the politicization of language issues may be the straw that strengthens the camel's back would be to take an important step in understanding language, politics, and ethnic violence.

ACKNOWLEDGMENTS

Much of the work that forms the basis of this paper was done in collaboration with James D. Fearon, who helped me think through the implications of the data presented herein. I would also like to thank Kanchan Chandra and Bruce Bueno de Mesquita for comments on a draft and the "Chicago on the Hudson" seminar (John Roemer, Adam Przeworski, Jon Elster, Steven Lukes, John Ferejohn, Brian Barry, and Stephen Holmes) for showing me how to better specify my argument. Finally, Paul Stern coherently conveyed the often contradictory advice given me by the review committee organized by the National Research Council.

This chapter also appeared in *Archive Européenes de Sociologie* 2000 (41):97-137.

NOTES

[1]Selig S. Harrison, ed. (1957), *The Most Dangerous Decades: An Introduction to the Comparative Study of Language Policy in Multi-lingual States* (New York: Language and Communication Research Center, Columbia University).
[2]The Ocalan quote is from a report in *The New York Times*, June 24, 1999, by Stephen Kinzer.
[3]Clifford Geertz (1973), "The Integrative Revolution" in *The Interpretation of Cultures* (New York: Basic Books), pp. 256-257.
[4]For a full description of the database, see Ted R. Gurr (1993), *Minorities at Risk* (Washington, D.C.: United States Institute of Peace). There are several worrisome methodological pitfalls in the construction and coding of this database, discussed in James Fearon and David Laitin's proposal to remedy them, funded by the National Science Foundation, grant no. 9876530, "Minorities at Risk Database and Explaining Ethnic Violence." The proposed changes will surely have some impact on the relationships discussed in this paper. The findings herein can therefore only be considered preliminary.
[5]Ernest Gellner (1983), *Nations and Nationalism* (Ithaca, N.Y.: Cornell University Press).
[6]Max Weber (1968), *Economy and Society* (Berkeley: University of California Press), pp. 71, 655, 809-838, and 1108 for discussions of different forms of rationalization.
[7]Eugen Weber (1976), *Peasants into Frenchmen* (Stanford, Calif.: Stanford University Press); Abram de Swaan (1988), *In Care of the State* (New York: Oxford University Press), chap. 3.
[8]This is a summary of David D. Laitin et al. (1994), "Language and the Construction of States: The Case of Catalonia in Spain," *Politics and Society*, vol. 22, no. 1 (March), pp. 3-30.
[9]Juan Linz (1974), "Politics in a Multilingual Society with a Dominant World Lan-

guage," in *Les états multilingues: problèmes et solutions*, J.G. Savard and R. Vegneault, eds. (Quebec: Presses de l'Université Laval), pp. 367-444.

[10]The Habsburg case is an archetype for the foundational figures in contemporary theories of nationalism, especially those who lived in it at the time of its dissolution: Hans Kohn, Karl Deutsch, Eric Hobsbawm, and Ernest Gellner.

[11]REBELLION, unless otherwise specified, is the variable "rebel90x" in the MAR dataset, reflecting a value of the group's rebellion against the state for the years 1990-1995.

[12]See David D. Laitin (2000), "What Is a Language Community?," *American Journal of Political Science*, vol. 44, no. 1, pp. 142-155.

[13]Barbara F. Grimes, ed. (1996), *Ethnologue: Languages of the World*, 13th ed. (Dallas: Summer Institute of Linguistics).

[14]For a discussion of the methodological problems in using a measure of language distance, see Laitin, *What Is a Language Community?*

[15]Gurr, *Minorities at Risk*, p. 18.

[16]Given the limitations of the MAR dataset, where language grievances are coded only for the 1990s and the latest scores for rebellion are also in the 1990s, I cannot now rule out the interpretation of the forthcoming results as rebellion causing a reduction in language grievances. This is rather implausible, and subsequent updating of the database will allow me to assure myself that the causal arrows as I interpret them are correct.

[17]James D. Fearon and David D. Laitin (1999), "Weak States, Rough Terrain, and Large-Scale Ethnic Violence Since 1945," paper prepared for the Annual Meeting of the American Political Science Association, Atlanta, Ga.

[18]Users of the MAR database will want to know: there is no rural base for rebellion (RURBASE = 0) if the group is primarily urban (REG5 = 1), or if the group is widely dispersed (REG6 = 1), if the group did not migrate to the country until the twentieth century (TRADITN = 4 or 5), or if the group members (even if it was primarily rural) were the descendants of slaves or are travelers (Romani). Meanwhile, the group was considered to have a rural base (RURBASE = 1) if the minority group could trace its origins in the country to the period before state formation (TRADITN = 1) or if the group had at least a majority concentrated in one region of the state (GROUPCON = 2 or 3).

[19]Other interaction terms—with race and class in particular—would be feasible elaborations of this analysis. Getting an objective measure of race prevents an exploration of its dynamic. I lack data on the class composition of the ethnic groups and cannot explore its impact here.

[20]The mirror is also true: religious grievances reduce the rebellious potential of language grievances, but this effect is far less strong statistically than the one reported in the text.

[21]See David Laitin (1989), "Language Policy and Political Strategy in India," *Policy Sciences*, vol. 22, p. 426.

[22]Under such conditions violence is more likely, as James D. Fearon argues in "Ethnic War as a Commitment Problem," paper presented at the Annual Meeting of the American Political Science Association, New York, 1994.

[23]This is the source of humor in Woody Allen's *Bananas*, when the leader of a Latin American guerrilla army, at the moment of victory, with cigar in mouth, announces that from that point on Swedish will be the sole language of all communication in the island nation.

[24]My research career has been devoted to this dilemma. I focus on the identity aspects of language in David D. Laitin (1977), *Politics, Language and Thought* (Chicago: University of Chicago Press). I focus on the strategic rationality of defection in David D. Laitin (1988), "Language Games," *Comparative Politics*, vol. 20, pp. 289-302. I focus on the "Janus-facedness" of culture, which has both an identity and a strategic component, in David D.

Laitin (1986), *Hegemony and Culture* (Chicago: University of Chicago Press). In this paper the identity aspect of culture plays only a bit part because the dependent variable is "violence" (where strategic action is more important) rather than "assimilation" (where identity issues play a major role).

[25]David D. Laitin (1986), *Hegemony and Culture* (Chicago: University of Chicago Press).

[26]For a compilation of the details for this aspect of corpus planning, see Government of Andhra Pradesh (1968), *White Paper on Official Language (Telugu): Preparation of Authoritative Texts* (Hyderabad: Government Secretariat Press).

[27]K. Ravi (1982), "Regional Separatist Agitations in Andhra Pradesh," in A. Prasanna Kumar, V. Linga Murty, and K. Ravi, eds., *Government and Politics in Andhra Pradesh* (New Delhi: S. Chand), pp. 54-65.

[28]R.V.R. Chandrasekhara Rao (1979), "Conflicting Roles of Language and Regionalism in an Indian State: A Case Study of Andhra Pradesh" and Dagmar Bernstorff (1979), "Region and Nation: The Telengana Movement's Dual Identity," in David Taylor and Malcolm Yapp, *Political Identity in South Asia* (London: Centre of South Asian Studies, SOAS, University of London), pp. 138-150 and 151-169. See also Myron Weiner (1978), *Sons of the Soil* (Princeton, N.J.: Princeton University Press), chap. 5.

[29]Paul R. Brass (1974), *Language, Religion and Politics in North India* (London: Cambridge University Press), p. 430.

[30]Jyotirindra Das Gupta (1970), *Language Conflict and National Development* (Berkeley: University of California Press), pp. 259, 266, 268, 270.

[31]David Laitin (1989), "Language Policy and Political Strategy in India," *Policy Sciences*, vol. 22, pp. 415-436.

[32]Stanley J. Tambiah (1986), *Sri Lanka: Ethnic Fratricide and the Dismantling of Democracy* (Chicago: University of Chicago Press), pp. 5-7, and Gannath Obeyesekere in a letter to the *New York Times* (April 24, 1984) hopefully lay to rest any lingering notion of such a divide in Sri Lanka.

[33]Tambiah, *Sri Lanka*, pp. 58-60.

[34]Stanley Tambiah (1992), *Buddhism Betrayed?* (Chicago: University of Chicago Press), pp. 49-57.

[35]Tambiah, *Sri Lanka*, pp. 20-27; Stanley Tambiah (1996), *Leveling Crowds* (Berkeley: University of California Press), p. 100.

[36]Tambiah, *Sri Lanka*, pp. 71-78; Tambiah, *Leveling Crowds*, p. 86.

[37]M.R. Narayan Swamy (1994), *Tigers of Lanka: From Boys to Guerillas* (Delhi: Konark Publishers), p. 21.

[38]S.G. Samarasinghe (1996), "Language Policy in Public Administration, 1956-1994" in R.G.G. Olcott Gunasekera, S.G. Samarasinghe, and V. Vamadevan, eds., *National Language Policy in Sri Lanka* (Kandy: International Centre for Ethnic Studies), p. 98.

[39]R.G.G. Olcott Gunasekera (1996), "The Implementation of the Official Language Policy, 1956-1970" in Gunasekera, op. cit., p. 32.

[40]Samarasinghe, op. cit., p. 105

[41]Gunasekera, op. cit., p. 45.

[42]Ibid., pp. 58-62.

[43]Samarasinghe, op. cit., pp. 79-91.

[44]The Houdini-like leader of the Liberation Tigers, V. Prabhakaran, became a militant largely because of the "standardization" decrees that were designed to advantage Sri Lankans who took official examinations in Sinhalese. In this way, language laws took young Tamils out of the education stream and into the guerrilla river. This relationship is incomplete, however. First, Prabhakaran had a fixation for explosives well before he thought about Eelam. Second, recruitment into militant groups was extremely slow until 1983, when the LTTE had fewer than 50 hard-core members. But when rumors spread in 1983 that the

Indian government was funding and training Tamil guerrillas, recruitment skyrocketed. At that time, however, standardization was hardly an issue. See Swamy, op. cit., chap. 4, and pp. ix, 96.

[45]Ibid., p. 294.

[46]Stanley Tambiah, comments at the National Research Council seminar to review a draft of this paper, October 22, 1998.

[47]James Fearon and I, in the context of our National Science Foundation grant, will include some groups not considered to be at risk in future analyses and in doing so may pick up the violence-decreasing aspects of the 3±1 missed in Table 13.4.

[48]B = .475264; SE B = .467966.

[49]B = −.438306; SE B = .449604. This is when the dummy for 3±1 is also in the equation.

[50]There are insufficient numbers of cases to analyze LANGREGIME = 4 or LANGREGIME = 5 for groups with RURBASE = 1 living in countries that entered the world system after 1945 (YRENTRY > 1945). Even under these conditions the bivariate correlation between REBELLION and MAXLANG is weakly negative.

[51]Users of the MAR dataset might want to note that the threshold for democracy of high quality is ndem89 = 8; the threshold for substantial language grievances is MAXLANG > 1; and the critical threshold for REBELLION is rebel90x > 3.

[52]For Lieven's position, see "No Russian Spoken Here," *The New York Times*, July 16, 1999.

14

The Organization for Security and Cooperation in Europe: Its Contribution to Conflict Prevention and Resolution

P. Terrence Hopmann

The Organization for Security and Cooperation in Europe (OSCE) provides an excellent case to evaluate the development of regional international regimes in the realm of security. This organization is currently composed of 55 member states[1] in Europe, broadly defined as extending from "Vancouver to Vladivostok the long way around," including the United States and Canada and all former Eurasian states that emerged from the breakup of the Soviet Union. It is the successor to the Conference on Security and Cooperation in Europe (CSCE), which produced the "Helsinki Accords" of 1975, often cited as marking the highwater point of the East-West détente that developed in the early 1970s. Since the end of the Cold War, it has evolved and adapted to the post-Cold War environment and has begun to play a primary role in the prevention and resolution of the many conflicts that have appeared in the Eurasian region since 1989.

My main argument here is that the OSCE has developed into a "security regime" for the Eurasian region. Its performance may thus serve to illustrate the power of liberal institutionalist ideas about international relations. Using the OSCE as a case study of a regional security regime, I thus propose to examine the proposition that regional security organizations can restrain anarchy in international political relations and promote cooperation to solve common problems and resolve violent or potentially violent conflicts. I will investigate the impact that multilateral organizations can have in managing conflicts and building security at the regional level.

Realists argue that international relations are inevitably characterized by conflicts of interest in which changes in the relative power positions of states within an anarchic international system make war and violence almost inevitable, especially during times when system structures become destabilized and power balances break down. Realist predictions about the end of the Cold War generally maintained that the collapse of a relatively stable balance of power founded on nuclear deterrence between the United States and the Soviet Union would inevitably lead to greater violence and war in contrast to the previous four decades of the "long peace."[2] Many realists feel vindicated in the validity of their theory and its resultant predictions by the many conflicts that have appeared throughout the region formerly occupied by the Soviet Union and Yugoslavia since 1989.

In contrast to the realists, most liberal institutionalists have argued that it is possible to construct cooperative arrangements among sovereign and independent states within an anarchic international "society"[3] on the basis of international "regimes." Regimes have been defined by Stephen Krasner as "sets of implicit or explicit principles, norms, rules, and decision-making procedures around which actors' expectations converge in a given area of international relations."[4] Most early treatments of regimes within the liberal tradition focused on their operation outside the realm of security, especially on issues such as the economy or the environment, and most analyses of security issues were largely conceded to the domain of the realists. A notable exception is found in the work of Robert Jervis, who has argued that it is possible to have regimes in the domain of security as well, defined as "those principles, rules, and norms that permit nations to be restrained in their behavior in the belief that others will reciprocate."[5] Jervis goes on to note that a security regime must facilitate cooperation that goes beyond following the dictates of short-run self-interests in order to qualify. At the same time, regimes are usually accepted by sovereign states because their leaders perceive that their long-term gains from fulfilling the expectations of a regime will exceed the losses they expect to suffer through forgoing temptations to follow short-term narrow self-interest. The theory of security regimes thus falls at the intersection of realist and liberal conceptions of international relations. This argument is stated succinctly by Keohane and Nye:

> International institutions do not call into question the core of the realist model of anarchy, since they do not have the power to enforce their rules on strong states. But they may challenge some of the implications of anarchy for state behavior, making less likely the competitive, worst-case behavior that realists predict. To the extent that international institutions provide information and coordinate actors' expectations, the security dilemma that states face may be less stark, and doctrinaire realist

predictions of state behavior may be off the mark. International cooperation will be affected by the richness and appropriateness of available international institutions.[6]

My principal contention in this chapter is that the OSCE came a long way during the 1990s toward forming the core of just such a security regime. It created many of the conditions necessary for regional cooperation to maintain European security since the end of the Cold War. It has articulated shared values to which all of its members have formally subscribed. It has constructed an institutional framework within which all member states may attend to the security needs of one another, exchange information, and facilitate the peaceful resolution of differences. It has also emphasized the development of common political, economic, and social principles based on the ideas of liberal democracy and market economies in an effort to create a "zone of peace."[7] Finally, the OSCE has created a set of structures intended to prevent conflicts, to mediate ceasefires in times of violent conflict, to manage and resolve those underlying issues that have produced violence, and to assist states and regions that have experienced violence to rebuild their security in order to rehabilitate their political, social, and economic structures.

The many roles that the OSCE has attempted to fulfill may be evaluated in terms of a model of conflict escalation and abatement, along the lines suggested by Michael Lund.[8] Although not all of these functions have been undertaken by the OSCE in the first decade since the end of the Cold War, most of them have been attempted by at least one of the OSCE missions or organs involved in conflict prevention. To the extent that the OSCE can successfully fulfill one or several of the functions identified in Table 14.1, it can make a significant contribution to reducing security dilemmas and promoting greater collective cooperation in meeting some of the many challenges to post-Cold War Eurasian security. Since the OSCE has undertaken virtually all of these tasks only in the period since 1992, it is important to keep in mind that this is an ongoing process and that some patience may be necessary before concrete results are forthcoming.

In this paper I propose to assess the overall contributions of the OSCE at this early stage in its history to limiting the escalation of conflicts and promoting the abatement and resolution of conflicts in the aftermath of violence. I will do this largely by comparing a few cases in which the OSCE undertook a significant role in regions of conflict during the last decade of the twentieth century. I shall assess the contributions made by the OSCE to promote more cooperative and less violent outcomes in several of these situations, and I will evaluate reasons for the failure of the OSCE to meet expectations in preventing violence or resolving underlying conflicts in other cases. Before doing this, however, a brief examina-

TABLE 14.1 Diplomatic Roles at Different Stages of Conflict—Potential OSCE Activities in the Management of Conflict

Stages of Conflict	Ladder of Escalation	Ladder of Abatement
Violent conflict	Humanitarian aid; protection of noncombatants	Cease-fire negotiation
Crisis (turning points)	Crisis management	Peacekeeping, prevention of conflict reignition
Precarious peace	Conflict prevention	Conflict resolution
Conditional peace	Monitoring, early warning, democratization	Postconflict security building
Stable peace	Peacetime diplomacy	Peacetime diplomacy

tion of the development and institutionalization of the OSCE since its inception will help establish the context for the subsequent analysis of the OSCE's performance in conflict management.

DEVELOPMENT AND INSTITUTIONALIZATION OF THE CSCE/OSCE

The stimulus behind the creation of the CSCE was a Soviet/Warsaw Pact proposal for an all-European conference intended largely to resolve unsettled issues held over from the end of World War II. Their primary objective was to ratify the postwar status quo in Europe, especially the division of Germany. The CSCE negotiations opened with a foreign ministers' meeting in Helsinki on July 3-7, 1973, comprising 35 delegations, including two North American countries—the United States and Canada —plus all states of Europe big and small, from the Soviet Union to the Holy See, with the sole exception of Albania.[9]

The working phase of negotiations took place in Geneva from September 18, 1973, until July 25, 1975. During this phase, issues were grouped together in three major substantive "baskets." Basket I focused primarily on a set of principles to govern relations among states in the realm of security and on specific "confidence-building measures." The latter are military provisions intended to create transparency and reduce tensions by requiring countries to provide assurances to potential adversaries that their military preparations are essentially defensive and nonthreatening. Basket II emphasized cooperation in the fields of economics, science and technology, and the environment. Basket III issues concerned cooperation in humanitarian areas, including human contacts, travel and tourism, information and cultural exchanges, and educational exchanges. It was this basket that covered many of the human rights issues, especially the freer movement of peoples, ideas, and information across national boundaries.

The concluding stage of the original CSCE was a summit conference at which heads of state of all 35 CSCE countries signed the Final Act in Helsinki on July 31-August 1, 1975. The Helsinki Final Act, first and foremost, contains the "Decalogue," 10 principles that should govern interstate relations: (1) sovereign equality of states, (2) refraining from the threat or use of force, (3) inviolability of frontiers, (4) territorial integrity of states, (5) peaceful settlement of disputes, (6) nonintervention in internal affairs, (7) respect for human rights and fundamental freedoms, (8) self-determination of peoples, (9) cooperation among states, and (10) fulfillment of obligations under international law. The elaboration of these 10 principles, and others subsequently derived from them, has created the normative core for a European security regime. However, the implementation of several potentially contradictory principles has given rise to considerable difficulty.

First, the issue of the relative priority of the sixth and seventh principles became a subject of dispute. The effort to enhance individual human rights and the rights of minority groups has necessarily brought the organization to intervene into what many states consider to be their internal affairs, and during the Cold War period the communist states especially insisted that principle six took precedence over all others. With the disappearance of the East-West conflict, however, a broad consensus has developed within the OSCE that, when states have freely accepted certain principles, including those in the decalogue, this gives other member states limited rights of intervention in order to uphold the agreed norms. Therefore, on matters ranging from intrusive inspection to verify compliance with military confidence-building and arms control measures, to provisions for human and minority rights, the OSCE has increasingly insisted on "transparency" and on the right to intervene in the affairs of a member state to implement those principles to which that state has subscribed. In short, the Helsinki decalogue weakened the absolute nature of state sovereignty to a far greater degree than was envisaged at the time the Final Act was signed in 1975.

The second value conflict became paramount only in the period since the end of the Cold War and the breakup of the Soviet Union and Yugoslavia. As the 15 Union Republics of the USSR achieved statehood while five independent states emerged out of the six republics of the former Yugoslavia, regional and ethnic groups in many of these new states also claimed the right to self-determination. Believing that they had been deprived of this right by the essentially arbitrary way in which the Soviet Union and Yugoslavia had been divided historically, many ethnically distinct regions in the new states also proclaimed their independence and sovereignty on the basis of the right to self-determination. This came into direct conflict with the desire of the OSCE to recognize the territorial integrity of all existing and new member states regardless of how their borders had been drawn in the past. The inability to reconcile the principle of the territorial integrity of new states with the claims for self-determination by minorities existing within and across the borders between these new states has been one of the most significant factors accounting for the widespread violence in the region since 1989.

In addition to the three baskets, the Helsinki Final Act called for a series of follow-up conferences to review progress in implementation of the Final Act and to consider new provisions to strengthen security in Europe. The first CSCE Review Conference in Belgrade in 1977-1978 was characterized largely by rhetorical attacks and counterattacks, with Western governments criticizing the human rights performance of the communist bloc countries, and the latter accusing the former of blatant interference in their internal affairs. Nonetheless, this meeting did set a precedent for legitimizing CSCE involvement in the internal affairs of member states when they might have consequences for regional security.

The second follow-on meeting began in Madrid in 1980 and lasted for more than three years. At the outset it, too, was stalemated by the intensified debate over human rights and intervention in internal affairs. The Western governments at first refused to move forward on proposals to reinforce confidence-building measures and other provisions to increase security until the situations in Poland and Afghanistan were resolved to their satisfaction and until the general human rights picture improved in the Eastern bloc. However, before adjourning in 1983, the Madrid conference did eventually take up proposals to strengthen confidence-building measures and establish machinery for the peaceful resolution of disputes. Of particular significance was the adoption of a mandate for negotiations in Stockholm under CSCE auspices, known officially as the Conference on Security- and Confidence-Building Measures and Disarmament in Europe. In addition, working meetings were set up to deal with human rights and fundamental freedoms in Ottawa, human contacts in Bern, the peaceful settlement of disputes in Athens, cultural contacts in Budapest, and Mediterranean security issues in Venice. While few actual decisions were taken in Madrid, the CSCE process at least regained momentum.

This momentum carried through into the third follow-on conference, which began in Vienna on November 4, 1986. Mikhail Gorbachev's ascent to power in Moscow only several months before was evident in the improved climate of East-West relations within the CSCE. Thus, the Vienna conference, which lasted until January 1989, responded to the rapidly changing political scene in Central and Eastern Europe and began to adapt the European security framework to the new environment even before the definitive end of the Cold War. Virtually all baskets of the Helsinki Final Act were strengthened, confidence-building measures were further extended, and numerous conferences were spawned to deal with the rapidly changing security environment.[10]

With the fall of the Berlin Wall on November 9, 1989, the CSCE rapidly began to adapt to the new post-Cold War security environment in Europe. Suddenly the possibility of creating a genuine system of "collective security" on the European continent appeared to be feasible. Two major documents were produced by the CSCE in the first year after the end of the Cold War that fundamentally changed the normative and institutional structure of European security.[11] The first of these was a report of an expert meeting held in Copenhagen in June 1990 on the human dimension of security that attempted to apply the essential features of Western democratic practices to the entire continent. Specifically, it called for free elections leading to representative governments in all CSCE states open to observation by all member states, equality before the law, freedom to establish political parties, and rights of accused persons.[12]

The second major document was the "Charter of Paris for a New Europe," signed at a summit meeting held November 19-21, 1990. In addition to reaffirming the *acquis* of the CSCE from the Helsinki Final Act through the various follow-on conferences and expert meetings, the Charter of Paris began the formal institutionalization of the CSCE. Having met as an itinerant series of conferences without permanent headquarters or secretariat, the Paris meeting established a secretariat in Prague (later moved to Vienna). In addition, a Conflict Prevention Center was created in Vienna, an Office for Free Elections (subsequently renamed the Office for Democratic Institution and Human Rights—ODIHR) was set up in Warsaw, and a Parliamentary Assembly, made up of parliamentarians from all member states, was created. Annual meetings were to be held at the level of foreign ministers, summits were to be held biannually, and a Committee of Senior Officials would prepare ministerial meetings and could call emergency meetings when required. In short, the CSCE began to take on most of the traditional features of an established international organization rather than a series of ad hoc meetings about security issues.

The next major milestone in the post-Cold War expansion of the CSCE came with the follow-on conference and summit in Helsinki in 1992. This was the first meeting at which all of the former Soviet and Yugoslav countries plus Albania participated as full members, increasing the total number of member states to 53.[13] The Helsinki conference was preoccupied with the wave of violence that was sweeping across the former Soviet Union and Yugoslavia, and it sought to engage the organization more actively both to prevent the future outbreak of such conflicts and to manage and resolve those that had already broken out. The flagrant violation of CSCE principles by the Serbs during the fighting in Croatia and Bosnia-Herzegovina led to sanctions being imposed on the Federal Republic of Yugoslavia, including its suspension from active participation in the CSCE.

One of the most significant accomplishments in Helsinki was the adoption of a proposal by the Netherlands to create the Office of the High Commissioner on National Minorities. Based in the Hague, the high commissioner was mandated to engage in early warning, preventive diplomacy, and informal conciliation in an effort to prevent and resolve some of the most significant conflicts that have emerged in Eurasia since the end of the Cold War, where the status and treatment of ethnonational minorities is a major issue. In addition, a Court of Conciliation and Arbitration was created, based in Geneva, with voluntary membership; many key member states have declined to participate, and in the initial six years of its existence it has not taken up any cases. Finally, the Forum for Security Cooperation meets regularly in Vienna to provide a venue for discussion of long-term issues of common security and to negotiate additional confidence-building and arms control measures.

Another major advance taken in Helsinki was the decision to establish missions in areas of tension to provide for "early warning, conflict prevention and crisis management (including fact-finding and rapporteur missions and CSCE peace-keeping) [and] peaceful settlement of disputes." The original intent of the heads of state assembled in Helsinki appeared to largely be to create temporary, more or less ad hoc, missions to deal with conflicts as they arose. However, especially because of continued worsening of the situation in the former Yugoslavia, the Committee of Senior Officials decided to create so-called missions of long duration, the first few of which were to be sent to monitor the situation in three regions of the former Republic of Yugoslavia—Kosovo, Sandjak, and Vojvodina.[14] From this time on these missions were normally mandated for periods of six months, although the mandates have generally been renewed every six months with the sole exception of the first mission in Serbia, which was not extended because of objections from the government in Belgrade.

The next significant stage in the institutional development of the organization took place at the Rome Ministerial in 1993, which created the Permanent Council, which meets weekly throughout the year to conduct all business between the annual ministerial or summit conferences. It is staffed by permanent delegations of the member states, usually headed by ambassadors, and carries on the continuing work of the organization, especially regarding conflict prevention, management, resolution, and postconflict rehabilitation. At the Budapest Summit in 1994 the member states agreed that the CSCE had become sufficiently institutionalized with a permanent secretariat and associated organs that it could be renamed the Organization on Security and Cooperation in Europe and declare itself to be a regional security organization under Chapter VIII of the United Nations (UN) Charter. This change, however, did not affect the status of the OSCE as a political rather than a legal organization, and it did not grant it a collective legal status under international law. In addition, the Budapest Summit adopted a Code of Conduct on Politico-Military Aspects of Security, which created a normative framework for all aspects of military activity in the region, including civil-military relations, the conduct of warfare, and the behavior of military personnel in combat.

Ever since becoming institutionalized formally in 1995, the OSCE has remained a small organization. Its entire budget for 1998 was about 950 million Austrian shillings ($76 million), over a third of which was allocated solely to OSCE activities in Bosnia (not including, of course, the costs of the NATO-led Stabilization Force, SFOR, which were many times greater than the entire OSCE annual budget). The largest single item, about 40 percent of the overall budget, went to support the 14 OSCE missions and field activities. The entire staff, including interpreters, amounts to about 160 persons, making the OSCE an extremely lean international organization in comparison with its responsibilities.[15]

The U.S. government, nevertheless, has generally assumed a cautious approach to the CSCE and its successor, the OSCE. Indeed, U.S. officials were skeptical about the process even during the initial negotiation of the Helsinki Final Act, where, as John Maresca notes, "the United States, deeply involved in bilateral negotiations with the USSR, relegated the CSCE to the second rank."[16] The U.S. government has remained cautious about the potential of the CSCE/OSCE ever since, even though, ironically, the United States subsequently became one of the organization's most active members and its largest financial supporter. Throughout the Cold War period the United States regarded the CSCE mostly as a forum to attack the record of the Soviet Union and other communist bloc governments on human rights. Even in the post-Cold War period there appear to be several reasons for the lukewarm attitude of the United States toward the OSCE, especially at higher levels in the foreign policy and national security bureaucracies.[17] The OSCE is often seen as a distinct competitor with NATO for primacy in providing for security in Europe. American officials frequently believe that whatever strengthens one organization weakens at least the relative influence of the other.

In this competition Washington usually prefers NATO for several reasons. First, U.S. policy makers generally believe that in times of crisis it will be easier for NATO to take a decision than the OSCE. Although both organizations require consensus to make decisions, the broader member-ship of the OSCE may make consensus harder to achieve in Vienna than in Brussels, where American influence has traditionally been more strongly represented. Americans especially fear that the OSCE may be paralyzed by a Russian veto on important security matters, just as the UN Security Council has been in the past. Second, U.S. policy makers generally perceive that the OSCE lacks appropriate means to implement its decisions. Although the OSCE has played an important role in political and humanitarian spheres in Bosnia, for example, it depended on the support of the NATO-led Implementation Force (IFOR) and subsequently the SFOR to provide security for its own personnel, especially election monitors, to say nothing of Bosnian citizens. Since the OSCE does not have and has never raised peacekeeping forces, these policy makers believe that the OSCE's depen-dence on other institutions for providing the muscle needed to carry out its decisions is likely to weaken its effectiveness.

On the other hand, the agreements on Kosovo brokered by Richard Holbrooke in October 1998 assigned a major role to an OSCE force that was intended to reach some 2,000 civilian monitors to observe Belgrade's withdrawal of security forces and the disarmament of the Kosovo Libera-tion Army, representing by far the largest mission undertaken to date by the OSCE. Indeed, it appears that the Serbs and their Russian supporters were willing to acquiesce in an OSCE role in Kosovo at a time when Russia was not prepared to support a UN Security Council resolution authorizing NATO to take military action to dissuade Serb leaders from attacking the Kosovar population. Even though this Kosovo Verification Mission had to be withdrawn in late March 1999, when NATO began a full-scale aerial assault on Yugoslavia, U.S. officials continued to envision a significant role for the OSCE to assist in the repatriation of Kosovar Albanian refugees following the cessation of hostilities.

Despite the skepticism of some U.S. officials, the OSCE had become by the end of the twentieth century an institutionalized European security organization. It is charged with dealing with a wide range of activities: preventing violent conflicts, mediating cease-fires, helping to resolve con-flicts in regions that had previously experienced violence, and helping to rebuild security in the aftermath of traumatic conflicts. How well it has performed these tasks is very much a subject of debate. As Stern and Druckman (Chapter 2) point out, evaluating the success of interventions in conflict situations is a tricky business, especially since the criteria for defining success are themselves so murky. Furthermore, apparent short-run failures may turn out over time to contribute to a long-term solution to underlying issues of conflict, whereas short-term solutions may break down readily and actually exacerbate conflicts over the long run. My task in this chapter is further complicated by the problem of equifinality—

namely, that any particular outcome may be accounted for by a combination of factors, and it is extremely difficult to ferret out the extent to which the involvement of the OSCE may have played a determinative role. Therefore, in the analysis that follows, it is neither fair to give OSCE all the credit for the successful outcomes of crises where it intervened nor to attribute exclusive blame for its apparent failure to solve other complex problems.

Nonetheless, in the remainder of this chapter I assess the contributions that OSCE interventions into conflict situations have made in avoiding or ending violence, on the one hand, or averting escalation to higher levels of violence, on the other hand. I focus on the principal instruments that the OSCE uses to intervene in conflict situations, primarily the missions of long-term duration, the high commissioner on national minorities, and the chairman-in-office. While I will occasionally discuss specific techniques that these OSCE representatives have used in their interventions, my main focus is directed toward an assessment of the role that a regional security organization may play to monitor and assist parties confronting different stages of the conflict process. Thus, this chapter does not emphasize assessment of particular intervention techniques, in contrast to other chapters in this volume, but instead concentrates on the general argument about the role of multilateral security institutions in lessening the extent and severity of conflict and in promoting the development of a regional security regime.

Finally, since this chapter deals primarily with conflicts in post-Cold War Eurasia, I focus mostly on intrastate conflicts, as opposed to interstate conflicts. The general OSCE role has been defined in terms of responding to internal conflicts that threaten the peace and security of neighboring states and surrounding regions. Indeed, most of the violence that has erupted in this region since the end of the Cold War has carried significant implications for regional security extending well beyond the borders of the states where violence has broken out. Sometimes this is manifested in irredentist claims to unify regions of newly created states with other states (e.g., Nagorno Karabakh with Armenia, South Ossetia with North Ossetia in the Russian Federation, Kosovo with Albania, Crimea with Russia). On other occasions, violence threatens to spread due to the presence of ethnic groups in regions that cut across international borders (e.g., Hungarians in Romania and Slovakia, Albanians in Kosovo and in the Former Yugoslav Republic of Macedonia, Russians and Ukrainians in the Transdniester region of Moldova). Finally, there is a more general concern about the apparent "contagion" of conflicts in unstable regions such as the Caucasus, parts of Central Asia, and the Balkans. In short, the neat distinction between interstate conflicts and intrastate conflicts has been blurred in the postcommunist region. Therefore, the following analysis treats the role of the OSCE as a regional security organization that has intervened in numerous conflicts in the Eurasian region, whenever those conflicts—regardless of their origins—have implications for regional or international security.

THE OSCE ROLE IN CONFLICT PREVENTION, CEASE-FIRE MEDIATION, CONFLICT RESOLUTION, AND POSTCONFLICT SECURITY BUILDING[18]

This section examines OSCE activities in four regions to illustrate some of the ways in which the OSCE has been successful in its conflict management activities and other instances where so far the outcomes have fallen short of expectations. These cases were also selected to illustrate some of the most important functions identified in Table 14.1 that the OSCE has undertaken in regions of conflict since the end of the Cold War: (1) monitoring, early warning, and conflict prevention to head off incipient violence (Crimea in Ukraine); (2) negotiation of cease-fires in ongoing conflicts (Chechnya in the Russian Federation); (3) preventing the reignition of violence and assisting the resolution of underlying issues in conflict situations (Transdniestria in Moldova); and (4) postconflict security building (Albania).

Monitoring, Early Warning, and Conflict Prevention— The Case of Crimea in Ukraine

Principles

The principal focus of OSCE's conflict prevention activities is to identity and respond to brewing conflicts to prevent the outbreak of violence. These activities are most intensive in times of unstable peace, including both conditional and precarious peace, when the possibility of violence looms somewhere over the horizon. The view that conflicts are easier to resolve before they become violent than afterward has been expressed forcefully by Max van der Stoel, the OSCE high commissioner on national minorities:

> It is evident from the experience of Bosnia, of Chechnya, of Nagorno-Karabakh, of Georgia and elsewhere, that once a conflict has erupted, it is extremely difficult to bring it to an end. In the meantime, precious lives have been lost, new waves of hatred have been created and enormous damage has been inflicted.[19]

As van der Stoel suggests, once Humpty Dumpty has fallen from his wall, it is extremely difficult to put him back together again. So it is with states; once conflicts reach the stage of violence, peaceful accommodation may become extremely difficult to achieve. Indeed, negotiation theory suggests that the situation may not be "ripe" for negotiation until a "hurting stalemate" has set in, at which time the situation "has become uncomfortable to both sides and . . . appears likely to become very costly."[20] At this point, by definition both parties have suffered great losses and have become sufficiently desperate so that solutions that previously might have been unacceptable become more palatable. Instead of waiting for the typical cycle of violence eventually followed by a hurting stalemate to run its course, preventive diplomacy seeks to identify an earlier point to intervene before a conflict turns violent in the first place. Intervention at this stage is more likely to lead to mutual accommodation than after a period of violence and even after a hurting stalemate is mutually recognized by the disputing parties. Lund has enumerated some of the most important advantages of early intervention:

> [T]he issues in the dispute are fewer and less complex; conflicting parties are not highly mobilized, polarized, and armed; significant bloodshed has not occurred, and thus a sense of victimization and a desire for vengeance are not intense; the parties have not begun to demonize and stereotype each other; moderate leaders still maintain control over extremist tendencies; and the parties are not so committed that compromise involves loss of face.[21]

One difficulty with preventive diplomacy, however, is that there is often only a very narrow "window of opportunity" during which parties may intervene to prevent the outbreak of violence. At early stages in a conflict, the signals of a developing confrontation may be so ambiguous that the gravity of the situation may not be recognized. Furthermore, premature intervention may create a "self-fulfilling prophecy" by focusing attention on the conflict in the minds of disputing parties or by legitimizing radical political leaders, such as extreme nationalists. At the same time, if outside parties wait too long before intervening, the threshold of violence may be crossed, delaying efforts to mediate until a hurting stalemate has set in. Timing the engagement of preventive diplomacy is thus an extremely critical yet elusive factor in the etiology of a conflict.

The first requisite for effective preventive diplomacy is "early warning" to detect situations that might lead to violent conflict. Protests, demonstrations, and riots may provide early warning, as may actions by governments to suppress dissent. Parties to disputes may come directly to OSCE missions and field offices to report threats to the peace that they have witnessed or experienced. Indicators of incipient conflicts may include nationalist claims to establish separatist regimes, irredentist claims of secession and unification with another state, concerns about the possible "spillover" of an ongoing conflict across international borders into neighboring states, and warnings about potential unauthorized external intervention in ongoing internal conflicts in member states.

Early warning is not enough to trigger an appropriate response, however. There must be a capability of separating real dangers from "false alarms." As George and Holl have noted, the problem for preventive diplomacy is often not the inability to identify potential trouble spots but rather one of "understanding such situations well enough to forecast which ones are likely to explode and when."[22] However good their intentions may be, states and multilateral organizations may antagonize important constituencies with too many cries of "wolf." They may alienate parties if they try to intervene in situations that do not seem to warrant such a drastic response. And they may exhaust both the willpower and the limited resources of regional security organizations if they try to intervene in more conflicts than they can handle at any one time.[23]

Once the incipient crisis has been recognized, the next and often more difficult problem is to mobilize inside parties to enter into direct negotiations or outside parties to intervene. As George and Holl have pointed out, "early warning does not necessarily make for easy response. On the contrary, available warning often forces policy makers to confront decisions of a difficult or unpalatable character."[24] The warning must be rapidly delivered to the central OSCE institutions in Vienna, the Hague, or Warsaw and to key member governments. Once they attend to these warnings, there must also exist a political will among member governments and the OSCE authorities to respond to those warnings. It is then necessary to decide on an appropriate response, whether it will take the form of verbal protest or denunciation, imposition of sanctions, creation of a mission of long-term duration, intervention by a third party to provide good offices or to assist in mediation, deployment of monitoring or even peacekeeping operations, or activation of any other means at the disposal of the OSCE.

The principal organs of the OSCE available to perform this conflict prevention function include the chairman-in-office, who may decide to call the OSCE into action or may intervene directly himself or through his special representatives; the Conflict Prevention Center, which receives warnings from the OSCE missions and offices in the field about brewing conflicts and offers suggestions or instructions about how to respond; the high commissioner on national minorities, who may travel to areas of potential conflict involving national minority issues on a moment's notice and issue warnings to the Permanent Council or, in cases of great urgency, may intervene himself to try to assist the disputants to resolve their conflicts; and the Permanent Council, which generally receives reports from the Conflict Prevention Center, the high commissioner on national minorities, and the field missions which may decide to authorize special mission activities, dispatch a special representative, impose sanctions on disputing parties, and even call for the creation of an observation or peacekeeping force, as was agreed to by the chairman-in-office, Polish Foreign Minister Bronoslaw Geremek, as part of the agreement regarding Kosovo in October 1998.

The Crimea Case

The OSCE has undertaken several conflict prevention activities in regions where conflict appeared to be escalating and where the risk of large-scale violence was significant. One such situation, where the OSCE appears to have played an important role in heading off escalating violence, was the situation in Ukraine. The region of Crimea, populated by about 67 percent ethnic Russians, had been part of the Russian Federation until it was given as a "gift" by Nikita Khrushchev to the Ukraine in 1954. This change in status made little practical difference until the Soviet Union collapsed, and the Crimean Russians suddenly found themselves to be a minority in the new Ukrainian state. Tensions between the Crimean authorities and Kiev reached a crisis level in January 1994 when Yuri Meshkov, a nationalistic Russian, was elected as the first president of Crimea. He immediately proposed changing the Crimean constitution and declaring independence, which set off a strong response among Ukrainians who wanted to preserve the territorial integrity of the Ukrainian state. The OSCE high commissioner on national minorities, Max van der Stoel, visited Ukraine in February and May 1994. As a result of those visits, he recommended the creation of an OSCE mission of long duration in Ukraine, with a branch office in Crimea. The mission was established in June 1994 with a mandate to assist in settling the status of Crimea as an autonomous region within the state of Ukraine.

In September 1994 Crimean President Meshkov unilaterally abolished the Supreme Council of Crimea as well as local councils. However, the Presidium of the Supreme Council of Crimea declared that Meshkov's actions violated the laws of both Crimea and Ukraine. President Kuchma of Ukraine also stepped in and told both Meshkov and Sergei Tsekov, chair of the Supreme Council, that he would "not allow the use of force to settle the conflict between the branches of government in Crimea." He ordered Deputy Prime Minister Marchuk to go to Crimea to mediate in negotiations between the Crimean president and parliament.[25] The Ukrainian Rada (parliament) simultaneously passed a law giving Crimea only until November 1 to bring its constitution fully in line with the Ukrainian constitution.

In early 1995 the Supreme Council of Crimea ratcheted up its defiance by declaring that the state property of Ukraine in Crimea belonged to

Crimea and by threatening to hold a referendum on independence during the April 1995 municipal elections. The Ukrainian Rada, in response, tried to dismantle Crimean autonomy altogether. On March 17, 1995, it annulled the 1992 Crimean constitution and abolished the Crimean presidency, its law on the constitutional court, and its election laws while also bringing criminal charges against President Meshkov. President Kuchma also decreed that the Crimean government was to be fully subordinated to the Ukrainian government. The two authorities appeared to be on a collision course with potentially violent consequences. In response, Sergei Tsekov, speaker of the Crimean parliament, called on the OSCE to make an assessment of the decisions taken by the Ukrainian parliament in the light of international law.

The OSCE mission began intensive consultations with Ukrainian officials, and a meeting of OSCE ambassadors was held at the Hungarian Embassy in Kiev. They arrived at a mixed conclusion. On the one hand, they found that Ukrainian authorities had generally acted within their constitutional authority and that many of the decisions taken by the Rada had been provoked by Crimean separatists. They noted that Crimean autonomy remained intact, even though the central government had substantially increased its veto power over decisions taken by the regional authority. On the other hand, they deplored the abrogation of the Crimean local election laws that had guaranteed multiparty representation, especially for Tatars and other minorities, far more effectively than the Ukrainian election laws. They expressed concern that the Rada's actions had provoked an escalation of tensions and the possible radicalization of Crimean Russians. They further urged the restoration of Crimea's autonomy status of 1992, concluding with the following observation:

> [N]o efforts should be spared by the OSCE, by the HCNM and the Mission to Ukraine, also by the Council of Europe, to point out to Ukrainian authorities the urgency of establishing a Constitutional Court system as guarantor not only of a meaningful Autonomy Status for Crimea but also for a substantive Ukrainian democracy based on Council of Europe standards. It is highly unsatisfactory to have the Ukrainian Parliament play lonely and supreme "judge" of constitutional frictions between Kiev and Simferopol.[26]

The OSCE head of mission, Andreas Kohlschütter, warned external parties not to interfere in the situation, presumably referring to the possible actions by politicians and military authorities in the Russian Federation to support the Russian community in Crimea. In this vein he argued for a major effort by the OSCE to promote dialogue and to introduce a voice of "moderation and compromise into the decision-making process on all sides."[27]

As a result, the high commissioner on national minorities stepped up his activity in the region and became actively engaged as a "go between" to help the parties make their constitutions consistent with each other. High Commissioner van der Stoel organized a conference in Locarno, Switzerland, on May 11-14, 1995, which came on the heels of an announcement by the Crimean parliament of its intention to hold a referendum on the reinstatement of the 1992 constitution. On May 15 the high commissioner proposed a formula that recommended drafting parallel language in the constitutions of Crimea and Ukraine to grant Crimea irrevocable autonomy in many key areas, a right to appeal to the Ukrainian Constitutional Court if it considered that Ukrainian legislation infringed on its autonomy, while also acknowledging Crimea's status as an autonomous republic within the state of Ukraine. He also proposed that the parliaments of Ukraine and Crimea create "an organ of conciliation with the task of suggesting solutions to differences arising in the course of the dialogue about relevant legislation."[28] These recommendations were generally well received in Kiev.[29] Based on this success, a second roundtable was held in September 1995 in Yalta focusing on the narrower topic of the reintegration of deported peoples (Tatars) returning to Crimea. In 1996 the high commissioner focused on both the constitutional issue and provisions for the education of minorities (both Ukrainians and Tatars) in Crimea.[30]

Meanwhile, the Crimean leadership began to acquiesce to most of Kiev's demands.[31] Not the least of the factors enabling Ukraine to preserve its territorial integrity was the fact that the Crimean separatists received little support from the Russian government. Crimea's almost complete dependence on financial support from Kiev also made autonomous action virtually impossible to sustain. The central government successfully gained control of the law enforcement agencies in Crimea, and Kiev successfully maneuvered to have sympathetic individuals selected to the posts of prime minister and speaker of the parliament in Crimea.[32] This more moderate Crimean leadership was also more inclined to follow the recommendations of the OSCE's high commissioner.

On November 1, 1995, a new constitution on the status of the Autonomous Republic of Crimea was adopted that incorporated many of the suggestions from the Locarno conference, although it failed to guarantee representation for the Crimean Tatar community as the high commission had encouraged.[33] The OSCE mission also urged the government in Kiev to institute economic development projects in fields such as tourism in Crimea in order to capitalize on the potential of the region. They also urged initiatives to privatize and restructure the extensive military industries located in the region that had declined following the end of the Cold War. In short the mission emphasized the importance of joint benefits from the great economic potential that Crimea offered that could enrich both the center and the region itself.

By 1999 it appeared that the OSCE's role in Crimea constituted one of its most significant successes in the field of conflict prevention. The situation was especially explosive due to the threat of Russian intervention, made more likely by the disputes between the Russian Federation and Ukraine over the status of the Black Sea Fleet based in Crimea and the city of Sevastopol, the fleet's headquarters, which had long been a bastion of Russian military influence on the Black Sea. By intervening rapidly, the OSCE mission, supported closely by Ambassador van der Stoel, was able to strengthen the forces of moderation on both sides and push for a solution granting substantial autonomy to the region without full independence. Thus, the territorial integrity of Ukraine was preserved at the same time that the residents of Crimea achieved a substantial degree of self-determination over the most important issues of everyday life, including education, language for the conduct of official business, and local police. In this explosive situation, violence was averted in Crimea that could have escalated rapidly in the already tense situation that existed between Russia and Ukraine.

Negotiating Cease-Fires—The Case of Chechnya in the Russian Federation

Principles

The OSCE has been generally reluctant to intervene in ongoing conflicts that have taken place in the formal jurisdiction of a single member state. Typically those states contend that secessionist conflicts are internal matters. In addition, the OSCE lacks the capability for coercive inducement that other parties, such as the United States and Russia, have brought to bear to impose cease-fires in places such as Bosnia and Abkhazia. It is precisely for these reasons that the OSCE has tended to intervene more often either before conflicts turn violent or after violence has been brought to a halt.

Thus, for example, when fighting broke out in the former Yugoslavia in 1991, the CSCE Conflict Prevention Center had just been created, and no adequate mechanism existed to engage the center in direct conflict prevention or resolution activities. Therefore, at a Council of Foreign Ministers meeting in Berlin chaired by German Foreign Minister Hans-Dietrich Genscher in June 1991, a resolution was passed condemning Yugoslav government activities in Slovenia and Croatia. The CSCE, however, was unable to take any action, so responsibility for future involvement with this conflict was passed on to the European Union, which sought to demonstrate its bona fides in dealing with conflicts on the European continent under the common foreign and security policy that was formalized in the Maastricht Treaty in December 1991. Subsequent efforts to negotiate a cease-fire in Bosnia were undertaken jointly by the European Union and the UN, represented respectively by David Owen and Cyrus Vance. Following the breakdown of their efforts, the task of mediation was taken up unilaterally by the United States under the leadership of Richard Holbrooke. The OSCE was assigned a major role in implementing the disarmament provisions of the Dayton Accords, which resulted from that effort, and in organizing, supervising, and monitoring the many elections that were to take place under the terms set out in Dayton, but it was not even represented at the negotiations that produced that agreement.

The Case of Chechnya

The only case in which the OSCE became a direct broker of a cease-fire was in the 1994-1996 war between Chechnya and the Russian Federation. Chechnya is a predominantly Sunni Muslim region in the northern Caucasus, with a population consisting largely of mountain dwellers who resisted Russian occupation for centuries. Its population in 1989 consisted of about 65 percent ethnic Chechens and 25 percent Russians, mostly living in the capital of Grozny. Following the Moscow coup attempt in August 1991, General Dzokhar Dudayev seized power in Chechnya. Shortly thereafter he declared Chechnya's independence from Russia and refused to sign Yeltsin's federation treaty. After a long period of political skirmishing, on December 11, 1994, approximately 40,000 Russian troops entered Chechnya, resulting in a full-scale war, by far the bloodiest of the post-Cold War conflicts in Eurasia. The war lasted off and on for some two years.

The behavior of the Russian Federation troops clearly represented a violation of many CSCE norms and principles. The massive military activity in the region, which was undertaken without the presence of international observers, represented a formal violation of the many confidence-building agreements most recently incorporated into the so-called Vienna Document 1994. Furthermore, the war began only days after the signing of the Code of Conduct at the CSCE summit in Budapest, which established extensive norms for military engagement and especially respect for the rights of noncombatants. The head of the U.S. delegation to the OSCE, Sam Brown, noted on January 12, 1995, the requirement, even in instances of internal security operations, to "take due care to avoid injury to civilians or their property." He argued that violations of this and other principles made Russian actions in Chechnya not only an internal matter but rather a "legitimate issue of international concern."[34] The government in Moscow, however, maintained that this was purely an "internal affair" and opposed any formal role for the OSCE in Chechnya. Given the apparent absence of consensus in favor of intervention, the OSCE was initially paralyzed.

After much discussion and debate in Vienna, however, the OSCE Assistance Group in Chechnya was created by the Permanent Council on April 11, 1995, with a mandate to "promote the peaceful resolution of the crisis and the stabilization of the situation in the Chechen Republic in conformity with the principle of the territorial integrity of the Russian Federation and in accordance with OSCE principles." In addition, the OSCE group was assigned to monitor compliance with the human dimension norms, including human rights, the unfettered return of refugees to their homes, and allowing for the operation of international humanitarian organizations in Chechnya. Finally, they were mandated to "promote dialogue and negotiations between the parties in order to achieve a cease-fire and eliminate sources of tensions," the first such mandate of this kind. The OSCE Assistance Group was initially headed by a Hungarian diplomat, Sandor Meszaros, supported by a team of six members.

At the outset they found that there was little space to open productive negotiations between the parties. However, Russian and international opinion against the fighting was mobilized following an attack by Chechen guerrillas on a hospital in Budennyovsk in southern Russia in June 1995 in which numerous hostages were taken. As a result, negotiations were opened at the OSCE offices in Grozny shortly thereafter. The Russian delegation refused to accept full independence for Chechnya but did discuss informally the possibility of a formula based on "constructive ambiguity." The Chechens agreed to a moratorium on the implementation of their declaration of independence for a period of two years while the formal status might be negotiated, whereas the Russians insisted on a moratorium of five years. The two sides then agreed to work out a military cease-fire and to leave final negotiation of a political solution to a later stage. Under the terms of this agreement, Russian forces in Chechnya were to be reduced to about 6,000 men. In exchange the Chechens would be allowed to maintain small armed self-defense units in every village until a new law enforcement organ was established. An agreement was thus signed on July 31, and a military cease-fire went into effect in the absence of a political settlement.[35]

The cease-fire soon broke down. Russian troops began to resume military actions against Chechen villages in the mountains, whereas Dudayev and his associates began to take advantage of the cease-fire to rearm their supporters in Grozny. The Russians refused to allow the Chechens to arm themselves in villages under their control, and Chechen appeals to the

OSCE to "interpret" the terms of the agreement allowing them self-defense forces in all population centers apparently had no effect. Reportedly the U.S. member of the OSCE team, Roman Wasilewski, became openly disillusioned with the inability of the OSCE to act as an assertive mediator and to insist on Russian compliance with the terms of that agreement.[36] By October the cease-fire had broken down altogether.

An election was staged by Russian authorities in Chechnya on December 17, boycotted by the opposition, in which the former pro-Russian leader of Chechnya, Doku Zavgayev, was elected as head of the Chechen republic. Although the OSCE did not endorse the elections, it also failed to condemn them vigorously, even though they were not conducted under international monitoring and appeared to fall well short of normal OSCE standards. Indeed, Russian human rights activist Sergei Kovalyov was quoted as saying: "If the OSCE had insisted elections were against the interests of peace, Moscow would not have been able to go ahead with them."[37] Even the OSCE mission head acknowledged after the elections that its influence had been severely limited and that it could only be effective in the near future in the fields of humanitarian aid and human rights, not in promoting further negotiations toward another cease-fire.[38]

In January 1996, however, leadership of the OSCE Assistance Group in Chechnya was turned over to Ambassador Tim Guldimann of Switzerland, who took a much more activist role as a mediator between the parties to the conflict. In February he went to Moscow and met with Interior Minister Kulikov and Emil Payin, Yeltsin's adviser on ethnic issues on the Presidential Council. The former took a hard line, insisting that Dudayev was essentially a terrorist and thus not an acceptable partner for negotiations. However, Payin was more conciliatory and appeared willing to consider negotiations with Dudayev as long as Zavgayev could also play a role and if the negotiations were mindful of the overall importance of respecting Russian sovereignty. Guldimann, on behalf of the OSCE, criticized efforts by Russian General Kulikov to create so-called zones of peace due to the disregard for human rights evidenced by Russian troops. Nonetheless the Russians continued to encourage villagers to turn over weapons in exchange for "assurances" that the Russian troops would no longer shell their villages.

On April 22, 1996, Dudayev was killed by a Russian rocket attack on the village of Gheki-Chu, which ironically came shortly after Russian President Yeltsin had indicated to Guldimann his willingness to meet with Dudayev. Leadership of the Chechen forces was then taken up by the vice president, Zelimkhan Yandarbiyev. Guldimann met with him on May 9 and discussed setting up a meeting with Yeltsin. After two quick trips to Moscow to try to obtain the Russian president's consent for such a meeting, Guldimann returned to Chechnya and informed the Chechen leadership of

Yeltsin's interest in arranging a meeting. On May 27 Guldimann accompanied Yandarbiyev to Moscow and, after a brief but tense dispute over the status of the Chechen leader, the two men signed an agreement on another cease-fire and exchange of prisoners. A second agreement was signed by the Russians and Chechens and witnessed by Guldimann on behalf of the OSCE on June 10 in Nazran, the capital of neighboring Ingushetia, calling for the withdrawal of all Russian troops by the end of August as well as the gradual disarmament of the Chechen side.

A few weeks later Yeltsin was reelected as president of the Russian Federation, and he appointed one of his primary opponents, former army general Alexander Lebed, as his chief security adviser. Less than a week after the second round of elections, Russian planes resumed bombing in Chechnya, and the Chechens retaliated by launching an attack on Grozny in early August and recapturing the city from Russian control. A few days later General Lebed traveled secretly to Chechnya and met with the Chechen chief of staff Maskhadov; they agreed to a truce in the fighting. Lebed abandoned all support for the puppet Russian regime under Zavgayev and made several subsequent trips to Chechnya. On August 22 he signed another cease-fire agreement with Maskhadov. Finally, on August 31, OSCE Assistance Group head Guldimann arranged for a formal meeting between Lebed and Maskhadov in Khasavyurt, in neighboring Dagestan.[39] The agreement signed there largely reflected the results of Guldimann's activity as mediator. It deferred a final settlement of Chechnya's future for five years, until the end of 2001, during which time the two sides would negotiate about their relationship. Russian troops would fully withdraw by the end of December, and a joint commission would be set up to govern the economy. The OSCE was given an important role in the implementation of this agreement. On January 27, 1997, presidential and parliamentary elections were held in Chechnya, monitored by 72 observers from the OSCE, and Aslan Maskhadov was elected president.

Subsequently, the attention of the OSCE mission in Chechnya shifted to postconflict rehabilitation. Tragically, however, this effort never really got off the ground. The damage done to the economy, infrastructure, and the social structure of Chechen society by the war was too much to overcome. For example, roughly 70 percent of the potential work force was left unemployed, most schools were closed, and large numbers of light weapons were widely dispersed throughout the region. Thus, while the peace agreement brought an end to fighting between Russians and Chechens and the election under OSCE observation of a new president and parliament, it did not bring lasting security to Chechnya. By the end of 1997 the security situation in Chechnya had deteriorated to the point where the OSCE Assistance Group remained as the only international organization—governmental or nongovernmental—to be operating in Chechnya with foreign personnel. The OSCE mission continued to report from Chechnya and to try to assist in securing the release of a significant number of international aid workers who had been kidnapped in Chechnya, but the governments of both Russia (which essentially withdrew altogether) and Chechnya were incapable of establishing law and order in the republic. In short, the OSCE's success in brokering an end to the war between Russia and Chechnya was not followed up by a successful effort to rebuild Chechnya in the aftermath of the fighting.

Responsibility for this failure, however, does not lie primarily with the OSCE. The feudal nature of the clan system in Chechnya had produced a strong warrior class, and the end of the war with Russia did not bring an end to this spirit of combat. Furthermore, the war itself, especially the way in which the Russian Army savagely attacked the civilian population and infrastructure of Chechnya, left the region in ruins after the end of the fighting. In the midst of vast destruction, a shattered economy, and an education system left in total shambles, little remained in Chechnya except a heavily armed population living in desperate conditions where survival was problematic. The state of anarchy that descended on Chechnya after the cease-fire thus appears to have been primarily a consequence of Russian action during the war. The net result, however, was that the cease-fire in Chechnya brought little in the way of security to the people living there, and conditions in postconflict Chechnya remained among the most desperate of any place in the world.

Any overall evaluation of the OSCE role in the Chechen conflict thus must remain mixed. Initially, the OSCE reacted hesitantly to violations of its norms and principles by one of its most important member states. The desire to achieve consensus and the fear of a de facto Russian veto largely paralyzed the OSCE during the first few months of the fighting. Early efforts to contain the conflict seemed to many critics in fact to legitimate Russian actions in defense of their territorial integrity. However, once Russian military excesses became apparent to all, especially as the OSCE mission was taken over by an activist mission head, the OSCE played a much more proactive and effective role in mediating several cease-fires and an eventual peace agreement between the warring parties. However, the disappearance of all Russian influence in Chechnya and the inability of the Maskhadov government to establish legitimate authority over the many factions in postwar Chechnya, meant that the OSCE was largely powerless to reverse the trend toward anarchy. Therefore, although the OSCE can justifiably claim success in mediating an end to the 1994-1996 Chechen war, albeit after several failed attempts, it was unable to move into the next phase of postconflict rehabilitation due largely to factors outside its control. Judged by the overall outcome as of early 1999, therefore, the OSCE mission can be viewed as having played a positive role in bringing an end to the intense fighting between Russian and Chechen forces but as having fallen short of its goal of restoring a secure environment in which Chechens can reestablish anything approximating a normal livelihood.

Prevention of the Renewal of Violence and Conflict Resolution— The Case of Transdniestria in Moldova

Principles

In those regions that experienced violent conflict followed by tense stalemate the OSCE has focused on managing the situation in order to avert the reappearance of violence and to resolve the underlying issues that led to conflict in the first place. The kind of situations the OSCE has confronted in the former communist countries have often been very challenging since they typically involve questions of ethnic or national identity. A person's sense of identity may be defined by the social group with which he or she affiliates subjectively, which gives that individual a feeling of having a place in the universe of social relations. Ethnopolitical conflicts almost always develop because at least one group thinks that its identity is problematic, perhaps even at risk of being extinguished. At moments of social and political upheaval these identities may be especially vulnerable. Such conflicts cannot easily be resolved through bargaining involving concessions, tradeoffs, or other similar methods. Instead, as Zartman has emphasized, it is usually necessary to establish an identity formula that guarantees protection of the identity of the vulnerable group. It requires "an identity principle to hold its people together and to give cognitive content to the institutional aspects of legitimacy and sovereignty. Without such a regime it will fall apart in continuing and renewed conflict; without an identity principle it becomes merely a bureaucratic administration with no standard terms for expressing allegiance."[40] And such an identity principle is more likely to be discovered through a problem-solving rather than a bargaining approach to negotiations.[41] In this method the parties must treat the conflict as a problem to be solved jointly with the other parties rather than as a conflict to be "won." Bargaining generally works best when a dispute involves values that can be traded and exchanged, aggregated and disaggregated, on the basis of well-defined interests. By contrast, when conflicts revolve around irreducible values and identities, a different process is required, one that encourages a creative search for identity principles.[42] Yet it is precisely this kind of search process that is most difficult for parties to enter into when they are in the midst of a conflict in which their identity as a "people" or "nation" is at stake.

Therefore, constructive intervention by a third party in situations of this kind can assist the parties to adopt a negotiating approach that stands a reasonable chance of resolving their differences. Third parties may assist the disputants in reframing the issues so that they no longer appear to be "zero-sum" in nature, help them to overcome stereotyped images of their adversaries, aid them to locate possible formulas that merge their joint interests rather than divide them, or even provide assistance in making concessions that will not entail losing face or opening oneself to exploitation by the other party.[43] Thus, the third party may assist the disputants to find ways to resolve their conflict that they would be unlikely to stumble on by themselves.

Within the OSCE, these third-party roles may be played by key individuals such as the chairman-in-office, the high commissioner on national minorities, or a head of mission, all of whom assume a special role as a representative of a regional international organization whose principles have been subscribed to by all states involved in the ongoing dispute. What matters in the eventual success of the OSCE intervention is usually the ability of the individual or team to assist the parties to move away from hard bargaining based on competing interests and into a problem-solving mode. The third-party role is thus primarily one of facilitating the negotiation *process,* although of course in doing so the third party may also assist in the discovery and formulation of solutions to the conflict or ways to prevent its mutually destructive escalation.

The Moldova Case

OSCE officials have played a role as a mediator between central governments and secessionist regions in a number of conflicts, especially in three cases—in Georgia (mainly South Ossetia), Azerbaijan (Nagorno Karabakh), and Moldova (Transdniestria). Here I shall illustrate this function with reference to the mission in Moldova, which was created on February 4, 1993. The mission's mandate called for it "to facilitate the achievement of a lasting, comprehensive political settlement of the conflict in all its aspects . . . " including "reinforcement of the territorial integrity of the Republic of Moldova along with an understanding about a special status for the Trans-Dniester region."

The history of the region on the east bank of the Dniester River made it somewhat distinct from the rest of Moldova, since it had been part of the Russian Empire as long ago as the eighteenth century, while the rest of Moldova had been part of the Russian province of Bessarabia and later part of Romania. Furthermore, about two-thirds of the population of this region is made up of Russian- and Ukrainian-speaking peoples, and a good deal of industry was built there during Soviet times, so that even the ethnic Moldovans living there were generally more "Sovietized" than their compatriots living west of the Dniester River. Finally, the Russian 14th Army was (and still is) stationed in this region.

During the Gorbachev period, Moldovan nationalists began calling for independence from the Soviet Union, and some even called for unification with Romania. The Moldovan language, which had been written in the Cyrillic alphabet in Soviet times, was renamed Romanian and written in the Roman alphabet. The residents east of the Dniester resisted these moves and responded to Moldovan calls for independence by declaring themselves to be the Transdniester Moldovian Soviet Socialist Republic within the Soviet Union, and their leadership continued to proclaim its loyalty to the Soviet Union even after its collapse. In the spring of 1992 the authorities in Chisinau, Moldova's capital, insisted on the primacy of Moldovan law throughout the country. When they attempted to implement this decision by force, fighting broke out between the Moldovan army and the Transdniestrian Republican Guard supported by elements of the Russian 14th Army.

A cease-fire was reached in Moscow on July 6-7, 1992, after approximately 800 people had lost their lives, and a peacekeeping force of Russian, Moldovan, and Transdniestrian forces was established to police the cease-fire. In the aftermath of the Moscow cease-fire agreement, the CSCE mission in Moldova was created to oversee the performance of the peacekeeping forces, report on the human rights and security situation, and assist the parties in achieving a permanent political settlement that would recognize some form of autonomy for the Transdniester region in the Moldovan state.

At the outset the CSCE mission had to be content with creating transparency and assuring that the "peacekeeping" forces would prevent a resumption of fighting along the lengthy border, which mostly coincided with the Dniester River. Nonetheless, the head of mission began informal consultations with officials on both sides of the Dniester, proposing that a special region be created as an integral part of the Moldovan state but enjoying considerable self-rule; it would have its own executive, elected assembly, and court, as well as assured representation in the national parliament, executive, and court system in Chisinau. The mission identified three governing principles for a settlement: (1) the need for a single economic, social, and legal space; (2) the principle of subsidiarity under which anything that does not need to be decided at the central level would revert to the regional or local levels; and (3) the promotion of mutual trust. It then proposed three categories of jurisdictions: (1) those residing exclusively in the central authority, (2) those shared between the center and the region, and (3) those falling exclusively within the regional jurisdiction.[44] Finally, it noted that Transdniestria should be given a right to external self-determination if Moldova should ever decide to merge with Romania.

Direct negotiations between President Snegur of Moldova and Igor Smirnov, self-proclaimed president of Transdniestria, based on these principles articulated by the OSCE mission, opened on April 9, 1994. They agreed to set up a working group made up of five experts from each party along with representatives of the OSCE and the Russian Federation. A second summit on April 28 concluded with the signature by Snegur and Smirnov of a "joint declaration on principles for the settlement of Trans-dniestrian dispute." The expert group's negotiations got under way shortly thereafter and continued to meet regularly. The OSCE's high commissioner on national minorities also became active in Moldova and Transdniestria in December 1994, concentrating mostly on problems faced by ethnic minorities in both regions of the country.[45] He especially focused on three Romanian-language schools in Transdniestria that claimed that their efforts to conduct instruction in the Latin alphabet had met with considerable harassment at the hands of Transdniestrian authorities.

After a hiatus in the negotiations between Chisinau and Tiraspol, as the two sides prepared for elections, negotiations resumed in the spring of 1995. Both sides expressed interest in a proposal to introduce Ukrainian peacekeeping forces along the cease-fire zone monitored by the OSCE. Ukraine also joined the negotiations formally as a third mediator alongside Russia and the OSCE in September 1995. However, the Tiraspol regime seemed to toughen its negotiating position whenever agreement appeared to be within reach. Hopes for a breakthrough were raised when Russian President Yeltsin invited the parties to meet in Moscow shortly before the Commonwealth of Independent States (CIS) summit scheduled for May 1996, and both sides set to work to try to draft a "framework document." After considerable delay, including concessions and retractions by both sides, the agreement was ready to be signed formally in Moscow on July 1. However, one week after initialing the document, the government of Moldova made an extraordinary request to renegotiate two articles of the agreed text. They wanted to replace the basic formula defining the status of Transdniestria within the Republic of Moldova by a vague reference to continued negotiations between the parties "to establish state and legal relations between them."[46] The Moscow signing was postponed, and the OSCE focused on trying to keep the expert meetings alive and urged the Moldovan side to make a new political initiative to try to break the stalemate it had created. In an effort to achieve a breakthrough utilizing the methods of track two, or unofficial, off-the-record, diplomacy, a seminar on the conflict was held at the University of Kent in Canterbury, England, from September 29 through October 6, 1996, attended by all members of the experts group, including the new OSCE head of mission, Ambassador Donald Johnson. At the official level, however, negotiations largely ground to a halt.

In the spring of 1997 relations also deteriorated between the OSCE and authorities in Transdniestria. The head of mission came under personal attack for his allegedly biased approach to the mediation effort, and the authorities in Tiraspol refused to allow mission members to enter Transdniestria to carry our their mandate. Despite the criticism, Ambassador Johnson remained an outspoken critic of the Transdniestrian authorities. These tensions and accusations of bias, also voiced by members of the Russian delegation in Vienna, eventually contributed to Johnson's replacement as head of mission by John Evans, also an American diplomat. Johnson had been caught in a difficult position. Absolute neutrality was virtually impossible for the OSCE to achieve in this case since Moldova is a member state with a vote on the OSCE Permanent Council and Transdniestria is not; furthermore, the mission's mandate emphasizes preserving the territorial integrity of Moldova, which presupposes that complete independence for Transdniestria is out of the question. Altogether these factors create a structural asymmetry that makes it virtually impossible for the OSCE to be viewed as a strictly impartial mediator. However, this also placed a special burden on the head of mission not to compound that structural bias by creating the appearance of personal bias as well. That perception at least temporarily reduced the OSCE's credibility as an "honest broker" in the eyes of Transdniestrian and even Russian and Ukrainian participants during a critical phase when agreement seemed to be just around the corner.

To compensate partially for the diminished status of the OSCE, Ukraine and Russia both began to take on an increasingly active third-party role throughout 1997. Ukrainian President Kuchma paid a visit to Moldova on March 11, 1997, and Russian Foreign Minister Yevgeny Primakov visited on April 10-11, 1997. On that occasion Primakov virtually dictated the terms of an agreement to the parties. He pressured them to add an article to the still-unsigned memorandum committing the parties to build their relationship "in the framework of a common state within the borders of the Moldavian SSR as of January 1990."[47] This agreement was signed in Moscow on May 8, 1997, by President Lucinschi of Moldova and Igor Smirnov of Transdniestria. In addition, the three mediators—the OSCE chairman-in-office, President Yeltsin of Russia, and President Kuchma of Ukraine—signed a supplementary joint statement, originally proposed and drafted by the OSCE mission, affirming their understanding that any agreement must respect the sovereignty and territorial integrity of the Republic of Moldova under international law.

The signature of these two documents at a high-visibility ceremony hosted by President Yeltsin appeared to unblock negotiations and to remove any ambiguity about the international status of Moldova as a single subject of international law. As a result, the OSCE mission wanted to redirect its attention to finding solutions to specific issues involving the relationship between the central government and Transdniestrian authorities, especially regarding a specific division of competencies that would define the precise nature of Transdniestria's "special status." On May 24 Lucinschi and Smirnov met and established a negotiating commission to meet once a week, alternating between Chisinau and Tiraspol; four working groups on foreign economic activities, customs services, education, and criminality; and an additional group to prepare a proposal regarding the role of the guarantor states, Russia and Ukraine.

In August 1997 several actions by the Transdniestrian authorities appeared to undermine the negotiations. First, they officially declared Transdniestria to be a separate customs area, thereby appearing to preempt one of the issues under negotiation. Second, they created an official commission to demarcate Transdniestria's "frontiers" with Ukraine and Moldova, thereby seeming to undermine the fundamental agreement arrived at in Moscow just three months before. The Russian mediators, however, tried to push the negotiations forward in the hopes of having an agreement ready for signature at the summit meeting of the CIS that was scheduled to take place in Chisinau on October 22-23. At a meeting held at the Meshcherino dacha in the Moscow suburbs in early October, additional documents were drafted and initialed for signature at the Chisinau summit. However, the Transdniestrian delegation began to criticize this document even before leaving Moscow, and the frantic efforts by the mediators to salvage something from the Meshcherino document failed to produce any results. Indeed, "President" Smirnov did not attend a meeting with Yeltsin, Kuchma, and Lucinschi during the CIS summit, as planned, and no document was signed.

By February 1998 OSCE Head-of-Mission John Evans (who had replaced Donald Johnson in September 1997) noted in a report to the OSCE Permanent Council that the negotiations between Moldovan and Transdniestrian authorities seemed to have become "institutionalized." Both sides appeared to lose any real enthusiasm for reaching a speedy agreement, and the Transdniestrian authorities gave every indication of trying to stall the process. Several factors may account for the apparent stalemate in the negotiation process that developed by the end of 1997. Despite severe economic distress, there was little evidence that the two sides had in fact become enmeshed in a mutually recognized "hurting stalemate." On the west bank of the Dniester the Moldovan authorities had become preoccupied with their own internal political squabbles with the parliament and trying to cope with the continually deteriorating economic conditions. In the absence of violence or of any real threat to their political position from the regime in Tiraspol, they had little incentive to reach a rapid solution. With the principle of the territorial integrity of Moldova, including Transdniestria, well established and endorsed by both Russian and Ukrainian leaders as well as the OSCE, they were confident in their long-run ability to preserve the formal status of Moldova as a single state, but they were less than anxious to force an immediate settlement. For their part the authorities in Tiraspol appeared to believe that the presence of the Russian 14th Army and an extensive cache of weapons under its supervision would assure their ability to retain at least de facto independence for the foreseeable future.

In summary, the case of Moldova illustrates the role that the OSCE can play as a third party in order to promote resolution of conflicts in the region where it operates. But it also illustrates dramatically the difficulties inherent in resolving conflicts in the aftermath of violence, especially when the parties to a dispute are not under strong internal pressure to reach an agreement rapidly. The division of Moldova and the appearance of a separatist regime in Transdniestria called into question the reality of the territorial integrity of the country despite the strong reaffirmation of that status in principle by virtually the entire international community. Yet the resistance of the authorities, especially those in power in Tiraspol supported by nationalist influences in Russia, prevented the OSCE from achieving a long-term resolution of the conflict, even though the OSCE undoubtedly helped to prevent the conflict from once again turning violent.

Postconflict Security Building—The Case of Albania

Principles

The OSCE has also frequently been engaged in promoting long-term peace and security in regions where conflicts have occurred and where a political settlement has been formally achieved but where the destruction of war has left a legacy of hatred and animosity, so that peace remains conditional. The effort to create a more stable peace usually involves efforts to promote reconciliation between the parties to the conflict that go beyond a formal settlement of the dispute and move them toward a deeper resolution of their differences. It may also involve assistance with building democracy in order to create nonviolent means to resolve differences that were previously settled by coercion and the threat of violence. The construction of civil society, holding of elections, assistance in the creation of new constitutions and the promotion of the rule of law, and all other aspects of the OSCE human dimension activities may be stressed in these situations.

In addition, the OSCE has assisted in the verification of disarmament agreements between disputing parties. It arranges and provides training for institutions required to maintain law and order, especially for civilian police. Since economic distress is frequently a major obstacle to post-conflict rehabilitation, the OSCE assists the parties in identifying donors to obtain external economic relief or in helping humanitarian organizations become established in zones where violence has created severe social needs. In short it provides assistance to help relieve the conditions that breed conflict and make reconciliation difficult to realize. Finally, in a number of cases the OSCE has assisted with the return of refugees and internally displaced persons to their prewar homes, for example, by advising governments on the legal provisions regarding property rights. In some cases, such as the Eastern Slavonia region of Croatia, the OSCE has worked directly with returning refugees to facilitate their return. All of these efforts are thus directed toward facilitating the further abatement of conflict and eventually the creation of a condition of stable peace.

The Case of Albania

The OSCE played a major role not only in resolving the conflict that broke out in Albania in early 1997 but also in the process of trying to rebuild political and social order after the fighting ended. This mission was created on March 27, 1997, in the aftermath of the collapse of civil order in Albania. The major precipitating event was the failure of a "pyramid scheme" supported by the government of President Berisha, which led to widespread chaos and apparently random violence throughout the country. In response to this outbreak of violence and a flood of refugees that crossed the Adriatic Sea and entered Italy, the Italian government led a "coalition of the willing" to create a small Multilateral Protection Force to enter Albania and restore order. Known as Operation Alba, it was sanctioned by both the UN and the OSCE.[48]

Shortly thereafter the OSCE decided to establish its presence in Albania, and one of its major tasks was to assist in the preparation, monitoring, and implementation of elections scheduled for March 9, 1998. The mandate adopted by the OSCE Permanent Council on March 27 was even broader, however, asking the mission to provide "the coordinating framework within which other international organizations can play their part in their respective areas of competence, in support of a coherent international strategy, and in facilitating improvements in the protection of human rights and basic elements of civil society." Specific areas of OSCE specialization would include, as in many other missions, responsibility for preparing and monitoring elections; oversight of democratization, media and human rights; and monitoring the collection of weapons. The fact that there was a relatively smooth transition between the military activities undertaken by Operation Alba and the new OSCE presence also contributed to the success of the mission, since the OSCE did not have to fear being dominated by this ad hoc military operation as it was to some extent in Bosnia where the large NATO-led force at times overshadowed the OSCE's political and diplomatic operations.

Former Austrian Chancellor Franz Vranitzky was appointed head of the OSCE presence in Albania. His status in European political circles gave him access to the highest-level officials of all major European governments, enabling him to secure the support that the OSCE presence needed from key member governments. The OSCE also worked closely with the Italian-led Multilateral Protection Force, relying on it to provide the security necessary to undertake its major tasks. Despite little advance warning, the OSCE reacted rapidly and creatively to a fast-developing crisis to which other organizations, more tightly bound by bureaucracy, were unable to respond so quickly. The ODIHR was able to prepare and mount presidential elections by the scheduled date of June 29, and the elections proceeded peacefully with the selection of the opposition leader, Fatos Nano of the Social Democratic Party, as prime minister. Following the election, the OSCE mission was reduced in size, and the Multinational Protection Force was withdrawn as political stability returned for the most part to Albania. The OSCE continued to make some progress in overseeing the return of some of the 1 million to 1.5 million light weapons, mostly Kalashnikovs, looted from storehouses during the violence[49] and in restoring some of the foundations for civil society in Albania. Although the situation in Albania remains precarious, there can be little doubt that the OSCE played a major role in coordinating the international response to a severe crisis in the volatile Balkan region of southeastern Europe. It thus represents the fulfillment of what Hugh Miall has appropriately characterized as "light conflict prevention," which aims to prevent escalation or "to bring about de-escalation without necessarily addressing the deep roots of the conflict."[50]

The primary reason for OSCE's success in Albania was perhaps ironically the same factor that has hindered its success in other cases, namely its flexibility, which is in turn a function of its small staff and resource base. Yet the ability to react flexibly, under the leadership of prominent individuals and concerned and willing states, gave the OSCE a capability to respond quickly to a crisis where an international consensus existed to act but where no other international organization was able to respond in a timely fashion. The personal representative of the chairman-in-office, Franz Vranitzky, and his deputy, former Austrian Ambassador Herbert Grubmayr, were given virtual carte blanche by the OSCE to take charge of the mission, and they acted promptly and decisively. Their leadership of the OSCE presence and the fact that their hands were not tied by the Permanent Council in Vienna were undoubtedly major factors in enabling the OSCE to play a significant role in putting "Humpty Dumpty back together again" in Albania. This case thus offers especially useful insights into the role that a regional security organization can play in managing crises in collapsing states located in tense regions such as the Balkans.

CONCLUSION

Strengthening the OSCE

As the preceding review of four cases of OSCE intervention in conflict situations suggests, the OSCE has successfully fulfilled several of the security functions with which it has been charged, though its record in some other activities is mixed. Two strengths of the OSCE have been evident in its most successful undertakings. One clear strength is OSCE's broad approach to security, linking the human dimension to virtually all of its efforts to prevent the escalation and to facilitate the abatement and resolution of conflict. The OSCE has thus contributed significantly to strengthening democratic processes and institutions in countries undergoing transformation, and this activity has been helpful both in preventing conflicts from escalating and in confidence building in postconflict situations in countries such as Albania. In addition to the cases surveyed above, this strength was evident in the OSCE's democracy-building activities in Estonia and Latvia and in its postconflict efforts in Central Asia, especially in Tajikistan.

Second, the OSCE has proven to be remarkably flexible in reacting to potential crises, which has made it possible to respond more rapidly than most other institutions and to adapt its responses more appropriately to the specific issues arising in particular cases. Innovative individuals have had the freedom to engage in problem-solving efforts to prevent and resolve conflicts. This may be illustrated by the rapid intervention by High Commissioner on National Minorities Max van der Stoel in the Crimean situation in Ukraine; the active leadership of Ambassador Tim Guldimann as head of the OSCE Assistance Group in Chechnya to mediate an end to the war with the Russian Federation; and the leadership shown by Franz Vranitzky as head of the OSCE presence in Albania to prevent the collapse of that country, which almost certainly would have further destabilized the fragile Balkan region. The OSCE has thus provided the necessary institutional support and legitimacy for the efforts of talented and innovative individuals to broker solutions to complex problems in several significant conflicts.

Conversely, the OSCE has been less successful in several of its other tasks. So far it has largely failed to mediate long-term solutions to issues underlying conflicts after large-scale violence has abated. In all fairness the OSCE has had to grapple with some very deep identity-based conflicts, which it entered only after a period of intense fighting had made resolution of the deep-seated differences extremely difficult. This was certainly true of the conflicts in Moldova, Nagorno Karabakh, and both the Abkhazia and South Ossetia regions of Georgia, all of which have proven extremely resistant to settlement efforts. Despite the inability of the OSCE to broker solutions to these difficult conflicts, the organization's presence has at least helped prevent violence from reigniting, and this is a significant accomplishment for which the OSCE deserves considerable credit.

There can be little doubt that the OSCE has failed to meet many of the expectations generated on its behalf when the Cold War came to an end and the Charter of Paris was adopted in 1990. In large part this is due less to the inherent inadequacies of the institution than to the unwillingness of member states to make the necessary contributions of human and economic resources as well as political support to enable the OSCE to be more successful in achieving its objectives. The chaotic conditions in the Balkans and in the peripheries of the former Soviet Union at the end of the Cold War made any easy success too much to expect, especially given that the OSCE was provided only limited leverage to affect the outcome by its most powerful members. It would thus be inappropriate to expect too much from a fledgling multilateral security institution operating in a political context that has tended either to favor unilateral action by hegemonic states or, in cases where multilateralism is preferred, to rely primarily on NATO, the European Union, or the United Nations. Nonetheless, with only a modest additional infusion of resources I believe the OSCE role in conflict management in post-Cold War Eurasia could be strengthened significantly. The following areas deserve special attention:

1. The OSCE needs high-profile leadership at the very top. Where it has been most successful in conflict management, individuals have stepped forward to assume creative leadership roles, but, with the exception of the high commissioner on national minorities, so far no such role has been institutionalized. Most leadership comes from the chairman-in-office, who rotates every year, and this person is selected according to nationality rather than because of any special leadership qualities. Above all the OSCE needs a high-profile secretary-general, who may also take a personal role in intervening in the most difficult conflict situations to try to promote resolution. The secretary-general also needs to be backed up by a highly professional director of the Conflict Prevention Center, supported by an enlarged if still

modest staff of professional specialists in conflict analysis and management, to take leadership of the OSCE activities in this vital area.

2. The OSCE missions need to be infused with more professional personnel, including the heads of mission and all professional supporting staff. Missions currently depend almost exclusively on personnel seconded by governments, typically for assignments of six months at a time. This means that there is some unevenness in the quality, preparedness, training, and knowledge of the region—including its culture and languages—of mission members. All missions likewise suffer from excessively rapid turnover of personnel. Furthermore, seconded personnel may feel less loyalty to the OSCE than to the governments that pay their salaries. This also occasionally inhibits the ability of OSCE personnel to remain (or at least to be perceived as remaining) neutral between the parties to a dispute. The OSCE thus needs to make financial and personnel commitments to its missions extending beyond the usual six-month mandate now authorized in virtually all cases. Almost all conflicts are too complex to be dealt with in such short periods of time, and long-term planning is required so that missions may build up the expertise and continuity of personnel that are needed to be able to perform their functions effectively.

In addition, a commitment to hire personnel for longer time periods, typically at least for two-year commitments, would reduce turnover and enhance the knowledge and experience of mission members. A core professional staff of conflict management experts backed by high-quality personnel seconded for significant lengths of time would be in a better position to engage actively in the tasks of conflict prevention and resolution with which the missions are charged. Furthermore, personnel are needed whose first loyalty is to the OSCE rather than their home governments. The criteria for selection need to be based on qualifications to manage conflicts of the kind that have appeared throughout the region, instead of the current practice of selecting individuals who can be spared for one reason or another by their governments, often because they are not those who are most needed elsewhere.

3. OSCE mission members need to receive high-quality professional training before going into the field. At present there is no formal training program, so mission members frequently have little knowledge of the situations in the countries where they are stationed. Even more significantly, almost none have any formal training in techniques of negotiation, mediation, and conflict resolution beyond what they might have picked up from training given by their ministries when they entered the service of their home governments. The OSCE thus needs to assign high priority to establishing formal training in negotiation, mediation, and other con-

flict management skills, as well as training about the important and sensitive issues of the regions in which its missions are stationed.

4. An analytical support staff at the Conflict Prevention Center in Vienna could provide expert backing and advice for missions in the field. Staffed by a small number of specialists in conflict management, who could be called on by field missions whenever their advice and assistance were needed, supported by good library and data-processing resources, an analytical bureau within the Conflict Prevention Center could go a long way toward providing mission members with the professional backing they so desperately need. What is needed is not a large bureaucracy but a small staff of specialists on conflict analysis and management who can respond flexibly to developing conflicts in whatever region they might appear.

5. The OSCE needs to strengthen both the mandate and resources of the Office of the High Commissioner on National Minorities without making it overly bureaucratized. The high commissioner is one of the OSCE's most effective tools for early warning and early intervention in potential conflict situations. At present the high commissioner is severely constrained by several provisions of the office's mandate and by the limited resources and relatively small staff available to draw on in fulfilling that mandate. Interventions are restricted to issues (a) where *national* minorities are involved, (b) where there is no terrorist element operating, and (c) where there is a significant threat that a conflict might spill over international borders.

These constraints largely explain why the high commissioner has functioned only in conflicts in former communist countries rather than in other parts of Europe, even though the incumbent high commissioner has defined his role broadly within the limits of the mandate adopted at the 1992 OSCE summit in Helsinki. This has created the unfortunate perception that the OSCE is largely an organization through which Western European and North American governments can manage conflicts in Eastern Europe and Central Asia but not the reverse.[51] It has created the impression that only some minority conflicts deserve attention and not others; for example, conflicts where the parties are divided along religious rather than nationality lines are not formally eligible to receive assistance from the high commissioner's office. And it means that terrorist activities by extremists associated with a national minority may prevent the high commissioner from interceding in disputes in which they participate, even when the vast majority of the members of that nationality may have refrained altogether from the use of violence. Ironically, the high commissioner may intervene in conflicts where parties have resorted to full-scale war but not where some individuals have resorted to terrorism, as defined by member governments. Thus, the high commissioner has intervened in the conflict between Abkhazians and the Georgian government, who fought a bloody war in 1992-1993, but may not do so in the conflict between Kurds and the government of Turkey due to government allegations of terrorist activity by certain Kurdish factions.

The success of the office of the High Commissioner on National Minorities since its creation in 1992 has largely been the result of the dedicated and brilliant work of its first incumbent, former Dutch Foreign Minister Max van der Stoel, and a small, hard-working, and intelligent professional staff. It is by no means certain that future high commissioners will interpret their mandate as broadly, engage themselves as actively, and perform to the high professional standards set by the original set of officials in the Hague. The office thus needs to be strengthened in terms of both its mandate and its resources—human and financial—in order to assure that its effectiveness is institutionalized after the first high commissioner leaves. Any efforts to weaken the office after van der Stoel's retirement must be strongly resisted by the most important countries in the OSCE. The high commissioner has enjoyed strong support from the delegations of the United States, the Russian Federation, and the European Union, and the continued support of all of these delegations will be essential to preserve and strengthen what has perhaps been the most innovative and unique contribution made by the OSCE to enhance security in Europe since the end of the Cold War.

6. The OSCE needs to enhance its cooperation and coordination with other organizations working in the field of European security, especially NATO, the European Union, the Commonwealth of Independent States, the Western European Union, and the Council of Europe. No one organization is likely to emerge in the near future as the sole arbiter of European security, since no single organization has the capacity to fulfill the full range of functions required to promote the building of a security regime.

The OSCE's dependence on NATO to provide military security (as SFOR does in Bosnia) so that the OSCE can carry out its activities, such as monitoring elections and assisting in the return of refugees, is evident in several cases. It is equally evident that there are many issues in which military force does not provide the exclusive answer, so that the OSCE rather than NATO was assigned to monitor the withdrawal of Serbian forces from Kosovo and disarmament of the Kosovo Liberation Army in October 1998. If NATO and other OSCE member states had been asked and been willing to provide armed protection for the Kosovo Verification Mission, operating as it did in a hostile environment, the mission might have been able to fulfill its mandate more effectively. Indeed, limited action by NATO and its partner countries, acting under OSCE auspices, to prevent violence on the part of both the Serbian and Kosovar Albanian sides in the early stages of escalation in the summer and fall of 1998 might have been able to head off the explosion of the Kosovo crisis into full-scale war in 1999 and the resulting humanitarian tragedy that unfolded throughout the Balkans.

Finally, as indicated in the NATO-Russian Founding Act, peacekeeping operations in which NATO troops play a prominent but not an exclusive role might be mandated by the OSCE. Since Russia has a voice in OSCE decision making, OSCE-mandated operations, perhaps with Russia and other non-NATO states contributing troops, may be viewed as less politically one sided and may have more widespread political legitimacy than actions undertaken unilaterally by NATO. In this respect the model of IFOR and SFOR in Bosnia might serve as a precedent but with the OSCE providing the mandate, especially if a UN decision is blocked by a possible Chinese veto.

The OSCE also needs to expand cooperation with the European Union, on which it often depends to finance many projects essential to fulfill its mandate in postconflict security building, for example. Finally, the OSCE needs to negotiate a clear division of labor with institutions such as the Council of Europe that perform overlapping functions such as democratization in the former communist states, so that the two institutions do not duplicate efforts much less get in one another's way in carrying out their activities.

7. Member states need to recognize that participation in a regional security regime like the OSCE inherently entails the sacrifice of some of the prerogatives of state sovereignty. Too often action on the part of the OSCE has been blocked or watered down by the necessity to maintain support for the work of its missions by countries that are parties to a dispute or by powerful states that back particular factions in some of the ongoing disputes. There are good reasons for maintaining the principle of consensus as the decision rule in the OSCE, since it acts as a safety valve to keep the organization from collapsing due to disputes among its member states. On the other hand, consensus should not be regarded as equivalent to a legalistic veto, and a "substantial" consensus among an overwhelming majority of the member states should be respected by dissenting states. This is especially true for some of the most powerful member states. The United States has occasionally resisted OSCE actions that might have impinged on its ability to intervene unilaterally in conflict situations. And the Russian Federation, which professes strong support for the OSCE as an alternative to NATO, has occasionally blocked consensus or prevented the OSCE from acting decisively in some of the most significant areas where it works, since most of these conflicts fall within Russia's "near abroad" or at least within its perceived "sphere of influence." If Russia wants to make a credible case for making the OSCE the centerpiece of the European security architecture,

its behavior within the organization will have to match its rhetoric more closely.

In short, although the OSCE has developed and promoted a number of important universal norms as a multilateral organization, it is simultaneously a political organization composed of states with their own interests. It has not totally overcome the obstacles created when the interests of powerful states take precedence over the interests of parties locked in conflict or the larger interests of the "international community." Nonetheless, it has undertaken a wide range of activities to realize common interests in preventing the escalation of conflicts, facilitating their termination and resolution, and aiding in the reconstruction of societies damaged by the ravages of war. In fulfilling these functions the OSCE has clearly surpassed the minimal criteria for a security regime identified by Keohane and Nye in the Introduction to this chapter, namely restraining anarchy and promoting cooperation in situations where peace is unstable and the risk for violence is high. Yet its strength has been in its ability to make modest incremental contributions, alongside other parties, often carrying out the detailed work necessary to make more publicized activities successful. It often operates quietly, outside the glare of publicity, so that the large number of significant contributions it has made to security building in Eurasia have frequently gone largely unnoticed.

For the OSCE to achieve its potential, member states must have confidence that their long-term interests will be better served by a stable and secure Europe in order to be willing to forego getting their way on issues that may negatively affect their narrow, short-term interests. The OSCE thus faces a "dilemma of expectations": if national governments were confident in the OSCE's potential and gave it the support it needs—not only material but also political—it could become demonstrably more successful in producing clear and recognizable joint security benefits for all of its members. This would reinforce the confidence that member governments and their populations have in the OSCE and their willingness to give it the support it needs. As a consequence, the OSCE might become even more effective at producing common security, in a positive spiral of mounting confidence and capability, perhaps eventually forming a full-fledged security regime.

Conversely, in the absence of such support the OSCE will inevitably fall short of the expectations generated for it. This will cause its critics to dismiss it as another weak and ineffective multilateral organization on which states cannot depend to protect their national security. States may consequently withdraw their support from the OSCE and put greater confidence in military alliances and unilateral "self-help." This would further weaken the OSCE and make it into the helpless organization that its critics said it was all along, reinforcing a negative cycle of diminishing expectations and ineffectiveness.

The OSCE alone, of course, is not a panacea for a new, stable, and secure European order, and excessively optimistic expectations could lead to almost certain disappointment and disillusionment. At the same time the denial by realists of the potential of multilateral security institutions like the OSCE undermines the ability of regional security organizations to reach their potential. What is needed is a recognition of the concrete accomplishments already made by the OSCE and support for the optimistic but not unrealistic belief that some modest efforts to strengthen the OSCE could make a significant positive contribution to a more secure common future for all Europeans "from Vancouver to Vladivostok."

The OSCE as a Model for Other Global Regions

Finally, I turn briefly to lessons learned from the OSCE experience in Europe that may be applied to other regions of the globe. The OSCE has become a full-fledged regional security organization as defined under Chapter VIII of the UN Charter. Although similar organizations exist in some other parts of the world—the Organization for African Unity, the Organization of American States, and the Association of Southeast Asian Nations (ASEAN) Regional Forum (ARF) in Southeast Asia, for example—no regional organization has taken on the broad security functions of the OSCE thus far. For example, the ARF has entered into confidence-building measures in dangerous regions, such as the South China Sea, but has been extremely cautious about intervening in disputes that might in any way be construed as falling within the internal affairs of states. Thus, it has avoided any attempt to develop an agreed set of norms comparable to the Helsinki Decalogue, to say nothing of relatively intrusive measures like the OSCE missions of long duration or the high commissioner on national minorities, even though such ideas may be of interest to some states in the region.

At the outset, therefore, several cautionary notes are appropriate about the generalizability of the OSCE experience. First, the OSCE has largely assumed many of the functions previously performed by the UN in Eurasia, and in several places such as Bosnia, Croatia, Georgia, and Tajikistan there has been some modest competition between the OSCE and the UN. Competition has faded since the early 1990s, however, as the UN has been overwhelmed by so many conflicts that many UN officials are relieved to see the OSCE lift some burdens from their shoulders. Nonetheless, it is far from clear that regional security organizations in other parts of the world will have the resources to replace the UN as the major guarantor of security. Fortunately, in recent years the UN has been able to focus its scarce resources on those regions that most need its help, such as Africa and the Middle East. It thus seems to be neither necessary nor desirable to create regional organizations that essentially duplicate the functions of the UN Security Council in every region of the world, unless it can be demonstrated that regional organizations are likely to be significantly more effective at conflict management than the UN.

Second, the OSCE at present is to some degree a creature of its history, especially its origin as an institution intended to overcome the divisions wrought by the East-West conflict. Prior to 1990 the OSCE had thus been a unique institution for East and West to discuss security issues. Since the end of the Cold War it has evolved into an organization that has sought to create order out of the chaos that accompanied the collapse of the communist system, and it is currently able to take advantage of the potential for post-Cold War cooperation to deal with those conflicts that have erupted in large part as a consequence of the end of the Cold War and the breakup of the communist bloc. For this reason many of the lessons of the OSCE are perhaps not relevant to other regions that were situated more on the periphery of the East-West confrontation.

With these cautions in mind, there are nonetheless several key OSCE functions that might be adapted and applied in other regions afflicted with difficult conflicts:

1. The OSCE has founded its security role on a firm basis of normative principles, including human rights and democratic governance, that make it more than a narrow security organization. These "shared values" have been accepted by European states despite the substantial diversity of values that existed in the region, at least until 1989. While other regions may find it even harder to identify shared values, this should not be an insuperable obstacle to overcome in regions such as sub-Saharan Africa or much of Latin America, for example.

2. The OSCE concept of "missions of long duration" might also be usefully applied in other geographical regions that have experienced long-simmering conflicts that threaten to boil over. These missions may provide early warning of potential conflicts on the horizon, and they may aid parties to a dispute to avert violence while pursuing negotiations leading to a more fundamental resolution of their differences. One might envisage such a role in locations such as South and Southeast Asia, for example, in Indonesia concerning East Timor and other regions populated by ethnic and religious minorities, in the Philippines with regard to the Moro region, and in Sri Lanka with regard to the Tamil-dominated regions. These multilateral activities might begin largely as observer groups and perhaps expand into formal activities, including mediation and conflict resolution work with the disputing parties.[52]

3. The regime of confidence- and security-building measures associated with Basket I of the Helsinki Final Act, the 1986 Stockholm agreement on Disarmament in Europe, and the Vienna Documents 1990, 1992, and 1994 might also be relevant in other regions, especially where traditional enemies face one another in tense circumstances. Confidence-building measures might thus be especially valuable, for example, between Israel and Syria regarding the Golan Heights, between India and Pakistan in the Kashmir region, between Taiwan and China in the Taiwan straits, or between China and its Southeast Asian neighbors in the South China Sea. In each of these areas routine military activities by one party risk being perceived by others in their region as provocative and thus might initiate an escalatory cycle that could spin out of control.

4. The high commissioner on national minorities is also one of the most innovative and successful of the OSCE devices for dealing with conflicts that might be imitated with appropriate modifications in regions of the world where nationality conflicts are present, including much of Africa, the Middle East, and South Asia. The key to the success of this model is selecting a high-profile figure of great discretion and impartiality as the high commissioner, so that he or she will be accepted as an authoritative and fair figure by most governments and leaders of national or ethnic groups. This eminent person must be granted considerable flexibility, supporting resources, and the power to intervene on his or her own discretion in issues that many countries will consider to constitute purely internal affairs. Again, it is not hard to envision literally dozens of nationality disputes in Africa, South Asia, or the Middle East where such an individual might act more effectively than national governments or even the UN, especially if the high commissioner comes originally from the region affected by conflict and thus can be sensitive to its cultural values.

While each of these specific functions from the OSCE experience might readily be applied in other regions, what will be most difficult to transfer is the entire set of interconnected issues and institutions that together make up the OSCE and even more broadly the institutional "architecture" of European security. The OSCE region possesses more of the background characteristics necessary for the creation of a security regime than any other area of the globe. Simply put, Europe is the most "institutionally dense" region of the world. Insofar as the OSCE is successful at contributing to European security, that is in large part because of its many complex linkages with other institutions such as NATO, the Western European Union, the Commonwealth of Independent States, the European Union, the Council of Europe, and so forth. Without these reinforcing institutions to assist the OSCE in fulfilling its functions or to fill in the gaps in the fabric of European security not covered by the OSCE, it is doubtful that the OSCE could have realized even the modest level of success that it has achieved since 1975.

Since this environment simply does not exist in any other global region, it is unlikely that any regional security institution can be developed that will be able to replicate all of the many attributes that the OSCE now possesses. That said, the OSCE has invented and developed more fully than any other regional organization certain techniques and institutional structures to deal with violent conflict that might usefully be applied elsewhere, either by regional security organizations or the UN in its activities in those regions of the world in which it still is likely to be the institution of first choice whenever threats to the security of states and peoples arise.

ACKNOWLEDGMENTS

This chapter was researched and a first draft was written while I held a Fulbright senior research fellowship to the OSCE in Vienna, Austria, and a Jennings Randolph senior fellowship at the United States Institute of Peace in Washington, D.C., from September 1997 through August 1998. I am grateful to both organizations for their assistance in making this research possible, especially to Richard Pettit at the Council for International Exchange of Scholars; Stanley Schrager and Ilene Jennison of the Public Affairs Division, U.S. Mission to the OSCE in Vienna; Otmar Höll, director of the Austrian Institute on International Affairs; Finn Chemnitz, Diplomatic Officer at the OSCE Conflict Prevention Center; and Joseph Klaits, director, and Sally Blair, program officer, of the Jennings Randolph Program of the United States Institute of Peace. I am also grateful to Simon Limage for research assistance and Daniel Druckman, Alexander George, James Goodby, Dennis Sandole, Janice Stein, Paul Stern, I. William Zartman, and four anonymous reviewers for comments on a draft of this chapter. Portions of this chapter are drawn from a larger work being prepared by the author for the United States Institute of Peace Press.

NOTES

[1]One of these states, the Federal Republic of Yugoslavia, was suspended in 1992 due to its actions in violation of OSCE norms in Croatia and Bosnia-Herzegovina. Prior to 1995 the OSCE was known as the Conference on Security and Cooperation in Europe (CSCE). In this chapter I refer to it as the CSCE when discussing its activities from 1973 through 1994, but when referring to it generically, or to its activities since 1995, I refer to it as the OSCE.

[2]For classic statements of this argument, see John Lewis Gaddis, "The Long Peace: Elements of Stability in the Postwar International System," in Sean M. Lynn-Jones, ed., *The Cold War and After: Prospects for Peace* (Cambridge, Mass.: MIT Press, 1991), pp. 1-44, and John J. Mearsheimer, "Back to the Future: Instability in Europe After the Cold War," ibid., pp. 141-192.

[3]Hedley Bull, *The Anarchical Society* (London: Macmillan, 1977) and Barry Buzan, Charles Jones, and Richard Little, *The Logic of Anarchy: Neorealism to Structural Realism* (New York: Columbia University Press, 1993).

[4]Stephen D. Krasner, "Structural Causes and Regime Consequences: Regimes as Intervening Variables," in Stephen D. Krasner, ed., *International Regimes* (Ithaca, N.Y.: Cornell University Press, 1983), p. 2, based largely on Oran R. Young, "International Regimes: Problems of Concept Formation," *World Politics*, vol. 32 (April 1980).

[5]Robert Jervis, "Security Regimes," in Krasner, op. cit., p. 173.

[6]Robert O. Keohane and Joseph S. Nye, "Introduction: The End of the Cold War in Europe," in Robert O. Keohane, Joseph S. Nye, and Stanley Hoffmann, eds., *After the Cold War: International Institutions and State Strategies in Europe, 1989-1991* (Cambridge, Mass.: Harvard University Press, 1993), p. 5.

[7]See Michael Doyle, "Kant, Liberal Legacies and Foreign Affairs," in *Philosophy and Public Affairs*, vol. 12, no. 3 (Summer 1983), pp. 205-235; Bruce M. Russett, *Grasping the Democratic Peace: Principles for the Post-Cold War World* (Princeton, N.J.: Princeton University Press, 1993); and Michael W. Doyle, *Ways of War and Peace* (New York: W.W. Norton, 1997), chap. 8.

[8]Michael S. Lund, *Preventing Violent Conflicts: A Strategy for Preventive Diplomacy* (Washington, D.C.: United States Institute of Peace Press, 1996), p. 38. I have modified Lund's "Life History of a Conflict" to take account of an additional distinction suggested by Alexander George and James E. Goodby, namely to divide "unstable peace" into two categories, "conditional peace" and "precarious peace." See Alexander George, "Foreword" to James E. Goodby, *Europe Undivided: The New Logic of Peace in U.S.-Russian Relations* (Washington, D.C.: United States Institute of Peace Press), pp. ix-x. Precarious peace refers to a situation that is highly conflict prone though not yet in a crisis stage, whereas conditional peace refers to a less acute situation where there is a potential for escalation but where acute crises seldom arise.

[9]At this point in the Cold War and under the regime of hard-line dictator Enver Hoxha, Albania had severed most of its ties even with other communist regimes in Europe, maintaining friendly ties only with the Peoples' Republic of China, North Korea, and Cuba.

[10]For an excellent and detailed analysis of the Vienna CSCE meeting by a member of the Austrian delegation, see Stefan Lehne, *The Vienna Meeting of the Conference on Security and Cooperation in Europe, 1986-1989: A Turning Point in East-West Relations* (Boulder, Colo.: Westview Press, 1991).

[11]Two other documents also were adopted under CSCE auspices in 1990, namely the Treaty on Conventional Forces in Europe and the 1990 Vienna document on confidence- and security-building measures. Since these documents dealt mostly with arms control measures, they had less of an impact on the normative and institutional underpinnings of European security while nonetheless strengthening the European security regime through greater transparency, limitations on military activities, and significant reductions of conventional armaments.

[12]Jonathan Dean, *Ending Europe's Wars: The Continuing Search for Peace and Stability* (New York: Twentieth Century Fund Press, 1994), p. 210.

[13]The number of member states increased to 54 when the Czech and Slovak Federal Republic divided voluntarily into two separate states at the beginning of 1993 and to 55 when Andorra was admitted in 1996; this includes the Federal Republic of Yugoslavia whose voting rights were suspended in 1992.

[14]Allan Rosas and Timo Lahelma, "OSCE Long-Term Missions," in Michael Bothe, Natalino Ronzitti, and Allan Rosas, eds., *The OSCE in the Maintenance of Peace and Security: Conflict Prevention, Crisis Management, and Peaceful Settlement of Disputes* (The Hague: Kluwer Law International, 1997), p. 169. These missions were subsequently withdrawn at the re-

quest of the government of the Federal Republic of Yugoslavia after its voting rights in the CSCE were suspended.

¹⁵This figure excludes the many individuals seconded to the OSCE by member governments, including the bulk of the staff of its missions and field activities. It also excludes the large number of people recruited on a short-term basis by ODIHR, for example, to supervise and monitor elections.

¹⁶John J. Maresca, *To Helsinki: The Conference on Security and Cooperation in Europe, 1973-1975* (Durham, N.C.: Duke University Press, 1985), p. 64. The author was deputy chief of the U.S. delegation to the CSCE negotiations during the period covered in this book.

¹⁷This skepticism has not necessarily extended to the working levels where there is often active engagement with the OSCE and support for its activities, especially by the large U.S. delegation assigned to the OSCE in Vienna.

¹⁸The analysis in this section is based largely on on-site research by the author at the OSCE headquarters in Vienna for two extended periods. In 1992 the author spent a total of about five months in Vienna and Helsinki, observing closely the work of the CSCE's Conflict Prevention Center at a time when missions of long duration were first being created. He also closely observed negotiations on the Vienna Document 1992 on confidence- and security-building measures; the final negotiations of the Open Skies Treaty; and the preparation, conduct, and follow-up to the Helsinki summit of July 1992. He interviewed senior officials in the CSCE secretariat and senior representatives (generally the head of mission) of most CSCE countries present in Vienna at that time.

The author also had a second extended period of close observation of the OSCE from September 1997 through January 1998. During that time he attended most formal and informal meetings of the Permanent Council, including reports by mission heads and the heads of OSCE bodies in both an informal setting and formal presentations to the council. He also interviewed all heads of the OSCE missions during their regular reporting visits to Vienna, and he visited on site the OSCE mission in Moldova, traveling with the mission head to Transdniestria. He interviewed senior officials of the Conflict Prevention Center, the high commissioner on national minorities, and the Office of Democratic Institutions and Human Rights in Vienna, the Hague, and Warsaw, respectively. He has obtained copies of all field reports from the 14 OSCE missions and other field activities since their inception, typically issued about once a month, although the frequency may be more or less often according to the demands of each individual situation. He also obtained copies of all official correspondence between the high commissioner on national minorities and governments where he visited, including all of his recommendations to those governments. Finally, he obtained materials from ODIHR, including all election evaluation reports.

The analysis that follows, therefore, is based largely on the author's personal observation, interviews, and reading of original documents concerning the field activities of the OSCE in several regions of potential or actual violent conflict.

¹⁹Max van der Stoel, "Minorities in Transition," *War Report,* no. 48 (January/February 1997), p. 16.

²⁰Saadia Touval and I. William Zartman, "Introduction: Mediation in Theory," in Saadia Touval and I. William Zartman, eds., *International Mediation in Theory and Practice* (Boulder, Colo.: Westview Press, 1985), p. 16. See also Chapter 6 in this volume.

²¹Lund, op. cit., p. 15.

²²Alexander L. George and Jane E. Holl, "The Warning-Response Problem and Missed Opportunities in Preventive Diplomacy," in Bruce Jentleson, ed., *Opportunities Missed, Opportunities Seized: Preventive Diplomacy in the Post-Cold War World* (Lanham, Md.: Rowman and Littlefield, 2000), p. 29.

²³In a personal interview in the Hague on November 18, 1997, Ambassador Max van der Stoel, OSCE high commissioner on national minorities, expressed concern about this

problem regarding the continuing crisis in the Kosovo region of the Federal Republic of Yugoslavia, where international agencies have been warning of a potential crisis since 1989 but where by late 1997 the crisis had not yet boiled over into widespread violence. The danger, he noted, was that the international community had become habituated to the crisis in this region and might not respond to new warnings that this crisis was on the verge of rapid escalation until it was too late. Unfortunately, his concerns in this regard appear to have been largely borne out by the intensifying conflict and increasing violence that appeared in Kosovo in 1998, more than one year before NATO began its aerial bombardment of the Federal Republic of Yugoslavia. One can only speculate about the lives, resources, and human misery that might have been spared had political leaders in the major states, especially in Washington, heeded the "early warnings" generated by several OSCE missions and officials such as Ambassador van der Stoel in late 1997, rather than waiting almost a year to act, at which time the cycle of escalation had become firmly entrenched and the potential for effective preventive diplomacy had been greatly reduced.

[24]George and Holl, op. cit., p. 24.

[25]Viacheslav Pikhovshek, "Will the Crimean Crisis Explode?," in Maria Drohobycky, ed., *Crimea: Challenges and Prospects* (Lanham, Md.: Rowan and Littlefield, 1995), p. 48.

[26]OSCE Mission to Ukraine, Activity and Background Report No. 5, 31 March 1995, p. 9.

[27]Ibid., p. 10.

[28]Letter from Ambassador Max van der Stoel to Foreign Minister Hennady Udovenko, 15 May 1995, OSCE Reference No. HC/1/95.

[29]Letter from Foreign Minister Hennady Udovenko to Ambassador Max van der Stoel, 30 June 1995, OSCE Reference No. HC/4/95.

[30]Foundation on Inter-ethnic Relations, *The Role of the High Commissioner on National Minorities in OSCE Conflict Prevention* (The Hague: Foundation on Inter-ethnic Relations, 1997), pp. 75-77.

[31]Tor Bukkvoll, "A Fall from Grace for Crimean Separatists," *Transition,* 17 November 1995, pp. 46-53.

[32]Ibid., p. 48.

[33]John Packer, "Autonomy Within the OSCE: The Case of Crimea," in Markku Suksi, ed., *Autonomy: Applications and Implications* (The Hague: Kluwer Law International, 1998), p. 310.

[34]Statement by U.S. Head of Delegation Sam Brown, 12 January 1995, to the OSCE Permanent Council in Vienna, in Commission on Security and Cooperation in Europe of the U.S. Congress, "Hearings on the Crisis in Chechnya" (Washington, D.C.: U.S. Government Printing Office, 1995), pp. 128-130.

[35]Carlotta Gall and Thomas de Waal, *Chechnya: Calamity in the Caucasus* (New York: New York University Press, 1998), pp. 275-282.

[36]Ibid., p. 284.

[37]Ibid., p. 288.

[38]Report of the OSCE Assistance Group in Chechnya, 8 January 1996.

[39]Tim Guldimann, "The OSCE Assistance Group to Chechnya," paper presented at the Carnegie Endowment for International Peace, Washington, D.C., 11 March 1997, p. 3.

[40]I. William Zartman, "Putting Humpty-Dumpty Together Again," in David A. Lake and Donald Rothchild, eds., *The International Spread of Ethnic Conflict: Fear, Diffusion, and Escalation* (Princeton, N.J.: Princeton University Press, 1998), p. 318.

[41]P. Terrence Hopmann, "New Approaches for Resolving Europe's Post-Cold War Conflicts," *Brown Journal of World Affairs,* vol. IV, no. 1 (Winter/Spring 1997), pp. 155-167.

[42]For a discussion of the difference between these two styles of negotiation, see P. Terrence Hopmann, "Two Paradigms of Negotiation: Bargaining and Problem Solving,"

Annals of the American Academy of Political and Social Science, no. 542 (November 1995), pp. 24-47.

[43]For a review of the literature on third-party roles, see P. Terrence Hopmann, *The Negotiation Process and the Resolution of International Conflicts* (Columbia: University of South Carolina Press, 1996), chap. 12.

[44]CSCE Mission to Moldova, Report No. 13, 16 November 1993, pp. 1-3.

[45]Foundation on Inter-ethnic Relations, op. cit., pp. 68-70.

[46]"Memorandum on the Fundamentals of Normalizing the Relations Between the Republic of Moldova and Trans-Dniestria," annex to Spot Report No. 18/96, OSCE Mission to Moldova, 11 July 1996.

[47]OSCE Mission to Moldova, Monthly Report No. 7/97, 22 April 1997, p. 3.

[48]See Marjanne de Kwaasteniet, "Alba: A Lost Opportunity for the OSCE?," *Helsinki Monitor*, vol. 9, no. 1 (1998), pp. 20-21.

[49]Many of these weapons, however, ended up in the hands of the Kosovo Liberation Army to be used in its struggle for independence from Serbia, which turned violent in 1998.

[50]Hugh Miall, "The OSCE Role in Albania: A Success for Conflict Prevention?," *Helsinki Monitor*, vol. 8, no. 4 (1997), pp. 74-75.

[51]The argument that the OSCE has tended to become engaged only in conflicts in the former communist countries of Eastern Europe and Central Asia rather than in Western countries (including Turkey) is made persuasively by Martin Alexanderson in "The Need for a Generalised Application of the Minorities Regime in Europe," *Helsinki Monitor*, vol. 8, no. 4 (1997), pp. 47-58.

[52]For example, the government of Indonesia has mediated in its role as chair of the Organization of Islamic States and as a member of ASEAN in the dispute between the Moro region populated primarily by Muslim inhabitants and the government of the Philippines, also an ASEAN member state. See Dino Patti Djalal, "The Indonesian Experience in Facilitating a Peace Settlement Between the Government of the Republic of the Philippines (GRP) and the Moro National Liberation Front (MNLF)," paper presented at the Preventive Diplomacy Workshop of the Council for Security Cooperation in the Asia Pacific, Bangkok, Thailand, 28 February-2 March 1999.

About the Authors

COMMITTEE

ALEXANDER L. GEORGE is professor emeritus of international relations at Stanford University. He is an author or a coauthor of a number of books, including *Woodrow Wilson and Colonel House: A Personality Study* (John Day Company, Inc., 1956), *Deterrence in American Foreign Policy* (Columbia University Press, 1974), *Presidential Decision Making in Foreign Policy* (Westview, 1980), and *Avoiding War: Problems of Crisis Management* (Westview, 1991). His most recent book, for the United States Institute of Peace, is *Bridging the Gap: Theory and Practice of Foreign Policy* (1993). He is preparing a book on the use of case studies for theory development.

JUERGEN DEDRING is an adjunct professor of political science at the City University of New York and at New York University and is a senior research associate at the Ralph Bunche Institute on the United Nations, City University of New York. From 1975 to 1996 he was a political officer in the United Nations Secretariat and worked specifically for the Security Council Department, the Office for Research and the Collection of Information, and the Department of Humanitarian Affairs. He published a critical survey of peace and conflict research in 1976 and more recently articles on conflict resolution, humanitarian issues, early warning, and the role and functions of the UN Security Council. He is currently working on a book-length manuscript about the role of the UN Security Council in peace and security matters in the post-Cold War era. He received a degree of Diplom-Politologe from the Free University, Berlin, Germany, and A.M. and Ph.D. degrees in political science from Harvard University.

617

FRANCIS M. DENG is special representative of the United Nations secretary-general on internally displaced persons and is a senior fellow at the Brookings Institution, where he helped establish the African Studies branch of the Foreign Policy Studies program, which he heads. Born in the Sudan, he attended schools in both the African-Christianized south and the Arab-Islamic north and holds law degrees from Khartoum and Yale universities. In addition to academic appointments in his home country and at several U.S. universities, Deng served as human rights officer in the United Nations secretariat; as Sudanese ambassador to Canada, the Scandinavian countries, and the United States; and as minister of state for foreign affairs. In 1996 Deng assumed the position of acting chairman of the African Leadership Forum following the imprisonment of General Olsegun Obasanjo, former head of state of Nigeria and founder of the forum. He is the author or editor of more than 20 books.

DANIEL DRUCKMAN (*Consultant*) is professor of conflict resolution at George Mason University's Institute for Conflict Analysis and Resolution, where he also coordinates the doctoral program. He formerly directed a number of projects at the National Research Council and held senior positions at several research consulting firms. He has published widely on such topics as negotiating behavior, nationalism, peacekeeping, political stability, nonverbal communication, and modeling methodologies, including simulation. He received the 1995 Otto Klineberg award for Intercultural and International Relations from the Society for the Psychological Study of Social Issues and a Teaching Excellence Award in 1998 from George Mason University. He currently sits on the boards of six journals, including the *Journal of Conflict Resolution* and the *American Behavioral Scientist*. He is also an associate editor of *Simulation & Gaming*. He received a Ph.D. in social psychology from Northwestern Unviersity.

RONALD J. FISHER is a professor of psychology and founding coordinator of the graduate program in applied social psychology at the University of Saskatchewan, Saskatoon, Canada. He specializes in the theory and practice of conflict resolution, with particular interests in unofficial third-party interventions at the intergroup and international levels. His writings include *The Social Psychology of Intergroup and International Conflict Resolution* (Springer-Verlag, 1990) and *Interactive Conflict Resolution* (Syracuse University Press, 1997). In addition, he has published numerous chapters and articles in interdisciplinary journals focusing on conflict analysis and resolution. He holds a B.A. (honors) and an M.A. in psychology from the University of Saskatchewan and a Ph.D. in social psychology from the University of Michigan.

JAMES E. GOODBY is a senior research fellow at the Massachusetts Institute of Technology and a nonresident senior fellow at the Brookings Institution. He has taught at Carnegie Mellon, Stanford, and Georgetown universities and held the Payne Distinguished Lecturer chair at Stanford during 1996-1997. He is the author of *Europe Undivided*, a book on U.S.-Russian relations published in 1998 by the United States Institute of Peace in cooperation with the Institute for International Studies at Stanford. He has edited or coedited four other books dealing with U.S.-Russian relations and is the author of many articles on Europe and northeast Asia. He entered the U.S. Foreign Service in 1952 and rose to the rank of career minister. His assignments included those of special representative of President Clinton for the security and dismantlement of nuclear weapons, 1995-1996; chief negotiator for nuclear threat reduction agreements, 1993-1994 (the Nunn-Lugar program); head, U.S. delegation, conference on confidence- and security-building measures in Europe, 1983-1985; vice-chair, U.S. delegation to START I, 1982-1983; ambassador to Finland, 1980-1981; and deputy assistant secretary in the State Department's Bureau of European Affairs and Bureau of Political-Military Affairs, 1974-1980. He is the winner of the inaugural Heinz Award in Public Policy, the Commander's Cross of the Order of Merit of Germany, and the Presidential Distinguished Service Award. He was named a distinguished fellow of the United States Institute of Peace in 1992. He received an A.B. degree from Harvard and an honorary doctor of laws degree from the Stetson University College of Law.

ROBERT H. MNOOKIN is the Samuel Williston Professor of Law at Harvard Law School and chairman of the steering committee, Program on Negotiation at Harvard Law School. In both his scholarly and his applied work, Professor Mnookin has taken an interdisciplinary approach to a broad range of questions relating to conflict resolution. He is the author of numerous scholarly articles and six books, including *Dividing the Child: Social and Legal Dilemmas of Custody*, with E. Maccoby (Harvard University Press, 1992) and *Barriers to Conflict Resolution* (W.W. Norton, 1995), with colleagues from the Stanford Center on Conflict and Negotiation. His current book projects include *Negotiating on Behalf of Others* (Sage, 1999), which he coedited with Lawrence Susskind, and the forthcoming *Beyond Winning: How Lawyers Help Clients Create Value in Negotiation* (Harvard University Press, 2000), with Scott Peppet and Andrew Tulumello. Professor Mnookin received his A.B. in economics from Harvard College in 1964 and his law degree from Harvard Law School in 1968.

RAYMOND SHONHOLTZ founded and directed the Community Board Program for 12 years and in 1989 founded Partners for Democratic

Change, an international organization of national Centers on Change and Conflict Management in Central and Eastern Europe, South Caucasus, Latin America, and the United States. Mr. Shonholtz has written extensively on conflict and change management theory and practice and serves on the editorial boards of *Mediation Quarterly*, a publication of the Academy of Family Mediators, and *Consensus*, a publication of the Harvard University Program on Negotiations. He received his B.A. and M.A. degrees from the University of California, Los Angeles, and his J.D. degree from the University of California, Berkeley.

JANICE GROSS STEIN is director of the Munk Centre for International Studies and Harrowston Professor of Conflict Management and Negotiation in the Department of Political Science at the University of Toronto. She is a fellow of the Royal Society of Canada and holds the title of university professor. Her recent publications include *Choosing to Cooperate: How States Avoid Loss*, edited with Lou Pauly (Johns Hopkins University Press, 1992); *We All Lost the Cold War*, with Richard Ned Lebow (Princeton University Press, 1994); *Powder Keg in the Middle East: The Struggle for Gulf Security*, edited with Geoffrey Kemp (University Press of America, 1995); and *Citizen Engagement in Conflict Resolution: Lessons for Canada in International Experience*, with David Cameron and Richard Simeon (C.D. Howe Institute, 1997). She received B.A. and Ph.D. degrees from McGill University and an M.A. degree from Yale University.

PAUL C. STERN is study director of both the Committee on International Conflict Resolution and the Committee on the Human Dimensions of Global Change at the National Research Council, research professor of sociology at George Mason University, and president of the Social and Environmental Research Institute. His work on international conflict issues has included coediting a three-volume series, *Behavior, Society, and International Conflict* (Oxford, 1989, 1991, 1993), and *Perspectives on Nationalism and War* (Gordon and Breach, 1995). His work on environmental issues includes coediting *Energy Use: The Human Dimension* (Freeman, 1984), *Global Environmental Change: Understanding the Human Dimensions* (National Academy Press, 1992), and *Understanding Risk: Informing Decisions in a Democratic Society* (National Academy Press, 1996) and coauthoring *Environmental Problems and Human Behavior* (Allyn and Bacon, 1996). He is also coauthor of *Evaluating Social Science Research* (second edition, Oxford, 1996). Dr. Stern is a fellow of the American Psychological Association and the American Association for the Advancement of Science. He received a B.A. from Amherst College and M.A. and Ph.D. degrees in psychology from Clark University.

STANLEY J. TAMBIAH is Esther and Sidney Rabb Professor of Anthropology, Harvard University. He is a fellow of the American Academy of Arts and Sciences and a member of the National Academy of Sciences. His most recent books include *Sri Lanka, Ethnic Fratricide and the Dismantling of Democracy* (University of Chicago Press, 1986); *Buddhism Betrayed? Religion, Politics and Violence in Sri Lanka* (University of Chicago Press, 1992); and *Leveling Crowds, Ethnonationalist Conflicts and Collective Violence in South Asia* (University of California Press, 1996). He received his Ph.D. in sociology, anthropology, and psychology from Cornell University.

M. CRAWFORD YOUNG is professor of political science at the University of Wisconsin-Madison, where he has taught since 1963. He has also taught and conducted research in Uganda, Congo/Zaire, and Senegal. Among his publications are *Politics in the Congo* (Princeton University Press, 1965); *The Rise and Decline of the Zairian State*, coauthored with Thomas Turner (University of Wisconsin Press, 1985); *The Politics of Cultural Pluralism* (University of Wisconsin Press, 1976, winner of the Herskovits and Ralph Bunche prizes); *Ideology and Development in Africa* (Yale University Press, 1982); and *The African Colonial State in Comparative Perspective* (Yale University Press, 1994, winner of the Gregory Luebbert prize). He received a B.A. from the University of Michigan and a Ph.D. from Harvard University.

I. WILLIAM ZARTMAN is the Jacob Blaustein Professor of International Organization and Conflict Resolution and director of the conflict management program at the Nitze School of Advanced International Studies at Johns Hopkins University. His research focuses on the conceptual study of negotiation and its application in various cases. His recent publications include *Power and Negotiation* (University of Michigan Press, 2000) and *Preventive Negotiation* (Rowman and Littlefield, 2000). Dr. Zartman received his M.A. in political science from Johns Hopkins University and his Ph.D. from Yale University in international relations.

OTHER CONTRIBUTORS

BARRY M. BLECHMAN is president of DFI International and chairman of the Henry L. Stimson Center in Washington, D.C., where he works on finding and promoting innovative solutions to the security challenges confronting the United States and other nations in the twenty-first century. His current work also includes analyzing markets and financial conditions affecting U.S. and foreign industry and advising companies on the defense, aerospace, telecommunications, and electronics industries. Dr. Blechman has also worked with senior U.S. government officials and

is a frequent consultant to Department of Defense agencies. He recently
served on the Rumsfeld Commission to Assess the Ballistic Missile Threat
to the United States. He has served as assistant director of the U.S. Arms
Control and Disarmament Agency, directed the defense analysis staff at
the Brookings Institution, and taught at Johns Hopkins University,
Georgetown University, and the University of Michigan. Among his publications are *Force Without War* (Brookings Institution, 1978), *Rethinking
the U.S. Strategic Posture* (Ballinger, 1982), and *Preventing Nuclear War: A
Realistic Approach* (Indiana University Press, 1985). He holds a master's
degree from New York University and a Ph.D. in international relations
from Georgetown University.

YASH GHAI is the Sir Y K Pao Professor of Public Law at the University
of Hong Kong. He has taught at the University of East Africa, Uppsala
University, and the University of Warwick (U.K.) and has been a visit-
ing professor at the Yale Law School, Toronto University, Melbourne
University, the National University of Singapore, and Harvard Law
School. His books on public law include *Law in the Political Economy of
Public Enterprise* (Holmes and Meier, 1977); *The Political Economy of Law:
Third World Perspectives,* edited jointly with Robin Luckham and Francis
Snyder (Oxford University Press, 1987); *The Law, Politics and Administra-
tion of Decentralisation in Papua New Guinea,* with Anthony Regan (Na-
tional Research Institute, Boroko, 1992); *Hong Kong's New Constitutional
Order: The Resumption of Chinese Sovereignty and the Basic Law* (Hong
Kong University Press, 1997; 2nd ed., 1999); and *Hong Kong's Constitu-
tional Debate: Conflict over Interpretation,* edited with Johannes Chan and
Fu Hua Ling (Coronet Books, 2000). A book edited and partly authored
by Ghai, *Ethnicity and Autonomy: Negotiating Competing Claims in Multi-
Ethnic States,* will be published by Cambridge University Press in 2000.
In recent years his research and publications have focused on constitutional settlement of ethnic conflicts, globalization and human rights,
and the transfer of sovereignty over Hong Kong to China. He has served
as a consultant on the constitutions of Papua New Guinea, Solomon
Islands, Vanuatu, and Fiji and is currently advising the government of
Papua New Guinea on peace negotiations in Bougainville. He is a member of the advisory boards of Interrights, the Minority Rights Group, the
International Council on Human Rights Policy, and the Asian Commission of Human Rights. He holds a B.A. degree from Oxford University,
a master's degree in law from Harvard University, and a doctoral degree in law from Oxford.

PRISCILLA B. HAYNER is an independent writer and consultant based
in New York City. She has written widely on the subject of official truth

seeking in political transitions. Her book on the subject, *Unspeakable Truths: Confronting State Terror and Atrocity*, will be released by Routledge in 2000. Previous publications include "Fifteen Truth Commissions— 1974 to 1994: A Comparative Study" (*Human Rights Quarterly*, 1994) and "Commissioning the Truth: Further Research Questions" (*Third World Quarterly*, 1996). Ms. Hayner has been a program officer on international human rights and world security for the Joyce Mertz-Gilmore Foundation and currently serves as a program consultant to the Ford Foundation on transitional justice issues and as a consultant to the United Nations High Commissioner for Human Rights on truth commission developments in Sierra Leone. She received a B.A. from Earlham College and a master's in international affairs from the School of International and Public Affairs at Columbia University.

P. TERRENCE HOPMANN is research director of the Program on Global Security at the Watson Institute for International Studies and professor of political science at Brown University. His research focuses on international negotiation and conflict resolution as well as security and arms control in the Eurasian region. His recent publications include *The Negotiation Process and the Resolution of International Conflicts* (University of South Carolina Press, 1996) and *Building Security in Post-Cold War Eurasia: The OSCE and U.S. Foreign Policy* (U.S. Institute of Peace, Peaceworks #31, 1999). In 1997-1998 he held a Fulbright senior fellowship to the Organization for Security and Cooperation in Europe based in Vienna, Austria, and in 1998 he was a Jennings Randolph senior fellow at the United States Institute of Peace in Washington, D.C. Dr. Hopmann received his B.A. from the Woodrow Wilson School of Public and International Affairs at Princeton University and his M.A. and Ph.D. in political science from Stanford University.

BRUCE W. JENTLESON is director of the Terry Sanford Institute of Public Policy and professor of public policy and political science at Duke University. He is the author and editor of seven books, most recently *American Foreign Policy: The Dynamics of Choice in the 21st Century* (W.W. Norton, 2000) and *Opportunities Missed, Opportunities Seized: Preventive Diplomacy in the Post-Cold War World* (Rowman and Littlefield, 1999), as well as numerous articles. His current research focuses on post-Cold War strategies of conflict prevention. In 1993-1994 he served on the State Department's Policy Planning Staff as special assistant to the director. Before going to Duke, Jentleson was on the faculty of the University of California-Davis and was director of the UC Davis Washington Center. He has received fellowships from the United States Institute of Peace, the Brookings Institution, the Social Science Research Council, the Council on Foreign Relations, and others. He holds a Ph.D. from Cornell University and a master's degree from the London School of Economics and Political Science.

DAVID D. LAITIN is a professor of political science at Stanford University. He has conducted field research on the relationship of culture and politics in Somalia, Nigeria, Spain, and Estonia. His most recent book is *Identity in Formation: The Russian-Speaking Populations in the Near Abroad* (Cornell University Press, 1998). He is currently writing a book in collaboration with James D. Fearon on large-scale ethnic rebellion. Laitin received his B.A. from Swarthmore College and his Ph.D. from the University of California, Berkeley.

BEN REILLY is a research fellow in the National Centre for Development Studies at the Australian National University, Canberra, and an external associate at the International Institute for Democracy and Electoral Assistance (International IDEA) in Stockholm. He has advised on issues of constitutional design to international organizations, such as the UN and OSCE, and in a number of divided societies around the world. His published works include *The International IDEA Handbook of Electoral System Design* (coauthor, International IDEA, 1997), *Democracy and Deep-Rooted Conflict: Options for Negotiators* (International IDEA, 1998), and *Democracy in Divided Societies: Electoral Engineering for Conflict Management* (Cambridge University Press, forthcoming), as well as numerous journal articles and book chapters. He holds a Ph.D. in political science from the Australian National University.

ANDREW REYNOLDS is an assistant professor of political science at the University of Notre Dame. He has written extensively on issues of democratization and constitutional design in southern Africa and consulted on issues of electoral system design for the United Nations and in South Africa, Guyana, Indonesia, Liberia, Sierra Leone, Zimbabwe, Jordan, and Fiji. His books include *Electoral Systems and Democratization in Southern Africa* (Oxford University Press, 1999), *Election '99 South Africa: From Mandela to Mbeki* (editor, St. Martin's Press, 1999), *Elections and Conflict Management in Africa* (coeditor, United States Institute of Peace Press, 1998), and *The International IDEA Handbook of Electoral System Design* (coauthor, International IDEA, 1997). He has also contributed articles to various journals. Dr. Reynolds received his B.A. from the University of East Anglia, his M.A. in South African politics from the University of Cape Town, and his Ph.D. in political science from the University of California, San Diego.

NADIM N. ROUHANA is a professor with the Graduate Program in Dispute Resolution at the University of Massachusetts, Boston, and an associate at the Weatherhead Center for International Affairs at Harvard University. At the Weatherhead center at Harvard University, he is chair of the Program on International Conflict Analysis and Resolution and cochair of the Seminar on International Conflict Analysis and Resolution. His work focuses on the role of power and identity in ethnic conflict and conflict resolution and on unofficial third-party intervention in international conflict. He is the author of *Palestinian Citizens in an Ethnic Jewish State: Identities in Conflict* (Yale University Press, 1997) and has contributed articles to numerous scholarly journals. He received his B.A. in psychology from Haifa University and a Ph.D. from Wayne State University and did his postdoctoral work at Harvard University.

HAROLD H. SAUNDERS is director of international affairs at the Kettering Foundation, a research and operating foundation where he conducts sustained dialogues among groups in conflict. From 1961 to 1981 he worked in the U.S. government on issues affecting the Near East and South Asia, serving on the National Security Council staff, as deputy assistant and assistant secretary of state for Near Eastern and South Asian affairs, and as director of intelligence and research at the State Department. After the 1973 Arab-Israeli war, he flew with Secretary of State Henry Kissinger on the "shuttle" missions that produced three disengagement agreements in 1974-1975 and was a drafter of the Camp David accords in 1978 and the Egyptian-Israeli peace treaty of 1979. He has received the President's Award for Federal Civilian Service and the State Department's Superior Honor Award. He has been a fellow at both the American Enterprise Institute for Public Policy Research and the Brookings Institution. He has participated in dialogues among Americans and Soviets/Russians; Americans and Chinese; Arabs and Israelis; Indians, Pakistanis, and Kashmiris; Armenians, Azerbaijanis, and Karabakhsi; Estonians and Russian-speaking Estonians; Tajikistanis; and black and white communities in the United States. He is the author of *The Other Walls: The Arab-Israeli Peace Process in a Global Perspective* (Princeton University Press, 1991) and *A Public Peace Process: Sustained Dialogue to Transform Racial and Ethnic Conflict* (St. Martin's Press, 1999).

STEPHEN JOHN STEDMAN is a senior research scholar at the Center for International Security and Cooperation at Stanford University. His current research focuses on implementation of peace agreements in civil wars, current wars in historical perspective, and the manipulation of refugees by warring parties. He is the author of *Peacemaking in Civil War*

(Lynne Rienner, 1991) and *The New Is Not Yet Born: Conflict Resolution in Southern Africa*, with Thomas Ohlson (The Brookings Institution, 1994). He received his B.A., M.A., and Ph.D. degrees from Stanford University.

TAMARA COFMAN WITTES is director of programs at the Middle East Institute in Washington, D.C. Her current research examines confidence building in the Israeli-Palestinian peace process and the role of ethnic diasporas in conflict resolution. She also writes and teaches on the use of force, complex humanitarian crises, international law, and U.S. counterterrorism policy. Her work has been published in *Political Science Quarterly, International Studies Notes,* and *National Security Studies Quarterly.* She has a B.A. from Oberlin College and M.A. and Ph.D. degrees in government from Georgetown University.